MICHAEL PALIN
TRAVELLING
TO WORK
DIARIES 1988–1998

MICHAEL PALIN

TRAVELLING TO WORK

DIARIES 1988–1998

Weidenfeld & Nicolson

LONDON

First published in Great Britain in 2014
by Weidenfeld & Nicolson

1 3 5 7 9 10 8 6 4 2

A CIP catalogue record for this book
is available from the British Library.

ISBN HB 978 0 297 84441 9
ISBN TPB 978 0 297 86961 0

Typeset by Input Data Services Ltd, Bridgwater, Somerset

Printed in Great Britain by Clays Ltd, St Ives plc

Weidenfeld & Nicolson

The Orion Publishing Group Ltd
Orion House
5 Upper Saint Martin's Lane
London, WC2H 9EA
An Hachette UK Company
www.orionbooks.co.uk

The Orion Publishing Group's policy is to use papers that are natural,
renewable and recyclable products and made from wood grown in
sustainable forests. The logging and manufacturing processes are expected to
conform to the environmental regulations of the country of origin.

For Helen, Tom, Will and Rachel

Contents

List of Illustrations

With Tracey Ullman on location for *A Class Act* [9]
With John Hall and Michael Hepworth at a *Pole to Pole* book-signing, Sheffield [2]
At Longueville Manor near Mallow, Ireland, 1993 [2]
With Freddie Jones, David Blount and the cast and crew of *The Dresser*, 1993 [2]

Section Three:

At the Equator on a research trip to Africa, 1994 [2]
Theatre billboard for *The Weekend*, Strand Theatre, Aldwych, 1994 [2]
With Elena Salvoni at L'Etoile, London [2]
With Lena Rustin at the Cambridge Theatre, London, 1994 [2]
With Travers Reid at the Cambridge Theatre, London, 1994 [2]
Sunday Times photo for *The Weekend,* Yvonne Arnaud Theatre, Guildford, 1993 [10]
Little Diomede Island in the Bering Strait, 1996 [3]
Turquoise lake in the Kamchatka Peninsula, eastern Russia [3]
Joining in with the Kodo drummers, Sado Island, Japan, 1995 [3]
On the Sado Island ferry [3]
Filming in the monsoon at Hue Station, Vietnam, 1995 [3]
With Iban elders, Nanga Sumpa, Sarawak, 1996 [3]
Filming during the tea harvest, Java [3]
Mount Bromo, Java [3]
Helicoptering onto the Cook Glacier, 1996 [3]
In Alcatraz, San Francisco, 1996 [3]
El Tatio geyser field, Calama, Chile [3]

Section Four:

With Robert Linsday in *Fierce Creatures*, 1995 [2]
With Jamie Lee Curtis in *Fierce Creatures*, 1996 [2]
With Michael Powell at the National Hospital, London, 1996 [11]
The Pythons, 1989 [12]
On-stage with the Pythons at the Aspen Comedy Festival, 1998 [2]
With notebook and pen, 1996 [3]
Party on New Year's Eve, 1998 [2]
Family visit to Greenwich, Christmas 1998 [2]
With Merron and Julian Schlossberg, Nancy Lewis/Jones, Simon Jones and Sherrie Levy [2]
With Alan Whicker at the National Television Awards, 1998 [2]
With Spike Milligan at the Talkie Awards, 1998 [2]
With John Cleese [2]

While every effort has been made to trace copyright holders, if any have inadvertently been overlooked the publishers will be pleased to acknowledge them in any future editions of this work.

[1] Pankaj Shah
[2] From the author's private albums
[3] Basil Pao
[4] Doug McKenzie
[5] Mike Prior
[6] David Appleby
[7] Nigel Meakin
[8] Sophie Baker
[9] FremantleMedia
[10] Tim Richmond
[11] Paul Meyer, The National Brain Appeal
[12] Chris Richardson

Acknowledgements

Putting together a volume of diaries is rather like assembling a car from a lot of spare parts. *Travelling to Work* would not have been roadworthy without a great deal of help. Fulsome thanks first of all to Katharine Du Prez who not only transcribed well over a million words from my hand-scribbled notebooks but was an enormous help in the long editing process. Ion Trewin painstakingly and patiently helped me reduce the text to a digestible level. Alan Samson, my editor at Weidenfeld & Nicolson, has been hugely supportive throughout and is probably the only one who knows how all the bits fit together. Paul Bird and Steve Abbott at Mayday have been, as ever, co-ordinators extraordinary. Thank you all.

Who's Who in the Diaries: 1988–1998

FAMILY

Mary Palin, mother, lived at Southwold, Suffolk. Died in 1990. Father died in 1977.
Helen, wife
Children:
Tom born 1968
William born 1970
Rachel born 1975

Angela, sister. Married to **Veryan Herbert** of Chilton Hall, Sudbury, Suffolk. Died in 1987.
Children:
Jeremy born 1960
Camilla born 1962
Marcus born 1963

Helen's family:
Anne Gibbins, mother
Elder sister, **Mary**, married **Edward Burd** in 1964, daughter, **Catherine**, born 1966
Younger sister, **Cathy**

FRIENDS, NEIGHBOURS AND COLLEAGUES

Clare Latimer, neighbour

Terry Jones and **Alison**

Terry Gilliam and **Maggie**

John Cleese, formerly married to **Connie Booth**, one daughter, **Cynthia**, born 1971, married **Barbara Trentham** 1981, one daughter, **Camilla**, married **Alyce-Faye Eichelberger** in 1992

Graham Chapman, partner **David Sherlock**. **John Tomiczek** (adopted).

Eric Idle, married **Tania Kosevich** in 1981

Robert Hewison, contemporary of MP at Brasenose College, Oxford, 1962–5, during which time he persuaded MP to perform and write comedy for first time.

Simon and Phillida Albury. Simon met MP after Oxford in 1965. Television journalist, producer and Gospel music fan.

Ian and Anthea Davidson. Ian met MP at Oxford. Encouraged him to perform in revue and gave him early work at the BBC. A writer and director and occasional Python performer.

Neil and Yvonne Innes. Neil, ex-Bonzo Dog Band. Worked closely with the Pythons especially on their stage appearances. Collaborated with Eric to create the Rutles. Sons: Miles and Luke.

Mel Calman, cartoonist and friend

George Harrison, musician, ex-Beatle. Married to Olivia Arias, son Dhani, born 1978.

Derek and Joan Taylor, Beatles' publicist and wife

Chris Orr, artist and printmaker

Geoffrey Strachan, editor at Methuen who encouraged Python to go into print. Also published the *Ripping Yarns* books.

Tristram and Virginia Powell. Tristram was director/collaborator on *East of Ipswich* and *Number 27* and co-wrote and directed *American Friends*.

André Jacquemin, recording engineer, Python recordist, composer (with Dave Howman) of some Python songs. Founder of Redwood Studios.

Trevor Jones/John Du Prez, musician and composer (Python songs, *The Meaning of Life, A Private Function* and *A Fish Called Wanda*)

Ray Cooper, legendary percussionist who became important go-between and general troubleshooter on all the HandMade films.

FILM REGULARS

Richard Loncraine, film director (*The Missionary, Richard III*). First wife, Judy. Married Felice 1985.

Patrick Cassavetti, co-producer *American Friends*

John Goldstone, producer of Monty Python films – *Holy Grail, Life of Brian* and *Meaning of Life*

AT MAYDAY MANAGEMENT/PROMINENT FEATURES

Anne James, management

Steve Abbott, financial management. Film producer (*A Fish Called Wanda, American Friends, Fierce Creatures, Brassed Off*)

Alison Davies, secretary/assistant

Kath James, secretary/assistant

IN AMERICA

Al Levinson, writer, poet, close friend. After wife Eve's death, he married Claudie in 1979. One daughter, Gwenola.

Nancy Lewis, publicist for Python in the USA, deserves much credit for getting them on US TV in the first place. Married actor Simon Jones in 1983. One son, Timothy.

Paul Zimmerman, screenwriter (*King of Comedy*), married to Barbara

Julian Schlossberg, theatrical and film producer, distributor of *American Friends* in the USA

Michael Shamberg, co-producer of *A Fish Called Wanda* and *Fierce Creatures*. Also produced *The Big Chill* and *Pulp Fiction*, among others.

AROUND THE WORLD IN 80 DAYS, POLE TO POLE AND FULL CIRCLE

Clem Vallance. Devised *Around the World in 80 Days* and *Pole to Pole,* producer and director on all three series.

Roger Mills, co-director of all three series

Nigel Meakin, cameraman on first half of *80 Days*, and all of *Pole to Pole* and *Full Circle*

Nigel Walters, cameraman on second half of *80 Days*

Ron Brown and Dave Jewitt, sound recordists on *80 Days*

Fraser Barber, sound recordist on *Pole to Pole* and *Full Circle*

'We're all fag ends in the gutter of life'

Frank Muir, 18 January 1990

Introduction

In the last entry of the last published volume of my diaries I was in my bed at home trying to salvage what sleep I could before leaving for nearly twelve weeks away on the most ambitious project I had ever got myself into.

It might well have been a dream then, the semi-wakeful fantasy of a would-be traveller who had reached his mid-forties with no great adventures to show for it. By the time this third volume of Diaries begins, it is no dream. In my first entry I'm just out of bed, washing my smalls, no longer in the comfort of my own home, but in a ship's cabin halfway down the Adriatic Sea. I'm a full four days into a very big adventure which will shape my working life for the next twenty-five years.

This volume charts my attempts to steer an often bumpy course between the emerging potential of the television traveller and the reputation as actor and writer which I'd built up over twenty-odd years of a professional life that had begun in 1965. Even as I'm crossing the oceans filming *Around the World in 80 Days,* I'm hearing snatched messages suggesting that *A Fish Called Wanda* could be the most commercially successful film I'd ever appeared in. As we struggle with the heat and grimness of the streets of Bombay, I hear that my screenplay *Number 27* is pulling in overnight figures of near to eight million on BBC One. Clear signs that this is not the time to give up on the acting and writing. At first, as these diaries reveal, I regard the travels as a diversion from my real work, and no sooner am I returning to London – seventy-nine days and seven hours after setting out in Phileas Fogg's footsteps – than I am hard at work on *American Friends,* the film based on my great-grandfather's diary, in which I was both actor and co-author. Almost simultaneously, I take on the biggest acting challenge of my life, as Jim Nelson in Alan Bleasdale's *GBH.*

The early years of these diaries reveal the roller-coaster ride as I try to hold three careers together. I can't quite believe I took on so much, and many of the entries remind me how the doubts substantially outweighed the delights. By the mid 1990s my head was above water and I was breathing a little more normally. My confidence, and my bank balance, boosted by good numbers on *Around the World* and *Pole to Pole,* I began to take faltering steps in completely new directions. One was to fulfil a long-standing desire to write a novel, and the other to try and make a go of my stage play, *The Weekend.* The creative chicanes I had to negotiate on both these projects flung me all over the place, and the birth pangs of *The Weekend* in 1994 and *Hemingway's Chair* in 1995 find me confiding my insecurities to the diary more and more. I make no apology for exposing my doubts and fears. After all, as has often been said, you learn more from failure than from success. And diaries can be raw and emotional places, unsanitised by historical perspective.

It became increasingly obvious to me during these years that I was addicted to travel and there was no point in resisting the lure of map and atlas. Not only had the books and programmes been well received, but my tolerant wife didn't try to stop me signing up again. Indeed, rather suspiciously, she encouraged it. Thus, *Full Circle*, the circumnavigation of the Pacific Rim, was born in 1996. It was the longest and most ambitious of the adventures so far, and did not altogether run a smooth course as my wife had to undergo a brain operation whilst I was on the far side of the world. I kept a little of my old life alive playing film comedy again as the head of the insect house in *Fierce Creatures,* John Cleese's long-awaited, long-delayed follow-up to *A Fish Called Wanda.*

As this current volume comes to an end I am still wandering off in all directions: trying my hand at an arts documentary, toying with a second novel, attempting to distil my interest in Hemingway into a book or a film, being seduced, once again, by Hollywood. This is the rough-and-ready, on-the-spot account of a fundamentally wary and conservative soul, drawn to risk like a moth to a flame. Someone who's convinced that his gut instinct is more important than all the advice in the world. Someone grounded and safe who can be tempted into almost anything.

The great journeys which underpin these diaries make me realise, more clearly than ever before, that I don't like to be confined to the main road ahead, that I'm drawn to the backstreets and the side alleys, to the quirky ordinariness of everyday life, to the unexpected and the unexplored. When I'm not travelling I experience something very similar. As soon as life looks predictable, or secure or straightforward, I hop off to one side, lured by whatever it is I've never done before.

All the entries were written at my home in London, unless otherwise indicated.

Michael Palin
London, 2014

Those looking for full accounts of the three journeys, Around the World in 80 Days, Pole to Pole and Full Circle, *which I undertook during the decade covered by these diaries, will find them in the published books of the same name. I shall not attempt to repeat them here. However, in all three of these adventures I kept scribbled notes of more private thoughts, often little more than quick sketches or anxieties mulled over late at night. They're irregular, quite brief, and not all of them have survived, but occasionally their immediacy touches on a raw nerve that reminds me how I really felt as I travelled the world.*

This first selection from these 'private' travel diaries begins four days out of England on Around the World in 80 Days, *as the full impact of what I've embarked on begins to hit home.*

1988

Wednesday, September 28th: Aboard Espresso Egitto *on the Adriatic*

I've just got up, washed two pairs of socks and pants and considered what to wear for the day. As we have shots that are continuity with last night, I have to settle for the trousers I've worn since leaving London on Sunday morning and my second shirt of the voyage.

The sea is calm, my cabin, which is one of the more comfortable, has two beds alongside each other and a shower and loo. A porthole looks onto the deck and a lifeboat hangs above.

The journey has been fast and furious until now. Yesterday we were up and filming at first light in Venice – we left the city yesterday evening.

I still find the nights a problem. Last night I slept six hours, but that was with the help of a pill which I took in a panic about two. I swear not to take them again except in extremis. They do so little anyway.

Occasionally the realisation that this whole project is supported on my shoulders and demands not just my survival but my wit, energy, exuberance and enthusiasm quite terrifies me. It is going to be a supreme test, and now, only onto my fourth day and feeling low on all levels, I just can't contemplate the same continuing for two and a half more months.

But I'm determined to pull this off. Failure is unthinkable.

Thursday, September 29th: Espresso Egitto

It's nearly one o'clock and clear skies outside over the Saronian Gulf. We've just completed the quite dramatic navigational feat of the passage of the Corinth Canal – a man-made gorge it took us an hour to pass through.

Feel in good spirits today after a long sleep.

Phone Helen after breakfast and, despite the crew crouching and filming every word, it is one of our better phone calls and Helen sounds clear and very pleased to hear me – and surprised too. I don't think she'd expected a call from the ship.

These boat journeys will, I think, be a necessary interlude between periods of intense rush and activity.

The crew of the boat are treating us nobly, though I suspect they could turn ugly if they're not enjoying themselves. Today I got up in my *Adriatica* T-shirt, which pleased them – I was promptly given a sailor's hat.

It's hot outside now – the scrub-covered mountains of Greece are all around. Glad of the air-conditioning on the *Egitto*.

Friday, September 30th: Espresso Egitto

This boat trip has been restorative. I'm eager and receptive to places – especially glad I stirred myself from bed this morning to run into Heraklion. I don't suffer, as yet, from seasickness or homesickness.

Fears about my adequacy for the journey persist. I don't think now that I shan't make it, as I did that gloomy first morning on the *Egitto* – my worries now are what I shall make out of it.

My style is friendly, humorous and laid-back. It isn't best suited for revealing things about people – whose right to privacy I respect, as I would want them to respect mine. How much of the time should I be acting?

Saturday, October 1st: Espresso Egitto

Slept fitfully until finally rising at 6.20 to watch us approach Alexandria.

A thorough break with Europe, which I suppose could have been disturbing, but which I find exhilarating and energising. So the day dazzles and everything, all the hard work and the rushing around from location to location and city to city, encourages and stimulates me.

All we need at the end of our first week is sleep. We've filmed well and interestingly on the whole – though it is hard to get people on camera to be as easygoing and informative and anecdotal as they are off.

Sunday, October 2nd: Cairo

Sour taste of tourism at the Pyramids, and back to film two interviews in the bar of the Windsor[1] (where many stars of Egyptian theatre and opera gather!). Conscious of asking easy questions, not probing enough, being almost too respectful. Always after the interview I think of the one question I should have asked.

---

1 The Windsor Hotel. Eccentric city-centre hotel. The air-con unit was noisier than the traffic outside. 'I now know why they laughed at me when I'd asked for a quiet room' (*Around the World in 80 Days*).

Monday, October 3rd: Suez

Seven o'clock at the Red Sea Hotel – the silence outside on the straight, empty avenues is quite a shock after Cairo. So is the hot water, even though it's only a shower – no bath since Venice. The room is quite characterless and depressing, as is Suez. Can't wait to get on a boat tomorrow and get moving.

This morning we completed various shots in and around the hotel and I didn't have to go out. As in New York City, one has to be fit and strong to go out into the streets of Cairo, and a two-hour lay-off in the morning to write cards and ring the office was much needed and appreciated. *Wanda* is over 50 million in the States now. [The film *A Fish Called Wanda* had been released in the USA on July 15th.] Terry J starts *Erik the Viking* in Malta on the 19th.

The journey by taxi to Suez was pretty grim. The heat, dust, traffic and fumes of Cairo for the first half-hour were as uncomfortable as anything I've experienced so far on the trip. Once out of Cairo we were in desert – relics of war, barracks and endless rubbish tips.

The hotel is dry and we're all meeting at 7.30 to seek out a place for beer.

Wednesday, October 5th: Aboard the Saudi Moon 2,[1] *on the Red Sea*

As of today the journey has become quite an adventure. Information reaching us from Jeddah indicates that all our options must be reconsidered. I might have to drive across Arabia – but our visas, we think, confine us to Jeddah. I may be dropped from a container boat to go ashore at Muscat, or we may be in Jeddah for four or five days, losing precious time.

The Arab world was always to be the most difficult, Clem Vallance[2] had warned. Even he is now lost for answers. So we move on a rolling sea towards Jeddah and uncertainty on a considerable scale. It will be very hot, we shall have our patience tested to the limits, and we shall have to work a hard and long day.

What's more, we have been eleven travelling and filming days in succession and a day off would be an orgasmic pleasure. None beckons. Add to this poor food on the boat and a delicate situation in my stomach. Still, thanks to Allah – *Insh-Allah!* – it'll be the longest time I've been without alcohol for decades!

Out on deck as I write (10 p.m.) are sleeping, like corpses, hundreds of Egyptian workers, many of whom are leaving everything behind for a year or more.

1 Danish-built ferry. Her sister ship, the *Saudi Moon 1*, ran aground and sank on a reef near Jeddah. The *Saudi Moon 2* caught fire and sank in May 1994 with the loss of nine lives.
2 Deviser and co-director of *Around the World in 80 Days*.

Friday, October 7th: Red Sea Palace Hotel, Jeddah, Saudi Arabia

Day 13, country number 9. Outside my fourth-floor windows to the left it is a modern cityscape that looks back at me, dual carriageways, roundabouts, traffic moving in plenty of space, tall, featureless concrete high-rise clusters. Move a little to my left, say, to pick up an apple from the complimentary basket, and I look down on a beleaguered, ill-kempt quarter of older houses, four storeys at most with balconies of wood and screens and carved details about the windows.

First thing to be said about Jeddah is that it has been a rest and renewal stop. Our arrival on an uncluttered dockside, even our efficient clearance through customs, thanks to Ahmed and the presence of young Nick from the embassy in Riyadh, was much less of a strain than doing anything in Egypt.

The hotel – affluent, international, but really conforming to American standards of comfort and service – may be nothing to do with the real Saudi Arabia, but it has provided hot water and a bath and space and service and laundry and room to move and gather wits.

Sunday, October 9th: Riyadh

It's 8.30, dazzlingly bright outside and two weeks since I left home on a grey, London autumn morning. Ironically, here in the middle of the Arabian desert, I find myself in surroundings as familiar, comfortable and un-foreign as I've known in those two weeks. English businessmen and English voices downstairs in the lobby of the Al-Khozama, and in the breakfast room croissants and coffee almost as good as any I might have been sharing with Rachel two or three weeks ago.

Perhaps that's why I woke with an unspecifically dissatisfied feeling. Not about the travel, which I'm thoroughly enjoying and responding to, but about this sort of place – it's like America. In my *Arabian Nights*-led imagination it's an exotic, romantic location on the map, but the reality is depressing. Neon bursting out everywhere, buildings everywhere. Commerce and no culture, except the Islamic culture which the West doesn't really seem to want to know about. Cairo was grottier, but it moved me, made me think.

Tuesday, October 11th: InterContinental Hotel, Dubai

Midway through our second day in Dubai. Very hot this morning as we filmed at the dhow-builders – 110 in the sun – sweat poured off us. I took the opportunity for a run this morning, half an hour from 7.45, along the waterfront, past dhows loading, past the small, wood-hulled boats ferrying people to work across the creek, past ancient, wafer-thin old gentlemen in white robes who remind me of my mother.

A pleasant, cosmopolitan scene – Indian, Pakistani faces and Iranians and Syrians, African faces and Semitic faces, fat noses and long, beaky noses. Dull eyes, frightened eyes and calculating eyes.

I've now run three times since we left and would like to have done more, but feel in good shape still and fit for tomorrow's real adventure – the dhow trip.

From tomorrow we have a week in another world, one much simpler and more rugged than our own. Instead of bending them to us (as places like the InterContinental Hotel do), we shall have to bend to them.[1]

Wednesday, October 19th: Taj Hotel, Bombay

It's late – 11.45. Later, by several hours, than I've been to bed for the last seven days. I feel a slight tiredness in the eyes, an ache, otherwise well. Have eaten today for the first time since my stomach turned on Sunday night. My bags are open and airing, laundry is being done, I'm spread out and reordering my life in this disorderly city after seven days and nights on the dhow.

The experience was unique. Never have I been in a situation where, for so long, I depended upon a group of people quite different from me in wealth, class, race, religion and circumstance. All of us unequivocal in our appreciation of the crew from Gujarat.

How I shall sleep without the stars and the sea remains to be seen.

Thursday, October 20th: Bombay

The end of my first night in Bombay. Post-dhow euphoria dissipated.

I realise in the unblinking light of the morning sunshine that I have days ahead as hard, in their way, as any dhow journey. There's not a day off as we record Bombay, the overnight train and Madras.

I must rise to it all. There's no way one can retreat from the demands of

1 The journey on the MV *Al Shama*, a dhow carrying goods from Dubai to Bombay, took us seven nights and eight days. We had no radio, radar or GPS and the crew consisted of eighteen Gujaratis, all from the same village in north-west India, only one of whom spoke English. The friendships I struck up with the crew over that agonisingly slow week convinced me that, from then on, it was to be the encounters with ordinary people that I felt most comfortable with and which seemed to produce the best television. A formula that was to hold true through my next seven travel series. In 2008 we returned to India to try and find the crew of *Al Shama*. We found many of them in the dhow-building port of Mandvi in Kutch. We sat down together and watched the journey we made twenty years earlier.

India, no way one can do it on the defensive. Unshaven, unrested and uncomfortable, I must up and face the day and hope I shall pull through. The next five or six days are the most testing of the whole journey.

Friday, October 21st: Bombay

Bombay is the most difficult place to film yet. The people who stare at camera, the dripping humidity, the extraordinary locations – today in amongst grinding poverty watching a mongoose driven to draw blood from a snake. It is wearing us all down. Roger [Mills, one of our two directors] drives us gently, considerately, but persistently on.

Monday, October 24th: Connemara Hotel, Madras

Thirty days have gone. We've been through twelve countries, spent two nights on trains, 13 nights on boats, including seven on an open dhow, and I've slept in 13 different beds since we left London. We've recorded our progress daily, on film, tape and in notebooks. Though there are still 50 days available, I think, on paper, the worst is over. Only six more countries to pass through, and 28 days and nights will be spent at sea.

Hopefully we have more than half of the series already shot. My contribution, I think, will not be precision, analysis and revelation, but honesty, directness, openness and enthusiasm. I hope I reflect the fact that anything can happen on a journey if you allow it to.

Is this enough? I think of seeing all this through Jonathan Miller's and Alan Bennett's and Terry Gilliam's eyes and how much sharper and more original it might all be. But the fact is I have the easy, untroubled character that will, I hope, make me an interesting victim rather than a cool observer.

As of midday on Day 30, at the Connemara in Madras, in my room which was once in the summer palace of the Nawabs of Wallajah, I feel I've achieved something.

Sunday, October 30th: Aboard Susak,[1] Bay of Bengal

It's a Sunday and Sundays seem to be the days most susceptible to the stirrings of homesickness. And today aboard the *Susak* I have time on my hands. We've

1 The *Susak* was a Yugoslav freighter chartered by Bengal Tiger Lines to transport goods between Calcutta, Madras and Singapore. They could take only two of us, so Nigel went aboard with the camera and I was handed the sound equipment. We were quartered in the ship's hospital.

filmed most of our sequences over the last three days of the voyage, so, at the time of writing – 9.20 in the morning – I'm on my bed in the sickroom with the indistinct but mountainous skyline of Great Nicobar Island on the port horizon, nearly a thousand miles from Madras and with two and a half more days' sailing down the busy shipping lanes of the Malacca Strait until we reach Singapore. So, plenty of time to think.

It was a Sunday, too, when I last saw the family, five weeks ago. Five weeks doesn't sound much to me now. Can all that we've done and seen and recorded thus far have taken less than half our scheduled time? All this to go through again and still not be home?

Allied to these thoughts comes the image of Rachel following my progress, pinning up another of my postcards and, I realise, with a guilty and inadequate feeling, that it's Rachel I miss most, because, in a sense, I'm sure she misses me most. All of this quite unfair on Helen, but then she's been through it before and she has such a well-organised support system of friends and activities.

What I do know, and what keeps me from ever feeling desperately sorry for myself, is that the journey is, at every stage, remarkable and memorable. I shall never travel like this again, I shall never see so much so quickly, and when I am home and with the family again, I shall miss moments like this, in the hospital bay of a Yugoslav container boat, crossing the Bay of Bengal with the coast of Great Nicobar Island coming closer, and I shall feel sick for travel – as potently as I ever feel sick for home.

Tuesday, November 1st: Susak

It's just after nine in the morning. I sit on deck writing at the table at which we enjoyed the great barbecue party on Sunday. Today the weather is markedly different. Skies are grey and the air is sticky, warm and humid.

Last night was my sixth night in the hospital with Nigel and it was a night of doubts and broken sleep.

Should I be doing this programme? Am I the right man for the job? Should I not be extending my acting and writing skills? Have I not taken a journey round the world as a convenient way of avoiding other career decisions?

As we move slowly by sea, I have plenty of time to think. I'm better when we're on the move, working fast. But I have to face a lot more of this slack-paced travel in the next few weeks and maybe good will come of it ... insights will be revealed.

Thursday, November 3rd: Aboard the Neptune Diamond,[1] *South China Sea, Singapore to Hong Kong*

Forty days out of London: quite a landmark. We're currently in 'moderate swell' for the first time since the English Channel, but the wind has grown over the last 24 hours to a Force 7, heading almost straight at us, out of the north, so outside my yellow-carpeted suite with its all-plastic bathroom and yellow flower-pattern chair cover with plaid/gathered fringes, there is a spectacular seascape.

All of a sudden the sea that has been for so long our firm, friendly, cosseting and encompassing supporter is agitated with ridges of water flying before the wind and smashing against the side of the ship, sending columns of spray high into the sky and waves upturning themselves against the wall and somersaulting backwards to crash back on the next wave, propelling a boiling white wash a hundred yards out to sea.

Sunday, November 6th: Peninsula Hotel, Hong Kong

Yesterday my bag strap broke as I stepped off the *Neptune Diamond* gangplank. Now it's mended, thanks to the Peninsula's expertise. This morning the task I have to set them is to try and plug the holes in my trousers which a parrot made in an unprovoked attack on yesterday's visit to the Bird Market. Well, all right, I had asked the parrot if he knew John Cleese.

Friday, November 11th: Aboard the Jian Zhen[2] *between Shanghai and Yokohama*

We're four and a half hours out of Shanghai at the mouth of the Yangtze River. The whirlwind week in Hong Kong and China is over, tiredness overcome by the fascination with what I was seeing. A sore throat has been threatening for two or three days.

In my cabin, and sipping the first of my three-day course of Chinese reinvigoration medicine – bought at the shop in Shanghai.

Clem has declared tomorrow a day off.

---

1 The *Neptune Diamond* was a container ship owned by Neptune Orient Lines.
2 Once-weekly ferry between Shanghai and Yokohama. A connection we couldn't afford to miss.

Saturday, November 12th: On the Jian Zhen

Second day off out of 49. It's welcome, of course, but I'm not terribly good at days off. I catch up with the experiences of the last extraordinary week – notebooks edited and clarified, tapes numbered. I'm glad to rest this niggling sore throat. Treat it to another Disprin gargle after lunch, which relieves, but the air-conditioning's no help.

I have one of the brown parcels of Chinese medicine and, at the time of writing (6.30), feel pretty good. Drew the curtains across and lay and listened to Billy Joel and Pat Metheny and emptied my mind for a couple of hours.

A month tomorrow I'm due home. Light at the end of the tunnel. Will be difficult to keep up the momentum with 19 of the next 31 days on board ship – hard to work feeling the hard work has been done.

Must resist temptation to regard it as over.

Tuesday, November 15th: Tokyo

In bed in the pristine, antiseptic whiteness of the Akasaka Prince Hotel.

Maybe now we're in more controlled, familiar Western environments we'll have to strain harder to find the original material which was all around us in India, Cairo and the Bay of Bengal. (I'm now at the stage where I feel deep pangs of nostalgia for those early days.)

Have made the phone contacts I have to when in the big cities – spoken to Tom who's been sea-cliff climbing in Cornwall, Helen and Ma, whom I got out of the bath.

Thursday, November 17th: On board MV Neptune Garnet,[1] on the Pacific

Safely out of Tokyo Bay at half past eleven. The last night in Tokyo not as bad as I feared. The karaoke bar was very lively and silly and the Japanese there were very courteous. Many autographs were handed out. I think they just accepted I was a television star of some sort, even though they had no clue what I did.

But I sang 'You Are My Sunshine' and it didn't feel embarrassing at the

---

1 Another container ship, sister to the *Neptune Diamond*. Indian captain and largely Singaporean crew. It took us twelve days to cross the Pacific, but it took Phileas Fogg almost three weeks, so we caught up valuable time on the *Garnet*.

time, though I'm sure it will when I watch it sober. When I finished there was much orchestrated applause from the young Japanese, who chanted 'Eng-land! Eng-land!' just as enthusiastically as they had chanted 'Nip-pon! Nip-pon!' half an hour earlier.

When the chant changed to 'Thatch-er! Thatch-er!' we entered the realms of Grand Surrealism.

Saturday, November 19th: Neptune Garnet

Back in from a run along the deck. Reckon I covered about 10,000 metres altogether up and down the 250-metre starboard gangway beneath the groaning, screaming and today even trumpeting containers – Pacific swelling beneath me, puffing itself up and heaving our 42,000 tons about with contemptuous ease.

Another squally front is chasing up on us from the south-west, so I'm running between last night's gale and the one that's coming.

Somewhere halfway round the world (for once the cliché is permissible as we approach 170°), William is waking up to his eighteenth birthday. I rang and talked to him from Tokyo and wished him well for his exams, which he takes on the 21st – the day I have twice!

Wish I was at home – either to console or celebrate, as well as to be a sounding board if necessary. Feel I'm somehow missing a vital time in his life. But this is traveller's melodrama, I think.

Sunday, November 20th: Neptune Garnet

Bingo evening. The captain takes these particularly seriously and buys blocks of five tickets (one Singapore Dollar per ticket) each game. This strains the concentration, but between myself and the long-haired, pebble-glassed, slightly manic second cook and steward win five dollars from five cards.

This morning the engines were shut down to repair a leak in a pipe, which gave me a restful lie-in until 9.15. But I could not really relax – the weight of the project still hangs round my neck sometimes, feeling like the albatross that Nigel Walters [cameraman on this second leg of the journey] claims he's seen off the stern, following us.

The storm and an early call (6.30) to film the moment of crossing into the Western Hemisphere is bad enough – but there's also the promise of a wholly unlooked-forward-to 'initiation' ceremony to mark such a crossing. This is said to involve ugly humiliations such as daubing with emulsion paint and drinking some foul liquid. It'll be hard to make it funny, graceful or, really, anything other than humiliating. And as I'm being thus daubed, my son will be taking his Oxford exam!

Monday, November 21st: Neptune Garnet

A first, and probably a last, for the diary. An extra, untitled day. It's not yet the 22nd, but we've already had the 21st, so it's called the 21st again. 'It will be Monday again tomorrow,' as Jason announced solemnly on the PA last night.

Rose about a quarter to eleven and made a cup of coffee and went up to the bridge. The officers were tracing a strange, zigzag course on the map table and only after a while I realised they were marking out a crown for tomorrow's Crossing the Line ceremony. At one point it was tried out on a sheepish electrical engineer. It looked fairly ludicrous against his oily blue overalls.

The wind has shifted to the north today and is cooler, also I think the chief engineer has put on the air-conditioning, after I mentioned to the captain yesterday that it was becoming unbearably fuggy in the cabins. The captain is extraordinarily solicitous and sensitive to our needs. He's lent me his dictionary for Scrabble, and this morning, as we passed a westbound Filipino freighter pitching and taking on water, he ran through the whole of his phone call to the other boat twice, so that we could record it.

Thursday, November 24th: Neptune Garnet

Mid-morning, Day 61, ninth day on the Pacific. Our position is 38.09 N and 138.44 W. Our speed 20.2 knots. A wind from the north-west, Force 6–7, flecks the sea with flying spray.

Everything that could slide about, slid about last night and glasses smashed in the day room. Roger's room developed a squeak he could never track down and Ann's chair broke loose and shot across her cabin with a crash they heard up on the bridge.

I slept badly, as did everyone else. Up a mile one minute and slithering down the next. I would nod off only to be woken by a swingeing change to my centre of gravity, or the sticky heat of the airless cabin, or backache from the awkward, semi-foetal position I'd concertinaed my body into.

But the journey is accelerating. At the time of writing, *Neptune Garnet* is 1,000 miles away from California and 4,000 from Tokyo.

Sunday, November 27th: The Queen Mary, Long Beach[1]

After six hours' sleep and the first call home for nearly two weeks, I was up and out with the crew to Venice Beach. A glorious morning. Hockney weather. Our amazing luck with good weather on land and some attractively bad weather at sea continues.

We filmed human robots and Muscle Beach and all the activity against a bright blue sky. I walked beside the Pacific, at the very limit of America, and we were all very happy when we bought some champagne and white wine and set off for the party at Michael Shamberg's. [Michael was one of the producers of *A Fish Called Wanda*].

I'd been nervous of this for some time. Its genesis came from a rather abrupt demand from Clem, when I was in my anxious pre-karaoke bar phase in Japan, to 'ring one of your friends in Los Angeles and get them to organise a Thanksgiving party'.

We rolled up Mandeville Canyon in our two hire cars – Nigel W driving myself and Roger.

Guests arrived. All were quite bewildered and no-one seemed quite sure what was going on.

A phone call from London and it's Cleese. I'd not been told that he was being recorded in the next room (the whole thing had been prepared without my knowing), nor did I realise he'd been tipped off I'd be here. So, poor bugger, he and I groped for laughs and wit whilst the light went and Nigel could hardly see my face.

Then, when the light had truly gone, Jamie [Lee Curtis] arrived. Michael kept asking about how much sex I'd had on the journey and the whole thing felt a huge effort. 'Was that an awful strain?' the Professor (aka Roger Mills) asked as we pulled away from the house, soon after five.

I'm now back in the slightly ridiculous environment of the *Queen Mary*. We've had three beers, sitting in the Art Deco bar, with its naughty mural of a cross-section of English society doing a linked-hands dance (by Thomson, 1936), and repair to our staterooms for an early night.

Saturday, December 3rd: Rensselaer, New York State

It's ten-thirty on a bright, clear morning and our Chicago–New York train is being split between the Boston and the Grand Central sections. Across the River Hudson, about a half a mile away, is the skyline of Albany.

1 Transatlantic liner, former flagship of the Cunard Line. Following her retirement in 1967 she was permanently moored at Long Beach, California as a tourist attraction and hotel.

I have just been filmed getting up and have already improvised a jokey feet-washing sequence (Nigel Walters is game for filming anything).

I've been filmed for 68 out of the last 70 days. This time tomorrow we shall, hopefully, be at sea – on the Atlantic, heading for Europe.

Now, as the Good Lord offers a last splendid day to remember America by, I shall watch Albany slide away to the north-west and enjoy the Hudson view. Very content. Not much more to do, so I'm now beginning to worry about what we've done! Suddenly all the talk is of editing.

Tuesday, December 6th: Aboard Leda Maersk[1] *on the Atlantic*

A good sequence sailing from Newark, past Liberty, Manhattan and out under the Verrazano-Narrows Bridge at dawn on Sunday, and deck shots and a fine Atlantic sunset the same day. We have filmed Lillian cutting my hair and some strange effects of steaming ocean yesterday.

But it's as if we're all, at last, repeating ourselves. Container ship life is much the same, except that it's less of an adventure on the *Maersk* than on the *Garnet*. The weather is grey, damp, but the sea quite restful.

The presence of J. P. Moller, son of the founder of Maersk, hangs balefully over the ship. Jesper [the company rep] speaks of him with reverence, respect and awe. When Jesper says 'he rules with an iron hand' I believe it.

So the more easygoing, down-to-earth atmosphere of the *Garnet* is missing here. The captain is a very jolly seaman and has little time for the bureaucrats, but he too seems inhibited by the head-office presence.

So we wait as the last days slowly and anti-climactically pass. My cold streams out, the sun is gone, *Bonfire of the Vanities*[2] is, at last, a book I want to read and isn't too demanding. I check my diary notes and drink coffee and contemplate some exercise on deck in an hour or so. I've ironed three shirts and we've had a telex to the effect that all Pacific rushes were excellent.

Friday, December 9th: Leda Maersk

So here I am, almost home and reflecting back. I certainly haven't been through a Gilbert Pinfold ordeal,[3] as in the early, hectic days in the heat of Greece and Cairo I imagined I might. In fact, far from throwing me into a bewildering

1 Container ship owned and operated by the Danish company, Maersk Lines.
2 Tom Wolfe's best-selling novel set in 1980s New York had been published a year earlier.
3 *The Ordeal of Gilbert Pinfold* was a 1957 novel by Evelyn Waugh, autobiographical in inspiration, about a Roman Catholic writer who mixes drugs and alcohol and is verging on a nervous breakdown. Much of the narrative is on a sea voyage taken by Pinfold as a cure.

world of unreality and causing my reason to waver, I think that the journey has, in a way, calmed and settled me. It's been much nearer to sanity than the phone-ringing, celebrity-conscious world I left at home.

As I ran beside the sea today, for the last time, with wind buffeting, albeit gently, and tugging at the tops of the waves, I felt how fond I've become of the sea. I have grown to respect it, and I feel soothed by its motion and its presence. I looked around me for 360°, nothing in sight, a wide horizon – 15 to 20 miles away – only sea and sky.

There was no noise, except for the throb of the engines and the swish of the water and the flapping of the wind. I shall miss that in the car alarm, police siren, drunken singing, car-skidding 'reality' of London at Christmas.

I have had a lot of time to think about myself and wonder how I've measured up.

I know there are people much better at this than I am. I like people and I want to be liked by them, so I have to make an effort to be the inquisitor. I prefer when travelling to take in what's outside by myself, privately, and I respect the same privacy for other people. This makes it difficult to grab people and interrogate them.

Also I find the camera and microphone, even when wielded by considerate and friendly souls like Nigel and Dave and Ron, an embarrassing intrusion. Not always – sometimes people love to talk, can't wait to talk. But to me, confronting someone with a camera crew is like shining a torch on them in the night.

I feel, for better or worse, that the best way I could make a contribution to the project was to be natural throughout – but going around the world with a film crew isn't a natural thing to do and this is where I've come a little unstuck. I try to be me, I try to be as natural as possible, and yet time and again I have to act. Either look happy when I'm bored, or interested when I'm tired, or enthusiastic when I'm feeling ready to quit.

I can act – I can act characters of all sorts till the cows come home – but I can't act me.

Monday, December 12th

Back at home. As I write it's 9.30 in the morning on Tuesday 13th and my 80 days are up. In fact I was at the Reform Club at 4.45 yesterday evening, having completed the journey with 17 hours to spare.

Extraordinary luck with the weather continued, the Channel was calm as a millpond and the sun rose off Felixstowe yesterday in a cloudless sky. But it was a tetchy, awkward last filming day.

We progressed slowly – by container truck to Felixstowe Station, then, after a long wait in a hotel bar full of old ladies with cigarettes and scotch and sodas, to Ipswich.

All too predictable was the British Rail steward's apology for lunch – 'We've got no chef and no food, but we can give you afternoon tea.' So we had afternoon tea and were taken at a commendable rate up to Liverpool Street. We picked our way through the wreckage of the reconstruction and down to the Underground.

All proceeded satisfactorily as far as Tottenham Court Road, where a terse announcement warned us not to alight from the train as there was a 'suspected parcel' and the station had been sealed off. Hurried on to Oxford Circus, and I was filmed on the escalator and way out.

A newspaper seller refused to be filmed and was abusive. The passers-by looked drab and poorly dressed. We moved, filming, down Regent Street. Nearly everyone we asked about filming was obstructive or, at least, defensive, and by the time we reached the Reform Club we were all tired out.

We were not allowed to film in the Reform Club, capping a very bad day for Britain. A meanness and a defensiveness and a fearful surliness marked our return. But our little crew are as good a bunch as you could ever find and we shook hands on the steps outside 104 Pall Mall to seal our achievement.

What do I feel? The usual euphoria of arrival. Reintroducing myself to the once-familiar, rediscovering my old life from a new perspective. I don't feel regret or nostalgia for the great journey – we did it and we'll never forget it.

The house is being painted, or has been painted, inside. The bathroom is being redone. Helen has worked incredibly hard.

My room is full of envelopes, full of the old life, which I shall ease myself into slowly.

Tuesday, December 13th

I think I couldn't have timed my eleven weeks off any better, especially as later, ploughing through two and a half months of press cuttings, it's clear that my profile at home has never been higher. *Wanda* – already at £8 million after eight weeks' release – then the much-publicised and generally admired *Number 27,*[1] TV showings of *And Now, Time Bandits* and *Meaning of Life* and the tenth anniversary of HandMade have had the hacks raking through the Palin files, and my name and photo is all over the place, all spiced by the fact that I couldn't be there because I was filming six documentaries for the BBC.

1 My second film for the BBC directed, like *East of Ipswich*, by Tristram Powell, with whom I went on to make *American Friends*.

So I manage to give the impression of being successful, in great demand and, most admirable of all – not available! There's a lesson there somewhere.

Wednesday, December 14th

To Hampstead Heath for first run since the first day of autumn. Wet leaf smell and a chilly edge to the air. Find the hills hard – realise that all my exercise on the journey was generally on the flat – once we passed the Alps there was no mountain scenery until the Rockies.

Much sorting-out of letters and offers. A quartet of interesting documentary prospects. *The Shape of the Earth,* a big Granada spectacular about the people who mapped the world, a 'By-Line' on transport, an examination of a British city. All enticing, but no time left for most of next year.

Then by cab to see Terry Gilliam's *Munchausen.* The cab driver has a sign up saying he's training in Chinese medicine and if any of his passengers can spare a minute, he'd like to take their pulse, as he has to have taken 600 pulses at least by the end of the week.

So in Goodge Street, he solemnly gets into the back of the taxi and takes my left- and right-hand pulse. 'You'll live a long time,' he pronounces cheerfully and off I go to the Columbia viewing theatre in Wells Street, passing my likeness in the UIP window on the corner, permed head poking up from a group of fellow *Wanda* stars.

The movie begins like *Time Bandits* – an eighteenth-century city torn apart by war, caught in the middle of chaos. Indeed it reminds me of *Time Bandits* too often. There are cinematic fireworks and magnificent set pieces, but the whole misses the binding of a strong story. There is an emotional involvement lacking.

John Neville is quite superb as Munchausen – old-fashioned acting, with dignity, gravity, humour, charm all portrayed effortlessly.

Thursday, December 15th

Joe, keen Telecom engineer, brings round new telephone receiver, which can be used without picking it up. Very strange feeling, speaking into the air! Will receivers eventually become redundant, like appendixes?

Into the West End for the second time since return. Northern and Victoria Lines to Green Park. Everything still benefiting from the glow of rediscovery.

Meet Tristram [Powell] at Green's Oyster Bar (he chose it as he said I'd probably have had enough 'ethnicity' for a while). We talk over smoked eel, dressed crab and champagne.

American Friends [the film project based on the story of my great-grandparent] has not progressed much further.

Out into Duke Street, St James's, at the sober hour of 3.15. 'It's still light!' exclaims Tristram, with some disappointment. Buy a book of work by Atkinson Grimshaw at Thomas Heneage, where the young assistants jest amongst themselves.

Then back home, reading a film script by Robert Jones on the way. Don't think I want to do it, but flattered I'm still offered parts for men in their 30s.

Call Terry J, but wake him up at about ten o'clock. He films *Erik* until the end of next week.

Friday, December 16th

A few more work offers – including Edgar in Jonathan Miller's *King Lear* – keep coming in.

Had some fresh thoughts on '*AF*' as I ran this morning. Centred round making more of the sexuality, and on casting Emma Thompson in it somewhere. I was impressed by her confident and compulsively watchable characters in her series, *Thompson*, last night.

Meet David Rose, head of *Film on Four*. He is delighted that he has a season coming up next year which will infuriate the Whitehouses – including *Rita, Sue and Bob Too*. He asks if I've seen the article in which Rees-Mogg refers to Michael Grade [Chief Executive of Channel 4] as an ass.

Saturday, December 17th

Swimming with Rachel at Marshall Street Baths. They've been put out to private management since we last went, and the lockers now cost 10p and are just as poky as before. Also the mechanism sticks. The water has been so heavily chlorinated that my eyes sting on contact with it. All in all, a move for the worse.

Sunday, December 18th

Broken night's sleep with Rachel unhappy and raising a temperature and Helen coughing. Wake and lie thinking for a while. All there is to do. Feel the problems of house and home and London life gradually creeping back into the empty spaces left by the 80-day cleansing!

A morning of half-hearted sorting out and planning ahead, Christmas organisation calls, then to Cleese's for lunch. A new lady is by his side, small as Connie, American as both Connie and Babs, but with a hard Southern twang which gives her an odd country-boy edge to the voice. She's called Alyce Faye and she is more like an Australian than an American, direct and funny, and says she knew hardly anything about John's work when they met. I think she vaguely reminds me of Aunt Betty Sheldon [my mother's sister].

The food is rich and plentiful and Montagny or Chablis is served. As usual I hardly have a chance to eat – balancing food, wine and interest in the person you're talking to is not easy.

Talk with Michael Blakemore[1] about work, writing and Maggie Smith. He feels that Maggie comes alive on the stage or when acting; that all the rest of her life is a sort of 'greyness' leading up to the burst of shining brightness when she performs. I like Blakemore. He is a perceptive but modest fellow, full of curiosity about how things are done and why people are the way they are, without offering pat solutions.

Surprise guest standing there as I enter is Nigel Greenwood [my first cousin], who has been brought into the Cleese orbit by Alyce. He is off to the Albert Hall, where Sarah, his sister, is organising some carol do. Talk about 'Uncle Ted' [my father]. Nigel feels he was someone who never really knew what he wanted to be. An eccentric, Nigel thinks. Aunt Katherine [his sister] always regarded him with a certain guarded respect.

Monday, December 19th

I see Steve, the postman, resting his bag on Clare's window sill and sifting our mail. The last few days have been lived under the tension of not knowing whether Will has been successful at BNC,[2] especially as others have heard already.

I can't resist a look through the stack of cards just in case. Nothing very promising. A red herring from the central admissions co-ordinating body at Cheltenham – but second-class and unsealed. Then a thicker letter, white envelope, sealed, addressed to William, postmark Oxford.

It's an extraordinary moment. It is like having my own exam results in my hand.

Should I open it or not? Only one answer and I push my finger under the flap. It takes a moment to focus clearly on the dense page of print, but then it becomes clear that the message is affirmative. He's offered a place. Rachel, who's been languishing on the sofa with a temperature, comes to the kitchen door and I'm thumping the table with joy.

1 Michael Blakemore, Australian-born director, who had the previous year worked with Maggie Smith on Peter Shaffer's play *Lettice and Lovage*.
2 Brasenose College, Oxford, where I read history between 1962 and 1965.

Tuesday, December 20th

Write a lot of cards, do some shopping, then off to T2000's[1] Christmas party.

General spirit of optimism. I notice transport issues being discussed in the media as never before. King's Cross fire (incompetence) and the Clapham disaster (also incompetence) have raised questions of safety and, wider than that, how public transport is financed, run and what we expect from it. Things that T2000 has been trying to raise for years.

A mad dash from the glare of Union headquarters in Euston to the more sophisticated, homely and comfortable surroundings of Stockwell Park Crescent for Tristram's Christmas party.

Melvyn Bragg (a suit and tie man, but with the tie knot hanging a button's distance down from an open collar) joins me. Both agree chief physical ordeal of pre-Christmas parties is all the standing. Someone should invent an indoor shooting stick.

Talk of TV. Melvyn, as one would imagine, stoutly defends TV plays and TV documentaries as works of art in themselves, conceding nothing in terms of status or prestige to the theatre, opera or films. 'I'd far rather spend an evening in front of a good TV play than sit in some cramped West End theatre watching second-rate material.'

He tells me about the Cleese interview. Long setting-up process on the day of the interview – JC kept asking if everyone was alright . . . much introducing, lot of flattery of Melvyn, then, as they began, he stopped them and suggested that they should first talk to his mother. She was only next door. It would be the work of a moment.

Dr Miller passes by with his son William. He pats me rather fondly on the head. 'Tried to get him for Edgar,' he sighs to Melvyn.

£228,951

Wednesday, December 21st

A Channel 4 news presenter and his team arrive to interview me about Prominent Features [the film company owned by the Pythons]. Why are they suddenly taking an interest in Prominent? He's quite disarming, says it's Christmas week, there's no news.

Two and a half hours later a 747 blows up in the sky over a Scottish village called Lockerbie.[2]

1 The pressure group Transport 2000 (later Campaign for Better Transport), of which I had been Chair since 1987.
2 A PanAm transatlantic flight was blown up by a terrorist bomb over Lockerbie, Scotland, killing 270 people.

Friday, December 23rd: London–Southwold

To the office to leave presents for all, which I bought yesterday. Then head out onto the M25 and eastwards to Suffolk.

Granny [my mother] is still shrinking, it seems. Her arms are bony and she continues to be less steady on her feet. But it's still as good as ever to see her and she's full of the mixture of humour and exaggerated fears and ear-wagging gossip which keeps her going.

Alice Murnane, a friend with whom she had become close – they regularly took Sunday lunch together – has just died, and her funeral was this morning. Mum seems to have taken it all philosophically, or else she's very good at hiding real feelings.

She has some lunch for me. Afterwards I fight against an all-embracing fatigue which is within a whisker of sending me into a deep sleep even as Ma is talking to me. The cure is exercise and about three o'clock I set off across the golf course and down onto the marshes. Hard work against a firm, westerly wind.

In the evening we go to the Crown. Ma insists we walk. The wind has dropped and the air is almost warm. The Christmas lights are on down the peaceful High Street and the Crown is almost empty. Susan serves – full of laughter as usual.

Take a walk to the shore of the North Sea, on which I sailed home eleven days ago. The bright orange lights of the Sizewell B nuclear power construction site sparkle to the south. The lighthouse beam sends out three stabs across the cliffs above me, then revolves away to the north.

Tuesday, December 27th: Southwold

As we are unloading the car outside Sunset House, a tall man with a saucer-shaped face and big ears looms over us. He turns out to be Roger Ward, Kathleen Ward's son. He grasps my mother's hand – what is it about ancient hands that draws the graspers so? – and apologises for having taken his mother away at such short notice. So profoundly overplayed is his seriousness that Mother gets the wrong end of the stick and assumes Mrs Ward to be dead. Roger's following remarks – about her being 'in a better place' (meaning Perthshire, near their home) – only make things worse.

Once we are safely inside, Mum, who had been wonderfully sympathetic, turns to me in bewilderment. 'Who was that?'

After our sandwiches I walk into the town to check on Daddy's grave. Southwold full of Bank Holidayers.

On the way home, between about 4.20 and 5.15, one of the most spectacular and prolonged sunsets I've ever seen. Far outdoing anything I saw around the world, both in length and intensity. Wide East Anglian skies as the arena, and a collection of various shapes and sizes of cloud, from long, wispy, horizontal to almond-shaped smudges higher, away from the horizon. All catching, reflecting and burning with reds, yellows, dripping golds, pink-salmon reds.

Wednesday, December 28th

To the Tate Gallery to the Hockney retrospective, very full. No-one quite sure what to say in front of the canvases. Botties of men protruding from shower curtains can't be analysed in quite the same way as the light on a Vermeer, or the snow in a Sisley.

Friday, December 30th

I would like to write or read or generally relax, but have to scour the house for Australian things to take to the Guedallas' lunch party.

Decide on the spur of the moment to go as Sir Les Patterson,[1] but can't find anything nasty enough to smear down my shirt. Stick Helen's pillow into shirt and trousers and borrow an awful pair of Dracula teeth from Rachel.

We make our appearances as the Patterson Family and are very well received – I even have a cucumber in my trouser pocket to give the authentic phallic detail.

Talk mainly to the Australians there. All agree that Prime Minister Hawke has quite cleverly dropped the socialism from his Labour programme. Joy [an Australian-born neighbour of ours] tells me how much Sir Les Patterson is detested by Australians!

Saturday, December 31st

Because of the *80 Days* journey, 1988 seems to have come to an end with a rush. A year of travel – eleven and a half weeks on *80 Days* being the longest single period I've spent away from the family, but only half of the 22 weeks I spent out of the country this year.

---

1 One of several personae created by the Australian actor Barry Humphries. The uncouth Sir Les Patterson could hardly be more different from his other creation, Dame Edna Everage. Patterson is overweight, with no social graces and offensive at virtually every utterance.

The winter and spring work done on writing and casting *American Friends* was inconclusive. The script is still not satisfactory. Attempts to float my play *The Weekend* also failed. *Number 27* was, quite successfully, floated, and has added to my reputation as a writer of plays as well as jokes and films.

The summer belonged to *Wanda* and the US publicity tour was made bearable by the growing awareness of how popular the film might be. Now, at the end of the year, it's reached 60 million rentals in the US and is the fourth-biggest movie in GB for 1988.

I seem to be better known than ever now. A mixed blessing. 'He's the famous man' I heard one seven-year-old boy tell his friend solemnly yesterday. But there's also *Bella* magazine ringing to know who I'd most like to do an April Fool on and sounding very aggrieved when I told them I wasn't interested.

The urge to move house, that somehow it's time for a change to the physical parameters of my life, strengthens, then ebbs. At Christmas the house was stretched to capacity, yet it coped and was warm and friendly and characterful and the prospect of uprooting and creating the same cordial feelings elsewhere is frightening. But also tantalising.

I have the feeling that I shall be mooning over the same problem in a year's time from my comfortable workroom in Gospel Oak.

1989

Sunday, January 1st

Mrs B [our cleaner] comes in for a drink and we talk about what Oak Village used to be like. Mrs B bought a pram from a lady who lived here. About that time our house was a 'sort of club' and Mrs B hadn't liked to ask further about it.

Also a wonderful story about the war. There was an air-raid shelter in Lismore Circus and one night a lady came in to find a friend of hers ... unfortunately the friend's name was Cass. She couldn't get any response so shouted the length of the shelter for her. 'Cass! Cass!' Mrs B says she never saw such a panic. Half-cooked food went flying as everyone scrambled for their masks.

Tuesday, January 3rd

I read that Harold Nicolson[1] said that a diary should be written for a great-grandson.

So briefly, great-grandson, and just for you, I woke about eight and was at the desk, with the phone off the hook, by ten o'clock, as I began work on the *80 Days* book. I only composed two sentences – but they were the opening two, so psychologically worth a lot.

Wednesday, January 4th

Jonas [Gwangwa, South African musician, ANC stalwart and, briefly, our neighbour] comes round for a drink and to bring back the £200.00 I loaned him.

Pour him some wine and talk about Botswana, which he says is a paradise, but he can never go back there. He was nearly arrested for setting up 'political' entertainment there some years back (i.e. getting local blacks together in a band) and chased by South African security people across walls and through gardens.

---

1 Harold Nicolson, diplomat and later MP, published three much-praised volumes of political and social diaries covering the mid-1920s to the 1950s.

Thursday, January 5th

Tristram arrives at a quarter to eleven. We discuss the future of *American Friends*.

Upshot of our discussion is that '*AF*' has much going for it, that this year (post-*Wanda*) it should be easier to finance than last, that we can be freer with the casting if we do it through the BBC (Connie Booth[1] rather than Ellen Burstyn, for example), that there are significant improvements to character and plot which have come up today, all of which point in the right direction.

We agree to go ahead. I feel energetic and positive and pleased with the decision. Ring Steve Abbott, who is as enthusiastic as I've heard him and he will go ahead with money-raising plans. Our filming dates will be September and October.

Friday, January 6th

Give an hour's interview to Debbie's nephew Michael,[2] who has set up an arts magazine at the University of East Anglia, which now sells seven or eight hundred copies. It's an un-elitist mag of catholic interests and I like it and him. I think in years to come anything worth really knowing about me will be in magazines like this and not in the publicity handout-fed pages of the daily press.

To dinner deep in the leafy hills above Aylesbury with Liz (née Manning) and Dick Johns. Dick is now an Air Vice-Marshal. (Helen always gets into a tizzy about his rank when sending Christmas cards. Every time she thinks she's got it right, he's promoted.)

Dick and I talk a little about his job. Revealingly, for they've just shot down two Libyan fighters, Dick confesses that he and most of his European colleagues are scared stiff of some of the gung-ho American attitudes.

Thursday, January 12th: Brussels

Brussels about midday.

My first exposure to the media since *Wanda* work in the UK in September begins with a lunch in the hotel.

---

1 Connie Booth, John Cleese's first wife: co-writer of, and played Polly in, *Fawlty Towers*.
2 Debbie Woolard was a dental hygienist who had looked after my complicated mouth for so long that we had become good friends.

Hear a tapping on the glass window of the restaurant and there is Charlie's[1] ruddy face and thatch of silver hair grinning at me. Good to see him and especially Nadine. Charlie anxious to tell me he's going to be very rude about me later on.

More journalists, then at four out of the hotel and down to the Grand Place.

At the florid Town Hall we are shown into the presence of the Director of the Brussels Film Festival, an oldish man with silver-grey hair and a strong, intelligent face. Of Russian parentage. We're introduced to an obsequious character with a red face from the Embassy. I later hear that the British Embassy, having seen *Wanda*, declined to be too closely involved with it – despite the fact that it is one of the country's better export-earners and that it will open a film festival in a country with great respect for British films.

Then we are ushered into the presence of the Mayor of Brussels.

The Mayor is wrapped in a colourful ribbon around his tum, and it's all rather stiff and formal. The room has lots of gilt mouldings and paintings of old Brussels. We're shown these lovely glimpses of how the city must have been without any evident sense of irony. 'There's a pretty square with a small market, is it still there?' 'No, that is now a big insurance building.'

The Mayor reads a carefully written speech, ponderously, but he's reading in English. Charlie, dwarfed by the huge fireplace behind him, leans on his stick and tries to look comfortable.

At the end of this interminable speech Charlie is presented with a medal of the City of Brussels for his work in helping the Resistance – he made a film in 1947 with Simone Signoret on this theme. Charlie briefly replies that on his last trip to Brussels he had a lunch with some army parachutists which began at twelve and finished at twelve the next day. And that's about all.

Handshakes, farewells to the girl who's shown us the building, then to a rather grim hall of culture where we are to hold a press conference. A translator called Dominique looks even more nervous than Charlie.

Nobody says anything. 'Don't all talk at once,' I try, to break the ice. The ice seems to grow thicker. 'Do you ask us questions, or do we ask you questions?' Still nothing.

The combination of Charlie's incomprehensibility, even to the translator, and the need to pause for regular translation into French, make the whole thing something of an ordeal. Banter, irony and throwaway jokes all die the death.

Eventually we're delivered from this, then three other interviews – press, radio and TV – before being rushed back to the Astoria to rest in the bath

---

[1] Charles Crichton, film director whose long association with Ealing Films (*The Lavender Hill Mob*, *The Titfield Thunderbolt* etc.) led John Cleese to hire him, aged 77, to direct *A Fish Called Wanda*.

(delightful), then don dinner jacket and return to the Palais des Congrès, or whatever the culture hall is called, to be present at the start of *Wanda*.

We're to be interviewed on stage by two presenters, a man and a woman dressed like Christmas presents. Video cameras follow us everywhere, lenses click. Then, flanked by a rather overdone and unnecessary escort of leggy, jolly girls in black, we're led out onto the stage.

I have a plastic fish tank with a mechanical fish in it. Jokes are made, translated, and Charlie flaps his arms and makes a brief speech in French, telling them he hasn't been to Brussels 'il y a quarante ans'.

Then, at last, a break. We're taken to a local restaurant where, without cameras, we meet various Belgian artistic figures, including a cartoonist called Frederic in Corbusier glasses, who is a great Python fan and interesting too. He and his friend have drawn a special cartoon for us to celebrate *Wanda*.

The cartoonists are desperate for more time with me and their patient, hangdog eagerness is much more acceptable than the pushiness of so many of the others, so end up drinking and talking over a bottle of champagne in the bar. They hold London graphic designers in great respect. Belgium a mixture of identities. Much of their surreal tradition comes from this cultural split personality.

Friday, January 13th: Amsterdam

To sleep about 2.15. Wake five hours later, am at Amsterdam Station by five past twelve.

Begin at one o'clock at the Amstel Hotel. Three and a half hours' talking and being photographed. I don't have a lot to say about *A Fish Called Wanda* – the stammer, the character of Ken, all can be dealt with in 15 minutes – so I waffle on, filling in details about John, about how the film was made, what it was intended to say, desperately trying to sound as if I care a damn.

Finish with a TV piece recorded in the Aquarium. Background of huge, plate-sized black and yellow mega-Wandas and an occasionally active pair of sharks. I sit on a high stool in front of the glass and questions are fired at me.

A bright light shines. Faces look at monitors as I speak. I feel as if I'm having a body scan.

Delivered at last from this nightmare and out along the motorways to Schiphol, where I have time to sit with a coffee and cognac and collect my thoughts. I conclude that film publicity becomes harder, not easier, as you become better known and that it is perhaps the most demanding aspect of this whole crazy business.

Monday, January 16th: London–Madrid

I've brought Buñuel's *My Last Breath* to help renew my appetite for a city in which I've never had a bad time. The book, like his films, is a very personal jumble of insights and anecdotes. I'd forgotten that the name of the only porno film he saw when young was *Sister Vaseline* and he had planned to hijack a theatre during a children's matinee, tie up the projectionist and substitute it for whatever was showing.

Madrid is the same temperature as London. Met by an overweight, funny, tragic Argentinian called Inez, who has had enough of Spain after 12 years, finds no emotional support from the increasingly Yuppie, materially obsessed Spaniards. With her is a slim American lady called Chaplin O'Grady.

It's clear both are intelligent and don't take the whole thing too seriously. Ideal companions for Madrid, for, as Inez is depressed with it, Chaplin delights in the things I like about it – bars, restaurants, variety of architecture and richness of decoration.

After six journalists and two TV interviews we reach Restaurante El Landó, where I have to sign a VIP book, just below some gushing praise from Mel Brooks – 'I love your restaurant, I love your food, I love you!'

Saturday, January 21st

To the shops, then with Will to Highbury for Arsenal v Sheffield Wednesday.

It pours with rain. We park about a half-mile from the ground and join the gradually swelling crowd flowing along the terraced streets. The houses are in much better condition than I remember from our previous visits – the dreadful semi-final defeat by Brighton in '82, and the heart-stopping night we nearly beat Arsenal in the Cup in '79. Money has moved into every corner of Highbury.

Good seats on the halfway line. Pitch soggy and pools of water in the goal mouths. Wednesday fourth from bottom and Arsenal heading the League, but of course it doesn't turn out true to form.

Wednesday are lumpen and completely uninspired in attack, but rather solid and consistent in defence – always winning balls in the air. They gradually wear Arsenal down to their level, then midway through the second half audaciously score on the break. Arsenal equalise quite swiftly, but that's as far as they get.

One of the more satisfying features of the game is the presence in the Arsenal half-back line of a lithe black boy called Gus Caesar (presumably Augustus Caesar). He doesn't play well and richly bizarre shouts like 'You're rubbish Caesar!' can be heard.

Wednesday, January 25th: London–Southwold

With Ma by a quarter to twelve. She seems to shrink a little more every time I see her. Eyes bright, but the legs and arms thinner than ever. Her face is heavily dusted with make-up, some of which has rubbed off onto her blue cardigan. She has trouble finding things – bits of paper, envelopes, old magazines lie in piles all over the place. I long to go through them and throw a few things away, but there is a sort of haphazard system to it all.

After lunch I set up my typewriter and enjoy a couple of hours of productive *80 Days* book-writing. It's so good to be away from the distractions of London.

Thursday, January 26th: Southwold–London

Leave Mum waving at the door of Sunset House and head back home. I can feel a little of her disappointment, though she is remarkably free of self-pity and only very occasionally makes me feel guilty at not giving her more time.

Arrive back about three o'clock.

An interview about stammering, for an outfit called 'Link', which I think makes programmes for the handicapped. The director is blind and the interviewer has a stammer. Both are quite tough and unsentimental, with a steady string of subversive one-liners.

Meet Kevin [Kline] and Phoebe and go to see Peter Hall's production of *Orpheus Descending*.[1] Kevin says the British have rediscovered Tennessee Williams – and this is an excellent production. Technically superb – sound, lights, music blend perfectly. Only the melodramatic ending full of screams and gunshots strains my credulity. Maybe it is because a woman behind me keeps hissing 'Oh, God ... Oh, my God, no.'

Friday, January 27th

Up to the shops. The litter caught in the grass and among the scrubby bushes by the new flats on Mansfield Road is thicker and more ugly than ever. The decay of 'socialist' London is painful to watch. The apathy and helplessness of those who live with this filth is utterly depressing. I feel like organising an

---

1 *Orpheus Descending* was the first production of the Peter Hall Company after Hall left the National Theatre in 1988.

anti-litter vigilante group – a sort of environmental Guardian Angels[1] - to try and jerk people from this mute acceptance of drabness and mess.

John rings from Heathrow. He's off to the Golden Globes in LA and sounds quite cheerfully resigned to progressing no further than his nomination.

He reels off the latest *Wanda* statistics. A million dollars in a week in Holland, No. 1 in Paris, with three times as many admissions as the next movie, and Italy looking promising.

For the first time since before my world trip, a game of squash with Terry. A good battle which I win 2-1 and am up in the last, gruelling game.

Later in the pub he shows me his half-moon reading glasses. He has had just the same difficulty with small print, bad light, etc. as I have over the last few months, and nothing makes us feel more middle-aged than sitting with a pint in the Flask taking turns with TJ's specs to read the small print in *Country Life*!

Saturday, January 28th

Helen leaves for skiing holiday in St Anton at half past seven. Her yearly departure almost a routine now. Back to bed, listen to the unfamiliar sound of falling rain. A warm, wet morning.

Simon Albury rings and extols the virtues of the Apple Macintosh. Everything I'm doing at the moment – crossings-out, substitutions, reordering of lines and paragraphs – can be done instantly, he raves, and it only takes 30 minutes to learn. I promise to go round and try it out. But at the moment every writing hour is precious.

Sunday, January 29th

Wake about 7.15.

Try to get back to sleep, but my brain is up early and has a lot to do today. Must work on the book and also work out a speech for the awards tonight. Feel very lethargic and not looking forward to either of these tasks.

Light a fire, for the weather's colder now, not far from freezing. The pressure's so high the barograph needle is almost off the graph.

Work in the garden and, as dusk falls, take a short run, then dress up and get down to the Savoy Hotel to face the photographers, TV cameras and lots of successful people [at the *Evening Standard* Film Awards].

Am sat at the top table! Duchess of Kent, Michael York (wearing make-up,

1 An international volunteer group set up in New York in 1979 to combat street crime.

which worries me until I realise he's compering the occasion), Billie Whitelaw, Mrs Charles Dance, Bob Hoskins.

An excellent tableful. If Helen had been there she would have fitted in very well. Billie and Mrs Dance and Mrs Hoskins all, like her, down-to-earth and quite undazzled by it all.

Most people a bit nervous as they're to give speeches, and our table collects three awards – Billie for best actress in *The Dressmaker* and Bob for best actor in *Roger Rabbit* and *Lonely Passion*[1] and I, by proxy, for *Wanda* as best film.

Michael York is very nervous and reads his appalling script with difficulty – but after a while rallies and is very charming, even when he can't remember Jack Clayton's name. 'A great British director, one of the foremost names of British cinema for several decades, let's welcome …' then, rather lamely, '… him.'

Charlie, expansive at the microphone collecting the Peter Sellers Award for Comedy. 'People are always saying how much they like working with directors. Well I enjoyed working with actors.' Touching really.

Bob Hoskins is as exuberant as ever and we enact our usual 'When will we work together?' litany. Bob comes up later, fresh from a trip to the loo, with an idea about a plumber who becomes a vampire in modern London. 'That's the one!' he enthuses.

Friday, February 3rd

Drive out to BBC Kensington House for my first glimpse of the rushes of *80 Days*.

Am struck by how much longer interviews seem on film than when you're filming them. That and my walk. Ron Brown was quite right, my feet stick out at 45 degrees when I'm not concentrating, my shoulders fall and I lead off with my stomach. Not a pretty sight. But I'm quite pleased that I never look quite as debilitated as I often felt and that my interviewing is more revealing and energetic than I feared.

Buoyed by what I've seen, I stay on for a quick lunch and a couple of hours more into the afternoon. The two editors have different assessments of what they've seen. The fair-haired, striped-shirted Howard Billingham feels that we are light on material. Dave Thomas [the other editor], on the other hand, says he's 'captivated'. He's been watching solidly for a week and is still caught up in the story. Roger and Clem talk in terms of a possible seven programmes.

It's all quite confusing. All I know is that the seascapes and the shipboard shots lose out on film. Well shot though they are, they mean little out of

1 Bob Hoskins starred in *Who Framed Roger Rabbit?* and *The Lonely Passion of Judith Hearne*.

context. The people and the faces and the land action are the strengths of what I've seen today.

Monday, February 6th

Lunch at Café Flo in Belsize Park with Connie B. I'm not sure how well I sell *American Friends*. It sounds confusing as I tell it, but Connie is interested and my approach is as candid as possible, indicating my doubts over the last two and a half years of the project and for the future as well.

Helen is very angry at supper about the filthy conditions at Gospel Oak School. Some cleaners are off sick. No money for replacements. The headmaster cleans the lavatory himself.

The demoralisation of everything we held dear and cared about in the '60s and '70s is tragic to see. Thatcher has turned us into a selfish, greedy country, supporting and rewarding those who want to make money at the expense of those who are happy to work for nothing more than pride in doing something good.

Perhaps I should be saying this. The trouble is, if I wrote a film about 'everything that's wrong', it would quickly date and I haven't the temperament to maintain anger about anything for very long.

Tuesday, February 7th

Connie calls; she'd been trying to ring me all morning. Says the screenplay is 'beautifully written' and is complimentary about the feel and the 'texture'. She would very much like to do it.

Promise to send her a couple of tapes of my work with Tristram – *Number 27* and *East of Ipswich*.

At 4.30 to William Ellis for Parents' Open Day for the sixth form. Chance to meet Will's teachers. The school does look very run-down. Tragic when you compare the money spent on corporate offices to the lack of money spent on something as vital as education.

My respect for the teachers is increased. Most of them are lucid, helpful and prepared to spend considerable time talking about the children. But it is a rather depressing world and Will's success in the Oxford exams seems all the better considering where it's sprung from.

To Odette's in Primrose Hill for dinner with JC.

He's off to California until mid-April. He wants some time to think, read, clear his mind and decide what to do next. 'I've done everything in comedy, Mickey, there's nothing else I want to do there.'

He tells me of his experience of writing party political broadcasts for the SDP/Alliance. One was all about admitting you've made mistakes. John incorporated some references to Steel's and Owen's differences of opinion on defence.

Owen saw the script and rang John to say he didn't feel that the defence differences should be talked about. JC asked then if there was any other sort of mistake or misjudgement which might be acceptable. Owen, after thinking for a while, said 'I don't think we've made any.' From that moment JC knew he and the SDP/Alliance would never really get on.

Kingsley Amis is at the window table, with three women. When it comes to putting his coat on to leave, he shuffles the length of the restaurant with it half off his shoulder until he can find sufficient room to swing the other shoulder in. One feels he'd rather go half a mile with it like this than have a waiter help him.

Wednesday, February 8th

Dream on and off about the Python meeting that lies ahead. Funny how we met daily, month after month, and now our get-togethers are so infrequent and our reputation so inflated that meetings take on an aura of significance – as if we're somehow affected by our own publicity.

A call from Steve to tell me that the BAFTA nominations have been leaked. *A Fish Called Wanda* has nine, and I have one for best supporting actor alongside David Suchet (*World Apart*), Peter O'Toole (*Last Emperor*) and Joss Ackland (*White Mischief*).

To the Python meeting, held in the echoey downstairs room at Prominent [in Delancey Street, Camden Town]. JC and Graham are there with TG. Graham's appearance strikes me immediately. Apart from looking dreadfully thin, he has red stains across either side of his face, from ear down to the neck, on the left side of which is what appears to be a billiard-ball-sized growth.

'How are you, Gra?' 'I'm fine.' And he goes on to tell me that he has cancer of the throat and is receiving radiation treatment, hence the red flush. He will have completed the treatment by the end of the week and it will, he is confident, have eradicated the growth. But with his pale, drawn face, and spasms of pain as he swallows, he looks very sick indeed. He is quite open about what's wrong and only asks that we do not let it out of the room, for fear of what the press will make of it.

To work and the various 20th anniversary options. No-one cares a great deal about 20th anniversaries, and my suggestion is that we let Charles Brand

and John Lloyd[1] loose on our material to make not only the documentary they pitched for, but also the clip-show which we ourselves are supposed to compile and link. We've all sent in our selection of sketches. 'Isn't it typical of Python,' observes John, 'that's there's no one sketch which all six of us can agree on.' Later he finds that there is one – 'Cheese Shop'!

Then much looking at diaries to decide on next meeting. GC will be in the States from May to August shooting 'Ditto', in which he will be playing the lead. John away until mid-April. TG off round the world. Everyone impossibly committed.

So we all disperse. I go across to the Edinboro Castle for a drink with Graham. He laughs. An ex-alcoholic, homosexual with cancer – he's become the perfect chat show guest. So many shades of the old Graham, dry, funny, wonderfully aware of the absurdities of life that I pray he will look better next time I see him. And an awful, sharp pinprick of doubt somewhere tells me I may not see him again. There is an air of doom about him. TG is characteristically blunt. Gay, alcoholic – he wants to be the first to die as well!

'After today I know we'll never do anything together again,' says TG over a scotch in the Edinboro.

Friday, February 24th

Graham C rings. He has just finished his course of radiation therapy. He sounds much happier and says that he was given a slightly stronger dose of radiation than is usual because his system was deemed strong enough to take it. This he was very proud of, but I suppose it begs the question of why it was necessary to give him more.

But it's now just a question, as GC puts it, of 'collecting up the debris' – meaning possibly minor surgery on glands in his throat. No permanent damage except a few hairs on the nape of the neck. His voice is coming back and he's off to New York at the end of the week to sort out 'Ditto'. Brave man. Find myself quite moved by his straightforwardness and practicality in the face of something as traumatic.

Monday, March 6th

Into town to meet Terry at George Akers' cutting room – De Lane Lea. Some glimpses of *Erik* on the Steenbeck are impressive. Looks as good as a Gilliam

---

1 Charles Brand is a film and TV producer. John Lloyd, who produced *Not the Nine O'Clock News* and devised *QI*, had made a previous documentary on Python.

film. In fact, it looks like a Gilliam film (which might possibly be a disadvantage). But strong on design and lighting and camerawork and performance and script (literate) and editing. Looks to be a winner.

TJ and I to Sutherlands.

Good talk about Prominent. TJ thinks it's finished and has virtually told Steve so. Terry will work with the same team that made *Erik* if he does another film. He's starting to work on *The Man Who Could Work Miracles* and we discuss some ideas on that.

The bill is enormous. TJ takes a while to arrive from the table; some rich Americans at the table next door buttonholed him to ask the name of 'the guy who was at the table with you'. They then went into a panegyric about my comic talents, which TJ had to listen to, ending up with 'I hope he paid for your meal'.

We laugh a lot at this, as we walk, on a warm, still, multi-odorous evening, down Broadwick Street, which is being recobbled.

Thursday, March 9th

Letter from Al L [Al Levinson, my New York writer friend]. Problems continue. He has a lesion on his liver, only discovered because he specifically asked them to check it out when going in for a hernia operation. It's operable, they say, and he may go into Mount Sinai Hospital. A surprisingly perky letter, though.

Like a driven man, I head on into the Pacific commentary. Enormous difficulty in maintaining enthusiasm and commitment, but haul myself up to the end of Day 57 before a run and then again into town – this time to see Alan Bennett's *Single Spies* with Eric and Tania.

The *Englishman Abroad* is a pale imitation of an almost faultless TV play and its revival on stage doesn't add anything. But the dialogue is always worth listening to. Alan has a Wildean wit and is excellent on observations of his fellow countrymen.

Blunt and Burgess not traitors in the political sense, no deep commitment to Marxism or the Soviet system, just an inability to fit in easily to British life, a feeling of alienation – the Russian connection maintained almost out of spite.

In the second play Prunella S[1] is magnificent as the Queen – this is a performance which transcends mimicry and caricature, it's terrific observation, not only sustained, but growing in substance as the scene goes on.

1 Prunella Scales, actress and married to actor Timothy West. Basil's wife in *Fawlty Towers*.

Friday, March 10th

By Underground to Leicester Square and lunch at Grimes with Tristram. Update on '*AF*'. Tristram is confident we shall make it this year and I think he will push me.

Out to Robert [Hewison] and Erica's.

Good talk, old photos of Oxford. Robert's warning on *American Friends* – I'm not to make it too 'heritage'! He reminds me of the typhoid epidemics in Oxford which almost closed the university at one time.

Monday, March 13th: London–Southwold

Ma says she feels 'very old all of a sudden'. She is undoubtedly thinner, but otherwise there doesn't seem to be much to justify the gloom. She says her feet are now completely flat and one of them is arthritic and making it difficult for her to move.

I usually feel tense and less receptive when I arrive, and unwind over the rest of the day, so I fear I'm not as sympathetic as I should be. I know I've lost a morning's writing and really all I want to do is to get down to it in the afternoon.

Make some progress and enjoy a windy run over to Walberswick. Two herons flap languidly over me as I cross the bailey bridge, long legs swept behind them, parallel to the ground. The gorse is out and the common very bright.

After a bath, a glass of champagne and watch TG [promoting *Munchausen*] on *Wogan*. The audience absolutely silent throughout. Pity, as TG quite engaging, but appears to work hard, and Wogan's only line of enquiry is: are you mad and why spend 43 million on a picture?

Tuesday, March 14th: Southwold

The weather has gradually worsened and when the time comes to take Ma to the Crown for dinner, a fierce, grasping wind is blowing up Godyll Road and bringing slanting gusts of rain with it. Park almost inside the front door and just get Ma in.

A drink in the bar – she a Dubonnet, me a half of Adnams. We're sat in the Parlour Bar, as the main restaurant's fully booked. One other couple and a group of eight, not quite at home here. The women all smoke between courses and the voices are strident, except when they recognise me, when they fall to even more distracting whispers.

I eat haggis and drink a glass of Tyrrell's Flat Red Wine from New South Wales, which is excellent and reminds me that I wrote today to Aunt Betty to congratulate her on becoming a great-grandmother. Notice that Ma had written, in her half of the letter, that there was no sign of her becoming a great-grandmother yet, in or out of wedlock!

Back home, the tempest still blowing. Finish *Jude the Obscure*, which ends in a torrent of tragedy.

Sunday, March 19th

Slow start to the morning. The children go up to Abbotsley for Granny G's birthday lunch, which Helen and I can't make owing to ridiculously early start for BAFTA.

Leave at 4.30, with Helen in a new and very elegant dark blue outfit. She looks in a different league from me! We're there far too early and our driver takes us round Hyde Park for a quarter of an hour. As the car is comfortable and the park about to burst into spring, it's a very relaxing prelude to a long, hot evening.

Masses of photographers as usual and have to stand, grin, turn this way, turn that way, step back a little and eventually, eyes seeing only green spots from the flashbulbs, we're let through.

Bump into Bennett. 'You're the first famous person we've seen,' he says on meeting. *Talking Heads* is up for all sorts, but Alan says he hopes *Tumbledown*[1] will win best play – 'for political reasons' he adds, a bit wickedly.

We're at a table with Jim Higgins[2] and his wife, Charlie and Nadine, a Swedish producer and English wife and Cubby Broccoli[3] and his wife. I think the fact that the evening is mostly dominated by British TV – and fairly radical TV at that – *Very British Coup, Death on the Rock* both winning awards – leaves people of Broccoli's taste rather high and dry.

And I note a sharp and disapproving intake of breath from Jim Higgins' wife when Shawn Slovo, accepting the Best Screenplay Award [for *A World Apart*], said that there was still much injustice in South Africa and a long way to go before a democratic, multiracial society is achieved.

Wanda fails to win Best Screenplay and Best Direction and when Best Actor in a Supporting Role comes up I feel oddly resigned to being part of an evening of disappointments.

1 *Tumbledown*, drama set during the Falklands War, written by Charles Wood, directed by Richard Eyre, with Colin Firth in the lead.
2 James Higgins, head of UIP (United International Pictures) Distributors.
3 Albert (Cubby) Broccoli, American-born film producer, long resident in UK, where he co-produced the James Bond films.

Susan Wooldridge reads the awards after some clips of powerful acting from Suchet and the other heavyweights, O'Toole and Ackland. And the winner is 'Mr ...' (Helen says that she knew it was me then) '... Michael Palin'. A genuine moment of great relief and happiness and as I went up to collect it, all I can recall feeling was how wonderful Susan Wooldridge was. All my absurd gratitude for this chunk of credit was personified in her dignified smile and even some clichéd comment she felt she had to make was not enough to break the spell.

Back to the seat, feeling rather hot and trying to be cool. Cleese won Best Actor and gave a long list of people he wanted to thank, including Sir Basil Smallpeice, Ann Haydon-Jones and her husband Pip, and the Tijuana Brass.

Monday, March 20th

Ring Mum early. She says she was so pleased she did a little dance around the room. That I would love to have seen.

Phone off the hook at ten and try to forget the head-swelling events of last night and concentrate on finishing the book. The Atlantic crossing is as anodyne to write about as it was to experience and I find it hard to breathe life into these last days or to say anything new about ships and oceans.

To the Halcyon Hotel in Holland Park to record a short video for Greenpeace, to promote their views in the US. Peter Ustinov flew in from Geneva to record his, Susannah York was in today, and I catch a glimpse of David Byrne's[1] hunted, raccoon-like eyes, looking up as I climb the stairs. He's doing promotion in England anyway and is staying in the hotel, so was roped in to take part. He hurries away before they can ask him to do anything else.

Back home by half past. In between hearing about Rachel's ski holiday, and preparing lamb chop supper, Michael Shamberg calls. He says he has rights to the old Three Stooges scripts, am I interested?

Wednesday, March 22nd

Up to Highgate to a meeting, called by Eric a 'creative meeting', of TJ, TG, himself and me to try and decide on the future of Prominent Features. The usual attitudes. Eric wants to keep Prominent Features and its cache of money ticking over, but only for us to use as and when we want it, for projects in which one of us must be closely involved. TJ agrees.

1 David Byrne, *Talking Heads* front-man until 1991.

TG wants Prominent to be involved in the making of other people's pictures without direct involvement from ourselves. His arms begin to flail and he rattles off various mid-European names and multi-million-dollar figures and Ray Cooper[1] and Wendy[2] and George[3] and asks why we don't have people like this running Prominent. 'It should be fun!' he protests.

We meet in the Cromwell Room, one of the oldest rooms at Terry G's Highgate mansion. Every time anyone steps outside, Bryn, the Irish wolf-hound which TG used on *Munchausen*, barks in fear. TG mutters gloomily ... 'We had to teach it to bark for the movie, now the fucking thing won't stop.'

Some talk of *American Friends* as the full moon rises into a cold, clear sky. The atmosphere always goes rather chilly when '*AF*' is mentioned. I think I know how they all feel about it, and agree on many of their worries. On the other hand it also brings out the stubborn Taurean in me and redoubles my determination to see it through.

A drink with TJ at the Flask. We've drifted apart a little – as happened when TJ was making *Personal Services*.[4] A film is such an all-embracing project that it tends to subsume one's private and personal life, so I understand.

TJ expresses reservations about '*AF*' being my *Missionary* role all over again.

Thursday, March 23rd

Maundy Thursday. Day of the washing of feet. The first I hear of it is an eight o'clock news bulletin which reports a terrorist threat to hijack a US airliner over Easter. Rachel will be at Gatwick now, preparing to leave for Florida. Are the chances of her arriving there safely increased or decreased by what I've heard? Better security? Not if the other stories about three youths being able to walk into the cockpit of a jumbo at Heathrow unsearched are true.[5]

Whatever, it's further evidence of the way the great problem-solving developments – cars, aeroplanes, battery farming or whatever – simply produce another set of problems.

To Prominent Studios at half past three. My first look at the new viewing theatre – very neat, and with eight sound speakers on the walls and two more at the screen it is a nice toy.

1 Ray Cooper, a musician, also a key figure in George Harrison's HandMade Films.
2 Wendy Palmer worked with Ray Cooper on marketing.
3 George Ayoub, also at HandMade Films.
4 *Personal Services*, 1987 film based on the career of Cynthia Payne, suburban 'Madam', written by David Leland and directed by Terry Jones.
5 Only three months after the Lockerbie disaster, three young men were able to board a 747 in Heathrow's maintenance terminal and sit in the cockpit without being challenged.

The Python scripts are being put together for Methuen to publish in the autumn.

Some interesting work coming in for me. The *South Bank Show* want to discuss something for the autumn, *The Times* has offered me a column (which I turn down) and Tim Bevan was asking about my availability to direct a Working Title film in the summer.

Tom goes off to spend the weekend climbing in Devon and Cornwall, Helen to badminton and me to see Alan Rudolph's *The Moderns* [set in 1920s Paris], which I like very much apart from a caricature of Hemingway which didn't feel right. Gertrude Stein terrifying. Keith Carradine excellent.

A BAFTA winner's placard has gone up outside the Plaza, where *Wanda* has been playing since I was on the dhow. Pass the doors of the Reform Club, locked for the Easter holiday.

Friday, March 24th: Good Friday

Normally I'm wary of public holidays – they leave me, like Sundays, a bit listless and aimless and occasionally depressed – but today and the Easter weekend ahead I welcome with open arms. They've arrived at just the right time. The pressure of the book deadline is relieved, but I'm still faced with the quite pleasurable task of reading the whole lot through at the beginning of next week.

I can ease myself into '*AF*' rewriting, knowing that every day's work I do on it between now and the end of next week is a bonus I hadn't allowed for.

Write a long letter to Al, who goes in to have surgery for his liver lesion tomorrow.

Dinner with Roger M and Susie. Will Wyatt[1] and wife Jane, who restores pictures, also there.

Roger and Susie have a little house in a low and unpretentious terrace at the back of Shepherd's Bush. They have two bicycles in the hall and four BAFTA awards on the piano.

Roger returns persistently to his theme of the evening – his determination to apply for the job of Head of Religious Broadcasting. He claims to be quite religious – 'I could dispute with the elders' – and a 'smells and bells' man, who would fight against the phasing-out of Latin and the phasing-in of women priests. Helen and Jane take him on quite successfully.

We end up singing hymns at one o'clock in the morning.

---

1 Will Wyatt, Managing Director, BBC Television.

Tuesday, March 28th

The Zimmermans arrive at quarter past seven. Paul[1] is now a rewrite man. He says the money's much better, he's good at it, it's less agonising and his Apple Macintosh reduces 12 weeks' work to seven!

After an excellent supper of tomato and mozzarella salad, chicken marinaded in herbs, white wine and garlic we sit by the fire and talk.

A '79 Pauillac delighted Paul Z and he is eloquent without being overpowering. Says interestingly about *Ripping Yarns* that, though he liked them very much, they lacked the 'killer touch', as he puts it. *Fawlty Towers* had that touch, had the sense that the writer had sweated and suffered to get it right. The *Yarns* were gentler and he felt they were written by someone who 'wouldn't die for them'!

I know what he means and it's revealing that the differences of personality, temperament and character between JC and myself should be carried through so clearly into our work.

Paul had not much liked *Wanda*. Thought it hard and cruel and redeemed only by comedy. It doesn't seem to be an East Coast intellectual's film. Which is probably why it made so much money in the States.

Friday, March 31st

A photo on Hampstead Heath for the *Sunday Mirror Magazine* to accompany an interview about the benefits of walking and the problems for pedestrians in London. This is conducted in our garden over a cup of tea. The journalist talks more than I do, which is quite a feat.

Then out to see *The Vortex*.

Full house at the cramped little Garrick, and an excellent performance. Starts mannered and predictable, with Tristram Jellinek doing a Coward take-off. My spirits sink for a while until revived by Maria [Aitken] and Rupert Everett, who are brilliant. Missing nothing – the teasing, the wit and then the awful pathos underneath. The final bedroom scene played at full blast. Best experience in a theatre so far this year.

---

1 Paul Zimmerman, wrote screenplay for *King of Comedy* and *Consuming Passions*, which he adapted from original Jones and Palin TV play *Secrets*.

Sunday, April 9th

Decide not to agonise over work decisions today but let the day pass with as little pressure as possible. Sport helps and play an hour's tennis with Helen in the afternoon.

Kevin K calls from Tacoma, Washington – he begins a movie with Joan Plowright, Tracey Ullman and Larry Kasdan tomorrow, [the film was *I Love You to Death*]. Kevin is funny about his Oscar speech. Apparently something about 'Charlie Crichton – one man and his dream' was censored by Hollywood. He'd originally written 'one man and his drink'.

Ring Eric and wish him well on *Nuns on the Run*,[1] which also starts shooting tomorrow. Eric sounds very calm and relaxed about the whole thing ... 'It's just acting, Mike, no big deal ... I just stand where I'm told to and move to the left and right and work with nice people, take the money and go home.'

Tuesday, April 11th

I drive at a quarter to ten out to Clem V's house in Ealing to look at the 75-minute compilation of episode two of *80 Days* and a 45-minute assembly of the dhow days.

Without music, or explanatory commentary or a sound mix, all of which act as useful cover, my misadventures are laid out nakedly.

Bons mots are equally matched by maux mots, and I am, as I suspected, far too readily agreeable and conciliatory about everything.

But I find the 'long edit' of the dhow quite beguiling. It is increasingly rare to have time for anything on TV. Information must be imparted ever faster to an audience presumed to be easily bored and constantly distracted. The dhow works better for being longer. Its unusualness and charm remain the single strongest impression of the journey and I think that, in order to put this across to an audience as faithfully as possible, we must accord it a fair share of the film. But it may mean seven episodes.

Home and look at the 'Great Railway Journey' to compare my efforts with what I've seen today. There seems little difference except that I've aged a lot. I look preternaturally schoolboyish and unblemished in 1980. Can I have turned into W. H. Auden quite as quickly?

A couple of phone interviews re *Wanda* for Australian video. To bed reading a good poem by Byron about ageing. He considered all his naughty times over at 30!

---

1 *Nuns on the Run*, written and directed by Jonathan Lynn. Idle starred with Robbie Coltrane.

Thursday, April 13th: Southwold

Mum's breathing is alarmingly difficult. Wonder when, and if, she will need oxygen, Dennis Hopper-style,[1] to keep her going.

Take her into the doctor's. As we get out of the car on the High Street she says 'Come again soon ... because,' and here she drops all pretence of perkiness, 'I feel very old.'

Beginning to worry about these moments when the effort of keeping going is too much and the defences come down. Compounded by the death of one or two of her closest friends – Alice Murnane, Joan Macpherson – she seems to have less to look forward to.

Back to London and to Prominent Studios. Coded security locks have been put on all the doors and we, who've paid for them, cannot get in because no-one's told us the code.

To a Redwood meeting. [Redwood Recording Studios were a joint project with André Jacquemin, myself and Bob Salmon, an accountant.] The elation and excitement of owning and setting up the studio has been replaced by the sad realisation that it hasn't turned into the butterfly we'd all hoped for. Profit margins are still tiny, so investment, let alone repayment of original loans, is currently impossible.

André seems to have lost some of his vivacity, persistence and urgency and, having never found anyone he'd trust to help him run the place, he's paying the price in overwork and we are reduced to giving half the facility to another company in return for a small guaranteed income.

But he's made a very professional job of the new Sheila Ferguson single 'Misty' and I hope and pray it works for him. Tom leaves his temporary job at the studio tomorrow – not a moment too soon, I fear.

Awful gloomy today. Neither Mum nor Redwood seem as likely to survive as I'd thought.

Saturday, April 15th

Late breakfast. Tennis in the sun at Parliament Hill and back by 4.15. Rachel tells us the news of the awful happening at Hillsborough.[2]

The story is still breaking and pictures that should have shown a classic struggle between two of the best teams in the League – Liverpool and Forest – show a battlefield of a different kind. Crushed bodies stretched out all over

1 In David Lynch's film *Blue Velvet*, Dennis Hopper plays Frank Booth, a sinister villain who wears a mask to breathe.
2 Ninety-six spectators died and 766 were injured during the FA Cup semi-final. The police were blamed in two public inquiries for lack of control and for the alteration of evidence.

the pitch, small knots of police, supporters, officials, all bearing that stunned, deadened look of anxiousness and disbelief. Ten killed. Fifty killed. Seventy killed. A crowd, out of control, ironically killing itself on the barriers only put there to prevent crowds getting out of control.

The cameras, all there to record happier things, caught filming an appalling disaster as it happens – as if in slow motion. Hillsborough, one of Sheffield's proudest attributes, will never mean the same again.

I haven't felt quite as sick about a tragedy as this, and Britain's been full of them these last few years.

Sunday, April 16th

Helen and I dress up in our black and whites to attend a gala performance of Chaplin's *City Lights* with score arranged and played live for the first time by the irrepressible Carl Davis and orchestra.

The rain is driven hard and cold at us as we struggle down Tottenham Court Road beneath the HandMade umbrella. A bank of photographers flanks either side of the entrance to the Dominion (which I hear some developer wants to remove).

'Michael!' 'Michael?'

A pushy young man demands to know how Chaplin has influenced my work – 'Just the walk, the moustache and the bowler hat, that's all.'

We're all in our seats for quite a while before the royal person – lovely Princess Diana – steps, head bowed, down the aisle to the front row, accompanied, of course, by Sir Dickie. Then a whole troupe of Chaplins – children, grandchildren, great-grandchildren possibly – follow on. They look interesting and all darkly attractive. The strength of the Chaplin gene evident.

A self-indulgent little short in which Chaplin shows off shamelessly for ten minutes is followed by *City Lights*, in which Chaplin shows off, more acceptably, for 90 minutes. The score big and full, but has inexplicable gaps.

However, quite a treat and, considering how comedy dates, a fitting tribute to the little man who was born 100 years ago, along with Hitler, with whom he shared perhaps more than he'd care to admit. An obsessive personality, extraordinary work rate and generally tyrannical attitude to those around him. In the end Chaplin was the one who achieved world domination.

Tuesday, April 18th

Anne James [my manager] rings and I have a long talk about Saturday and the implications of all the Python 20th anniversary stuff. She has told the lawyer negotiating for us in the US that there will be 15 minutes' worth of new material. Without this the network won't touch us. Why the hell are we crawling to the network all of a sudden? Find myself experiencing considerable revulsion for the whole 20th anniversary thing.

With Terry and Al to Langan's Bistro.

Terry still as angry about things as ever. He quotes *Libération*'s judgement on the Hillsborough disaster that it is a symptom of the class war in England. This seems altogether too simple. The success of a team in a city whose morale and pride had received such a buffeting over the last 30 years is responsible. The Liverpudlian passion, channelled into football and ignored, fatally, by the FA and the police. They did not begin to understand what they were dealing with. The aftermath of the tragedy dominates the news and sobers everything. Ninety-five now dead. The impact seems greater than anything since Aberfan.

Wednesday, April 19th

Yesterday morning's '*AF*' work hamstrung by demands of my Prince's Trust appearance in the evening. Having agreed to do a quick intro, I now have to do two intros, both almost a minute long. This before a London Palladium well-heeled charity audience, the royals, Chas and Di and, later, an international TV audience.

It's not until midday that I have two links I feel satisfied with.

American Friends writing suffers dreadfully after this. I cannot pull it together. I pace the room; wander downstairs at the slightest excuse and generally experience classic symptoms of writer's block. And always lurking at the back of my mind is the suspicion that no project should be as difficult as this to bring to fruition.

Collected by a car and taken to the Palladium.

We are all assembled in a backstage passageway and sorted into a line, along which royalty will pass. I'm at one end between Kiri Te Kanawa, big and jolly, and Maureen Lipman, thin and less jolly (Jack Rosenthal, her husband, is in hospital having a hip replaced) on the other.

Sean Connery, who is chief host, is brought to the line last. Nigel Havers cracks golf jokes with him.

When we are all, rather gracelessly, marshalled into line, we are moved up to the Cinderella Bar and deployed in a wide semicircle as if about to take part in some strange parlour game. The lights are switched on, the cameramen stand ready, but the royals do not arrive for another 20 minutes. 'Five minutes!' We're told ... 'Three minutes ...' 'They're downstairs ...' 'Here we go,' and Charles is working the line; he looks smaller than Diana, who stands rather imperially – she's definitely becoming the part.

Charles is very good indeed at this sort of thing. Considering he has to move around 40 people – some from pop groups, some from films or telly or stage – and find things to say to all, he is amazingly cool and relaxed. Low-key and informal and appearing genuinely pleased to see people.

He asks Kiri Te Kanawa if she'd seen me in *A Fish Called Wanda*. He'd liked the chips.

Diana is less jokey; her skin quite beautiful – pale, but just tinged with a soft, attractive pink. Though it has to be said that both of them could be impersonators.

Off they go into their box and the show kicks off about eight. My first link, introducing Wet Wet Wet, goes smoothly.

There is now a two-and-a-half-hour wait before my next appearance. There's no Green Room, but we're all directed to Connery's dressing room. Here, in an unattractively furnished and cramped space, said to have been re-designed to Yul Brynner's requirements, I sit with Sean, Marie Helvin, Jerry Hall and Rosanna Arquette, sparkling, squeaky and oddly helpless, who's with Peter Gabriel.

Jerry H fixes me with her big bedroom eyes and reveals, amongst other things, that Mick is a different man in his letters than in real life. To illustrate this she does what I think is rather a cruel impersonation of the great rocker's public utterances, but says his private epistolary utterances are very romantic.

I end up grabbing a snooze in the dressing room. By the time I come to my next link I've relaxed too much and fluff my last line. As I stand out there with my hand mike I'm aware of how vast the Palladium is.

I find the LWT transport service has broken down, so I trudge up Oxford Street, collect a cab and am home, having done my bit for the future king, at half past one, almost eight hours after setting out.

As I make up for a lost supper I remember other moments of the evening. The restless, almost snarling vigour of Sandra Bernhard, and Charles Fleischer, a small, energetic, simian figure with thick curly hair who did the voices for *Roger Rabbit* and who prowled the Cinderella Bar as we lined up, shouting, doing voices and rolling a pair of Chinese balls in his hand.

And Princess Diana frowning a little as she met me and opening with 'Aren't these lines awful?' I told her it was like being back at school again.

Thursday, April 20th

Ready to write, by mid-morning. Better progress than yesterday, but as the notes pile up around me and the aubergine script jostles with the yellow second draft and the blue first draft, I feel myself submerged by the material rather than on top of it.

I think back to all the advice that I've been given about the film but what sticks most in my memory is Helen's observation that the things I write best are written fast – from Python material like 'Blackmail' or 'Spanish Inquisition', which spilled out in an hour or so, through the better parts of the *Ripping Yarns*, like the first half of 'Tomkinson', or the whole of 'Golden Gordon', to the best scenes in *The Missionary* (the butler at Longleat sequence).

Helen's always had a gut feeling for my own gut feelings and this afternoon, as fierce, hailstone-hurling showers appear suddenly out of the east, her words make up my mind. I have no choice but to set *American Friends* aside, possibly indefinitely.

Friday, April 21st

Tristram arrives about eleven. He's clutching a huge and elaborate scroll which he unfolds to reveal a painstaking breakdown of characters and scenes. This doesn't make it any easier to say what I have to say.

Tristram listens sympathetically, but his response is stubborn and tenacious and he will not allow me to let it go. He suggests an alternative approach, which is that he works full-time on it for the next three weeks, relieving me of the pressure of sole responsibility.

By lunchtime he's convinced me that I should not turn my back on it, and shown me that, though the road ahead may not be entirely clear, at least it's not a cul-de-sac.

Then on to see David Pugh[1] in Shaftesbury Avenue.

He likes *The Weekend* and wants to put it on. He has some worries, but his approach is rather like mine when I look it through – much of it is very funny, funnier than most other West End comedies (as Bennett observed a year ago) and it should work.

He asks me some questions which I can't answer as I've forgotten most of it, but I leave at 5.30 agreeing to talk further and for him to organise a read-through. He had the same thought as Colin Brough in suggesting A Bennett as director. I don't think it's likely.

Drive over to Chez Moi restaurant in Addison Avenue to dine with JC (fresh back from LA), Alyce Faye (who adores him) and Steve Martin and Victoria Tennant – his English wife.[2]

John stares round the table at each of us. I think this is something he might have learnt from encounter groups. How do we all look? My hair is mocked

1 David Pugh, West End producer.
2 Steve Martin and Victoria Tennant married in 1986, two years after they acted together in the film *All of Me*. Her mother was a Russian ballerina, her father a talent agent in London. They divorced in 1994.

– I can't quite see why, but Steve Martin is very complimentary and says I look the way he always wanted to look.

None of the men can read the menu because of failing eyesight, but only Steve (who is nearly three years younger than me) has glasses. He lets me try them – tortoiseshell half-moons.

Victoria is rather good fun. She and I are the two at table who've never been in any form of psychoanalysis.

Saturday, April 22nd

A full Python turnout with Terrys G and J already there with Graham, looking thin, pale, tight-skinned, but much better than a couple of months ago. JC arrives in his great Bentley which can be parked nowhere but in the central courtyard, with Eric ambling in unhurriedly and helping JC to back it very gently into the wall.

John Lloyd and Charles Brand with lots of bits of paper and Martin Hone, their editor.

First we have a group photo taken, the first for about four or five years. Chris Richardson is the photographer – a recommendation of mine, as was Charles Brand for the compilation.

Then to the screening room and watch about 90 minutes of Python material in three segments. Their choice is interesting, well-linked and -edited and vindicates the idea of having outsiders in, instead of attempting the impossible and making a selection ourselves. Rather heavily leaning on JC, but then he had the pick of the parts in Python and rarely wasted a chance.

It made me laugh a lot and there are one or two scenes, such as the ant salesman in Harrods, which I'd completely forgotten I'd played.

Monday, April 24th

Ma rings me in late afternoon to tell me that the doctor is admitting her to Southwold Hospital tomorrow afternoon, for a week. Then the doctor rings, 'Bill Thom', as he introduces himself. She may have suffered some vertebral collapse, owing to the thinning and brittle state of her bones (due to old age and not eating enough). This isn't quite as distressing as it sounds and may well 'settle down' within a week. She will be able to 'be cosseted and spoilt' in hospital and it will give her the maximum rest and recovery opportunity whilst enabling him to sort out some support for her when she comes out.

All very reassuring, but I can't help feeling that things will never be quite back to normal, that the word 'collapse' is something I'd foreseen as her body shrank and folded and reduced so that it has so little resistance to such an emergency.

Wednesday, April 26th: London–Southwold

At 11.30 I pack my bags and my '*AF*' script and set off for Southwold to visit Mum in hospital.

I sit with her in a small day area, nothing much more than an extension of the ward.

A handsome and undoubtedly well-bred lady sits in one corner and receives visitors in plus fours. A cat perches on the wall outside and Granny and I laugh about the view of the graveyard.

Thursday, April 27th: Southwold

Mrs Kiddy [a recommended carer] could be the salvation, as she seems competent and efficient and energetic and will be able to 'take on' Ma when she leaves hospital.

Round to the hospital and find Mum in better control of things, but still holding her aching back. An hour later I leave her and walk into town, laying some of her surplus flowers on Dad's grave.

At six to see Dr Thom, a young man in a tweed three-piece suit. He says the X-ray revealed the least serious of all the possibilities – a vertebra has crumbled and slipped a little; pain for a week, then three weeks' discomfort. Talk about aftercare. He doesn't think she'll need someone all night, so Mrs Kiddy should fit the bill.

Saturday, April 29th

Off to a Python meeting – the follow-up to last week's. A photo for the *Sunday Telegraph Magazine* set up in the shooting studio. Young local photographer called Gered. JC, in his grey Nike tracksuit, is in imperious form. 'Gered? That's much too difficult. We'll call you Norman.' The session is quite brief. Gered patient with our awfully short attention spans.

A quick business meeting and agreement on most of the minor problems.

There is naked enthusiasm for a Soviet Union stage show from JC and Terry, less from myself, Eric and Graham – 'Who's it for, all the English-speaking Russians?' he asks, pointedly.

We split up at 1.30. John to begin the long process of extricating his Bentley,

TJ to Cambridge to open, he declares rather mournfully, 'An Arctic Festival. Lots of Eskimos really.'

Tuesday, May 2nd

Warm and summery at last. Sue Summers arrives at 9.30 for an interview re 20 years of Python for the *Sunday Telegraph*. Pontificate on the Python years and become pretentious.

Then a run, then to the BBC for lunch with Colin Cameron – an amiable, solid young Scot who is head of Clem's department. He asks me before we leave to let him know if there's anything else I should like to do in the documentary line.

Wednesday, May 3rd

Down to Tristram's – 50 minutes through knotted traffic, but it's a warm and pleasant day and Tristram's artfully disordered house is looking its best in the sunlight. Whilst Virginia mows the lawn, we work through the script, looking at all the new ideas, new locations, new dialogue.

TJ rings to ask me to lunch but I'm really too deep in the material. He walked out of the *Erik* dub yesterday because he was so frustrated with the slowness and incompetence of the studio. I think he needs cheering up and I feel bad about being too busy.

We work for seven hours, winding up after six o'clock, the resurrection of 'AF' confirmed.

Friday, May 5th

Good, deep sleep takes me into my 47th year. At eight o'clock, as I'm about to attack the pile of presents on the table before Rachel has to leave for school, the telephone rings.

It's Mum to give me birthday greetings for the 46th time, but she sounds unhappy and the celebratory call turns into a problem call. She hasn't been sleeping well and her legs are bad and she has to get up two or three times each night. It sounds depressing and worse since, at a distance, I'm helpless.

Back to breakfast and the presents and cards, when Kay Kiddy rings with her assessment of the last few days. 'Four things you should be aware of. One …' She's well-meaning, thorough and working superhumanly hard, but I do find her delivery grates.

A lunch meeting with Mary-Anne Page, a potential American source of 'AF' money, and her partner – who make up High St Films.

Mary-Anne P (ex-Yale) is effusive in praise of 'AF' and cannot quite understand why I'm rewriting a script which she found almost perfect. Even if I only believe half of this it's quite a nice birthday present.

Sunday, May 7th: Southwold

Mum, supported by a stick, is waiting upstairs. As is often the case with her, the first impression is worse than the last. Mrs Kiddy has just left, and Mother looks tired and tiny and tense.

The inescapable fact is that she is in considerable pain and cannot find any comfortable position, and until the pain begins to subside she will not be able to eat or sleep well, therefore have less energy for doing all the things she used to do and now can't – like going to church and walking to the shops and running her house her own way.

The rest of the day improves a little. I give her a glass of champagne and we have a talk over things. She says she remembers being taken up to London at the age of five and being asked to strip in a very cold room whilst a doctor examined her back. He diagnosed some inherent weakness and she was ordered to drink lots of milk.

Wednesday, May 17th: London–Cannes

Steve and Patrick Cassavetti, the two bearded ones, come round to the apartment and we walk together along the Croisette.

The first 'pitch' is to Harvey Weinstein[1] of Miramax, who have two of the few films to have created any interest here – *Sex, Lies and Videotape* and *Scandal*, so is bullish. He works out of a tiny, cluttered room, with three assistants. Patrick greatly approves of this economy.

Surprise myself at how good I make 'AF' sound after all these years. Real Dale Carnegie stuff. Not a doubt in sight. The new work, largely helped by Tristram, does come out sounding fresh, new and bright. Harvey listens intelligently and asks the right questions. We leave over an hour later with his exhortation not to talk to anybody else!

---

1 Harvey Weinstein backed both films, which marked the debuts of two directors: *Sex, Lies, and Videotape*, written and directed by Stephen Soderberg, and *Scandal*, inspired by the Profumo scandal, directed by Michael Caton-Jones.

Thursday, May 18th: Cannes

I'm collected by the beards at half past eight and am surveying other early deal-makers at the Majestic dining room.

At our own power table – with a lady called Sara (specs, Yale-educated) and her assistant Mitch. Problem of pitching at table is that the waiter and his comings and goings become subtly interwoven with the story. It's difficult to pick up the intensity of the film's subtext after a three-minute break to survey the muesli table.

We walk to the Croisette and sit in the sun looking out over a flat, exhausted sea towards Dino de Laurentiis' galleon.

Lunch is at the Majestic again and is interrupted not just by waiters and trips to the buffet, but by the regular fly-past of aircraft trailing the Salkinds' latest – *Christopher Columbus* – which drowns out most other deals.

In the afternoon, in room 131 at the Carlton, I tell the story all over again to Donna Gigliotti of Orion Classics, and in the evening to CBS/Fox – Francesca and a young, rather podgy rich boy called Steve.

Activity of this sort demands rest and respite, which comes in the form of a three-and-a-half-hour session at the Petit Carlton with TJ, Anne, Steve and others. Harvey Weinstein appears, shakes my hand very warmly and introduces Michael Caton-Jones, who confuses me by being Scottish. I'm just telling him that no English directors come here anymore when David Leland walks in.

Friday, May 19th: Cannes–London

Walk round to the Cristal, encountering the redoubtable Ingeborg Hansen and her Norwegian sidekick. *Wanda* doing extraordinary business still; she can hardly let go my hand, such is her enthusiasm.

To the sixth-floor restaurant of the Cristal. Terry Glinwood[1] and his wife sit together beside a long table at which Simon Relph,[2] host, arranges myself, an Indian lady financier from Guinness Mahon called Premila, whom I like a lot better than most bankers, Derek Malcolm of the *Guardian*, the Wingates who run the Curzon, Steve A and a couple of others.

Derek M good value. He won a competition at the Carlton for the best recounting of a first sexual experience. 'Mine was the only one that was gay,' he explains. 'I think they gave me marks for bravery.' 'Gay? ...' 'Well, you know, public school, almost bound to be.'

1 Terry Glinwood, producer (*Rentadick*, *Merry Christmas Mr Lawrence*).
2 Simon Relph, founder and chief executive of British Screen Finance.

Michael Williams-Jones, head of UIP, enthuses 'It's a real-life drama!' and is so much taken with the existence of my great-grandfather's diaries that he thinks we should publish them a year before to build interest.

The day is bowling along commercially, but then thick, cloggy, humid air begins to drip viscous rain as we thread our way past the building sites to the Virgin office to make a final pitch to Mike Watts.

Out to the airport and home by 8.30.

The script is waiting – fifth draft of '*AF*' on which all my enthusiasm of the last few days is based. Read it through before bed. Find it lean, but too severely pruned. Much of the Palin character of the script lost.

Monday, May 22nd

Another look through the screenplay with Tristram.

We work at a table in Café Flo until nearly five o'clock, as I explain my changes. Discuss what we both feel is the unfinished area of the script – that is the filling-out of the three main characters, especially Miss Hartley, in Oxford. The shape, direction and line now simple and clear, but more flesh I think needed.

We both agree that this is make-or-break time for the project. In two weeks nothing will be quite the same again. We'll be either on a roller-coaster ride to a September start, or back, with tails between our legs, having these convivial and creative lunches.

Back home to devote the rest of the evening to proof-checking of *80 Days* book. A similar exercise to *American Friends*, but with emphasis on cutting rather than adding.

Thursday, May 25th

'*AF*' corrected screenplay arrives mid-morning. Make some good fresh coffee and set to reading. Pleased with the result. Tight, with a strong, simple structure. All the characters clear and ready to be developed further over the summer and in rehearsal.

Sunday, June 4th

Look through *The Weekend* prior to lunchtime read-through.

With Rachel to Prominent by 12.30.

Then the actors – Edward Hardwicke, Stephanie Cole, who arrived on her bike from Swiss Cottage with a plastic black helmet. Like her immediately. As I offer a glass of champagne to Julia McKenzie, she says with great enthusiasm, 'Wonderful, we can drink to the death of Ayatollah Khomeini' (who snuffed it earlier this morning). Ben Whitrow, who is to read Stephen, arrives later with a worried expression and a suitcase – he's driving on to Sheffield for a Friends of the Earth benefit.

The reading goes very well. Ben Whitrow softer, less bullishly angry than I'd seen the character, but able to sustain well and in the end very funny and moving. Julia McKenzie quite excellent and Stephanie Cole faultless. Rachel [Palin] too is very accurate and funny.

At the end David Pugh says he is now even more keen on putting it on and everyone seems encouraged.

Steve A calls in the evening re *American Friends*. Miramax are interested but they're worried that the lightness and humour of my pitch are not so clearly there in the script. Jim Higgins of UIP thought it very good. Simon Relph and Michael W-Jones should report over the weekend.

Monday, June 5th

Clem V rings with the encouraging news that Colin Cameron liked the *80 Days* rough cuts enough to recommend to Jonathan Powell that the series be extended to seven shows, and Powell's reaction is awaited.

As Will labours through the first of ten days' A Level exams, I embark on an unscheduled rewrite of *The Weekend*, adding a new last scene which works quite pleasingly.

Wednesday, June 7th

Miramax have asked if we would be prepared to look at Sally Field or Diane Keaton instead of Connie. I see no point in such compromise. I know Connie is not a name, but I also know she will give a performance at least as good as either of them and she is here and can write and is a friend and we've worked together – all enormous assets to the film.

Friday, June 9th

Into town, park car and run through the West End to the Wardour Mews offices of Palace Pictures – small, cluttered premises with only some cans of film, VDU screens and Steve Woolley's ponytail to distinguish it from some

Dickensian underwriter's office. It looks like *Hard Times*, but with *Scandal* heading for a ten-million gross in the US and even *High Spirits* reviving in Europe, they're bullish. They have David Leland's pic *Big Man* opening in September and they were courting Roger Pratt[1] as lighting cameraman only today. He's our first choice as well.

Pitch the film, but Nik Powell comes clumping in with his mobile phone, 40 minutes late, in the middle of some vital sentence, so I wouldn't say Steve was riveted. We leave the script and, like brush salesmen, troop out into the street.

Patrick shows me Miramax's seven pages of 'notes'. 'The terrific screenplay caused much discussion.'

Scanning quickly through it I'm depressed by the lack of subtlety (make Ashby more physically comical – a stutter perhaps?), but basically they worry about it being more drama than comedy.

Tuesday, June 13th

Complete typing of commentary, then try to knock off a 1,500-word piece for *Good Housekeeping* on *80 Days* – telling the story through the eyes of my shirt.

Writing seems not to present a great problem at the moment. Maybe I've developed a style at last, or maybe I know my strengths and weaknesses better, but I find I can turn from commentary to fluent 'feature' piece quite smoothly. And I have to, as there's no time to dawdle.

Helen and I are to go out to dinner with Steve Martin and Martin Short, but only I go as Helen is struck down with some fierce stomach pains which double her up.

To the Hiroko at the Ken Hilton. Not really my idea of somewhere convivial. The service and atmosphere are about as intimate as a refrigerator. And there is a kind of cultural unease about Steve M. Lingering at table is not his thing – nor indeed an American thing.

Enjoy talking with Victoria T. She took Steve up to see her very county cousins in Yorkshire. It was two days before anyone referred to what Steve did for a living.

Wednesday, June 14th

The hottest day of the year, with the thermometer at 84°, high pollen and very sticky.

1 Roger Pratt shot Terry Gilliam's *Brazil*, later *Fisher King*, *Twelve Monkeys* and *Harry Potter*.

I have been lumbered with two requests tonight – the first being the publication launch of David Day's book *Eco Wars* at Canada House. TJ originally got me into it and the invitation adds that 'there will be a statement on ecology by Michael Palin and Terry Jones'. Now, this morning, a harassed David Day calls to say that TJ can't be there. So I cobble together a short address and, taking a taxi which edges slowly through thick traffic in St Martin's Lane and Trafalgar Square, arrive at Canada House at about 7.20.

Am introduced, do my bit, leave by taxi for the NFT where JC has asked me to attend a Directors Guild interview after *A Fish Called Wanda*. JC to be interviewed by pink-cheeked Michael Winner, on stage. Not at all sure of my function there, nor is Stephen Frears, whose cheerfully bleak, baggy-eyed face looms up beside me on the way in.

He says that *Dangerous Liaisons* has 'changed my life ... changed my life ... I've got a house in Somerset. I don't have to work all the time'. He looks just the same, like an unmade bed. I can't imagine him ever becoming a country squire.

A very large man emerges from the crowd going to listen to John and, taking him to be Leslie Hardcastle, the Falstaffian figure behind MOMI [the Museum of the Moving Image], I grasp his hand and accept his praise of the film gratefully. Am just about to ask leading questions about his life in theatre admin when I realise that he's not Leslie Hardcastle at all, but Norman Willis, head of the TUC.

Frears and I slip in at the back and I realise I've been remiss when someone asks 'Where were you?' – we 'celebrities' having been introduced at the beginning.

JC in complete command – dauntingly articulate, full of ideas and observations which he expands with the care and authority of a great teacher – a man who feels he has worked it all out.

Norman Willis is asleep after ten minutes. A lot of people fanning their faces. The whole thing, with questions, is over by half past ten and I am not required to take part.

JC leaves with Winner in a big limousine and I walk up onto Waterloo Bridge and take a taxi home.

Thursday, June 15th

It's an almost perfect summer's day and I have to stop at Highgate Ponds to watch a crested grebe, who has nested in open water only a few feet away from a busy path, standing and rearranging her nesting materials before easing herself down onto two white eggs. Also see a heron drifting over the ponds and a rabbit, very fat and comfortable, that doesn't even move out of my way.

To Julie's in Notting Hill for lunch with David Pugh and discussion on *The Weekend*.

We decided that it should go forward – to John Dove[1], to cast a directorial eye over it, and to Denholm Elliott for Stephen.

Saturday, June 17th: London–Southwold

I'm on the road by nine. Heavy traffic, but moving, and I'm not at Sunset House until just before midday. Granny moves quite quickly, and unaided, about the house. She has a loose summer dress and cream cardigan – both symbols of the new regime.

She eats a good lunch and we walk out along the Common later in the afternoon. I find that her hearing is quite a lot worse and that she has suffered a loss of confidence in herself, which it will be very hard to replace. She knows that she is slowing down, she knows that she is less in control, and occasionally I see a look in her eyes which I've never seen in my mother before – it's a look of momentary resignation, as if she has an inkling that things are coming to some sort of conclusion.

So, despite all the sunshine and sitting out on the balcony together watching the cricket, and the love of gossip and the digs at her minders, that's why I leave with a heavy heart.

Tuesday, June 20th

Tristram rings early, just after I've sat down to start a day's work on commentary. He is frustrated with the lack of information, drive, energy and direction in pursuing '*AF*'.

This, from a generally calm and tolerant man, galvanises me into calling Patrick. He confirms what I have been left to presume, which is that responses have not been as good as we'd hoped. But as details of any response, good or bad, are valuable, he suggests, and I readily agree, that we should all make time this afternoon to meet and discuss progress. We are eight working days away from our deadline on finance.

The heat builds up in my room as I sit by the screen. It must be almost as hot as the footage I'm looking at – Dubai shipyard, 100°, about the hottest and most uncomfortable working conditions on the whole *80 Days* trip.

Begin meeting at five. General feeling of disappointment/confusion on part of investors. They liked pitch more than script (honourable exception of

---

1 John Dove, director with long-standing Hampstead Theatre Club connections.

Simon Relph). Not antagonism, but bemusement. Also very uncommercial line-up – no stars, except me, new director, etc. etc.

TJ is staying with us tonight. He's mixing at Elstree and, as there is a complete close-down of public transport tomorrow, fears he won't get across London.

TJ has read '*AF*' and before telling me about it says ominously 'I don't want to depress you.' He still feels the film doesn't know what it's about, and that accommodating Miss Hartley and Elinor at the beginning was wrong as it diverted attention from the central figure – Ashby – whom Terry likes.

Friday, June 23rd

Tristram arrives to write at 10.30. Discuss the script again, as he has implemented TJ's suggestion that we lose American scenes at beginning and end.

To Prominent for a hasty meeting with Mark Shivas[1] and Lynda Myles.[2] Not awfully satisfactory – Mark late, Lynda has already seen a copy of the script. 'More passion' she feels is what it needs. I agree.

Have to rush away, eating lunch as I drive, to get to the BBC for the third of my *80 Days* commentary recordings.

At half past two a Xeroxed sheet is delivered warning that the unions have called a strike for three o'clock. About five minutes later another, type-written, sheet announces that the Director-General will talk to the workforce on the internal systems at three o'clock.

No options but to abandon the session and go back to Prominent. As I walk along the corridors of Kensington House, people are either leaving or sitting in groups lounging back in chairs as the monotonous voice of Michael Checkland [Director-General] drones out of the speakers urging negotiation. A scene reminiscent of *1984*.

Saturday, June 24th: London–Abbotsley

Armed with a thick assortment of '*AF*' drafts, I catch the 8.40 local train from King's Cross to St Neots for a final, concentrated assault on the problem script. I have to leave London – the continuing heat is spawning drought talk from the water authorities and disaster from the cereal farmers.

Granny meets me, and I'm at Helen's father's desk by ten o'clock. The garden is rich and full of colour and a thick haze of midsummer smells. The

1 Mark Shivas, film and television producer, including *A Private Function*.
2 Lynda Myles, former director of Edinburgh International Film Festival.

only irritation is the periodic eruption of batches of parachutists from a plane above. They fall, shouting and yipping shrilly and imitatively, whooping with excitement which it's churlish to say is a real fucking nuisance.

I dig away at the Elinor/Ashby relationship, searching for 'more passion' for Lynda Myles and a less perfunctory ending for TG and almost everyone else.

Wednesday, June 28th

Another rail strike, but traffic not too bad as I drive in to Ken House mid-morning to work through fitting commentary for show four with Roger M.

At lunchtime I encounter Colin Cameron, who tells us to go ahead and make the series seven shows.

Thursday, June 29th

At home all day writing commentary for show five, Hong Kong and China. Rather like the journey itself, the commentary gets tougher the further on I go. My eyes ache with the concentration on the small screen, my brain aches with the concentration on *le mot juste*. I feel as if I'm playing some elaborate machine in an amusement arcade.

But I complete by early evening and begin to type it up. Finish at midnight. Reeling.

Sunday, July 2nd

Clear desk and letters in the first half of the morning, after breakfast in the garden. *Monty Python and the Holy Grail* is No. 1 in Athens! *Wanda* still in the Top Tens of Amsterdam, Copenhagen and Stockholm. In Denmark, a doctor died of laughter whilst watching the film.

Drive over to a meeting with Patrick and Steve on this crucial weekend for finance.

The situation is as follows. Nice offers from BSB, CBS/Fox and British Screen; Palace will come in, Virgin deciding. But all the combinations of these offers will not make up the three and a half million needed. However a most unlikely saviour could be LWT [London Weekend Television], who would arrange a cash flow of three million for three UK TV screenings, leaving us to sell the rest.

We still await a definite decision from them and the beards would like me to see Sky TV tomorrow.

Monday, July 3rd

To David Pugh's office to talk about *The Weekend*.

Pugh very keen for me to play Febble and says he can see every reason why it's better to make Febble 55 instead of 65. Then John Dove, a prospective director, arrives. I like him immediately. He talks in sharp bursts, then clutches his face and grins.

He's only read the play once. Finds it 'interesting'. He wants to know a little more of the whys and wherefores, as if he's half suspecting a catch. Why have I written this when I could be making comedy films?

Wednesday, July 5th

Verity Lambert has sent me four scripts from Alan Bleasdale – *GBH* – and she rings to ask if I will play one of the lead roles. Twenty-six weeks' shooting, for Channel 4.

I go to see Rachel's play, *The Godmother*, at Parliament Hill School's 'Drama Space'. She looks to have overcome first-night nerves and plays a difficult part well.

Take the Bleasdale script to bed to start reading. It's a tough part. He's described as early forties, blond, blue-eyed and big. He moves arrogantly and intimidates people unpleasantly. In short, some acting required.

No word all day from anyone involved with *American Friends*! Am now hoping that the whole tortuous process will end, very soon.

Thursday, July 6th

Ring Patrick early.

Nearly two million available from the UK, but it's not enough and Prominent, unlike a Palace or a HandMade, does not have the collateral to borrow a million.

Back to Patrick's office. Feel the oppressiveness of the weather conditioning my views. Feel frustrated and make it clear to the beards that the money must be in place by Friday evening, the 7th of July, or *American Friends* is not made this year. No-one disagrees. Our heads are low enough, and I'm in no shape to take a long call from Margie Simkin re our American casting trip. Who do we want? When do we fly out? It's all squeezing us and we've no room to move or respond.

Home. Read the latest script. It isn't bad. The relationships are richer. It's worth making.

Friday, July 7th

A dense, thick blanket of steam outside. The night temperature fell just below 70°, and a cracking thunderstorm and downpour the only relief.

A run is vital and I leave the house about half past seven. Very atmospheric up on the Heath, which is dripping and steaming. Through the woods it's oddly, unnaturally dark, thick, claustrophobic and unreal. Expect to find strange three-headed beasts or knights in armour battling in glades.

The only people I pass are Frank Bruno[1] and his small, white-haired trainer, walking very slowly up towards Kenwood, deep in conversation, like a pair of dons.

To the BBC to record another commentary. We have done half a dozen cues when a strike is declared and the whole effort has to be abandoned once again.

Monday, July 10th

Simon Relph wants to speak to me. His message is simple. Never has he seen a film that is nearer to being made. We have come so far, done so much. Everyone at British Screen wants it to go ahead. We mustn't give up now. He will put his money where his mouth is, etc. etc. The tide of enthusiasm is unstoppable. Within half an hour Patrick and Steve are confirming our US casting trip and *American Friends* is on.

Tuesday, July 11th

Alan Bleasdale calls. He sounds a quiet, intelligent and modestly self-confident man. He pushes nothing and is anxious not to pester me, and this deadly combination, combined with the strength of the scripts, and the fact that I seem to be his personal choice, make for a cordial conversation and I give a firm as possible commitment to making it.

He says that I must read shows three and four, the ones he's really most proud of, which will reveal why he particularly thought of me. Billy Connolly is his choice for Jim Nelson.

Of course, I sit right down, push '*AF*' to one side, and begin to read shows three and four. Halfway through three I can stay awake no longer.

---

1 Frank Bruno, British heavyweight boxer, who went five rounds with Mike Tyson in February 1989.

Wednesday, July 12th: London–New York

Leave for the airport by car at three o'clock. Flight isn't until seven, but it's another rail-strike Wednesday and we move slowly out to the M4, collecting Patrick on the way.

To the TWA desk. Security tighter. My passport raises queries. 'For what reason were you travelling in an Arab country?' I tell her I was filming for a BBC series ... 'Oh, yeah, I saw it,' she replies agreeably, before going on to warn me that the 1-11 we shall be flying to New York on is a Gulf Air plane – 'but completely staffed by TWA.' Did I have any worries?

To the Mayflower Hotel on Central Park West. A short, squat, middle-aged porter with 'Wilson' on his lapel takes me to my suite. 'The world needs comedy,' opines Wilson, and we crack a joke together about 'smoking seats' on aeroplanes. All very New York.

We take a walk round the corner for a couple of beers at a sidewalk café on Columbus Circle.

A good chat, but Tristram and Patrick are beginning to swap names I've never heard of and it is a quarter to five a.m. UK time and we do have 15 girls to see tomorrow.

Thursday, July 13th: New York

Meet Margie Simkin, mid-30s, grey- or perhaps silver-haired daughter of Russian and Polish Jewish grandparents, now one of the leading casting agents in the US (*Beverly Hills Cop*). She is keen to do it all properly and keeps coming up with new names to put on the list for here and LA.

Interviews in my apartment take the form of cheery hellos, comments on the moment – how they got here, where they bought their dress, the time in England, and so on, followed by my telling of the story. As usual I try to do too much to start with and it's drastically pruned by the time I talk to the last girl nine hours later.

The very first girl we talk to, Brigitte Bako, makes a good impression. Few previous films, but Scorsese used her on *New York Stories*. At the end of the day she's co-favourite with Trini Alvarado, pale, dark-haired, curiously prudish about the 'sex scenes', but very appealing, a good height and match for Connie.

Friday, July 14th: New York/Los Angeles

Wake at 3.30 (still jet-lagged) in my room in the Mayflower Hotel knowing, with absolute certainty, that 'AF' is not ready to go ahead.

Yesterday's gruelling ten-hour casting session revealed a lot:

1. After describing the movie ten times I realise that I am telling them what is not yet in the script. So much of the Hartley/Ashby/Elinor relationship is clear only when I describe it, and not in the script.

2. Martha Plimpton, one of the exceedingly bright girls we saw, was describing a movie she'd been in in Germany. 'It wasn't quite right, I could tell that ... but they all said, it'll be OK ... it'll come right on the day. And, of course, it never does.'

3. Another girl asked if it was going to have any present-day element, any character looking back. This, it occurred to me in this early-morning brain-storm, is exactly what 'AF' needs.

4. The long list of girls in LA means that we shall cut even more into our limited rewriting time back home.

Breakfast time: eight o'clock. Called TP and PC together to dis-cuss my concerns. Neither share my worries or seem at all inclined to share them. They listen politely then tell me that the film is certainly not in 'no shape to shoot by September', but quite healthy. Is my time the problem? My part the problem? My clarity of 4 a.m. desperately hard to remember.

We recall four actresses this morning and then prepare to leave for Los Angeles. Jamie L-C's[1] screeching Cockney greeting echoes along the lobby. She's soon embracing me, much to the amazed delight of a party of Mid-Westerners checking in. Full of beans, she goes quickly into an energetic rap about nannies which bewitches Tristram and Patrick.

Saturday, July 15th: Chateau Marmont, Los Angeles

We find a big, round table in the gardens of the Chateau at which to conduct our interviews. Instead of lunch, I take a dip in the pool, which improves things even more and, for the first time since it was mooted that we should go to America this week to audition, I've unwound enough to accept and even enjoy the idea.

We're just going over our choices after a ten-hour session when Helen rings to tell me that Tom has had a nasty accident and has been operated on at the Royal Free after he fell from his bike and got the handlebar stuck in his

1 Jamie Lee-Curtis, who had appeared in *A Fish Called Wanda*.

stomach. He's conscious, no head damage, no bones broken and no word of any interior damage.

Sunday, July 16th: Los Angeles

Eight o'clock in the evening at LAX. Our TWA 747 for London has pushed back two hours late from the jetty. Tristram immersed in 'The Art of the Screenwriter'.

Steve A has flown in from London. We all met in the Ambassador Lounge in late afternoon to discuss the latest financial position on 'AF'. A final solution still seems, frustratingly, to be just out of reach. An abrupt, unsigned fax from LWT appears to have doused any hopes there – cash-flow problems, they say. But we are to keep going as if all was well.

We discuss a further week's postponement of principal photography.

Thursday, July 20th

All going well until a phone call from Patrick. Sounds grave. 'Steve's had no luck in the States,' he tells me.

Only one shot remains, and that's HandMade – PC and Tristram both agree that we should not accept defeat without at least a call in DO'B's[1] direction. But he's in LA and can't be disturbed until 3.30 UK.

Go up to the hospital to see Tom. He is in a state of constant discomfort and can only get up and walk with extreme difficulty. Some dispute as to when he can come out. An American doctor, whom he describes as 'ruthless', says tomorrow, the staff nurse two or three days. Leave him at 3.30 and return home.

Patrick rings to say that Gary Oldman[2] may be susceptible to the personal approach for Syme. So, just when the film seems to be tottering unsteadily into the 15th round, I find myself talking to an extremely approachable Gary Oldman in New York, where he's making State of Grace. Agents get in the way, he agrees, and he does not give a damn about doing leads or not doing leads. If it's a part that intrigues him he'll do it. A script is to be dispatched fast.

Then DO'B rings. He's at the Bel Air, about to rush out to a day of meetings. To his credit, no gloating or 'I told you so's. His last two million presently tied up in the court case with Cannon and is not fluid enough to hold out

---

1 Denis O'Brien, American lawyer and business partner of George Harrison in HandMade Films.
2 Gary Oldman, English actor who played Joe Orton in Stephen Frears' Prick Up Your Ears.

much hope, but he takes it seriously and asks for scripts, budgets and schedules.

The dreadful uncertainty continues – agonisingly; though now I feel strangely serene and detached from the whole process.

Sunday, July 23rd

A call from Graham C. He's in the Wellington Hospital. His movement became so impaired last week that they brought him in, explored a bit, and found a lesion behind one of his vertebrae. Another outbreak of cancer, in fact. They operated yesterday.

After lunch I go in to see him. He's on his side, but talking quite clearly. Sunday papers scattered around, but no evidence of his having read them. He's puzzled as to why the cancer (which, I note, is the last word he ever uses) should have moved from his neck to his spine. He sounds admirably detached and phlegmatic about it. His colour isn't bad, but there is still an angry red patch on his left lower jaw, running down his neck.

Monday, July 24th

With TG and Maggie to Peter Hall's *Merchant of Venice* at the Phoenix. Dustin Hoffman is playing Shylock (quite a coup for this unfashionable end of the Charing Cross Road) and has secured the tickets.

TG is not sure what the etiquette is. Hoffman doesn't like to know who's out there on any particular evening, and consequently it's difficult to fix up any rendezvous afterwards. However, TG's booked Orso's and hopes to lure him there.

The heat weighs heavily inside. The 'Phoenix' ironic for conditions tonight. A regular Shakespearian production – difficult to follow until Hoffman comes on. He plays his scenes with an excellent Jessica [acted by Geraldine James], very movingly and completely without displays of pyrotechnics or fussy Method touches. He is Shylock, and now always will be in my mind.

At the end of the show we are led round the back, across the compact little stage, and up to Dustin's compact little dressing room. A line of celebs is being introduced, and just to be in the same room as Mel Brooks and Dustin Hoffman on the night one of them has played the Jewish outcast Shylock is wonderful in many ways.

The Brookses leave and eventually there is only us, Dustin, his admirable lady minder and Geraldine James and a couple of the cast left. It's suggested we go to eat round the corner at a Greek café.

We all squeeze out of a back door to avoid the fans. Terry and I are quite seriously asked by his minder to walk on either side of Dustin just in case. As it is, Charing Cross Road is deserted of all but drifting litter, and our rather pathetic Praetorian Guard act soon evaporates.

The restaurant is way off the *Good Food Guide* circuit – in an unfashionable street opposite Centre Point, but the food is fine and there are only two or three other tables occupied.

Hoffman is enjoying himself tonight. He apologises for not recognising me on the first handshake, and proceeds to enthuse about my performance in *Wanda*. He admits this is the first time he's done Shakespeare and he doesn't understand what the play's all about.

After he's gone, Geraldine J, in a cheap denim jacket with badges, says that he's sensitive to criticism – and that people are constantly arriving backstage to offer suggestions. Connery, and, last weekend, Zeffirelli, who thought the whole production was wrong.

Friday, July 28th

Lunch with Tristram and Patrick.

By the end of the meal we have agreed on a postponement [of *American Friends*], rather than a cancellation, and will try to shoot in March/April next year.

Back home, via the Wellington, where I dropped in to see the doctor [Chapman]. He clearly felt hard hit by not being well enough to attend his mum's funeral two days ago ... 'But they gave me Amoxapine in the evening and I thought about her.'

We discuss mothers, childhood (how important it was to value it, remember it, relish it in the way that GC feels Eric nor John ever did), the choosing of partners, exclusion of others, jealousy, etc.

The office has sent him videotapes of classic comedy shows, but the ones which gave him most pleasure were the last six shows of Python. Series 4. His face squeezes into a very contented smile as we discuss these.

He's worried about Terry Gilliam. 'All that energy ... he really must try to slow down.'

Tuesday, August 1st

Patrick Cassavetti calls to give me the encouraging news that his rich friend who deals in antiquities (as opposed to antiques) has read 'AF' and likes it enough to offer a half-million. He'd told the story to a group of friends at a dinner party and it had gone down well. It now sounds as though we might have enough equity pledged to secure a bank loan to make the film. Have a slight suspicion that, even at this late stage, the tenacious Cassavetti would like to have a last crack at the autumn dates, but I'm now more convinced than ever that a postponement is the only course.

Friday, August 4th: London–Southwold

Unable to get to Southwold for the last, rushed month, and feeling that show seven commentary is within striking distance of completion, I take the day off to visit Ma.

She walks well, without a stick, and can get up and sit down without pain. Her voice is brisker, crisper, less laden with the weariness of coping.

Sit awhile out on the balcony. The tents of the Boys' Brigade out on the common resemble a World War One scene. The Scripture Union are running children's games, the cricket square, watered day and night, is a lurid green, reminding us of what the countryside was like in the days when it rained.

The sun is still hot when I leave at six. Straight to a party at Julian Charrington's[1] in Parsons Green.

Talk on until 11.30, then drive home. Someone has changed the sign on Gunter Grove to 'Cunt Grove' so well, I nearly drove off the road.

Tuesday, August 8th

Down to South Ken for lunch with Joyce Carey [90-year-old star of *Number 27*]. Impossible to park, such is the prosperity of this part of town, so am late and find TP and Joyce lingering over a Kir at Bibendum.

Joyce – pink hearing aid (with, I swear, an earring in it), mousy brown wig not quite concealing strands of the silvery-grey original beneath, lipstick applied vigorously, but not quite accurately – is delighted with our company. She's convinced I've just walked in from Saudi Arabia and I give up trying to correct the impression. 'Did you like India?' she asks querulously, in a perfect, if unintentional parody of Noël C.

I ask her what her plans are for the rest of the year ... 'Staying alive,' she returns, with great amusement. Show her the *Times* review, which she hasn't seen. She slips it in her bag most gratefully, but later I notice her take it out and read it.

1 Julian Charrington. Julian was the camera assistant and stills photographer on the first part of *Around the World in 80 Days*.

She remains absolutely on the ball, matching us in food and drink, and clasping both our hands about three o'clock and declaring that it's time for her to leave us alone.

I drive to the Cromwell Hospital to see GC. He's having radiation treatment on his back. In last week's *Time Out* he told all about his condition. Evidently the *Sun* and *News of the World* were onto him immediately after. He told them the truth as well.

Wednesday, August 16th

A taxi to TV Centre to be present at the launch of the BBC Autumn Schedules.

Colin Cameron, head of Doc Features, greets me with a strange left-handed handshake. He is clutching a massive computer printout in his right hand, which is presumably too valuable to let go. He draws my attention, with great enthusiasm, to the figure for the repeat of *Number 27*: 6.7 million, which he thinks very good indeed. As it's nothing to do with his department I am touched.

Then into the studio and escorted by Colin C and Paul Hamann – the other main Doc Features man – to become part of the studio audience for the Jonathan Powell show. Powell sits at a desk with his name on, as if he was an actor in an LE sketch whose partner had failed to turn up.

Clips are shown. The usual unabsorbable mishmash of drama (wife being smashed across the face by drunken husband), documentary (drunken husband being interviewed) and LE (drunken husband jokes).

The hype is greeted with the usual cynicism from the weary hacks, who are given the chance to ask questions of Mr Powell. How much did it all cost, had the strike cancelled programmes and was colour footage of Hitler 'colourised'? It wasn't.

Then the screens are raised to reveal tables groaning with wine and chicken curry. The hacks go for the wine, then fall upon the celebrities. Peter Sissons, looking burlier and more like a Mafioso than I remember, is most popular. Sue Lawley and Esther Rantzen and Anneka Rice and Victoria Wood are the most photographed, and I never have time to eat, nor to talk to any of my fellow thesps.

Thursday, August 17th

To William Ellis to pick up Will's A Level results. I park in the grounds whilst Helen goes in. A boy, white-faced and in shock, wanders trance-like from the school. He sits nearby and buries his head in his hands. A girl comforts him. I've never seen more intense and desperate grief on a face and long to tell him it's not worth it.

Will has three passes, in English, History and Biology.

Friday, August 18th

To the modest home of Tom Phillips, the artist, who is painting the Pythons' portraits. He was described as a 'polymath' in the paper the other day, but is in person not as forbidding as this sounds.

He's done the two Terrys. TJ looks like his mother. He's given them both anagram names – TG is Emily Girlart. Can't think of a female anagram for Eric Idle – but a good male one – Eli Lides.

He sits me, or rather lets me sit, on an African chieftain's chair. Tom goes off to Africa once a year 'at least' and potters about collecting bits and pieces. He likes the Africans and especially their 'quite open and blatant way of trying to con you'. Also he's impressed by the fact that they are nearly all multi-lingual. No lingua franca as in India.

The two hours of being examined and painted pass easily. Slightly disappointed that he's not painted me smiling. (Which I've been trying to do, desperately!)

We go for lunch to a magical place in the Walworth Road – unpromising location, but the name – 'Secret Garden' – for once really describes a place. At the back of the Camberwell antiques gallery, along passages and down stairs to what looks like a sort of artists' canteen. There is a wartime feel about it. Nothing spent on decor, but run by women of great friendliness, in a sort of inspired amateurish way. We sit in the garden, overgrown and run-down, but a wide and serene space which is quite remarkable when you consider the drab blandness of the busy road outside.

We talk about pictures, paintings, dealers. He likes Pissarro, who was a good-hearted man and looked after all his friends, whereas Monet would 'whip your wife away from under you'.

Wednesday, August 23rd

Irene[1] rings with encouraging news that Gary Oldman likes the 'AF' script and will do it, if free. With a positive also from Alfred Molina,[2] we're all set for

1 Irene Lamb, casting director I first worked with on *Time Bandits*.
2 Alfred Molina, actor whose work has ranged from *Raiders of the Lost Ark* to *Prick Up Your Ears*.

Prick Up Your American Friends.[1] I should be delighted if these two can come in, as this will help the film look different from the Merchant Ivory repertory production line.

Ring Al L – because I feel guilty at not having written for a while. He says I've rung at 'one of the better times'. He is still having treatment for his liver cancer (which Helen says is incurable) and has had trouble walking. Takes water pills. Things don't sound too good and I find myself waffling my way through an apology for not fitting in a trip to the US until December.

With Rachel, Will and Tom to Pizza Express in Dean Street. All my children together again for the first time since the start of July.

Will fell in love with Venice and thinks James Morris's book on it the best thing he read in two months. He says he wants to buy a flat there! This strikes me as absolutely the thing to do, and now is the time to do it!

Thursday, August 24th

Taxi to Tom Phillips, for ten o'clock start on next instalment of the portrait. Today he has a video camera set up on a tripod. In his usual diffident way he affects not to know quite how to use it, and says he's only used it on Lord Scarman[2] so far. Lord Scarman rests on the wall to my right.

Tom thinks Scarman 'a lovely man', but thinks that the government probably got 'the wrong man', as far as they were concerned, to report on Brixton. Scarman a great Africophile and knew and greatly liked black cultures.

At eleven Tom switches on the cricket from the Oval. Great excitement from the commentary box when Concorde flies over, and a moment later we see the beautiful and noisy creature fly past the windows of Talfourd Road.

Friday, August 25th

I'm chasing the Venetian contacts given me by Robert H. One, Jane Rylands, is American and sounds confident and crisp. Property? 'Very expensive here.' About how much was I prepared to spend? Throw a figure out. '200,000 ... pounds.' She pauses, only thrown for a moment and soon her enthusiasm is greatly increased. This would offer no problem. A garden ... did I want a garden? A lovely place in Dorsoduro ... Contact definitely made.

---

1 *Prick Up Your Ears* had been one of the big hits of 1987.
2 Lord Scarman. Retired judge, who enquired into the Brixton riots of 1981.

Monday, August 28th

BBC invitation to the Proms at the Albert Hall. This time to see Berlioz' *Damnation of Faust*.

Up to the Council Room, where the rest of quite a large group are assembling.

David Attenborough (is he a 'Sir'? I can't remember) has just returned from Russia looking for the Siberian hamster, 'which I could have bought down the road at Harrods'. He's full of infectious humour and an easy companion amongst all these Arts and Features heavies. He says that when they did find a particularly fine example of the Siberian hamster, his Russian colleague became so excited that he dropped his torch on the creature and killed it.

The performance is magnificent. The Chicago Symphony Orchestra play beautifully and with great assurance, and the massive black-and-white-attired ranks of the Chicago Symphony Chorus are superb. A rich, mellow sound capable of attack as well as the long, gently modulated passages. Quite a wild, romantic story, but everything performed rather decorously, without losing any energy.

Later, the cast come by for a drink. Not the chorus, which numbers 184, but soloists and the conductor, Sir George Solti. Solti, his well-polished head and an almost yellow complexion, appears and is asked whom he might like to meet. No-one seemed particularly to interest him until he set eyes on me. He rushes up and grasps my hand. 'I have seen *A Fish Called Wanda* three times' – here he holds up three of his priceless digits. He asks me how I got the stammer so well, and so on, and for a while I bask in the envy of the great and good around me.

Thursday, August 31st

Blearily, to Tom Phillips' studio for ten o'clock.

He now has a name for me: I'm Milli Panache – and take my place alongside Emily Girlart and Joy Sterner.

Sunday, September 3rd

At Twickenham Studios by 10.45 [to film the Python 20th anniversary TV piece].

Our Jaguar is met by an awkward, respectful crowd of Python workers, Tiger TV personnel and, always hovering, the documentary crew. Too many people, too much respect.

Terry J, fresh back from holiday, is combative as ever. He says he only read the script on the plane back from Tuscany, and clearly had the same sinking reaction that I experienced. It starts well, but goes on too long, and is not Python. TJ doesn't even like what is Python, and isn't at all happy with the inclusion of 'Hearing Aid Sketch'. His view is that the compilation works very well and anything else that goes in will only reduce it.

JC is the last to arrive before GC. He brings his two daughters, a shy but beautiful Camilla, somewhat upstaged Cynthia ('If you've anything for her in your next film, Mickey, she's not a bad little actress') and Dingbat, as he calls Alyce Faye.

GC arrives about 2.30, about three and a half hours after TG and I got into our schoolboy outfits. He looks very frail and his eyes are staring out of hollowed sockets.

His presence is inspiring, but somehow the sight of him in a blond wig and schoolboy cap sums up the whole misbegotten day.

GC, carried and put into position by two nurses, is tremendous despite weakness. He talks and laughs and, even when squashed in a cupboard with the rest of us at six o'clock, is still uncomplaining.

Monday, September 25th

In the post today two double-page spreads from the *Sun* tell Graham Chapman's own story – the alcoholism (GC's claims for his drinking grow more prodigious each time he tells the story), the homosexuality (which seems to be by implication a sort of disease) and now the cancer. Pictures of him pitifully thin, but back at home. Is talking to the *Sun* and being photographed all over your house really the best thing to do on your first week out of hospital?

Anne rings with an unsettling request. The *Guardian* want me to write an obituary for Graham C. Cannot believe this is the *Guardian* and feel very uncomfortable. Do they know something I don't? Are any other Pythons being asked? Anne confirms it's just me. I cannot go along with it. GC must only be thinking in terms of the future at the moment, and so must I.

Friday, September 29th

To Prominent Studios. TJ not able to make the meeting as this is *Erik* launch day, but JC (wearing glasses, I was relieved to see), Eric and the Gilliam are there. Elaborate and confusing figures are disregarded and Anne, who chairs, asks us directly who is in favour of a move (at the right price), from the studios, and who against? Myself and TJ (whose vote I have) are in favour. JC and Eric against. TG wavering towards our side.

I think the Cantabrigians are surprised. Elaborate my reasons. The place has not developed into a Python film-making community, as idealistically intended; the facilities seem to be administratively cumbersome and financially unpromising; André definitely, and Mayday I think, would welcome the move. I would rather keep my involvement with Redwood than be the landlord of some editing rooms and offices.

'Mikey's bored,' John accurately paraphrases. Eric wavers. If we get a decent price – £2.6 million is suggested as a minimum – how much do we make? It works out that we save, and make, up to £70,000.

TG reiterates the arguments, that it's not fun any more, like Neal's Yard was (Anne's eyebrows up here). JC, who really likes the viewing theatre and being able to park his huge Bentley, refuses to agonise and eventually an agreeable consensus is reached that we should proceed into the projected sale, but should accept no less than 2.7 million.

Tuesday, October 3rd

Time Out is the first journal to sow seeds of doubt in my mind over *80 Days'* appeal. A humourless review which whines about the shame of having to 'pour cold water' over the programme and proceeds to do so with great glee.

Anne rings to say Graham has had a bad night and may go back into hospital. He certainly won't be able to attend the anniversary party tomorrow.

Down to the Holiday Inn Hotel in Mayfair to fulfil a series of interview obligations. First an appearance in a documentary about *Viz*, defending the magazine, then a piece about Python's 20th for Australia's Channel 7. The TV crews are so typical of their countries. The Australians grin a lot, are rather like big schoolboys and seem anxious to get it done and go round the pub.

Then hare off home to a longish chat with CBC – the non-aligned, apologetic, intelligent Canadians.

Establishing shots of me in garden. Squirt what I think is water from one of Helen's garden sprays into my mouth as a joke. Later told it's highly poisonous!

Granny G has arrived for Mary and Edward's 25th wedding anniversary party.

We eat late – it's almost ten by the time we are all assembled at Mon Plaisir, Mary's and Edward's favourite restaurant in courting days, now benefiting from the Covent Garden renaissance and no longer having the rather squashed, cosy, plain and unpretentious French presence it had in the bad old days.

Will rings sounding grave. He's heard from TG, who's heard from Anne, that Graham is seriously ill in hospital. He has secondary cancers all over his body and is not expected to last the night. All this over the noise of popping corks and laughter reminds me of my father dying during the football results. There's precious little dignity around. Ring Terry J. Sal [Terry's daughter] answers. He and Alison have both gone down to the hospital.

Back home. It's half past twelve and been a long evening. There seems no point in my rushing down to Maidstone. I'm legally too drunk to drive anyway. Phone the hospital, but can never get through. Sometime after one I give up and get to bed, expecting to be woken any time.

Wednesday, October 4th

Anne rings at a quarter to eight. Graham has stayed alive through the night. The anniversary party this evening is to be cancelled. I agree. There will be nothing to celebrate.

After breakfast I call David [Graham's partner]. Can't keep back a choke of emotion on the phone and feel rather feeble having to curtail the call, but the moment of regret for Gra suddenly so intense.

Sit for a few minutes in the sunshine on my balcony. The telephone rings. Drag myself back in. It's Alison at the office. She's had a call from JC who has just spoken to Graham's brother, John. Gra has only a few hours left to live. John is on his way down to the hospital. I um and ah for a moment. What can I do? Will I be in the way? Consult Helen, who says I should go. Suddenly the tiredness disappears and, I suppose, a shot of adrenaline revives the system as I grab whatever I may need, check the directions and leave for Maidstone.

The traffic is going home all across South London and it takes me over one and a half hours to get to the hospital. It's set in fields outside Maidstone, has some bright, post-modernist pavilions at one end, and a big, heavy Victorian workhouse at the other. Around it a quiet and spectacular sunset is fading.

Long walk to the Cornwallis Ward. Graham is in a private room at the end.

At Graham's bedside are John, his brother, heavier, a quite different shape from the megapodal Graham, and on the other side, holding the hand above which the bandages conceal a drip feed which is keeping Gra alive, is John C.

We talk a while, then they go out and I'm left alone with Graham. He breathes laboriously but regularly.

I'm told that the faculty of sound is known to be the last to go and so I rattle on about everyday things. About my lousy review in *Time Out*, the sunset, the fountain being removed from Prominent courtyard.

David comes in, smiling and relaxed. He kisses Graham's head and smoothes his sallow brow, closes the window a little, tells me that their house is the next one to the hospital, just across a field. He's happy to leave me with Gra. David says a room has been cleared where we can go. I say I'm all right … 'You Yorkshiremen,' grins David.

I walk round to the window then come back to his right-hand side; take his cold hand in my hot one and tell him, quite loudly, that we all love him.

The regularity of his breathing is broken. A long pause, then a long inhalation. His lower jaw rises, his mouth closes and bares his lower teeth. I reach for my cup of tea. He breathes heavily. I start to talk again. A single tear emerges from his right eye and rolls down his cheek. The mouth is set. The great ridge of Adam's apple is still. There is no more noise from him. Nothing dramatic, no rattles or chokes or cries. He's not moving any more.

I don't want to leave him, nor do I want to make any noise or sudden movement. It's a moment out of time. All I can feel is that I shouldn't be here, that David and John his brother should be.

There's noise outside. The clatter of patients and visiting friends. I call John and David to go in. They re-emerge a minute or so later. Graham is dead. It's about twenty past seven. John C, David Sherlock and I hug one another together. Tears but not in torrents – just filling the eyes. David S is quite magnificent. He makes it easier for everybody by being genuinely pleased and relieved that Graham's suffering is over.

I drive him back to the house at Barming – ironically the first time I've been there.

David shows me the house. It's unreal to be talking as if it's an ordinary day, but then what should one do? This is his way of celebrating Graham – the rooms he lived in, the chaos of newspapers and magazines.

There was an easel with a rough-and-ready oil painting of the garden gate – did I know Graham had taken up painting? He showed me the pool and the squash court and pulled two Coxes off the apple tree – 'Organic, of course' – for me to eat on the way home.

I left David cutting an Arctic Rose off the tree by the gate to take to Graham – 'His favourite thing in the garden' – and headed back to London. David said as he hugged me goodbye that he felt elated … 'I know it seems silly.' It doesn't really. I feel something similar as I drive back up the almost deserted A20. Much more tranquil, much more comfortable and at ease than I have been for days. Graham has, after all, been delivered from months of great pain.

I drop in on TJ, who's at home with Al and the children. He's very pleased to see me. He's just heard the news from JC who was lost somewhere near New Cross.

Drink a glass of red.

As I leave, he observes Graham must be the greatest party-pooper in history. I can hear Graham laughing at this all the way down Camberwell Grove.

Switch on the eleven o'clock news. The train of refugees still coming out of East Germany. Odd to know that one is sitting on a headline story which the press still haven't got hold of.

I hardly have time to talk to Helen before the phones start ringing. (In fact as I sat with Graham in the little room he died in, David entered and showed me a name on a piece of paper ... 'Baz Bamigboye[1] rang'.)

I don't want to talk to anyone tonight. Rachel has deflected the *Mail*, Helen copes well with the *Mirror*, and, repeatedly, the *Sun*.

To bed about one with both upstairs phones unplugged.

Thursday, October 5th: London–Southwold

The headline in the *Sun* on the day of the 20th anniversary of our first broadcast is 'Python Star Dies'.

The phone is ringing downstairs when Rachel goes to feed the cats at 7.30. Ask no-one to pick it up until I'm up, washed, dressed and fed.

Then to my desk, at 8.30, and open up the shop. The phone calls come without a break. Fifteen times I tell of my reaction, give my assessment of 'Graham Chapman's contribution' either to the phone, or the tape recorder and camera or, later, in the form of two instantly written pieces for the *Guardian* and the *Telegraph*.

Three TV crews visit the house. I've no time to pour boiled milk for a cup of coffee, and it burns away, filling the house with a frightful pong.

The activity subsides about six o'clock. My first interview was with CBS News in New York, my last with CBC in Toronto. I feel emotionally unmoved today. This is a job of work, but I feel I must do it to make sure the right things are said about GC, the introverted extrovert.

I hear, via Anne, that both TJ and Eric have given up and gone to bed. My way of getting away is to leave for Southwold in mid-evening, just as more American interview requests are coming in.

Book a room at the Swan. Am up at Sunset House by a quarter to ten. Mum fit and well, but needs her hair doing. It lies drably across her brow. Nice hour with her, then to the Swan for a drink with Dudley Clarke, the manager, and his staff before bed.

Friday, October 6th

Clear skies as I wash and shave at a quarter to nine. To breakfast and read three obituaries for GC. My *Guardian* piece reads well, but has three glaring mistakes

---

1 Show business correspondent of the *Daily Mail*.

due to hasty dictation. JC has written a short and well-expressed piece in the *Independent* which, thank God, makes up for an appallingly insensitive piece by their own man which ends up revealing why Graham 'was the one who was ultimately dispensable'. My *Telegraph* piece has had the last sentence about 'why we all loved him' removed.

Sunday October 8th

Tom's 21st birthday.

Rachel makes a 1968–1989 poster and Will does some very silly things on the photocopier with Tom's head and other bodies.

Show some early film of Tom which is riotously received. It's almost uncannily appropriate, too, that one of the Super 8 films shot in the very first days of Python shows Tom as a baby at Remenham climbing over a sleeping, supine Cleese and Connie whilst Graham does handstands in the background, and wanders across frame smoking his pipe!

Monday, October 9th

More parties ahead today, but have to rise early for appearance on *Start the Week*.

At BH by 8.30. Melvyn is dapper in a nattily fitting pin-stripe suit, tie and matching handkerchief. Others on the prog are gathering, including Mark Lawson of the *Independent* – one of my favourite journos, funny, informative and enthusiastic. In jest – well, partly in jest – I complain that the paper I've supported since the day of its birth should rap *80 Days* so severely over the knuckles in Saturday's preview, before anyone's had a chance to see it. He asks after the name of the journalist ... it was one Stephen Pope ... 'Oh, Pope Stephen, as they call him in the office.'

To a viewing theatre at CFS [Colour Film Services] in Portman Close.

People already arriving at the *80 Days* screening. George Harrison, looking on good form with a big, flowing mane of hair, John Cleese, with his mum, and a present of a *Three Men in a Boat* picture, Michael Barnes,[1] looking thinner and more patriarchal than ever. Most of our regular friends there.

I watch it in a sweat of embarrassment, noticing for the first time the dull, intrusive music, the plodding, heavily delivered clichés of commentary, the overlong sequences of Venice and the preparations. Can see quite clearly what

1 Michael Barnes. Director of the Belfast Festival who encouraged me to do my first one-man show there in 1981.

the critics are on about and retreat from the applause at the end to grab a cooling glass at the bar.

Thursday, October 12th

Mark Lawson is the first critic I read and sure enough he leads with *80 Days*. Beneath the rather unkind headline 'Travel Sickness', is a not unkind review.

He opens with the line 'Is it possible to be too nice to be a television presenter?' This 'niceness' is clearly to be used as a stick to beat me with ... What a world. But I like the review for its detail, constructiveness and wit, though I would have liked its conclusions to be a little more favourable. I write him a note and send him a book!

Collect a fat wad of other papers and am quite shocked at the intensity of feeling. *The Times* is a two-line dismissal of all our work, written by Rhoda Koenig, a lady I met in New York some years ago. I remember her as clever but eccentric. (Apparently she dismissed *Miss Saigon* as well.)

The *Express* and the *Mail* both disliked it with a strange vehemence. Nancy Banks-Smith [critic for the *Guardian*] said I'd preserved, into middle age, 'the bright-eyed charm of a baby chipmunk'.

For a couple of minutes my senses smart from the unexpected virulence of these reactions. It's like being spat at in the street. The hurt is quick but does not go deep and my swift surge of anger subsides.

Down to GLR, formerly Radio London. Johnnie Walker is in the chair. An esteemed name from the pirate ships, by way of Radio 1 and now a nicely mellow survivor playing his own eclectic selection of music. Phone lines busy when my presence is announced. One man asks me how drunk I really was in the *Orient Express*. He said he'd been off the booze for a week and really envied me.

A gossipy lunch with TG. He goes on about this last year, which I think has been a blow to his pride – *Munchausen* largely dismissed as an expensive failure; 'Watchmen' never getting off the ground and Prominent Features, his brainchild, in disarray. He variously refers to these misfortunes as a year of doing nothing ... a year off ... a year out. To the restless TG there can be little advantage to what others might consider a welcome break.

Friday, October 13th

Early call from Granny. Most concerned about Lady Collett's vehement reaction to my denunciation in the *Mail*. Apparently Lady C is wild about this slight to her neighbour's good name and, what's more, is convinced that Alan Whicker wrote the review!

Drive to Shepherd's Bush and meet Verity L, David Jones, her fellow producer, Peter Ansorge, commissioning editor of Drama at Channel 4 and, at last, Alan Bleasdale. They have been in a smoke-filled room for a week, going through every one of the six episodes. Verity is anxious to assure Alan that nothing has been lost that shouldn't have been lost. Bleasdale begs, in a gentlemanly way, to differ. But it's good to see the project still strong.

Bleasdale is talkative, funny and gives off a palpable air of worry and insecurity which is attractive and affecting.

He fortifies himself with very large vodkas and is clearly a fish out of water in London. He's staying at the Kensington Hilton – 'A terrible place.' Has he sampled its restaurant, the Hiroko, the best Japanese in West London? 'I didn't know it existed ... anyway, I've never eaten Japanese.'

GBH is going to be some adventure, and after two hours with these shell-shocked writers and producers I feel a breath of cool, fresh air blowing over the next 12 months.

Saturday, October 14th

I spend the afternoon writing a 1,300-word piece on 80 Days for Arts and Entertainment's 'TV Guide' in the US before leaving for Helen's surprise birthday evening.

For company, Mary and Edward, Ian and Anthea and Terry and Al, for hospitality, L'Escargot, for entertainment to Ronnie Scott's, where Hugh Masekela is playing.

Ronnie's, especially on a busy night like tonight, has an exciting, sweaty, smoky feel. It's still a triumph of passion over environment, and the hot, densely packed atmosphere is lively and carries a welcome hint of minor decadence in an increasingly 'styled' and designed world.

Masekela begins with a recital of some impressive lists of jazz greats, beginning with the Deep South cotton fields and on up to Chicago and then into South Africa. The music is played with tremendous attack and great virtuosity, especially from the sweat-dampened Masekela and his slim, high-foreheaded, white saxophonist, who hurls the sounds out with seemingly not a bead of perspiration.

Excitement fulfilled and it's a magic hour's set, which none of us wants to end.

Monday, October 16th

Heavy traffic and don't arrive at Tom Phillips' studio until half past ten. 'If you think your reviews are bad, listen to these,' he greets me, with a clutch of cuttings about his recently opened exhibition of 'portrait works' at the National Portrait Gallery.

A man called Richard Dorment in the *Telegraph* is particularly enraged by what he perceives as Tom's overweening ego. 'He even writes his own labels for the pictures.' And why not? I side with Tom.

But it's a cold morning in the studio and I don't feel in sparkling mood. I look at his watercolour of me on the wall behind him, alongside Terry and Terry and now Eric (Di Celeri). I look rather thin and tense.

Only one man he has painted in his studio whom he really disliked – Professor Owen Chadwick, who, on entering, saw a half-finished canvas. 'Ah, painting ugly old women are we?' It was Tom's mum.

Tuesday, October 17th: London–Southwold

A couple of uninterrupted days in my workroom is the least I need, but I have promised to go up to Southwold, where it is no longer as easy for me to work as before.

Ma more demanding now and less flexible, so lunch has to be quickly served up.

Then take her out for a walk, followed by a visit to Lady Collett, to whom I present a copy of *80 Days*. She is delighted. The two of them, both slightly deaf, have oddly unconnecting conversations ... 'How's Mrs Hurran?' 'She fell over.' 'Is she better?' 'You know she fell over?' Lady C gives us sherry at 4.30 and has to draw the curtains across against the piercing bright sunlight. She suggests my mother and she get together to play Scrabble.

Then the best part of the day – a glorious run across the marshes in the still-warm, vaporous haze of a lazy autumn day.

Wednesday, October 18th: Southwold

Described today in the *Independent* as the 'terminally nice Michael Palin'.

Walk across the Common on a day almost as perfect as yesterday. A harassed master struggles to teach Eversley boys outside Ma's window how to play football.

The fact is, she is bored. She has nothing much to do but sit and wait to be fed and walked. She tries to find things she can do on her own, but these all seem to require more and more effort.

Watch the second episode of *80 Days* together. It's the Egyptian and Saudi Arabian section and I feel it all works much better than episode one. Ma nods off as I enter Jeddah.

Thursday, October 19th

After breakfast, round to Ma's by 9.15. Her *Telegraph* bears the headline 'Palin for Prime Minister' on the arts page. I'm now very jumpy about reviews and sure enough this one, with gushing praise suggesting I have all the qualities for getting on with people that Maggie T hasn't, eventually slides into some mild but wearisome stick! Ma has seen no further than the headline and is quite delighted!

Farewells, feeling a little less guilty this time, and into the car.

To Clem's office to sign books for the crews. Roger quite perky about the reviews. 'What they don't realise is that this isn't a serious documentary, it's a stunt.' I don't think Clem likes this. I think all of us waiting for some unequivocally good news. With anything less than this there is the faint smell of blood in the water at Ken House.

Thursday, October 26th

A warm review from Lawson in the *Independent*, recalling his early doubts, but withdrawing them after this third show, which he described as 'high-class'. Also noted that part of my 'charm' was an 'unsneering' way with foreigners.

A message from Stanford's to ask if I could come in early for my book-signing as they have had a surge in orders after last night's programme.

At Stanford's just before twelve, and continue signing until 2.30. They have never experienced anything like it. Trolleyloads of my book wheeled in like piles of bricks. The queue still full an hour after I was due to stop.

Fight my way out of the shop to lunch with Clem at Grimes in Garrick Street, pursued and accosted by locals bearing books or just scraps of paper. Clem confirms that there is now better feeling about the series in the corridors of the Beeb. Oysters and Sancerre and slowly cool down from the excitements of the morning.

I've promised I will go back to Stanford's and sign the rest of the stock. This takes a further one and a half hours, and by the time I fold myself into the back of the taxi I've signed over 650 copies.

Friday, October 27th: London–Stocks House, Hertfordshire

Clem calls with the best news of the *80 Days* transmission thus far – the viewing figures actually built, on the second episode, to 8.6 million.

Back home and into a hectic hour of packing for JC's 50th birthday party.

JC's present, a 1939-bottled Armagnac, arrives, as well as his Margaret Thatcher plate. Neat timing in view of Lawson's resignation.[1]

Leave for Stocks at 7.15, arrive at the house less than an hour later. We've been given a room with a waterbed. Already guests gathering in the hall with their obligatory funny hats on.

Jeremy's sheep on my head is easily the biggest and silliest and most inventive. David Hatch later says it's a hat which grew more silly as the evening went on.[2] Every time he looked up and saw me talking earnestly or toying with white wine and smoked salmon, the sheep on my head, wobbling and nodding, gave him more and more pleasure.

The 'entertainment' works extremely well. All my props, especially the parrots and the spangly jacket I found at the last moment, are greatly appreciated, and I read the *This Is Your Life* joke intro smoothly, despite this being the first time I've worn my specs in public. David Frost, John Lloyd, David Hatch (very, very funny in a deadpan BBC way), Stephen Fry ('Some men are born great, some achieve greatness and some have greatness faxed through to them') and Peter Cook – not as good on his feet as he is at table – make the awards, and Shamberg shows some video tributes, including one from Jamie who is seen at home greedily apportioning her *Wanda* money – 'house', 'education', 'divorce'.

It's all a great success and it's a quarter to two before Helen and I climb aboard the waterbed, bringing on distinct memories of the dhow.

Saturday, October 28th: Stocks

Strong winds assault the house and rain is hurled against the windows. We're at breakfast just after Peter and Lyn Cook and just before the Frosts. David and Carina are rather a lovable pair. Carina wipes egg from David's lower lip as he rises to pay us a gushingly appreciative goodbye.

We read the papers in the soft-cushioned hall, then walk a while in the sunshine. Then some table tennis. I beat Helen, but lose to Peter C, who is a very large man now. He was the only one who sported fancy dress at the party last night. He came as Demis Roussos.

We all go to lunch at the Bell at Aston Clinton. Feuilleté of mushrooms, stuffed salmon en croute (always too rich and yet I always fall for it) and sweet puddings.

1 Nigel Lawson, Chancellor of the Exchequer in Margaret Thatcher's government since 1983, resigned over the role played by Sir Alan Walters, the Prime Minister's economic adviser.
2 David Hatch was an ex-Cambridge Footlight and close friend of John's who rose to become Head of Radio at the BBC. He died in 2007. The upturned sheep on my head was made for me by my nephew Jeremy Herbert.

Alyce Faye's birthday evening more subdued than the night before, but some fresh blood – Kevin K, the Hutchisons, M Winner and the lovely Jenny Seagrove. Winner makes a speech in which he says how nice it was to meet everyone at lunch, even if 'the sole topic of conversation was Michael Palin's hat'.

The lights go down mid-meal and we all prepare to sing 'Happy Birthday', but it turns out to be a power cut.

Sunday, October 29th: Stocks House–London

We are down at breakfast at nine.

Peter C arrives, looming, shambolic, cigarette held rather daintily in right hand, hair awry and one trouser leg suspended mid-calf. He says he was woken in horrific circumstances when the electric current came back on in the middle of the night. Apart from the lights, his radio and TV came back at full volume and his hairdryer began to writhe across the floor.

It's a very funny breakfast. At our different tables in this elegant dining room, united by the music of Kenny Rogers on the PA, discussing bribery and smuggling. Peter observes that the first rule of bribery is to bribe the right people. Carter DeHaven, the *Yellowbeard* producer,[1] spent large sums from the budget lavishly entertaining locals in Mexico City who had no influence over anything at all.

Leave a message for JC, who has not yet appeared, and drive down leaf-sodden lanes into a brilliant blustery morning.

Only cloud on an otherwise clear horizon is from my Ma. She says that her back has gone again. Dr Thom who was so excellent in May has gone to Australia. So she's back on painkillers and sounds a bit low.

Saturday, November 4th: Glasgow–London

Wake, at the Caledonian, in much the same state as I awoke last Saturday at Stocks. In a room verging on the vulgar, much bigger than any room at home, with a soft wash of luxury and indulgence about it, and in my mind a clear and clean feeling of work done, of tests survived successfully, of the calm after the storm. All that and the hint of a headache.

To breakfast, then catch the eleven o'clock shuttle south.

Since Monday morning I've signed 3,110 *80 Days* books. BBC Books have

---

1 *Yellowbeard* was a 1983 comedy produced and co-written by Graham Chapman. One of the cast, Marty Feldman, died during the filming.

authorised a 45,000 reprint, larger than the original first run, and Clem told me last night that a further 300,000 have been added to the viewing figures, taking it up to 8.9 for the bowels and bum episode on the dhow.

Sunday, November 5th

The *Sunday Times* best-seller list is required reading (meaning I have to make a special journey to fetch it and all its concomitants), showing me in there at No. 3 on the Hardback Generals. Any great feelings of literary achievement tempered by the fact that the book above me is the complete *'Allo 'Allo!* scripts. Denis Healey is top.

Long, slow unfolding over breakfast. Thatcher really does seem to be wobbling now. The look in her eyes on last week's Walden show was that of a trapped rat. Today in the *Correspondent* she is, for the first time, equivocal about staying on to lead the party.

Monday, November 6th

More confirmation of the *80 Days* effect from Anne – Tesco want me to go to various parts of the world to extol their food products, and have offered me £200,000.

In mid-afternoon I go for a run. It's cool today and harder work than expected. Meet Denis King, who is playing at Maureen Lipman's Joyce Grenfell show, *Re: Joyce!* Says it's packed every night.

Now Maureen did ads, and they didn't do her any harm. But somehow it would be such a letdown. Q: What are you doing after *80 Days*? A: A series of commercials for Tesco. Not really on.

Friday, November 10th

Clem calls at 11.30 with the viewing figures for programme four. Good news indeed – a hoick in the audience of 1.3 million to beyond 10 – 10.2. 'We've made it,' says Clem. 'Time for the champagne.'

I don't think I've ever done anything that's pulled in a 10-million audience. For Clem today must be the vindication of all his work. We could fall back, but to have passed 10 on the fourth show represents unequivocal success.

Give an interview to three Arab women – living in England – for a magazine about Muslim affairs. They loved the dhow episode and felt it showed the best of the Muslim way of life – the hospitality, the food, the prayer, the simple values, etc. I was pleased and must write again to Dave Thomas, the editor, who first said the dhow should be an entire episode.

I wash and shower and come down to find a bottle of champagne from Fortnum's and a note from Suzanne Webber to say that my book is No. 1 this week on the best-seller list!

Then TJ rings from Berlin. Almost speechless. *Erik the Viking* opened in Germany on the night they began to pull down the wall. Extraordinary times, he says. The streets full of people in an emotional state. Complete strangers clutching each other. Euphoric happiness.

Tuesday, November 14th: London–Southwold

The fog grew thicker the nearer I came to Southwold. Last few miles very slow. Arrive to find Ma looking like Joan Crawford in her later days, haunting the top of the stairs. 'Oh, Michael! Oh ... I was so worried,' and so on.

Bite my lip – what good would it do to tell her I was driving carefully in fog, that I had said teatime? Anyway, calm and restore her to her chair. But she is not in good shape. The wretched back pain seems to keep her in perpetual discomfort.

As always happens, no moment is guaranteed sacred and the *Mirror* tracks me down to ask some footling questions about Python. As I try to recount 'how we thought of the title', Mum grunts and clutches herself in pain beside me. The room's very hot. She's short of breath.

Eventually we settle to eat supper on our knees. I hate to see her spirit break. She has always been so strong, so stoical, so composed. But humour creeps in ... 'Kiddy came in the other day dressed like the Ayatollah ... some great long thing.' She smiles. She is really most happy watching an episode of *Dad's Army*. This does her more good than any food, drink or drug.

About a quarter to nine, feeling somehow I've failed, I call Kay. Ma wants a painkiller and she wants to go to bed. She can't hear, she can't connect, but her brain knows well that she is in a sad state.

I write all this in the impersonal neutrality of my hotel room, unable to stop making useless comparisons that, at the peak of my own celebrity, Mother is at last beginning to give up.

I hope I'm wrong. I hope the pain and indignity will lift with the fog, that we'll all be fresh and everything will seem less bleak in the morning light.

Walk to the sea. Southwold is much quieter now – reverting to its winter ghost-town status. I think about ghosts, about strong and yet insubstantial things. My sense of regret for the days when Will and Tom sat astride the barrels of the cannons in their green duffle coats. Time cannot be held. It slips away, always eluding the grasp.

Wednesday, November 15th: Southwold

To Ma on time. She is uncomfortable, often acutely so, and being with her is like being beside a hospital bed, which is where she would surely be without 'Kiddy'.

A lady reporter rings up and Granny comes back from the loo with such groans and 'Oh, Michaels' and clutchings at the furniture that I have to put the phone down. Then she's quite happy. This technique creates apprehension bordering on panic in those around ('What were you doing? You looked as if you were going to die!') and immediately calms the perpetrator, who then becomes almost sheepishly apologetic.

Thursday, November 16th: Southwold–London

Leave for London at half past ten.

To Dean Street to discuss my involvement in a video to help parents of children who have speech problems – especially stammers. Awfully nice man, middle-aged, called Travers Reid. A stammerer, now almost cured, he remembers 'the day I unlocked my T'. The teacher had gone out and he had taken over and had the class roaring with laughter … 'I've had to tell jokes ever since,' he admits, a little unhappily.

Friday, November 17th

Granny has just rung, sounding clear and confident, to say Dr Hopkins has diagnosed a great recovery. There is almost no sign of the crackle of fluid in her lungs and she went for a walk (in her chair) almost as far as the Harbour Inn today.

The *Independent* has a piece by Peter Kellner on 'The Alternative TV Ratings'. These are the ratings of Audience Appreciation rather than just viewing and result from door-to-door surveys of 3,000 punters. Top of the ratings for the week ending 29th October was … *Around the World in 80 Days* with 85 (anything over 80 he judges 'a clear success').

Audience figures for show five are up to 11.3 million, which makes us bigger than all three other channels put together. This leaves me temporarily disorientated, as if I've just been flung round a spectacular corner on a fairground ride. Exhilarated, a little light-headed and a tiny bit sick.

In the evening I begin to assemble material for the Belfast Festival.

Sunday, November 19th: Belfast

To the Arts Theatre at half past ten.

Over the next hour I sort out an opening, with Michael Barnes as a psychiatrist asking me why I wanted to be a lumberjack and getting me from there into a rap about anniversaries, looking back and then into an autobiographical piece from birth to Python.

Second-half opening and closing worked out. Then to a lunch party at respectable, safe Myrtle Wood Road, where the Troubles seem very far away.

Bath, rehearse new bit in my mind, then, hoping upon hope that I will feel right on the night, I set off up Great Victoria Street, past the latest rash of newly opened restaurants in a city whose revival, as I have seen it over eight years, has been constant, and that despite a continuing emergency.

For a moment in my dressing room I experience a sinking feeling that I am not going to be able to pull off the trick again, but the energy returns, the moment passes and, though the first half has some less successful moments, it is 80 minutes long and I never noticed. Cracking second half and back to dressing room at 10.30, elated and very damp. Glorious moment of relief spreads on into the evening and if I could only bottle this blissful state I'd sip a little each day of my life.

Wednesday, November 22nd

The last of my *80 Day* programmes goes out tonight. Stephen Pope continues his war of attrition to the end – refusing to like it much, but refusing to give up on it, but the other *Independent* preview is wholehearted – 'The last in MP's splendid series. Quite why some have seen his ease in front of camera, professionalism and apparent "niceness" as a handicap is a mystery.' Jeremy Novick joins Mark Lawson on an honourable roll!

Then to Kensington House for champagne with Colin Cameron. Almost two years since his predecessor Will Wyatt first put the idea to me, we have come to the climax of the realisation of the project. Cameron clearly delighted at its success – the figures, etc.

Then on to Angela Elbourne [Production Assistant on *80 Days* and *Pole to Pole*] and Jeremy's small house on 'Chiswick/Acton Borders' to watch the last transmission.

It goes down well. I almost have tears in my eyes at the end.

Thursday, November 23rd

A clutch of final reviews. The *Guardian* is lengthy and quite sensible, selecting the dhow as favourite. *The Times* re-reviews with muted enthusiasm. Peter Paterson of the *Daily Mail* remains grumpily unconverted.

I am asked to do a phone-in to the TV programme *Open Air*, who have never received as many letters for one series. Today all sorts of nice things said. People will miss it ... 'Tears in Dewsbury!' Will Wyatt calls and gushes for nearly 15 minutes. He says 24 calls of support on last night's duty log. Unprecedented.

It's a delicious feeling to have risen above the critics – to feel completely invulnerable. I run, on a cool, bright day, with a wide, stretching peace of mind.

Sunday, November 26th

Read the rewritten first episode of *GBH* and am confirmed in my interest in the part of Michael Murray. Nagging feeling that perhaps the subject of the corruption of socialism in the '70s is not as pertinent as the political changes going on in Europe (and hopefully the UK) at the moment.

Monday, November 27th

Some early Christmas present shopping this a.m.

I feel tired and rather scruffy and am most surprised at the number of people who recognise me until I remember that my on-screen appearance at the end of *80 Days* last week was exactly the same – tired and scruffy and even in the same bomber jacket and trousers. Smiles, hoots from cab drivers and general enthusiasm all round.

Suzanna Zsohar [my publicist from BBC Books] calls to say yet another reprint has been organised, bringing the total number of books in the shops by Christmas to 155,000.

Watch another episode of *Boys from the Blackstuff*. Alan Bleasdale, Alan Bennett, probably the two playwrights whose work moves me most. The chance of working for both is not to be missed.

Tuesday, November 28th

Up and to first appointment, which is at Parliament Hill School. I've offered them a chunk of my ill-gotten gains. Wait in the main hallway – quite pleased to find it clean, painted and friendly.

Judy Base, the head teacher, gives me a list of areas where money might be spent – computer lines to some of the classrooms, carpets in the clattery language classrooms, etc. After yesterday's news on the book reprint, I up my donation to £4,000. Cheque signed then and there. Why do I feel vaguely guilty, seedy, apologetic about bringing out the chequebook and signing? Is it because such behaviour goes against all my parents' attitudes to money – that, like sex, it's something that goes on, but not in public?

Friday, December 1st

To lunch at Odette's with Clem V. Last prog's viewing figures 12.8 million, an increase of one and a half million over last week.

We talk about future plans. Clem assumes that I shall work with him again and that our destinies are now irrevocably entwined. Not unhappy with this, but would like Roger's presence there somewhere. With 'AF' and Bleasdale the front runners for '90, we're talking autumn '91. For the first time Clem comes up with the excellent, almost too obvious suggestion that we should do it independently of the BBC.

Saturday, December 2nd

Call Al L to check it's all right to visit him next Thursday. He has just heard bad news. The tumour on his liver has not responded to the chemotherapy. It's still growing. He has lost 25 lbs with the treatment and they are now taking him off it in order to let his body recover before another course of poison is unleashed on it. More so than I ever knew with Graham, I know this is the end for Al. What a goddamned motherfucker of a year. A beauty and a beast.

Sunday, December 3rd

Drive down to Bart's for Graham's memorial. Rather like arriving at the run-through of a charity show. Groups of people standing about, mikes being tested.

Barry Cryer is to MC. JC has bought himself a leather cap, just when they're going out of fashion in East Germany. Terry J, tanned and fluffy-headed and beseeching, is fresh back from Hong Kong.

Alan Bennett and Jonathan Miller are sat behind us – modestly lurking in overcoats like Russian Secret Service men.

Barry hits the right tone from the beginning – avoiding sententiousness, but not necessarily discouraging it. John is outrageous and does the 'Dead Parrot' sketch. 'Graham Chapman, co-writer of the "Dead Parrot" sketch is no more …' etc.… . 'He is an ex-Chapman.' It's a fine piece about shock and in praise of Graham's use of it as a weapon. 'I also want to be the first person to say fuck at a memorial service … (pause) but I daren't.'

No-one puts a foot wrong. There is nothing insincere or not truly felt in the 11 or 12 readings, reminiscences and songs. David is very good – celebrating Graham's giggling and remembering how GC and Cleese were banished from a Trevor Nunn production after an afternoon spent miming climbing a glacier.

I was the last, but my remarks about GC being incorrigibly late were well received. 'I'm sure that Graham is here with us today … (pause) or at least he will be in about 20 minutes.'

Eric ended with a communal singing of 'Always Look on the Bright Side'. An excellent occasion, managing to be funny, silly and moving at the same time. As the throng began to stand up and move away, John sat for a moment, silently, his eyes full of tears. That I shall remember for a very long time.

Monday, December 4th: London–Southwold

Gather together my slide sheets and speech notes [for an *80 Days* talk], throw overnight clothes in a bag and set off on my travels again. Yesterday morning's fog not repeated and the drive up is uncomplicated and I arrive an hour early, which takes Ma by surprise.

She is sitting with Anne and Kay – a tiny, shrivelled presence in one chair while these two healthy, strong women watch over her, like birds beside a nest.

I walk round to the church hall to sort out the slides and the sound system. All looks efficient. Arrangements have been made to have my mother there – in her wheelchair – along with Mrs Pratt and Lady Collett – combined ages of 250 years!

The hall filled beyond its 200 capacity – at least 240 there. Talk goes well. I have inserted two slides of Mrs Pratt, Granny, Snowy the dog, and Rachel at the door of Victoria Cottage in amongst the dhow sequence – as dreams of home.

It's quite a shock to see someone below the age of 50 come up to the book-signing desk, and especially schoolgirls – three of whom bring up the rear with much blushing and shifting from foot to foot. 'You're a sex symbol at our school,' says one. She is referring to St Felix, the expensive private school where my Aunt Katherine was educated. 'Oh, yes … the bit where you enter the hot baths in the Rockies, we play that bit and stop the tape, just as you're entering the water.'

Tuesday, December 5th: Southwold–London

It briefly flashes through my mind that the thin little face frowning and waving vaguely from the upper window as I drive away may be the last living image I shall have of my mother. I wish I knew if she was happy or not. Then I would really know whether these lurking feelings of wanting her to be soon delivered from this imprisonment were justified or not. But I'm an optimist and I want her to be there again at the window when I next call – frowning, anxious or not.

Wednesday, December 6th: London–New York

To Heathrow for 10.30 Concorde. Journey uneventful. Usual impressions – the size of the plane compared to the size of the passengers – huge men moving about bent double. The rocket-like acceleration at take-off. The heat of the sun and the friction at 50,000 feet keeps the little tube boiling despite the fierce cold outside.

Nancy [Lewis] has found me a room at the Plaza Athénée. Small, prettily decorated hotel in French Rococo style. My room is spacious. Dark, but quiet, overlooking a blank and characterless New York back wall.

Make calls and walk round to Nancy and Simon. First introduction to Timothy, who favours me with fetching smiles and then joins us at Jean Lafitte for lunch. Nancy hasn't really changed or become overtly maternal and yet she seems a perfect mother – unhurried, unworried and full of the sheer delight of having this new thing in her life. Simon is off to do voice-overs – he is in a suit and hoping to get some Volkswagen business.

Wander the streets getting blown along by the unceasing flow of New York. Buy various things to take up to Sag tomorrow. Call Al. His voice sounds weak. He says I couldn't be coming at a better time, though I'm not sure what this may mean.

Thursday, December 7th: New York–Sag Harbor

Riding out onto Long Island in perfect conditions helps me to set aside some of my apprehensions as to what I shall find at Sag. As it is, I draw up Henry Street feeling optimistic and, as usual, feeling comfortable in and charmed by this good-looking little town.

No-one seems to be about in the house. Then Claudie emerges from the bedroom. She looks well, I'm relieved to see – slim and attractive without make-up and with damp hair. Al is down in the Hold and after some bright pleasantries we go down.

My first reaction on seeing him is one of relief. The fine Levinson head is as strong as ever. He hasn't lost hair and even the marked loss of weight has not distorted his handsome face. But when he speaks the voice is low and does not come clear from his mouth.

He has been asleep. His brow furrows and he reproves himself for falling asleep too easily. 'These drugs ... Mike ... these drugs.' He tells me later that this has been a bad week. Last night he was awake for hours scratching at his itching skin. The doctor says that the tumour may be pressing against the bile duct and preventing it from emptying properly.

He is overjoyed at the *80 Days* tapes I've brought him and the 'Palin Belfast '89' T-shirt. He and Claudie have loved the *80 Days* book and he relates several times the pleasure he got from being woken by Claudie laughing at a passage she was reading in bed.

He has asked if I will allow a local reporter from the *Sag Harbor Express* to take my picture and do a short interview. Al dons his Breton duffle coat and we drive down to the corner restaurant. His pace reminds me of my father and the occasional confusion is sad to see. But we sit down by the window looking out to the bridge which figures on so many of the cards he sent to me, and the wind-flecked cobalt-blue waters of the bay.

I eat boiled scrod and drink a Boston beer of taste called John Adams. With the sun shining in I notice that Al's eyes look a bilious yellow. He tries to concentrate and occasionally chimes in with a very good line – a flash of the old Al – but mostly he's suffering and trying not to show it.

I like Joe, the reporter – he's an ex-professional musician. Now he paints and does a bit of everything and his jolly, extrovert wife runs a framing business. He takes photos of myself and Al together.

Later I go out to the bank and there is Claudie just getting into her car. She tells me that she is very frightened. That Al was responding so well to the chemotherapy until two weeks ago when the deterioration started. And Al won't accept it's that serious so they can't plan ahead. She wipes the tears from her cheeks and we stare out at the neat, clean tidiness of Main Street and it seems suddenly offensive to me that no-one else seems to care.

I take a walk then go back to Henry Street. Talk to Al down in the Hold. He has high hopes, as I do, of someone from the hospice who is seeing them tomorrow.

Gwenola keeps bobbing her head round the door to get me to come up and open the presents I've brought her (a book of Greek legends and some Christmas socks). She is full of life and shows off and makes up to me and gradually gets closer and sits on my knees. Claudie cooks a meal of chicken and pumpkin pie and we drink some of the champagne I bought this morning in Noyack.

Soon after eight, having embraced Al and kissed Gwen and Claudie, I slide the wide door of the kitchen open and let myself out. As long as Al is there I don't feel sad or deprived. I want him to live only as long as he can see, hear, talk and enjoy himself.

Long drive on a conveyor belt of vehicles west to New York, down into the Midtown tunnel and back into an icy-cold city at half past ten.

Sunday, December 10th: New York

Cold and bright. Brunch and chat with Trini A at a small, check-tablecloth basement. Taking her clothes off in front of a camera is still her big worry. Mum possessive, but she loves her. A good and honest and truthful girl. Definitely the best casting.

Tuesday, December 12th: New York

Have just called Al to thank him for his latest half-written MS 'Matchpoint' which arrived c/o Federal Express in my room this a.m. He and the family watch an episode of *80 Days* each night before bed. Al cannot get out of his mind the image of old Kasim hugging me at the end of the dhow journey. I'm the same. I can never describe it without tears welling up.

Recorded 12 interviews back-to-back via satellite to Orlando, Kansas, Dallas, Atlanta, Hartford, etc. Lunch with 'top' TV writers at Villa d'Arte.

Back, as snowflakes drift down, to Associated Press interview. Now to the Rainbow Room for the fourth meal in succession at which I have to sparkle, charm, be poked and prodded, be the star attraction.

Friday, December 15th: Los Angeles

It's five o'clock. I'm writing in the Ambassador Lounge at LAX.

The *80 Days* juggernaut continues to roll. Helen told me yesterday that a further reprint of 15,000 has been authorised, reaching the 200,000 mark, and the Royal Family has ordered a set of tapes for the holiday! And the BBC are to repeat *Ripping Yarns* in January after 12 years of prevarication.

Breakfasted by the pool. The Sunset Marquis is small, low and laid-back. Many Brit guests and quite an assortment of rock musicians still persevering with '70s hairstyles. One band were from Canada and awestruck to meet me. 'Your tapes, man ... We play 'em all the time ... they keep us going in the tour bus.' Shades of '69/'70 all over again. Python and the rock world's strange compatibility.

This time yesterday I was being exhibited at the Western Show – a vast gathering of 13,000 cable execs. I was doing duty at the Arts and Entertainment booth where people could 'have your photo taken with Michael *A Fish Called Wanda* Palin'. There was an old balloon-painted backdrop and the front of a basket on a raised dais, and here I stood while those who wanted to were given a Polaroid snap of us together.

I looked on it philosophically and tried to do what I had to do in an optimistic frame of mind. It was really no worse than a book-signing without the books. There weren't that many takers – maybe 30 or 40 in the hour – and they were all good-natured and ranged from hot-handed girls to three-stripe military men.

Then out in a limousine, away from Anaheim's convention sprawl, to the more glamorous smog of Burbank and the NBC studios. Arrived an hour and a half before taping at the *Tonight Show*.

I showered; my shirt and jacket were pressed, the questions and Johnny Carson's answers, prepared after yesterday's long and tedious pre-interview over the phone from JFK, were handed to me and I briefly encountered Carson himself down in the gloomy, grubby wardrobe room. He was reciting the 'Parrot Sketch' and I told him how John used it at the memorial service. Later Carson used this as a spontaneous lead-in to the questions, which showed that he's not entirely in thrall to his researchers.

Saturday, December 16th: Los Angeles–London

Manage four or five hours' sleep on the plane, which leaves me in good shape for landfall at Heathrow. The fierce gales forecast do not materialise. The big lady beside me has 'Jesus' in pearls on a brooch prominent on her left breast. She read the Bible during the flight and didn't drink. She smiled a lovely, wide, infectious smile and told me that she'd prayed that the weather would clear up and it had.

All the hostesses have dreadful hairstyles and worn faces. One senior one came up and asked me if I would like them to lay on anything special in London. I assured her I would be fine ... 'You won't be mobbed, or anything?' she asked, in all sincerity!

As the plane bumps down its heavy load onto a wet tarmac, the Bible-reader beams at me and says she will pray for my career.

Wednesday, December 20th

To lunch at Chez Victor. Anne J, David Pugh and John Dove already at table. Time to plan ahead on *The Weekend*. Pugh still very interested. Most of all with me in it. Would I commit to 20-week involvement sometime in '91?

At the moment it sounds tempting. I would enjoy live performing – but is this the best vehicle? Will I really want to do a play I wrote ten years ago for half of a year – when there are bound to be exciting things offered?

Continue trawling through the shops. Rain pours down as I dodge into Hatchards. Am welcomed with open arms. 'Best-seller of the year' I'm told. They've three copies left. As I'm signing them a woman laden with books catches sight of mine and asks eagerly if she can buy one. The assistant manager clasps them protectively – 'These are spoken for, I'm afraid.'

Friday, December 22nd: Southwold

Kay is not prepared to take on day and night supervision of my mother. She tells me of a couple of incidents recently when Mother has been rude to people – she was 'appallingly rude' to Mrs Anstey, and though Kay loves her in a way, she is quite rightly not going to allow her to take over her own life.

I hardly recognise in all this the mother who never let things get on top of her, who was always efficient, hard-working, generous and tolerant – who looked after others impeccably and who can no longer look after herself.

The decay all around seems more real than any of the success. Graham's death and the reduction of Al and my mother to weak, flickering points of light. And my own loss of 100% eyesight, the sudden awareness that I can no longer see everything unaided, brings a whiff of their decay close to me.

Wednesday, December 27th: Abbotsley–London

Up while it's still dark, for we have to return to London and prepare and pack for a ski trip to the Pythonically-named Crap Ner Hotel in the resort of Flims.

Helen and Will sound to have done a sterling job at Southwold. They spent five hours with Granny, on her own. Helen is quite firm with her when she has one of her turns, and I think can deal with them in a more detached way than myself – pulling my own mother's knickers up on the loo doesn't come easy – though how many times do I remember her doing the same for me!

Try and anticipate what will come up over the next few days and call various people. The most difficult call is to Sag Harbor. Gwenola answers, very correctly and confidently, but when she asks if I want to speak to Mummy I momentarily fear the worst. Claudie says Al is eating very little now and finds it very difficult to move from his bed ... 'He's so tired, Michael ...'

But Al does manage to come to the phone. His voice is faint and weary, hardly there at all. I find myself telling him all the things I gushed out to Graham as he lay unconscious in the hospital in Maidstone – that we loved him, and were with him and thinking of him.

Kay Kiddy doesn't think it a good idea to tell Ma that we're going to Switzerland. But I've never lied to her over such things and don't feel at all comfortable starting now. So I ring, with some trepidation. But she sounds fine. Helen's visit had been a great time, she has been off drugs for three days, and is quite well aware of the impending arrival of a BUPA Home-Care nurse … 'Another creature,' as she puts it, a trifle ominously. I tell her that we shall be away, but keeping in touch, and she seems to take this in without confusion or anxiousness.

Friday, December 29th: Hotel Crap Ner, Flims, Switzerland

I hear the alarm go. It's a quarter to seven in the morning. Still dark of course, but the near, military-moustachioed Crap manager (sorry, I can't resist a bit of that), has advised us to be up the slopes early and to come down early to avoid crowds of day-trippers desperately seeking snow.

I curl up in bed, really feeling rotten, and hear Helen moving around trying to organise all the rest of our party and then deciding she's perhaps started too early. At eight o'clock the bedroom door bangs shut for the last time, the noise of our army on the march recedes and I drift off in and out of sleep until after eleven o'clock.

I take breakfast of a roll, butter and some tea in the Giardino Café, part of this well-scrubbed, fussily decorated but warm little hotel. Don my big Irish overcoat and walk up into the backstreets of Flims to get some idea of what the place is like away from the conveyor belt of a through road.

Quite attractive mixture of town farm buildings – wood-framed, balconied, etc. and a number with cows shedded on the lower floor. If the main road smells of nitrous oxide and carbon monoxide, the parallel 'old road' smells of woodsmoke and farm manure.

To the church, dating from 1517. Nice tall tower and onion dome.

Sit in the sun on the terrace of the Crap, drink a mineral water and a tea and begin to re-read the diaries of Edward Palin, who passed very close to Flims on his Swiss trip of 1859 – 130 years ago. Struck as I read by Tristram's observation that Edward P has much the same attitude to life as myself. He's humorous, given to doing silly things (like bathing naked in rock pools), rather pedantically accurate in things to do with time and topography, clearly enjoys women and their company and often gets carried away with his prose.

1990

Monday, January 1st

What surprises me is how long the eighties have been going. I had not done my first train documentary when they began, nor even *Time Bandits*. What slightly depresses me is how little I've really moved on. I've ended the eighties with another travel documentary and Python and *Yarns* repeats. Nothing very new.

I've survived well, professionally, with clutches of awards, but aside from, I think, learning how to write longer and more sustained drama, there's nothing much I've done in the '80s which I hadn't done better before. Except skiing, of course, and it's this strange and punishing sport which marks the start of the new decade.

Thursday, January 4th

Sitting, pleasantly exhausted by all this day's effort, catching the last of the afternoon sun on our concrete balcony and wondering just where the smell of fresh manure was coming from, when the telephone rings.

It's Kay Kiddy. 'I make no apologies for contacting you by telephone. It is with reference to your mother.' The call reveals little of the nature of the crisis, just enough to make me worry considerably without knowing why. She says she'll ring later after the Doc has been, but it's her opinion that my mother should be in hospital and that I should return at once.

Swissair and the hotel extremely helpful and efficient in reorganising my schedule to catch the midday flight from Zurich tomorrow. Walk up the road to the Cantonal Bank to cash traveller's cheques. The last of the sun has turned the snowless rock face behind the town a golden brown and I feel suddenly quite sad. Sad for my mother, sad to leave Flims and the good times we've had here, sad that things have to come to an end.

Friday, January 5th: Flims–London–Southwold

Arrive soon after five o'clock and go straight to Kay K's. 'I'm sorry you have to see your mother in this state,' Kay keeps repeating, not particularly help-fully. Yesterday morning she had thought her so weak and ill that she feared she wouldn't last until I got back. The current BUPA help is criticised – for smoking, for having a radio with headphones in her room at night and generally ignoring my mother. Dr Hopkins is felt to be another villain of the piece and K suggests I transfer my mother to another, more sympathetic practice.

Approach Sunset House with misgivings, which are quite confounded by what I see. My mother, propped up in her armchair, holds a half-full glass of sherry. On one side of her sits my favourite amongst her friends, Kay Gibson, to whom she is chatting – and a stocky, slightly masculine lady with blonde hair brushed in a parting sits opposite with a paperback.

Saturday, January 6th: Southwold

Am at Sunset House by 9.30. Ma not so good. She can only move now when supported and the question-mark shape of her body is sharply pronounced. The strain on her spine from her bowed back must be considerable. She seems very drowsy and again I notice the slurring of the speech.

I sort out some of her papers and write letters to a number of people who have written to her over the last few months. Time passes slowly in this hot little flat for, whilst Ma can do very little for herself, she dominates the room and one can never relax. She groans, sighs and readjusts her position, then tugs at her dress again. But we get through and by early evening she's more relaxed than I've seen her all day. At 7.30 a big, jolly nurse called Chris arrives, who will look after her for the night.

I leave her about 8.15. Outside the rain is blowing about inhospitably. Dudley, the manager at the Swan, has asked me to dine with him and his fiancée, but I haven't the energy. The day with its constant minute attendance to the fine detail of keeping my Ma interested in life has exhausted me as much as a day on the slopes.

Sunday, January 7th: Southwold

One of the first in the breakfast room. *Sunday Times* best-seller list shows *80 Days* to be the first Non-Fiction No. 1 of the nineties ... 'This book has sold 180,000 copies in two months.'

Feeling vaguely better for this reassurance I walk across the Common to see what I shall find at Sunset House.

There is a note on the table from last night's nurse. 'Your mother had a really good night. She slept through until six o'clock.' Ma is upstairs. The note has raised my hopes, but her appearance is a shock. She looks tired and moves with difficulty. A new face – Sarah, young and spiky blonde hair – is guiding her.

At one point she gives me the look I've seen more than once this weekend – the look of someone who's stuck in the audience at a long, bad play ... 'Oh Michael, let me go,' she mutters at one point.

But the woozy morning gives way to a much happier afternoon. The weather is, by Southwold standards, unusually seductive. Mild, with a sun diluted only by high, white cloud. Kay and Sarah get Granny into her wheelchair and, swathed like a Christmas present, she is pushed off to the sea.

On return she's altogether more alert. She picks up a romantic novel in big writing which Kay Gibson brought her from the library. Out of the blue she asks 'And what is going to happen with your film ... the one about the American girl?' And we discuss it as if the last six months had never happened.

The nurse Anna who arrives at a quarter to eight is slim, soft-spoken and immediately sympathetic. I show her around upstairs and then we sit and talk for a while until Ma dismisses me. She knows I'm staying till tomorrow and is much buoyed by that and she bustles Anna to the stairs and mounts the chair-lift, which she controls herself with considerable assurance.

The air is crisp. Fresher than last night as I walk across the Common. I think that the changeover from Kay is not going to be half as bad as I feared. My clothes, packed to last until Saturday night, are drummed into another combination for dinner. I order a glass of champagne and marinated goat's cheese and venison.

Have just finished the goat's cheese and my mouth is watering pleasantly, when a receptionist approaches.

At the hotel door is an agitated Michael Kiddy, Kay's son. ... 'Your mother's collapsed!' He runs with me up the High Street, I cut across the Common. Everyone is upstairs. Mum lies on her left side on her bed, her face drained of colour, her body rigid. Kay is soothing her and comforts Anna, who looks distraught. Apparently she had been bathing my mother, who was in high spirits. Jokes were exchanged and then quite suddenly she collapsed.

Mum's features look set, her eyes are wide and fixed and unseeing. There is no reaction to the pressure of my hand in hers. A Doctor Sanger arrives and examines her.

My mother has had a stroke. A brainstem stroke, which is the most severe. She is unlikely to recover, but could last the night or even for a couple of days. I sit with her and talk on things, knowing that something may be going on inside the shell.

For two hours I sit. Anna has recovered with the help of a couple of cigarettes and she sits and works on some embroidery.

At eleven I leave them to turn Mother onto her right side. Sit downstairs. Thumb through the *Mail on Sunday* – surprised to find a thorough condemnation of the parsimony and unfairness of the government's educational policy.

The kitchen door opens. Anna announces that my mother's dead.

I go upstairs alone. The little body is crouched round like the Tollund Man, but her strong face remains beautiful, though sallow now and silent. I bend and kiss her and thank her for giving me life.

I hear the door shut at the bottom of the stairs. I know Kay and Anna don't want to intrude, but nor do I want to be any longer with a cold shell. I go downstairs. Hug them both.

The rest is practical. The clearing-up. Doctor comes to ascertain time and cause of death: 11.04 p.m. Cerebral thrombosis. The undertaker arrives softly with a friend and a van and asks if we would clear the house whilst the body is removed. Kay, Anna and I walk in the darkness, eased occasionally by a moon scudding between the clouds, down towards Lorne Road, talking between us about the exquisite timing of my mother's death – and how good it was that she had probably been driven to her death by elation rather than fear or agitation. Of course only Anna knows that – and I trust her and it makes her somehow special, this girl who walked into our lives four hours ago and has seen so much.

Kay goes home. I shut off the lights and lock the door. I'm at the Swan at ten past one. The Irish night porter says he'll say a prayer for me.

In all this I forget that Norman Rosten phoned Helen in the afternoon to say that Al Levinson had died the day before Mother. I'd rung Claudie. She sounded strong. As my mother kept saying earlier this evening – 'This is all extraordinary.'

Monday, January 8th: Southwold

Wash, dress, pack and make my way over to Sunset House in order to head off the new girl who will be arriving to look after Granny at eight.

The telephone rings at a quarter to. It's Anna, the nurse from last night. She has done her best to notify the girl who's coming that Ma is dead. As she signs off she asks if she can send me the fish she was embroidering by Granny's bedside. I'm moved to tears and choke for the first time this morning.

Back to the Swan for breakfast. Alone in the big dining room reading of the death of Ian Charleson (of AIDS at 40) and Terry-Thomas (of Parkinson's, alone and penniless at 78). Nice that Mum should have gone at the same time as two others who brought me pleasure.

Then back to the flat to begin a succession of explanatory phone calls, interspersed with the practical business of death – involving undertakers, vicars, doctors and solicitors. Cancelling Mother's newspapers seems the most bathetic moment. She must have received the *Daily Telegraph* every morning

for at least 60 years and now I find myself calling Chapman's ... 'I'm ringing on behalf of Mrs Palin ...' 'Oh yes ...' 'She died on Sunday night.' 'Oh
dear, I am sorry ...' 'So ... I'd like the papers cancelled from tomorrow.'
It doesn't sound final. It doesn't have an apocalyptic ring, but in a way it's
definitive.

In the afternoon I have to drive into Lowestoft, to a '60s office building of
no charisma, to register Mother's death.

I'm called in by a friendly registrar in early middle age. Help with questions
of Granny's provenance, all of which are handwritten onto a form marked
'Death'. My eye strays to files on the window sill marked 'Removal of Bodies
Out of England. Deaths at Sea. Bodies Brought Into England. Bodies Never
Recovered.'

Armed with legal confirmation that Mother has ceased to be, drive back to
Southwold. Now it's getting dark and the flat seems empty and sad.

Some more calls, arrangements for the rest of the week, then drive home.
No-one to wave from the window tonight.

Wednesday, January 10th

Morning on letters, 50 or 60 requests for openings of preserved railway lines,
woodlands, etc. participation in various forms of agitation.

Lunch with Tristram at Alastair Little.

Talk about deaths. Virginia's mother died in the kitchen, preparing dinner
for a friend. Next morning they were all up at the house consoling each other
when V asked what had happened to the dinner. It was found, intact, in the
oven, so they ate it for lunch.

TP has generous memories of Mother – calls her The Queen of Southwold.

Friday, January 12th

To Central St Martin's School of Art, where British Screen is holding its
annual dinner. Just before leaving Steve A calls to say the money is theoretically in place. Believe it or not, LWT has come in with an offer of £500,000,
Greg Dyke reportedly liking the script.

Simon Relph welcomes me. He beams like a schoolmaster and promises
everything will be all right. Recognise a number of those to whom we went
for money and support for 'AF' and who turned us down.

Opposite me is David Hare. He's very gloomy about prospects. 'If you
can't get money for your film, who can?'

At the end of the evening talk briefly to Relph. He begins to tell me about his alternative strategy – with the BBC. I've seen Lynda Myles, Mark Shivas and Richard Broke[1] there tonight and none of them have said anything positive about the script, so I have no grounds for hope.

Back home by 11.45. Feel as if some stuffing knocked out of me tonight. A faint air of hostility.

Sunday, January 14th: Southwold

The first January 14th in my lifetime on which my mother will not be around to enjoy her birthday. But her admirable sense of timing last week means that we can still give her a party.

The service goes well. The church itself is a fine setting. TJ was waiting for the coffin to appear and when he saw them raise the casket of ashes he was taken aback ... 'I know she'd shrunk,' he said. I can hear Mother laughing at that.

The choir was out in force and the hymns sung lustily. 'Guide Me, O Thou Great Redeemer', 'The King of Love My Shepherd Is', 'Immortal, Invisible' and 'Morning Has Broken'.

The choice of lesson worked well ... 'There is a time to every purpose under heaven' seemed to suit her departure so well. 'He hath made everything bootiful in his time,' reads Joe Hurran, in unconscious parody of the well-known turkey farmer. I read my address clearly, though received a bit of a shock when I mounted the lectern to find a piece of paper with 'Cleese' written on it. It turned out to be Joe's aid to pronunciation of Ecclesiastes!

Then we repaired to the Swan for a tea – scones, fruit cake, smoked salmon sandwiches. Lizzie [my cousin] and I talked of being Taureans who ate a lot. Lizzie gloomily ... 'As you get older your worst enemy is gravity.'

We were all in good spirits and it's a last tribute to Mother that the tone of the day was as if she had been there herself.

Wednesday, January 17th

To lunch with Eric at L'Aventure. He's sprouting a little moustache for a part as an American homosexual in a 'cult film' he's going out to LA to shoot. How a film can be a cult film before it's made, I'm not sure, but I think it means no money.

Eric, so often the catalyst (I think it was he who really pushed me into writing *American Friends*), comes up with a neat idea which catches precisely

1 Richard Broke. BBC Drama executive in long-time working partnership with Mark Shivas. They produced Jones and Palin's black comedy *Secrets* in 1973.

my mood at the moment. Telling me that he's just signed our development deal with Universal, giving us each $100,000 to bring films on, he suggests that he should be my producer and commission me to write a modern comedy screenplay. The thought seems so close to what I want to do with the next few weeks that we shake hands on it.

Scribble some thoughts down. An agency which offers culture tours to foreigners, many of them completely specious. Thatcherite Enterprise Britain – screwing the past to keep a business going. Full of enthusiasm.

Call Cleese, just back from the Danube. Did he enjoy the Eastern bloc? 'It'll be fine in five years, when Hilton have built a few decent hotels.'

Thursday, January 18th

To lunch at Langan's Brasserie with Ken Stephinson, his wife Marjorie and Maria Aitken.[1] Maria is wonderfully laid-back and incapable of being dull. Peter Langan had been a house guest of hers in the days before he died. 'Always setting fire to things then ...' He utterly charmed her children, though.

We talk about the problems of telling strangers what you do – especially if one is an actor. Maria was stuck next to someone on a long flight and when the inevitable question came up, for some reason she replied, presumably to shut him up, that she worked in a bakery. He was a baker.

Last call of all is from Patrick Cassavetti. Granada are interested now in 'AF'. They want to see a budget. I'm afraid I almost howl with frustration and despair. All I feel is another dreadful grating of the mental and emotional gears as we go from reverse into first again. Patrick straight-bats creditably – 'I just don't want to see the last nine months wasted.'

Change into DJ then with Helen to the *Publishing News* Awards Dinner. Am shortlisted, with Newby and Peter Mayle's *A Year in Provence*, for Travel Writer of the Year.

To the Park Lane Hotel, confusingly located in Piccadilly. Hanif Kureishi and Michael Rosen have both come in everyday shirt and sneakers. Frank Muir is affable. 'We're all fag ends in the gutter of life,' he replies cheerfully to my observation that the timing of success is quite unpredictable ... 'One realises that all those things like talent, looks, skill and hard work really don't get you anywhere.'

We, the BBC table, have been sat right across the entrance, probably a fire risk. I am on the main road from the kitchen and am dug in the back endlessly. Quite nice when shapely award-winners squeeze by, but piles of plates not so good.

1 Maria Aitken, actress, who played John Cleese's wife in *A Fish Called Wanda*.

We are the second award ... and the winner is ... 'Peter Mayle'. Desultory applause which cannot sustain till he gets to the podium. Suzanna Zsohar horrified. I'm a little relieved. Living with the title 'Travel Writer of the Year' in a world of Theroux, Thubrons, Lewises and Newbys would surely be fraudulent. But it's clearly not a popular choice; nor it seems is a creepy Author of the Year Award to Prince Charles for *A Vision of Britain*.

The ceremony, full of missed cues and cheap fanfares, is at moments plain embarrassing, as when P.D. James is silenced in mid-eulogy by a premature fanfare, at others enormously funny – Lord Lichfield discovered taking a quick pull on a fag when the lights are cued early – and only once does it strike an uplifting note, when Robert McCrum of Faber, accepting Publisher of the Year Award, reminds us of the existence of Salman Rushdie for the first time that evening.

Sunday, January 21st

Simon A arrives about four and takes me down to the HQ of Campaign for Quality Television – to brief me before the 'crucial meeting' with David Mellor on Wednesday evening, into which I've been corralled as Rowan Atkinson and John Cleese are both too busy. Not really my cup of tea. I can't get worked up and indignant about something that I know is being fought for perfectly well by others more qualified than myself. Nor is it like transport – a cause that runs deep.

Still, I will help my friend out and it will be another experience. SA even shows the place settings he's already worked out for dinner. 'This is a good place for Terry (meaning TJ) to blow up from, and you'll still have eye contact with the Minister from here.' Then there's an element of subterfuge. 'I can't tell anyone else, but ... the ITV companies have all put a considerable sum of money into the campaign, but it's much better if it's assumed we have very little.' This leads to a suggestion that I should be seen to pay for the meal and SA would pay me back.

Tuesday, January 23rd

To Vasco and Piero's[1] (for the first time since Piero's premature death) for lunch with Alan Bennett and Barry Cryer. 'The Three Yorkshiremen' as Barry calls us.

Barry quotes Peter Cook on the Yorkshire Ripper. The police and

1 Our favourite family restaurant run by two friends from Umbria.

Private Eye became quite thick with each other over the libel case and Peter remembers a policeman recounting one of the killings. Sonia Sutcliffe was obsessively house-proud and her husband wasn't. One night she turned him out of the house for making such a mess of the place, and ... 'in the half-hour he was away from the house, he went out and strangled a dwarf.' Peter couldn't apparently contain himself when he heard this. Probably the way the police told it. I asked Alan about corpsing in *Beyond the Fringe*. Apparently Dud went so easily that 'Some nights he'd start before the curtain had gone up.'

Alan sits so low on his back that at times his head is only just above the table top. When he laughs, which he does readily and enthusiastically, he manages with one swift movement to bring hands up to his face, whip his glasses off and then cover his face almost entirely, pushing up his absurdly boyish fringe like a fright-wig impersonation.

Barry sits upright, leaning forward. He occasionally scribbles a key word on his Consulate cigarette packet. 'Peppermill' he wrote after I'd done a bit about Italian restaurants whose status is determined by the length of the peppermill. I remark on the fact that he's smoked Consulate as long as I've known him. 'That's because there's plenty of white on the packet for writing on.'

Wednesday, January 24th

To a party hosted by the editor of the *Correspondent*[1] magazine. This is in an art gallery in Cork Street.

Meet John Brown, the editor of *Viz*. Agreeable, young and unassuming. They were greatly encouraged, at the beginning, he says, by my letter comparing the mag with Python. 'What we all thought, but didn't dare say.' They sell over a million every two months and as it's on 'crap paper' it's incredibly cheap to produce and everyone makes a lot of money.

The champagne flows, the chattering classes greet and kiss and tout for information. I feel it wholly right that I should be going on later to meet the Minister of Broadcasting and do some lobbying of my own.

Our venue is L'Amico restaurant in Horseferry Road – within sound of the division bell.

David Mellor arrives in a blaze of bonhomie. Am struck first of all by his old-fashioned haircut, long and straight like boys at school.

The menu, indeed the restaurant itself, looks a little dusty and depressing, but it is the only restaurant in London where Gorbachev has eaten, and in his

---

1 The *Sunday Correspondent* was a national broadsheet. The first edition was on September 17th, 1989, the last on November 25th, 1990. Much missed.

Twenty-seven days away. Much-needed head
treatment on Chowpatty Beach, Bombay.

With Nigel Meakin, my cameraman. A working partnership that has lasted twenty-five years.

Attack on my trousers in Bird Market, Hong Kong. 'Well, all right, I had asked the parrot if he knew John Cleese' – November 6th, 1988.

Halfway round the world. The crew in Hong Kong harbour. At back: co-director Clem Vallance with our Hong Kong fixers, MP, and Angela Elbourne, production assistant. Foreground: Simon Maggs, camera assistant, and Dave Jewitt, sound recordist.

Day 79: Weary warriors on the steps of the Reform Club, having made it round the world with seventeen hours to spare. Clockwise from back left: MP, Nigel Walters, cameraman on the second leg, Maggs, Jewitt, co-director Roger Mills, Ann Holland, production assistant. And they wouldn't let us in.

On Michael Aspel's show with Maureen Lipman (on his left) and Wendy James, founder member of Transvision Vamp.

With Charlie Crichton, my director, collecting a BAFTA for Best Supporting Actor for *A Fish Called Wanda*, March 19th, 1989.

Being silly with Gilliam. Edinburgh Film Festival, 1989.

Python's twentieth anniversary filming with Steve Martin, September 23rd, 1989.

Publicising *80 Days* at the Western Show at Anaheim, California. 'Have your photo taken with Michael *A Fish Called Wanda* Palin' – December 15th, 1989.

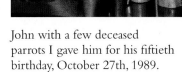

John with a few deceased parrots I gave him for his fiftieth birthday, October 27th, 1989.

Mum on her terrace at Southwold, summer 1989.

At La Residencia, Deyà, Mallorca, with Helen, daughter Rachel on the right, and her friends Kate and Sylvie Lewis, August, 1990.

With Terry Jones, posing as characters from the *Ripping Yarns* as publicity for a new combined volume of the scripts. January 25th, 1990.

As Reverend Francis Ashby (based on
my great-grandfather) in *American Friends*,
Oxford, 1990.

Gordon Ottershaw in Barnstoneworth
United strip. At *The Complete Ripping Yarns*
shoot, January 25th, 1990.

memory there is a Spaghetti Gorbachev at £5.50. We are in a private room, decorated like a sauna.

Food and wine ordered, Simon gently but firmly begins to put our case: that the granting of a licence for Channels 3 and 5 to the highest bidder, without some positive definition of a commitment to quality programming, will result in a lowering of television standards. After some discussion a concession is granted by the Minister over 'exceptional cases' – whereby a bid of less money, but higher 'quality' might be, and should be, accepted. He says he will do all he can to push this through, but will need all our help to get it past the four or five diehards, who presumably are Thatcher and her ideologues.

Terry J asks why the auction system had been chosen in the first place. Mellor flannels. TJ invokes the Middle Ages ... 'A gift from the King.' We all know that Terry's question is the heart of the matter, and everything else is trimming.

Mellor, who drank red wine, left at eleven, with much cheerful banter. He thought *The Life of Brian* the best thing he'd ever seen and requested a tape to be sent to him.

Thursday, January 25th

Anne J rings. I've been asked to play Gulliver in a film this summer. Script, by Simon Moore of *Traffik*, on its way to me.

Meanwhile, stirrings at *GBH*. I have all the rewritten scripts, but the unavailability of Billy C for the other main part sounds, according to Anne, to have given Bleasdale other ideas about casting.

Saturday, January 27th

To dinner with JC and Alyce Faye at Cibo – an unfussy, new Italian restaurant off Holland Park Road. We go with the Hutchisons. Excellent company – Alan and Sarah are the most natural of JC's friends, quite unaffected by his fame.

Sarah says that the Treasury is awash with money and certainly doesn't need the money from the TV auction. As she points out, it will suddenly start spending at the Budget before the election. So we bleed and suffer for the Tories' survival instinct. Eat lots of wild mushrooms.

Interesting sidelight on *GBH* when JC asks me ... 'What's this I hear about you and Robert Lindsay doing a Bleasdale series ... 26 weeks!'

Monday, January 29th

Talk to Bleasdale, briefly. He says that Connolly has left the project and he now wants me to do 'a straight swap' – Jim Nelson for Michael Murray. 'Jim Nelson, Michael Murray and Jim Nelson are three of the best characters I've ever written.'

I make it clear that I am not asking him to hang onto me at all costs, and if the Connolly/Palin pairing has fallen through then maybe he'll want a fresh start. Robert Lindsay isn't mentioned.

Thursday, February 1st

To Ken Hilton to meet Bleasdale, Verity and David Jones.[1]

Bleasdale, dark-eyed and dark-browed, emerges from the bar looking like a Romanian defector. We talk and by the end of an hour I've agreed to play Jim Nelson, subject to the 'Gulliver' script being less tempting. They all seem to breathe a sigh of relief. Bleasdale reassures me that he's one of the producers and will make sure we have the best people around.

The 'Gulliver' scripts have arrived. A beautiful adaptation by Simon Moore – bringing Gulliver back home at the beginning – to a world which mistrusts and disbelieves him – and keeping his fight for credibility as one of the two stories running in parallel. And I could do Gulliver well.

To bed after twelve – bleary from reading, with sore eyes and confusion about the future.

Friday, February 2nd

News is coming through of de Klerk's liberating speech from Pretoria, unbanning the ANC and the Communists and promising Mandela's release. As Helen says, it's easy to forget, amidst all the paraphernalia of our day-to-day lives, that we are living in momentous times.

Monday, February 5th: London–Lancashire

Have chosen a garlanded venue in the *Good Hotel Guide* – the Old Vicarage, Witherslack – for rest and relaxation and writing of 'The Adventure', named after the restaurant in which Eric and I came up with the idea. The train is

1 David Jones was Verity Lambert's co-producer.

remarkably empty and Lancaster Station neat and quiet as a museum. On the way up I complete my reading of *Gulliver's Travels* – which is excellent and intelligent and impassioned to the end. *GBH* remains the one original piece of work I've been offered this summer, but the competition is hotting up.

Collect a white Maestro and sign autograph for Europcar girl and then a 35-minute drive north and then west to Witherslack. My room is in an annexe. Tall and very spacious and only just commissioned. The smell of fresh paint and the tang of polyurethane in the air.

The decoration is a little fussy. Flounced curtains in the bathroom, florid wallpaper with pheasants and a lot of Tiffany lamps. A fire crackles in the hearth, but it's a fire constructed of fireproof materials. Two fireproof logs lie beside it.

Start reading *London Fields* and am reminded how funny Martin Amis is. He's flash and nasty as well, but the constant and dazzling humour (I hate to call it wit) keeps me hooked. Beside the solid soul-searching of Margaret Atwood, it's the cocktail after the long, bracing walk.

Tuesday, February 6th: The Old Vicarage, Witherslack

An orgy of banging and drilling from the next-door room, shortly followed by the screaming roar of low-flying aircraft, makes me feel that this is a sign I should not start on 'The Adventure'. But I persevere, the noise lessens, and by one o'clock I've an opening sequence and some character ideas.

Drive to a recommended local pub – the Mason's Arms, which overlooks the hamlet of Bowland Bridge. This is a small but popular pub, most tables full, over 200 beers available.

For me it's a minor ordeal – heads turning, smiles, stares, whispers. I've lost that most precious commodity, anonymity. Sometimes, as when compliments fly along with the recognition, it's quite exciting, most of the time it's like being the idiot or the leper. Still, worth it for a succulent pint of Thwaites, a roll of thick, fresh-cut ham and a view over the lumpy, hummocky valley that runs north/south from the High Lakes to Morecambe Bay.

Wednesday, February 7th: Witherslack

More crowded tonight. A party of 30-year-olds – 20 years ago everyone in this sort of 'Good Food'/'Good Hotel' Guidey place would be older than me. Now it's almost the opposite.

Also dining tonight, a wonderful couple – she handsome, carefully well-dressed, with a fine string of pearls at the neck, he ancient, craggy, crusty, with thick glasses, a hearing aid, a stammer, a fierce bronchial cough, both somehow communicating throughout and demolishing one and a half bottles of wine and a cocktail between them. County folk, as resilient as the rocks.

Amis continues to make me laugh out loud on every other page. It's all quite shallow, but doesn't half glitter on the surface.

Back in my room, stuffed, I switch on *Newsnight*. In Russia, Communists no longer the single, lone party – they will fight elections like the rest.

Never has history moved so fast in so many directions. Momentous and fascinating. But still treated by the media as Heroes and Villains. Current Heroes, Mandela, de Klerk, Gorbachev. Current Villains, Ceauşescu (obscene on every level now), Stalin, of course.

To bed and sleep by midnight. The wind sighs outside, comfortingly.

Thursday, February 8th: Witherslack

My friends of the first two days have been replaced by another couple from Leeds – he a barrister. Wince a little at the opening gambit at breakfast, 'Ah, good to see another *Independent* reader' (the paper having been going for two years), but we get on well after that.

They talk about books, easily and without pretension, and Salman Rushdie. He knows some of the Pakistani Muslims from the Bradford area who burnt the books. They wanted a little local publicity and were as surprised as he was that the issue assumed such international proportions. One thing clear in the whole issue is that hardly anyone has read the book.

Saturday, February 10th

Call Patrick Cassavetti and listen in disbelief as he tells me that he thinks he has the money for *American Friends*.

I now have to bring the film – and my obligations of conscience to all who have spent time on it – back into the reckoning, just after I've breathed the fresh air of a new screenplay.

Anne is pressing me into 'Gulliver', which sounds so efficient, well-organised and easy. *GBH* dates still unspecified as they bargain for budget with Channel 4.

Give up. Watch Rossellini's *Rome, Open City*. Now there's courageous film-making. 1945 – a cataclysmic year in my lifetime, perhaps to be only rivalled by 1990.

Already, this week, the Russian Communists have yielded a 70-year-old monopoly on power. Enormous arms cuts are proposed. The reunification of East and West Germany could be set in motion within a month and today the momentous news came through that Nelson Mandela will be released tomorrow.

Sunday, February 11th

I settle down with calendars and coloured pens to plot various possible schedules, breaking off to watch the live coverage of the release of Nelson Mandela after 27 years.

If I am to carry out my gents' agreement with Eric to provide a first draft screenplay, *and* do '*AF*', then I shall not be able to start *GBH* until August. 'Gulliver', with its 12-week shooting, beginning in June, means I could not start *GBH* until September.

Sunday supper and repeat of the *Murder at Moorstones Manor* Ripping Yarn. Family howl with laughter when the BBC announcer heralds me as 'that awfully nice chap, Michael Palin'. This is becoming quite seriously derogatory.

Monday, February 12th

Patrick Cassavetti here at 9.30 to discuss the feasibility of making the film this year in the light of my commitments.

He says he's worked himself to 'fever pitch' over the last nine months and it shows. He's pale, tired and has a thick cold he can't shake off. Though he personifies all I try to avoid – 'film as suffering' – I respect his dedication greatly, find his constancy to the project moving, and want nothing more than for his energies to be rewarded. 'If I'm not making a film ... then I die ...' he said. 'I am only in this world to make films.'

Wednesday, February 14th

To lunch with Clem V at Cibo.

In the course of it Clem suggests a future Palin journey. Emerging beneath the North Pole in a nuclear submarine, I would follow the 30° East meridian south across Lapland, past Archangel and down through Leningrad, past Kiev, Odessa, the Black Sea, Turkey, Cyprus, Cairo, down the Nile, the Rift Valley, the length of Africa to Port Elizabeth, then across to Antarctica, where, hopefully, some adventurers or some expedition could be found to take me over an 11,000-foot mountain range to the South Pole. Time wouldn't be such a governing factor, so I could linger in interesting places.

Our plan should be to make it independently, but approach the BBC and A&E for funding.

Buoyed by an excellent meal and a gut feeling that at last I've heard of a viable follow-up to *80 Days*, I drive home to give an interview about my childhood to Ray Connolly of *The Times*.

Ray has good stories from rock 'n' roll's heyday. He was at LSE a year before Mick Jagger and remembers Jagger saying of the group he'd just founded 'All we're short of is a vocalist.'

After supper I call Alan Bleasdale back. The money has been found for *GBH*. A deal has been struck with Channel 4 and it's on. 'I wanted you to be the first to know, after the wife.'

Thursday, February 15th

Now I have the longest, sustained acting role I've ever been offered lying ahead of me in five months' time. It's when I get to worrying about what lies in between that a mild panic lurks around. A draft screenplay to write and a major film to shoot and rewrite. All manner of other small things: offers flood in every day and just sorting through and fighting them off is work enough.

I try to concentrate on 'The Adventure', but I'm half expecting the phone to ring with news of '*AF*'. It doesn't.

Saturday, February 17th: London–Southwold

Must visit Southwold today – mainly for diplomatic and social reasons. There isn't a lot to do at the house. It's a mild, damp day. Helen and I leave at 10.15 and reach the house in two and a quarter hours. Fierce wind wrenches at the car doors.

Home, bearing an inkstand which Ma has left to me in her will. It bears an inscription – to 'Edward Palin, from his grateful parishioners at Summertown – 1861'. Now is this a sign that we should do *American Friends*, or not? Its arrival in the house two days before a decision is given is oddly coincidental.

In the *Guardian* Whicker has been stung into public utterance about my interview in which I revealed that he was the first presenter to be offered *Around the World in 80 Days*. He is asked, 'Why did you turn it down?' He calls my journey a seven-hour ego trip, and pleads that in his progs we only see 'the back of my head'. But he's too wise to knock popularity – even if it's a competitor … 'He did do it very well,' he concedes. Between fiercely clenched teeth I should think.

Monday, February 19th

Steve calls at 6.30 to relay the wholly predictable news that another deadline on 'AF' has passed without resolution. Alan Howden at the BBC met with them this morning, together with his reader and their lawyer, and such good progress was made that Steve feels that only two, very small, hurdles remain, and both should be cleared by tomorrow. Extend the deadline yet again.

Thursday, February 22nd

A clear writing day lies ahead. Call Patrick, who still sounds under pressure, but convinced the end, or rather the beginning, is in sight.

I've put the inkstand presented to my ancestor in 1861 in front of me on the desk. Hope this will help.

To dinner at David Attenborough's. Jane cooks a splendid meal – boeuf en croute. Liberal wine. Barry Took, with two of his favourite people, is almost embarrassingly adulatory. 'Why are the two of you so loved by the viewers?' sort of thing. Attenborough brushes it aside in his case and jabs a carving knife towards me ... 'And, for him, it's because he's funny.'

After dinner we are shown up to a small library, then up another flight of stairs to a huge open-plan gallery, running the length of the three bays of the house, neatly organised, walls covered with books, beams rising above a semi-circular slab of a desk which puts me in mind of mission control somewhere. No word processor, but everything else, including fax, of course. What's more, the books all look as if they are continually used. David very concerned that he couldn't find reference to leaf-eating ants for a whole day – so the system isn't perfect.

Tuesday, February 27th

We begin to get 'AF' back on the road again. Contact made with Irene Lamb, our casting director, who says Colin Firth will do anything for me! She is warmly, spontaneously happy at the end of the conference phone, to hear that we are under way again. Trini is still available.

Into the crowded West End to a sardine-packed theatre to see one of the great hits of the day – *Jeffrey Bernard Is Unwell*.

O'Toole holds sway, just about makes the first half bearable and triumphs in the second. He is a Grand Performer, effortlessly charismatic, a tall, athletic figure in complete control.

Talk to Annabel [Leventon][1] afterwards. They hated him at the beginning of the rehearsal. He only looked after himself and made life very tough for them. Now they would die for him. He leaves the show next week after four months to be replaced by Tom Conti. Brave man.

Sunday, March 4th

To a building in Farringdon Road, which has been acquired by Frontliners – the AIDS organisation run by AIDS sufferers which impressed me so much a couple of years ago. Twice they've been on the verge of buying or leasing premises only to find the sellers panic because of the AIDS association. One of them had to be convinced by a doctor that a building could not catch AIDS, as it's impossible to have sex with one.

Interesting that the patrons nearly all women – the Frontliners themselves nearly all men.

Tuesday, March 6th

Slept deeply and it's a quarter to eight when I wake from pleasant dreams. Gird my loins and set off, via King's Cross, for Leeds, where I am to do a piece on homelessness for the ITV charity telethon. Carole Tudor, the Yorkshire TV producer, meets me off the train.

Unfortunately the interview she had lined up with a homeless girl cannot now be done, as the girl killed herself yesterday. She was the third suicide in a week at this hostel. Apparently when one goes, there is often a 'domino' effect.

At the hostel, in the undistinguished Beeston area of West Leeds, I am to interview Ronnie and Les. Many of the other inmates will not be around today for the cameras, as they're wanted by the police.

Ronnie and Les, both in their 60s, are regulars here. They're very well behaved and obliging in the short interview, in fact too much so as they keep interrupting my summary by agreeing with me loudly and making remarks out of the blue like 'We do have a problem, we drink you see.'

Anyway, this is a hard half-hour. The whole set-up resembles a Python sketch. At the end I remark to the excellent trio who run the hostel how agreeable were Ronnie and Les. 'Before they've had a drink,' they warn, chuckling at my eager naivety.

Their point is proved in spectacular fashion when Ronnie returns from the

---

1 Annabel Leventon, actress who also appeared in the original London productions of *Hair* and *The Rocky Horror Show*.

pub within ten minutes, a changed man. No shaking hands and thank yous, he is on the warpath and the enemy is Carole Tudor, who gave him and Les a pound for a drink ... 'What do you think we are?' 'A bloody insult.' 'One pound, for all the money you've got.' Carole seems not much shaken. She has a sort of detachment from it all which I suppose she's learnt from 25 years in television.

Wednesday, March 7th

Down to a studio off Great Portland Street to be beamed live by satellite to a morning show in Melbourne. The security man downstairs asks me if I'm the cab driver they're waiting for. The 'studio' turns out to be an office with a swivel chair set in a wilderness of coffee cups and faxes, with a six-by-four-foot cardboard-mounted colour photo of the Houses of Parliament propped up on a desk behind me. On camera it looks as if I'm in a luxury penthouse 20 storeys above the Thames.

Friday, March 9th

I make my way to Verity's office to meet Robert Young,[1] who will be directing *GBH*. The hallway dominated by the languid bulk of Verity's Great Dane licking his balls into rawness.

A mild-looking middle-aged man, with a soft, just-woken look in the eyes, is at the office doorway. Momentarily take him for a cab driver – it's that sort of week!

Dates are discussed. I find myself almost apologising for *'AF'*s sudden resurrection.

I feel enormously reassured by our brief meeting. Young is friendly and approachable, he says he read it and felt the part could have been written for me. So far no big bad wolves on the project. All the main players nice and uncomplicated.

Friday, March 16th

To the BBC for meetings with Clem and Colin Cameron to make an early pitch for 'Pole to Pole with Palin' as Clem has titled it (embarrassingly as far as

---

1 Robert Young, director, who before *GBH* directed five episodes of the Hugh Laurie-Stephen Fry *Jeeves and Wooster* TV series.

I'm concerned). Despite news today of sales of *80 Days* to Russia, Saudi Arabia and about 20 other countries, as well as a Broadcasting Press Guild Award for Best Documentary Series of 1989, Cameron listens coolly and certainly betrays no excess of enthusiasm for the 30° longitude journey.[1] But neither is he hostile.

All in all, we remain knocking at the door, with no more certain chance of admission than anyone else.

Saturday, March 31st

A day of work on *'AF'*.

Knowing that we are to make the film and knowing that we, as good as certain, have Connie and Trini to play the other two main parts, makes these rewrites different, closer, more intense.

On the news, pictures of familiar streets smashed up. There has been a poll-tax protest and riots have broken out on the periphery of the demonstration. A sunny, comfortable day ends with ugly scenes of flying truncheons, crowds trampled by police horses, faces contorted with hate, cars set alight in St Martin's Lane.

Pick Rachel up from the Lelands'. David has a cast and crew screening of *The Big Man* tomorrow at the Lumière in St Martin's Lane. 'I just hope there'll be a theatre left.'

Sunday, April 1st

The evidence of yesterday's wanton destruction begins at the top of Shaftesbury Avenue, but is clearest in St Martin's Lane, where nearly every window shows signs of damage, either cracked, partially broken or, in the case of the Renault garage, completely boarded up. A burnt-out Porsche is being examined by passers-by, tall-sided glaziers' vehicles work their way down the street. The Salisbury pub is boarded up.

Into *The Big Man*. Simon Relph is sitting just behind me. He grasps my hand ... 'Now we really are in business.' Feel much perkier and more self-confident now the millstone of doubt and apology for *'AF'* is off my neck.

The Big Man starts with images of police and riot shields and the same looks of anger and protest and snarling hatred we saw yesterday filling the street outside. Its central story, of the setting-up and execution of a bare-knuckle

---

1 The 'discipline' of *Pole to Pole* was to try to stick as close as possible to 30° east line of longitude, as we made our way south.

fight, very well presented, with strong images and Morricone's music giving it a world-class feel. But underneath this hard film there's a soft and sentimental centre, and the Liam Neeson character hardly changes from beginning to end. One feels these are characters whose destiny is quite predetermined and I felt pleased that '*AF*' at least sets out to make its characters change and develop.

Wednesday, April 11th

To supper at Simon A's.

Clive Hollick is also there and the talk is of the possibilities of setting up a TV company to bid at the next round of licence grants, incorporating the values propounded so successfully in the Campaign for Quality Television. TVS [TV South] looks the weakest of the present franchise holders and Simon and Clive have plans, either to buy the majority of shares in the existing company or to make, as they call it, a 'green field' bid, starting from scratch and creating a totally new company. They are keen on pursuing Nigel Walmsley as Chief Executive (my original suggestion) and Roger Laughton as Head of Programmes.[1]

I sense a whiff of the burning rubber of the fast lane, as Clive, clearly, precisely and tantalisingly, sets out the various ways in which TVS, the limping, wounded prey, will be stalked by the new, strong, seemingly unstoppable predator.

The only problem, as far as I am concerned, is my inclusion as an important member of a prospective board, representing the 'values' of CQT.

I could not commit the amount of time required of a serious board member of the new company. In addition I have prog commitments to the BBC (though Simon didn't think this important) and an inclination and a sympathy towards the North, rather than the South.

Hollick very much in cahoots with the Labour Party and tells me that they are going to propose a new high-speed rail link up the spine of England, bypassing London and connecting with the Channel Tunnel. It will be financed, they hope – 'funded' is the word used – by allowing private operators, such as SNCF, to rent out the track.

Thursday, April 12th

At ten Connie here, and a little later Tristram. We work through the script. Connie seems more relaxed and at ease with her part, maybe because she

1 Nigel Walmsley was a contemporary at Brasenose and Roger Laughton the executive producer of the *Great Railway Journeys* series.

knows it's happening now, and she suggests little line changes which work well and remind me of one reason I wanted her in the first place – because she could write.

I leave this productive and concentrated morning at one o'clock and drive over to Don Pepe in Frampton Street to meet with Clem V and Mirabel [Brook, Location Manager] re *Pole to Pole*. He has worked out a schedule which involves four months' travelling. Suggest a two-week break on the road somewhere, possibly around Luxor or Aswan. Still looks an amazing trip, but the nuclear sub opening beneath the North Pole looks exceedingly problematical and the journey to the South Pole debatable.

Then down to LWT for a Michael Aspel show recording with the Princess Royal as one of the guests.

In my dressing room there is a typewritten protocol sheet which notes that the Princess Royal should be addressed as 'Ma'am' ... 'rhyming with Spam'. Led then to a makeshift 'green room' behind the set and the Princess, shapely and composed, face looking a little older close to, arrives and greets me with extreme affability. 'We passed your dressing room,' she said, 'looking for mine, which we never found.'

She goes on first and astutely refuses to give away family information, except inadvertently ... 'Was there much conversation at dinner when you were young?' 'We weren't allowed down to dinner.' An impression, possibly inaccurate, of a rather tight-lipped, serious lady emerges.

But she is very subversive in her little off-camera asides. A revolving stage, to move us into another position, worries her ... 'I hate these things ... if we go too fast I may well throw up.'

Nigel Kennedy, the extraordinary, Mozart-like genius and wide boy combined, plays Bruch beautifully, spellbindingly, in bandana wrapped around cropped hair, a 1707 Stradivarius clutched to a jacket studded with giant safety pins. He tells a great story of inserting a naughty magazine between the pages of the score of the conductor of the Vienna Philharmonic.

Friday, April 13th: Good Friday

Day at home. Last of our children leaves us. Will is in Portland, Oregon, Tom sleeping rough in the mountains behind Barcelona and at lunchtime Rachel joins her friend for a week in Norfolk.

Ring Alan Bleasdale and fix a couple of days in May to go up and see him and a school for difficult kids and a psychotherapist (at A's suggestion!).

Quiet evening before the box, sobering too, as we watch a programme based on letters home from troops in the Vietnam War – sobering to be reminded that the average age of the 58,000 Americans killed in Vietnam was

19. Those troops, heavily armed and screaming as they raced out of Hueys, were mostly William's age.

Friday, April 27th

Flying back from a short 'AF' writing trip in Ireland. A surveyor in the oil-freight business asks if I will sign his sick bag. He says he has quite a collection of celebrity-signed sick bags. The hostess tells me they don't call them that, they call them cuspidors.

Monday, April 30th

To the launch party for Elena's[1] book at L'Escargot. Elena surrounded by her admirers. She seems to have gracefully put on weight. Her hair looks golden and wonderful. Her husband Aldo hovers, far more nervous than Elena.

A chatter of celebrities – Melvyn there, lock of hair jauntily falling across forehead, looking about twelve. Alan Yentob of course, but John Birt it is who attaches himself to me. We talk about our mutual friend Mick Sadler[2] who has written a radio play with a character who some think, say Birt, is modelled on me, others on him. This is quite disturbing as I've never thought of Birt and me as having anything in common. Success is the common denominator, he reveals, modestly.

He's very chatty and expansive and so is Yentob – realise that I'm a bit of a lucky charm at the moment, as the success of *80 Days* appears to be lasting. My shirt much admired by Yentob and Birt, who is quite a fashionable dresser and not at all as dour as he's made out.

Tuesday, May 1st

Drive down to Hammersmith, to the *AF* Production Office in Macbeth Road. The offices are located in a big, empty old primary school – Victorian and quite fine, with rows of washbasins only a few feet off the ground.

Out with Irene, Tristram and Patrick to a drink with David Calder, a Pollitt possibility. A dauntingly impressive list of credits, and he is an agreeable and companionable man.

1 Elena Salvoni, long-time manageress at L'Escargot in Greek Street, Soho.
2 Mick Sadler, fellow revue actor and writer at Oxford, now living in Paris.

Thursday, May 3rd

I arrive at Cosprop at two for a fitting with our costume designer, Bob Ringwood. He looks a little like Lawrence Durrell and is keen, eager and loves all the scenes we've just removed – the soirée, the cycling through the woods and the parting of the ladies at the end.

I'm enormously relieved to see from contemporary photos that dog collars didn't come in until the 1880s and '90s and white neck 'stops' were worn, which look more attractive, less clichéd and take me well away from *The Missionary*. Hair and whiskers were worn in a variety of wild and wonderfully fanciful ways, and I look much more like a Regency figure than a modern clergyman. Bob and his assistant, Graham Churchyard, seem well pleased.

In the evening, with Helen at badminton, I go to the Renoir to catch the last night of *A Short Film About Love* [by Kieslowski]. Compulsively watchable. A careful film, tight shooting and editing and absolutely believable performances.

I come straight home and in the balmy night – warm as 60° outside still – read with care the first of the *GBH* scripts. Look at Jim Nelson as a piece of acting; think how I can make it as successful as the leads in the film I've just seen.

Friday, May 4th

'You've got no pressures any more, have you?' Peter Lewis asked me as I lay upended on his dentist's chair this afternoon. 'I mean, everything's easy now, isn't it?'

Tuesday, May 8th

To lunch in Gloucester Crescent with Colin Haycraft, at Lyn Took's behest. Haycraft, a jolly, bustling, cheerful, donnish man (he loves Oxford and found the name of Edward Palin in a dusty copy of the Oxford Register – 'Honours Degree in Literae Humaniores 1848 ... MA, First Class, one of only 8 awarded that year').

They have one of those charming, rather magically overgrown houses, rather dark inside, but full of atmosphere and a soft, warm comfort, like a patched but favourite dressing gown.

Anna Haycraft, alias Alice Thomas Ellis, is introduced to me. She has big, dark, unavoidable eyes and must have been very beautiful. And still a powerful, heavy-lidded presence. Beryl Bainbridge is there, small-framed, bird-like and amused, a smile always about to happen. A beautiful young son who leaves early to get down to Wandsworth to rehearse Shakespeare.

They all agree Alan Bennett is the best of neighbours, though Haycraft, whilst being immensely agreeable, fires in brisk controversial shafts, and thinks Alan 'very limited as a writer'! Yes, but who wouldn't die for such limits.

Ostensibly I'm being wined and dined because he regarded my foreword to Barry Took's autobiography as a work of near-perfection. 'You can write,' he advises me bluntly ... 'It's as simple as that ... some people can, some people can't.'

Beryl leaves to have her verruca attended to yet again. Someone had told her that banana was good for ridding oneself of verrucas, so she'd slept with a banana in her bed feeling rather silly, before being told it was only the skin.

Wednesday, May 9th: London–Liverpool

Catch the 7.50 Merseyside Pullman and, after a breakfast served in leisurely style over one and a half hours, arrive early in the slime-green canyons that lead into Liverpool Lime Street.

Bleasdale, pale suit, floral shirt (a combination he likes), greets me with apologies for the fact that Gerry, his driver, has turned up in a white stretch limousine. 'The Liverpool limousine,' I jest, but realise too late that this is probably true. Gerry remembers driving Maggie Smith and me in the same car during *The Missionary*.

We drive out to the 'Mal-ad' school in Wigan.

The school is residential, with a high teacher-pupil ratio and a sensible, tolerant, flexible approach to the children which seems to have paid off, for they are polite and receptive and enthusiastic. In only two of them do I see the lowered brow, intense concentrating eyes and set mouths that suggest something bottled-up.

We sit at lunch tables with them, then afterwards sit in on classes. I play draughts with one boy whilst his friend, a small lad with a crew-cut, offers mad advice and pops any draught removed from the board into his mouth.

One of them asks Alan if he's Engelbert Humperdinck.

Then a beer in a pub, where I meet a tight, lean-faced, charismatic teacher on whom AB has drawn for some of Jim Nelson. His toughness and wry, quick Lancastrian wit put him in a class of his own and remind me further of the task I've taken on.

Then on to see a hypnotherapist called Sam Beacon, who looks Anglo-Indian. His neat, fragrantly perfumed wife brings us endless small platefuls of fruit and sandwiches whilst Sam shows us a video of him working a lady with an awful fear of supermarkets into a trance.

Alan tries to pin Sam down to what we need to know for Jim Nelson's character and the approach Sam used to treat Alan's own fear of bridges. Alan asks Sam to try his hypnotism technique on me. I just tense up and have to pretend to be affected.

Second time around I decide not to act and so my right arm, which I'm holding in the air and which is supposed to become heavy, never does.

Eventually Sam gives up. 'Well, we've not much time, so I'll put your arm down anyway.'

On the way back in the car Alan and I laugh, wondrously, about it all.

Thursday, May 10th: Liverpool–London

Wake around six. The demands of the part, the scale of my involvement, my inexperience of this kind of drama, all seem heavily negative this morning. I contemplate telling Alan, at breakfast, that I am not the right person to take on this pivotal part, that, all things considered, I will only be a disappointment.

I'm downstairs in the long, bright kitchen at twenty to nine. Radio 2's playing. Bleasdale senior is busy. He smiles, we exchange a greeting and he's off upstairs.

Alan appears apologetically five minutes later. I don't mention any doubts, and doubt I will until it's all over.

Monday, May 14th

This is my first working day on *GBH*: the day I shall meet the actress who is to be my wife and to spend time with Robert Young.

Robert lives on Kew Green, a peaceful and attractive spot, bordered by Jacobean and Regency houses and later terraced houses, spoilt only by an almost continuous squash of traffic heading for the bridge.

Alan is smiling and smoking and a slim, neat woman with short hair cropped at the back of her head is sitting with the two of them tucking into breakfast. She is Dearbhla Molloy, my Laura, and though my first impression is of a possibly severe and serious sort, she has a warmth and above all an easy, unforced, untheatrical naturalness which attracts me.

After a mug of tea we all move into a dining room and sit at a round table with the tallest glass vase I've ever seen stuck in the middle of it, and read through our scenes from the beginning.

Robert is sage, measured and never talks unless he has something to say. He's pleased that I can show anger well – he hadn't expected that. In fact my shortcomings are, ironically, in the humour department: I've not yet found a comfortable way of delivering the Scouse wisecracks that Alan dots generously around for me.

Tuesday, May 15th

At Robert's today are Julia St John, a pretty girl with big eyes who plays Diane Niarchos and Mike Angelis who plays Martin Niarchos. At the reading Angelis is solid and very funny and his immediate rapport and ease with the material leaves me trailing behind. I can't seem to get the light and shade into Jim yet, though occasionally I hit it and it feels very good.

Meet Robert Lindsay for the first time. He quickly indicates that he knows I was offered Michael Murray first. Daniel Massey, immediately likeable, warm, charming and delightfully silly, is there and Lindsay Duncan who plays Barbara and Julie Walters and the lighting cameraman, also delightful.

The sun shines and it's all very auspicious. Alan smokes, drinks and pads about nervously. He does seem to suffer for his art.

Wednesday, May 16th

Bob Lindsay is reading with me today. He's arrived on a bicycle, with a child seat on the back. He's in quite good shape and I should imagine does some weights. He is reading Murray with writer, director and co-star for the first time – going through what I went through on Monday.

Technically he is good, and his timing is impressive; how he will cope with the introspection of Murray, the personal desolation and inadequacy inside, I don't know.

He asks many and detailed questions which make everything go on a little slowly, but I deliver my final uplifting peroration and we have lunch.

I know that when I hit it – when I am absolutely truthful, I am, as Jim Nelson says, the best. But I need technique to get me there. I fear that the workload (of everything) might just fight against relaxation and ease and enjoyment. In short I have to rediscover the old eagerness – the spirit of the Edinburgh Festival Revue of '64.

Thursday, May 17th

Another fine, warm, dry day. An *American Friends* morning. Blinds down in my workroom and calls to various people. Alfred Molina is back in England. Can he play Syme with a beard and an Icelandic accent? He sounds busy.

I call up Eric and go to lunch with him. This is just what I needed. A break from the twin projects weighing in on me at the moment, a chance to talk with an old friend – and these Python, pre-Prominent relationships seem all the more important now. We have 'The Adventure' to talk about, and Eric is so enthusiastic that he would like to set it up for mid-summer filming next year! We have a long and therapeutic laugh at the thought of playing two ex-RAF types.

Eric's off to France for two weeks, I head towards Camden Town and recycling and some shopping, then home to work on episode two of *GBH*. There is no short cut through Alan's scripts. They are dense and complex and I'm only halfway through the second when I have to shower and change for an evening out with David Frost.

To his house in Carlyle Square, quite a grand London mansion with stripped pine and bare floors adding a touch of character to the dark but carefully chosen decor. Frost has a fetish for photos which proliferate on every surface – all in thin silver frames, and all of himself or famous friends.

His son Miles, who's only about six, asks questions with all the acuity of the master. How much older is my daddy than you? Answer six years. Can interviewing technique be hereditary?

We watch the tape of *How to Irritate People*, in which I took part in 1968. Frost, whose company produced it, wants to put it on sale. It's too long, is appallingly directed and exudes cheapness in sets, titles, etc. However, it has wonderful Cleese/Chapman sketches and some of Graham's most brilliant performances; his Mountie coming backstage for compliments is a wondrous, cringingly painful gem.

Friday, May 18th

A short time working on *GBH* three, then up to Hampstead for dinner with Peter and Lin. Cook and Chung. Peter says he'd very much like to be called Peter Chung. His stomach is huge and pendulous, like Mr Punch's and, when it peeps out from beneath his T-shirt as Peter does some athletic piece of mime, it's like having another person in the room.

Peter is a big, genial presence, but not a solicitous host. Lin gets the food on the table and keeps it all going. Peter eats very little, drinks, but to start with not heavily, and smokes gazing round at everyone inquisitively as if assessing where he should take us all next. 'I'm going to get absolutely plastered, I think,' I hear Peter say to himself as he delves about in the fridge, in the same functional, unsensational tone that one might use if you were going to run a bath.

He sprawls into memories, often very funny, but, like some boozers do, loses sight of us, in absorption in himself. Peter becomes maudlin, sentimental, sharp, bitter, concerned in rapid succession. How cruel he was to Dudley in *Derek and Clive Get the Horn* .∴. He shakes his head, 'I was so cruel.' How he would love to work with Dudley again, but it would have to be on something quite different.

The evening sort of crumbles, but we're not away until 1.30. Find ourselves driving back through agreeably empty streets after second night on the trot with a 50-year-old Cambridge satirist!

Thursday, May 24th

At the *American Friends* production office. David Calder, who's to be Pollitt, comes in this morning and we inch through his scenes together. He tends to RSC dramatics and doesn't quite find a way to cope with the inadequacies, the bufferishness of the character; but his commitment and positive attitude are very encouraging.

After lunch I work with Trini. The 'rehearsal' room is quite accessible – it's just a big, empty, echoing schoolroom, and I suppose Mike the unit driver was not to know that Trini and I were wrestling with one of our more intimate scenes when he walked in with a black plastic bag and began to empty the remains of lunch.

At six o'clock I throw a champagne party for cast, crew, actors and anyone else who can make it. It's at the school and the investors are out in force – two from Virgin, Ceci and Andy Burchill from BSB, Felicity from the BBC and Relph from British Screen. In the plaster-peeling seediness of an old primary school, the final signatures go down and the picture is financed, almost four years after I first thought of the idea.

Sunday, May 27th

Connie comes round to rehearse the restaurant scene which we shoot on Wednesday.

Useful rehearsal. The scene feels as if it has a direction and a purpose and we reduce the 'stodgy historical' dialogue. Then TP and I have a good talk over Ashby. I feel I must play him with less movement and fewer facial mannerisms if he's to avoid being a clone of Fortescue in *The Missionary*. Stillness and seriousness will provide the humour – and this goes for all the potentially 'comic' characters. TP endorses this, and I know that we basically share the same taste.

Trini arrives for supper. I walk with her over the Heath to Kenwood. Her boyfriend Robbie is coming to join her next week, but her mother would disapprove and mustn't know. She looks pale and tired, but so completely Elinor.

Tuesday, May 29th

Picked up at ten and taken to the location at Twickenham. They're filming in Strawberry Hill, Horace Walpole's elaborate and delicately decorated Gothic re-creation, now some sort of educational centre.

At eleven o'clock I witness the first take of *American Friends*. Trini and Connie both looking perfect, wading into the emotionally charged evening before the night-it-all-happens scene, which has been words on the page for so long. Now, today, its realisation on film is work for 50 or 60 people.

Encouraged by what I see. The two rooms which represent the mythical 'Angel Hotel' in Oxford are striking and lightly elaborate, the performances seem assured. Connie and Trini both have trouble with their corsets.

Wednesday, May 30th

My first day as actor on a film set for two and a half years, in a house on Kingston Hill got up to look like an Oxford restaurant of 1861.

My hair is tonged into curls and swept away to one side. I contemplate the state of my face eight years after *The Missionary* and find it wanting. Lines deeply etched on my forehead now rivalled in magnificence by a starburst of creases travelling out from my eyes. I can't remember feeling quite as old and tired for a long time, an almost laughably poor state to begin seven months' acting.

Fred Molina is in today. Fred is full of life and bonhomie and humour and takes a bit of keeping up with. Connie is worried, but then she always is. The set for the restaurant is very effective and with the other diners and the harpist in it feels completely right.

My voice is an octave or two lower than usual – husky through tightness perhaps. I rather like it. The day feels immensely long and there are so many people to be jolly to.

But I manage without incident to do my stuff. I can't say I felt relaxed, though, and I hope this will not show.

Friday, June 1st

Hardly time to register a new month, or look at a paper. Out to Hadley Wood, arriving about seven-twenty. No-one races up with compliments about the rushes so I assume either that they think I don't need them or that there is nothing to say. Suspect the latter. There was nothing extraordinary about my performance.

Work on through the afternoon. Jimmy Jewel,[1] who is very friendly to me but less so to anyone else, smokes almost continually, flicking the lighted end of his cigarette off with swift dexterity just before a take. 'Make your fucking mind up,' he says at one point and I feel Tristram flinch a hundred yards away.

I'm driven to rushes in the Prominent viewing theatre by Steve A.

Champagne is produced by Patrick and Steve afterwards and there is mellowness and relief and, though I have been in these post-first-week euphoria sessions before, I know that this is genuine – for they are a very good crew. I forget in my solipsistic trance that others have been tested this week – especially Tristram, our lighting cameraman Philip Bonham Carter, and Connie too. All have come through with flying colours and everyone is happy for a moment in the damp courtyard below lowering skies at Prominent Studios.

Monday, June 4th

Difficult emotional scene with Trini – in my Oxford room. All much easier and more fun than I'd expected.

Trini grows in confidence and seems able to switch easily to whatever performance is required – apart from earthiness or coarseness. Bryan Pringle is ebullient. Always laughing. Tristram asks delicately if he could take his performance down a bit ... 'Wrong actor!' booms the weather-beaten Welshman and roars with laughter.

Tuesday, June 5th

Awake at six. Up at 6.30. Car at seven. On set at 8.30, hair crimped, calves gaitered, body frock-coated to play my half of the tender, moving scene we embarked on yesterday.

Then into another night-time confrontation. TP very good in his notes to me. It seems I nearly always start too big, and too predictably. He asks me to

1 Jimmy Jewel, Yorkshire-born comedian, who had a thirty-year partnership with Ben Warris (his cousin); also an actor.

reduce the level and vary the pace, which is of course the way to a much more interesting performance. This is only my fifth day back down the acting mines and I realise that instinct can only achieve so much.

Finish with Trini in the afternoon and begin the scene with Cable, played by Colin Firth's brother Jonathan. I hadn't expected the pace to be quite as sustained. Another seven o'clock finish. Ten and a half hours on set.

Friday, June 15th

A BSB Film Programme unit have been brought along by our publicity lady, and they keep making incursions into the unit and carrying one or other member away into a far-off part of the garden to be probed.

Apart from the actors, all come back a touch self-conscious, as if they've just had a rather intimate medical examination. Only Connie, of the actors, is terrified of being interviewed. Her self-doubt is so appealing I only hope she never overcomes it!

I'm interviewed after lunch. A swan climbs quite fearlessly out of the water and wanders inquisitively amongst the crew as I talk! My cold seems to be developing nastily as the day wears on. The soft, windless, airless atmosphere doesn't help.

Try some rowing on the river in preparation for tomorrow. Alter some dialogue. How can it be, that after two years of raking over every syllable, Tristram and I are making it up a minute and a half before the take? Beginning to appreciate the organic nature of a film. This one is like cooking some delicate dish. It could be quite ordinary – the ingredients are not exotic – but if they're mixed and added in just the right way it could be unforgettable.

Sunday, June 17th

A delicious prospect of a day when I need feel no guilt at not working, when I can legitimately ease off and give my system a chance to recover. And it's warm and there's some sunshine outside.

Bleasdale rings – they start shooting *GBH* tomorrow. Like us, they're starting in on the emotional hard centre – with Michael Murray, Barbara and Murray's mum.

Try to think of myself as part of them, but it's too remote.

Work in the garden, watch World Cup football and enjoy pork roast for dinner – all of which makes me feel very content.

Tuesday, June 19th

Drive across Central London and down to the old St Thomas's Hospital operating theatre beside Tower Bridge, which is generally open to the public, but which today Prominent Features has hired, to shoot Elinor wandering in to Syme's lecture on dissection.

The character of this old part of London is now quite schizoid. Many fine buildings like the George Inn and the various Wren churches are set amongst attractive, interesting shop and warehouse buildings. All seems to have been well until the late twentieth century and the discovery of the new technologies. Now enormous blunt, anonymous skyscrapers tower over the area – like the huge and unwelcome feet of a giant in a garden.

Watch a couple of shots after lunch, look round the gory museum of old knives, saws, etc. Note that patients in hospital in 1830 were prescribed eight pints of beer a day.

Wednesday, June 20th: London–Oxford

Leave for Oxford at ten to three. Arrive in reasonable shape at the Cotswold Lodge Hotel.

A cup of tea with TP and Alun Armstrong, on for the first time. He's exercised that he's not remembered his father's birthday. TP suggests a telemessage. 'No, they always know you've forgotten them.' I suggest he goes early to the location and finds a card in Oxford. 'What would I find in Oxford for a retired miner?'

In the evening I'm filmed walking up past Brasenose, with the lamps illuminating St Mary's and the Radcliffe Camera: staking claim to a piece of my past in rather a grand way. Reminds me of Charlie Bubbles.[1] The boy made good. Almost 25 years to the day since he finished his full-time education, he returns in a blaze of light!

Patrick and Steve have seen assemblies of the material so far. Patrick voices a slight fear that it may become Bergman in Oxford and emphasises our need to keep the lightness. But apparently the investors are all pleased.

---

1 *Charlie Bubbles* (1968). Albert Finney's only film as a director. He also starred as a self-made man returning to his roots.

Thursday, June 21st: Oxford

To the location for supper at six, but am not required for first shot (in Merton Street) until it's dark at ten. Much hanging around – but that's what film is. Long periods of waiting, interspersed with nothing to do.

In the library of the building which has become our 'Angel Hotel' a crackly old TV with a blizzard-strewn black and white picture is propped up on a rubbish basket.

We watch England's clumsy toiling against Egypt. Am out in Merton Street, negotiating the awkward cobbled surface and trying to avoid foot contact with Trini's crinoline when an assortment of cries from various ends of the street heralds England's goal, which puts them through into the second round of the World Cup.

Saturday, July 7th

Returned from Oxford at 11.30 last night, having gone to the Rolling Stones 'Urban Jungle' concert at Wembley on the way back. A week of total and time-consuming involvement in the film.

Tuesday the busiest day of all, as we filmed the Lear sequence in the cloisters. First shot at nine, last shot at 9.15. The weather held, which was as well for there were film crews from BBC's 'Film '90' and ABC New York as well as a smattering of freelance journos amongst the visitors.

Wednesday began wet and windy and spirits drooped accordingly. But it was decided to go ahead and use the conditions by shooting the funeral sequence in the rain with umbrellas and all. A long but successful morning, despite choristers at the front running amok and shouting 'Action' in shrill voices – gratified by the Pavlovian response of the rest of us who immediately begin to shuffle forward.

Watch England's semi-final game against Germany with many of the rest of the crew, including boisterous sparks who really do like to sing 'Here We Go!'. England at last hit form and hold the Germans to a 1-1 draw, before being beaten on penalties.

The saddest aspect of the defeat was the sudden puncturing of what was likely to be a hysteria of delight. I really just wanted to see what everyone would do to each other if we won. But it wasn't to be and a complete and deflated silence greeted the successful German kick. After four years and four weeks it was unbelievable to see the stuffing knocked out of people so quickly.

Sunday, July 8th

At four to George Akers' cutting rooms. We watch a couple of assembled sections which TP feels will be a helpful indication of the film's mood and the story development, and how the Swiss stuff can best be played.

See the Oxford section before Switzerland and the Ashby/Elinor night at Oxford. Both delicately and atmospherically shot, certainly a joy to look at. The Syme/Ashby rivalry, the slight mystery about A's hols, but above all the intimation that something is to happen comes out strongly. There is an emotional intensity, and once again it's about the things not said.

This is a great send-off before Switzerland and will help fortify me over the next two hard weeks.

Monday, July 9th: London–Fiesch

Up the Rhône valley, through Sion and Brig, to an archetypally neat Swiss mountain town called Fiesch. (Check in Ed P's diary and find he passed through here in July 1861. He went up the Eggishorn Mountain behind the town and spent two weeks laid up there because of his heel.)

Our hotel, the Christania, is new and clean and family-run. I have an attractive double room under the eaves with a quiet view onto what Tristram calls 'Heidi-like' pastures and the slopes of a mountain.

Not much time to rest as TP, Patrick and I go to the production office, a low-ceilinged old house in the town, to meet the Swiss crew, make some script changes and then drive to the location, the tiny hamlet of Im Feld, which has been transformed over the last two weeks by our construction and art dept into the romantic haven where E and A meet.

Like all Andrew McAlpine's[1] work this is not a chocolate-box set, not glossy or in the slightest twee. It's quite steep too, which adds character. Another great success for location finders and art dept.

Saturday, July 14th: Fiesch

I went up on the cable car to the top of Eggishorn with Bob Ringwood and Armstrong and son. High up, above the tree line, on a worn shelf full of building materials, stands the Jungfrau Hotel, in whose predecessor Ed P spent two weeks 129 summers ago. He noted how thin the partitions were 'which

1 Andrew McAlpine, New Zealand-born production designer whose films include *The Rachel Papers*, *The Piano*, *The Beach* and *An Education*.

did not suit the honeymoon couples'. At the top of the mountain, snow still lingered and on the north side the Aletsch glacier, grey, crevassed ice, swept round and down to the south-west in a curve of imperceptible motion.

Called for the night shoot. First shot at seven. The last at about ten to five this morning. About 60 extras, much dancing – very muggy and uncomfortable conditions – and finally the kiss. In the middle of all this I signed my *GBH* contract in an upstairs room!

Walked back down from the village as grey dawn turned white, for breakfast in the meadow by the river. Felt like a soldier after battle.

Thursday, July 19th: Fiesch

7.45 a.m. A helicopter comes in to collect cement from the electricity company's cable-car station where I have dressed as Francis Ashby for the last full day's filming.

Later. I had been doing a series of walking shots towards the waterfall. Every couple of minutes the helicopter roared overhead, shattering the calm of a beautiful natural location – bucket either hanging low, or empty, trailing out in the slipstream.

Then there was an odd noise, a sort of irregular and more vehement acceleration of the engine. Did not register any emergency though, and, resting in the generous heat, beneath a bush, I was gently nodding off, whilst the crew moved up to take another shot. Made no connection between my ability to nod off and the absence of the ferrying helicopter.

We hear that the helicopter has crashed – down at our base camp, a few yards from the make-up bus where Connie and Trini are being prepared for later shooting.

But work goes on and soon I'm scampering up warm rocks to the base of the waterfall, pulling down my mid-Victorian underwear and exposing most, if not all, to the camera far below.

As I splash the mountain water over my body I at last understand what could have made Edward Palin pull all his clothes off and plunge into an Alpine pool. The natural basin of rock, the seduction of flowing water, the fields thick with butterflies and the silence from protecting mountains all around.

Walk slowly back down the hill, away from this paradise, quite reluctantly.

First I see Trini and her mother Sylvia sat beneath the trees, Trini working on her crochet, her mother knitting. T's make-up smudged with lines of tears. She had looked out immediately after the impact and seen a man hanging from the helicopter.

Connie B, in dressing gown with hair up, looking every inch the actress, sits reading. I notice she has a glass of red wine beside her – unusual, but probably a reflection on the morning's events. Connie very self-contained, small, bird-like, back straight, never sloppy. I envy that sort of ability to hold things in, to coolly conserve.

Bits of the helicopter rotors scattered all over the landing strip. Holes sliced in the Perspex walls of the cable-car station. A miracle that the make-up bus, or any of our crew, avoided injury.

The day hotting up. Cloudless sky. Must be in the upper 80s. In the p.m. we squash into the electricity co.'s rugged little cable car, and are hauled up to 2,094 metres, nearly 7,000 feet. A bleak, rocky area with tremendous view of the Finsteraarhorn to the north.

The last shot is, most unusually, the last shot of the story – myself and Trini on our honeymoon in Switzerland. Great-grandfather and great-grand-mother arm in arm walking across the splendid, dominating landscape of the Alps.

Eventually the sun descends behind the mountain to the west. The light is turned gently but firmly off. Thirty-seven days of filming are complete.

Friday, July 20th: Fiesch–London

In response to requests, I have had the Edward Palin diaries copied and have brought them along, rather like song-sheets, for those who want to them take away.

They are probably all leaving about now – Trini to fly direct to New York, and half of our crew to London via Geneva.

In my bed I turn over in relief at the sudden loosening of the film's grip and relax until half past nine, when I go downstairs for a breakfast of coffee and hot milk, thick honey and fresh brown bread, taken solitarily, apart from a French family.

After a bath I slowly gather together my possessions and am packed by midday.

Then into the Espace and we make for Geneva.

Thursday, August 2nd

To Mister Lighting's new studios out on the A40.

Akers day, we call it, as most of what we're doing has been requested by George Akers. So for a couple of hours, they pick up things in close-up. My Oxford study and then my Swiss chalet room are recreated. Reminds me how much of filming is an industrial process, how little is romantic. Yet there is something romantic about our little band today. A quiet, happy feeling of achievement which cannot be specifically quantified but binds us all together.

Into Central London, to the Royal Academy for a shot of myself and Connie walking away from camera between two rows of statues. At least it's cool in here amongst all the hefty classical figures with arms and penises missing.

Then back into the traffic jams and out to the studios for Connie to change – all for a back-of-head shot in Jimmy Jewel's garden.

And in a small and unpretentious little park in Acton our small and unpretentious film finally comes to an end.

Tomorrow at this time I should be in Majorca with Helen, grabbing whatever holiday time I can.

Eric Idle has become a father again, and there is very good news from Anne on the next big project after *GBH* – the BBC has decided to back our independently produced *Pole to Pole* and we've been given a BBC One transmission slot of January 1993.

Friday, August 3rd: London–Deyà

Up at 7.15. Outside the heat waits, indolently and inevitably, as in some southern city. We leave home at eight o'clock. Newspaper headlines scream Saddam Hussein's promise to 'turn Kuwait into a graveyard' if his invasion is countered with force. For the first time there appears to be an international consensus that his action was unjustified, but ominous silence from the rest of the Arab world.

We are at the hotel in Deyà by three. About half past three I begin the laborious process of hacking away at my Ashby-esque mutton chops with a GII razor, when a cut-throat and a barber's in Jermyn Street are really what's required.

I do shed a year or two as the hair disappears down the basin.

Sunbathe, read deeper into the delightful *Mohawk* by Richard Russo, then out into the village. Look at Robert Graves's grave and marvel once more at the situation of the church and panorama of Deyà coiled below us.

A play is taking place in the open air, there's music in the church and the lizards wait, toes splayed, in the street lamps.

Saturday, August 4th: Deyà

Helen to the sunbeds and me onto our little terrace overlooking roofs and hillsides to read through more of *GBH*.

Richard Branson, who owns the hotel, is about, playing chess with a friend whilst friend's girlfriend watches (later he's on the tennis court with a friend whilst girlfriend watches). He's always engaged in some sort of competitive activity; I never see him sit and read. But then he hasn't got *GBH* or *Mohawk*.

Sunday, August 5th: Deyà

Breakfast at half past nine, as the sun edges up over the mountain rim. I sit outside on the patio and plough on through *GBH* – around me light, sounds and the muted colours of the terracotta tiles and the silvery grey of the olive tree leaves.

See Branson making his way to the pool with a sheaf of files and papers. Later I see him lying in the shade going through them, dropping those he's finished with into a child's blue rubber dinghy.

Finish my latest read-through of *GBH*. My long, final, triumphant speech on socialism prepared in these privileged surroundings.

Tuesday, August 7th

To the Crown viewing theatre for my first look at an assembly of '*AF*'. For some reason I feel elated anticipation. Not un-to do with my conversation with Virginia P on the phone last night. She had seen the video of the assembly twice over the weekend. She'd loved the look of it and thought I was 'brilliant'. This has kept me in good spirits most of the day.

There is no doubt that it is an appealing film – the photography, the performances and the story all very watchable and involving. At the end smiles all round. 'Delightful' is the word most often used. 'Everything I hoped it would be,' says Irene Lamb.

Over supper I make a list of Helen's observations. 'Don't make the film any shorter,' she says. It's currently about 100 minutes.

Wednesday, August 8th

Wake to hear the milk van shuffle to a halt and the bottles being collected. It's six o'clock and that means my mind is waking too early.

Try to confuse it, or at least keep it dulled with the most soporific and boring images. But it's no good, it wants action, and it soon finds it in analysing, in the cold, or in this case rather muggy, light of day, my performance in '*AF*'.

Find myself wanting. Feel that I am absorbed into the story without dominating and dictating its direction. I do not change enough, or as dramatically, as perhaps I should.

But the day's commitments beckon and at ten minutes to nine I'm at BUPA's new medical centre in Gray's Inn Road.

Usual tests: eyes, ears, blood, lungs, as well as an abdominal X-ray, then the fitness assessment. Though I may feel mentally off-colour, I'm in good physical shape.

I run for nine and three-quarter minutes on the treadmill at seven miles an hour on ever-increasing gradients. This is longer than two years ago when I was filmed having a medical for *80 Days*, so I can assume I'm fitter at 47 than I was at 45. Most memorable moment was Dr Goldin's exclamation as he took his finger out of my bottom – 'You have the prostate of a 21-year-old.'

Autographs and messages for the nurses. I have the sneaking feeling as I leave that to give me any bad news would have so spoilt this morning that they just invented the results.

Sunday, August 12th: London–Abbotsley–Manchester

To Abbotsley for the first time since the Sunday before 'AF'. We walk round the garden – the pond has almost disappeared in the drought – then Rachel hears some of my lines for the week in the little room next to the kitchen, then a bottle of champagne rosé on the lawn and lunch, coffee and loll half asleep on a rug in the sunshine. Then tennis – Rachel and I take a set off Tom and Lisa [Tom's girlfriend] – then some more lines with Rachel and it's time for me to start back home to pack and leave for Manchester.

They're all on the tennis court when I say goodbye, providing the most idyllic tableau. Rachel waves from the drive and at half past four I turn out into the village and head for three or four months of the most challenging work since *80 Days*. Miss them all as I drive the familiar back lanes to the motorway.

Meet Robert Young and Bob Lindsay at the airport. We share a row of three on the Manchester shuttle. The row opposite is entirely taken up by the almost inconceivably massive bulk of Giant Haystacks – the wrestler. He's the largest man I think I've ever seen.

Once at Manchester I'm driven to a meal with Robert Y and Alan B at a restaurant called the Lemon Tree. Alan arrives late, looks harassed. His play *Having a Ball* goes into the West End next week. It's broken box office records in Liverpool, but he's worried about the London critics. Both men seem pleased with the shoot so far. Julie Walters has been marvellous, they say, quite brilliant.

Monday, August 13th: Manchester

Collected at ten and driven south to the location – an old technical college of some kind being turned into a high-tech modern industrial estate.

All the 'major' actors share a Winnebago. Comfortable, but no privacy. Like a common room. Tom Georgeson, Bob Lindsay, Drew Schofield, Paul Daneman and myself in there as well as Alan B, who occasionally joins us to watch the cricket. The rest of the day's cast – including 30 'assorted lefties' – either sit on the grass beneath warm, cloudy skies, or are squeezed into a grubby, dilapidated double-decker bus.

I meet the selection of Welsh collies which are here to audition for Beulah. The first one is called Spike: an older dog than required in the script, but wonderfully, abjectly, lovable. Head turned up and nuzzling into my crotch. Hard to resist. We run, stop and heel around the gardens. Robert and Alan are summonsed and Spike is unanimously chosen.

After lunch I have my hair cut by Jane then am driven back into Manchester. My time is suddenly my own. A situation I often desperately crave, but now, here, at this odd time, I'm a little frightened of.

Walk down to Sunlight House and the site of 'Herriot's Turkish Baths'. Probably once rather grand, now a health club with impressive tight-shirted exec. girls wearing lots of make-up at the door. Downstairs is a pool of irregular shape into which enamel-tiled columns disappear, giving it the feel of a flooded basement. However, manage 30 lengths and feel better. Keen girl signs me up for fitness assessment tomorrow.

Tuesday, August 14th: Manchester

Leisurely rising, then driven out to Oldham to a drama workshop where most of our children have come from. The head man, David Johnson, is a stern teacher, but produces some impressive performances.

Meet two of those who will be my children. They're lovely – Anna Friel, the confident, attractive 15-year-old daughter of a teacher, and Edward, with a broader accent, a reassuring face – a 'Just William' lookalike.

Meet David Ross, who is to play scenes with me next week; he's also the lead in *Having a Ball*, which opens to previews in London on Thursday night. A gentlemanly figure, soft-spoken, like a slightly more pert Alan Bennett.

I make my way to Herriot's, where Sharon tries me out 'to find my limits'.

Wednesday, August 15th: Manchester

My first acting day on *GBH*.

Taxi collects me at 7.15. He asks me where the location is, can't find it on his map. It's raining. We drive up motorways towards Bolton, and eventually find ourselves in Lostock; vehicles parked in station yard. I'm taken to the Winnebago.

Because of the rain we first do a scene I haven't even learnt. (As I've been learning manically for the last few days this is quite ironic.) So I bring Jim Nelson to life in a small headmaster's study at Lostock School, Glengarth Drive in Bolton. Phone-answering sequences.

We do a scene at the end of the day almost uninterrupted, with camera on tight long lens following us everywhere. The cut-ins are shot in a businesslike way. Robert Young's vitality and rather patrician control obviously the secret. He looks as if he started yesterday, not eight weeks ago. Alan is there and, I think, pleased by the last scene – when I turn the press hacks away. Because of rain we work until eight.

Thursday, August 16th: Manchester

More rain, so my telephone conversation with Frank Twist is done first. The pickets, and the thugs who will be jumping on the roof, sit mouldering on the bus. The Winnebago is home to five or six speaking actors. Bob complains.

I have the feeling that things are beginning to fall apart a bit. The weather is clearly putting some of the arrangements under pressure and we shall film some of next week's material tomorrow, including one of my important showdown scenes with Murray.

As we're filming in the early hours of Sunday morning it doesn't seem worth my while going home for the weekend. Talk to Will, who's back from France – apparently Tom's new house in Kentish Town is looking very good. Rachel is concerned for me, and how the acting's going, and I miss them.

Friday, August 17th: Manchester

The confrontation scene with Murray seemed to go well, though I did not approach it with sufficient confidence at first. I hope I did it well. I feel I'm too old and too physically slight for Jim. But at six we wrap and my first week is over.

Back at the Portland Hotel. *Newsnight*. War sounds to be closer over Iraq and Kuwait. Sleep while watching most of it. Light out on week, finally, at a quarter to twelve.

Saturday, August 18th: Manchester

Wake about six o'clock. Lie in bed until eleven. Very occasionally I drift into dreams. In one of them, I'm looking out of a corner window, the shutters are opened a crack. I look down as I hear a noise, figures run away, soil and dirt are flung through the shutters and hit my face. I wake sharply, heart beating hard.

I will not succumb to the self-pity of a tired actor alone on a warm, busy day in Manchester, and I take myself off to the Whitworth Art Gallery.

Friendly inside. Much communication with the visitor. Three Camille Pissarros and many Pre-Raphaelites including a voluptuous Rossetti and a weird Millais. Exhibition of landscape painting with good notes relating landscape to the human factor. Generally informative.

Taxi back down the Oxford Road to the health club. Just time for a run on the treadmill. I miss my Hampstead Heath.

At the hotel, I read through all the script for next week. Hard work for me. Two Weller scenes, one with the children and a big one with Murray before I see home again.

Walk down to the Cornerhouse, passing an array of chunky hookers in the streets behind the hotel, cruising along streets lined with chunky buildings and right below the splendid mock-mediaeval façade of the old Law Courts.

Back at the hotel the manager has requested I join him for a drink. He's a nervous, youngish man, and no sooner has he ordered champagne and sat down beside me than the fire alarms sound everywhere. A frightful din and complete confusion. Turns out that the flambé trolley set off the restaurant alarms. 'I'll be skinned alive for this,' mutters the manager, as firemen mingle with guests as if in some sitcom.

He apologises for the absence of his wife who really wanted to meet me. 'She had the vomits.'

Tomorrow morning's pick-up call is four o'clock.

Wednesday, August 22nd: Manchester

Robert Young came into make-up first thing yesterday and said how pleased he was with the confrontation scene in the gymnasium. He talked enthusiastically of 'the strength' in the performance. His word of caution was almost the same as Tristram's, that occasionally I let Michael Palin, with too ready a smile and too expressive an eye movement, through into the performance. Most of the time Jim Nelson dominates and is strong and solid, but I must watch the Palin-isms.

This morning I have a five-and-a-half-page, quite tricky scene with David Ross. David was playing in *Having a Ball* at the Comedy last night, arrived in Manchester at 2.15 a.m. and had four hours' sleep. He's already in make-up being aged, spectacularly well, when I arrive at the Winnebago.

The drizzle means that they are going straight into the common room scene. Robert plans it in one take, running over four minutes. Though tired as we both are, the final result is greeted by all as a success.

As I walk back to lunch, Alan B shouts after me 'That was magnificent.'

Friday, August 24th

Feel cool, calm, relaxed and relieved. Wish I could always be like this. I've appeared as Jim N for nine days now. I know and feel the character; I know that Robert Y is pleased, but the challenge to produce my best in all circumstances is daunting. I simply pray I have the ability to rise to it.

At present, as I experience the pleasure of seeing my house again, and wandering, free from cameras and scripts, into the overgrowing garden on a thick, hot, windless afternoon, I have no fears, and I feel that I have already overcome the darkest worries I had before going up to Manchester.

Tuesday, August 28th: Manchester

Richard picks me up at 7.15 to go once again to the school. Grey drizzle. Morning spent on scene with the children in which I have to entertain them for an end-of-year treat. The mad science experiment. It must be energetic, improvised, and funny. I feel like Jim Nelson's supposed to feel in the script – ground down. Dragging himself/myself to an enormous effort.

It is one of the hardest half-day's filming I've ever done, and at the end of it I feel hot and only half successful. All I want to do in the Winnebago at lunch is to rest and hopefully sleep. But a deputation from the producers – tall, rich-voiced David Jones and large, friendly-faced Caroline Hewitt, the Production Manager, squeeze themselves in and discuss 'problems'.

Evidently Bob L has talked to them about on-set accommodation for actors, co-ordination of calls on set, etc. etc. and it's all been taken very seriously. I make my points and they are concerned and appreciative and say I must always say if anything is wrong. On busy days a second Winnie will be provided.

When Caroline's gone David J lingers. He says the rushes are brilliant. 'I always thought Jim Nelson was an interesting character, but you've made him even more interesting.'

Because I like him and feel that he is approaching this from a writer's point of view, his compliment fell most happily, and, together with Alan's endorsement over the weekend, combined to reinvigorate me in the afternoon.

After wrap go with Lindsay to the gym. I do four and a half miles in 35 minutes on the treadmill and row for five minutes. Then we both overeat at a Japanese restaurant where flamboyant chefs cook at your table and throw eggs in the air.

Friday, August 31st: Manchester–London

Sleep until six o'clock. This is now quite a late awakening for me. Up at 6.45; oh, how hard it is to roll back the bedclothes!

Check out of the Portland; then to Runcorn Bridge with Richard and Julia and Dearbhla. Mike Angelis there too. All day spent on completing the final shot which is really my moment of glory, redemption, self-discovery, the apotheosis of Jim Nelson.

End the day emoting and elating and triumphing and overcoming, with the car parked beneath the viaduct's immense concrete supports surrounded by props men rocking it and local children looking on incredulously. 'I'm alive!' 'Ha-Ha-Ha!' Not my most natural and I can tell from faces of Alan and Robert that it's good. Only good. Robert's cousin Julia seeks me out and looks at me in some admiration. 'You're so patient.'

Home about 9.30. Sit and watch Michael Caine talking about techniques of film-acting. Resolve not to start worrying about next week's work until next week.

Thursday, September 6th: Brockwood Hall, Cumbria

2.50 in the afternoon. In the Winnebago at Brockwood. Dan Massey asleep. His book *Not Prince Hamlet* by Michael Meyer on the table in front of me. Annie Spiers read my Chinese horoscope while making me up ... 'A good year, if you do not forget old friends.'

The Winnebago is rocked, as I write, by 50–60 mile-an-hour gusts. The tail end of a hurricane, due to blow into tomorrow. It's continuing the bad run of weather luck which has hit the film from the day I began. Robert Y confesses that we are two and a half days behind. (They were half a day behind when I joined.) This week has progressed untidily.

Began with a strong emotional scene with Dearbhla on Monday to get the juices going, and have also completed the tennis-racket-smashing which I'm glad to be free of. For all the planning and choreographing, in the end I went at it with a frenzied lack of control, which was the only way to do it.

Sunday, September 9th: Trinity House Hotel, Ulverston

It's late afternoon. My shutters are closed against the noise of traffic from the Barrow–Lancaster main road, just outside this uncomplicated, handsome little Georgian rectory.

I am aware that I am running on overdrive. This is a test of stamina as punishing as any since *80 Days*. I knew it would be. My body and mind prepared themselves at the beginning of May. Somehow they keep me together. I learn and remember my lines, I have completed difficult physically and emotionally demanding scenes to what I sense to be general satisfaction.

I wish that I were always on top form. I wish the effort wasn't quite as hard. I wish I could always wake up positive, fresh and vigorous.

I am happy with the crew. There is not a single bad egg amongst them. Robert is everything Robert Lindsay said he would be. Enormously patient, supportive and the complete director.

However wound up I may be at the beginning of the day (and maybe this is just the price of giving a good performance) I relax almost ecstatically at the end and the homecoming drive over the low ragged fells, and the whisky and the bath and the meal, generally with Dearbhla and Julia and Dan Massey, are times of unqualified happiness.

I don't read much outside of the newspapers; I find I can't concentrate. My mind is full of *GBH*, except when I turn off the light and the short but blessed sleep clears my mind of everything.

Monday, September 10th, Ulverston

Think back over a painful but satisfactory night shoot. Rain was to fall throughout the long scene, and I had only thin pyjamas and a pair of Y-fronts against the elements.

The first time we played it the rain was such a surprise to Dan that his voice rose several octaves and he sped through the scene almost halving its time. Robert took him aside afterwards and said he felt he'd missed some nuances. 'You must remember that it's warm spring rain,' tries Robert. 'But it isn't!' says Dan with feeling but not hostility.

A wasps' nest is discovered in the middle of shot and has to be dealt with. A cable burns through, but by six we have the sequence, though one or two cut-aways are abandoned.

The crew applaud Dan and myself after we manage a third long take under the hosepipes!

Up at one o'clock to meet Alan B for lunch at the Bay Horse Inn. A picturesque spot by the Duddon Estuary.

Alan's a great storyteller and we sit out with a light wind taking the edge off a warm day by the mudflats.

He tells us his Princess Margaret story. How she made a beeline for him and Willy Russell at an Everyman Theatre do.[1] How she drank four whiskies in swift succession. How nice she was when Alan spat a piece of vol-au-vent onto her, and how she just wanted to meet actors.

Tuesday, September 11th, Ulverston

Shoot the car chase sequence in our rotten old Volkswagen Variant. Most of the morning taken up with stunt-driving. Andy Bradford, who fell down a mountain as Ashby in Switzerland, now risks his life as Jim Nelson on the back roads of Cumbria.

The commissioning editor for C4 and his assistant are visiting. Alan has to entertain them. A long, very noisy meal.

Remark of Dan's makes me laugh longer and more helplessly than I remember for months. I say that I can control the dog quite easily and it will obey whichever command I give it ... 'Come!' or 'Kneel!' ... 'Oh, kneel, surely,' says Dan with anxious distaste. For some reason we all collapse.

To bed at one o'clock. Two and a half hours later than I meant to be.

Friday, September 14th, Ulverston

Pick-up at 7.15. The milk and vegetables wait to be collected outside the back door. Travel in with Dan. Pass valleys filled with fluffy white mist. All quiet and untroubled by wind or rain.

Once again to Woodlands, the house Jim and his family have retreated to, bouncing along the field up to the small group of those in the crew who arrive even earlier than ourselves.

Full complement of holidaymaking extras here today – including Anna

---

1 Opened on Hope Street, Liverpool in 1964. Gave first break to many left-leaning writers and actors.

Ford's father, a very fine, white-bearded gentleman, who looks like an old Boer, and Chris Erwin, whose portrayal of the hero in some performances of *Having a Ball* left audiences gasping ... 'Cock like a baby's arm,' was Angelis' description.

Apparently some of the film of the stunt-driving sequences shot on Tuesday has been lost on BR. Depressing news when we're fighting to keep ahead.

Work with horses, dogs and children. Eleven takes of one shot with the dog. But short scene when I burst out onto the balcony with an envelope full of photos screaming for Laura works well. I hit full intensity and dog lady Sue admits to being much moved.

Monday, September 17th, Ulverston

John Cleese on morning TV, hands raised with Paddy Ashdown on Liberal Democrat conference stand! No wonder Alan couldn't get hold of him. Alan wanted to ask John to play the Scottish doctor part, but was very nervous of approaching him.

Shooting more car stuff this morning: a bridge over the river Esk which lies in a most beautiful valley – not spectacular, but low, gentle, wooded and empty. Sellafield Nuclear Power Station is just up the road and the river is, I'm told, seriously polluted, with five times more radiation than anywhere else in the country.

I manage an impressive emergency stop in the roadway, hitting the mark twice. Peter Jessop, the lighting cameraman, most impressed with my stunt-driving.

Tuesday, September 18th, Kirkstanton

To Kirkstanton, a small village on the coast near Haverigg. Featureless apart from a scruffy green, a pub and a farmhouse which is being renovated, expensively and tastelessly.

This is a nuclear neighbourhood – 14,000 are employed in the Trident programme at Barrow and many more reprocessing nuclear waste at Sellafield. A railway line runs close by and every now and then a Plutonium Special rumbles past, the characteristic brown flasks slung on flatbed bogies, full of spent plutonium in rods.

The weather is closing in – gales forecast for tomorrow. So we shoot inside first. Two scenes, one of which is among the most demanding I've done. I have to tell Martin (Mike Angelis) that I'm going mad. When I rehearsed it it moved me to tears, but Robert Y discourages a strong emotional reading.

So, at the last minute, I find my approach changed. I go along with Robert but I feel less sure of myself and the dry joke at the end – about Diane having it off – doesn't play. Robert thinks it does, Alan, whose gut reaction I trust, feels it could be better.

A long, hard scene which takes most of the day, and leaves me sobered.

Sunday, September 23rd

Feel drained of energy. Halfway between worlds. *GBH* on one side and London life on the other. Make an effort to shift myself in some direction. Call TJ and fix some squash and leave message for TG inviting myself round to tea.

In the evening a full house for Sunday dinner. Tom and Will spar like five-year-olds. Tom very funny with his banter about Will at Oxford. 'Have you got your monocle?' etc. etc. He must have taken in more of the Tom Merry world than I'd expected.

A lovely, boisterous dinner, and, through it all, a poignant sense that with Will at Oxford and Tom having left home this month marks quite a sea change in family life. But for tonight – we're the same as we always were.

Sunday, September 30th

The *Sunday Correspondent,* after a brave start, has gone tabloid. *80 Days* book seems to be fading – down to No. 10 in its 45th week. Funny how one is never satisfied. A year ago I'd have been delighted to see it touch the charts at all. Now I shall be very aggrieved if it doesn't hold in there for 52 weeks.

Friday, October 5th

A screening of '*AF*' to check out the sound. Terry J there and thought it the most beautiful film he'd ever seen; his laughter helped the atmosphere.

I like the music by Georges Delerue and feel it adds to the quality. Still have misgivings about my playing of Ashby. I think too consistently and persistently severe. Not much burning off him. It's a measure of how good Trini and Connie's performances are that they make my emotional involvement seem convincing.

Wednesday, October 10th: Brookfield Hall, near Buxton, Derbyshire

Alan has agreed to three days of cuts to keep us on schedule. The weather at our location – a house up on the most exposed part of the moor, near Hayfield – has been grey and inhospitable and not at all right for the summer scenes we're shooting. A complicated interior of the four of us took over 20 takes to complete.

Rang Patrick Cassavetti from the house. Stan Fishman of Rank has seen *American Friends* and 'quite' likes it. Will give us the Odeon Haymarket in March or April next year, though. He doesn't think it will do business outside London. Patrick thinks he's wrong. Whatever, I feel badly in need of some unequivocally good news.

Saturday, October 13th

Maggie T used the 'Parrot Sketch' in her speech to the Conservative Party Conference yesterday and I'm rung by the *Correspondent* for a quote.

Patrick says the 50-person 'random' audience research screening of *'AF'* went off well on Wednesday. No-one hated the movie and there were one or two excellents!

Sunday, October 14th

Present-opening at the breakfast table. Give Helen a long silver necklace, UB40 tapes, a book on witchcraft in south-west France, and one on Indian cooking, and a big basket of winter-flowering jasmine.

She goes to tennis. I take two signed books up to the William Ellis auction, then back home to find Will has just arrived on his first break from Oxford. Rachel has made a wonderful birthday card, with all Mum's activities and habits noted!

Then we all go off to lunch at Mary and Ed's, after I've spent a very satis-factory hour with Rachel going over the seven big scenes I have next week.

Saturday, October 20th: Brookfield Hall, Derbyshire

One of my most difficult scenes comes up before lunch. It's the Robbie Burns death description – myself and Dearbhla. On the page it's described as enraged – 'tears flow'. I'm aware as I do it, cruelly cold for the crew, that Alan and Robert have reservations.

They take me away to a quiet room – dressed as the children's bed-room with posters of Jason Donovan on the wall – and Robert at some length gives me the wise note that in the retelling of a dreadful experience the emotion is often suppressed and does not need to spill over the surface.

As I walk back to the Winnebago I feel a heavy weight; I'm cross at not having thought of that myself. But maybe I'm the last one to see how I come across.

Dearbhla takes my arm and says I should tell the story in the same way I told her about Angela's death, which she said was calm and matter-of-fact. This helped me enormously – provided the key.

I do several takes with minor script errors – though only Alan spots them. But being a writer myself I know how much accuracy matters, and I'm hugely relieved when, despite the heat and the fatigue, I manage two good and complete takes which they are pleased with.

I walk outside. The light's fading. The line of trucks shields the view on one side, but to the east the wide, bare slopes of the Pennines begin. Alan joins me. He has tears in his eyes. He says there are certain scenes he can't watch without crying.

Fly back to London feeling muted. Less euphoric than seven days ago. It all came harder this week.

Sunday, October 21st

To Simon A at six for a meeting re his idea of getting together a group to bid for one of the new TV franchises.

'Basically, we want you to be a part of it,' says Simon, who claims I am the first person he sounded out, after first hatching his plan in the bath, 'but what role can you play?' Both decide to think about this further, to see if my desire not to become administratively involved or even contractually involved can be reconciled with the desire of him and Clive and Roger Laughton to have me on board.

Monday, October 22nd: London–Derbyshire

Out to see latest version of 'AF' with Patrick, Steve and Tristram at De Lane Lea. Improvements (including dawn shots beneath opening titles) all seem to the good. The music enriches and seems better each time I hear it. Last half-hour almost trouble-free. Some of the middle section still sluggish. I can see extra cuts I would have made but the picture is being neg-cut at the moment so confine my notes to one or two observations about soundtrack which TP will look after later today.

Recycling, checking through latest offers, including a Barclaycard ad – as the new Alan Whicker! (To be directed by John Lloyd, but, that apart, I've not the slightest compunction in turning it down.) Wonderful relief of not having to learn heavy speeches again this weekend. A call from *GBH* to say that they have decided to use myself and Dearbhla tomorrow after all. Could we come up on the late flight?

Thursday, October 25th

Plunged into a silliness over Python's reaction to Thatcher's recital of the 'Parrot Sketch'. 'The Parrot has Twitched' said Paddy Ashdown after Eastbourne and in a sense the by-election slap round the face has made Thatcher look very silly and the Parrot indeed will not be mentioned by her again.[1]

TJ is the only one who still wants to sue her. Anne has come up with a press release reflecting Eric and JC's wish not to sue but to issue a silly statement about Thatcher being 'tired and shagged out after a long squawk'. Too late to sue anyway. Impact lost now I feel. But I have to ring TJ and tell him this. He doesn't push his view and we make amicable arrangements to meet next week.

Friday, October 26th

See an *Evening Standard*. There on the front page is a picture of Derek Hatton being led away by detectives, and the news that he's been arrested in a massive fraud operation involving 300 police.[2] *GBH* is now given another dimension, as the story Alan has written is being played out for real. Extraordinary.

Two small children come trick-or-treating. I tell them to come back on Halloween. They depart, one of them muttering indignantly, 'Going on 'oliday!'

1 Only two weeks after the Liberal Democrats were likened to a 'dead parrot', their candidate David Bellotti overturned a Conservative majority to win the Eastbourne seat, which had become vacant after the death of Ian Gow, who was killed when the Provisional IRA put a bomb under his car.
2 Derek Hatton, unofficial leader of Liverpool City Council when it was controlled by the Trotskyist Militant Tendency, a far-left socialist council grouping.

Sunday, October 28th

Call Alan B. He says that, even more than Hatton's arrest, life has imitated art with the revelation that Wimpey, major contributors to the Conservative Party, are alleged to have funded Militant[1] through Derek Hatton's PR company. Alan is rewriting the ending.

TG comes by. Quite like old times – tea and gossip in the kitchen. He confirms that he loved the look of *'AF'*, but felt it was not dramatic enough. Time passed pleasantly, but there were no highs and lows, no 'emotional Alps'.

A long rambling chat leads into Sunday supper – delicately disposing of a chicken whilst Attenborough's *Trials of Life* shows a squad of chimpanzees hunting a luckless monkey and then tearing it apart and eating, as far as I could see, every bit of it.

Monday, November 5th: Manchester

Day 100 on *GBH* goes unremarked. It's the start of another week's work, the 21st in succession, which promises some of the most busy and complex scenes.

Re-meet everyone in the cinder-covered car park of the Taylor Brothers Sports and Social Club in Eccles. There is a high and cloudless sky and it's been a cold night.

Colin Douglas, who has a heavy week as Frank Twist, is in bad shape. He's a big, warm, lovable man you want to hug, but the rewrites of his scenes with me have devastated him.

Colin is 79, his wife died at the start of filming. It had taken him many weeks to learn the lines – he'd write them out time after time – and then suddenly to be presented with a scene, or scenes, demolished and rebuilt had sent him into shock. 'I can't do it … I've not slept since I got the rewrites.' He shakes his head and it's a desperately unhappy sight to see a big man's pride laid so low. Just like the character he's playing, that's the uncanny thing.

But Robert is sensitive and adapts without fuss, even to the extent of secretly shooting a scene I thought was a rehearsal. This led to Colin giving a fine performance and me drying!

---

1 Hatton was cleared of any impropriety after an eight-week trial.

Tuesday, November 6th, Manchester

Colin is in a dreadful state again. In the Winnie I find myself holding his great shoulders, feeling the heat and stickiness of the sweat through his shirt, as he sheds some tears and says he's not slept and had thought of throwing himself over the banisters at the Britannia Hotel.

I go over the lines as often as he wants, and when we start to shoot Robert end-boards and never shouts 'Action!' Colin rolls easily through the speeches that have been driving him near to banister-hopping, and we complete work scheduled for one and a half days before day one is out.

Thursday, November 8th, Manchester

Jim's apotheosis, and my single most important contribution to this whole nine-hour epic, looms.

Dealing with Colin D, though nerve-wracking in a way, has helped me to forget my anxieties. They are exactly the same as Colin's, of course, fear of letting people down, fear of failing to meet the high standards expected of you, fear of physical inability to meet the demands, but Colin's are felt so much more intensely and appear so massive that in comforting him I'm able to put my own fears into proportion.

As the afternoon wears on I pace around the car park trying to keep the lines fresh. It's getting dark by the time I'm asked into the hall. Robert explains to the crowd about the next part of the sequence and then I'm thrown to the wolves.

I do it, and because it is such a strong speech, it fires me and carries me along and after the first minute or so I know I'm launched and that passion and conviction and belief is what I can put across much better than the comedy asides. At the end they applaud spontaneously, and a number of people in crew and crowd come up and congratulate me. John Maskell, the camera operator, says that it's just what people need to hear in politics today. It's not the performance so much as what I was saying that has caught people.

Friday, November 9th, Manchester

We work through the speech again. I run it five times in succession with only minor hiccups.

The day warms up, the hall is hot and smoky under the lights. Robert L's afternoon, as he plays his breakdown very movingly. Then round onto the reverses of my speech for all the audience reactions. My concentration holds and we finish at seven, with nine minutes of story in the can.

We go to a Pizza Express.

Talk about early sexual experience. Dearbhla reveals she used to put socks in her bra and only whip them out at the last minute. Lindsay Duncan, who has a lovely, rather wistful way of telling a very rude tale, reflects on the number of times she had some sexual encounter with a man 'just to be polite'!

Alan calls late to ask how it went. I'm able to convey the enthusiasm he wants to hear. He's in London, where *Having a Ball* closes tomorrow night. I ask him if he'll be with us next week. I hear ironic laughter, which worries me.

Monday, November 12th, Manchester

Anne James at Mayday tells me that *80 Days* has won four nominations in the American 'ACE' cable awards. Best Doc, Best Editor, Best Script, Best Presenter. The ceremony is on Rachel's 16th birthday – 13th January – and I agree to go over to LA. It will also be my first weekend clear after the end of *GBH*.

Wednesday, November 14th, Manchester

Leave the hotel at 7.40. Collect Colin D from the Britannia for his final day. Once again, deep gloom. And yet this time he cannot blame the rewrites. The Frank Twist phone call scenes he has learnt long ago. But he is as maudlin as ever ... 'I haven't slept since two o'clock the night before last ... I'm leaving the profession after this.'

I can't see much to cheer him up as we drive out to a location somewhere beyond the Manchester Abattoir, a modern concrete complex, unnervingly similar in design to an airport. The bus depot is a bleak and inhospitable place, wind whistles through, though it's still quite mild. As he loves cooking, I've brought Colin a last-day present of one of the glossy Roux Brothers books, but he's in too much distress right now to accept anything other than his fate.

As it is, he once again defies the bogeymen and turns in a big, strong, word-perfect performance.

Saturday, November 17th, Manchester

Day off before Sunday shooting. After breakfast catch up on diary and organise myself before Simon A comes to my hotel room at eleven. He wants to bring me all the latest news on the franchise project.

The trouble is that Simon is much more enthusiastic about the whole thing than I am. He loves the world of wheeling and dealing and fixing. I don't much, except when it relates directly to the fulfilment of a creative project. So I listen and Simon bubbles, as has been the pattern over this matter since it was first mooted. Try as I do, I cannot seem to communicate the real basis of my caution to someone who can see nothing better than to be involved in such a scheme as winning a franchise.

He, Clive and Roger have found a way of involving me, which is that Prominent TV should have shares and a place on the board. Knowing my reservations, he suggests that rather than me (an absentee explorer for much of next year) I should depute someone from Prominent to sit on the board on my behalf.

It's a sunny day outside now, I am still preoccupied and indeed fatigued by *GBH* and I don't really want to waffle on, so I agree to Simon's strategy and about one we break up.

Sunday, November 18th, Manchester

Filming today at the school in Lostock, in which I began my career as Jim Nelson last August.

Feeling of déjà vu as I walk past pickets and slam Michael Murray against the bonnet of his car. Then an assortment of 'on the way to school' shots, which are supposed to be late summer.

Back to the Portland, and settle on the bed and immerse myself in the Sunday papers, all of which are full of Heseltine's bid to oust Thatcher. She comes across, as always, as a friendless person, and if she loses then nemesis will be swift and probably very painful.

Out to eat in the evening with Dearbhla and RL. We wander round deserted streets where everything seems closed and emerge into Albert Square to the bizarre sight of the vast £15,000 inflatable Santa flapping lifelessly against the columns and arches of the Gothic tower of the City Hall. Father Christmas has burst.

Wednesday, November 21st: Brookfield Hall, Derbyshire

The huge St Bernard sprawls in the doorway of the small breakfast room. He buries his head in his paws in a hopeless attempt at invisibility.

The papers are all brimming with the details and speculation surrounding the greatest political upheaval since Thatcher came to power – in the year *Life of Brian* opened. Most of the comment judges her decision last night to fight on and win as being a typical Thatcher knee-jerk reaction. Ill advised, indeed unadvised.

Thursday, November 22nd: Derbyshire–London

Alarm at 6.45. Leave Brookfield at 7.15. There's frost on the car roofs and the climbing sun illuminates the bare Peak hillsides with a pinkish glow. It's going to be a spectacular day.

Work starts at 8.30 with a long walking shot – me talking to Spike. Spike behaves very well and we do two versions and print both takes. Then to the gory sequence in which I discover Robbie Burns (played by Daniel Street-Brown) with left foot melted and bleeding.

Daniel lies, his exposed foot being rigged for pumping blood. A tear or two wells up in his eye as he waits with extraordinary patience. Someone fetches a fan heater.

Then Carl, the second assistant, comes up to me, holding a walkie-talkie to his ear. 'Did you know Margaret Thatcher's resigned?'

The dreadful injuries to the boy are now of only secondary interest to the rest of the crew, as the news filters onto the slopes.

The clouds, and even a light flurry of snow, pass by, and the sun emerges powerfully making the next few hours, until late lunch ('Lunch will be at the end of the day,' as the 1st Assistant puts it) easily enjoyable, with the spreading views dramatically detailed by the low, bright sunlight.

Alan and I shake our heads in disbelief as we sit in our layby near the Lamb Inn eating fish and chips as, on TV, Margaret T enters the Commons. She sits behind Richard Needham so the cameras catch the two faces in juxtaposition. The toppled leader and the minister now renowned for his remark on a car phone that he wished 'the cow would resign'. The drama of the occasion is breathtaking.

Neither of us can believe that the days when daily and nightly we heard her voice dictating to the nation are over. It could be that the theft of the 'Parrot Sketch' precipitated this last slide. Python may, after all, have a greater place in history than we ever imagined.

Rick drives me from the celestial hills of the Peak District on to the murky motorways round Manchester and I catch a delayed 4.30 shuttle back to London.

Rachel and I eat together. She shows me a copy of the *Express Sunday Magazine* – 'Decade of the Nice'. My name there, needless to say!

To bed at 12.30. Thatcher is out. I'm out, about one o'clock. I should be owed hours of sleep, but life, for now, is too exciting.

Friday, November 23rd

The five books I have to read for the Whitbread Book of the Year Award arrive – *Hopeful Monsters*, Nicholas Mosley, *The Buddha of Suburbia* by Hanif Kureishi, *AK* by Peter Dickinson, a biog of A. A. Milne by Ann Thwaite and Paul Durcan's poetry *Daddy, Daddy*. I have to read them, carefully, before January. A lovely task, which demands a break of a week at least. Am toying with Italy.

Tuesday, November 27th

Watching the drama of Thatcher's successor unfolding. John Major two short of absolute victory. Heseltine's quick to make the speech he must have prepared with considerable distaste – a concession that he will never now be Prime Minister. His great bid to lead the party has failed.

Fascinating stuff. Rich in its coincidences and twists of fate.

Wednesday, November 28th

I go to Prominent Studios for a meeting with Simon A, Anne and Roger Laughton re the implications of SA's suggestions about board representation on the franchise. The *Mirror* financial page has got hold, a week late, of the story of my involvement. A picture of myself as the It's Man, dressed in rags and tatters, dominates the page together with the headline 'Mad Mike Wants His Own Show'. Roger L takes this well – in fact he roars with laughter. For me it's all the proof I need of why I shouldn't ever have been involved!

To dinner with Tristram and Virginia down in Stockwell. They have two new kittens they've christened Ashby and Elinor.

Sunday, December 2nd

In mid-afternoon to the Tricycle Theatre to help out at an auction of pictures to raise funds. Mostly very ordinary, but I do buy an original Ken Livingstone watercolour of Thatcher in a coffin with a Struwwelpeter-like Heseltine looming over her. Painted the day she resigned! Outbid someone at £110.00.

Monday, December 10th

Out to dinner at the flat of Julia St John in Chiswick. Dearbhla arrives shortly after, then Alan, big, smiling shyly underneath the single long eyebrow. Too big for the little flat, every time he turns he hits something.

At one point we're talking of Derek Hatton and how close Murray is to him, and Dearbhla observes that Murray is Hatton and Nelson is Alan. Alan shakes his head and smiles ... 'Oh no, he's Michael Palin now ... that's what's so good ... that's what I'm pleased about ... It isn't me.'

Tuesday, December 11th

Up at eight to discuss lights in No. 2 with electrician. Then, full of beans, down to Brompton Road to look for presents at Conran.

Two or three ladies come up and are complimentary about the *80 Days* series. One says she wrote me a letter, but that I didn't reply. I apologise, but she says ... 'Well, I did say some rather naughty things ...'

Patrick reports back on progress of *'AF'* selling in America. There has been no explosion of enthusiasm or rush to buy, but Miramax were very complimentary and are negotiating, though will not pay the advance of 2.7 million dollars that P and S were asking. Atlantic, Avenue, Fox and Paramount still keen. At Warner's the two people sent to see it walked out halfway through.

Wednesday, December 12th

To the Hiroko restaurant for an *'AF'* interview with *Tatler*, personified by Jessica Berens. She doesn't talk about the film much, or gush with praise, but is quite bright and sparky in that confident way that the owning classes have.

We then go on to a photo-session. This takes place in one of the huge, almost Muscovite-scale apartment blocks set in a strange no man's land off the Cromwell Road.

The photographer looks about 18, a tall, pale, rather gawky girl called Arabella. Their flat is what used to be called bohemian. Scattered with objects, paintings, unmatching chairs, all in dark, high-ceilinged rooms.

Ari (as she's called) and her assistant have a little finger puppet for me to play with. Lots of enthusiasm and swirling hyperbole ... 'Oh, you're great ... no, you really ... this is such a joy, to have someone who can just do it.'

They are such a weird lot these rich, young, well born. There's a whiff of decadence about everything, a sort of hint that as soon as the doors close drugs and dressing-up will not be far away.

Finish my session and, feeling old and awkward, am quite glad to leave. Taxi home, then time for a phone call or two before setting out for an evening of parties – John Birt has invited me for drinks at BH, and *Private Eye*, the British Council and Jonathan Cape are all partying tonight.

Off to Broadcasting House. It's really a BBC News and Current Affairs do, so lots of familiar faces of interviewers, newsreaders and politicians and celebrities.

John Birt, like a father figure, welcomes me … 'Now who would you like to meet? …' Janet Street-Porter kisses me and carries on talking.

Chat to Ned Sherrin, mention *American Friends* and mishear him when he asks when it's coming out. 'I thought you asked when I was coming out,' I apologise. Ned seems to like this and I promise him he'll be the first to know.

Anna Ford and I chat a while. She would rather be singing and writing than reading the six o'clock news. She's disarming and honest.

Politicos arrive, Cecil Parkinson and Ken Baker especially egregious and smiley. Prof. Carey[1] from Oxford gushes to me about how much his sons love and admire me. Ken Baker smoothly says how rarely anyone ever says that to him. I've had a glass or two. 'Don't worry,' I assure him, 'there must be someone somewhere who loves you.' Have I really said that to the Home Secretary? Am impressed that he remembers the film we saw at the reopening of the Electric Cinema many years ago. *Vertigo.*[2] New print.

To *Private Eye* in Carlisle Street, but no-one answers the doorbell.

Friday, December 14th

To Hampstead to buy more Christmas cards. Hopeless. Nothing but boutiques: expensive shops cursed on the area by the accumulation of wealth nearby. As the rich have got richer so has Hampstead become poorer – in choice, variety and spirit.

Another working lunch, this time with one Susan Jeffreys from *20/20* magazine. She had worries about the women in the film. Not knowing enough about them. She was nice, intelligent and candid. 'I'd have come out absolutely raving about it, if only I'd been given a little more background.'

To the Greenwood Theatre to record a Jonathan Ross show – to be played on New Year's Eve.

We are both dressed in Victorian costume – smoking jackets and tasselled hats.

Best part of the evening is after the recording when I'm asked if I'd mind

1 John Carey, Merton Professor of English Literature at Oxford University, also principal book reviewer of *The Sunday Times*.
2 A film directed and produced by Alfred Hitchcock in 1958.

doing some trailers with Jonathan. We ad-lib with props – things like bananas – which they unaccountably produce. For a few minutes I taste the pleasure of fooling about in front of an audience again. Jonathan is sharp and funny, but generous too. All in all we make a good team for a while.

Saturday, December 15th

In the evening to the latest of Jeremy H's[1] productions, this time at the ICA.

The piece was called *A Few Small Nips* and was devised by J and Renee Eyre (after their trip to Mexico) as a way of illustrating how a Mexican artist's work was affected by a dreadful accident on a trolleybus 'A copper rail … entered her abdomen, shattered her spinal column and exited through her vagina,' as the cheery programme note informed us.

There were four girls and Renee who interpret or recreate in dance and movement the sufferings of the woman. Very graphic, with bare, twisted bodies and a relentless and effective soundtrack (by the man who does music for Derek Jarman, Simon Turner). Moments of calm, then fierce, angry, physical pain. J had done bold work with very limited resources, including a wall that bleeds.

Tuesday, December 18th

A day I am not altogether looking forward to. Taxi at 8.45 to London Bridge and Adelaide House for the first meeting of the franchise bid 'core' group.

I'm early and before going in think I might walk to the middle of London Bridge and see how much has changed since we shot *The Missionary* down at Shad Thames. But there is such a solid body of commuters coming towards me that, rather than try and climb the waterfall, I go with it, into the building.

Both Simon and Roger Laughton emphasise that this is to be a 'lean and mean' exercise. Simon gives a short, inspirational opening speech. A fine and rousing vision whose delivery owes much to SA's fondness for gospel music!

TVS, Television South, is the region we will be going for.

Then Fiona from accountants Coopers & Lybrand analyses all the info we shall need for the bid, which must be made, backed with considerable detail, in about three months' time. Allan McKeown of SelecTV and myself ask a

---

1 Jeremy Herbert, my sister Angela and her husband Veryan's oldest child, who was making a name for himself as a theatre designer.

number of questions. McKeown sounds keen and well informed. He looks dangerous though.

Lambie-Nairn, the branding agency founded by Martin Lambie-Nairn, then give us their thoughts on names. A not very impressive shortlist of names are rolled out. The quiet, pale youth from Charles Barker PR almost apologetically suggests what feels to me the best name so far: Meridian. Better than Downland or Southstar or Star TV.

Wednesday, December 19th

To Shepherd's Bush. Meet Roger Mills in the Duke of Edinburgh, a seedy, smoky, unreconstructed working men's dive. Roger, swathed in pipe smoke, sits with the *Daily Telegraph* crossword almost finished on the table in front of him.

Together we traipse up Richmond Way and into Kensington House for Colin Cameron's Documentary Features party. Colin not very happy with the state of things in the department. Cuts in progs and personnel.

Clive James[1] is friendly. He's very keen on Japan. Visits often, is learning Japanese and has just written a novel about London, seen through the eyes of a Japanese man. James works ferociously hard. He looks leaner in the face, more purposeful, more successful, I suppose.

Gerald Scarfe,[2] on the other hand, looks as if he's been living a bit hard. Reminds me, with his boozy bonhomie, of how these sorts of parties used to be before everyone became health-conscious and job-conscious. We are laughing like schoolboys but, as always, one is interrupted by bores and we never finish whatever it is we're laughing at.

Down to Walkden House for the T2000 Christmas party.

New man from BR very different to Grant Woodruff. Soft and rather dreamy ... 'What are the two things you think British Rail should be doing to improve their image?' is his most incisive question. 'Stop killing passengers' is what I want to say, but I waffle politely and don't mention faulty doors and bad signalling.[3]

1 Clive James, writer, presenter, television critic of the *Observer*. His latest novel was called *Brmm! Brmm!*
2 Gerald Scarfe, cartoonist, *The Sunday Times*.
3 Five recent high-profile accidents, including the Clapham Junction crash in December 1988, had resulted in 240 deaths. Signalling problems were a common factor.

Friday, December 28th

This time of the year is rather like one long Sunday, a period when the life of the country is in limbo. A limbo of food or television. Few interruptions. I aim to finish *Hopeful Monsters*, which I do, and am much impressed.

Monday, December 31st

Drink to the New Year, which I feel ridiculously optimistic about since reading a letter in the *Independent* which points out that 1991 is a palindrome. 1991. Our year!

Tonight, looking out over the roofs of Gospel Oak on which spills light from a full moon in a cloudless sky, I know that I can still enjoy myself, express myself and, I hope, look after myself. If I avoided a nervous breakdown in 1990, I think I shall be able to avoid one at any time. A big, busy, bruising year in which I learnt quite a lot about myself.

As for the loss of Mum and Al – I've yet to account for their effect on me. Perhaps the problem is that I never had time to really think about it.

1991

Saturday, January 5th

During filming yesterday Robert Y did not seem quite his enthusiastic self. He told me that he had not been able to put out of his mind at Christmas the prospect of an imminent war, and whenever he looked at his daughter Kate, he had been filled with dread at what may be about to happen to the world.

How like 1939 is this? Hussein has clearly all the dangerous mixture of convictions, charisma and cruelty which most dictators enjoy. He has few allies, but the more he can skilfully paint America as the centre of the aggression, the more he will be able to fuse all sorts of blinkered and rabble-rousing 'anti-colonialists' who see hope only in disorder.

The Americans are flexing their muscles, obligingly showing that they are as simple-minded as anyone else. I only hope that beneath the rhetoric there is some diplomatic skill and sophistication at work, otherwise we may well be doomed to see the body bags come home and another celebration of hatred and bigotry.

I must say it puts *GBH* in perspective and Whitbread prizes too.

Monday, January 7th

John Shrapnel, who is to play Dr Jacobs in six scenes with me over the next two days, appears, dressed in black and almost merging with the darkness. I'd expected a rather grand figure, but he is very down-to-earth and untheatrical. Remembers being directed by Eric Idle at Cambridge.

I think he finds the opening scene quite demanding. He has to slide into a Scottish accent almost imperceptibly and also into a working unit who have been together for seven months.

Alan B appears briefly in the passage beside our 'surgery' as we are lining up for the camera. He looks baggy-eyed and bleary and makes gestures of apology before disappearing. Later I hear he's come down with a bug and retired to the Richmond Hill Hotel.

But it is neat that the writer of a scene about a man who always thinks he has something wrong with him should indeed have something wrong with him on the day we film it.

Thursday, January 10th

Talks between Iraq and the US have broken down in Geneva. A photo in the *Guardian* of a handshake between Tariq Aziz and James Baker across the table speaks volumes. Aziz looks almost debonair, faintly smiling, the man in control. Baker looks tense, unhappy and lost.

But first I must clear the final hurdle on *GBH*, which is not an easy one. Almost a page-long speech, of great anger and passion. I suppose one of the most important of Jim's speeches. One of a handful in which Alan's most deeply heartfelt views are articulated. I have to try and resist the party mood and the almost tangible pressure of the prospect of an early finish and rise to the occasion.

Uncharacteristically I make two false starts. Take 2 works well, Alan gives me a thumbs-up, but I feel I have the bit between my teeth, am relaxed and confident with the lines, so I should try once more. I do, and miss the feeling, the rhythm.

On the close-up I'm given, on Robert's instructions, a blow of menthol into the eyeballs to make them water. This feels like another failure. There is a lot going through my head as we finish the scene – mainly centring on my own inability to deliver the speech as powerfully and finely as it deserved.

It's only midday. Robert has suddenly decided not to shoot my reverse and he's making an announcement that this is my last shot and everyone is clapping, and I'm hot and not prepared with words or emotions.

Friday, January 11th

After breakfast begin to tackle the many and various problems that litter my desk, whilst it pours down outside.

Discuss the dates for delivery of book and the eight progs now proposed to make up *Pole to Pole*. Must make sure that I don't fall into the trap of rushing it again. The whole project will tie me up for at least 15 months.

News on *'AF'*. Miramax are not offering anywhere near what we wanted for US distribution. Virgin's 'men in suits' are prevaricating over payment in UK and if they have not paid up by January 23rd we may have to sue them and try to get the film back. This would threaten the April opening day. If ever a project was cursed, *'AF'* is the one. Its agonising birth was bad enough, now it seems to be unable to walk.

Saturday, January 12th: London–Los Angeles

Arrive at LA in mid-afternoon for the Ace Cable TV Awards. Take a taxi. The driver is a Ghanaian accountant whose home turf is Liberia. He's driving a cab as a temporary job. Doesn't much like LA, but laughs a lot. The day looks fresh and fine.

Quartered at the Mondrian. Noise rising from Sunset Boulevard below, but the hotel's quite fun – a homage to Piet Mondrian, with his colours and motifs and patterns reproduced throughout the building.

All the Arts & Entertainment people are there. Abbe Raven gives me the news that we won none of our three awards yesterday, but they have high hopes for me tomorrow.

Sunday, January 13th: Los Angeles

Run along Sunset then dive down and south towards the green and affluent lawns of Beverly Hills. This litter-less, pristine and orderly grid of long, straight avenues is perfect for running. Traffic's light and the houses present a constant eye-catching variety of styles. The neat manicured lawns all bear the black-on-yellow warning 'Armed Response'.

Relevant indeed as we are within 48 hours of the expiry of the UN deadline when American troops from very much poorer neighbourhoods than this will doubtless be sent into action to fight for capitalism, seen here on Oakhurst, Palm and Hillcrest at its most seductive and potent.

Later, as the limousine takes me to the Wiltern Theater for the ACE Cable TV Awards, I see it's 81 degrees. But I'm in a dinner jacket and won't see much of the rest of the day. Along red carpet and into a big, impressive and wonderfully old theatre. Art Deco at its best.

The Python Showtime special doesn't win and I and others are pipped by Billy Crystal's Moscow film for best writer of an entertainment series.

A&E are not downhearted and continue to be excellent hosts. Nick Davatzes says he's really looking forward to *Pole to Pole*. 'We have a deal!' he enthuses.

Tuesday, January 15th: Los Angeles–Santa Barbara

Sleep through until 8.15. Long, recharging rest. Day of the expiry of the UN deadline. Day of foreboding, but deceptively pleasant here above Sunset Boulevard, probably about as far from Iraq as it's possible to be – until you turn on the TV of course. But I don't – yet.

I take a run round the Armed Response neighbourhood, then back into shoddier West Hollywood. Bathe and breakfast. Hot coffee, granola and berries and an unhurried read of the *LA Times* in the sunshine.

A local newspaper piece tries to explain this feeling of remoteness from the Gulf War fever, as evidence that the real decision-making happens on the East Coast. California may supply the technology that will be decisive in the war, but it remains outside the executive clique.

A stocky man in black T-shirt and worn black-leather jacket approaches. I think for a while it might be Joe Cocker. With a shock of recognition I hear him mention *GBH*. He turns out to be Declan, alias Elvis Costello, who has co-written our music score. He has all the *GBH* tapes and says he thinks my performance is wonderful. He rushes off shouting hopes that we'll see each other again … 'At the awards,' he laughs.

Long drive down Sunset to the ocean. Temps lower perceptibly and it's quite chilly when I eventually turn onto the Pacific Coast Highway where the wind whips the dust around me.

Reach Santa Barbara at 3.30. The Four Seasons Biltmore is a sprawl of low buildings, carefully landscaped, in the Spanish style. A coach outside with Shriners all standing around in white conical hats.

Walk across the road to the seashore. Firm sand. Lots of joggers, walkers and surfers – though the waves seem modest.

Worry what will happen when the deadline expires – nine o'clock our time. War seems such a ludicrous waste – just for Kuwait – and once it begins how many people and countries and lives will be dragged in? Momentous times.

Wednesday, January 16th: Santa Barbara

At half past three, I switch over to CNN. There is no moving picture, just a map of Iraq and the voice and face of a reporter called John Holliman, but from the sound I know instantly that war has begun.

As Holliman speaks, unhysterically, but with measured excitement, his voice is interrupted by thumping explosions. He is not sure what's going on, but he and his two colleagues are on the ninth floor of a Baghdad hotel. It's 2.30 in the morning, Baghdad time.

So, this incredible situation – of the sounds of war being relayed all over the world from a single microphone hanging out of the window of a hotel in Baghdad, before anyone in the world, bar military commanders, knows the war has started.

Only at four o'clock, when Marlin Fitzwalter[1] is seen hurriedly at the White House to declare 'The liberation of Kuwait has begun', is there official confirmation of what we have heard from Holliman's hotel room.

After an hour and a half I take a walk along the beach. Life goes on. Joggers, surfers, dog-walkers. The mournful sound of a railway siren rings out from the Southern Pacific Line just behind the hotel. Everything seems muted.

This is how it continues – even in the tone of later reports. This doesn't seem to be a jingoistic war. There is none of the jubilation of conflict or the swaggering macho tones of revenge or the triumph of force. It's as if everyone is hoping that perhaps it can be a war unlike other wars; that it can be a short, sharp, technological triumph.

Friday, January 18th: Santa Barbara–London

Scud is the word of the day. Scuds are the missiles which Hussein is still able to fire despite the sophisticated bombing of the last two nights. Scuds are Russian-made and look set to become the equivalent of the Exocets in the Falklands War. Saddam Hussein has Exocets as well.

Walk by the ocean. Clear blue skies, a gentle breeze, a big, bright beauty of a day.

But I have a lunch booked in LA with Eric and Steve Martin, and a plane to catch this evening and a family waiting in London.

It's 1.40 by the time I'm at table with Eric and Steve. I apologise for taking so long. I'd been told it took only 90 minutes from Santa Barbara. 'But you drove on the left,' quipped Martin.

He's currently shooting a two-week appearance in a new Larry Kasdan film.[2] 'A cameo.' We decide two weeks must be more than a cameo. 'A hameo,' Eric suggests.

At the airport at four. Plane is delayed. There have been two bomb scares at LAX since the war began. A number has been given out on the radio which you can ring to report anyone or anything suspicious.

In the small, box-like room which passes for the Speedwing First Class Lounge, they apologise for the lack of a television, but tell me I can go into Qantas next door ... 'They let us use it.'

By rich coincidence I'm prevented from immediately doing this by the arrival of Melvyn Bragg, followed swiftly by Leon Brittan[3] and his little assistant,

---

1 White House press secretary to George H. W. Bush and previously to Ronald Reagan.
2 *Grand Canyon*, with Kevin Kline.
3 Leon Brittan, former Conservative MP and Minister, now a member and Vice-President, European Commission.

followed by Steve Morrison of Granada, who is profusely apologetic about turning down *'AF'* two and a half years ago, followed by Kenneth Branagh, who's just finished directing a film for Paramount[1] and is flying back because he wants to be with his family.

Melvyn can't understand why there has been so little retaliation by the Iraqis. I think he would like to think that we all panicked and overestimated their resources. I think SH is lying low, soaking up as much as he can, knowing that unless his people start dying in large numbers, he can gain kudos merely for surviving day by day.

Saturday, January 19th

Young, remarkably young, rosy-faced lads in army uniform holding machine-guns at gates of Heathrow's Terminal 4, and outside, instead of limousines, two army personnel carriers. I see no tanks, but I'm told they're about. Police marksmen can be seen, but unlike the army they keep a much lower profile. It's like Belfast.

Everything reasonably calm at home in this funny little amateur, apologetic, ancestor-obsessed country.

A note from the office tells me that last night's Python repeat was cancelled. Ypres sketch in it. Second casualty of war is comedy.

Monday, January 21st

A BBC car down to Broadcasting House.

Marina Salandy-Brown,[2] whose character is stamped on *Start the Week* more than Melvyn's, is at the front desk to greet me. An elderly white-haired gentleman who turns out to be Sir George Trevelyan has arrived for the programme a week early.

Melvyn wanders in after we've all sat there, a little awkwardly, for about 20 minutes, and dispenses his ironic smiles and professional bonhomie. 'In view of what we shall be talking about in the programme, I'm going to ask you all a quick question at the beginning, just so listeners know you're there.'

Well, the question Melvyn has chosen for this light-hearted warm-up is, 'Do you think that sexual liberation necessarily follows political liberation?' From that moment I know I am in the wrong place.

---

1 Kenneth Branagh had just completed starring in and directing a thriller, *Dead Again*.
2 Marina Salandy-Brown, Trinidad-born journalist who was editor of BBC Radio 4's *Start the Week*. She returned to Trinidad in 2004.

Marina warns us not to talk about the war, as the frequency has been split so that Radio 4 on long wave reports only on the war.

Everything this morning, from the spectral presence of Sir George Trevelyan behind the glass, to the instruction not to mention the one thing everyone is talking about, seems designed to create unease and destroy good humour and harmony.

And if none of these is enough, Melvyn has the services of Catherine Bennett, who is brought in, at the raise of an eyebrow or the flick of wrist, to have a go at the guests.

I notice the bottle of champagne remains unopened on the table as we leave.

Tuesday, January 22nd

Down to Whitbread's Brewery for the Book Prize evening.

We're shown into the chairman's sitting room. Norman Willis appears, bows to Helen and introduces himself as 'Robert Redford'.

Sybille Bedford,[1] who has that manly mutter and skin like some latex compound, announces with ratty indignation that someone on the radio yesterday had said the award was as much about beer as books. 'Absolute nonsense!' she rumbles ... 'Who was it said that?' I confess it was me and Sybille is far more put out by her indiscretion than I ever expected and keeps apologising, despite my entreaties.

Shown into a dining room, with a big Sheraton table, writing pads and pens. Here the eleven of us judges sit, myself opposite Gerald Kaufman and beside Jeremy Isaacs. Bill Kellaway, the Awards organiser, relieves us all with the news that there is a clear winner and that is, it turns out, Nicholas Mosley's *Hopeful Monsters*, which five of us chose as the winner, though none chose it as runner-up. Paul Durcan's poetry was second. So my choice conformed with the majority.

We all troop over to dinner (sworn of course to secrecy, even with our wives and friends).

I'm sat next to Penelope Fitzgerald, kind, grey-haired lady who won the Booker Prize in 1979 for *Offshore*. She's very modest and shrugs off my interest in her and how she writes in favour of questions about *80 Days* and Python.

But I persist and am rewarded. She lives with her daughter and son-in-law in what was Arnold Wesker's house in Highgate. 'What happened to

---

1 Sybille Bedford, German-born writer, long resident in England. Her most recent novel, *Jigsaw*, had been highly praised.

Arnold? ...' 'Oh, I think he had a lot of friends ... you know ... he was always very generous ... and I think eventually, over-generous.'

She's quite enjoying writing a thriller. It started as a detective story, but 'it wasn't quite clever enough, so it ended up a thriller'. She is lovely company.

Nicholas Mosley stammers attractively and speaks gently and self-deprecatingly. It's only tonight that I realise he's Oswald Mosley's son. His wife, a pretty blonde, is clearly very fond of him and holds his hand before the vote is announced. I look over in their direction. It's odd knowing what I do.

Wednesday, January 23rd

To the New Connaught Rooms in Great Queen Street, complete with yellow carnation and label announcing that I'm the President of Transport 2000. The occasion is the Best Station Awards.

There can be few awards in which rows of urinals figure as prominently. I think it quite right too, as decent toilets on stations are probably what everyone wants.

Sometimes, as the pictures flick on and off in remorseless succession, I begin to confuse this with some kind of horticultural occasion, such is the emphasis on flower beds and hanging baskets. The eventual winner, Aberdour, looks like a magnificent garden with a railway line just about visible.

To Parliament Hill for Rachel's open day. Rachel is predicted, as a result of her mock exam results, to hit A in every subject except French. All speak highly of her ... 'pleasure to teach', etc. etc.

Later, as we have supper together, we talk about school. Rachel says her class not much involved with boys. Whereas Caitlin [Shamberg] had ventured that a third of her classmates in LA had slept with boys, Rachel thinks that probably only one of her class has lost their virginity, but there is a 15-year-old who recently became pregnant by her 24-year-old partner. Rachel very wise and thoughtful about it all and doesn't condemn or endorse.

Wednesday, January 30th

'Happiness stops the moment you know you're happy' or something like that, is how Bonnard, who looked a very morose individual, put it. And today I feel in that delicate state of being, almost totally content with my life.

Considering there is a war on, and that we haven't seen the sun for a week, and that a cold, leaden gloom is settled over the city, my resurgent spirit is very welcome, and I organise myself a day in town.

The smart shops around Covent Garden are full only of assistants. Their windows, no longer stylishly minimalist, are now as desperate as any in the Holloway Road, screaming 'Sale' and 'Reduction' and 'Further Reductions!' Bad times.

Thursday, January 31st

Unmoving weather now for almost two weeks. General sense of stasis – not just as represented by the weather, but in the Gulf War as well.

Casualties on the allied side still low, the impression still of a controlled war in which superior technology is remorselessly stamping out evil chemical facilities and nuclear weapons plants. The tone of most commentaries is to endorse this view and the glowing attention given to the military hardware must be delighting the arms manufacturers whose livelihood had been so threatened by the end of the Cold War.

To the National Gallery for another look at the Impressionism in the Making exhibition – detail worth seeing ... sand in the paint of a Monet done at Trouville beach – then walk across the Strand, down past Charing Cross Station which is now capped with a bulky, rather silly Terry Farrell office development.

Going down a blank-faced concrete walkway on the south side of Waterloo Bridge and suddenly I catch my breath in shock. From being alone on a concrete bridge I'm now looking down on a busy world, but one completely different from that on the surface. Of course, it's Cardboard City, home of the homeless. A glimpse of the Third World less than a mile from Parliament, a river's breadth from the Savoy.

It's like a scene from a film. Indeed for a moment I think they may be filming – this must be a set. A series of boxes draped in scraps of various materials. A group of about a dozen are clustered round a fire, hair wild and clothes shabby. Four or five dogs scurry and chase around barking, then return to the fire.

It's quite a shock to the system. A glimpse of a strange and foreign land. I don't dawdle, I don't stare ... I feel threatened, morally rather than physically, in my big Donegal tweed coat with my Filofax crammed with credit cards and twenty-pound notes, on my way from the National Gallery to a smart restaurant.

Friday, February 1st

On the one o'clock news, report of de Klerk's speech committing himself and South Africa to the abolition of remaining apartheid laws. Apartheid, like communism, is one of the most emotive political keywords of my lifetime. It looks now as if both will have disappeared by the time I'm 50. Extraordinary and, so recently, unthinkable. And the sun slips through the clouds after many days away.

Monday, February 4th

To TV Centre for a screening of Donald Woods' 'Assignment' prog about his return to South Africa after 12 years.

Donald and Wendy and children there. He smoking and trying not to be nervous.

Donald is the perfect host – from both sides people talk and confide in him. The formidable 'Pik' Botha, bull-like and dangerous, calls apartheid a sin, and Nelson Mandela, gentle and courteous, on being told what Botha has said, smiles minimally and replies ... 'Well, that's very nice.'

Lunch with Geoffrey Strachan. Octopus Books – another child of the big-business, acquisitive, 'growth-oriented' '80s – is now faintly shabby. A book is on show in the foyer with the 'Whitbread Book of the Year' card on it. I think it's meant to be *Hopeful Monsters*, but the cover's missing and the book that's left behind it is John Ardagh's book on modern France.

Geoffrey S very apologetic about the inadvertent printing of my address in the latest editions of the *Holy Grail* book, and is having the unsold 1,700 books doctored accordingly.

Tuesday, February 5th

Virgin have refused to accept *American Friends* as delivered, citing some trivial points, and will take steps to cancel the opening at the Odeon Haymarket.

Steve seems completely baffled and is not able to give me any cogent reason for their behaviour other than that Virgin's owners are in financial trouble.

To my first Russian lesson with Paul Marsh, who lives in Muswell Hill. He has a flat which indicates few luxuries, and is enthusiastic in a clever, self-deprecatory way, peppering the lesson with what I imagine are quite regular gags. But I like him. He's clearly consumed with the subject of Russia and Russian, and I think I shall enjoy his softly authoritative approach and become used to the slightly oily scent of perspiration which pervades the room.

Drive across to the Kensington Hilton where I've fixed a drink with Will Wyatt. He talks of *80 Days* as a great success, largely due to me and my 'faux-naif' approach. Never thought of myself as 'faux-naif'. The Henri Rousseau of the silver screen.

Wednesday, February 6th

Steve rings to say that the bank, supported by six legal opinions, is moving tomorrow to wind up our distribution agreement with Virgin. Steve hopes that we will force Virgin to release the film to us; worst scenario is that they will suddenly find the money and we will be left to pick up the pieces of a distribution plan with a company in whom we have all lost confidence.

The irony is that there should be this great row over money when 'AF' was made so cheaply.

Thursday, February 7th

Snow lies around, crisp and even. The winters we'd forgotten, the Christmas card winters that seemed to be victims of the greenhouse effect, are back. Sweep paths and clear snow with the same mixture of effort and pleasure as did my father.

To Jeremy Gilkes in Devonshire Street. As I drive through the swirling snow I hear on the radio confused reports of a mortar bomb attack on the Ministry of Defence in Whitehall.

Dr Gilkes looks at what was an irritating and sore spot on my back, pronounces it non-cancerous, gives it a name I can't begin to remember and applies liquid nitrogen – 'This is so cold you'll feel a burning sensation.'

As I leave the snow is thickening and the news is that the mortars were aimed at 10 Downing Street and one has gone off in the garden. Expecting Iraqi terror attacks, it's almost a relief to hear that our old enemy the IRA are being blamed.

The snow gently falls for most of the day and my workroom becomes more like a cocoon as the windows are gradually covered.

The last thing I see before bed is a fax of a piece in *Broadcast* re the Meridian TV bid. There I find myself described as 'former Monty Python star turned film director (*sic*) and actor. A "Mr Nice-Guy" with a high PR profile and a bit of money in the bank.'

My epitaph as at February 7th 1991!

Friday, February 8th

Parliament Hill is a Bruegel snow scene. Several hundred on the crown of the hill sledging, skiing, or just sliding down on old sheets of cardboard. The schools are closed and the North London Line seems rather feebly to have given up the ghost.

Walk beyond range of the sledgers and sliders, down to Highgate Ponds. The Men's Pond completely frozen, but above it on the next pond there is an area of clear water on which Canada geese, ducks, coots and pigeons fight for space. A viciously cold wind.

Tuesday, February 12th

Press launch of the Stammering in Children campaign.

Very well attended. I do TV interviews for BBC, Capital and later LBC. The press conference is filmed. I'm asked to speak and produce quite an articulate volley without notes which I'm pleased about.

The relief at being able to talk about stammering after a childhood spent without mentioning it keeps me going and keeps me articulate and enthusiastic.[1] The two boys who stammer and appear in the film are there. Great boys, full of fun, intelligence and indomitable character.

On way home in taxi put headphones on and practise Russian alphabet.

Ash Wednesday, February 13th

Patrick C rings to tell me the news that Virgin have capitulated and agreed to pay over the money for distribution in full. Should we rejoice? Is a company that's just 'capitulated' the best place to do the best for the film? Is a company that has treated us appallingly badly over the last few months suddenly going to turn sweet? It seems as if we stumbled up the wrong path with Virgin from the very beginning and it would have been better if we'd found our way out and started again.

Thursday, February 14th

Lunch at the Great Nepalese with five members of T2000 staff. The cheerful Ghurkha is still there and remembers me. Food is wonderful: delicate and original. Ludicrously cheap too.

General update on T2000 business, and embarrassed request for more money for laptop computers, etc. As T2000 still has so much good sense to impart I agree.

On the way home I have a cab driver who cannot talk – not a stammer, just grunts. Didn't realise at first and he had to write down the word he was trying

---

1 My father stammered for all the time I knew him.

to say; later I notice a sign, 'Sorry The Driver Cannot Speak'.

Feeling like staying at home and stewing by the fire, but we are asked out to David Frost's for a Valentine's Day dinner.

David answers the door, very charming and welcoming. We're offered pink champagne and led eventually into a small drawing room with French windows giving onto the snow-covered garden. Present are Tim Rice, the Owens – David and Debbie – and others I don't know.

Debbie Owen is Delia's agent and says Delia has been watching my experience with BBC Books with interest. Debbie says her latest book about Christmas cookery is 'still selling in February!', but that she has no foreign sales at all.

As she's talking her eyes swivel to the latest arrival. People shift positions, men feel their ties. This is obviously quite a guest. Turns out to be the Duchess of York, née Sarah Ferguson, looking rather fine, in good shape, with clear, open features and a striking pile of red hair.

At dinner we are divided onto two tables in two rooms. Helen is spirited away to Carina's room, along with an ex-SDP leader, and I find myself next to the Duchess, with Frost at the head of the table.

Fergie says that she saw me publicising the Stammering campaign and asks how she can become involved. Though her interest is obviously genuine, I feel she is anxious to be taken seriously and to have some moral ammunition to throw back at the press whom she so clearly hates.

She, rather sweetly and awkwardly, asked at one point, with much hesitation ... 'I mean ... may I ask you a question ... do I ... do I appear to you as the same person you've read about in the press?' I mumble something about not reading the papers and embark on a compliment.

She paints a depressing, almost frightening, picture of the royal life. She is monitored and controlled by a group of 'men in brown suits' – the palace staff who, it seems, are forever hauling her over the coals for breaches of protocol.

Friday, February 15th

Apparently the Iraqis have agreed to withdraw from Kuwait. On my way to lunch it's clear that the offer is highly conditional but at least it's the first time in this whole crisis that Iraq has even mentioned the word withdrawal ... and indeed they don't often mention Kuwait.

Lucinda Sturgis, our Production Co-ordinator, made me very worried when she said *American Friends* may be a title we regret in view of the way things are going on in the Gulf (600 civilians killed in a bomb shelter).

Lunch with Jonathan Powell and Colin Cameron, for whose department *Pole to Pole* is being made.

Anne embarks on the hard sell, chiding Jonathan for not agreeing to put out *Pole to Pole* before Christmas 1992. (Powell says it's penned in for January, and always has been – this of course is not good for the book sales, as Anne points out firmly. Powell looks uncomfortable, not sure quite how to assert himself.)

Eventually though we have a good meal and in the end have achieved what I had hoped – an opening of doors, an assertion of our desire to work with the BBC but equally of our desire to be treated as we deserve – as a potentially very successful show.

I switch on the news to hear, I hope, that this morning's Iraqi withdrawal offer may really be the good news we've waited for. Well of course it isn't. Bush has dismissed it out of hand, and the bombing goes on.

A piece in *20/20* – the first of a salvo of '*AF*' articles – depresses me. Susan Jeffreys seems at pains to make the point not only that I don't understand women but that, like most other British male comedy writers, I don't like them.

It told its audience that the film had a serious flaw and suggested I probably did as well. My flaw was being born white, male, middle-class and going to public school and Oxford and never having to suffer.

Monday, February 18th

Drag myself very wearily from bed in time for the eight o'clock news. Reports of explosions at Paddington and Victoria stations. All London main-line stations closed, which sounds a bit drastic.

Fearing dreadful traffic congestion as people travel by other means, I leave plenty of time for journey to Shepherd's Bush for meeting with Virgin Distribution.

We discuss date of release. We might have been discussing the date of a funeral. Virgin's Bill Tennant feels that we are being rushed into a theatre – the Odeon Haymarket – which he feels is too big for us. He would like to open in a 300-seater, not a 600-seater in the West End. The bombs that went off this morning, especially if they indicate a new IRA campaign of disruption, will only make matters worse.

There is to be no TV spend on the film.

Back at home an *Express* photographer is ready, set up in my room. Shots of me on the balcony against a sunset. Though I find these photo-sessions the most unjustifiably time-consuming aspects of publicity, the photographers are usually quite interesting – craftsmen with some of the same characteristics as musicians – streetwise but not boastful. Barry Lewis, today's lensman, knows Spitsbergen well and whetted my appetite for the place where we start the

Pole to Pole journey. We sit in my room, his assistant, Barry and myself, and drink tea and talk travel.

Tuesday, February 19th

Another interview re *'AF'* – this is the tenth national newspaper piece I've done so far. A bright, tall, upright young man called Andrew Davison.

We talk for an hour and a half. As I tire my mind slips into woolly over-drive. I find it very difficult to stand back and talk about myself and I feel I shall probably be punished in the article for any unguarded slips or intellectual looseness.

By taxi to dinner with JC, Alyce Faye and Len Deighton[1] and his wife. Deighton is a slight man, slim and more donnish than the '60s hard black and white image might suggest. Easy to talk to, unassuming and keen to give and learn information. I thank him for once writing a fan letter to the BBC about *Number 27* ... 'Oh, I do things like that,' he said, 'writers need to be told they've done well ... otherwise everything on TV's going to be game shows.'

Sunday, February 24th

Switch on my radio as I wobble, blearily, from bed to bathroom prior to a run at nine o'clock, to hear that the allies, or the coalition forces, or the infidels, are deep into Kuwait and even Iraq, having begun their offensive as we were getting into bed early this morning. So far 'the mother of battles' has been without the enormous and dreadful loss of life they predicted and the Iraqis are backing off or surrendering.

Monday, February 25th: London–Glasgow–Dunoon

Up at 6.15. Surprised to see dawn light outside. Winter receding, already. Taxi to Heathrow at a quarter to seven. On the news, buoyant reports on the progress of the allied advance. Very few casualties, all targets reached well in advance, little resistance.

Yesterday the *Independent on Sunday* carried a brief article by a man describing what it's like to be bombarded or shelled. He drew a graphic picture of the

1 Len Deighton, writer, whose first novel, *The Ipcress File*, was turned into a film with Michael Caine.

sensory distortion and damage. The sucking-out of eardrums by the constant changes in air pressure, the adrenaline-filled fear that brings sleeplessness and confusion. The Iraqis have been subjected to the heaviest bombardment since World War One, probably ever. One can realise why they're surrendering.

Flight to Glasgow almost full – no evidence of fear of terrorist attack here. But Hamish MacInnes[1] meets me in Glasgow with the news that all London main-line stations were closed again this morning and a bomb had exploded on a railway line.

Hamish drives me in to the BBC where I record my commentary for *Palin's Progress*.[2]

Back onto the motorway, heading along the south bank of the Clyde, past the massive, and in most cases rusting, cranes of Port Glasgow and Greenock to Gourock and the ferry across to Dunoon, where I've selected a *Good Hotel* entry called the Enmore Hotel to spend two or three days on 'The Adventure'.

Hamish smiled broadly when he heard I was away to Dunoon. 'Oh, y'll get some peace there,' he grinned, 'people only go there to die ...'

My room has a four-poster bed whose posts are wrapped in chiffon and tied with a pink ribbon.

The menu for the evening is rolled up like a scroll and to be found in a silver urn on a tray in the corner of the room. On the bottom of the night's menu the guests' names are printed.

Short but good menu – cheese and herb roulade, carrot soup, a real mother of an Arbroath smokie and plum tart. A glass of Glenfarclas malt and a half-bottle of Sancerre render me pleasantly drowsy.

Tuesday, February 26th: Dunoon

Watch the news as I wash and dress. Saddam Hussein ordering a withdrawal from Kuwait within 24 hours and claiming victory – maybe this lost something in the translation from Arabic, but it does sound to be an exaggeration, as the faces on thousands of surrendering Iraqi soldiers show only exhaustion, fear and relief at being taken prisoner.

To breakfast, where I first encounter the formidably extrovert Angela, wife of the proprietor. 'And what do you do Mr McLennan?' Her voice rings round the small dining room as she interrogates the only other diner.

Then retreat up to my room to begin work on 'The Adventure', which I haven't touched for ten months.

1 Hamish MacInnes, founder and leader of the Glencoe Mountain Rescue Team.
2 *Palin's Progress*, a film of me and Tom making a father-and-son climb along the Aonach Eagach ridge above Glencoe, shot by Hamish.

Watch the news, bathe and down to dinner. Angela in charge tonight. We all learn quickly about herself, her body, her retiring husband and her inability to play squash. Her husband had evidently reproved her for thinking I was a commercial traveller. 'He's the "Fish man",' he'd said. This gave Angela a chance to launch into a further riff ... 'But the fish man only lives in Tarbert ... I couldn't think what he'd be wanting to stay here for ...'

Thursday, February 28th: Dunoon–London

1.15 shuttle to London. Pilot has wonderful dry sense of humour. 'Do sit back and try and relax. This is my first flight ...' pause '... to London.' 'If we can find Manchester we then should find Coventry, then we shall fly into London past Aylesbury and pick up the A41 to Berkhamsted ...' 'For those of you on the right there is a fine view of Welsh clouds, whilst those on the left can see their English equivalent.'

Friday, March 8th

To lunch with JC at L'Aventure.

Little small talk for JC wants to talk seriously about the film – the new film for the *Wanda* team that is.

Film to be about the importance of humour v bigotry and prejudice. He says he probably won't be making it until the early autumn of '92. Not with Charlie. He found it heavy going with Charlie towards the end of *Wanda*, especially, JC says, in the editing stage. Checking out Robert Young. Of course I give him a big recommendation.

We adjourn at a quarter to three. The prospect of having a Cleese-Kline-Jamie Lee collaboration to embark on at the end of *Pole to Pole* is very satisfactory ... 'Give me the occasional lunch between now and when you leave,' JC requests.

Sunday, March 10th

To Camden Town with Helen, Rachel and Will for the cast and crew screening of *American Friends*. Already people are converging on the Parkway Cinema in a practically unbroken stream – as [Helen's sister] Mary said later, 'like people going to church'.

Connie's and Trini's performances are so delicate, so full of precise, carefully controlled meanings. I watch in sheer pleasure, and am often moved.

Rush out at the end. Generous applause from within, at beginning and end of the credits. Then the crowd spills out.

Very strong commendations from Richard Loncraine [director of *The Missionary*], who raved for quite some time, and D Leland, as well as Barry Humphries, who gave me a big hug and pressed me against his smooth, fleshy cheek. All around were heartfelt congratulations. Terry J had 'cried again'. The crew all seemed very happy.

Later Robert Young rings and becomes the third director of the day to rave about the film. He is so fulsome I only wish he were not a film director but a film critic. Nicest remark is that he feels it is such a 'truthful' film. Also a brave film, he says, referring to the uncompromising way in which we've avoided playing the story up, or milking it for comedy.

All this highly satisfactory, even bearing in mind people want to be nice.

Monday, March 11th

Lunch with David Robinson of *The Times*. David is no longer the *Times* film critic. A new young arts editor elbowed him out, and though David does not tell the story accusingly, it sounds as if he's been disgracefully treated.

Geoff Brown is the new critic. 'He's a trasher,' warns David ... 'a good or bad man, nothing in between' and, ominously, 'he doesn't like period stuff'.

Tuesday, March 12th

Two interviews in the morning, including a very good Radio 5 chat with a bright man called Mark Kermode – who notices the dark side of almost any comedy I've been involved in.

Lunch and a chat to Iain Johnstone for *The Sunday Times*. I can answer almost everything except the personal stuff ... 'Are you nice?' 'Of course I'm not.' 'What's the least nice thing about you?' – and there, pathetically, I'm lost for words.

At seven o'clock round to Barry and Lyn Took's. He has Paddy Ashdown[1] and wife Jane to dinner.

Paddy is as one would expect an ex-Marine to be. He is in good physical shape, with a big, ready, eager laugh; he's direct and fires off questions as if he were interrogating one of his men after a reconnaissance raid ... 'How do you sell a film?' 'Who makes the film what it is?' 'At what stage do you know you have a success?'

---

1 Paddy Ashdown, leader of the Liberal Democrats from 1989 to 1999.

But we do eventually get on to politics and Ashdown is characteristically candid. He's complimented by Lyn on being honest and not trying to deceive or dissemble in order to get on. Ashdown protests ... 'Look, I am like that at fifteen per cent' – 'Sixteen per cent,' his wife corrects him – 'Fifteen, sixteen ...what the hell ... but if I were up to forty per cent or forty-five per cent I would have to behave very differently.'

He thinks the House of Commons is a dreadful place, but loves being a constituency MP.

Like most politicians I meet they know much less about our business than actors and writers know about politics. They really are in an hermetically sealed world. But I liked them both. He seems enormously sane and sensible ... but he is still only at fifteen per cent. Sorry sixteen.

Tuesday, March 19th

At 12.15 I'm deposited at the Ivy restaurant to await those of the critics and the critics' screening audience who have accepted our invitation to lunch. This is another of many nervous moments in the history of *American Friends*. But there are smiles on the faces of the first arrivals – George Perry and Chris Tookey – and they come bearing warm praise.

Dilys Powell is here; she's unable to move much and sits, bowed over in a chair, reading the press kit. No-one seems to be minding her. I go to talk to her. She turns her sweet, bewitching eyes to me and I feel the same emotional wobble as I did when I met her last at the *Private Function* do.

She tells me that she's followed my career with great pleasure. She had been in trouble at Oxford herself, she said, for being caught climbing back into her college. When she leaves, prodding forward on a stick, I notice she's sporting a pair of scarlet socks and sandals.

About half past two the last critics and friends leave – unhurriedly – Davenport of the *Telegraph* going off to drink with the man from the *Morning Star* – and I can have a rest from two hours' almost non-stop talking.

Time Out carries a full-page colour ad, an article and a review which commends the film as being 'full of small pleasures'. Could be worse.

Out in the evening to Parly Hill to see Rachel's play which she and others in her drama group have written and performed and staged as part of their GCSE. It's a thoughtful, serious piece about a political prisoner – his conscience, etc. Rachel takes quite a dominant role and shows clearly that there is an actress in there. Other plays treat with child abuse, cancer, the Gulf War. Not a lot of laughs.

Wednesday, March 20th

At eight o'clock a car collects me and takes me to TV-am. The interior of Terry Farrell's light, bright, successful building looks sprucer than I remember. There's an air of confidence about the place which may be deceptive. Is this just a conscious effort to appear attractive, knowing that bidders are at the door, eyeing the franchise?

Paul Gambaccini gives the film a robust review and an eight out of ten rating. He also, I notice, does his piece to camera ad-lib, with great confidence. Very unusual.

A half-hour with Michael Parkinson at LBC in Hammersmith. He seems a lonely figure, almost imprisoned in this quiet, soulless, modern ambience. But we have a lively chat. I like him. He's easy to strike up a rapport with (maybe the Yorkshire thing helps) and one feels that he's intelligent and sympathetic.

Away from Parky to St Pancras, and a train ride up to Nottingham.

Here my optimism begins to weaken.

The location of the Showcase Cinema does not seem to be in Nottingham at all but in an industrial estate a mile or two outside. The Showcase is a multiplex of 13 screens surrounded by a car park. There is a cheerless emptiness to the place.

The Showcase operation is run from America, all decisions on 'events' at the cinema have to be cleared through a lady in Boston. I can't, as I look around the bland, pop-corn dispensary that is the foyer, feel anything other than a sinking feeling that I would rather not be here, and that ironically *American Friends* will not spend much time here either.

Thursday, March 21st

Lie in or read the reviews? Only one answer, so up and buy the *Guardian*. Nice, warm piece from Derek Malcolm, protective of the film 'so gentle it almost hurts to think what will happen to it in Des Moines'.

Call Tristram. Virginia says he's smarting from some cruel mention in *The Times*. Reassure her that blood was expected from the *Times* reviewer after my lunch with David Robinson, whom he replaced.

I pass by a newsagent in Marylebone High Street and pick up likely publications. Best reviews from unexpected sources – a rave in *What's On*. '*Total Recall* it isn't but aren't you glad of that.' Hugo Davenport obliges in the *Daily Telegraph* and even *The Times* is less severe than predicted.

The overall impression is of fondness for the film and respect for its values and qualities, tempered in some reviews with 'buts' ranging from the condescending to the derogatory. Nigel Andrews, who Patrick says 'doesn't like films anyway', concludes a not unpleasant *FT* review with the phrase 'utterly pretty, utterly charming, if also utterly minor'.

Friday, March 22nd

A tonic at breakfast. Rave reviews in *Today* and the *Daily Express* ('better than *Room with a View*'), glowing review from Shaun Usher in the *Mail* and approval and a lot of space on the review page from Kevin Jackson in the *Independent*.

For a time I feel as if I'm on a settled plateau after climbing a difficult mountain. That all the hard work and the gruelling trips to the US and the let-downs from financiers and distributors are worth it.

Saturday, March 23rd

Two unpleasant reviews in the post – one from the *Good Times* opines that 'if one film can bring Michael Palin's career down in rubble this is it'. More abuse, ending by calling the Ashby character 'snivelling'. Another, though less in the category of hate mail, calls it 'so slow as to be almost invisible'. But after yesterday's thick dose of praise these are not enough to rattle me.

What does rattle me far more is a phone call to Patrick at 11.30, an hour before we leave for the airport and a skiing week. Even allowing for Patrick's customary disinclination to exuberance, this is a grim leaving present. Friday night at the Odeon Haymarket was worse than any of us had ever considered. No rush to either of the early performances and only 250, considerably less than half the house, for the main evening perf. Nothing much either of us can say.

I stare out of the window, realising that I'd prepared myself for everything but this. By any standard a first-night failure.

No time to mourn, or even ascertain more information, as we have to organise departure to Heathrow (two taxis) and then flight to Zurich, for seven of us.

Monday, April 1st

Finish unpacking and sorting through letters. Find a lovely, generous review of '*AF*' by Dilys Powell in the latest *Punch* which cheers me considerably.

Alan Bleasdale rings, late. He's under the weather again after weeks of editing and won't be able to make tomorrow's post-synch session. He carefully and dutifully warns me in advance that two scenes of mine have been shortened – neither, he assures me, for acting reasons – the panic attack, now contained in a montage, and fuck, fuck, fuck ... which he said just looked as if the writer had kept it all in for no other reason other than to hear the character say fuck repeatedly. 'Apart from that,' he rasps, 'I think you're untouched ...'

Tuesday, April 2nd

To Adelaide House for a briefing meeting on the present position of the MAI [Mills & Allen International] franchise bid. Quite a shock to see the number of people round the table since our meeting of six weeks ago. The boardroom on the eighth floor is packed. Upwards of 30 people, including Allan McK and his Managing Director, a quiet, neat man called Michael Buckley, who have just flown in from New York.

Roger Laughton seems very relaxed in the chair. Nice to see someone doing the job they really want to do, and he lends the whole enterprise an air of quiet, efficient determination.

As we are introduced I'm described as the man responsible for the choice of the name Meridian, which is not entirely true, though I did champion it very strongly.

Allan McKeown, another man who clearly enjoys his job, pitches the various ideas which he and his clients Marks and Gran and Clement and Le Frenais[1] had come up with at their recent weekend at Chewton Glen. They include a half-hour sitcom for me. Nice of them, but I groan inwardly as I hear my character described as a charming, likeable ... etc. etc. It's a two-hander with a cat!

A mythical week's schedule is revealed. Roger rather sweetly admits that the 'In Search of Railways' idea put into peak time on one of the nights is his own.

Meeting winds up after about two and a half hours. The strength and seriousness of the enterprise, what began as a thought in Simon's kitchen one night, is impressive. But I know it's not really my world. The game of winning the bid and running the station doesn't really interest me. I want, as always, to be able to take a step back and observe all this ironically. Yet it could affect thousands of people's jobs and livelihoods.

---

1 Two writing partnerships: Maurice Gran and Lawrence Marks, best known for *Birds of a Feather* and *The New Statesman*, and Dick Clement and Ian Le Frenais for *The Likely Lads* and *Porridge*.

Wednesday, April 3rd

Letter from Ron Eyre[1] brightens my breakfast time. 'I've just had the best possible evening at *American Friends*' ... a film 'straight to the heart and the senses ... and your performance showed presence being present rather than acting being acted. A rarity.'

So this morning, with my back niggling and precluding any running, I turn to the problem of '*AF*'. Various ideas, thoughts, suggestions flying around including doing a series of radio ads and if necessary paying for them ourselves. I ring Pete Buckingham from Virgin, and suggest that he and I should meet.

First person I see as I walk into an almost empty Cibo (London is civilised and unrushed this Easter week) is Harold Pinter. He greets me with warm praise for the film, which he had been to see on opening night with Lady Antonia. I know he's a friend of Tristram's but he gushed most gratifyingly. I said I hoped he would proselytise and he recruited the man he was dining with, a small, reddish-brown American who was introduced as Michael Herr,[2] the writer. The three of us bemoaned the macho demands of the box office, much sympathetic head-nodding.

Pete B is very nervous and jumpy, almost his first words are 'You must be having a terrible time', but once he's settled down and had a cigarette and a glass or two of wine (Umbrian by Lungarotti) we have a good sensible conversation. I tell him of the radio ad plan and of course he's enthusiastic.

Home, make calls to Lucinda and decide to go ahead with the radio campaign as soon as possible. To expedite matters the Gumby Corporation, my own company, will produce them. Assemble some good quotes.

To Camden Lock for supper with Rachel, then home and look through Clem's notes on the Egypt–Tanzania leg of the *Pole to Pole* journey.

Sobering schedule shows the filming to be seven weeks longer than *80 Days* – 43 days to Aswan, then 90 to Antarctica and home.

Thursday, April 4th

Tristram has heard very little about the film's performance, but confirms that for many who have seen it the experience was pleasing – including his father, who saw it on video at the weekend. Much taken with Switzerland and the notebooks and all the detail of travel and very complimentary about my performance.

I ask TP if his father has been in demand following Graham Greene's death

---

1 Ron Eyre, director mainly in theatre (*London Assurance* for Royal Shakespeare Company).
2 Michael Herr wrote *Dispatches*, one of the major books of the Vietnam War.

yesterday. 'Actually it seems to have reinvigorated him,' says Tristram. 'He hasn't been in such good form for a long time.'

Friday, April 5th

To the Haymarket to check the cinema. Very difficult to make out the identity of the film at the Odeon. Small corner frontage – no lettering around the marquee – only bland pink neon stripe. Closer examination: pics of me looking severe and only two quotes, both quite unsensationally placed in cheap Letraset.

Inside, no-one about. Knock on door to box office. A face eventually peers round. 'Yes?' 'I'd like to see the manager.' 'What about?' I point vaguely at my likeness on the big poster opposite, then, apologetically, 'Er ... I'm ... er ... I'm in the film.' Then the penny drops and a few moments later the manager, shirt-sleeved, appears. Youngish man, looking uncomfortable.

Some quick talking to reassure him that I only want to help and I haven't come with any personal bodyguards. He is very sad about the performance, saying that they all like the picture very much, and there's nothing worse than seeing the demise of a film you want to succeed. I query the lack of review-flaunting in the foyer and at the entrance. Suggest having boards made up. He thinks this a good idea and I promise to get the quotes sent round. Ask him about the neon around the marquee instead of the name of the film. He blames this on a previous manager's keenness on the corporate Odeon image!

Monday, April 8th

Drive over to the *Pole to Pole* production office. In Smiley-esque anonymity in the Uxbridge Road looking out over Shepherd's Bush Green. The windows murky with traffic-stirred dust.

This is the first meeting of the *'PTP'* team. I meet Nigel Meakin and his new assistant Patti Musicaro on the road outside. Patti is Italian-American and I think will be a good foil to our Englishness. She's quiet but obviously together and competent.

Roger arrives in a very large coat and immediately the difference between a room with and without Roger is evident. With Roger there's an air of danger, an edge of risk, a hint of provocation. Straight away we're naughtier, riskier and a touch more passionate. He talks about the Eye-ties in Ethiopia and Patti flashes her big dark eyes in disapproval and the place comes to life.

Clem's news of the evening is that there is some hope we shall have a nuclear submarine to take us to the North Pole.

Tuesday, April 9th

It's now two and a half weeks since we received the first good reviews and still the Odeon foyer looks dead as a doornail. A punter is studying the pictures as I walk in.

Down the unlit stairs – light on in the manager's office, can hear him talking. Knock on his door, call 'Hello! It's Michael Palin.' Poor man nearly has heart failure for second time in a week. He says Chris Bailey of Virgin has promised the board and review splash and it should be here today. He brightens on mention of last Saturday... 'had all the feeling of a first night ... very good atmosphere in the bar'.

Tuesday, April 16th

At seven o'clock all the weekend secrecy over our presents from the children is explained. With Rachel and Lisa the ringleaders, they've provided us with 25 separate presents. I'm in my new Margaret Howell flannel suit and Helen's in her new black dress and we both look good and suddenly I'm enjoying the prospect of our 25th anniversary party.

Out in the garden is a silver birch tree which Helen's badminton-playing friend Kathryn Evans delivered by taxi this morning and now the children are all around to watch us open the Great 25 before we leave for L'Escargot. Wonderfully chosen selection – all marked so we open them in the right order.

Begins with the mundane – kitchen foil, refreshers, a bar of Toblerone, works up through lovely pottery cats and mugs to old prints of the Arctic and Egypt for me, and then little silver pieces – for me a silver bubble-blower, and ending up with a framed set of photographs showing the two of us, and three pictures of each of the children when young.

Terry J, still in Australia, at the Melbourne Comedy Festival, is the only Python missing.

My speech is well received and, I must say, well delivered. Start by pointing out that it is a very special night – the first night (pause) for 13 years (audience a little uneasy) that Monty Python's Life of Brian has been shown on network television! Applause, as four of the main cast are here, plus others like McKeown and Neil Innes.

The gathering is always noisy but not loud. Elena, London's greatest maitresse d', keeps a maternal eye and it's all a great success.

It's five to three by the time we're both in bed – the passing of our 25th year together could hardly have been better marked, or happier.

Friday, April 19th

By three I'm at Paul Marsh's in Muswell Hill. Eleven hours of Russian and I've not much to show for it. Paul is sympathetic and helpful and does not condemn. I'm growing quite fond of him.

He tells me he was Bernie Grant's[1] secretary at Haringey Council during the Broadwater Farm Riots in 1985. Paul is measured, reasonable and not the slightest bit Spart-ish,[2] so the tales he tells have some weight. Winston Silcott's father, a small, inoffensive elderly man, described to Paul the police raid to pick up Silcott. Mr S arrived with the door key just as police were beating on the door and about to use a sledgehammer on it. He told them that he had the key and he'd let them in. They sledgehammered the door anyway.

I asked Paul if he thought Silcott was guilty. He said he wasn't sure but the two who were put away with him were definitely innocent. [All three were acquitted on November 25th 1991.]

Sunday, April 21st

With Will sporting his Wednesday scarf, we set out on the road to Wembley for the final of the Rumbelows Football League Cup. Down Oak Village to Gospel Oak Station, Willesden Junction, change to Wembley Central.

Apart from a flurry of autographs at one point and a longish speech of appreciation for *80 Days* from one of the senior police officers on duty, we get to our seats without much interference soon after two o'clock.

The Wednesday end is already full and the supporters are putting on an impressive display. 'We love Carlton Palmer, he smokes marijuana. Da-Da-Da!' 'Ron's Arm-ee!' 'Ron's Arm-ee!' And 'Always Look on the Bright Side of Life'.

The game itself is not attractive and Manchester United always more likely to score. But we keep them out, and then quite unbelievably a speculative crack at goal by Sheridan spins off Sealey's outstretched hands into the net. The Wednesday fans, who have been throwing teddy bears and stuffed toys around the stand and chanting non-stop, deserved this and we are all of us part of a mighty roar of delight.

The second half is 45 minutes of the most exquisite torture. Seldom are so many people in the same place at the same time enjoying the same emotions – whatever their age or sex or background. We are united in our dreadful anxiety, we shout and sing and chant to exorcise the doubt.

1 Bernie Grant, Labour politician, MP for Tottenham.
2 Dave Spart, voice of left-wing activism, was a character created by *Private Eye* magazine.

The referee suddenly raises his hands, it's the end and we can at last release everything. A shock of collective pride, relief and unequivocal joy.

The Manchester United fans don't stay, but Wednesday's blue and yellow explosion rolls on and is still rolling 15 minutes later when Will and I begin to find our way out.

Man U fans are dead-faced, surly and suddenly scruffy and downtrodden. Wednesday's supporters, yobs and all, can enjoy the victor's role, for the first time at Wembley for 56 years.

Monday, April 22nd

There is a phone call from Patrick C to tell me that the weekend figures on 'AF' are not bad. Despite the misinformation in the *Standard* and the lack of information in the *Ham and High*, we took over £7,000 in London, as good as we ever did at the Odeon with fewer seats. Oxford respectable, Brighton reasonable, only Birmingham hopeless.

Monday, April 29th

Up early – today another connection added to my pre-'*PTP*' physical preparation prog. A regular workout (something I've never done before) suggested by osteopath Andrew Harwich to strengthen my back. So I'm walking past Selfridges at nine o'clock on my way to the Danceworks building in Balderton Street.

The Pilates class is up on the top floor. Small, high room with six or seven people quietly exercising on equipment or on mats. No sounds of sweat, no grunts of effort, and quiet classical music plays, so completely unlike most gyms, which seem to work on a combination of thudding disco and galley-slave atmos.

Tuesday, April 30th

Back home via dry cleaners to find Michael Coveney at my front door. He has come round to tape some impressions, views, info from me for a book on Maggie Smith. Says he's just been to see Alan Bennett who judged Maggie not to be 'the stuff of anecdote'.

Switch on TV. On Channel 2 Ranulph Fiennes struggles to the North Pole, on Channel 4 I'm shouting at Andrew McLachlan in *The Meaning of Life*. *Brian* topped Channel 4's ratings last week at 4.4 million. That was in the 'Banned' season. I think *The Meaning of Life* will offend far more people.

Thursday, May 2nd

Will arrives from Oxford and we go together to the 150th anniversary party of the London Library – neither of us quite knowing what to expect.

They have been given permission to use the gardens in the middle of St James's Square, and two or three marquees have been erected.

Norman Lamont shepherds the Queen Mother around, and we catch glimpses of an erect, pallid and cadaverous Enoch Powell, a neat Jim Callaghan slowly proceeding into the tent with no retinue, only his wife. Thatcher is reported to be there, as is Anthony Powell (though I never see him or Tristram).

Someone in the know tells me some Queen Mother gossip – she apparently did not have much time for Edwina Mountbatten, and when Edwina was eventually buried at sea, the QM, sitting with the family at Windsor, watched dispassionately as her coffin hit the waves. 'Typical Edwina, always did things with a splash.'

A lady with a foreign accent tells me that she has seen and enjoyed *'AF'* and leans in confidentially, 'You have a tremendous body.'

Tuesday, May 7th

Take bull by the horns and call Roger Laughton. He is surprisingly agreeable to my suggestion that writing my film script is a more urgent priority than attending tomorrow's Meridian board meeting. 'Of course we'd love to see you, Michael, but we do understand.' Well that's enough for me and I feel relieved to have that off my plate.

My head is muzzy and I'm not on sharpest form. Everything seems to take so long, papers litter my workroom floor, the telephone rings and I find myself shouting at it as the answerphone stands in for me. Radio Kent want to interview me re Meridian – straight away please. Clem wants to know why Anne has not yet signed the BBC contract for *'PTP'*. Will comes back from Oxford and needs ideas by tonight for a revue sketch on freshmen.

Thursday, May 9th

Up to Muswell Hill to see Paul. Good session; am learning about Russia as well as Russian.

Though I have a blind spot about being taught things (reaction to my father always telling me what to do?) I feel better for having listened and learnt and I enjoy and revel in the expansion of my knowledge in these hours in Muswell Hill. He's put me on to some Isaac Babel stories. I'm suddenly aware how much there is to read in advance of the Great Journey – now not much more than two months away.

Back home to do letters with Kath. Twelve charities alone in less than a week – Womankind, Oxfam, Film Centre at Sussex University, Linda Mc-Cartney for Lynx and Anita Roddick for Amnesty – not to mention the schizophrenics and the Samaritans and the Writers' Trust and Tom Stoppard. To care and be rich – well you're staring into the headlights.

Friday, May 10th: London–Cork

Head out to Heathrow for flight to Chris Orr's show in Cork.

The Crawford Art Gallery is a large, solid building with an excellent space downstairs in what was the old sculpture gallery.

They'd let Chris put a few sculptures around – so there's a figure with a discus and a marble baby at his mother's breast beside the imposing figure of William Crawford on a plinth: 'One of Ireland's worthiest sons – from his youth upwards his heart throbbed for her prosperity.' One or two of Chris's more scatological works have not been hung, including the copulating warthogs.

I'm poured a glass of Murphy's – the local stout. A beautiful colour and somehow its taste and effect are very comforting. Feel myself slipping into Ireland, but remain clear-headed enough to say a few words, with Crawford looming behind me.

Then we're all taken off to some ceilidh dancing in the Metropole Hotel.

About 50 people of all ages taking part. They are rather serious about it (majority of them are women) and the drunken antics of some of our party – among them a bone-thin sculptor who was once a baker in Lincolnshire, who dances on his head – are rather rightly, and indeed literally, looked down on.

Murphy's flows dark as the River Lee outside, which I find myself peering into with Chris at half past one.

Saturday, May 11th: Cork–London

Up at nine and at 9.30 down to breakfast at the 'Clouds' restaurant. Thick clouds seem to have come down over the service.

A shiny-headed, elderly maître d' passes helplessly amongst us like the only doctor at a disaster scene. Eventually, though, I get my muesli and strangely unreal orange juice and brown toast, done for about three seconds. Pick cutlery off other tables.

Read the papers – Frost/Branson almost certainly co-bidders and rivals for TVS – and then walk up South Mall and over various bridges and into a bookshop and then a tailor specialising in Donegal tweed – wonderful cloths at ridiculously low prices. Order a suit that will come out around £250 and buy two coats. The owner/cutter is an Englishman. Says David Puttnam was in recently and bought a whole lot of stuff – 'all loose-fitting'.

Walk round the upper rooms of the gallery. The bone-thin sculptor, more subdued now, sits surrounded by his hideous collection of ceramic hats and straitjackets and plastic dustbin lids, not a single visitor in sight.

Wednesday, May 15th

At half past twelve, half an hour after the deadline, a motorbike rider hands me the Meridian bid document. It comes in a box – rather like a *Reader's Digest* offer.

With Helen to the Ivy for a Meridian dinner. Roger L, dark-eyed from the nights at the bid document, Clive H, very perky and bright, Simon A and Bill Cotton, Allan McKeown and Tracey Ullman plus some late arrivals – Baroness Flather,[1] Sir Richard Luce and a smattering of local media.

General feeling is that we have prepared an excellent bid. Frost and Branson's company are competitors, as are Carlton (but Carlton will go primarily for Thames). We have done a more thorough job than anyone else – having not only found an HQ site but made an offer and designed a building to go on it.

Thursday, May 16th

Nigel Walmsley rings. His Carlton bid for TVS also went in yesterday. It's somehow neat that the two people I championed as prog heads to Clive and Simon a year ago now face each other as the two heads of the most likely bids. Nigel and Roger have been in amiable contact throughout. Nigel betting Roger an undisclosed sum that he couldn't get the word 'oleaginous' into his bid document and Roger betting Nigel the same about 'mountain greenery'.

---

1 Baroness Flather, Indian-born lawyer, first Asian woman to receive a peerage. Sat as Conservative in the Lords. Prominent in race-relations work.

I haven't looked at the bid doc yet, but the quest for the word 'oleaginous' makes it a much more appealing prospect!

Friday, May 17th: London–Brighton

Read some of the Meridian franchise bid in the taxi to Victoria to meet Simon A for trip to Brighton.

To the Grand Hotel where the first journo arrives. He's an obliging and good-humoured man from the *Argus*. Seems to think that Meridian have done their homework best.

Phone interview then a merciful half-hour to lie down before leaving at 6.45 for the independent cinema in Brighton – the Duke of York. Simon Fanshawe, with the smoothly curved profile of a 1930s toff, joins us together with a comedian called Eddie Izzard who once interviewed me in Sheffield.

Q and A with a full house after *American Friends*.

Fanshawe buttonholes me to go and watch Eddie Izzard. He's transformed from the quiet boy at the dinner to a very funny, un-rabid stand-up performer, working a large audience well. Nice piece about the people in Hove all being about 80, and how, as a kid growing up there, the youngest person he could find to play with was 76.

Sunday, May 19th

GBH cast and crew screening at 10.30. It's held at BAFTA and consists of episode one, all dubbed, but without the opening titles – 'Being finished in Vienna,' I'm told by David Jones – and some scenes from the end of episode three, including the doctor/Jim scene when the doctor declares he's dying.

It is unquestionably powerful stuff and the audience is dazzled, mesmerised and excited. Nicely, there is a lot of laughter too, at the right places. It works on all the levels it set itself to work at, and I think the vigilance and tenacity of the post-production period has paid off. There is hardly any drop in the tension and the good and bad both come across powerfully.

Alan revealed to Helen that he had ordered up all my work before seeing me and made his mind up on two performances – one, as he said 'in a film I hate', was Jack Lint in *Brazil*, and the other, when I decided to buy the dress in *The Dress*.[1]

1 *The Dress*, a short film with Phyllis Logan directed by Eva Sereny in 1984.

It's a lovely feeling to walk out across Piccadilly on a lazy Sunday afternoon with Helen buzzing with suppressed delight at her first look at what took so much out of my life last year!

Sunday, May 26th

At the Hay Literary Festival. Narrow streets full of cars and people.

Am whisked away to be photographed by the *Western Daily Press*. 'They don't want anything literary,' the photographer assures me, without irony. Then back to a hotel 15 minutes' drive away – very posh, English, sorry Welsh, for we are in Powys now, country house converted for rich people with pompous waiters of 17 who come out with lines like 'Half-bottles will be found towards the rear of the wine list, sir.'

Here meet up with TJ, Sue Townsend and, later, Patrick Barlow. In a very spacious and agreeable snooker room with leather armchairs we rehearse the 'Aladdin' panto from *Dr Fegg's Encyclopaedia of All World Knowledge*.[1]

Rushed lunch of wild mushroom soup, quails' breasts and other expensive standards, then with Geoffrey Strachan, our publisher, getting increasingly anxious, we're driven back into Hay to be picked up by the local HTV crew stepping out of the car.

Our talk, called 'What's So Funny', is in a tent which is full to overflowing and very hot by the end.

We are then rushed (one is always 'rushed' at things like this) to a book-signing outside. Fegg books by far the most popular and Patrick and Sue very patient.

To remain in my mind above all others as an image of these crazy five hours in Hay is a Lauren Bacall-signed cricket bat! She had been staying at our hotel.

Lovely drive to Oxford for Playhouse talk, along quiet, isolated Border valleys that stretch for miles.

Spot a sign for 'Linton' and pay quick homage to Ed P.[2] No-one about as I walked beneath the gnarled yew tree into the churchyard. In the porch are stills from the film. Fred's bearded Renaissance Syme regards me calculatingly.

Walk round beneath the tower and its soft-red stone spire and wonder if I did the right thing by Edward. Well yes, I decide, I think he would have enjoyed it. Pause a while in the graveyard where he's buried, then continue my journey to Oxford.

---

1 Palin and Jones comic book published in 1974. Illustrated by Martin Honeysett.
2 My great-grandfather Edward Palin was given the living of Linton in Herefordshire when forced to leave Oxford for marrying Brita.

At the Playhouse at 8.30. Dressing room is empty. Hear Ned Sherrin being witty over the tannoy and David Kernan singing witty songs and feel rather lonely for a moment, for this isn't quite my thing.

I get to read 'Biggles Goes to See Bruce Springsteen' after about an hour and a half of waiting. Behind me, at a table, are ranged Ned and Victor Spinetti and Sir Ian McKellen and Dame Judi and Michael Williams and other performers.

Miss a few moments but generally read tight and clearly and good laughs – especially from behind me.

Afterwards Ian McKellen, who looks about 22, welcomes me to the table and fetches me a glass of wine. Elizabeth Welch[1] finishes the show and is magnificent. Her voice so effortless and her interpretation of the songs immaculate – hitting the right note in every way.

I eventually get away back to the Old Parsonage Hotel – open only four days. Very tasteful and *World of Interiors* at reception, but the taps in the bath have the last laugh today. One completely comes away in my hand and a fountain gushes over me, and later the hotel manager who comes to investigate.

Monday, May 27th

JC has purchased more Burmese cats – he gets them all from Somerset – the latest are no bigger than his hand – as he pursues the search for the meaning of life. He meditates twice a day and one of his current jobs is as writer to the Dalai Lama, whom he met in London. JC says that they didn't exchange a word to start with – they just looked at each other and started to laugh. 'Then I brought Cynthia in and they had a laugh ...'

Thursday, May 30th

To Gascogne for lunch with my producer. Eric looking healthy, he's the last Python to need glasses, but he admits the time is getting close.

We talk over 'The Adventure'. EI's view after a quick read this a.m. is that 'it's a good first draft'. Characters are rich and the basic idea of the story works. He feels that the structure and shape of the story now need to be examined and motivations tightened to lose any feelings of arbitrariness.

Useful chat. We agree to sleep on it through June. EI will read it again

---

1 Elizabeth Welch, American-born singer ('Stormy Weather' and 'Love For Sale'), long resident in London.

and make suggestions and we'll meet up in early July to decide on the next step.

Friday, May 31st

Tristram and V and Hermione and Robert Young to dinner.

Earlier this evening Alan and Robert were on *Wogan*. Asked about me, Alan said that I hated, above all else, being called nice … 'but he is so nice!' he went on and told the story of the only time in the whole of *GBH* when he'd seen me in a sulk, which was when I'd asked for an *Independent* and been delivered a *Guardian*!

Saturday, June 1st: London–Brookfield-on-Longhill

June comes in cool and severe. Determination to follow all the advice to get fit for *'PTP'* pushes me out of bed and down to Marshall Street for a swim.

Home to find my face, lean and ascetic, staring up at me from a fashionably grainy b/w photo in the *Independent Magazine*. Accompanies a pre-*GBH* piece on me by Mark Lawson. Most of it is about my being nice. It's like an actress being only known for the size of her tits.

A podgier Palin photo sloshed across the front of the *Daily Mirror* TV page: 'Bleasdale Blockbuster Turns Two Softies into Boys from the Bash Stuff'. Hilary Kingsley leading off with my pleasure at being able to throw a punch on TV!

Early afternoon departure for Helen and myself, arriving at Brookfield-on-Longhill about 5.30.

Stay in the room I had during *GBH*, with the wide swathe of yellow curtain giving the impression that the sun's shining whatever the weather outside.

Sunday, June 2nd: Brookfield Hall–Sheffield–London

A slow and perfectly served breakfast surrounded by glowing previews for *GBH*.

The Sunday Times talks about it becoming a 'modern classic' – Alan's 'conviction fuelled through two magnificent performances' by Lindsay and Palin. Alan's wide, hairy, smiling visage beams out at me from every paper, as it used to from across this table over half a year ago. Somehow it seems the right time to be here.

Followed, kind of appropriately, by a dip into the more distant past, as I drive Helen over the Snake Pass from Glossop along the Rivelin Valley and via Hagg Lane, Crosspool and Whitworth Road [where I was born] to Graham and Margot's.[1]

Memories stirred of bike rides to Ladybower Dam ('Did you really cycle as far as this?' asks Helen), of asking for beer mats in pubs, blackberry-picking with Daddy in the fields beside the Rivelin, of playing football in days as chill and inhospitable as this at Hagg Lane.

In fact it was all as if nothing had changed. Graham stood up a lot and talked loudly and Margot wanted to know what it was like to kiss someone whilst acting.

Monday, June 3rd

At Hammersmith by eight to see Billy Connolly at the Odeon.

Keep thinking of how he would have done Jim Nelson as he starts, a little awkwardly, then warms into two hours of sometimes inspired raconteuring. His ruderies less good when they're direct ... 'I love the word wank!' and much better when they come incidentally and unbidden into his stream of consciousness. 'I don't know where these ideas come from. A wee idea will just come into my mind saying "Use me ... use me".'

Laugh constantly, with breaks; sometimes in tears. Much nostalgia – lots of jokes against modern technology. Lament for the 'on/off' switch. Quite male-oriented, I would think.

Tuesday, June 4th

The glorious fourth of June. It's 5.15. I'm sitting in the garden. Strong sunshine whose heat is moderated by a north-easterly breeze.

On my lap Jonathan Keates' seductive *Italian Journeys*. Below me the lawn I've just mown, beside me a Chambers dictionary to help me with Keates' penchant for the recondite word or phrase.

The commuter trains whine and clatter out of St Pancras and into Belsize tunnel, but I'm here and I don't have to move. A five-minute phone interview re *80 Days*' forthcoming repeat is the only immediate shadow on this very satisfying horizon.

Happiness – a good title for a film and one I was starting on five years ago.

---

1 Graham Stuart Harris, a neighbour in Whitworth Road, and a friend since the age of three. Married to Margot.

Alan Bennett said in an interview that he could only recollect being happy on four occasions. Keates writes of himself – the lonely traveller – 'he finds it so much easier to be wilfully miserable than to acknowledge a genuine happiness'.

I just can't be miserable here on my balcony in Julia Street at this moment, however hard I try. And, as if to add an unexpected extra to my non-misery, the smell of woodsmoke drifts over.

Thursday, June 6th

At nine o'clock, after all the ads, the trailers, the ubiquitous Alan Bleasdale reviews which make my publicity efforts seem positively Trappist, after 18 months of worrying, soul-searching, depression and elation, the first credits entwine – Robert Lindsay and Michael Palin. The second credit is a most enormous red 'in'.

At the end the phone rings like in the old days. First Ron Lendon[1] to say that he understood just what my character was going through – he too had been intimidated at Gospel Oak. Parts, he said, 'moved me to tears'. Tom rang, genuinely and warmly appreciative – perhaps the call that meant most.

Friday, June 14th

A nit-picking *Independent* review of last night's episode – 'the series is becoming more and more Michael Murray's'.

Experience a sudden squeeze of self-pity, which hits the same raw spot – that easily bruised corner of my ego which has so often seen me become a very good second, but never quite a first.

Lunch at Fontana Ambrosia in St John's Wood with JC.

JC asks me what I want, period ... my reply 'to know everything' strikes a chord with him. He wants to do a series of comedy films throughout the '90s.

We talk a little about *GBH*. He likes my performance and all the ingredients, but is not quite happy about the way they're put together, wants to know more about why things happen.

We talk for two and a half hours, like friends, and about friends.

Home to deal with letters. Hear from the office that *GBH*'s first episode had cumulative figures of 5.95 million. Doesn't seem quite as much reward

---

1 Ron Lendon. Charismatic headmaster who guided all our three children through Gospel Oak Primary School.

for all the pre-publicity as one might have expected, but Channel 4 are very happy.

Sunday, June 16th

The newspapers today are full of Liverpool. The death of Eric Heffer[1] has prompted a vital by-election in Walton on July 4th which will bring out all the Labour divisions. There is a £700 million debt in the city, the binmen are on strike, and Hatton is due to come up for a hearing on embezzlement/ corruption charges. The police have requested the *GBH* tapes but Channel 4 has refused to release them.

Alan is in the thick of it again. His uncanny knack of relevancy has worked in a way none of us could have expected. Alan wanted to put the finger on the evils of Thatcherism. She's gone, and his finger is now pointing, with frightening pertinence, at the incompetences of the loony left in Liverpool.

Monday, June 17th

To Cibo to meet Donald Woods for lunch. David Puttnam and Jeremy Thomas[2] sit opposite. Puttnam over a mineral water, Thomas over a wine.

Donald wants to use me 'as bait' (twinkle in the eye here), to try and lure the likes of Paul McCartney and Elton John into providing money for scholarships to help educate black children in S Africa. Of course I'm happy to help. He's quite influenced by American methods, I think, and the idea of a 'star' to draw in the rich and impressionable is one he learnt there, where celebrity is used much more shamelessly than here.

Cleese, also in the restaurant, sends us a half-drunk bottle of mineral water with 'the compliments of Table 1'. I send him back a half-empty salt-dish. Steve Abbott is dining with him. He finished *Blame It on the Bellboy* yesterday and looks harassed. I mention *'AF'* and he promises to check out the latest.

Puttnam, as he leaves, offers me use of his house near Skibbereen, and knocks over the water bottle John has sent us. Donald is too shell-shocked by this rash of celebrities to notice Harold Pinter slip out a moment later.

1 Eric Heffer, Labour MP for Liverpool Walton.
2 Jeremy Thomas, film producer of *The Last Emperor*, which won 1987 Academy Award for best picture.

Monday, July 8th

I begin to feel dreadful guilt about my approaching Russian lesson. It's nearly three weeks since my last, rushed, session and I have done no homework. Apply myself as best I can, but can do little but mouth the phrases I learnt in my first three visits.

Paul seems a little disappointed. He is really such a specialist, such a linguistic egghead that it must be of little interest to him to teach at this level. But he's also very decent and polite and doesn't let me know the full extent of his disappointment.

We descend from the heights of grammar to the mundane plain of phrase-book Russian.

Go to car wash on way home. One of the cleaners recognises me as I'm trapped inside whilst the car's being covered in suds from many hands. 'Monty Python ...' he points and screams exultantly to his colleagues ... 'it's the man from Monty Python!' Now, at last, I know what it's like to be a goldfish.

Tuesday, July 9th

A lunch at Fetter Lane with Robert H. He felt moved to ask me, he said, because of his mother's death, less than a month ago. Thoughts of mortality, long journeys and wills came into his mind and he wanted to see me before I disappeared.

He'd bought two plates of smoked salmon salad from what used to be the butcher's downstairs, and I've bought a bottle of Rongopai Sauvignon. We sit, flanked by his leather-bound volumes of Ruskin, in this little room, devoted to writing. It reminds me of Eisenstein's flat in Moscow.

As he is my literary executor he wants to know if I would mind a) having my diaries published and b) edited for publication. No to the second (within reason) and no to the first.

Surprise myself how quickly I reply – it's as if I'd made the decision long ago.

Thursday, July 11th

A session on Russia with Roger Mills. We sit in the garden with glasses of iced water and coffee and talk through Leningrad to Odessa.

For me the first half of this *Pole to Pole* journey is dominated by Russia. It's Russia I want to know about, read about, experience, see. Roger feels the same. It is so strange, magnificent, mysterious and flawed. I feel that I may have an uncomfortable time there, but somehow that's what I expect. That's what makes it so unusual and unfamiliar. Russia fascinates me with the same intensity as India did.

Shower, then to meet David Jones for a drink at the Ladbroke Arms.

The full story of the Lindsay/Palin casting. Alan had a photo of Lindsay on the wall as he wrote first draft. Then Lindsay couldn't do because of dates. Billy Connolly charmed the pants off Verity and came in as Nelson. Verity suggested me for Murray and everyone delighted. Then Connolly backed out. Alan goes home and tears up Connolly's photo. Lindsay's plans fall through. He becomes available, but I'm in as Murray and they keep it that way rather than ask me to change. David Jones it was who eventually suggested the swap round and though at first it was resisted, it later became a wonderful idea.

Home and settle in to watch episode six. I thought it so good – a different pace, a quietening of the plot and a tightening of the tension, but the humour and the tragedy constantly, exhilaratingly clashing. All the principals now as confused as the audience.

Rang Alan up afterwards to congratulate him. 'Your ears must be burning,' he said, and with a shy prelude of apology paid me a lovely compliment ... 'You made me proud.'

Head swells, but sinks much too late to the pillow.

Sunday, July 14th

Betty starts being very pleased to see us at about five a.m. She purrs louder and more consistently than at any other time of day – kneads the duvet and stares at us from very close range for signs of life. Then she disappears. There is brief silence and just when you're falling asleep she begins sharpening her claws on the underneath of the bed.

Up to lunch at Gilliam's. Richard Broke and Elaine there.

Richard B says that the effect of *GBH* on the Beeb has been profound, along with ITV's *Darling Buds*, etc. BBC now cancelled £175 million building prog to invest instead in drama!

Monday, July 15th

Books to sign, then some Russian homework.

To the Renoir to see *Andrei Rublev*. It is a long, uncompromising film, using wide sweeping shots and long takes; so it proceeds very differently, say, to the sharply edited modern product like *Thelma and Louise*. But it's a road movie too, with a fine, self-effacing but hypnotically watchable performance by Anatoly Solonitsyn.

'Russia endures' says one character after some spectacular cruelty and devastation has left bodies littered in a burning church. 'Yes, but for how long?' asks Rublev. 'Probably for ever,' replies the other.

Thursday, July 18th

A letter coolly and dispassionately shows the figures for Prominent Facilities' last three months. Costs were about 30,000; income 12,000, deficit 18.

To Pilates.

A fond farewell to Hannah and Sue. I have learnt a lot from them – exercises which I can do as I go, exercises which run completely counter to the punish-yourself theory of British PE drummed into me at school. My back feels stronger and straighter and, as with Alexander Technique, I feel I know my body better, and will from now onwards treat it better.

Meeting at Prominent at five with Terry Gilliam, Bob, Justine and Kevin and Ian. We sit in the viewing theatre, the worst loss-maker of them all. I'm quite wound up and angry, but don't want to direct it at anyone, though I'm generally disappointed that no-one let TG or myself know what was happening. After my work on reorganising the place in February I feel let down.

I've then promised to view *Blame It on the Bellboy* – Steve's latest exec production. Good first half, then a little plodding, but light and agreeable farce. Richard Griffiths on top of Patsy Kensit must be one of the most extraordinary couplings in screen history.

Met Ken Livingstone last night at Vasco and Piero's: 'Michael Murray was too nice to be Derek Hatton,' he told me.

My private notebook for the period 20th July–November 5th, 1991 was lost by Zambian Airways at Lusaka. No personal diary kept again until December 11th, 1991. The travel diaries I kept were not lost, and form the bulk of the Pole to Pole *book.*

Thursday, December 12th

It's midday. I'm up in my workroom surrounded by piles of letters, notebooks, films, cassettes, boxes of presents, new books kindly sent to me. A huge mess. Half of the room taken up by the word processor Helen has bought and which I know I shall have to learn to use. Try to view it as a friend and not a baleful technological bore itching to change my life!

Though I was standing on the South Pole a week ago, I feel that the whole journey is oddly transitory, almost as if it never happened. Certainly the enormous effort, the upheavals, the trials and tribulations and ineffable pleasures have all merged into a sort of homogenous blur.

I suppose that as soon as I have cleared my desk and can start looking into the diaries and at the photos things will be different. But at the moment I feel this spatial numbness, as if I'm not quite anywhere. A temporal limbo.

I've lost about five pounds in weight, largely due to a mixture of unexciting food and an unsettled stomach (possibly affected by the malaria tablets I've been taking daily for over 12 weeks), and my ribcage continues to be painful after the battering in the Zambezi on 9th November.[1] I can still only sleep comfortably on my back.

In the evening joined Terry and Al and Basil at Mon Plaisir. It seemed, once again, as though no time had passed. TJ at one stage, however, regarded me carefully and said, 'You know, Mikey, I think we're beginning to look grown-up.'

Sunday, December 15th

Spend a couple of hours on the word processor. Not as daunting as I'd expected. In fact it promises well. Quiet and smooth, an easy keyboard, no paper to insert, no crossing out or Tippex-ing. At the purely basic level I can work it, but will just need practice.

Don't much feel like leaving the house tonight, but have promised Rachel a trip to Vic Reeves' stage show.

Audience mainly consists of what Rachel calls 'Channel 4 students'. They are, I'm sure, the natural successors to the Goon Show and Python audiences. Brighter than they like to look, also fairly affluent. It takes a certain confidence and a degree of achievement to laugh at the absurdity of life.

Vic and Bob do their stuff well. They are more original than most.

Wednesday, December 18th

The news on *American Friends* is not as bad as I'd thought. Had virtually written the film off as I heard that post-Venice business in Italy was bad. [The film was shown out of competition at the Venice Film Festival.] I was glad to hear from Steve today that it held on and improved in Italy and may well still be

---

1 I cracked a rib whilst filming a whitewater rafting sequence.

playing. The film opened the Dinard Festival and has been well reviewed in Australia.

Sunday, December 22nd

In the middle of the night I wake up lying comfortably on my right side – the first time I've been able to do so without pain for six weeks. This is exactly the time I was advised it took a rib to heal. Talk to Chas McKeown, who had his ribs crushed whilst filming *Young Indiana Jones* for TJ in the summer. Since then he has had bronchitis, near-pneumonia and a series of debilitating colds. Like many others who've wintered in London, he sounds unhealthy.

Ian MacNaughton, director of the Python TV shows, rings from Germany having just seen episode one of *80 Days*. Apparently I'm now one of his mother-in-law's greatest favourites – along with Pavarotti and Boris Becker! She's 86.

Christmas Day. Wednesday, December 25th

Woke, I must admit, with that unsatisfactory feeling of doubt as to whether I shall psychologically be able to live up to the day. The piles of presents, the tablefuls of food and drink, the bonhomie expected all put demands on a system which really craves a quiet day in the study.

Helen has to get up and start cooking and I'm aware that she is probably as apprehensive as I am. But Rachel comes into bed with us and we open our stockings and this irrational Christmas spirit begins to flutter and grow.

Soon we're up and the house is full of the bright colours of the wrapped presents, and cards cover the kitchen walls and the family silver is on the table and all the weight of tradition and all the happy associations of Christmas begin to work, and then as Granny and Auntie C arrive and, much later, a Palin, Burd, Gibbins, Christmas rolls remorselessly into action.

And it works. We get hot and we eat and drink too much and the present piles are bigger than ever – 'Obscene!' says Helen when she sees them all together.

I am given a Norman Lewis book on India, a marvellous series of old French jigsaw maps, a new watch, a print of 1688 maps of the hemispheres by Tom and Lisa and a CCCP T-shirt from Will, on the day Gorbachev resigned as President and in the week the Soviet Union ceased to exist. Momentous times.

Walk up Parliament Hill in the dark. Long chat with Rachel, who loves the sixth form and is obviously great friends with a group of boys and girls rather than being exclusively with one. I enjoy her company and am proud of her openness and enthusiasm and common sense.

Friday, December 27th

At six go round to the Idles for a drink – first time I've seen my producer since before *'PTP'*. His house seems even more *Dallas*-like than I remember, big, empty, warm rooms – the hangings and decorations impressive rather than cosy. Lily is walking now.

As if on cue, Jerry Hall, swathed in a showy scarlet dress, and much larger than I remember her, appears down the stairs. She's pregnant, that's why she's so big. I ascertain she's three weeks away from having Mick's third child. She doesn't look like someone who likes looking like this.

Eric's mother appears. Even Norah glitters expensively, as if she too has just come out of Aladdin's cave. She looks well and sounds strong and I'm pleased to see her.

Then Mick appears – impish, puckish – all the clichés really do apply. He's one of those people with a cheeky face – Eric being another.

Jerry and Mick seem fond of each other. Jerry is dreamily Texan, Mick quickfire English. He bemoans, insincerely, having three children – and about to have a fourth. 'I'll 'ave to become a house husband ... give up going to work.'

1992

Monday, January 13th

Up in time for the eight o'clock news. Algerian elections cancelled as it seems the Arab fundamentalists will win, and at home politicians trying to talk over each other in macho encounters which leave the listener bewildered and embarrassed.

Rachel is 17 today. We've given her a black-leather school bag, books, a Cure T-shirt and a Mont Blanc fine-point pen. She's still in her room when I start work on the *Pole to Pole* book at nine. I'm pleased I'm here, having been absent for all the three other family birthdays last year.

Back to work. A thorough scan of all the source documents and a very slow start. Rachel and her friends fill the kitchen with the smell of toasted cheese sandwiches.

Tuesday, January 14th

To lunch at Odette's with TG. He's off to Madrid tomorrow and then on to Hollywood for the Golden Globes, for which his latest film *Fisher King* is entered in Comedy and Musicals section!

I tell him that TJ has rung me this a.m. to let me know, amongst other things, that he feels Roger Saunders is unfairly shackled in his Python sales efforts by our refusal to have the programmes dubbed or sold to commercial stations. TJ having been the prime supporter of the anti-dub position – this comes as something of a shock. But he feels the shows have now made their impact on all the people who need to know about them in their pristine form – and it no longer seems worth safeguarding them so jealously. In short, he wants the money, which is fine. TG says he doesn't feel motivated in any direction.

In the evening receive good news re *American Friends* French release. Ring Michel Burstein, our French distributor, to confirm. He says that they are all pleased, the reviews were generally good, but returns in the provinces significantly lower than in Paris.

Wednesday, January 15th

Taxi to Adelaide House for my first Meridian board meeting. Things seem to be going well. TVS messed up their judicial challenge to Meridian, and just before Christmas our licence to broadcast was assured. Meridian bought TVS' studios in Southampton for 13 million, which is considered by those in the know to be a bargain.

Thursday, January 16th

Humiliation at the Post Office today. I have forgotten my glasses and cannot see to fill in a Recorded Delivery slip. Bassant, behind the counter, gently takes it from me. 'I can do that, Michael.'

At eleven o'clock William is packed and ready to be returned to Oxford. Another grey day, but at least his two flatmates are installed already at 35 Jericho Street, so there's someone to welcome him. He sounds more optimistic about this term – resigned to the flat, looking forward to work he enjoys – the Romantics – and determined to get out and involved in more things. I ask him about plans after Oxford. He still seems to like the idea of film school, but travel and writing come in there too.

Tuesday, January 21st

Have jolly chats with Beryl Bainbridge re Polar matters. I ask Beryl if she'd been anywhere near the Pole. 'Oh God, no!' she says ... 'I was once going to spend the night in a tent on the Heath.'

Tuesday, January 28th

To Cleese's for dinner. Things have changed there – the trees outside in the front garden have gone and been replaced by paving. Houses appear to have been knocked together – the swimming pool is operating, paintings plaster the wall.

Talk to JC about *GBH* – 'Fifty-five per cent absolutely marvellous ... and' JC pauses seriously, as if calculating the price of coal ... 'thirty-five per cent rubbish.' But it sounds as if Robert Young is restored to favour as the preferred director of a *Wanda* follow-up.

JC wants me to go and hunt the yeti with him; sometime in spring '93.

Saturday, February 1st

Helen up at the hospital to see her friend Greta who was taken in on Friday morning with serious breathing problems. Helen can only talk about the other occupants of the ward. The man who clears his throat horribly and always concludes his performance with a deeply felt 'Fucking hell!' He's known as Fucking Hell. There's a farting woman opposite, and a lady who isn't quite the full sixpence who takes her clothes off all the time.

Helen goes out to dinner with the badminton group, Rachel to the cinema with her 'posse'. I go to Cibo, to dinner with Michael Barnes. He's asked to go Italian ... 'My left hand isn't all that good at the moment.'

He likes to be early, so at seven o'clock opening time he's ensconced with a scotch and water, and the wine ... 'anything, so long as it's red'. He does seem genuinely relieved, as well as glad, to have me back, and reminds me that there was an element of danger to the journey, there were risks, which I'd become less aware of once we were working. Was Helen worried about me? I've never asked!

Michael's physical condition seems to have deteriorated. He sits heavily and stands with difficulty. His concentration is not as acute as I remember and he is quite alarmingly unsteady when leaving the restaurant and uncoiling himself from the taxi at his hotel in Tottenham Court Road.

One of the problems of going out by cab is that most of the drivers now know me and want to talk. One has caught a glimpse of our sitting room ... 'I thought you must be a brain surgeon with all them books ...'

Tuesday, February 4th

Good writing weather and I do get on, head down on *Pole to Pole* and hoping crises will not intrude. By the time I stop, I'm through Novgorod and heading for Dno! Pile of letters and requests as usual. A fine new book about Shrewsbury School places me (chronologically) as the last on a list of selected Old Salopians, but has my name wrong. So the list begins with Andrew Downes (1549–1628) Regius Professor of Greek at Cambridge, described by contemporaries as 'a walking library', and ends with Michael Edwin (*sic*) Palin (1943–): comedian, actor, writer. I share a column with Ingrams, Rushton and John Peel.

Thursday, February 6th

Lunch with Beryl Bainbridge at Trattoria in Parkway. She chose the place, I set up the lunch. Both of us try and read the menu blackboard they stick in front of you without our glasses, both admit we can't see a thing.

Beryl is very funny, easy, entertaining, gossipy company. She's being rung up by Terry Waite.

He's writing a book on his experience and has approached Beryl for help and guidance. But lately he rang so late that Beryl confesses she had to have a scotch or two to keep up with him. They discussed captivity ... '"Go on Terry," I said, sort of joking, "you probably really enjoyed it all a bit ... being chained up to the wall"' to which TW had apparently replied that he had found much of the experience beneficial and he was a better man because of it.

She's writing a book about the Crimea at the moment, but has no idea where the Crimea is.[1] 'Up near Leningrad isn't it?' For once I can use the European fold-out map at the back of my diary to good effect ... 'Oh, right down there!'

Letters and calls, then a determined sprint on the writing before going out to dinner with Robert Young. Hugh Laurie and wife Jo and a neighbour, an older man, are there already. Stephen Fry arrives a little later having flown in from Los Angeles that morning. There's talk of doing his book *The Liar* as a film.

Stephen tells me at dinner that *Round the World* has started something called The Palin Effect – actors and comics wanting to do documentaries.

Sunday, February 9th

Watch Colin Thubron on *South Bank* talking about why he travels. Though he's very serious and intense, I like what he says about the urge to travel. It's not escape, it's more about enhancement of your life. Widening horizons, physically and mentally. And the video footage of his entry into Bukhara was magical. A real feeling of a search.

Tuesday, February 11th

Drive across town to the Ladbroke Arms in Notting Hill Gate to meet Roger for a spot of 'beak-dipping' over our pints.

R tells me that Paul Hamann, the new head of current affairs, called the

---

1 Beryl Bainbridge's novel was published as *Master Georgie*.

department producers together and announced that they must search for a new Palin, as the current one would obviously be working for Meridian in the future. I'm a little hurt at this. After all, I've announced no public commitment other than to remaining freelance. The fact that no-one at the BBC has ever approached me about a future working relationship is quite odd.

Anyway, the name that came up as the new Palin was ... Ruby Wax.

Thursday, February 13th

Dinner with Alan Bleasdale at the Halcyon Hotel. He's lost weight, after dieting, and looks good. At dinner he tells us, prefaced with 'I don' wan any glass-clinking or anything like that', that *On the Ledge*, the play he's been working on for almost the same time as *GBH*, has been accepted by the National Theatre 'on the sixth rewrite!'[1]

Only Alan could describe so candidly his delight at receiving the fax from Richard Eyre. 'I just wanted to hug someone, to lift them up in the air, but there was no-one there. Not even me dad was in. So I just went round the house doing war-whoops!'

Whilst writing this up, I hear from Kath that I have been nominated for Best Actor at BAFTA, along with Lindsay, John Thaw and Tom Bell – and there's no-one in the house to tell!

Tuesday, March 10th

Started on Sudan writing at nine. Well into flow now. Feel that there is a chance of reaching my goal of Equator by BAFTA.

Receive a nod from LWT, who are broadcasting the proceedings this year, to the effect that if I should win an award I am permitted to make a short speech of thanks. In view of the length of the proceedings they would be obliged if it could be confined to '0.20'.

To a party at Methuen's new HQ in Kendrick Mews, South Ken. Interesting turnout. Michael Frayn, beaming and friendly, Peter Nichols, almost a Frayn lookalike, guarded and not forthcoming. Robert H, Patrick Barlow, Terry J, David Nobbs, the same as ever. Ivor Cutler,[2] formidably eccentric – Geoffrey has to find guests to talk to him, rather like finding meat for an animal. Champagne out of plastic cups. Jolly nice group of authors, I decide.

1 *On the Ledge* was eventually first presented at the Nottingham Playhouse in 1993.
2 Ivor Cutler, Scottish poet and songwriter.

Friday, March 13th

An interesting film idea via Angela Elbourne. A proposal that I should be seen in the US trying to track down Bruce Springsteen; using his songs as clues and as an excuse to visit various unvisited parts of the US, viz. Asbury Park. In the end we would meet and exchange whatever. The idea that intrigued the authors of this proposal is the difference between English public-school, middle-class comedy writer and American working-class rock idol – or the similarity. Also on my desk, a treatment called 'Orphans of Empire', a look at the remaining island colonies.

Monday, March 16th

By cab to lunch in Brompton Road with Teddy Warwick and John Peel. This is one of those events which has taken the best part of ten years to come to fruition. It's been mentioned so often on our Christmas cards as to become a joke, but today here we are, gathered together in the almost religiously neat and silent offices of Melody Radio, who are paying Teddy good money to come out of retirement and help them with some of his BBC expertise.

I ask about the station. It turns out to be owned by Lord Hanson, very much as his private plaything. DJs have strict instructions to announce only the record and the artist – anything more, any statement of opinion or per-sonal prejudice, is spotted by the Lord himself and noted in a cautionary fax.

J Peel lives in Suffolk most of the time and, beyond his own show, mixes not at all with fellow DJs. He remembers less about himself at Shrews-bury than I do, but says he owes an enormous amount to Hugh Brooke, our housemaster, who appreciated humour and spirit and, in a way, non-conformity. JP says that Brooke purposely gave him Study 13 because it was near the library and it would annoy all those people listening to their classical music.

We talk about Zimbabwean music and his inordinate (this is one of those words he's very fond of using) love for The Four Brothers, who his wife Sheila got along to his 50th birthday as a surprise. We share an inability to dance – crippled by shyness at early dance classes, and a predilection (that's another word he might use) for football.

By the end it feels as if the three of us have had lunch every week for the last ten years. John Peel Ravenscroft – as he was known when we both, briefly, were in the same house at Shrewsbury School – has very clear likes and dislikes (Springsteen is one of the latter, Lonnie Donegan one of the former) and is a storehouse of odd facts about the kitsch of the music biz – e.g. that somewhere in the USA there is Twitty City, dedicated to the life, work and good name of Conway Twitty.[1]

Thursday, March 19th

To Adelaide House for my second Meridian board meeting.

Clive, who clearly doesn't like board meetings and finds them a tiresome necessity, bustles through, but every now and then questions are raised which manage to halt the proceedings.

Lots of figures, and a nice human moment at the end when Shreela Flather persists in pushing her 'help for the community' suggestions. Meridian's execs firmly try to put the lid on this, saying that our duties extend only to making television programmes, but Shreela persists ... 'For just £50.00 we could have a minibus to take old people out.' She is so patently sincere, and yet it is so touchingly far from what Clive is in the business for, that I have to smile.

Sunday, March 22nd

I edit the Ethiopian section. It does not excite as it should do. I think I have description fatigue.

Off to BAFTA at 5.45 in an LWT Jaguar. The journey is smooth, but the arrival a mess. In the back way, so we miss the bank of photographers which Helen and I rather look forward to once a year. Instead, as we step out, a ferocious woman shouts at us: 'Picture with the Jaguar, please!'

Then an uncertain researcher leads us to the stage where I'm shown what is required of me as an award presenter.

I begin to pick off a few celebs including Cliff, who is the most extraordinary 50-year-old I have ever seen. Only a trace of tightening skin indicates that he's anything more than 13 years old, and his neat, eager, clean manner all contribute to the feeling I have that he must be kept in a box. That's right, he is like a living doll.

This is a good time to be a nominee, as you can rake in a few congratulations before becoming, most likely, an ignored loser. Stephen Fry cautions me not to leave early as there is a special award which he's presenting which will be of interest. He's looking quite debonair and has lost weight ... 'Not eating, really. Well, I was 17 stone!'

The table is left to right – Helen, who was sat elsewhere but has moved her

1 Conway Twitty, American country and western singer. Born Harold Lloyd Jenkins.

name-place to be next to me, Beth Worth from Channel 4, then Dan Massey, sporting a hussar's moustache for *Heartbreak House* and lady friend, Di and Robert Lindsay (hair cut, blow-dried, immaculately styled, beard trimmed), Alan and Julie, Michael Grade and his perky new girlfriend. Alan has his head down already, a bull against the world.

Lindsay Duncan, who I wish had been on our table, is very funny. She'd seen my photograph, she says enticingly, before adding 'at the car wash'. I remember just after Christmas going into my favourite Afro-wash place under St Pancras arches and suffering the embarrassment at having to be photographed for their celebrity board. 'You looked very happy,' says Lindsay.

I'm backstage with Dame Edna and Hale and Pace and a nervous, quite sweet Jason Donovan, when I hear that *Prime Suspect* has taken the Best Drama Serial Award from *GBH*, *Coronation Street* and two others.

We win Best Music and Robert takes the Best Actor so we have our celebrations.

Our director Robert Young had had the best thing happen to him, which was to be given the special award that Stephen Fry so elegantly presented.

Friday, March 27th: Stranraer–London

Returning from Glasgow, after a *Pole to Pole* writing blitz, I find the flight is full and by extraordinary coincidence many of the passengers are people from Channel 4 whom I last saw at BAFTA, six nights ago. Beth Worth brings me up to date on the scandalous goings on over *GBH*'s 'Drama Serial' defeat by *Prime Suspect*.

Knowing that Alan had heard he had won, Michael Grade rang the jurors on Monday morning. Four of them – a majority – confirmed they'd voted for *GBH*. The non-voting chairman of the 8-strong jury was Irene Shubik,[1] an avowed enemy of Verity Lambert. It all sounds absolutely in the spirit of *GBH*.

Thursday, April 2nd

Out to Shepherd's Bush to see the rough cuts of episodes three and four of 'PTP'.

Disappointed by a 'holiday' programme feel to the start of episode three. The pictures are fine, but it lacks much quirkiness – just endless shots of me walking, travelling, and in the company of conventional characters in

---

1 Irene Shubik, television producer associated with *The Wednesday Play* and *Play for Today*.

surroundings which most people know about anyway. It's the Mediterranean travel brochure world, and doesn't come alive for me until we reach Egypt – after which there is no problem.

But it is the Sudan episode, number four, which will, I think, become a classic; like the dhow, it has the elements of unfamiliarity, danger and improvisation. Nigel's photography on the roof of the Sudanese train is breathtakingly beautiful. Best of all, as someone said afterwards, it needs the minimum of music or commentary, a simple structure holding together a feast of rich material.

Saturday, April 4th

The story of the potential BAFTA scandal over the *GBH* vote is now public since four members of the jury broke the confidentiality rule, claiming that they wrote to the BAFTA chairman saying they had voted for *GBH* and it should therefore have had the majority without any casting vote being needed. An inquiry is under way, but *The Sunday Times* is already calling it Baftagate.

Saturday, April 5th

To dinner at TG's invitation with Ray Cooper and Robin Williams at the Caprice.

Robin looks younger and calmer than when I last saw him. His hair has been dyed a sort of light chestnut for his latest film, and I notice he barely drinks. Robin is one minute the earnest, interested conversationalist – a good listener and a good laugher – and the next the demon of improv grabs him and he wrestles in the grasp of what appears to be an elaborate and spontaneous beast of invention.

Sometimes he can extricate himself, but only with considerable effort. Usually he just lets himself go with it – sometimes raising his voice to a shout, but generally not involving anyone other than those immediately around him.

It is a wonderful gift, sometimes eye-streamingly funny, such as his quite magnificent creation of the Indian warrior who rings Kevin Costner about *Dances with Wolves* royalties ...

But generally it makes for an awkward evening. Conversation is possible, but everyone is waiting for the fire to start blazing.

I don't really remember the food.

Monday, April 6th: London–Mountrath

To Dublin, from Heathrow, on the 9.05 flight. Collect my car, and begin to pick my way along the maze of roads to the west of Dublin.

The Irishness of things appeals to me. Ireland may try to look like any other bland and prosperous Western European country, but it is neither. Instead of 'Dual Carriageway Ahead' it has signs saying 'Dual Carriageway Now'.

Turning in the gates of Roundwood House an hour and 40 minutes after leaving the airport.

Carry my bag into a strip-wood-floored hall hung with old portraits, doors on either side and ahead a staircase and a Venetian-style window letting in plenty of light and matching its companion above the front door. A lop-eared middle-aged man with an ironic smile emerges unhurriedly from a side door. 'You're the Cleese man,' he greets me, not at all disagreeably, but I'm a little huffed. 'No, I'm the Palin man.'

No harm done, he shows me upstairs – rooms off a curious criss-cross-balustraded gallery. Big room at the front – yellow, mustard-yellow, chosen in preference to violent-green one on the other side.

They make me a basket full of sandwiches which I eat downstairs in another tall, airy room, with some tea. There are no curtains at Roundwood – all wooden shutters and few soft furnishings – everything is good, old, antique but gone to seed.

But am very happy about my broad Georgian writing desk, which I move across one of the deep-set windows so I can look out onto the lawn, across which ducks potter periodically, to a field with big, oddly pollarded trees, in which three racehorses while away the day.

Down for a drink at a quarter to eight. An English couple – he with Denis Healey flying eyebrows, grey hair, probably late 50s early 60s, both very nice *Good Hotel Guide* types.

A log and peat fire has been lit and I order myself a Bushmills malt and settle down with the curiously cold *Kindness of Women* [by J. G. Ballard]. We are to eat communally, which I must say is something I dread.

A third guest, besides myself, joins us. She's a gnomic little American lady. Quite a bluestocking – possibly even a writer. Even the most inconsequential story delivered in measured, elegant tones and richly ornamented with figures of speech and self-conscious irony. In short, a bit of a pain.

The owner then takes them all off to the pub – but I'm tired and must make a good start at nine tomorrow, and I know that when he says they'll be back at 11.30 he's Irish and doesn't mean it.

Friday, April 10th: Mountrath–London

My week at Mountrath produced a lot of words and I only hope the quality matches the quantity. By one o'clock today I've added nearly 15,000 words to my *Pole to Pole* tally, and am within striking distance of the end. In fact, totting up on the plane on the way back, I have now written over the 93,000 total that I had set myself.

At breakfast, Rosemary, the owner's wife, tells me that my premonition about the election result was right. The Conservatives have won and with a working majority. Major's last-minute appeal to the voters to go with the trend 'in almost every other country in the world' and reject socialism seems to have worked.[1]

On the plane back read Raymond Briggs' *The Man*, which they want me to read for audio cassette. Absolutely marvellous.

Rachel very cut up about the return of the Tories, but Glenda Jackson has taken Hampstead and Frank Dobson, our local man, has not suffered from the lack of my vote – he's in with a five per cent swing.

As if to rattle me back into city life, there is an explosive boom, with an after-boom, from somewhere outside. Helen rushes upstairs. It's reported later as a massive bomb in the City, the biggest ever used on the mainland. A bit of Ireland has returned with me.[2]

Saturday, April 11th

Another distant but frighteningly powerful blast just after we have gone to bed. I make it eight or nine minutes after one o'clock. Switch on the radio for information. Nothing official, but callers, mostly from the Cricklewood, Hendon and Finchley districts, ring in to tell the same story – windows rattled, houses shaken. I'm asleep by the time Helen hears the news that a bomb has exploded under a flyover near the M1 junction with the North Circular.

Thursday, April 16th

To work at nine o'clock, and after an hour I know I shall finish today. Which means that the morning is a little more relaxed than usual. Will, Rachel and

1 1992 Election result. The Conservatives, led by John Major, retained power with 336 seats against Labour's 229.
2 The Baltic Exchange bombing: three people were killed and £800 million worth of damage was done.

Helen are all around. Rachel has drawn us a wonderful wedding anniversary card – my nasal hairs, penchant for pottery shops and dark-brown bread all noted.

I began writing *Pole to Pole* in January – on Rachel's birthday – sharing the book with the rest of my life, trying to fit it in with people, ideas, half-projects, scripts to read, etc. This meant that I never allowed myself time to become absorbed in it, to feel the pace and weight of it, to address the subject matter as anything more than another chore after five months of heavy work.

But since the end of March, and especially through the week at Mountrath, I gave it the priority and the total commitment it needed – and, as I say, I feel on top of the work, and sort of cleaned out; cleansed by a period of three weeks of, for me, monastic solitariness.

And I know that I never want to go back to the world of trying to satisfy everyone else's demands. I have achieved much of what I want to achieve. Though I don't feel I'm out of the rat race – I no longer believe in it enough to want to win. And that's a start.

At a quarter to four I type 'The End'.

Thursday, April 23rd

An interview with a very bright, chirpy ex-air hostess who now edits the BA staff magazine. One thought-provoking question. If I was able to travel in time would I go for the future or the past? I unhesitatingly plump for the past, which I suppose betrays my literary and artistic preferences over scientific curiosity. Choose Ancient Egypt or Elizabethan England – tempted by the prospect of going to the world premiere of *Hamlet*.

Monday, April 27th

Graphic dream that Helen was having another baby. Couldn't get the mid-wife, so there was just her and me. (I think I blame *Kindness of Women* for graphic description of something similar.) H lying on a bed with placenta and afterbirth all in amongst the duvet – telling me quite cheerfully that the baby is 'in there somewhere'. I find it but am unable to tell its sex without my glasses on.

Thursday, April 30th

Lunch at Odette's with TG before collecting manuscript. TG good company as ever, but he is working under pressure on the *Quixote*. 'I'm getting boils and my back is going ...' he says cheerfully.

He has two offers of finance – 20 mill dollars from Jake Eberts[1] and 23 mill from 'the richest man in France'. Now he's suffering doubts about whether the script will be ready for his projected October shoot and if it is ready, whether it will be any good. He says that J Edgar Hoover would make a wonderful subject for a film. Calls him possibly the most important and influential figure in post-war America!

He's touchingly keen to do something together again, and promises to send me work so far on the 'Defective Detective' idea, which he says that Richard LaGravenese – his *Fisher King* writer – has not been able to get right.

I feel almost guilty at having completed a book when TG is having such a struggle with his script – but that's the way it goes – we inspire each other and keep each other going forward.

Saturday, May 2nd

Wake Rachel, as instructed, before I go swimming. 'I think I'll give it a miss,' she says, before quite rapidly changing her mind – and we end up with a swim, followed by coffee, orange juice and croissants at Patisserie Val's – first performance of this ritual for a long time.

Then to the bookshops of the Charing Cross Road for Rachel's Shakespeare and trade union books and my Arctic exploration literature. Feel rather pleased to be able to go to Stanford's and ask for maps of the Arctic, when everyone else is scrabbling over the South of France.

May 4th to May 23rd: North Pole journey as described in Pole to Pole. *Unable to shoot this section last summer because of the fragile state of the sea ice.*

Wednesday, May 27th

Have put all other activities on hold – shopping, lunching and cinema-going – until I have completed the Arctic chapter.

I looked into Simon Brett's *Faber Book of Diaries*, and found V Woolf for May 25th 1932 – almost 60 years ago today – in dreadful state of self-doubt.

1 Jake Eberts, Canadian-born film producer, co-founder of Goldcrest with David Puttnam.

'What a terrific capacity I possess for feeling with intensity. I'm screwed up into a ball, can't get into step ... see youth, feel old; no, that's not quite it; ... hatred of my own brainlessness and indecision; the old treadmill feeling, of going on and on and on for no reason; contempt for my lack of intellectual power ... reading without understanding ...'

Both these passages were relevant to how I felt and therefore curiously comforting. I even checked on Virginia's dates and found that she too was 49 years old at the time of writing.

Friday, May 29th

Ken Stephinson rings and tries to persuade me to rejoin him for a second *Great Railway Journey*. None of the foreign trips appeal – all too soon after 'PTP' – but, just as I've decided on a positive negative, Ken mentions Ireland. Now that is tempting. Easy to get to, a country I like and which interests me, a country in which the railway is part of the political drama and a country in which there is no danger at all of a dull interview! By the end of the call I have virtually committed to my first job in 1993.

Thursday, June 4th

I am to spend the day ahead reading Raymond Briggs' latest book, *The Man*, for audio cassette.

To a small studio set back off a side road in Shepherd's Bush. Mike Carrington-Ward is producing the tape. Raymond Briggs is there. He is less assertive and outspoken in the flesh than in his writing. Gentle, really, and immediately likeable.

A small 13-year-old, smaller than 13-year-olds are normally, William Put-tock, is there with his mother. He's being taken through his paces by the indefatigably ebullient Mike Ward, and after a coffee the two of us go into a hot little room where we are observed on closed-circuit TV, and rehearse about two-thirds of the story.

Others arrive during the day, including Raymond's long-term publisher, Julia MacRae, whom I liked a lot, and who was very complimentary about the reading, and a marketing lady who had a mock-up of the cassette sleeve with the words 'Read by Michael Palin' across it. William Puttock's mother spotted this straight away and said she hoped William's name would appear alongside mine. The marketing lady looked startled and smiled unconvincingly. She clearly thought the woman was mad.

Friday, June 5th

A programme called *A Stab in the Dark* has put a rather nasty little note through my door, informing me that in 'light-hearted' vein they have not only 'observed' my rubbish but have taken samples to form the basis of a film on their prog tonight. The reason being that I am, according to them, 'an environmentally conscious individual in the public eye', and it is my fate to have my 'commitment' tested.

I ring them up and they cheerfully admit to trespass and say that they won't be using any of my rubbish in the prog. They think they'll have more fun with Sting and Anita Roddick. 'A little squirt of malice' is how the producer put it. I think it just about sums him up.

Sunday, June 7th

Read of the latest lurid details of the Prince of Wales' marriage. Aside from the unhappy, if true, evidence of Diana's suicide attempts, the story seems to be so uncannily close to *Private Eye*'s Mills and Boon spoof of the couple as to further increase the case for the *Eye* being the most prescient and accurate organ of its generation.

Thursday, June 11th

To lunch at San Lorenzo with Robert Fox and David Pugh. Both very good company – we share similar likes and dislikes. They have contacted three directors for *The Weekend*. Mike Ockrent's secretary didn't ask about who or what the play was, just said he's busy for the rest of his life.

Alan Ayckbourn is Fox's front runner and the script will be sent to him. Fox's suggestion for the lead is Nigel Hawthorne, with which I very much concur.

Thursday, June 18th

At midday Steve A comes round, partly as my financial adviser, partly as producer, partly as friend.

Would like to have heard better news on the production side, but the *'AF'* story is now so like a long, dull, grey day that the merest break in the cloud is reason for some celebration. Castlehill, the US distribution company, were enthusiastic at Cannes and should be coming up with an offer 'very soon'. Some money has come back from France after a Canal Plus sale, and the Antipodes saw its biggest success.

To Will Wyatt's BBC party for 'writers' at Leighton House. Jimmy Perry[1] looks splendid in cream suit, shirt and tie and shock of reddish-blond hair. He's very complimentary about *GBH* – says that, at the very least, I should have shared the Best Actor Award.

Ken Trodd says he has something for me – 'September ... vicar with a bit on the side?' and Alan Plater wants to propose me for the Writers' Guild. 'Is it a lot of work? ...' 'No, just money.'

Tuesday, June 23rd

I'm due at the Groucho – for an hour with *Me* magazine, and then a 'profile' or 'in-depth' for *She*. The *She* interviewer, Suzie Mackenzie, asks to be alone with me.

Suzie Mackenzie's style most disconcerting. If she wanted to put me on my guard and see my defences go up, she could not have done better.

After an hour and a half of largely uphill work, we adjourn to the bar, and both of us are immediately easier and more comfortable – she less inquisitorial, me less guarded, and for an hour we find ourselves talking about everything. She asks whether I have a sister and what she's doing and she's the first journalist I have told about Angela's suicide. I always want to talk about Angela – and it's women who can talk more openly about it. I can tell she desperately wants to use this in the interview, but I ask her not to.

I'm bumped into by Colin MacCabe,[2] who wheels me back into the Groucho for another glass of champagne and a proposal to write a series of five essays on the films that BFI has in its archives.

Later still, finish Ray Connolly's book about the Beatles' generation and, later still, lie awake worrying about how I could have been so indiscreet with a journalist. Had I been had – by flattery and feminine skills?

Saturday, June 27th

To St Margaret's Hall in Bethnal Green where I am to address the AGM of the Association for Stammerers. (I'd been warned by Travers Reid[3] that I might be there a long time.)

---

1 Jimmy Perry, deviser with David Croft of *Dad's Army*.
2 Colin MacCabe, writer and academic on film.
3 A stammerer himself and President of Action for Stammering Children.

A small hall full of, I assume, stammerers, would be many people's idea of a great comic event. Considering the disabilities they come across with a certain dignity, considerable bravery, and otherwise just like any other gathering-together of people to make rather footling rules.

I read a three- or four-minute piece which I hastily assembled last night, then face questions from the floor. Pleased to find that I don't feel at all un-comfortable waiting for the questions to come, nor is there any shortage of them.

To an upper room for a drink (non-alcoholic). Two men I spoke to said that alcohol, far from loosening their tongues, makes their stammer worse. Developing techniques to avoid stammering is what they're all about and that's fascinating. Winston Churchill, one of the great orators of history, had a stammer and his rumbling start to sentences was not an oratorical tool but a stammer-avoidance technique.

Men are about five times more at risk than women.

Thursday, July 2nd

At the cutting rooms by twenty to ten.

We set to work on the commentary for *Pole to Pole* number one. Most of my timings are accurate and the words usually fit, so much of the time is spent examining and dissecting the lines themselves. There is a lot to say in this first episode – route and ground rules to be explained – and a lot of Frozen North to be described owing to lack of the right conditions for recording synch sound.

Mimi O'Grady from the Production office appears regularly to take pages back and have them retyped. Then into the recording studio.

The first hour in the hot little box is dreadful. I find it difficult to be as spon-taneously lively and involved when I'm surrounded by technical equipment, headphones, green lights, disembodied voices from the control panel – 'He could do that better ...' 'Can you get rid of his breath?'

It requires a great effort of stamina, concentration and sheer will-power not to shout 'Do it yourself then!' But I remember this is the way it was before and I know that it is important for every utterance to sound right. That's the pressure, but also the job I'm paid to do. So I drink water and more coffee and get my head down and gradually the effort decreases and the ease increases and we coast quite quickly through the last half.

Finish by a quarter to seven. Nine hours of almost unrelieved concentration leave me quite drained. All I want is a pint somewhere, far away from the hot theatre air.

End up in the Ladbroke Arms with Roger.

Roger is very special – full of life and the wisdom of experience without any of the superiority that might go with it. He's schoolboy and headmaster rolled into one.

Wednesday, July 8th

Trying to crack the commentary for show three. I cannot get the words to fall right; sentences are half formed, a sort of intellectual dyslexia sets in. I know what I want to say but I can't find how to say it.

Some progress. To lunch with JC. First time we've seen each other since his trip down the Nile and mine to the Pole.

I ask him about the therapy. He confesses to being very bored by it now. I decline the yeti film and JC reckons he will not have a *Wanda* follow-up ready now until spring of 1994.

I work on at episode three and suddenly the knack of commentary-writing returns. I remember lightness of touch – thoughts and observations glancing off the films themselves, not trying to compete or over-expand them. This is what will ultimately carry *Pole to Pole* as it did *80 Days*. I've all too often been intimidated by commentary – I've fallen into the trap of reproducing the sort of stuff I used to be so good at parodying.

Sunday, July 12th

Up at Chilton Hall to celebrate Veryan and Valerie's wedding.[1]

Chilly wind. Chilton looking more spruce – and the garden richer and more prodigious – this seems to be Valerie's influence. Derek and Joan Taylor are there, which is all the better for being unexpected.[2] They loved *80 Days*. Derek says George has gone rather serious about Natural Law and things and rather rubbed Derek up by ringing and asking if he was happy with his life and did he want to keep 'floundering around'. 'Not floundering, thank you George,' D had replied a bit testily.

Ann Hollis, wife of the vicar who gave the address, says to me at the end 'This must have been difficult for you.' In all honesty I have to say I haven't thought of it as being difficult. I'm pleased that Veryan is happy and Chilton seems to have lost some of its coldness. Angela never really liked it. Valerie loves it.

---

1 Veryan, my brother-in-law, married for the second time to Valerie Stevens, a journalist.
2 Derek was the Beatles' publicist.

Friday, July 17th

Unduly worried about what I said to Suzie Mackenzie, the *She* journalist, about Angela – tried to ring her this week but she's gone on holiday. Talk to the features editor. Not a pleasant encounter. She suggested that nothing is ever 'off the record' with a journalist and irritatingly mentions Lynn Barber as a sort of role model and reference point.

I tell her what I've told Suzie – and my concerns for the Herbert family once it's into the cuttings and the hands of less scrupulous journalists. The features editor won't agree to let me see the copy in advance and puts forward silly objections.

Return a call from Puttnam who wants me to be a judge on the NCR non-fiction panel next year – with Princess Di. I accept. It only means reading four books.

Then by pick-up car down to Chelsea Harbour to be photographed for *She*.

Chelsea Harbour is one of the late-'80s boom developments. Half empty, like Docklands. Isolated and soulless. The Penthouse, on the market at over £3 million, has never been sold.

Monday, July 20th

Rachel leaves for the first day of a week's summer school history course, for which she won a bursary from Camden Council. She is diligent without ever being self-congratulatory or smug; she quietly organises her life (she quite independently has taken out an Amnesty subscription) and I admire her ability to be successful but retain her natural self-deprecating sense of irony. Which is a rather verbose way of saying I'm ever so proud of her.

Will has gone up to Oxford to clear the last remains out of the flat in Jericho Street which I think never brought him great happiness. Tom is working at Redwood Studios while André has two weeks' hols. H is helping restock the sitting room and Martin the painter has moved on to the stairs and hallway – all empty-walled and shrouded in dust sheets by mid-morning.

Work on with lightning flash and thunder rumbling and the rain is still coming down when I finish commentary four at midnight. When we get to bed a half-hour later, both cats are hiding under it.

Wednesday, July 22nd

Collected by car to go to the President's Evening of the RSNC/Wildlife Trusts Partnership.

David Attenborough wrote to me some weeks ago to ask if I would become one of the vice-presidents. The cause of nature conservation and the no-nonsense persuasiveness of David's letter must have combined to catch me on a good day and I said yes – and now I find myself in the only suit I have – a dark-brown wool-worsted quite unsuited to a sticky day like today – being welcomed into this large, marble and chandeliered chamber by Sir David and Lady Att. He's off to the Antarctic soon – but he's never yet been to the Pole.

He says the job of 'high-profile' officers like me, Julian Pettifer and himself is very often to attract and assuage sponsors . . . 'And of course – the more they pollute, the more they give us,' he confides with a broad grin. He is quite an operator – able to play the establishment using flattery, humour and enormous charm, yet to hold the credibility of old cynics like myself by his intelligent self-awareness.

Friday, July 24th

Seizing the day, I write a letter resigning from the board of Meridian. Not confrontational or critical in any way – give myself more time to make programmes, which is what I feel I'm really good at.

Awkward, distracting morning in which I try to make a start on show three but find it difficult whilst the Meridian thing remains unresolved. Have to keep going into the garden, where Will is reading *Foucault's Pendulum* in the sun, to find Helen and check with her that I'm doing the right thing.

I never was that interested in running a company, or helping run a company, least of all one in the dull Southern area, or being confined to one particular company. H pinpoints the area that has really prompted my withdrawal – 'You don't want to be bothered with the internal politics.'

Roger Laughton calls back after lunch. To my great relief he is understanding, even humorous about it. He makes no attempt to persuade me to stay, makes a joke about my writing 'the letter we all want to write' and compliments me on expressing my feelings so 'elegantly'. He suggests I send the letter on Monday, by which time he will have been able to prepare Clive [Hollick, the chairman] for the news.

Saturday, July 25th

Read in a weekly TV paper that *GBH*'s repeat audience is just over two million – which surprises me, as did the low figure for the first screenings. I can only conclude that audiences prefer good, clean, escapist fun and have lost their appetite for controversy. TV is sold much more nowadays as a branch of advertising – reflecting its values and techniques. I think that the nineties are for *The Darling Buds of May*, not *GBH*. No-one wants to change the world any more.

Tuesday, July 28th

At St Paul's Covent Garden for Joan Sanderson's[1] memorial service. Glorious summer's day – bright sunshine, cloudless skies, dry air. At St Paul's the vicar is escorting a muttering, grubby man out of the church and trying to be nice to him at the same time. 'Yes … you wait outside …'

Quite full, Alan Bennett next to Jo Tewson at the back, Tim West gives an address. Good, rousing, uncomplicated hymns – 'Fight the Good Fight', 'He Who Would Valiant Be'. The batty man remains outside shouting 'Wankers!' at us, occasionally quite loudly.

Suzanne Webber rings to say that, following big orders, the first print run of *Pole to Pole* will be 130,000. (It was 15,000 on *80 Days*.)

Sunday, August 9th

Carol Cleveland rings – very pert and perky. 'I expect you know why I'm ringing.'

… No idea. 'I read about your film "The Adventure" with all the Pythons in it, and I hear it's going ahead, and well … to be blunt, I hope there'll be a part for me.' Turns out it's some snippet she's read in *TV Quick* giving a lot of completely fabricated information.

Best of the letters: request from Auberon Waugh for me to present the third Literary Review Poetry Award (Alec Guinness and Lucinda Lambton did the first two). 'You are the only people in public life whom the entire staff of *Literary Review* admires'!

Thursday, August 13th

To Liverpool Street by nine to catch the 9.30 to Norwich.

Driven to Richard Clay, the printers, where a machine is churning out sheets of *Pole to Pole*.

Five thousand sheets an hour flop gently onto the stack. Extraordinary to

---

1 Joan Sanderson, imperious actress of comedy, particularly remembered for one *Fawlty Towers* episode. She starred in the *Ripping Yarns* 'Roger of the Raj' and 'East of Ipswich'.

see the fruits of my solitary labour now being processed by half a dozen men, and occupying a million-pound machine 24 hours a day for more than a week.

Then on to Bungay, where Clay's have their HQ.

Satanic Verses was printed here in Bungay. A perfect place to keep it quiet. Apparently they approached the local constabulary to discuss possible security problems, but the threat of Muslim fundamentalists in Bungay was not considered likely.

Friday, August 21st

Drink at lunchtime with Roger M to discuss a Meridian project. Roger Laughton has asked if we could supply four 30-minute documentaries. Over a pint or two at the Ladbroke Arms, with black pudding lunch and sun warming us pleasantly through the open window, I agree to a start date of October '93 – that is presuming we can come up with some ideas drawn from the region.

Tuesday, August 25th

Clem rings early to say that he's just watched programme one with nearly all its bits sewn together and he is very, very pleased. 'It works in the living room,' he enthuses.

Also, have received word that John Hughman[1] is in hospital after a fall and a serious illness (some sort of blood poisoning) and I go over to see him in the afternoon. He's at St Mary's Paddington in what appears to be a geriatric ward. The premises are run-down and the whole place has a scuffed and demoralised appearance – but the staff are cheerful and patient.

John is lying, in a rather theatrical pose, on top of his bed, with a blanket draped ineffectually across his stomach. He has a clipped white beard, which rather suits him. But there is no disguising the fact that he has, in the year since I last saw him, become sad and old. His eyes wander unless he makes a real effort of concentration – the long, thin hands he was always so proud of twitch at the bedclothes. He's pleased to see me, but he is confused and obsessive about his 'financial problems' – rather like my mother was in the last years of her life.

An old Irish woman has lost her hearing aid and her visitor has to shriek to make her hear. 'No, you're not coming out tomorrow!' Across the way, an elderly man with watery eyes and a bowed head (a head which must have been

---

1 John Hughman, actor who was one of the cast of Jones and Palin's *Complete and Utter History of Britain* TV series in 1969.

stoutly handsome and upright once) is being asked by the doctor 'How do you feel about an artificial limb?' – this again in a bellow.

Talk for half an hour. John remembers odd things but mainly looks wistfully unhappy. 'I've lost my zest for life,' he says.

Wednesday, August 26th

Turn my mind to finishing my speech for the *Literary Review* lunch. For some reason I can't crack it as I'd like to.

Down to the wine cellars of the Café Royal – amazing act of trust by the management to allow so many boozy hacks so close to endless racks of wine. Quite dark and rather confusing as a nice American girl introduces me around, apologising that Auberon Waugh, who invited me with flattering letters, has this morning been taken ill – some internal haemorrhage.

After a glass of wine we're all led into a dungeon laid for a banquet.

At various moments during the meal a vivacious and apparently supremely self-confident girl who looks like the young Mia Farrow gets up and announces that she will sing – then goes into Kurt Weill songs.

Richard Ingrams then sets the ball rolling. He is very funny – big and grumpy but neither churlish nor ill-mannered. Tremendous Les Dawson-like delivery. At one point, after mentioning Julie Burchill's name, he shakes his head and mutters darkly and incomprehensibly for almost 15 seconds. Lynn Barber watches adoringly.

Sunday, August 30th: London–Norwich

Gale-force winds blowing as Helen and I leave Oak Village about 10.30 to watch Tom's Hapkido black belt grading in Norwich.

Two others besides Tom are doing black belts, three others 1st Dans. There is a certain formality to the procedure, with bows to the Union Jack and pledges to the flag at the beginning and then much oriental bowing before every stage of the grading.

They must jump over six people and end with a roll, they must break three wooden boards in one movement, break tiles with their feet after jumping up and off a wall, and finally leap over three people and kick-break a breeze block.

It's painful to watch, what with all the time willing Tom to do well and not hurt himself. At intervals a fierce wind shook the building and sent leaves streaming past the window.

Tom was duly awarded his white jacket and black belt.

I watch, like a father in a maternity ward, as the new belts line up for a photograph, all a little awkward apart from Tom, whose great Cheshire Cat smile breaks out and seems to affect everyone.

Friday, September 4th

Kath[1] comes round at five with a fresh supply of work. Lots of letters done. She warns me of the massiveness of the BBC Books publicity campaign. 'You'll need a disguise after this.'

Tell her my idea for a play on the explorer theme. Small expedition, all men, setting out on long and arduous five-month journey together. After three weeks discover one of them is a woman. Kath said they should perhaps all turn out to be women.

Monday, September 7th

Work through the final commentary. I find all sorts of holes in it. It wrote itself quickly and smoothly over the weekend, but in the cold light of Monday morning much of it seems slight and insubstantial.

Out with H to dinner with Dan and Laura Patterson[2] in Chalcot Road. Gary Lineker and Michelle and Stephen Fry and his sister Jo the other guests.

Gary L is laid-back, agreeable. His skin is fascinating, very smooth and soft. He's like a young Samburu boy.

He tells the most wonderful stories of the evening – quite late, when everyone's about to go – usually about Gazza. 'He's a 12-year-old, always will be.' He sounds worse than any 12-year-old I've ever met. He would do his business, almost anywhere, often leaving a steaming offering on the bench in the changing room. He would shoot at people with an airgun, and could be brutally carried away with paint-sprays. His mischief was continuous and, from the sound of it, vacuous – but sometimes horribly funny.

Gary professed great admiration for the player Steve Sedgley, who could fart the tune of 'When the Saints'.

Wednesday, September 9th

Out in the evening to see *Someone Who'll Watch Over Me* – Frank McGuinness' new play transferred to the Vaudeville. David Pugh is greeting his first-night audience.

1 Kath James, my PA, later Kath Du Prez.
2 Dan Patterson is a writer and comedy producer who created *Whose Line Is It Anyway?*

I ask David P about *Weekend* casting. Denholm Elliott was our new choice, but David tells me that he is dying of AIDS. Can hardly take this in amongst the swirl of well-wishers and starers. The agent who told David this, ever the opportunist, has suggested another client – Ian Richardson.

Thursday, September 10th

On several occasions yesterday I was told by various readers of the *Guardian* that I had been called 'boring' by Lynn Barber (along with Norma Major and Felicity Kendal). I must say I wasn't much concerned – but a letter from Lynn arrives this morning – full of apologies – she'd been misquoted, of course it wasn't true. 'Nice, sane, straightforward' people are not those she can write about without it becoming a bit boring. I'm quite chuffed by the whole episode – and a letter from Lynn Barber bearing the words 'Oh God I am sorry' has to be valuable!

Tuesday, September 15th

The next two days are high-profile, Meridian Broadcasting days.

The first production meeting on *A Class Act.*[1] Meet, for the first time, Jo Wright, warm and welcoming, Kim Fuller and director Les Blair, a compact, bearded Mancunian who made *Law and Order*.

The meeting is quite low-key – we all say how we're looking forward to it. There are 12 days to shoot everything, which is tight. Blair, on the other hand, is agreeably loose about the actual shooting.

Then a rehearsal ahead of tomorrow's Meridian advertisers' launch.

Drafts of speeches are read at a podium resembling as closely as possible conditions at BAFTA tomorrow. Notes are given by a pair of women who seem to be in charge. 'Alan, sound as though you mean it ...' 'Richard, don't look down' and so on.

Wednesday, September 16th

To BAFTA by eleven o'clock. The Rogers and Richards look tired. This advertising bullshit is not really what they want to be spending their time on. There has been some technical problem with the video inserts.

---

1 *A Class Act*. Meridian TV's first in-house comedy series. A vehicle for the many talents of Tracey Ullman and written by Ian La Frenais and Dick Clement.

At 12.45 the first showing – largely for advertising managers of the major companies – Sainsbury's, Weetabix, etc. – gets under way. All goes smoothly except the sales director's speech which is incomprehensible.

The second presentation goes more smoothly. Clive and Sue Hollick very enthusiastic afterwards.

No-one asks about my resignation from the board.

Friday, September 18th: London–Sheffield

Packing and preparing for Sheffield this p.m.

At half past one we set off. The sun disappears and a stickily warm haze of low damp cloud comes down.

To the university – main building. I'm greeted by Professor Blake, the Public Orator, who is to commend me for a doctorate, then sidetracked away to the main quadrangle of this tall, classically red-brick, university building to be photographed.

Five or six hacks offer me parrots on sticks and Australian bush hats with corks. As I'm wearing the red robe and mortar board of a Doctor of Letters I think they can hardly expect me to hold parrots.

The Vice-Chancellor is a Welshman with a naughty smile who twice played for Manchester City Reserves. He's now a big influence at Sheffield Wednesday, and has been called in to try and improve Trevor Francis's 'man-management' techniques.

At seven o'clock the V-C takes me away to be robed up. Procession very efficiently organised by the Marshal and his assistant, both of whom carry long rods. We wind our way into the Firth Hall – tall, imposing space, well-filled with graduands and their supporters.

I am the first to be installed. I have to stand on the stage whilst a five-minute paean of praise is read out. It's a nicely judged piece, and ends quite touchingly after a quick run through 49 years of my life. Then I'm led to the V-C, who formally installs me as a Doctor of Letters 'in honoris causa'.

I've been grinning manfully and patiently for so long that I now need a few minutes' break. Only get it when I'm in the car, Helen driving, on the misty M1 back to London.

Back home we both agree that it was a very enjoyable occasion – quite undaunting – and the people amazingly friendly. Helen says it's the first time, she thinks, that she's actually been in bed with a Doctor.

Saturday, October 10th

JC rings to ask if he can bring his 93-year-old mother to the *'PTP'* screening on Friday. Also reveals that his latest film idea is based on the old Zoo saga that I wrote with TJ all those years ago – the big animals v the small. Wants to know how I would play the keeper of the insect house!

Friday, October 16th

At half past ten down to the Groucho with a driver who does things like nod at my scraped Mercedes wheel trim and tell me 'You'll have trouble with that later.' He's a member of a caravan club and for some reason wants to haul his caravan up to the North Cape of Norway. I tell him it's not worth it. He seems to have been everywhere but has no idea how to get to Dean Street.

Apparently another batch of mags are out with interviews I did last July; among them is *Me* magazine. Feel rather a fool going into one of the busy little Soho newsagents and asking if they have me.

Home and read the articles. Never feel it's a healthy pastime reading about myself. Do it out of fearful curiosity.

To CFS by seven for *Pole to Pole* cast and crew party – another screening, another evening to try and 'sparkle'.

All the Pythons there. JC prominent in row two. When, in my North Pole camera piece I say I could go 'that way through Japan ... down that way through India ... but we've chosen the 30-degree line down through Russia and Africa', John lets out an audible 'Oh dear!' – very naughty as it does break everyone up.

But most people seem very satisfied afterwards. JC feels it is a much stronger start than *80 Days* and others say I seem much more relaxed without the pressure of the 80-day deadline.

Saturday, October 17th

Derek Taylor faxes – asking me to turn all my lights off for ten minutes at nine o'clock tomorrow night as a gesture of solidarity with the miners.

Monday, October 19th

Start the Week, on a cold Monday morning.

This morning I have two massive egos to lock horns with – Anthony

Burgess and Broadway director Hal Prince. We're to be given 15 minutes each and the thought of Burgess and Prince having to stop what they're doing and listen to me for 15 minutes fills me with something approaching panic.

Delivered to BH at 8.40.

There, the most pleasant thing awaits, a complete surprise.

Burgess, lean with the bloodless skin colour you see on old people in hospitals, and a dry thatch of grey hair, belies his appearance with a bubbling, overflowing delivery, full of enthusiasms.

In little more than a minute he tells me of his admiration for everything I've been involved in, particularly *Life of Brian* – 'a profoundly religious film' – 'You were the centurion weren't you?' interrupts his wife, Liana – small, keen. *GBH* he thought the best thing of all – 'that brought a whole new performance out of you'. And so on.

He had sharp words of criticism for Zeffirelli, with whom he worked on 'The Life of Christ', when Zeffirelli expressed anger that Python should have been allowed to film on the same set as his in Monastir in Tunisia.

Tuesday, October 20th

To lunch at Odette's in Primrose Hill. First, business with Anne, then Roger, fresh-biked from Acton, joins us for a discussion about the documentary commitment to Meridian, provisionally called 'Down South'.

Roger comes up with a very strong idea – which is that I should join four of the region's local papers for a week.

Thursday, October 22nd

Prepare speech for my appearance as T2000 President at launch of Platform – rail users against privatisation – and out into action at eleven o'clock. A sunny morning, less bitter than of late; quite quickly down to the House of Commons. The security guard checks my bag – 'No mosquitoes in here, you know.' This is the first case of post-*Pole to Pole* street banter, which I shall have to get used to.

Walk down the towering, grey, imposing stone passages past groups of schoolchildren and lost foreigners. Rather reassured that in these days of IRA bombs and general twitchiness so many people are still allowed to poke around Parliament.

Up to Committee Room 12. Almost full. Read my piece – part Stephen

Joseph's[1] work, part my own gut feelings. A few laughs. Afterwards I'm about to leave when a blind man next to me holds my scarf up – 'I think you forgot this,' he smiles.

Then across to LBC for appearance on Frank Bough's prog. Poor old Frank, now a fallen angel since he admitted visiting a bondage parlour, only a couple of years after admitting drugs and infidelity. He's sporting a ruddy tan though, and seems to have added a few pounds. He reminds me for some reason of an old sea captain, weathered by the storms. No longer in charge of the big liners, but quite happy in an old tub.

Sunday, October 25th: London–Norwich

A pile of Sunday newspapers – none of which have much good news for *Pole to Pole*. Only the curmudgeonly opinions of a bored, snapping Jeremy Paxman in the *Mail on Sunday*, a clever, moderately enthusiastic Craig Raine in *The Times*, a tired and bored John Naughton in the *Observer* and finally a fairly savage book review by Adam Nicolson in *The Times* again. He saw glimmers of good writing but felt the whole book had been sacrificed on the altar of TV programming.

Up to Norwich on the train. At the huge Gardners warehouse within sight of the cathedral I am besieged by booksellers. 530 are attending the open day this year – a record number. Delia Smith, a solid, funny gardener called Geoff Hamilton and myself are the three speakers.

The gathering is treated to lunch and speeches, after which more hysterical signing before just catching the 4.05 back to London. Whingeing and grumpy though the day's reviews may have been, over 800 *Pole to Pole* books have been sold – and most of them signed – today.

Monday, October 26th

Start of the *Class Act* filming week. My first creative obligation to Meridian.

Collected at seven by Art Wilmot, a besuited Jamaican in a powerful BMW 5 Series which he drives fast, crossing from lane to lane as we negotiate the swift dual carriageways running north out of London into affluent, but not very beautiful, Bushey bungalow-land. We turn down a narrow little side road called Titian Avenue and into a red-brick Catholic girls' school which is home for the next two days.

1 Stephen Joseph, executive director Transport 2000, later Campaign for Better Transport.

Tracey arrives about the same time. She's refreshingly untheatrical and very funny.

Terry O'Neill is here to take photos of us, which kills some time. Terry a great royalist – and like Tracey and Allan McKeown, two other working-class talents - hates the unions, the miners and especially Arthur Scargill's appearance at the head of a 150,000-strong protest rally in London yesterday.

Home by nine. No-one in, but a message scrawled on a yellow pad on the kitchen table says viewing figures for '*PTP*' one were 8.76 million.

Tuesday, October 27th

With Art to Bushey, leaving Julia Street at the dark and unconscionable hour of 6.15. Bald cap takes the hour to put on. Heavy rain delays shooting; we lose some of the day's scheduled sequences. Les B is attractively laid-back and never even begins to be ruffled by the turn of events. His son tries to teach me some chords of 'Johnny B Goode' before the scene on Thursday.

We soldier on substituting interiors for exteriors and sending a whole crowd of extras and their cars home. Tracey and I rather enjoy playing Jackie and Frank Pillsworth – we call them 'The Pathetics'.

Saturday, October 30th

I was walking in the school grounds, learning my lines, dressed as old Frank Pillsworth – bald cap, hair grey and stringy, looking down-at-heel – when a groundsman/gardener shouts across – 'Love your *Pole to Pole* programme.' Then he takes a closer look at me before saying 'You look quite different in real life.'

Later I'm playing a biker in his 30s and I have long, greasy blond hair and tattoos and leathers. We do some improvising – a quarrel between the two of us. Tracey is excellent to play against – she listens, times her line, and always with respect for the partnership.

There's a general feeling that the last two weeks have been happy and productive and that *A Class Act* will be something more than just a fulfilment of an obligation, a rush job between Tracey's court case, over royalties from her work on *The Simpsons*, and her musical with Nick Nolte to which she returns on Monday.

Wednesday, November 4th: Leeds–Edinburgh

7.45: Clinton is the new American President. Despite Peter Snow's manic computer graphics which make me feel ill to look at and which at one time gave Ross Perot several states!

Along traffic-crushed Princes Street to The Caledonian Hotel. Before checking in, I have to be interviewed by the police – give evidence of identification, place and date of birth and details of visit. A Scottish receptionist is trying her best to explain to a Japanese tourist that this is because of the EEC Summit which is to be held in the city in mid-December. As it is believed that the Brighton bomb was planted in Thatcher's hotel weeks before it was activated, and as all the top European leaders will be staying at the Caley, no chances are being taken. The Japanese lady is utterly confused.

Some good news from Anne in London – the viewing figures for 'PTP' episode one have been revised upwards to 9.7 million.

Quite a rush to sign the books, then grab a bath, change and over to the huge, gloomy rooms backstage at the Usher Hall.

They've sold the place out – 2,200 people. Probably the largest single audience I've played to in my life – stacked up in two balconies. Strangely it's less unsettling than talking to a small group of 20 or 30.

Sunday, November 8th

Pole to Pole is my second No. 1 best-seller, having deposed Madonna and held off the challenge of Mr Bean in 3rd place. Once again I'm among the literary giants!

Sweep up leaves in the garden, clear drains and gutters and generally roam the territory!

Monday, November 16th

Very cold and damp, so hardly tempted away from correspondence until it's time to go and meet Rebecca Eaton from Masterpiece Theatre at the Hyde Park Hotel. Read some more of Auberon Waugh's *Will This Do?* on the way, including an account of his being taken for lunch at the Hyde Park Hotel ... 'At every other table in the restaurant there sat a single, rich, obviously unpleasant elderly person of one sex or another, eating alone ...'

This evening the surprisingly unmajestic tea room with its low, oppressive ceiling and curiously anodyne decor is filling rapidly with Japanese. Find Rebecca in a corner. She is a handsome, strong, American woman with regular features and a disconcertingly rambling way of speaking which almost makes me feel she's under some kind of sedation.

Over tea and fruit cake she continues to gently work away at my reluctance to get involved in replacing Alistair Cooke as host of Masterpiece Theatre.

Once Rebecca has accepted that she can't ensnare me, she produces, with appealing candidness, a list of other runners. They range from Stephen Fry and Melvyn Bragg and John Mortimer ('Don't you think he looks funny?') to Mike Nichols ('Not a hair on his body') and Meryl Streep and Peter Ustinov (she turns her nose up) and Tom Stoppard, Alan Bennett and John Cleese.

Going through the list is great fun. I speak highly of John Updike. Rebecca smiles with disapproval ... 'He is a terrible flirt, you know ... I mean just terrible.' We discuss for a moment whether there might be medical or psychological reasons for such determined skirt-chasing. Maybe it's something to do with his itching and stammering and generally low self-esteem, as described in his book *Self-Consciousness*.

In the end we both plump for Ken Branagh.

Tuesday, November 17th

Schizophrenic weather continues. The rain has cleared and bright sunshine cuts sharply in through the windows.

Rachel looks pale and tired as she sets off for the first of her two Oxford exams.

Third show figures confirmed at 9.7 million for Wednesday night, a jump of almost a million from the Russian episode. Suzanna rings with latest book figures – subscriptions now up to a total of 354,000. Reprints will keep Clay's running at full stretch until December 4th.

Back home and another phone interview, with a US travel magazine. He asks me what my favourite direction is, which is a nice question. After some thought I have to confess it's south and west. Why not north? Feel a direction traitor!

Sunday, November 22nd

Wake up, it must be said, feeling a little surly. A cluster of reasons, I suppose – tired, faced with a day of demands rather than dozing, my social life ill-adjusted after 16 months avoiding friends to concentrate on my work, and so on.

Wrap up a fine-looking book on fairground art for Terry G's birthday and take it up to his surprise party at the Old Hall. Apparently it wasn't a surprise, but I don't think he expected quite such a crowd.

Pole to Pole. The last months of the Soviet Union.
With two Lenins in Leningrad, summer 1991.

LEFT: *Pole to Pole.* Preparing to take on the white waters of the Zambesi, summer 1991.

Comparing pencils with Basil Pao's daughter Sonia, London, 1990.

With Helen and big friend in Thailand, 1993.

LEFT: Journey's End. Me and various poles at the South Pole on the last day of *Pole to Pole*, December 8th, 1991.

LEFT: Thinking up another ridiculous journey with Clem Vallance.

Early selfie. Polaroid taken before the North Pole trip, 1992.

LEFT: *Pole to Pole* sheets ready for cutting and binding at Richard Clay, August 13th, 1992.

Dearbhla Molloy, MP, Julia St John and Mike Angelis, Derbyshire, 1990.

Jim Nelson and his school kids, Bolton, August 1990.

Rain acting with Dan Massey. 'The rain was such a surprise to Dan that his voice rose several octaves' – Ulverston, September 10th, 1990.

A Class Act

ABOVE: A chance to extend my repertoire.

Mr Pilsworth and daughter:
MP and Tracey Ullman.

LEFT: *Pole to Pole* book-signing in Sheffield with John Hall, my geography teacher at Birkdale School, on my left, and Michael Hepworth, the headmaster, on the other side.

RIGHT: Trying out the pipe and slippers, presents from my office on my fiftieth birthday. Longueville Manor near Mallow, Ireland, May 5th, 1993.

BELOW: With Freddie Jones as 'Sir', my director David Blount (behind me) and the cast and crew of *The Dresser*, at the BBC, February 1993.

George Harrison has had himself detoxed and now no longer smokes or drinks.

He and I talk about Indian sects and how batty and surreal they can be. George is keen on the Tantric practitioners who can pleasure ten women in one night without coming. He's more intrigued by the fact that they can apparently ingest water, milk and lukewarm drinking chocolate through their penises.

Tuesday, November 24th

To lunch at Zen W3 with Malcolm Mowbray [director of *A Private Function*].

We talk about *An Immaculate Mistake* and Malcolm asks if I would like to play Paul Bailey.[1] I think *Days at the Beach* and *Private Function* are two films of great, quirky character – and I like Malcolm's ability to produce something unusual. He in turn says it's the 'sweet and sour' he likes in a film. Comedy can be tragic and awfully serious moments can be unintentionally and often savagely funny. So I say, yes, let's talk about it when you have a script, and I add it to the intriguing possibilities for next year.

At home an adaptation of *The Dresser* for radio has arrived with a request for me to play Norman opposite Freddie Jones as 'Sir'. I'm intrigued all over again.

Wednesday, November 25th

Run on the Heath and to lunch at the Halcyon Hotel with John C, Cynthia and Iain Johnstone, who is helping JC put the new film together. Iain is deputed to tell me the Zoo story – a large part of which is the old Zoo script Terry and I wrote in the '60s for GC and JC.[2]

I suggest Ken Pile make a brief appearance as an animal rights liberationist who frees a wild animal which promptly eats him. JC sees me as small-mammal keeper, Kevin as a sort of Murdoch maniac who has come to control the zoo via some conglomerate he's acquired. Jamie would have 'a tougher role' than in *Wanda*.

And so on. The Zoo is a winner, I'm sure of it. So many different strands of current thinking and so many different aspects of twentieth-century life

1 Paul Bailey, writer (*Peter Smart's Confessions* shortlisted for Booker Prize in 1977), whose autobiography *An Immaculate Mistake* was much admired.
2 John was cast as Mr Burster, the man who wanted to keep only the violent animals, and Graham as Mr Megapode, one of the keepers.

– greed, sentimentality about animals, green politics, marketing, sponsorship of every area of life – can all be covered.

Tuesday, December 1st: Los Angeles

It's a quarter to eight in the morning. I'm writing this in my bed at the Sunset Marquis.

My half-wakeful night was scattered with snatches of a speech I have yet to write and which I will have to deliver twice today at occasions in which I shall be the centre of attraction – a lunch in Los Angeles and a dinner and special screening at the Western Convention in Anaheim.

I feel so much that I need a breather from *Pole to Pole* now. I have lived it, travelled it, written it up, described it in commentary and now for a second successive autumn travelled and talked about it, and I'm pretty close to exhaustion point.

I long to sit all day and read a book, and be at home and share breakfast time with Helen, back in grey, squashed, chilly London.

I can hear the thud and rumble of traffic, unseen beyond the carefully watered screen of trees that rings the pleasant garden here, creating a passable illusion of Eden. It's five past eight. Birds are trilling outside my window (their richness always a bit of surprise in this city of concrete); I'll have a soothing hot bath, breakfast on the patio, write the speeches that I hope will last me the next week, and later, after the interview with *The Sacramento Bee* is done, maybe I'll snatch a swim and the pleasure of strong sunshine.

Later – half past six in the great wide wastes of my suite at the Anaheim Hilton – a Pentagon of a hotel, flooded at the moment with the 10,000 delegates to the cable convention. I've hauled myself quite successfully through the day.

Thursday, December 10th

Back home, Rachel kisses me goodbye as she leaves for her Brasenose interview at 8.30, but I don't get out of bed until the end of the morning.

News comes in from Anne of our highest overnight viewing figure for the series – 10.2 for number eight. No surge to the dizzy heights of 12.8 as for *80 Days*, but the last three shows have hit a plateau of around 11 million for Wednesday night only.

The announcement of a separation between Charles and Diana delays 'PTP' by 15 minutes, with a special news bulletin.

Wednesday, December 16th

Arrive at the HQ of NCR in Marylebone Road for the first meeting of the Book Award judges.

To the boardroom with a huge mahogany table, around which 30–35 people could easily be accommodated, leaving room for secretaries. David Puttnam, the chairman, sits himself at the head of this massive piece of furniture. Despite his best efforts, Princess Diana is not going to be on the panel after all. I sit on one side with Diana Rigg.

Opposite me Margaret Jay,[1] tall, dressed in a suit, soberly. She is voluble in her praise of *'PTP'*. Next to her is Richard Hoggart,[2] a markedly accented Yorkshireman, his tie awry, looking benignly from behind glasses – a little bewildered, it seems, but I'm sure this is a front. 'Have we agreed? ...' he keeps asking anxiously. Heads nod. 'About what?'

I fought to bring *Fever Pitch* out from the oblivion of the 'Not Recommended' category of readers' reports and now it's on the shortlist.

Finish by eleven. I leave having promised to read 19 books by mid-March!

To Classic FM to be interviewed re the Stammerers. Bomb has gone off in John Lewis and I watch their video screens for signs of the scale of it. Quite small, but Oxford Street closed off.

Thursday, December 17th

Out of the house at 7.15 to London Bridge Station. A minicab with a disagreeable old driver. He began to talk about the IRA – 'The only way to deal with that lot is to line them up and shoot them,' he maintained. For the first time in a long while I was driven to uncontrollable anger and found myself telling this man old enough to be my father that his solution was ridiculous, dangerous and didn't solve anything. 'That's what we used to do in Malaysia,' he went on doggedly, but he didn't really have the courage of his own bigotry and I felt oddly embarrassed, not by what I said, but by showing up what was not aggression so much as ignorance.

This and a long traffic jam on London Bridge, causing us a last-minute sprint to the station, certainly got the morning off to a lively start.

Met the film crew aboard the 7.50 and proceeded to Brighton, Portsmouth and the Isle of Wight, recording interviews with punters as we went – to be used to bind together a 'What's On Meridian' prog for New Year's Day.

1 Baroness Jay of Paddington, journalist and politician, daughter of the former Prime Minister James Callaghan.
2 Richard Hoggart, academic and writer, best known for *The Uses of Literacy* (1957).

Most of them made no distinction between BBC and ITV, many didn't watch much TV and others, when asked about preferences, plumped for comedy and nature programmes. 'More programmes like yours, Michael,' one lady kept saying.

On the hydrofoil to the Isle of Wight, a good group of locals – the further one goes from London the more relaxed people seem to be about talking. But it was not really what I wanted to be doing at the end of a year like this – trying to talk to seven-year-old girls on a double-decker bus from Ryde to Newport and elicit their views on television whilst trying not to look like a molester.

Friday, December 18th

At 6.30 picked up by Naim Attallah's chauffeur in a large Mercedes and driven down to the Mayfair Hotel where I've agreed to draw the raffle and present prizes at Asprey's Christmas Party.

What surprises me first of all is how many people work for Asprey's – there must be 300 there. Sign some books, then draw the raffle, whose prizes seem rather paltry for an outfit like Asprey's – one of them is Naim Attallah's own book, signed, which he presents without embarrassment of any kind.

His generosity, however, evident in the presentation of a beautifully bound leather-backed copy of *Pole to Pole*, decorated and inlaid with a gold design.

Then rush back home, where I'm greeted by Rachel, eyes wide, who says she has had a telephone call from the head of History at BNC, to tell her that they have a place for her, and that her interview in particular had been very good. She'll be receiving written confirmation but he wanted to put an end to her waiting before the weekend.

After so many days of having to appear delighted to see people and interested in everything they're doing, it's an enormous pleasure when real, spontaneous, natural happiness takes you by surprise.

Monday, December 21st: London–Liverpool

Train from Euston to Sean's[1] 50th birthday party in Birkenhead.

A Kenyan-Asian ticket collector on the train is quite bowled over to see me. With a complete lack of self-consciousness or discretion of any kind, he indicates me with a sweep of the hand – 'I can't believe this ... on my train! ...

---

1 Sean Duncan, close friend since we were contemporaries at Shrewsbury School. Became a judge.

Michael Palin ...' He won't let it lie ... 'This is like a dream to me ...' By now the other passengers are shifting about and grinning nervously ... 'Did you see his programme? ... Mm?' Various heads nod sheepishly. He then conducts an impromptu interview ... 'Tell me, which place did you like best? You like Kenya? I come from Kenya.'

The upshot of it was that the girl opposite confessed she'd bought my book for her brother, and the man in the seat in front actually produced a copy for me to sign.

Tuesday, December 22nd

A quick and easy journey from Lime Street to Euston, through the largely unspoilt and quintessentially English landscape of rural Cheshire, Staffordshire and the Midlands. Canals, hump-back bridges, low hills, fields and all sorts of trees. Today everything is made hauntingly beautiful by a thick layer of frost, creating a soft, silvery effect, as if the countryside had been artificially pre-served. Nothing seems to move. A line of sheep crossing a frozen field towards a trough of hay is about as vigorous as the activity becomes.

Wednesday, December 23rd

There have been no serious explosions over the last few days, but the bombs in John Lewis and yesterday evening in Hampstead Underground Station have been enough to keep a jittery, emergency atmosphere alive. My Christmas shopping is conducted to the accompaniment of police sirens and hurtling fire engines.

Most eerie of all was to drive down Gower Street after lunch and to find Malet Street cordoned off. Looking down its broad sweep beyond the blue-and-white plastic police strip was uncomfortable – the cars all in their places, but no-one moving. It's a picture seen so often on TV. It usually preludes an explosion.

This time no explosion, but it did set me thinking that whereas New York, one of the world's most dangerous cities, was wrapped in ribbon for Christmas, dear old Dickensian London is wrapped in police barrier strips.

Monday, December 28th

Take Granny G down to see the Sickert retrospective at the Royal Academy.

On the way home Granny tells me that H used to be known as 'Drip' when she was young – largely because of her vagueness. She got left behind one day when they were all shopping in Cambridge. The rest of the family waited in a tea shop for her and as the door opened shouted with one voice 'Hello Drip!' In walked a clergyman and his family.

Sun reporter rings to inform us (and glean a reaction) that John and Alyce have married in Barbados. Send them a fax saying that the *Sun* let me know, therefore it's obviously not true.

Tuesday, December 29th

Granny G leaves this morning after spending five nights with us. A tall, cloudless sky. The weathervane points ESE and doesn't move much. It's becoming colder by the day.

A Mrs Miller rings from Denville Hall, the care home for actors, to say that John Hughman is very unwell. He has a cancer 'deep down' and the doctor doesn't expect him to live out the week. She sounds a sympathetic woman – she was quite touching when she described the letter of recommendation I'd written for John ... 'I'd love someone to write a letter like that about me.' But she knows what I meant and says everyone there has fallen for him!

Wednesday, December 30th

Out to Denville Hall to see John Hughman. It's more accessible than I was led to believe, and looks more like a hotel than a hospital.

His room has a Turkish carpet, attractive curtains, a wing-back armchair, and his Christmas cards, about a dozen of them, are set out on the wall and the table. It's a warm room, in every way; he lies well covered up, his head profiled against clean, soft pillows. It's probably the best home he's had for a long time.

He wakes briefly; displays his familiar smile of welcome and apology and takes in my presence. He then falls back to sleep.

I talk to Mrs Miller over a cup of tea. She has 36 ex-actors, of both sexes, here. There is another home nearby for variety artists. They regard Denville Hall as a bit snobbish. I ask if Joyce Carey is in here. She was here a week ago, evidently, but in her official capacity as one of the council who run the place! Word got around of her presence and she was very soon surrounded by the inmates, who regarded her with great awe and respect.

Back to John. I put a hand on his bony shoulder and tell him what I feel, and what he was probably never told enough ... 'You're a great man, John ... a great man.' His eye flickers open and he startles me with a reply. 'Thank you,' he says quietly, clearly, politely. Before I go we exchange suitable last words. 'Goodbye John.' 'Goodbye,' he whispers, clearly again.

Thursday, December 31st: London–Southampton

H and I set out for Southampton. Along the crowded M3, slowly as fog closes in. Ghost story weather – the mist forming sheer walls of darkness beneath the lamp standards.

Fetch up eventually at the Botley Park Hotel and Country Club. It's an upmarket motel, really – with lots of sports facilities and a sub-Colefax & Fowler-decorated double room called the De Montgomery Suite. Simon and Phillida, both in dressing gowns, join us from the De Wriothesley Suite, which Simon can't pronounce. He apologises for the dressing gown, but wants to put his party clothes on at the very last minute as he's grown rather too big for them!

By taxi through the damp, chilly fog to the TVS studios. Studio 2 has been decorated for the party. A band (live) is playing and black drapes have been slung from the roof giving a tented effect, and little holes cut out to create the illusion of a ceiling of stars.

It's an awkward occasion. To celebrate Meridian's victory would be in-sensitive as there are many old TVS people who are visibly moved as the last ten minutes of their ten-year reign come up on monitors after a statesmanlike 'healing' message from Lord Hollick.

At midnight a studio show called 'Goodbye to All That' patters to a close and frankly Meridian's opening debut is a great relief. The logo looks good; it's boldly delivered. The first ten minutes flow well and there are some good vox pops. A child says 'I want peace in Yugoslavia and Disneyland in Britain.'

1993

Sunday, January 3rd

Piercing sunlight behind the red blind in my room, the fiercest frost so far makes the grass and rooftops glisten.

After the Sunday papers – one of which observes pithily that 'John Major has all the qualities except leadership, with Margaret Thatcher it was the other way round' – I retire upstairs and begin my NCR reading with Simon Loftus' Puligny-Montrachet.

Watch some of the progs I recorded last night – a piece about Sickert, a man who loved being in the public eye, who sent scribbled instructions to Winston Churchill on how to paint – 'wear old clothes'; then a chilling film about property development in the City of London during the Thatcher years when 96% of all the schemes were approved, resulting, ten years later, in mediocre office space equivalent to 14 Canary Wharf Towers standing empty in the City.

Supper with Rachel and H; a blazing fire and John Betjeman's *Metroland* film to end the day. Better than a cup of Horlicks! Though of the same vintage.

Monday, January 4th

A man arrives to replace our neat, once-efficient, now defunct, BSB squarial with a bigger, less efficient but more commercially successful Sky/Astra replacement. The quality of pictures will never be as good from the Astra satellite, but there we are. Murdoch 1, BSB lost.

Tuesday, January 5th

Restful day in prospect. Weather warms up, bringing rain.

Ring Denville Hall to see how John Hughman is, and am told that he died last night. Mrs Miller rings later to apologise for not calling personally, but it was the day of a big committee meeting. My visit cheered him, she says, but his pain increased and so did his sedation. He died peacefully. It's almost a week since he wished me goodbye.

Wednesday, January 6th

To a studio across the road from Parliament where I do a down-the-line TV piece with an unseen Anne Diamond in Southampton for a show called *TV Weekly* (originally TVS, now made by Meridian). The cameraman tells me that my earpiece has just been used by Virginia Bottomley[1] – 'but it has been washed'. Pity. I was rather excited by this vicarious intimacy. ('I Shared an Earpiece with Virginia Bottomley' – Python reveals.)

Pole to Pole's last episode was seen by 11 million on Wednesday and two million on Saturday's BBC 2 repeat, pipping *80 Days*' highest figure by 200,000.

Thursday, January 7th

To the BBC to record one of the new *Wogan* shows. I'm on with Neil Kinnock[2] and Sheila Hancock.

A grim Green Room in the basement of TV Centre. Kinnock small and wasted, two stone lighter evidently than when he fought the election. He behaves like a bigger man, trying to transmit buoyancy and bonhomie, but it doesn't convince. His world is not showbiz. He tries to talk knowledgeably about it, but cannot remember anyone's name. In short, he's trying hard, but gives all the signs of still being in shock.

Terry W is in make-up at the same time as me. He pats his growing stomach. He exudes a comfortable confidence, based on little more than the fact that he is, unchallengeably, Terry Wogan. He looks like a minor royal uncle, secure and enjoying the good things of life.

I'm first guest on. On the desk in front of him, Terry has a series of cards. On top of the one I can see is printed in large letters 'South Pole – Anti Climax?'

Kinnock comes on and tries hard to be the life and soul.

Politicians need Parliament. They need their club. They seem to think they can manage to move effortlessly into showbiz. Kinnock's performance tonight shows just how difficult it is. 'Showbiz' tightens its ranks, and has its rules, just like politics.

---

1 Virginia Bottomley, Secretary of State for Health since the General Election.
2 Neil Kinnock resigned after Labour's General Election defeat after nine years as leader of the Opposition.

Saturday, January 9th

First dinner party of the New Year. Sepha and David Wood. Sepha Neill grew up with my sister Angela in Sheffield. Haven't asked anyone else because I know shop will be the order of the evening – Angela, Sheffield, etc.

She feels that she and Angela were friends because they were so different from one another. Angela lacked confidence, she remembers, despite being at the top of one class whilst Sepha was bottom of the other. My father was clearly remembered as a strict man – always a stickler for punctuality, imposing times so inflexibly that Angela used to start getting worried half an hour before she had to be home. (I too remember that source of fear.)

Tuesday, January 12th

A dilemma came into my mind as I ran this morning. Someone – was it Clem? – mentioned a Palin journey round the Pacific, and the suggestion was reiterated in a recent letter to the *Radio Times*.

As I fought the south-westerlies to the top of Parliament Hill, I traced in my mind a route starting on the easternmost tip of Russia, looking across the Bering Strait to the westernmost tip of America, and taking on the challenge to get from one to the other the long way round – taking a route down through the Kamchatka Peninsula, Vladivostok, the northernmost islands of Japan, Hokkaido, Korea, China, Vietnam, the islands of Indonesia, New Guinea, the Great Barrier Reef of Australia, New Zealand, across the Pacific to Easter Island, Southern Chile, then up South America through Peru, Ecuador, Colombia, Central America, Mexico, West Coast USA, Canada and Alaska.

The scope of the journey, the pattern of the journey, the newsworthiness of the journey (Hong Kong to China in '97 – earthquake prophecies in California) is attractive, as is the convenient and not entirely arbitrary parameter of the Pacific. It may seem premature, but after a year vowing never to do another mega-journey, I can see 'Palin's Pacific' on the screens in '96.

Wednesday, January 13th

A pale, wet morning. Rachel's eighteenth birthday. A Technics music system was her chief present, which she spent most of yesterday fitting up. There are a lot of time-consuming things to clear up this morning and I get no Whitbread reading done. Will to be packed off to Oxford – he leaves at lunchtime – prior to leaving with TJ for John Hughman's funeral.

To Holy Trinity Church, Northwood, a short distance from Denville Hall, where he died over a week ago. The weather grows wilder by the minute, with terrific winds roaring outside the stout, well-kept little church.

About 15 of us there. The vicar moves us into the front rows to help the singing. The door opens and the wailing winds rise to a screech as the coffin is brought in. Not for the first time, but undoubtedly for the last, I am struck by John's size. It is a long coffin, and maybe it's a tribute to my memory of John that an unbidden comic thought springs to mind – that John's final appearance is like a sketch, a sketch in which a coffin is so long it just keeps going, with no end in sight.

It's laid in front of us, at the end of the nave, and the flowers that Terry and I brought along are placed on top. They are the only flowers.

A short service with two lusty hymns, a fairly half-hearted address from the vicar, who clearly had very little to work with – son of two generations of military men, joined the army in the '30s, never very happy, seconded to the Pay Corps, then a job in the civil service and some difficult times before he started acting in 1968. A life that doesn't lend itself to the usual orations – no roll-call of achievements.

Tuesday, January 19th

To Denholm Elliott's memorial service at St James's Piccadilly.

I squeeze into a row at the very back. The size of the turnout and the lusty singing of 'Praise My Soul, the King of Heaven' are in marked contrast to the funeral of John Hughman six days earlier. Denholm was a very naughty man but marvellous at his job and much loved.

John Mortimer, possibly the most reassuring figure in British public life, spoke elegantly and with feeling through an open letter – 'Dear Denholm ...' Then a marvellous rendition of 'The Owl and the Pussycat' by Leslie Phillips.

On the way out a deep, breathy voice behind me asks how my reading's getting on. It's Diana Rigg. Lionel Bart and Clive Swift are both very friendly. I congratulate Leslie Phillips. 'Quite nervous, you know, with so many of your betters out there.'

More talk with Diana R over the NCR books. *In an Antique Land* by Amitav Ghosh, I suggest, was good. 'Oh, marvellous, but never a winner.' She speaks with such positive authority, such decisiveness, that I can only nod and agree. She turns her impressive attentions to two men who were in a prison camp with Denholm. He once acted Eliza Doolittle whilst chained up, one of them remembers. 'Some of the actors had to wear handcuffs.' Diana hoots with laughter at the recollection.

Friday, January 22nd

An hour on *Dreams of Exile* – the book which H found me so fast asleep over yesterday evening that when the phone woke me I picked up a mug of cold tea and said 'Hello' into it.

Reading it still in the taxi, I go to lunch with Clem.

I tell him that I don't want to do another *80 Days* or *Pole to Pole*. He asks why. I veer between the argument that we did two very successfully, we had luck and good fortune and a third journey of such scale would be tempting fate, and the feeling I have that my career has been successful because I've always moved on – always kept one step ahead of those wanting to typecast me.

We agree to keep thinking and despite all my worries I know we know that somehow, somewhere, we'll travel again.

Tuesday, January 26th

Dinner party – with the Cooks (Peter and Lin) and the Cleeses (even more recently married than the Cooks).

Peter chain-smokes and displays great knowledge of current affairs, scandals and goings-on which befits the owner of the *Eye*! Lin is quieter, but they're both clearly devoted.

JC presents me with a book of some old buffer's reminiscences of Bechuanaland.

Then there is an enormous crash as Peter, on his way upstairs to the loo, tries to walk through the glass door to the hall. He's momentarily stunned as the thick glass smashes, leaving behind an imprint of the great man. Fortunately he's not hurt, apart from a few minor scratches, which are bound up and plastered.

The talk got on to autobiography – Peter dismissed the idea, said he'd only ever got as far as a title. 'Retired and Emotional' was one – 'A Woman in the Body of an Armadillo' was another. I asked him about his ill-fated chat show in the early '70s. The problem was not the guests, but what to say to them. 'They were all my friends you see, or people I'd really wanted to meet like S. J. Perelman, but once they were there I really didn't want to ask them anything.'

Saturday, January 30th

I approach the days of reckoning on *The Dresser*. Called upon to prove myself once again. In at the deep end. The Tom Courtenay replacement.[1] Feel reasonably perky though.

To Broadcasting House for 10.30. Meet Sue MacGregor at the desk as I collect my pass for the day. She asks if Angela was my sister – as she can remember an Angela Palin reading letters on *Woman's Hour* years ago. So I tell her about what happened. She is very responsive, sympathetic, and I should like to have talked longer.

When at last I reach Studio 6A, a large barn of a place, and the only drama studio still in use at BH, I find the cast all sitting around, scripts at the ready. David Blount, his PA Sarah, a half-dozen actors from the Radio Drama Company, another two or three contract actors – 'OAs' (Outside Actors) as they call themselves. Freddie Jones, with his W. C. Fields strawberry nose, rubicund face, a less raddled version of Anthony Burgess – even to the scarf tied round the neck. David introduces us. Freddie is polite but not effusive. I feel like a new boy at school.

Sunday, January 31st

Down to BH. We set to the first half of the play. I find everything unfamiliar – the process of moving around as if acting in a real space, preceded by a studio manager making your noises for you – the difficulty of turning script pages silently – the chummy bonhomie of the radio actors.

Freddie remains oddly enigmatic. He never joins us for lunch or tea breaks, preferring, as he puts it, 'to go for a cocktail'. He smells of whisky after lunch, but not immoderately so, and his relish of the part is wonderful to behold. He is 'Sir' ... or is 'Sir' Freddie? ...

He lards his conversation with rich theatrical hyperbole. 'My position is quite vile, I realise that,' he says at one point, 'knowing the play, having done the part ... it really is a loathsome position.' He does seem to be genuinely concerned not to seem like the old hand, to play down his seniority and the fact that the play is almost his property.

David Blount takes me into the gallery at six. 'I want to play you something you did really well,' he says ominously. Indeed this prefaces the playing of two or three speeches I did very badly. They have no sense, no unity of delivery;

---

1 Tom Courtenay had appeared as Norman in Ronald Harwood's play *The Dresser* in the West End (opposite Freddie Jones) and in the film version (opposite Albert Finney) about a great actor (assumed to be Donald Wolfit [1902–68], actor-manager).

they wander. As he says, radio performance is about concision and precision; no gestures, no grimaces can be used to augment the delivery, the attention and concentration is all in the words – the sense of them is absolutely of paramount importance on radio.

'You know what to say,' concludes David, 'but at the moment it's only coming out at half-cock.'

I take the criticism hard, because I know it's true.

Monday, February 1st

I learnt something from yesterday's playback. I was trying too hard. I was performing Norman rather than letting the part speak for itself. I was starting too high and too violently; the only way was to reduce the initial effort, which, given the size of the part, I couldn't hope to sustain.

All the actors are in this morning – the studio used to the full as we record the Lear scenes. Tympanist, thunder sheets ('Return to Room 608' painted on them), a wind machine, peas rattled in a drum for rain. Actors tell endless stories ... Of one famous name: 'Never knowingly underplayed.' The landlady who apologised to her theatrical lodger after she'd found her being rogered by the milkman on the kitchen table – 'You must think I'm an awful flirt.'

Reminiscences of Wolfit. Asked whether playing Macbeth in the afternoon and Lear in the evening took its toll. 'When I play Macbeth in the afternoon and Lear in the evening ... there is no junket for Ros[1] that night.'

So it goes on. I just listen. But the day's work is good. Though I don't have a lot of lines, I do them efficiently and I'm aware of a gradually growing confidence as I become familiar with the surroundings and the technique. More positive all round.

Home, at last, in higher spirits. Work till my eyes ache on the speeches and the songs.

Tuesday, February 2nd

To BH by ten o'clock. Set to work straight away. David very pleased at the work we have done on it, and, buoyed by his relief and pleasure, I never really look back. 'You've got it,' he says like a Henry Higgins and he's right. I still have to make every line count, I still have the example of Freddie hitting every intonation, drawing every ounce of emotion and humour from

1 Rosalind Iden, his third wife.

his lines, to aim at, but at least I'm no longer intimidated. I can begin to enjoy myself.

Wednesday, February 3rd

A *Radio Times* survey throws up some unexpected results. Trevor McDonald is considered the television personality most readers would like to see in the Cabinet. Michael Palin tops the poll of those they would most like to see representing Britain at the UN (24%, ahead of Kate Adie at 17%!).

By ten, I'm at Studio 6A for the fifth and final day of *The Dresser*.

In the last section I'm required to break down as 'Sir' dies. We can't leave Freddie on the set as the microphone may pick up his breathing, so I end up emoting to an empty studio chair. From somewhere I find the ability to act grief and tears quite believably.

Freddie comes across from the other side of the studio. 'Marvellous, absolutely marvellous,' he says. Though I have to go through it twice more, this moment of unequivocal praise from Freddie is when I know that I have done the right thing in taking the part.

I've joined the club, as it were. I'm no longer the new boy.

Thursday, February 4th

Hunter Davies, wrapped up like an Iranian spy in black fedora and multi-coloured sweaters, has come to do me for the *Independent*.

Once Hunter has chosen to do you, you have entered his world. There is little I can say which will affect the agenda. His style is to rush at you like a bull at a gate, prodding behind comfortable answers towards the uncomfortable truths he hopes to unearth. The pace is brisk. He doesn't use a tape recorder, he prefers a small red soft-back notebook in which he scribbles every now and then, like a policeman interviewing a witness. His redeeming feature is his twinkling good humour, and his audacity, well cheek really – to which I respond. Despite all my best intentions I'm led into areas I've sworn to avoid – 'niceness', attitudes to critics, and so on. Hunter's juggernaut rolls on.

Wednesday, February 10th

Tom has good news of the rap track. KISS FM 'love it' and are playing it. The video shoot over the last couple of days went well, and there is a lot of interest in using his mini-studio. As usual I ask the clumsy but relevant parental question about money and rewards for all this work. 'That'll happen,' Tom assures me, and I like him so much I don't push.

Thursday, February 11th

Set aside the books and concentrate on writing a speech to match the auspicious occasion of Sheffield's 100th anniversary as a city tomorrow night.

At 6.30 we're collected and driven to the *Publishing News* Book Awards at the Royal Lancaster. A good crowd.

In the gents Roy Hattersley,[1] with whom I'm sharing a bill at Sheffield tomorrow, asks if I'd like tickets to the Wednesday–Southend FA Cup match on Saturday.

The Travel Writer of the Year Award is announced by none other than Peter de la Billière.[2] He makes quite a tension out of it, but then that lovely cathartic moment when I hear my name called, and I'm being clapped and smiled at by 500 people and given a 'Nibby' and I'm embarking on a speech of thanks which I only half expected to have to give. 'This is almost the greatest moment of my life ... the greatest was being offered tickets for the Wednesday v Southend game by Roy Hattersley in the gents.'

Friday, February 12th: London–Sheffield

Wake with a worse than usual headache, probably the result of drinking worse than usual wine.

Onto the three o'clock train and complete the speech somewhere beyond Luton.

In Sheffield on time. Driven to the Cutlers' Hall, which is quite a lot older than the city itself and rather fine, with tall marbled columns and walls hung with portraits of Sheffield worthies – including a Duke of Norfolk looking very sexy in tight white satin hose.

After a drink in the Master's office we're led by a toastmaster in a red coat up the wide, high-Victorian staircase into the Hall itself, via an ante-room where 100 guests who couldn't get tickets are to sit and watch the speeches on closed-circuit. The 'guests' applaud us to our seats with a slightly sinister regular hand clap which I assume is part of the ritual.

1 Roy Hattersley, former deputy leader of the Labour Party, retired as MP for Sparkbrook at the 1997 General Election.
2 General Sir Peter de la Billière. Retired as Commander-in-Chief, British Forces Middle East in 1991 after serving in the SAS and leading the British forces that retook the Falkland Islands following the Argentinian invasion in 1984.

It does seem an extraordinary turn of fate, that one who knew Sheffield best as a fairly shy schoolboy, well away from the world of civic power and influence, should, 36 years after leaving Birkdale School, be making the main speech at the 100th anniversary celebration of the city – with a white-haired Derek Dooley (legendary footballer of my youth) sitting a half-dozen yards away from me. Derek Dooley was one of Sheffield Wednesday's most prolific goal-scorers. In February 1953 he was injured in a match. The wound became infected and his leg had to be amputated.

Well, I don't think I let the city down. The time and care I took with the words pay off and, at the end, quite unexpectedly, I receive a standing ovation. This is quite something. Guests along the rows of tables on their feet, turning towards me, beaming and applauding. The Master Cutler grasps my hand, the Mayor too.

Tuesday, February 16th

Hunter Davies piece in the *Independent* is quite a relief. Good photo – office looks suitably cluttered and I'm not given the searching full close-ups they sometimes deal in. Written in Hunter's staccato, breathless style, it includes a memorable description of the neighbourhood in which I've spent most of my life: 'Gospel Oak, a nowhere place on the wrong side of the Heath.'

By twelve I'm entering the sheltered forecourt of the St Ermin's Hotel in deepest Westminster, for a meeting prior to the Vice-Presidents' lunch for The Royal Society for Nature Conservation.

David Attenborough is deep in conversation with a formidable elderly lady. Her face is deeply lined and wide, strong and healthy at the same time. D introduces her as Miriam Rothschild, Doctor Miriam Rothschild. Daughter of Lord Rothschild.

'I gather we must no longer call you nice,' David teases, referring to my *Independent* interview. I suggest that it's quite a good way of getting things done. Dr Miriam disagrees ... 'I never get anything done by being nice. I swing my battleaxe.'

We adjourn to a small, very warm private room as the other Vice-Presidents assemble, three of whom are Right Honourables – one an Earl, two Lords – and all of whom have either MCs, CBEs or OBEs.

Dr Rothschild takes the lead once we are all sat down. She's shocked by the revelation in the *Observer* that about 250 Sites of Special Scientific Interest are threatened by the new Government Road Building Programme. She demands quick and positive action from the RSNC/Wildlife Trusts. When someone counsels a cautious approach ... 'there could be difficulties' ... she waves them wearily away. 'I don't believe in difficulties.'

Home by 3.30. Start reading Victoria Glendinning's *Trollope* [for the NCR Awards].

Thursday, February 18th

Complete *Trollope*. Victoria G is very interested in T's interest in women – evidenced by the number of women in his novels. Her attempt to get to the bottom (*sic*) of his sexuality is rather exciting. Through Victoria's eyes we look beneath the skirts of mid-nineteenth-century morality.

To BAFTA to see one of the four films from which I and others have to select a Best Adapted Screenplay Award. Odd thing to have to do, because really one should read the work from which the screenplay is adapted to be able to judge.

Sit through *Howards End* and enjoy its lush good taste, and am beguiled by the sets and the costumes and the crisp performances, but my heart is not moved, nor do I wish anything on the Wilcox family but to get them off the screen. I think it's a case of using a work of art to crack a nut.

Sunday, February 21st

John's and Robin Skynner's new book *Life and How to Survive It* has gone straight to the top of the best-sellers, displacing *Pole to Pole*. The two notices I read are not polite.

Ring John to congratulate and abuse him. He is weary. Weary about the reviews, weary about the press generally. 'They will not make any attempt to listen ... they are not the slightest bit interested in anyone who appears to be making an effort, however small it might be, to make life a little better.'

We talk for half an hour. Every now and then there is an interruption – a cat walks across the phone, JC coughs scouringly ... 'Oh this bloody virus', and, most disconcertingly of all, appears to be taking notes ... 'You know that phrase you used earlier, which I've written down ...' If only I felt worthy of being a Doctor Johnson.

We've been invited round to Will Wyatt's for lunch. Half expect a respectable, besuited affair, but couldn't be more wrong. Will's house in Chiswick is modest, and pleasantly disordered.

Meet Molly Dineen, who has just received rave reviews for *The Ark*, her self-shot, self-interviewed doc series about London Zoo. She is Irish, bright, quick, restless, and, if she doesn't burn herself out with her own energy, likely to go far. Her stories of the zoo could write 'Death Fish Two' on their own. Gorillas breaking out and attacking chimpanzees; a pony from the children's zoo fed to the wolves. The war between the keepers sounds absolutely plausible!

Tuesday, March 2nd

Cold, bland morning, low cloud, east wind. Opening of the Michael Palin Stammering Centre. Drive down to BH for an appointment with *Today* prog. Am taken straight into the studio. 'John Smith's[1] in there at the moment, and we want a bit of light relief,' confides the PA before apologising '... well, you know what I mean.'

After my remarks on stammering I'm asked to comment on the news of the death of Joyce Carey at 94. Having had no time to prepare I say my bit and then, with some mad rush of blood to the head, go on to make a point about the number of great old actresses who have died this week – mentioning Lillian Gish and, for some reason, instead of Ruby Keeler, Jessye Norman. I'm told later that an apology had to be broadcast after alarm calls from fans of the very much alive and kicking Jessye Norman.

Wednesday, March 3rd

To BAFTA for the meeting of the Best Adapted Screenplay jury.

We sit around a table, wine and snack provided. After the *GBH/Prime Suspect* debacle last year, strict new rules apply. No-one must leave the room once discussion has begun; choice of film must be marked by signature. The chairman must keep result confidential.

Our discussion was full but quite enlightening. Peter Nichols was the only one who'd hated *Strictly Ballroom*[2] – 'but I'm like that,' he admitted. Tony Palmer and myself spoke with one voice on most of the films – though he was a trifle more vituperative about *Howards End*.

I think *Strictly Ballroom* is a classic, one of the best adverts for modern film. Rich and complex and far less respectable (*Howards End*), preachy (*JFK*) and introverted (*The Player*) than the others. We vote. There is a clear winner. Charles Wood, our chairman, who naturally, I feel, tends to indiscretion, wants to tell us. It'll be *The Player* or *Strictly B*.

News comes from Howard Schumann of the death of Paul Zimmerman. I hadn't expected him to live, but I still find it hard to accept I shall never see

---

1 John Smith, succeeded Neil Kinnock as Labour leader.
2 *Strictly Ballroom*, 1992 film directed by Baz Luhrmann.

him again. As I tell Terry in a phone call later, I want, above all, to hear Paul tell me his side of the story.

Sunday, March 7th

About ten o'clock Nigel Meakin rings from the BAFTA Craft Awards at Nottingham to tell me he's won the award for best documentary photographer. In view of the fact that the BBC didn't even suggest him as their nomination (he had to be pushed by Clem), this is a tremendous pleasure, relief and so entirely well-deserved a success that I feel I've won something myself.

Tuesday, March 9th

Sunshine again. In my light, bright, glowing workroom (blinds down for first time this year), lose myself in the world of fossils and human origins – Leakey's *Origins Reconsidered*. Realise that we travelled, on *Pole to Pole*, through 'the cradle of mankind', the African Rift Valley, and were hardly aware of it.

After almost two years in which *Pole to Pole* has meant work, I find myself thinking about it with pleasure. Leakey's descriptions of a Kenyan dawn filled me with longing.

Friday, March 12th

Lunch with JC and Iain Johnstone in St John's Wood. Cartoon about JC's book in *Private Eye* ... 'Ello Miss, I wish to complain about this book ... it has ceased to be interesting.' JC hadn't seen it, and ventured the opinion that *Private Eye* had always treated him well. He'd found Craig Brown's parody of the Skynner/Cleese banter funny. John is definitely less prickly these days.

We have some good discussion on 'Death Fish Zoo'. Must remember to get JC together with Molly Dineen.

A fine spring night. Scent of hyacinths in the cooling midnight air.

Saturday, March 13th: London–Abbotsley

Rake through Waterstones in Hampstead for something to give Granny for her 80th.

Helen back quite late with a dozen helium-filled balloons which we have to try and pack in the car. 'Will they make the car lighter?' a neighbour asks helpfully. Clare [Latimer] brings round the 80th birthday cake. Unfortunately she's spelt Gibbins 'Gibbons', so before we can leave she has to make fresh icing and correct it.

Up at Church Farm, our first glimpse of the marquee. Sits very well in the front garden flanked by Granny's showpiece borders of purple hyacinth, primrose and primula with daffs hurrying forward in the quite unseasonable warmth.

Inside it's lined with flounced yellow nylon. Even the tent poles have been stockinged. Electrically lit sconces add a weird country-house-boudoir touch, and a plastic undersheeting crackles beneath one's feet like some giant incontinence garment.

Thursday, March 18th

The day that ends the reading programme that I've been put through (for £2,500 expenses) for the NCR. Twenty-two books read, about twice my yearly rate, in two and a half months!

At the NCR office by nine o'clock. In addition to the five members of the judging panel, a further four are present. The lady marketing the whole business, two other women, and the literary agent who acts as a sort of court of appeal and whose name I'm never told.

David Puttnam, apologising for his low voice and state of health, deals, with disarming ruthlessness, with the early 'drop-outs'.

The last seven are quite easily arrived at, but from this point on there are two main areas of disagreement. One is over Fred Inglis' *The Cruel Peace*. David stays quiet on this, but I suspect his silence is not one of approval. I am on awkward ground, disliking it for some emotional reason, possibly because Richard Hoggart won't even discuss *his* dislike of *Fever Pitch*, but I cannot be persuaded by Diana Rigg, who found it 'audacious' and Richard H, whose admiration for the work seems to lie uncomfortably close to his admiration for the author. As it's removed from the last four he mutters 'Poor Fred.'

But the nearest we come to blows is over the Iris Murdoch. Once again I'm first to talk about it and I have to put the shaky case for incomprehensibility. Richard Hoggart reveres it, but it's Margaret Jay who puts up the most spirited case. We need a new value system. Never have morals and ethics been so important. Religion has failed us. Age of apathy and uncertainty. New lead needed. Who better than Iris to supply it?

David confesses he was lost with it. Couldn't understand what she was getting at. It was the first book for a long time to remind him that he only got three O Levels. Hoggart cannot conceive of such a major work being set aside.

Diana reveals that she thought it very difficult and not fulfilling the criterion of 'available to a wide readership'.

Then up speaks the agent, whose name I must find out. He is respected by all and his words carry weight. 'Iris Murdoch is one of our greatest writers. She has made a living from some of the finest modern novels in the language. If she has written a book which three well-educated, intelligent people at this table cannot understand, then she has perhaps not written a very good book.'

Jay gives in and Hoggart is left muttering and shaking his head as *Fever Pitch* lines up ahead of the Iris Murdoch. But at least I no longer feel quite such a philistine.

At 12.15 *Fever Pitch* (unchallenged except by Hoggart), Wolpert's *Unnatural Nature of Science* (not much liked by Jay), *The English Bible* (not liked by Jay and Hoggart as much as the Trevelyan) and *Never Again* by Peter Hennessy (compromise) are stood up on the table as the four shortlisted books. We have our photos taken with them. I'm given *Fever Pitch* to hold. I think it's understood to be my crusade.

Sunday, March 28th

The IRA have made a lot more enemies after the Warrington bomb killed two young boys out shopping for Mother's Day. Waves of indignation, but the saddest news of all is that in Belfast, where the IRA turn out their terrorists, the Protestants slew five Catholics over the last week, instantly ensuring that the IRA win back sympathy.

Watch Eric being perky on *Aspel*. First evidence of any pre-publicity for *Splitting Heirs*.[1] He's 50 tomorrow. Same age as John Major. Seems unbelievable.

Monday, March 29th: London–New York

Concorde across the Atlantic in 3.27. Listen to *The Dresser*. Unfortunately the noise of this expensive aircraft is such that a lot of the quieter, throwaway lines cannot be heard unless the volume's turned right up. Then Freddie immediately goes into one of his roars, giving the eardrums a terrible battering. Tears in my eyes at the end. I do the last speech well.

Whisked to the Ritz-Carlton by limo. My second rush hour of the day.

TG is in the hotel, two floors down. This seems to be the way New York always is. A great meeting place. Never a dull moment. So I end up having,

---

1 Written by Eric Idle, directed by Robert Young, starring Eric, Rick Moranis and Catherine Zeta-Jones.

as my third meal of the day, a breakfast with TG and Ina. The 1976 Pythons v ABC team.[1] Very jolly.

He goes off to write. I go up to unpack and ring Samantha Dean, Castle Hill's PR lady. She says response continues well, reads me a great review of *American Friends* in *Rolling Stone*.

The sore throat lingers and I have a stomach ache.

Ask at a drug store about vitamin C. A very Jewish pharmacist points straight away to the strongest dose – 1,000 mgs. 'Linus Pauling took *two of these every hour* until he'd squeezed the life out of whatever had gotten into him.' When I take them home I notice it recommends one a day!

Tuesday, March 30th: New York

A call from the Letterman office. I tell them that the story of *American Friends* is not a comedy and that the most interesting thing about the movie is that I play a serious role. 'Well, maybe we have to find a way of saying this from a comedic perspective.'

Saturday, April 3rd: New York

The rain's stopped, there's some sun poking through the clouds. At ten I'm in a taxi to the Met and wandering happily around the Lehman Collection, which includes Vuillards of distinction and some lusty Bonnards too. Then around the American Wing – looking mainly at the paintings – Caleb Bingham's 'Fur Traders' one of my great favourites. Difficult to tear myself away.

Onto the subway to Union Square. Investigate the Quad Cinema where *American Friends* opens in six days' time. A modest, unassuming theatre in a pleasant, unostentatious neighbourhood. Just around the corner is a Gothic Revival church whose tower (erected in 1846) is said to be a replica of Magdalen College, Oxford. I take that as a good omen.

Sunday, April 4th: New York

After breakfast call Julian [Schlossberg, our American distributor]. He's in candid mood. 'If we don't get the *New York Times* we're dead.' The *Times* and the *Village Voice* are key to our success in the city, it seems. If either is critical or even lukewarm life will be hard.

---

1 Ina Lee Meibach acted for the Pythons in the case against ABC Television.

Despite all the work of last week, we are still vulnerable. Only hanging onto public awareness by our fingertips.

Thursday, April 8th: New York

Welcome Helen at 10.30. Very happy to see her; it's nice to be on neutral territory, in a comfortable hotel, away from the anticlimactic realities of home.

To add to the pleasure of our reunion, there is an unequivocally fine day, and to celebrate it I've booked a table at the Boathouse Café. Nancy comes along with Timothy. He's very good, but given to standing on his chair and saying 'Excuse me!' very loudly. Simon is stricken with back trouble two nights from opening in *My Fair Lady* out in New Jersey.

At 9.30 I find myself down at one of the halls of NYU for Richard Brown's Film Class. Richard Brown's acolytes prepare me to go on stage. The event, I'm told with pride, is being televised. (It seems nearly everything in America is televised nowadays!) Half an hour on stage. Feel comfortable and relaxed and the adulation helps.

Afterwards give Tristram, Virginia and Archie a ride back to their hotel. On the way we pick up a *New York Times* from a news-stand. Though it's only 10.15, Friday's edition is out. Tristram scans the review page faster than I can. 'It's not good' is all he says.

By the time I've reached Canby's review[1] I have heard enough to know it's very bad. In fact it's the only kind of notice I really am not prepared for – a vicious clubbing to death of the film. There is no quarter given. Every aspect irks him – acting, photography. Well it's impossible to read at one sitting.

Though the Powells must be exhausted, the Canby mugging has roused them sufficiently to suggest we all go for a drink and a bite to eat. We end up at Fiorello's on Broadway – where I seem to remember eating with Patrick and Tristram in the days of doubt about the film three or four years ago.

We can think of no explanation for Canby's virulence. Funnily enough, a few hours earlier at the Cleeses', JC had suggested calling my character Canby – to get back at the critic for his savaging of *A Fish Called Wanda*.

From the heights of praise and approbation at ten o'clock, we're plunged to the depths 20 minutes later; now, at midnight, I walk back along the edge of Central Park, past huddled sleeping figures on benches and in the crooks of walls, feeling curiously light-headed and carefree.

---

1 Vincent Canby, chief film critic of the *New York Times* since 1969.

Friday, April 9th: New York

Phone calls to Steve, Patrick, who arrived yesterday, and of course Julian S, who cannot conceal his disappointment. But during the morning word comes in of good reviews in the *News*, the *Post* and *Newsday*.

In the evening I've organised a get-together down in the Village for all friends of *American Friends*. Important not to let it become a wake in the wake of Canby's review, and in fact it works well.

H survives until 11.15; we're the first to leave, apart from Julian S.

A cold wind blowing down 5th Avenue tightens the breath as we walk past the church with its tower modelled on Magdalen College, Oxford, which I had hoped would be a good omen! Not on this Good Friday.

Monday, April 12th: New York

Wake early and, despite myself, fall to worrying about the work that lies ahead – the proximity of, and my unpreparedness for, the Irish *Great Railway Journeys* shoot; the pile of letters that will be awaiting my arrival at home. I wish we could stay in this happy limbo for a while longer, but all too soon it's coming to an end.

Julian calls. He sounds much more cheerful. Says that the *Washington Post* article is coming out this Easter weekend, but not Sunday. Business in both Washington and New York has been sufficiently good to ensure a second week in each. (How we clutch at straws! That this should be good news.)

Run round the Reservoir whilst H goes for a final blast of shopping; in the two weeks I've been in New York, the Park has begun to blossom. Cherry and hawthorn and what looks like magnolia, but the trees generally are still bare.

To Nancy and Simon for a drink and to say goodbye. Simon is on his third or fourth chiropractor and has been assured he will be ready to take his role on Wednesday, but he still stands against walls with the half-startled, half-agonised look of someone preparing to face a firing squad.

On by taxi to 77th and supper with JC.

Talk over thoughts on 'Death Fish Zoo' which have occurred to me over the weekend. Also try out on him my thought on a two-hander. That it should be set in a foreign country, probably in Africa, that we should play diplomats representing the old and the new school thrown together to evacuate the country of Brits in some crisis. JC likes the thought that it should involve the politics of international aid – about which there is much to be said.

Friday, April 16th

Helen has bought me a card, some artificial red roses and a seal cub paper-weight for our 27th anniversary. We still get on pretty well, neither of us being confrontational, but both of us being stubborn! As Helen says this morning, it's not been a claustrophobic relationship.

Tom comes round later in the morning. He has been working some 24-hour shifts with Rhythm and Bass, and his studio at Charlton King's Road is in demand. He seems to be finding new confidence – he's playing piano on some of the mixes, and is well on top of the new recording technology.

To a much-put-off lunch with Tony Laryea. After we worked together on *Comic Roots* [1983] he rose fast in the BBC, without compromising his radical tendencies, and was in line for No. 2 at BBC Manchester when he decided to leave and go independent. He has gravitas, but no pomposity.

I chat to him about my vague thoughts on a religious slant to my next pro-ject. Been festering in my mind as I found myself becoming more interested in Islam as a result of my travels. Wouldn't such a prog be helpful, as well as giv-ing a new slant to my travels? He was very encouraging. Apparently religion is an area many prog-makers are thinking about now.

Monday, April 19th: London–Derry

Meet Nigel and Julian on flight to Belfast to begin filming our Great Railway Journey. There meet up with rest of the crew at a local hotel. Ken, Hilary, Fraser.

Drive on the pleasantly un-busy roads to Derry, or Londonderry as the Protestant, Unionist, Loyalists call it. A striking city. A little reminiscent of Toledo in its situation on a hill above the river, with the still-solid grey walls built 380 years ago enclosing a tight cluster of roofs and tall spires.

We're the guests at a Lord Mayor's reception. Despite Derry now being 70-30 a Catholic city, the post of Mayor rotates on a power-sharing basis and our host tonight is actually a member of Paisley's DUP.

Lots of city councillors drop in to shake hands. No women, I notice.

Tuesday, April 20th: Derry

Filming delayed from the start by news of a security alert in The Diamond, the central intersection of Old Derry. Where our BBC hoist should be in position.

At Bishop Gate, where armour-plated doors block vehicle access from the

Fountain area, there was an explosion at 3.30 a.m. The frighteningly young, smooth-cheeked English squaddie we talk to is philosophical. It was timed to go off at 6.15, he says, when the side door is opened. He observes what it's done to the door, which is completely blown out, and adds 'It was my turn to open the door this morning.'

Thursday, April 22nd: Belfast

This afternoon, as the bright periods diminish and the rain sets steadily in, we visit the Falls and Shankill Road.

I spend a gruelling and uncomfortable afternoon squeezed into the unit Toyota with Ivor Oswald – businessman and guide – in the front, and Nigel and Fraser in the back. The car windows keep steaming up. The steady rain reduces visibility. Ivor drives erratically, but there is no sign of any impatience from other vehicles as we travel up the Falls Road.

At first the surroundings are nothing like as bleak and desolate as I'd expected. Apart from the notorious Divis Flats, there is little high-rise, and a lot of new terraces are under construction mirroring the red-brick Victorian character of the rest of the city. Schools, hospitals, joggers, ice-cream parlours, all the usual trimmings of late-twentieth-century life, not affluent, but by no means uncomfortable or desperate.

The shock is the sight of the police stations and army bases. Façades of concrete and sheet metal garlanded with cameras on infra-red control, from which the eyes of the authorities can observe the seeming normality of streets and gardens. These quasi-military presences must be as much a provocation as a necessity. They represent institutionalised force, embattled and dug in against the outside world. No wonder the men of both sides who attack them have a chance of becoming heroes.

The long streets off the Shankill where Catholic and Protestant communities face each other are uncompromisingly depressing. No amount of neat, brick housing can disguise this awful human mess. For three miles a 'peace line' runs across the city, separating the sides. The price of 'peace' has been the destruction of buildings, the blocking-off of roads, and the erection of more of the big, brutal fortresses which serve to both intimidate and protect.

Even Ivor Oswald, who has good to say for both sides because he 'believes in Belfast', admits that the two will not be reconciled in his lifetime. Ken thinks that being in Europe may hold the key to some sort of readjustment – Catholic Southern Ireland becoming more prosperous – closer links, less isolation. Ian from BBC Belfast newsroom says that as the Catholic birth rate is now so much higher than the Protestant, there could be a majority democratic vote for independence – but that won't be for 20 years at least. In the meantime the emotion and anger of rivalry remains painted on gable ends and written in graffiti. 'No Surrender.' 'Our Day Will Come.'

Tuesday, April 27th: Belfast–Dublin

Take the three o'clock Enterprise train service for Dublin.

The coach is scrubbed and still hung with a hint of disinfectant. The windows all have 'Reserved for the BBC' stickers plumb in the middle, preventing us filming anything until they've been removed.

So out of Northern Ireland, and into the less obsessively neat atmosphere of the Irish countryside. Hedges ramble, fields are lumpy and unused, the dwellings of the poor shabbier than anything seen in the North, but the heart lifts to be away from the video cameras and the steel fences.

Fax from Kath shows *'AF'* quietly slipping into oblivion in NYC and Washington.

Wednesday, April 28th: Dublin

The hotel is filling up with football supporters – a big World Cup qualifier with Denmark is being played at Lansdowne Road Stadium, five minutes' walk from the hotel. All around the streets are filled with salesmen, and a live jazz band plays on a traffic island.

We extract ourselves from the seething mass and drive out to Bray Station, south of the city, to film an interview with The Edge[1] of U2. He has requested that it be shot on the DART train service that runs along by the sea, into and across Dublin.

After all our nervousness that he will attract adoring crowds, Edge turns out to be quite mild and unsensational. No dark glasses or army of minders. He emerges from a Citroën BX, diminutive and pale. Been working hard. Six months in the studio completing a new album prior to a tour that begins May 6th.

He says he dreads the thought of touring until it happens, then he just lets it carry him along. Bono is the opposite, he says. Can't wait to get on the road, but discontent sets in as soon as he's on it.

The interview is more like a conversation – he's laid-back, eloquent and modest with a good sense of humour. Likes Ireland, obviously, finds it the best place to live and work and retain a sense of proportion. 'Let's face it,

---

1 The Edge played guitar and keyboard in the band.

no-one in Ireland can ever be more famous than Gay Byrne.'[1]

He's anxious to avoid getting involved in politics. Perhaps once bitten, twice shy. Ends up ruefully with a send-up of himself – 'It's hard work being an icon, you know.'

Thursday, April 29th: Dublin

A splendid day. We film at the National Library Reading Room, trying to fill out the 'Michael's Irish roots' aspect of the documentary.

Tom Lindert the genealogist has news for me though. At 11.30 last night he heard from his contacts that a copy of the marriage certificate of Edward and Brita Gallagher has been traced. They were married at the British Embassy in Paris by Chaplain Cox on 2nd October 1867. No note of the parentage of either party, which he thinks is odd.

In the afternoon up to Glasnevin Cemetery to walk amongst the graves and talk to a very laid-back American from Orange County who is also looking for his Irish ancestors. He doesn't hold out much hope. His name is Kopnowski.

Tuesday, May 4th: Ardmore–Mallow

We make for Ardmore, down the coast towards Cork. It's a small village on an impressive bay.

Then along the western arm of the bay to interview Molly Keane.[2] She lives in an unpretentious house set on the edge of the cliff, obtained by a long, steep stairway. She is frail and thin and walks slowly with the aid of a stick. All the time I'm there I'm haunted by the thought of her trying to ascend those steps to the road.

Once she's sorted us all out and relaxed a little she begins to show off as only a glamorous 80-year-old can – shamelessly flirting with the men, revelling in her stories of Noël Coward and various raffish horse-owning ancestors.

She cannot really be interviewed fast – her stories stretch out and naturally expand, occasionally she goes hacking off into the undergrowth of some half-remembered episode – usually to re-emerge triumphantly.

Despite sounding quintessentially English, she claims to be Irish. But she despairs of present-day Ireland – all the 'burglaries' and 'break-ins' seem to

1 Gay Byrne, Irish broadcaster, famed for his long-running televsion programme *The Late Show*.
2 Molly Keane, Irish novelist, who also wrote under the name M. J. Farrell. Her 1981 novel, *Good Behaviour*, was shortlisted for the Booker Prize.

give her great cause for anxiety. What we shall get from the interview is debatable, but she charmed and bewitched everyone there.

Ken leaves with tears in his eyes. He knew her, through Russell Harty,[1] who was a terrific friend of Molly's, and thinks that may well be the last time he will see her. She calls Ken her 'nephew Ken' and me 'baby Michael' – which is another reason to like her, as I meet her on the last day of my forties!

Train filming takes us through to Mallow and at six o'clock to the handsome Georgian country house overlooking the quiet rural landscape of the Blackwater River – Longueville House.

Surprise arrival of Anne James from London. At midnight Ken orders champagne, and Anne gives me the office present – slippers and a pipe!

Wednesday, May 5th: Longueville House, Mallow

Lift my blinds to reveal a gorgeous morning. Still, sunny, mist clearing from the low valley, cows and sheep contentedly grazing right up to the forecourt of the hotel. Magnificent and ancient trees adorn the view (evidently planted in the configuration of British and French troops at the Battle of Waterloo). There could really be nowhere better to raise the spirits on a change of decade.

A busy day's filming, based at the small town of Buttevant, about 20 miles north of Mallow.

Tony O'Neil's bar, which is at the back of his grocery shop, is our base for much of the day, and I salute the passing of my forties, at a quarter to twelve, with a glass of Guinness in his excellent company.

Much filming in graveyards as we search for Gallaghers. It seems that the deeper one goes into all this ancestor-hunting the more opaque the waters become. I really don't know where I am now – caught on slippery ground between fact and fiction.

But the weather stays dreamily warm, the locations are magical and Tony O'Neil is a great host, in a village where everyone is constantly introducing you to someone else.

It's a long day, and made longer when one of our two vehicles runs out of fuel in a dangerous part of a busy main road. At 8.15, I'm directing oncoming vehicles to slow down whilst Fraser leaps around organising relief.

We arrive back at Longueville – quick bath and at last down to order dinner. Sitting in a magnificent room, order myself a glass of champagne. For some reason it takes a while to arrive. Jane, who runs the hotel, tells me that she has a new waitress and she hopes we'll all be understanding. This only increases my impatience. I've earned this drink, for God's sake.

---

1 Television presenter of arts and chat shows, who died in 1988.

At that moment the tall doors of the drawing room, mysteriously closed, are pulled back to reveal Helen, bearing a tray of champagne glasses. A great coup, in the most theatrical of surroundings. I had already rung Rachel and suppressed a certain irritation on hearing that Mum was at badminton!

A complete and wonderfully welcome surprise. I thanked Fraser for his part in procuring me a woman on this sad day in my life!

Then we eat, splendidly, in the library, a table away from the other guests; presents include an old map of Ireland from Fraser, Nigel and Julian, a silver container for the 'tooth fairy', a big Guinness jug, and, from Patti, via Nigel, a caricature of the *Pole to Pole* team. Flowers from George H and Olivia too.

To bed on one of the best of days.

Wednesday, May 12th

By bike to the Lansdowne in Primrose Hill. A converted pub, which now resembles a cross between an Amsterdam family bar and a Viennese café. Bare boards, tables scattered about, a blackboard menu strong on aioli-assisted dishes. Music, good wines and small selection of draught beer.

Meet Roger Mills there. A little too trendy for him, I think, but a good pint of Everards settles him down.

The Meridian documentary series I've agreed to do now looks set to be on the Isle of Wight – on video, each episode shot in seven days; intro and outro, no commentary ... very different already from the long journeys.

Friday, May 14th

Documentary proposal arrives in the post from the TV Trust for the Environment. Would I host a big series on 'The Aid Game'. All over the world and talk to bankers, politicians, UN people, etc.

Sit on the loo and regard the prospect – hard work but a good chance to make a serious impact on people's thinking. The trouble is that I feel I would be driven in a certain direction – my communicative talents used to someone else's ends. Tempting, but later in the day write and decline.

Saturday, May 15th

Set off for Wembley at 12.45 in a BBC car, supplied by Radio Sport, who have also provided me with three £100 tickets for the Arsenal–Wednesday final. All in return for a live appearance on the Cup programme.

Great anticipation and excitement. Rachel hasn't been to a football match before and I've never been to an FA Cup Final.

Wembley Stadium boasts enormous 'SEGA' sponsorship signs and, like British Airports Authority, seems happy to sell every nut and bolt if there's a company name that can be slapped on them.

Met by BBC PA and led, through the dining (sorry, 'banqueting') room and right up onto the network of metal struts and tubes that holds up the roof. Pick our way across the underside of the roof frame, narrowly avoiding decapitation. I'm quite impressed that anyone gets up here alive.

The sun comes out for the kick-off. Wembley becomes the centre of the whole world, walled-in, caught in a time warp singing 'Abide With Me'– the ghosts of 69 previous finals around.

Wednesday are poor in the first half and lucky to be only one behind, but the recovery of confidence they so desperately need comes in the early second half. Hirst goal – then suddenly we start to play. But never incisive enough. Both teams look tired, short of ideas. Nail-biting goes on into extra time. A draw.

Massive feeling of disappointment, doubtless compounded 80,000 times. To be prepared to give so much, then to be cheated out of the madness, the spontaneous, unfettered joy of victory, leaves an odd numbness.

Fans leaving the stadium are generally quiet, as if they'd seen something they didn't really want to talk about.

Wednesday, May 19th

To the office with the other shortlisted NCR books for final reappraisal. Tonight we shall choose the winner.

Down to the Savoy by seven to meet the rest of the judges. Any hopes I might have still harboured of persuading them round to *Fever Pitch* as winner scotched by Diana Rigg's absence in South Africa, leaving behind a preference order of *Never Again*, Wolpert, Hornby and Christopher Hill.

We repair to the Iolanthe Room, a small, high-ceilinged, timber panelled and pillared side room. Puttnam gives us all a present for being good judges. It's a much more agreeable atmosphere than the boardroom at NCR and there is conciliation and courtesy in the air.

Richard Hoggart says that he has made every effort with *Fever Pitch* – 'I took it to Poland with me'– and whilst he sees qualities he had once closed his eyes to, he wasn't won over. Odd that such a man of the people should find it so hard to support a book that deals so well with a neglected area of popular culture.

Margaret is on good form. She can be formidable – viz. her defence of Iris

Murdoch; tonight, with Iris out of the way, she's much more relaxed and professes great enthusiasm for *Fever Pitch*, but seems set on *Never Again*. Still, I say my bit. *Never Again* is a safe bet – another academic work which I find only as good as several other works of historical research we've sidelined. *Fever Pitch* is an original, a book of passion and personality.

Puttnam's enthusiasm for *Fever Pitch* has waned, and I find myself acquiescing in the selection of *Never Again*, reminding myself that I've once more been hijacked by the intellectuals. I lost *My Life as a Dog* to *The Sacrifice* and, though it worried me less, *Strictly Ballroom* to *The Player*.

Thursday, May 20th

Around four a.m. the alarm goes and Helen gets up. She's organised a week's holiday on a Greek island with three friends from her bereavement class. Tickets have to be collected two hours before the flight, etc. etc. I'm barely conscious of her bending towards me in the gloom and planting a farewell kiss and later, when I hear the taxi door slam, I realise that in all the rush and tumble of this week I don't even know which island it is she's going to.

The likelihood of a third travel series comes closer with the writing of a letter from me to Clem expressing my own intentions, in writing, for the first time.

I have suggested a delivery date of October '97, and three filming periods of three months each, out of which we make ten programmes.

Important in my decision is the realisation that the travel series option offers the greatest chance of personal control over a project. The experience of *American Friends* – my own film, yet played at a lot of other people's pace, and to a lot of other tunes – has made me wary of film-making.

Arrive at the Savoy just as Nick Hornby, his fiancée and bevy of publishing ladies also appear. It is an extraordinary coincidence that Arsenal, Nick H's team – the team to which he is so totally, slavishly devoted, the team which caused him to write the book – should be playing Sheffield Wedensday in the FA Cup Final replay at the very moment when the announcement of the NCR Award is going on.

Nip out every now and then to keep an eye on the game. Nick H is sat at a small table near the kitchen, with a bottle of wine and the telly. Some of his minders become a real nuisance, endlessly telling me how lucky we are to have him here tonight. As I'd done so much to get his book into the last four, I felt I didn't need this.

Arsenal go 1-0 up in first half; Wednesday equalise midway through second! Hornby looks hot and distracted. 1-1 at full time.

The meal trails on, video presentations have to be gone through, then as extra time is being played, the judges are at last called up.

My tribute to *Fever Pitch* goes down well. Much laughter and I feel very relieved. Patrick Mill, the NCR man deputed to run the Award, announces Peter Hennessy to be the winner – and Hennessy is lapping up the applause when Mill slips me a piece of paper. Arsenal 2–1.

I think of Rachel out there in the rain, at Wembley for the second time in a week, and I can't, I'm afraid, enjoy any of Hennessy's triumph. I didn't want his book to win, and to see celebration at this time makes me feel oddly as though I'm at the match. A loser amongst winners.

Friday, May 21st

Awful news in the papers; in fact my first reaction when I see a blurred photo in the *Guardian* of the Opera House in Belfast, gashed down the side as if a huge ship had run into it, is that I must be reading some anniversary account of the bombing of 1991. But it happened again yesterday. The IRA left a 1,000lb bomb on a truck at the site where Michael Barnes and I did our interview less than a month ago. Most of the windows of the Europa are broken, the remains of the truck resemble a giant piece of liquorice, and the Opera House has been shattered again.

Later in the morning I call Michael – there's little one can say. He said it was better yesterday when he had to do 17 interviews and there was no time for the full weight of what had happened to sink in. They will not know for a few days how serious the damage is, but the auditorium is intact.

Catherine Bailey, who tried to get me to do a series called 'Orphans of Empire', is now getting different presenters for each one. They've just been to see Alan Bennett. Apparently he liked the idea but was worried that he might be expected to do more than he wanted to – 'I can't be like Michael Palin ... I can't talk to people'!

Saturday, May 22nd

A sort of loose schedule has arrived from Clem today which I see bears the title 'Palin's Pacific'. More excitingly for the future, I have a letter from David Pugh which bears the first good news about *The Weekend* since our last 'preferred' actor turned it down. Pugh had sent it on spec to Richard Wilson, whose agent says he likes it very much 'and would be available to do it next February'.

Thursday, May 27th

Compile some thoughts on the Pacific project. Have to think quietly and firmly about my own ability to take it on. The trouble is one forgets very quickly the awkwardnesses and privations of travel. Must be severe with myself – and remember sleepless nights in filthy huts and remorseless early-morning loading of gear and the runs for days on end.

Out to the Royal Academy Annual Dinner. It's all well stage-managed with guardsmen in bearskins sounding a tremendous fanfare to announce arrival of star guest – Mary Robinson, the President of Ireland. She enters, slow, cool and very regal; good-looking but not beautiful, turning a lot of intellectual heads. Her impressively large husband, Nick, walks deferentially behind.

Paul Smith is at our table. He introduces himself saying 'You don't know me but I know you.' To which I'm able to reply 'Of course I know you and I'm wearing your dinner jacket.' Flash the Paul Smith label back at him.

Eric Clapton is also there. I tell him that I'm easing up on commitments for the year. 'So am I ... So am I ...' he enthuses. 'I've finally made the decision ... I'm not doing anything at all ... for two months.'

Philip Sutton is opposite. He's an RA [Royal Academician]. They all tend to behave a bit like naughty schoolboys. Leonard McComb sketches faces in the throng and knocks over glasses of wine. A lefty sculptor called Bruce McLean heckles Virginia Bottomley, who gives a dull, school-mistressy speech which is politely received.

Roger de Grey the RA President is cheered to the rafters and halfway through his speech, which he aims cleverly at Peter Brooke, the Heritage Minister, he talks about state aid coming too late to plug the holes in the roof. At that point mock snow falls from on high and sprinkles the top table.

And Tom Phillips RA is sporting a wooden bow tie.

Sunday, May 30th

To Oxford, where Will is only a few days away from his finals.

Will in good form. He shows us two 8-mill films he's made with friends – just larking about, but they remind me of what Terry J used to make at his home in Claygate in 1965.

Will loves the 8-mill camera – without my pushing him towards it – and sounds to have found an aptitude and appetite for making films. 'They listen to me,' he says, with some pride ... 'I tell them what to do and they listen to me!' He now wants to be a film director.

Monday, May 31st: London–Llangoed Hall Hotel, near Hay-on-Wye

Looking at the Hay programme I notice that our event is titled 'Poles Apart'. For some reason I'd thought it was only about Antarctic travel, so, wearily, I must readjust the opening as well as finish the thing.

Catch the one o'clock train from Paddington.

Driven into Hay. Meet Daniel Snowman, who could hardly be anything other than an expert on Polar travel, and Beryl Bainbridge, a little nervous. At half past five she orders a large scotch with water – I follow her example.

Freddie Raphael is waiting to give his six o'clock writers' class, but Bernice Rubens bounces in announcing, without seeing him, 'They can't fill up Freddie Raphael's talk for love nor money.' I shush her just in time, but Beryl, bless her, has not noticed and blurts out 'So no-one's going to Freddie Raphael then?'

'Poles Apart' has attracted 900 people, and was the first of all the events to sell out.

We're driven to a tent in the middle of a field. Mud-gouged tracks make our car slither about, but there's a fine view of Hay on its ridge.

The event goes very well. The wind slaps the tent in a very passable imitation of Antarctic conditions, so I feel at home.

Though fearing I would be a lamb slaughtered by wolf-ish experts, I seem to know an awful lot about the place when I put my mind to it.

Wednesday, June 2nd

George H rings ... 'George here ...' he drawls '... Giorgio Armani of Henley.' He tells me that HandMade Films has finally ceased to be. He and Denis O'Brien have had a big falling-out.

George says he theoretically owes £28 million now.

He laughs about it, a little grimly perhaps, but it's clear he's been going through a tough time.

The HandMade Film catalogue – comprising most of our works – is to be put up for sale. He wants to let us know this in advance – just in case, I suppose, we can find the money to buy it. Trouble is our films tend to be the gems of the catalogue and we'd have to buy a lot of dead wood as well, to get at them.

Wednesday, June 9th

Work on my speech to launch Enviroscope tomorrow. Maybe it's the tremendously muggy heat, but I feel quite grumpy at having my time taken up with this Wildlife Trust project. I don't like the name Enviroscope. It looks extraordinarily confused and complicated in practice; I've not been adequately briefed, and Kath is critical of the vast amount of paper this so-called environmental organisation pumps her way.

Thursday, June 10th

Down to the Enviroscope launch. First a photocall in Hyde Park.

A group of well-spoken, healthy-looking schoolchildren from Thame, photographers, and a bevy of reporters. But nothing like the response to the Stammering launch. I think people have been numbed by endless environmental initiatives. Some men in suits from Heinz, who have put money into the production of the Enviroscope pack – which actually looks quite fun – a sort of I-Spy. The youth 'arm' of the Wildlife Trusts Partnership is called, a little sinisterly, 'Watch'.

Most of the time spent signing autographs for the children. I like them, they're bright, but not knowingly clever. At one point the photographer suggests I hoist a young schoolgirl onto my shoulder. Nowadays, of course, this is not at all the correct thing to do. But I do it all the same. Hope she isn't traumatised for life.

Then we troop across to the sombre surroundings of the Royal Geographical Society.

Robert Falcon Scott stares at me from the other end of the room as I take my place at a long table and make one of four speeches. Tell the audience (of 20–30 people) that Enviroscope is not a painful medical instrument. No applause to any of the speeches – but then they are the press.

Back to the office.

Read 'Open Verdict', a script sent to me from Jon Blair. I'm offered the character of a businessman in Hong Kong who sets out to find the reasons behind his 21-year-old daughter's suicide back in England.

Seemed conventional to start with but as I read on I became drawn into the story, largely because it avoided cliché and sensational revelation and generally rang true as a tale of compromises, inadequacies and little mistakes rather than big crises. No underlining of good or bad, hero and villain – but managing to keep the excitement that comes from nothing more than the human predicament.

Decide to think about it over the weekend – the first serious consideration of an acting role since JC decided to begin work on 'Death Fish Zoo'.

Out in the evening to Will Wyatt's BBC Writers' Party, held this evening at the Mall Galleries. From the top of a flight of steps I look down over a sea of hot writers. Will makes a speech. Les Dawson has just died. 'Just my luck,' muses Ian Davidson, when I catch up with him. 'I've just signed a contract for his new series.'

Monday, June 14th

In the evening to the Finnish Embassy in a corner of Belgrave Square for a sauna party to which I was invited, along with Jeremy Paxman (who cancels at the last minute).

Met by a harassed, rather browbeaten Finn, who is head of Public Affairs. He admits me, with many keys and many security locks, to a basement room – table, chairs, massive television screen and two men with the build and slightly seedy worldliness of blue-film actors. One is from a prominent Finnish paper and the other a German from *Die Welt*.

The German is most voluble. I ask him what the German status symbols are nowadays – 'Oh, probably, an abandoned Trabant in the garden.' He is critical of the way Germans travel 'always in groups', and resorts to speaking Swedish when there are too many of his countrymen around.

We sit and sweat, then drink some beer and take some refreshment, talk, wrapped in towels, then another session. The beer is weak and the conversation civilised. It's far from being an orgy.

Out into Belgrave Square about eleven o'clock. Rainer promises to send me an invitation to his crayfish and vodka party!

Realise how much I've enjoyed being the only Englishman in the group tonight and how much I enjoy hearing foreigners talk about the world.

Wednesday, June 16th

To Oxford to attend the Pitt Rivers Museum celebration for Wilfred Thesiger.

The traffic snarled up right along Westway from the flyover almost to the Polish War Memorial.

By the time I reach Pitt Rivers the speeches are under way. I'm thrust into TV interviews beside mammoth skeletons, and photographs with Thesiger himself.

Thesiger, with his superbly ridged aquiline features, is being pushed around as well, and the two of us are brought together, blinking in confusion before some display board, beamed at by a gawping crowd. Very uncomfortable.

Thesiger shows me the goatskin bag in which he kept his camera. He started with a Leica, went on to a Lutz. The photographs (25,000 of them) which he has presented to the museum are magnificent. Black and white, clean, clear, strikingly powerful images. Nothing seems random – every study is a little work of art in itself.

Then I'm moved on to the President's Lodgings at Magdalen where Thesiger is staying before returning to Kenya next week.

We're invited upstairs to the Old Library to see maps drawn by T. E. Lawrence.

Thesiger examines the text through a magnifying glass. We're also given a glimpse of the oldest handwritten book in existence in Britain – by William of Malmesbury, 12th century. Someone tries to get a learned discussion going as to whether a manuscript can be a book.

A chance to talk to Thesiger without the pressures of celebrity. He doesn't think such a journey as his [across the Empty Quarter of Saudi Arabia] could be done nowadays – all the Bedouins have pick-up trucks. I ask him about his health on these trips. He claims to have eaten everything put in front of him and drunk from wells and locally filled flasks and never to have suffered any problems.

Thursday, June 17th

To Feltham, to present my *Pole to Pole* talk at what used to be the Borstal there, but is now signposted as the Young Offenders' Institution.

The entrance is newish, red-brick, trying not to be daunting, but by the time you've been through three pairs of security doors – one locked before the other can be opened – and smelt the slightly musty bitterness in the air, you know you are in an institution. Two 15-foot-high fences topped with razor wire and separated by a 'dead area' – treated so that no cover can grow – surround an otherwise quite pleasant, campus-like arrangement of 'houses' and wide stretches of grass. The houses are called after birds – so there are men behind bars in Albatross or Lapwing.

Tea with the Governor, Joe Whitty. He's blunt, opinionated, but basically decent, I think. Reminds me of John Prescott; and in fact both served their time in the Merchant Navy.

Whitty and his deputy have just returned from Kentucky, where he found much to envy. Only 46 maximum in each institution – almost one to one with warders. Here he has 800 (500 on remand, 300 convicted) and 270 warders. In Kentucky they needed no fences or razor wire and, unlike Britain, sentences could be reduced by good behaviour at regular intervals, if there was a prison officer able to speak up for the offender. This gave incentive for the offender to better himself rather than, as Whitty put it, 'sit around all day with dirty books and the television'.

Our English penal system does sound very primitive. Still geared to giving everyone involved a bad time.

Meet some of the inmates. Nearly all working-class, about 50% black. Most were friendly, very little hostility. Confusion, resignation, listlessness.

Overall impression is of waste – waste of human potential – the indescribably depressing feeling of lines of communication being shut off – clanging shut like the barred cell doors they can't disguise here.

As I leave a boy calls out to me from the slit window of his cell. He thrusts a copy of *Pole to Pole* through the bars for me to autograph.

Friday, July 2nd

Lunch with Robert Fox, Pugh and our newest candidate for Stephen Febble – Richard Wilson – now a considerable 'oldie' star from *One Foot in the Grave*.

Wilson is quiet to start with, not over-eager – but I think genuinely likes the work. 'It's a very good first play,' he says, carefully; then realising just what he's said, adds, rather less carefully, 'It's a very good *second* play.'

After a cautious, not altogether comfortable few minutes fencing around his enthusiasm for the script and our enthusiasm for him, Richard appears to have a very difficult thing to say. It turns out that he feels the play is too tough and concentrated a piece to be played more than once a day ... 'It's a long journey,' he says – the only bit of luvvie-speak from him all lunchtime.

I'm not quite sure where we are at the end. Does he or doesn't he want to do it?

Taxi to the zoo, where I meet Cleese and Co. in the small mammal house. John is taking Robert Lindsay, Robert Young, Iain Johnstone and various children round the small mammal and insect houses. His hope is that Lindsay will play the small-mammal keeper and I will be, as had always been planned between him and me, in charge of the insects – or invertebrates.

We are allowed into the bat enclosures in the nocturnal areas. A cloud of fruit bats dart and dive around us, full of curiosity, but always just missing contact.

Friday, July 23rd

Down to Waterloo for a day 'auditioning' landladies in the Isle of Wight. My first close look at the new Eurostar platforms – inside a glass-and-steel-sheathed shed designed by Grimshaw. Quite splendid – a stirring piece of design and engineering made attractive without gimmicks. It blends well with the existing Waterloo complex and has a sweep and grandeur which harks back to Barlow's St Pancras. Concrete cut down to a minimum, steel tresses and ribs take the weight.

Meet the indefatigable Robyn, our location manager, and Roger Mills, our director, and onto the 9.32 to Southampton.

First landlady, Miss Wright, is in her 80s, runs the small terraced house without help and clearly is very fussy about whom she likes and doesn't like. She puts on a tape for us in the little back room she calls her 'kennel'. 'Do we like Patsy Cline?'

She then, under Roger's smooth and scalpel-like probing, tells us that her life has been 'marred by tragedy'. The man she was to marry died when both of his lungs collapsed, only days before the wedding. Her father had some problem with a vein in his leg ... 'then one day, just after he'd taken my mother some tea, he sat down to tie up his shoelace and his vein burst ... you know that blood can drain out of the human body in two minutes'. We sit, fascinated, but appalled... 'My mother had to walk to him, through blood.'

Robyn suggests we go for a different landlady each week, instead of one for the series. The more we talk the better this idea seems.

Last landlady is Wendy – an Islander, wry, bright and down-to-earth. Her place is more isolated but kept immaculately and the single room I would have has a view of the Needles.

It's sunny and warm when we return to Cowes to catch the five o'clock boat back to what they all call 'the Mainland'.

Home soon after eleven, greeted by Rachel with the news that Will has passed out of Oxford with a 2:1 degree. Great relief, tremendous news. All the weariness of the day disappears.

Thursday, August 5th

A recce day in the Isle of Wight.

To lunch with Peter Hurst, the editor of the paper I shall be writing for, the *Isle of Wight County Press*. We meet at a small Georgian house hotel with a view across the bush-bordered, nicely irregular lawns to the River Medina, and on the hill above it the long, hard angles of Parkhurst Prison.

Peter wears a well-cut suit and sports thick, well-groomed silvery-grey hair. The editorship sounds a comfortable and prestigious post which enables him to play golf and be respected and quite powerful in a community of 125,000 people. It's produced from well-equipped new offices in the centre of Ryde by a staff of 90 people.

As one of the biggest stories this week is the charging of 150 people with parking offences, one could be forgiven for thinking that the *Isle of Wight*

County Press must be a front for the CIA or possibly some American evangelical group. The image is clean, efficient, and rather dull.

We meet our next landlady in Victoria Street, Sandown. She's likeable, but the place looks like everything my taste – cultural, gastronomic, aesthetic – has fled from. We'll see. Rog, I think, is aware of my disappointment and reminds me, robustly, that it was my idea to go into bedsits.

As I drive back across the island I feel a little better. I must be philosophical about this. If the series is to be different, to have an edge, then it can't just be me sitting around with the *Good Hotel Guide*. I must lie back on the nylon sheets and think of Meridian.

The train back is slow, and has no buffet. Fifteen stops, at one of which a little bevy of BR staff spot an unaccompanied bag. They feel it, squeezing gently. 'Well if it goes bang, it goes bang,' says one of them, which makes us all feel better.

Wednesday, August 18th: London–Isle of Wight

I went to bed quite relaxed about the prospect of *Palin's Column*, but something keeps me awake for much of the night.

Palin's Column is all about personal exposure – in front of camera as actor, with people as interviewer and with the added emphasis on writing as the raison d'être of each programme. So, although it is only the Isle of Wight, my subconscious is readying me – making me alert, forcing me to concentrate, making sure I know that whatever I've done before doesn't make a scrap of difference – from the moment I stand before the camera for the first time today I shall be judged all over again.

A grindingly hard first day – besides getting used to a new place and new crew, we shoot in and around Newport, which is full of holidaymakers all agog. 'Round the Isle of Wight in 80 Days, Michael?' Laughter. On to the next.

Then out to a crowded beach to interview and follow an obsessive fossil collector. Despite the fact that he walks us out across a usually submerged petrified forest off the south-west coast and raves about the tide being further out than at any time this year, I cannot raise much interest in the fossils and the filming in his cluttered council house is a real ordeal.

But energy is still required for 'the arrival at Miss Wright's'. Because our opening day has been so long and because we had to eat on the way home from the south of the island, Roger and I are not delivered to Seaview until almost 11.30. Miss Wright understandably a bit distressed.

And she forbids either of us to have a bath 'at this time of night'!

Saturday, August 21st: Isle of Wight

According to Roger, Miss W calls me Fairy Feet. We are now allowed to call her Dorothy. Yesterday morning we filmed a scene in which I offered to stand her the stake money for a bet – she chose two horses and I went into Ryde and put the bet on.

Halfway through breakfast, with Rog and me weighing up chances of our teams in this afternoon's football, she comes up and gives me a smacking kiss. Her horses came one and two.

Like all old women she's obsessed by money, and throughout the morning she alternates between trying to work out how much she's owed by the bookie and how much I owe her for my two telephone calls. Then it's discovered that a cold tap has been left running and, though it produces hardly more than a steady drip, she says she'll 'kill me'.

At lunchtime we make our way to the Ryde Inshore Rescue HQ in preparation for the Trans-Solent Swim. As it turns out this is another case of something I don't want to do becoming one of the best things I've done. It's well organised, the sun pokes out for quite long spells, and as soon as I see our first swimmer plunge in and come up doing breaststroke I know that perhaps I won't make a fool of myself after all.

My turn comes in what I'm advised is the coldest stretch of the crossing, almost in the middle of the Solent. Our opponents are well ahead, so I don't feel I have to win anything, but the water is getting choppier and there is a lot of traffic building up. In I go (on film) and swim for over 20 minutes.

The only vaguely frightening moment was when my support boat hared off to pick up the last swimmer, leaving me alone, feeling very vulnerable in the face of an advancing hovercraft.

Tuesday, August 24th: Isle of Wight

We rendezvous at the *County Press* office.

The column is handed in and after lunch Peter and I are filmed looking it through.

Wednesday, August 25th: Isle of Wight–London

Into Ryde to interview a police spokesman about black magic, etc. He's not been helpful thus far. But Roger persevered with him and today, in Newport, when I asked him the question 'Who runs the Isle of Wight?', he nodded across the road to the Town Hall. 'Those bozos in there may think they run it, but if you want to see who runs the Isle of Wight, go to the County Club in Newport and the Masonic Lodge in Shanklin.' Freemasonry is strong here, he confirms. Parkhurst is full of 'people the police stitched up'. He's refreshing stuff after the cagey, non-committal editor.

Thursday, August 26th

After breakfast, work through letters, make a phone call to Tom P to ask him if he's interested in writing some music for *Palin's Column*. It's something I'd already discussed with Roger. There is such a tiny amount of money in the budget that we could not afford any established name and would have to have relied on library music. Tom has the equipment, and I hope the ability, without the price. It would be very good experience for him.

Good news from David Pugh – Richard Wilson has signed up for *The Weekend*.

Wednesday, September 1st

Tumble out of bed at 7.20. The dreaded man from Corian kitchen worktops is our early-morning guest today, and H warns me that he will undoubtedly get some of the way up my nose. She's right, well, quite spectacularly right. He arrives 25 minutes early, before I've had time to break the day in with a cup of tea or a glass of orange juice, and causes immediate disruption.

He is a Python character – usually played by Eric Idle with a nasal voice, a jarring egocentricity and an unerring ability to put backs up. 'Name by name, but not by nature.'

I'm 'Michael', straight away. 'Is this a rest period for you, Michael?'

'Is my little man here to turn the gas off?' I tell him that he will be here at eight. 'Oh, these London boys, they don't know what work is.'

So it goes on ... 'D'you mind if I smoke? A cigarette and a couple of drinks and I'm happy.' Yes, but who else is, I long to say.

Saturday, September 4th

My definition of having time to myself is to be able to pick up a book which I don't have to pick up – to read something which I don't have to read. Simon has sent me his copy of *Borrowed Time* and I'm learning a lot about my teenage hero Bobby D. He chose the name 'Darin' from the faulty neon sign of a

Mandarin Chinese restaurant in New York. He doesn't sound an awfully easy man. He had a goal – to be rich and famous and successful by 25 years old. And he achieved it. What is my goal? Did I ever have one? I don't think so. I rarely ever made plans more than two years ahead.

Monday, September 6th

TG persuades me to go to a live reappearance of Pete and Dud, as Derek and Clive, at a Working Men's Club in Kensal Road.

There are photographers clustering round the door of the club in what has always been a rough borderland between Maida Vale and Ladbroke Grove. Upstairs to a crowded room with a stage at one end and camera crews, lights shining like Cyclops, moving about picking off celebrities.

Bodies jostle up against us – Peter, a much slenderer figure than the one who went through our sitting room door. I'm told JC put him onto his private trainer.

Bubbling with good cheer and looking like a couple of naughty schoolboys, Keith Richards and Ronnie Wood greet TG and me with great warmth as if they'd just met lifetime heroes. Very odd. I remember telling Keith he should be Alistair Cooke's replacement on *Letter from America*, but not a lot else.

It's a good, old-fashioned, boozy evening and we all regress to our '60s behaviour. Keith and Ronnie, adept at crowd avoidance, get themselves and select others invited downstairs to the rather plush bar and lounge where the working men sit sipping their beer. Some seem happy with the intrusion, others sit close to their pints whilst Keith and Ronnie chat them up.

Pete and Dud, as far as I could tell, never performed, though Peter did occasionally leave the bar and reappear, claiming they'd done 'another nine and a half seconds'.

Tuesday, September 7th

To the Lingfield at five for squash with Terry J, who leaves in a week for the first of his *Crusades* filming trips.

We part on Rosslyn Hill with a hug – me to the Isle of Wight, Terry to Turkey. Back home I have to pack. The house is still in bandages – the smell of paint hangs in the air. Quick supper as another meeting is still to come.

At nine o'clock David Pugh and Billy and Richard Wilson pick their way over the black plastic sheeting in the hallway. Drink wine and discuss direct-ors. Richard W keeps mentioning my name as a possible – or as a double-act with him, and by the end of the two-hour meeting, when all the other names become a blur (Blakemore not available), it seems to have some sense to it. But no decisions taken.

Wednesday, September 8th: Bembridge, Isle of Wight

Met by Roger and Sally at Fishbourne. Settle ourselves in on the converted Second World War gunboat, which is now painted, bedecked with flowers and sits, the smartest of a line of veteran auxiliary craft quietly rotting on Bembridge Bay.

The top deck is light and airy. My cabin below is tiny and I keep cracking my skull on low beams as I unpack. There is one loo/bathroom amongst us all. The owner is a perky Brummie and it costs £15.00 a night B&B. It's called the Floatel Xoron.

Friday, September 10th: Bembridge

I sleep long and deeply. The creaks of the old timbers don't bother me at all, nor did I hear the rain that apparently fell heavily.

This morning we're taking Dorothy Wright for a coach trip.

We take her on a paddle-steamer trip down the coast. Long walk to the end of Sandown Pier.

I'm trying to remain calm whilst escorting her at a snail's pace and being frequently approached by autograph hunters. I sign rather tight-lipped for one boy, but his mother is very happy – 'Val Doonican was just bloody rude.'

We all eat a cream tea at Godshill, then on to film a spiritualist meeting in Ventnor.

The meeting is another first for me as I've never ever directly experienced what goes on behind the doors of a spiritualist church. It's a little disappointing. The medium is a popular, cheeky son of the Midlands, an ex-jockey who learnt that he had 'powers' after a serious fall which nearly ended his life. The hall is packed, not with impressionable old ladies but with impressionable people of all ages (there is one family with young daughters) and all walks of life.

Mark the medium sets about introducing people from beyond to people present. Many attempts sounded unconvincing – 'Venice means something to you right? ... Vienna? ... No, we can't settle for that. Psychics might but we can't (laughter). I see anemones next to you ... d'you like them?' Most people try to be helpful and he himself is unfailingly bright and optimistic. Little pain seems to come through and absolutely no recrimination, only reassuring little messages about looking after the garden and eating a balanced diet.

He picks me out at one point. 'I see a little boy called Brian ... does the name Brian mean anything to you?'

Monday, September 13th: Bembridge

A wild night, rain and wind. Roger knocks at seven to say my sailing sequence is off.

Lunch at a wonderful café beside Bembridge lifeboat station – multi-coloured Formica table tops and home-made crab sandwiches. *East of Ipswich*, Southwold in the '50s.

The gale blows fiercer as the afternoon goes on, providing a dramatic barrage of sound behind our afternoon interview in the lifeboat shed.

Quick drink afterwards in a pub full of wild, long-haired alternative lifestylers. 'Best marijuana in the island here,' shouts one of them as we leave.

Tuesday, September 14th: Bembridge

Roger knocks at seven. Sailing is on for nine o'clock.

Into *Blue Jay II*, a Bembridge scow – a tough, broad-bottomed, clinker-built sailing boat. The wind is still brisk but has turned from the exposed east to the slightly less exposed north. The rain has stopped.

Well covered against the weather, my instructor Victoria and I bob around. For about half an hour she supervises as I learn to tack and turn. It's impossible to head straight out of the harbour today as the wind is blowing us back in, so manoeuvres are of the essence and, with a quick wind, quick reflexes are necessary.

Roger, filming from a sandy spit, asks if I will now go solo. Apprehensive but unexpectedly carefree, I agree to have a go. Victoria is taken off and I'm on my own. The waves are now quite sharp and after one good turn I fly across the harbour so briskly that I hang on, pulling in the sail tight. The little scow stands almost on its side. Realise that it's filling with water in these unforgiving waves. Pull tighter, lean back, but still it rises as if to capsize. Within a minute there is so much water sloshing about the boat that I'm worried if I shall get out of this. Make another turn, more wind, more tight sail, more water.

At last I give in and call over Vernon, the boat's owner, and Victoria, only just in time to stop it from sinking. Quite a dramatic minute or two as rudder and tiller float away to be picked up by a support craft and the three of us drag the almost helpless (and highly expensive) little boat to shore, and empty out the water.

Roger and the others applaud me; Vernon thought I was deliberately sailing spectacularly, but I feel rather a fool. All of my incompetence, of course, is faithfully captured in sound and vision.

Friday, September 17th

At the house Hamish and the building team are rushing round like head-less chickens cleaning up after another week of 'finishing' and before going to Prominent for a party and showing of *Riff-Raff* that I've laid on for them.

Film screening for 22 people. Realise as the film progresses that all of us in there approach it from different ways and I'm not exactly certain whether all the builders enjoy it. Feel doubts suddenly – is Ken Loach, despite his working-class sympathies, still producing a patronising left-wing, middle-class view of the masses? Does anyone want to identify with the exploited – are Clive's boys at all embarrassed at being thought to be working-class? All I can tell is that the ones who laugh most are those who are the most comfortably off.

Leave them all at ten to nine and whizz down to Vasco and Piero's. H and I entertain Julian Schlossberg and his latest flame – a lady called Merron. Rather striking, with long ash-blonde hair and a pale, thin face. Turns out she is a psychic.

He's directing three short plays he's commissioned from Woody Allen, David Mamet and another. Says that I must meet Barbra Streisand – she's good company, unlike her big-screen persona, and anxious to make my acquaintance!

Saturday, September 18th

Begin the first movement of box files from my dusty eyrie to a more per-manent, less airy, but hopefully infinitely more capacious area – library and workroom combined. The first file to go up is Python, Series 1, 1969.

JC and Alyce Faye come round, in Alyce Faye's wide Mercedes 230 with the hood down.

JC is about to do a week's filming in *Frankenstein* for Ken Branagh. John claims he's only doing it so he can be stabbed to death by Robert De Niro – I remind him that my death in *Brazil* was also at the superstar's hands!

Alyce Faye has just heard 'Always Look on the Bright Side' being played at a Conservative Party Conference and is rooting around for Eric's phone number so she can leave a message on his machine.

Out to Odette's. John is on one of those diets only he seems to find which allow him to eat almost anything in large quantities. Says he's very close to finishing the first third of the latest 'Death Fish' script, but that my character, Bugsy, fades out a bit and will need to be looked at. He's leaving the UK in the winter, he thinks, and going to California and Hong Kong and points beyond for three months.

Wednesday, September 22nd

'I have Sir David Frost for you,' says a voice on the other end of the phone and after a brief pause the ebullient tones of the Great Man fill the earpiece. David always sounds like a man who's enjoying what he's doing. I haven't detected a moment's self-doubt since that call in the spring of 1969 when a rather anxious Frostie tried to grill me about what he regarded as the defection of JC and Graham from his production company, Paradine, to Python. In short, why were we not doing Python with him?

Sir D wonders if I would be interested in a series of programmes about the parliamentary process which he's putting together next spring. In one of them he would like to have me experience the election process first-hand. Not sure how to say no (as it's quite an idea), but David is sowing the seed, that's all. 'If you fancy running for Parliament just give me a ring,' he bubbles.

Sunday, September 26th

Out to Cibo for their fourth anniversary party. Apparently they give a party at the end of every year to celebrate with and thank their favourite customers. We're on a table already occupied by the Cleeses and Michael Winner and Jenny Seagrove.

Winner has just come back from Dublin, which he loves. (He either loves or loathes things, there seems no in-between.) He and Jenny had lunch at Claridge's, which he loves ... 'I was brought up there.' He smoked a big cigar, drank sparingly and was very complimentary about the journeys – 'your walkin' programmes', as he referred to them.

Monday, September 27th

Write a letter to JC to apologise for calling Paddy Ashdown 'meretricious' at dinner last night. Well, not to apologise but to explain why I accepted the words he put in my mouth. I know John cares about these things, but after a long day's entertaining I didn't have much concentration left for political discussions. John, I know, regards me as woolly in this area and I usually try and avoid politics with him, except in the most general terms.

Lunch with Travers Reid at the Overseas League – extremely well-situated club beside the Ritz with gardens bordering St James's Park and a room with bath costing less than £100 a day. Travers, who evidently started the Perfect Pizza chain – country's first takeaway pizza service – wants to know if I will do 'An Evening With' to help Stammering Centre funds. It's become a victim of its own success with 150 families currently waiting for assessment. I promise to help.

Sunday, October 3rd: Ventnor, Isle of Wight

Everywhere we set up the camera people come to talk to me. A simple shot at a telephone box in Ventnor – at nine a.m.! – becomes a distinct effort as I'm besieged by a coach party from Leicester.

All in all, by the time I've driven over to Freshwater Bay to attend a harvest festival at St Agnes Church, I just want to be ignored. Impossible. Little taps on the car window from people asking favours, and a congregation waiting to see me.

At Blackgang Chine a conker festival has been organised. More poking and prodding as I sit waiting in the car. 'You were supposed to be here at eleven ... can you sign to Susan? ... ooh look, he's got his own pen.'

I'm very near breaking point. I'm not in favour of filming the conker championship. I have a sixth sense that it will be a publicity stunt in which I shall be the bait.

Failed miserably to hit my opponent's conker and hoped only that the earth would open up beneath me.

Monday, October 4th: Ventnor

This morning I'm much more on top of things. We drive back to Ventnor to film around the Botanical Gardens – meet Simon Goodenough – the engaging, enthusiastic director who plays Baroque music in the Temperate House because he believes that plants grow better in a conducive atmosphere. He's a feet-on-the-ground dreamer, devoted to his gardens and his plants but with a much wider and non-parochial interest. After a fluent interview, I tell him he ought to do this himself. He's a natural communicator. He could be the Keith Floyd of gardening.

Then suddenly, as a result of five days of Herculean effort, we are finished. I complete my column and read it to Rog over a couple of pints before supper. He's complimentary and I'm relieved. A 2,000-word column and a half-hour programme in five days isn't bad.

Tuesday, October 5th: Isle of Wight–London

Home just after twelve to be told that there is a story on page three of the *Sun* about my cheating at conkers on the Isle of Wight. It seems that the misbegotten episode is not altogether behind me and that Simon Dabell, entrepreneur organiser of the festival and the man who owns a theme park that is slowly slipping into the sea, has manufactured a tale of my disqualification and sent it to the *Sun*.

This prompts a solicitous enquiry from Peter Cook on the answerphone, full of mock concern over the conker story and had I taken leave of my senses? Damage like this not easy to repair – sort of stuff. Within half an hour of my return the *Evening Standard* has picked up the story and rung me for comment.

Friday, October 8th

Ring Eric, he's just packing for a trip to the USA. He and I discuss 'The Adventure'. His view is that I have to set the running by deciding what I want to do with it – and exactly how I want to be part of it. Neither Eric nor myself very keen on directing.

To dinner with Richard Wilson at the latest restaurant on the Keats site. Richard told me it was called Beth's and was run by Fay Maschler's sister (he has an endearing habit of getting names wrong – Downshire Hill becomes Devonshire Hill, Fay Maschler becomes Fay Mailer).

The restaurant is actually called Byron's. They chose the name because of the large, ornate 'B' which hangs outside. 'It had to be a name beginning with B.'

What I could not believe is that Richard has the old script. He has been reading the one without the final scene and without substantial cuts in some of the speeches. Unbelievable. I read him the new last scene at table. He likes it. Richard Eyre is interested in directing – so that decision remains in the balance.

Wednesday, October 13th

Clem arrives to talk about a route for the Pacific project in greater detail. Almost immediately the phone rings – whether it's filing cabinets or alternate cries of help to BT to restore my fax line, or the Miele engineer, or Rab cutting through wires and pipes downstairs, or Nigel scattering paint shavings all over the garden where he thinks we can't see – it is a morning of classic Palin house activity.

Clem sits stoically beside the map and when we do get to talk about the route, the possibilities are beguiling and exciting. It's like planning the world's most wonderful holiday – at this stage anyway. We have five programmes on the western side of the Pacific alone.

To Odette's and lunch and a gossip with Terry G.

'Defective Tec' is, with current rewrites, before the studio heads – with Bill Murray hopefully linked to it. TG thinks JC has been tempted into the Hollywood Butler Syndrome – playing opposite Macaulay Culkin. Hollywood's Joel Silver estimates the casting to be worth 200 million box office and apparently JC will, if he signs, make up to two million! This, TG feels, is real reason why 'Death Fish II' has been postponed.

Thursday, October 14th: London–Isle of Wight

Go over the schedule for our last five hectic days. Tomorrow is perhaps the trickiest day of all – a visit to Parkhurst Prison from which Roger hopes to gather enough material for one half of the show.

To bed, but a broken and disoriented sleep. Never quite sure where I am, or what time of the night it is. Roger's pipe smoke drifts along the carpeted passageway and under my door.

Friday, October 15th: Isle of Wight

At Parkhurst by eight. The Governor, John Marriott, accompanies us round the prison. He is an energetic extrovert, full of expansive hand gestures, jokes, but beneath it all deadly serious about his co-operative rather than coercive approach. A thatch of white hair, a bright red tie, a loud, grunting, braying laugh.

Apart from the IRA prisoners, he allows us to meet, and if the 'inmates' consent, to film, anyone. Indeed we visit the high-security Category A prisoners first. These are murderers, considered to be among the 60 most dangerous men in the kingdom and most of them here for life.

Suddenly I'm in amongst them, in a workshop, and they're shaking my hand and asking me when I'm going to make another of my programmes.

I cannot really comprehend the evil and the violence – because here, now, it's rarely manifest. Only once in the day do I notice a moment of nastiness, and that wasn't much more than a gesture.

At the end of the afternoon I'm 'banged up' in a cell in order to get the feel of the isolation that is twelve and a half hours of every man's 24. Roger and I have planned that I should do a sort of summary of my feelings alone with the video camera – and segue into a summary of my feelings about leaving the IOW after four weeks.

We finish after almost eight hours' continuous filming. All of us rose to the occasion – any tiredness evaporated once we got going. We have shot enough for a whole programme.

In the evening over to Marriott's house in Brightstone for dinner.

It's an old, messy, lived-in, friendly house. Candles, log fire, chaotic family atmosphere, vegetarian food and some extraordinary tales of prison life – the man who changed his name by deed poll to Charles Bronson, the last escape from Parkhurst – Reg Pewter, who got out in the laundry and rang Marriott from Australia.

Tuesday, October 19th

Anne has had a very good meeting with Clem and Paul Hamann this a.m. Paul delighted to receive news that a Pacific project is going ahead. Of course the BBC would like me to start a year earlier. Five years is a long time to wait, they say, between Palin travel spectaculars.

Good news too from D. Pugh. Robin Lefevre[1] – much admired by A Bleasdale and D Molloy – loves *The Weekend* and wants to direct it. So, as one project begins to recede into the past, others are today given strong forward momentum.

Sunday, October 24th

I come to 'Death Fish 2', first draft. Though very funny at times, seems to suffer from the icy hand of good old Cambridge intellectual detachment – people talk and speak because they are the mouthpieces of an argument. My

---

1 Robin Lefevre, theatre director, whose work includes the Alan Bleasdale musical *Are You Lonesome Tonight?* (1985).

character, Bugsy, could be good, but for my mind there are almost too many keepers.

Monday, October 25th

The news from Northern Ireland is back to its worst – ten people killed in a fish shop in the Shankill Road. Oddly enough I was running through the transmission tape of the railway journey yesterday and there is a brief glimpse of the Shankill Road and Ivor Oswald is talking, drawing up at a pedestrian crossing. Look at my *Independent on Sunday* and there is the crossing on the front page. Right beside it is the blasted remains of the fish shop.

Sunday, October 31st

A message that Angela Thorne[1] loves the script of 'Weekend' and wants to do it. This is one project that does seem to be leaping ahead.

Tuesday, November 2nd

Meet with Pugh and Lefevre at The Union to discuss the script. David is wonderfully supportive or uncritical – whichever way you look at it. 'I've read the play again, very thoroughly,' he announces, a little ominously ... 'and really, all I can say is ... it's wonderful.' Robin nods, his dark brow and piercing, intense gaze combining in agreement.

As we work our way through the script Robin has queried only a few minor areas. Scenes that I've broken up should be run on, and there is some work to do on the end of Act 1 and the end of the play.

An harmonious session except for financial implications arising from Richard W's decision not to do matinees and his availability for only eleven weeks in the first West End period.

Friday, November 5th

Sunshine as I run – the beams of low sunlight breaking from behind early cloud to illuminate the delights of autumn leaves, in intense shades of yellow,

1 Angela Thorne, actress best known for appearing alongside Peter Bowles and Penelope Keith in the BBC series *To the Manor Born*.

red and brown. In West Meadow a gentle gust of wind causes leaves to fall from a tree as I run by. They're shed vertically, like a shower, accompanied by a whispering rustle.

Help Will prepare a Bonfire Night party – barbecue and mulled wine for about 20 friends. It's a clear, quite warm night – the temperature almost reached 60 today.

Will's friend Chris works at the Dept of Transport and we talk about the rail privatisation. No single line can ever pay for itself – so any bidder will have to receive government subsidy. So why the expense of changing what's happening already? He can only come out with something rather unconvincing about BR not putting the traveller's needs first.

Monday, November 8th

Out, mid-morning, to lunch with my cousin Judy Greenwood apropos of decoration/furniture for the house. Go via Cleese's to have a quick chat about my reactions to 'Death Fish 2' before I go away.

Arrive outside No. 82. Grin manically into the video security camera, largely for Alyce Faye's benefit, only to be screened by a lady with a foreign accent who doesn't think it's funny. The door swings open. No-one there. Wander into the hall, smiling expectantly as one does when about to meet friends.

A blank-faced young man appears from a side room. Is he one of Alyce Faye's children I don't know about? Is he one of John's new writers? No, it turns out that he is going to 'vacuum the driveway'. An invisible presence at the top of the stairs screams down to us 'You wanna Misser Cleese?' Louder, more impatiently ... 'Hello! I up here – you wanna *Misser Cleese*!'

By now thoroughly disoriented, H and I are told (still by someone we can't see) that we must go to No. 84. As we go, the young man, who isn't a new writer or a son-in-law, gestures to me to move my car so he can clear the leaves.

Eventually we are let into No. 84. A vast staircase stretches ahead. I suddenly remember what all this reminds me of – a fairy story – the entry to a giant's castle. I am Russ Tamblyn in Tom Thumb. I thought our houses were now spacious enough, but compared to this we are still living in a matchbox.

JC shows us around – everything is immaculate, not a gap or a piece of bare wall. One room John regards rather bleakly – it's expensively, luxuriously furnished in New York fin-de-siècle taste, but John cannot remember quite what it's for ... 'We thought we'd better give the designer one room he could just go to town on,' he says before closing the door on it, without much regret.

Tuesday, November 9th

A request from Random House Audiobooks that I read Roald Dahl's auto-biography for them – but what was very nice was that the Dahl estate had asked me to be the reader.

To Pizza Express with Rachel. Paul Foot, wife and son at next table. The *Mirror*, his old paper – the paper that fired him – has sunk pretty low this week, paying £100,000 to the manager of a gymnasium who had secretly installed cameras to take pics of Princess Di exercising. Pretty depressing – that the *Mirror* should be fighting for press freedom with a tawdry, unnecessary endorsement of blatant dishonesty. Foot says the men who run the paper now are morons.

Monday, December 6th

Whilst running this morning, I conceived a plan to write a novel as soon as possible, certainly over the next year. It would be called 'Uganda' and would be about two men, complete opposites, thrown together by the Foreign Service in some distant but photogenic outpost – Uganda. A framework that could hold comedy, travel, sex and malaria. It's the same sort of idea as I came up with in New York for JC and me.

Somehow feel that this next year would suit the writing of a novel – and the production of *The Weekend* has given me a boost of confidence in my writing.

Saturday, December 11th

A short, sharp dose of flu. I lay in bed for most of Wednesday, Thursday and Friday. There was little question of doing anything else. Either my throat ached (this was the first and worst phase of the illness) or my stomach ached or my head ached. Or else they all ached at the same time.

Was heartened in my misery by hearing that *American Friends* is to make its UK TV debut on Christmas Day on BBC Two. Barry Norman's little piece in the *Radio Times* awards it four stars and calls it 'a gem'.

David Blount calls. *The Dresser* is to be repeated this afternoon. In my present state I feel I can listen to it as part of my recuperation!

He wants to know if I'm interested in playing Mole in a radio version of *Wind in the Willows* (A Bennett's adaptation) to be done for Christmas '94. I have a certain reluctance and don't quite know why. I think he takes that as a yes.

Tuesday, December 14th

To the reopening of the London Transport Museum. Escorted into the old Floral Hall in Covent Garden (whose intricate Gothic ironwork upstages any of its exhibits) and shown around like royalty. Photographers snap away at me as I sit next to dummy drivers, various people grab interviews as we move around.

Sir Wilfrid Newton and many of the old directors of LT, including Peter Masefield, arrive.

There are quite a lot of bigwigs and my speech must have ruffled a feather or two with its endorsement of Ken Livingstone and the GLC and its lament for the public service ideals which made London Transport great.

Anyway, it goes better than I could ever have hoped. I am very glad that I threw in a few jokes this morning.

More interviews and photo opportunities then at last home, armed with an old Gibson ticket dispenser as a present.

Monday, December 20th

This morning I rang Geoffrey Strachan and enjoyed very much telling him I wanted to write a novel for him. Anne seems excited; she is cautious about how much of an advance I might get – she reckons she could get half a million easily if it were a travel book tied to TV, but for a first novel, even with my name, she estimates Geoffrey's offer to be around £50,000 based on 25,000 sales.

More important is a schedule. I don't want to be pushed into Christmas '94 publication – but want to have the book finished by the end of the year. There will be quite a lot of research, which I feel could be complete by May.

Tuesday, December 28th

Spend most of the afternoon preparing the Roald Dahl autobiographies which I'm reading on Wednesday and Thursday. There are lots of characters. Dahl's boyishly enthusiastic style sometimes palls, but once he's on a roll – usually describing something dreadfully painful – a beating or an accident – the pages come to life. Hope I can achieve that effect tomorrow.

Wednesday, December 29th

Paul is recording technician – a bit lugubrious, but the atmosphere is pleasantly low-key and I'm able to concentrate on the text. A little tight and tense to begin with – feel my voice being scrutinised, I suppose; then it begins to flow and by half past five we have completed *Boy* and the more reflective *My Year*, which I read almost effortlessly.

Thursday, December 30th

Despite feeling in more energetic form today, I make quite a meal of *Going Solo*. Unlike *My Year*, which was largely prose and recollection at peace, *Going Solo* is full of action stories and Dahl's brisk and wide-eyed enthusiasm for everything and everybody. Occasionally it comes to life easily, but at other times becomes a bit bogged down in aircraft names and details.

A man from Random House is present. He seems callow and very young. Why isn't Will doing something like this, I ask myself.

We finish around six. He (the young man) is complimentary, I think. He said he found my voice 'very hypnotic'. I took him into the story. Blame Dahl's writing for that, I say, though I'm pleased he's pleased – I'm always on the lookout for compliments!

1994

Tuesday, January 4th

To Broadcasting House to take part in a 50-minute prog about Terry Gilliam for Scottish BBC radio. 'If you ever want to talk about yourself for 50 minutes, we'd love to do it,' I'm assured by a voice in Edinburgh.

Meet Michael Barnes in the BH foyer and take him to the Regent Hotel beside Marylebone Station for lunch. He seems the ideal companion to share my first glimpse of the grandly restored hotel – largely because he and I appreciate the significance of its origins as the London face of the Great Central Railway. The Great Central was the last of the northern railway links with London to open, and the first to close.

A central courtyard is now an atrium with soaring columns, eight storeys high, supporting a glass roof. The size and scale is a little intimidating, but the lunch is good and we celebrate our reunion with a glass of champagne.

Michael keeps the bad news to the end. On top of the second bomb blast at the Royal Opera House came news from the Arts Council in Northern Ireland that they thought it was time for him to step down. The administrator, a QC of 'nationalist tendencies', did the deed. Michael faced the realisation that targeting the Opera House was perhaps not as arbitrary as was once thought – it is seen as the cultural flagship of Unionism. Not fair, surely, I said. 'What do they expect you to do, put on *The Plough and the Stars* every week?' 'Well, actually, we *are* doing *The Plough and the Stars* next month,' says Michael, rocking with laughter at the irony of it all.

Last year, he says, ended on the most savage note of all with some suggestion that he relinquishes the Festival as well. It seems, in short, that Michael is being pushed out. Some would say, at last, others, after *all* he's done. I have given him a *Great Railway Journeys* book in which I have thanked him for being 'Mr Belfast'.

On a wet, unfriendly day outside the Regent, we make our farewells, which seem poignant. We nearly always have left with something to celebrate.

Wednesday, January 5th

Across Trafalgar Square and into Uganda House. Not much on the walls but a picture of President Museveni. Beaming smiles. I'm assured I will not need a visa to visit the country.

I ask for a copy of Museveni's book *What Is Africa's Problem?* which is modestly advertised on a noticeboard. Whilst I wait for it to be brought down, I sit and read some of the magazines which are in hard covers, chained to the table. Also chained to the table is a brown folder whose contents are scrawled on the front in marker pen. 'Draft Constitution of the Republic of Uganda'.

Friday, January 7th

To Piccadilly to meet Major Grahame, author of *Amin and Uganda*, at the Cavalry and Guards Club. Feel doors opening onto the novel as I climb the steps and into a pillared lobby. A uniformed man looks up unhelpfully.

Iain Grahame emerges from a reading room. He is pleasant enough but radiates caution and unease. As we sit down in the Ladies' Room on the third floor ('only place you can get tea after five'), he fills me in a little about Uganda, about Amin and tribalism and how the madness happened, as he tucks into fruit cake and sandwiches – toasted teacake, his preference, being off. At the end of an hour he politely moves me downstairs. I think he is less suspicious of me than when we started. He encourages me to ring and talk to him again if I want more help.

Saturday, January 22nd

David Pugh signed up the Strand Theatre yesterday, which is very good news, as it seemed to be everyone's favourite choice. Tickets are rapidly selling out for Guildford and there are plans to set up a national tour in the summer whilst Richard W leaves the show to film another series of *One Foot*. All very positive.

I've suggested that Tom P might be able to provide sound effects and Robin seems to like the idea so have put them both in touch. Also rang Attenborough yesterday. He was just back from Africa 'filming plants', but was tickled by his inclusion in *The Weekend* and very happy to rewrite and record the piece of TV commentary.[1]

Called David Blount and turned down *Wind in the Willows*. He says I've been nominated by BBC Drama for a Sony Award for best radio acting perf in *The Dresser*.

---

1 At one point in the play Stephen Febble turns the television off in disgust, as a voice describes insect copulation in some detail. Very sportingly, David agreed to record it himself.

Monday, January 24th

Sleep well and happily. The daylight offers less comfort. It is drizzling stead-ily, but mild for midwinter. Struggle up and into a tracksuit for my last run before Uganda trip. Rachel smiles tragically at me from the top of the stairs. 'It'll be the last time you can take me,' she appeals. She finishes her job at the government health survey on Friday. I fall for this and run her to Belsize Park Underground – damp, dull streets, disagreeable drivers hurrying to work.

Will's new regime has begun. He was apparently up at 7.20, and running on the Heath. He tells me proudly that 'I nearly killed myself, Dad, I nearly *killed* myself.'

Tuesday, January 25th: Entebbe, Uganda

Squeezed on a small bus with a very nice batch of Americans – adventurous, quite elderly. All on a Museum of Natural History tour. Their leader, a tall, lanky man with a prominent chin and a wide, high forehead like an Imax screen, turns out to be John Heminway, who does a lot of travel progs for American TV and Arts and Entertainment.

We're driven round to the Lake Victoria Hotel.

Lots of staff in lots of different coloured uniforms but I still have to wait nearly two hours for a ham sandwich. Don't object. I order a Tusker beer and talk to a man who is selling educational books in Uganda. He says great improvement in last two years, but infrastructure still very poor. The hotel is clean and well kept and my room has everything working.

Martin Hardy, who helped organise some of the African leg of *Pole to Pole*, introduces me to a young Ugandan, neatly dressed in yellow shirt, green tie and brown jacket, who is called George and is to be my guide over the next two weeks.

I take a swim in the pool, to wake me up after a short night, and then walk, with George, out onto the streets of Entebbe, ending up at the Botanic Gardens.

It may say at the airport 'Pepsi welcomes you to Uganda', but life is very Hardyesque, lived in fields and side roads where houses have chickens and goats and a few crops like cassava outside.

The Botanic Gardens rather melancholy. Few funds for their upkeep and many of the trees look tired and worn. But little pleasures such as a troop of Colobus monkeys, with their long black and white tufted tails, springing gracefully from tree to tree. The crashing and cackling of hornbills and at the lakeside an abundance of sandpipers and hamerkops and terns.

Wednesday, January 26th: Entebbe–Kampala

A Catalina flying boat will leave Entebbe Airport at 9.30 to fly onto the lake, land and collect the Natural History Museum party; I've become, in less than 24 hours, almost an honorary member of the party, and Pierre, the owner of the Catalina, has suggested I might like to fly the short hop from airport to lake before the main group sets off.

So I find myself, with George, climbing into an A&K Land Cruiser to be driven to the flying boat.

On the way out we pass the old airport building with a burnt-out DC-7 beside it – the scene of the Israeli raid in June 1976. Depends who you talk to here. One local says it was an outrage – 'it felt as if the country had been raped'. Others see it as an embarrassment inflicted upon them by Idi Amin's policies.

Pierre, smoking his pipe, greets me and takes me through to the airstrip where the Catalina stands, blue and red and looking very sharp. Pierre goes round with the Pledge and puts finishing touches to the windows. The plane is 50 years old.

As we take off, pulling into the air at 70 knots, I speculate as to whether the white line along the runway could be the Equator. It must be very close. My Michelin map shows it running slap across the low headland on which the airport is situated.

Exciting few minutes as we bank and turn steeply, almost dizzily around the bay, low over the tree cover and clusters of round, thatched huts and finally smack down on the surface of Lake Victoria. No locals can remember a flying boat landing here since the 1940s so there's a small crowd lining the jetty.

The first lot of Americans climb aboard, with difficulty, from a coastguard dinghy.

Farewells and photos and I'm taken back to the jetty.

When they're all aboard, the Catalina roars along the water, but seems unable to take off. She kills her engines and aborts. There's no communication between plane and land save through the control tower at Entebbe, so no-one knows quite what's happening.

After an hour or so, and another two attempts at take-off, the dinghy is commandeered again (its two crew have to be woken from sleep) and Martin H goes out to the stricken plane.

Back at the hotel all is confusion. The pilots blame the heat and the strong swell out on the lake. The Americans, all so excited this morning, have been taken off the Catalina before their journey has begun.

Thursday, January 27th: Kampala

Up in my room, begin to make some contacts. British Council man is in Nai-robi, back tomorrow. The High Commissioner sounds cautious and a touch severe; he cannot meet me until the day I depart Uganda, which is almost two weeks away.

I walk out into Kampala. The city buzzes vigorously. Crowds fill the bro-ken pavements of Kampala Road. Fine, tall, straight-backed women in the traditional 'Busuti' – long, flamboyantly colourful, frilly-shouldered dresses – pick their way over fallen traffic lights and the empty, twisted remains of parking meters. No-one seems to bother about me as I stand in the shade and make notes – they're all too busy.

The bookshops are a little depressing. They all seem tied to religious organ-isations and sell much Sunday School stuff and very little about the country.

Back to the hotel where George is quietly, patiently waiting. We go to lunch – tilapia once again, with rice and matoke.[1] Ask George about himself – for as yet he will neither volunteer personal info nor question me. His surname is Byomuhumuza – which looks formidable on the page but when spoken has a mantra-like rhythm to it. He's from Kabale in the deep south-west, on the border with Rwanda. He's 28.

We decide on a seven-day safari to the west, beginning Monday. Then down to the Rhino Bar to have a drink with two American journalists. Talk about the AIDS epidemic here. Government runs condom campaign, Pope, head of the RC Church to which 49% of the population belong, comes here and forbids them.

A chance offer of a flight on a light plane to the wild, remote north-east of the country is gratefully accepted.

Friday, January 28th: Kampala

Lunch with Zahid Alam, an Asian businessman who stayed here throughout the bad years. In 1972 the Asian community was expelled by Amin (still con-sidered by the Ugandans to be about the only good thing he did). There were 70,000 in the country then. Zahid says there are now 12,000 or 13,000.

We eat at the China Palace. As we eat he talks – Amin seems less of an evil in his mind than Milton Obote. In Obote's second term of government it is conservatively estimated that 300,000 were killed, compared to 100,000 who died under Amin. Zahid's father stayed throughout by keeping a low pro-file. The Nile Hotel, which I can see from my window, was Obote's torture

1 Matoke is a starchy plantain banana.

centre; Amin, according to Zahid, dealt with people at the State Research Bureau behind the Kampala Club, which I can also see.

A trip out of town. Down onto the Kampala Road and left opposite the long, colonial façade of the railway station. Turn off the main road and through landscaped estates of large '30s-style suburban villas, some well kept, but most others sadly dilapidated, with windows broken, drainpipes hanging from walls and gardens left to decay.

An indicator points to 'The Source of The Nile' – surely one of the great signs of the world, beaten only by a second sign beside a metal pole barrier which announces 'Source of The Nile. Entrance Fees'. It costs 3,000 for the vehicle and occupants – about £2.00 – then the pole is raised and we drive down a red murram track to a parking area. From here, steps lead down to the site of the Ripon Falls, which Speke was the first white man to look on, in 1862.

A fisherman waits in his old boat in the lee of an island. It does seem incredible that this should be the start of the same river as flows beside the Cairo Sheraton.

Saturday, January 29th: Kampala–Karamoja

Met at the hotel at 7.15 by Samantha Dunn, she of the Emma Thompson eyes and pilot's stripes on the shoulder, and an Irishwoman called Ann Masterson.

Find myself, as last Wednesday morning, being led through the almost deserted airport building and out onto the tarmac. The Catalina which I flew in three days ago is still there, its defunct starboard engine being dismantled prior to replacement.[1]

Sam taxis the Cessna and we take off at nine o'clock.

The gentle green hills of the Lake Victoria littoral gradually give way to great swathes of papyrus swamp on the eastern corner of Lake Kyoga, then to patchy grassland – much of it scarred by burning – and finally into semi-desert. This is Karamoja – an area which has still to be 'subdued' by the government and which the UN still don't consider safe enough to operate in.

The runway is an earth strip with a hut beside it. Even the wind sock has gone. Sam grins. 'Someone's probably wearing it.'

Karamojong youths with a single striped cloth draped over one shoulder stand nearby – holding spears. A group of naked children rush out to watch us disembark. An old man who looks as if he has a cataract shuffles up. He it is who is paid to look after the plane.

---

[1] None of the Natural History Museum party ever got to fly on the Catalina as a new engine had to be brought out from America some weeks later.

Coffee is made then Ann takes me to see a typical manyatta. The Kara-mojong are a nomadic people – many of the men still walk naked. Central government has never really been able to bring these warlike, cattle-rustling peoples into the administration.

We're shown all the components of the community – an arable area, the ekals, or domestic areas, where families eat and sleep, the area where cattle and calves are kept. When I take notes the children watch fascinatedly.

Women do most of the work here. They build the huts and the fences, they prepare the food and till the ground and sow the seeds. The men seem to sit beneath trees and gossip. They eat meat regularly and don't share it with the women, who eat mainly maize and milk.

It hasn't rained here since last April and water is one of the main topics of any conversation. We visit a borehole nearby and there are tall, graceful men washing and children splashing about and an elder who takes me for someone who knows about water supply. He takes me by the hand to the edge of the borehole drain-off area and bangs on about the hole being in the wrong place.

Sam is anxious to get away before too late. Strong winds are blowing off the mountain and the take-off, as she promises us, is quite hairy. The little plane never reaches more than halfway up the airstrip before winds blow us sideways up and away.

More visual splendours on the way back – not least the long silver Nile, catching the light between grey storm clouds.

Wednesday, February 2nd: Mountains of the Moon Hotel, Fort Portal

Written by torch (between teeth) and candlelight. It's 9.30 at night. I'm on day three of my safari. A mosquito buzzes around.

There is no power in Fort Portal and has not been for three days. This is one of the many colonial hotels fallen on hard times but at least it is operational and the Ugandan flag is raised and lowered every morning.

My candle is burning down – my huge yellow water container waits in the bathroom, there are muted voices and twittering crickets and some noise of cars along a road. Otherwise it's a pleasantly cool night in the tea country at the foothills of the Mountains of the Moon.

Saturday, February 5th: Buhoma Gorilla Camp, Bwindi Impenetrable Forest

It's 6.15 in the evening. I'm writing on the verandah of my tent (set on a firm wooden base) looking out at the steeply forested slopes wherein the gorillas can be found.

For a time it seemed as if our day of gorilla-tracking would be as abortive as the six o'clock game drive at Mweya yesterday morning, when for half an hour we saw only rabbits.

Diana, the Director of the AWF [African Wildlife Fund], found the going very hard, and after two and a half hours we left her with one of the trackers and pressed on, through dense, vine-covered forest floor, hacking our way with a machete until we reached the crown of a hill which our guide said was the line of the Uganda/Zaire border. He found gorilla camp traces just the other side of the border, so they were very probably now in Zaire, and rules say that visitors must stop at the border.

Our guide asks Barbara, myself and Gordon, a local boy, to wait on the ridge while he goes ahead to look for any sign of the group.

After almost half an hour, during which I became a little apprehensive – for we were several kilometres deep in the forest and I had no idea which direction would lead us back to camp – they returned. As they had suspected, the gorilla group was moving into Zaire, but he had located them and they were only 200 metres away. As we had been tracking them for nearly four hours, the decision was taken to stretch the rules and to go after them.

A slippery, awkward, heavily wooded and vined slope fell steeply from the ridge. I could see the silvery reflections off a tin roof in Zaire, beyond the forest. We slithered and slipped awkwardly down. There were blue flowers all around giving off a smell like lavender.

After much crashing and thrashing of leaves and bushes, a serious black face peered up at us from about 50 yards away. Later this same black female climbed a tree obligingly, then leaned on a branch which broke and she fell with it to the ground and that was the last we saw of her.

As we resigned ourselves to returning up the hill, we heard some crashing away to our right and turned in time to get a view of a huge, full-grown Silver-back swinging, Tarzan-like, on the branch of a tree. He was suspended there, enormously and quite splendidly, for a few precious seconds, before the huge branch snapped and he, too, fell out of sight.

Sunday, February 6th: Buhoma Gorilla Camp

Around the middle of the night, I'm woken from dreams to find my tent shaking violently. Quickly conscious, I experience a few almost unbelievable moments of not exactly fear but complete disorientation. Have time to grab my torch and shine it at the walls of the tent before the shaking stops.

In the pitch darkness I already feel vulnerable. I think first of all that there are people out there shaking the timber base on which the tent is set. Perhaps they're locals who resent this luxury camp taking over their land. Could it be that the Silverbacks have followed us into camp and are registering their displeasure?

I unzip my tent flap and poke my head out into the night. I hear a zipper go in one of the tents lower down – which is reassuring, and there are voices and lights where the staff are quartered. There is no sign of anyone near my tent.

I switch off my torch and slide into a dozy state. Twice I'm aware of my bed moving; trembling. Is it just me trembling? Are they back?

At 3.10, 35 minutes after the initial shaking, my tent shakes again, violently enough for the mirror to rattle. The sensation lasts maybe five seconds, a lot less than the shuddering which woke me at half past two, but it's enough to get me out of bed, looking rather desperately for a pair of underpants (I shall die in a blazing building one day looking for my underpants!). Pull on trousers, and go out and check underneath the timber base to see if anything could be trapped there. There was nothing. The night was serene.

At breakfast, I was looking forward to having the first line 'Did the earth move for you?' but James, the Kenyan manager of the camp, got in first. There had been an earthquake.

It was a big one too, 6.7, with its epicentre at Fort Portal where we'd stayed four days earlier.

George and I set off soon after eight. Not bad, mountain gorillas and an earthquake in half a day.

Monday, February 7th: Kampala

I have arranged a last meal with George. He told me he'd never eaten Chinese food so I suggested I take him to the Shanghai, at the Kampala Club. He agreed with his funny, slightly dopey smile, 'Oh yes that would-er be good.'

Well the intention is better than the meal, which is rather a disaster. It isn't very good Chinese food – sticky, heavy dumplings and floury spring rolls. I'm tired and quite full, and after catching a chilli in his throat quite early on, George is not happy. So we leave dish after dish.

I give him a copy of *Pole to Pole*, 25,000 shillings in an envelope inside, and a Prominent Features T-shirt which he loves. He also takes the Travel Channel bag, which wasn't really on offer but I'm quite happy.

Thursday, February 10th

A jumble of African images feed through my subconscious during a broken, unrefreshing night and I'm awake long before it's light.

A long session with Kath. We are about to begin when there is an ominous phone call. An *Evening Standard* hack who asks me, politely enough, if I had indeed read several of Dahl's books for Talking Books. I said yes, quite proud of the fact. To which he replied by asking if I knew that there was some problem with Felicity Dahl and they were not being issued. I said I wasn't aware of any such problem, but that if she didn't like the way I read them that would entitle her to a say in this release.

Kath then admitted that they had heard there was a complication. I rang Anne – yes she was going to talk to me about it. I know I've not exactly made myself easily available these past two weeks, but I resented having to learn of this hiccup from the *Evening Standard*.

Walk up to Hampstead in the increasing cold to the Air Studios in Lyndhurst Road for Larry Adler's 80th birthday party.

Made the acquaintance of George Martin, the Beatles' producer, who told me that he didn't think the talked-of Beatles reunion was a good idea. Paul had evidently returned from New York with some Lennon off-cuts given to him by Yoko, which he hoped to mix in with new material. He says Paul wants any new Beatles material to be recorded at his home studio and George wants it to be at Friar Park. Martin suggested dinner sometime and I think I'll take him up on it.

Friday, February 11th

H and I out early to look at a sofa in John Lewis. One or two other errands and home by 10.30, to the news of Mel Calman's[1] death. I can't really believe it. I have a letter in front of me dated 2nd Feb asking me to address his design congress and, better still, to have lunch together. Mel, whom I've known since *'Now'* days – my whole working life – who influenced me to write children's books, who introduced me to Ballymaloe, and Caroline Holden and Pat Huntley and Debbie Moggach – a ladies' man, in the best sense. A wonderfully dry and funny companion. A life force. I really can't believe it. Long talk with Caroline H. Mel died after being taken ill in a cinema. Debbie was with him; which, as far as Caroline was concerned, was the most important thing.

This and the Dahl piece in the *Standard*, 'Dahling – you weren't wonderful!' and Gwen Watford's[2] death and Harry Nilsson's[3] death, all make me a little depressed.

1 Mel Calman, cartoonist, best known for his 'little man' character. His work appeared widely in the press, including *The Times*, up until his death.
2 Gwen Watford, actress who made her reputation in the theatre, but was widely seen also on television. She won a Society of West End Theatre award in a revival of Noël Coward's *Relatively Speaking* opposite Donald Sinden. She played Tomkinson's mother in the first of the *Ripping Yarns*.
3 Harry Nilsson, American singer-songwriter and very big Python fan.

Monday, February 14th

The Weekend takes a step nearer to reality with the press launch this morning at the Strand Theatre.

Arrive only to find that the black poodle which is to be the focus of the press photos (between myself and Richard) hasn't got there yet.

Richard W takes advantage of the delay to show me the theatre. 'It is very big,' he sighs. 'I saw Dawn French at a dinner last night, and she said she'd lost her voice.' (French and Saunders are in here at the moment.) 'Mind you,' he adds mischievously, 'she did matinees.'

Wednesday, February 16th

By taxi to the first rehearsal of *The Weekend* at Petyt House just along from Carlyle's House, by the Chelsea riverside.

A large crowd of people are gathered, some of whom are the cast. Two others are 'runners' and several others seem to be stage management. A man from the Yvonne Arnaud Theatre confirms that two weeks have already sold out there – before a word is read, this is rather alarming.

'Are you nervous?' asks Richard, straightening the collar of my coat. 'You jolly well ought to be.'

Robin Lefevre, who wears the intensely concentrated look of a man about to free-fall from 15,000 feet, has flown over from Dublin this morning, having opened a play there last night. He was up at 5.30. Richard W looks as if he too might have been up from 5.30 – his expression naturally hangdog, though he's making a big effort to be jolly. Pugh, Stirling[1] and Fox[2] are there to fly the investor/producer's flag.

The nerve-racking process gets under way around eleven. Richard is good. He's playing it low and soft as he searches out the character. Marcia Warren as Bridget and Yvonne D'Alpra as Mrs Finlay are spot-on. The rest all groping a bit.

Robin is brisk and businesslike. He plans, he says, to rehearse from 10.30 to 3.00, with a working snack/lunch. No-one demurs.

At three I drive back with Richard. He has a smooth and powerful new BMW – but then almost everything about Richard looks new and quite expensive. He's good company, though tends to whinge a bit about conditions. He had wanted no matinees except for Sunday – which would substitute for the evening – giving us six performances a week and two nights off. Pugh

---

1 Archie Stirling, married for eight years to Diana Rigg.
2 Robert Fox, producer, youngest brother of the actors Edward and James Fox.

hasn't fallen for this one yet. Richard drives a little distractedly, narrowly avoiding knocking over two pedestrians – on separate zebra crossings.

Saturday, February 19th

A night hovering on the lighter levels of sleep. Have to rise repeatedly, such is the discomfort within.

H suggests a visit to the doc as she fears that it might be the result of some African bug. So, unable to face breakfast, I drive down to the James Wigg practice and sit with a lot of other ill people, reading old copies of the British Museum magazine and *Harpers & Queen*. After 50 minutes I'm seen by Dr Posner, young, neat, with a relaxing surgery manner. Feels my stomach – nothing nasty there. Thinks it may just be gastro-enteritis, suggests some suitable antacid and says that, as a precaution, I should take a stool sample – a 'hot' sample as he graphically describes it – to the Hospital for Tropical Diseases on Monday. Just to be sure there are no parasites at work.

Feeling colder than can be accounted for by the weather, I collect my script and drive down to Chelsea.

Manage to last through rehearsal. Afterwards, as we're all packing up, I mention to Richard and Marcia that I shall have to take my droppings into hospital on Monday and Richard reveals that he has seen many a stool in his time. He was a lab technician once. Looking for tapeworms was the worst. There was no hygienic alternative to just prodding your way through it.

Monday, February 21st

Off to Chelsea via the Accident and Emergency Unit at UCH to drop my dropping. Not as easy as this of course. 'No not here, third floor.' On the third floor, 'No, not here, Microbiology.' I throw a short, gabbled fit and the lady behind the counter relents. 'What is it then?' she asks. I mumble something and she waves the transparent package around as if it's a Christmas bauble and drops it into what looks suspiciously like a rubbish bin. 'That *will* get to Tropical Diseases?' I enquire. 'Oh yes!' I'm assured. 'Leave it with us.'

At rehearsal Angela Thorne reveals that she is 'the world's worst with props', which I hope is thespian hyperbole for her part is almost entirely dependent on them. Richard reveals that he's never done a part of this size on stage before.

But after the first few faltering steps there is a hint of that magical process of transformation which makes this often overrated, over-indulged business so special. Angela begins to play, not just an upper-middle-class woman, but

Virginia, wife of Stephen. Richard responds accordingly and with this new-found confidence they begin to enjoy themselves and play the lines, and the lines, having stood up to four days' intense scrutiny last week, still provide laughs and unexpected little satisfactions.

By the time three o'clock comes I'm rather happy – *The Weekend* is not just moving forward but growing as it does so. Now the question is how all this can be nurtured, contained and released at precisely the right strength at the right time.

Saturday, February 26th

Drive Tom and his colleague Sheridan down to Petyt House to meet Robin and play the music they've so far assembled for the play. Fortunately Robin likes the first theme very much, and though he has criticism of the others it's generally because they're incompatible with the tone of the play at a particular time rather than uninspired. He likes the 'wit' and congratulates them both warmly at the end.

Afterwards I take Robin for a drink – he has Guinness, I have Brakspear's, but he refuses to eat anything.

He's an interesting man, self-contained, steely, controlled yet with great re-serves of humour. I haven't yet seen the warm side but that's probably because he hates false sentimentality – which makes him so good for the play!

Tuesday, March 1st

This evening I'm going into the Lister to have my bottom looked at and am not allowed to eat or drink for five hours before.

There is something unsatisfactory about going into hospital when you feel not only well, but better than you've felt for several weeks.

I remember being in a room outside the operating theatre and listening with some effort of concentration to a nurse in a green cap telling me how he personally brought in the classical music CDs, one of which was playing in the background as I lay there. In what seemed part of the same conversation an anaesthetist pumped something into my right arm and Mr Scurr, the surgeon, was telling me it had all gone very well.

I was trolleyed upstairs again, into my room, feeling very little pain or dis-comfort other than the wooziness of the anaesthetic, but a soft-voiced, effete Scottish male nurse was unduly concerned that I should not suffer and jabbed some Pethidine into my left leg. Fell into a peculiar time-disoriented sleep. At times very deep, at others fitful. My legs nearly buckled as I rose to take a pee.

This was the one moment in the whole business when I felt frightened.

The night passed slowly. A cup of tea at 6.30, a very good breakfast, *The Times*, and finally, at nine o'clock, Mr Scurr to tell me that the examination had revealed a fissure which had healed itself, two piles which he had injected and nothing further to worry about. I was free to go home.

Thursday, March 3rd

Uncomfortable night, though was rewarded towards dawn with a lovely, satisfying dream of a romance with Jennifer Saunders.

At rehearsal today there is a spat between Julie P[1] and Angela over the brown bread. Angela wants to change some of her moves at the start of the dinner party, Julie immediately defends her own role, digs her heels in. 'Do what you like, so long as I can pass the brown bread!'

Friday, March 4th

Another full-cast day. Robin pushes them on through the second act and the dinner party scene to the point where Richard protested quite fiercely. 'Not again!' he muttered, tramping back and forth across the room like a baited animal. But he did it again and did it very well, and watching this big, busy scene play – with props and without books – was exciting.

Lunch with Sally Vincent, a *Sunday Times* journalist, at Bibendum (my choice of venue). She is already at the table. Not a promising sight. She looks very bleary. A woman of my age, smoking and with something resembling a bloody Mary at her right hand.

Her opinions are strong and dismissive. She's not going to ask any stupid questions about my niceness, she wants to talk about sadness and loss. She produces a huge and dusty old tape recorder – the sort that looked neat and compact in pre-Walkman days but now lies on the white linen tablecloth like a sarcophagus.

She asks about Angela, without apology or any false sentimentality – just to find out. I don't think she is playing tricks. I think she is upfront.

She and I put away two bottles of Sauvignon and it's 4.15 before we notice that we've overstayed our welcome. We've talked for three hours – I really can't remember what about but she still wants another session.

Her reaction to the play, which I was pleased she'd read, worried me though. She felt that it all just came round full-circle – things were exactly the

1 Julie Peasgood, actress who made her name in the television soap *Brookside*.

same at the end as they were at the beginning. If this is what audiences think then I've got it wrong somewhere.

Saturday, March 5th

When rehearsals finish I invite everyone, including the young stage-management crew – four lads – along to the pub. I tell Michael Medwin[1] he should write his autobiog – or at least have a TV programme made about him. He has wonderful stories – like being introduced to Edith Evans – well, not introduced, but finally noticed by her – 'What's your name, young man?' she asked. 'Michael Medwin.' 'Oh,' she replied, quite impressed, 'any relation to Yehudi Menuhin?'

Wednesday, March 9th

Day away from rehearsal. Have to spend a morning on 'long-lead' publicity for *Palin's Column*. Then to St Ermin's Hotel where I'm due to meet Attenborough and others for the Wildlife Trust's Vice-Presidents' lunch.

Three lords, four knights and a minority of commoners, of which I'm the only one without a tie. David A is not here – mix-up with the diary – he's in Costa Rica.

Sit next to Julian Pettifer, at the end of the table. He, like me, is writing a novel this year. He's getting up at five o'clock to work on it. We talk about the BBC and the restricted market for good documentaries. He clearly feels rather miffed that there isn't a place for him in the schedules.

Discussion afterwards. Sir William Wilkinson is kindly and very articulate, only afterwards do I realise he's blind. Lord Cranbrook – 'Gaythorne' to everyone but me – speaks with that utter confidence which comes from being expected to be listened to, and being expected to speak too. Most of them have this gift of confident articulation. The RSNC is really there to preserve more than wildlife – it's also there to preserve these fine old species of British rural aristocracy.

Out to dinner with the Frosts. David's star guest tonight is the Prince of Wales, and we have been previously warned to arrive no later than a quarter to eight.

H and I are at separate tables. I'm in the Carina room, opposite the Prince and between Carina and Linda McCartney.

In the short chats that PC and I had together I was aware very much that

1 Michael Medwin, producer, actor and co-founder with Albert Finney of Memorial Films.

he enjoyed laughing and being made to laugh quite as much as he enjoyed having to look grave and serious and dutiful. One or two avenues were firmly closed though. When asked what his reaction was to all the press intrusion, etc. etc. he said quite firmly that he never reads any newspapers any more. I can't quite believe this, but it certainly cut down shared subjects of conversation and reinforced what I'd felt about the royals when I met the Duchess of York at Frost's – that they are being boxed into a corner, and likely to become Howard Hughesian if they go on like this.

As usual, these gatherings feel oddly posed – like those group paintings of famous citizens. Hierarchies are observed and in the end real companionship is stifled by the weight of fame, achievement and significance.

Thursday, March 10th

Today is the first full-length run-through. In fact it is run twice. Looks to be around one hour for the second act and 45 minutes for the first. It seems a mite short to me but I'm assured that a two-hour evening is fine. As Robin says, 'If it's longer than two hours pal, you'd better have a good reason why.'

Home, utterly worn out, to find the baleful presence of Sally Vincent in our kitchen waiting for the second part of our *Sunday Times* interview.

She dismisses most of what was poured into her hefty tape recorder at Bibendum on Monday. 'You're a good listener,' she observes after admitting that most of the tape was taken up with her talking.

She begins to dig. What do I think of prizes? What does feminism mean to me? I was unprepared for the latter and squirmed a) at being asked and b) at the aggression with which it was asked and c) the contempt with which my messy, confused reply was greeted. She became exasperated at her lack of progress – 'I've got nothing on you,' she kept saying … 'I don't know anything about you.' I was rather pleased at this.

Friday, March 11th

Meet Dan Patterson at Groucho's. He rang yesterday to enthuse over 'The Adventure'.

His feeling is that it is very healthy, has a number of well-drawn characters and intriguing situations and comedy locations on which to build. He, like me, sees the end as a confusion to be made sense of, but thinks that this is not a problem – the problem is having too many good ideas, not a lack of them.

In short, it's about the best thing he's read in a long while, he thinks it should be produced as soon as possible and in this country and as a British film – not an American. He wants me to try and rewrite the end, with him as a sounding board and ideas man.

His energy and enthusiasm catches me at an awkward time. I'm delighted by it, but I hear the distant rumble of overwork, rush and hassle in a year which had seemed so clearly devoted to play and novel.

Saturday, March 12th

Drive to rehearsal. For my money, the best run-through so far. Without fail Angela manages to move me. I know it's Stephen's helplessness we focus on mainly, but Angela's unerringly well-recalled and poignant readings of the lines about Driffield and their past always bring tears to my eyes at some point.

So we all break up for the weekend and will reassemble in Guildford, with opening night only three and a half days away. The text and structure have not changed radically since we began. My work has been in detail, and in fighting, in the most productive and discreet way, to get the actors to speak the lines as written.

Buy Paul Durcan's poems inspired by the National Gallery for Doug Adams'[1] 42nd birthday tonight.

It's raining and windy when we arrive at Duncan Terrace soon after half past eight. The invitation said 'Dinner' but not how many people would be there. A cavernous, echoing house with stone-slab floor and not a carpet to be seen. I ask Terry J where Douglas and Jane put all their furniture at a time like this and he says they haven't got any.

Sunday, March 13th

Down to the RAC Club, at Richard W's invitation, to play squash. His regular squash players are all on tour he says.

Yesterday Patsy, Richard's 'voice coach', came to see the run-through and she gave Richard a note which he thought a good one – that Stephen is a man who loves words – because the ability to use words and language is all that he has left. I thought this astute and hopefully it will help cure what I think is Richard's only real fault – a tendency to paraphrase occasionally, to lose precision and clarity. The words are, oddly enough, very carefully chosen!

1 Douglas Adams, author best known for creating *The Hitchhiker's Guide to the Galaxy*, which began as a BBC radio series.

Monday, March 14th: London–Guildford

The day is bright, with a low, dazzling sun – put on sunglasses as I drive out west. Long, slow journey. It seems every main road between here and Guildford is being torn apart.

Have to ask a policeman for the theatre, at which I arrive about half past two. It's a compact, mid-sixties building around which the fast-flowing River Wey swirls. It has cafés, restaurants and bars filling almost every available corner. The auditorium is tight, steep and well-raked, rows of red-covered seats with precious little to offer anyone over six foot.

Eileen's set fills the stage. Nothing spectacular, but it feels right except for the problem with gauze back walls to the sitting room. The gauze is there so that rooms in the rest of the house can be lit up when required, but it does mean that when not lit the walls look to be crying out for some kind of ornament.

Tom is there when I arrive, and his music is very much admired – it has class – unobtrusive yet stylish, it helps the transitions no end.

I drive to the hotel.

Tuesday, March 15th: South Lodge, Lower Beeding

The 'invited audience' for the dress rehearsal numbers around 30.

Two sound cues don't work at all, lines are all over the place. To my incredulity, the line after 'sexual drive' – 'depends what sort of car you've got' – proves to be an absolute belter, instead of the intentionally bad joke it's meant to be. The dog shit section at start of Act II is enormously well received, but apart from that it's a ropey old rehearsal.

Rush backstage for notes. Robin rather touches me by telling them – with his customary lack of any sentimentality – 'Do it well for Michael.'

'Full House' sign has been up all day, and will indeed be up for both weeks, so a good buzz inside the auditorium. The audience look like regulars – middle- to old-aged, but decent British types. I fear for the 'fucks'.

Well, all goes well. The laughs are more or less continuous and much to my pleasure, and surprise, they spread right through to the end of the second act. Even the speech about failing to be able to commit suicide has laughs which give the whole play a feeling of unity. It *is* a comedy. It's a comedy about someone who has made a mess of his life. Hancockian, someone said.

Wednesday, March 16th, Lower Beeding

Euphoria a little punctured – or should I say reality restored – by Robin's phone call. Robin goes straight to the point. 'Talked to the lads last night ...' (I only realise a moment or two later that the lads he's referring to are Pugh, Fox and Stirling, with whom he drove home to London.) The end needs to be changed and Robin has a suggestion – that Stephen should not be able to find the tea. Good idea.

More drastic, at first hearing, is Robin's feeling that the first half should be restructured.

As he rehearses the sound levels again and various scene changes I tinker with the script. It all feels like *Saturday Night Live*, or the day of a Python recording. A heightened sense of urgency. We tell the cast of Robin's new ending for the play and try it out.

Thursday, March 17th, Lower Beeding

Watch the performance, as last night, from one of the usherette seats at the back of the circle. Last night a group of women sitting in the café upstairs congratulated me on writing a play 'from a woman's viewpoint'; tonight at the half a woman watching with elderly parents and husband asks me for an autograph. Someone asks what she thinks of the show ... 'It's just like home,' she says.

I watch couples nudging each other or women casting sidelong glances at their male partners and in those moments I feel a curious sense of power – the power to draw something out of people – without drugs, without a psychology degree – just by showing them someone else's invented experience.

It's a much better show tonight. The dog stays on stage for the first time and, especially in the second act, I feel a consolidation, a solid feeling that comes from actors who are no longer scared of whether they will remember their lines.

Friday, March 18th: Lower Beeding–Guildford–London

Watch them rehearse the new order at end of Act One. Everyone seems pleased with it. Robin credits me with its success, though it was he who suggested something was wrong.

These long days at the theatre – nine or ten hours at a stretch – mean that little other work gets done. I have no base, not even a dressing room. I clutch my bag and shuffle around between the theatre auditorium, the café and the offices – I look forward to seeing my own workroom again.

I watch tonight from a single seat at the back of the stalls. There is a dreadful cueing mistake on the newly reordered section, plunging the stage into darkness just as Richard is about to deliver one of the funniest lines of the act. Generally the first half is patchy.

The second works well and there is generous applause at the end. The week has proved that there is much to like in the play. It does hold an audience's attention throughout. But how good does this make it?

I wish sometimes I had the blithe confidence of the convinced. But then I wouldn't want to be Margaret Thatcher or Ian Paisley.

A review, our first, in the *Surrey Advertiser*, calls it 'A good play. Funny and moving.'

Monday, March 21st: Guildford

At half past two leave for Guildford, with Rachel in attendance. Slow journey through the cone fields of Surrey, arrive a few minutes after four.

Show Rachel around backstage. Good to see the new first-half order in place. It's much more effective. Applause at the end of each scene tonight which helps the changes. Second act really settling in well.

Richard is compulsive in the whole section from the herbal cigarette onwards. He keeps the audience with him throughout his descent, and when they've reached the bottom he effortlessly brings them up again.

I'd quite like to be opening in London next week.

Tuesday, March 22nd

Helen has a persistent cough that is wearing her out. Doctor puts her back on antibiotics. But she isn't well enough to accompany me to a meal at the House of Lords with Shreela and Gary Flather and the Alburys.

I have been told to go and meet Shreela in the Peers' Lobby.

No sooner have I been directed to sit on one of the dimpled red-leather benches than I am hissed at to stand up. 'The mace is coming out!' The house has just risen and slowly, solemnly, the uniformed Serjeant at Arms, followed by a man in a suit and spectacles (Leader of the House), emerges from the chamber. I am one of a half-dozen standing, frozen to attention, as a short exchange takes place and the mace-bearer turns and walks past me down the corridor.

We move on eventually to the dining room. Gary points out a slim, stooped, grey-haired figure at the far end of the room, underneath one of the huge portraits of some great man. It is Lord Barber, once plain Anthony Barber,[1] who will always remain in my mind as the first candidate on Python's 'Spot the Loony'. 'Please, don't press your buttons until you've seen all the contestants.'

The food is a mixture – good crab bisque, but lamb so rare some of it remains on my plate like a bloody handkerchief.

After dinner we go on a tour of the building – up the Content, down the Not-Content corridors – the Peers' division areas; into the great chamber with massive murals of Waterloo and Trafalgar.

Beyond the red carpet, where the green carpet of the Commons begins, a growing noise – it's the din from the Commons Bar, loud and raucous as a Millwall pub after a home game.

Friday, March 25th

David Pugh rings to tell me that the head of the agency who does all his publicity saw the show last Wednesday and was so impressed that he wants to redesign the poster to reflect the 'quality' of a play which he had wrongly dismissed as zany comedy. David wants me to think of an ad-line to describe the work – not just a comedy, but, he suggests, 'a comedy of bad manners'. That sounds like asking for trouble from the critics, but I promise to have a think.

Precious little time left to look at 'The Adventure' and decide on my attitude to it as an ongoing project.

Meet Dan Patterson at Groucho's. Dan feels guilty at putting me under pressure. I feel guilty at stringing Dan along then suddenly panicking! What is to be done? Well, I suggest we make it as a TV series! The gallery of characters could then all be kept and developed. I would much rather work closely with Channel 4 or even the BBC than some American-backed film company.

Saturday, March 26th: Guildford

I have said I will go and see both shows at Guildford today – Richard specially urged me to come to the matinee – as it would give him that extra spur to the performance!

During the break I have my photograph taken in Dressing Room 9 for *The Sunday Times*. The photographer has some odd idea of me sitting in a dressing gown and eating Mars Bars. It seems to bear no relation to anything, but

1 Anthony Barber, Chancellor of the Exchequer under Edward Heath.

in the end the effort of not doing it is much more draining than just getting on with it, so I borrow a dressing gown from Richard and sit and eat Mars Bars.

Whilst they're shooting, two enormous bumble-bees fly around the dressing room and eventually into the huge spotlight, which they hit with a horrible fizzing noise.

The evening is a good show – the laughter and response rolls on. From my vantage point at the back of the stalls I watch the audience. Sometimes they literally rock with laughter, sometimes they howl quite violently (during discovery of the dog mess). I've rarely been in the position of being able to observe the effect a line I've written might have on people. There are moments tonight when I experience, with a very rare directness, the joys of being able to make people laugh!

Sad to be leaving the Yvonne Arnaud – it has been a most pleasant, comfortable and hospitable home.

Drive back, giving a lift to Robin. He thinks that whatever the critics say the play will be around in 200 years' time. Because, he says, there will always be Stephen Febbles. It will be done for the same reason that they still do [Sheridan's] *The Critic* 200 years after it was written. I nod intelligently as the cones flash by on the wounded A3 and make a mental note to read *The Critic*.

We talk about the appeal of Stephen. I admit that there's more of me in him than I might like to think. I can't shoulder all the blame onto my father. We both agree that we hate dogs and dinner parties – in the latter case Robin is almost fanatical. 'I don't do them any more! ...' Dinner parties I presume he means.

Tuesday, March 29th: London–Brighton

Start to read Terry Jones's 'Miracle Man' screenplay, in taxi on way to Victoria, then on the train to Brighton and finally in my hotel room with its fine seaside view filtered through salt-caked windows.

It makes better reading than the *Brighton Argus*, under whose encouraging headline 'Moaning Meldrew passes a tough test' lurks an irritatingly nit-picky review. Mourning the lack of silly walks and funny voices.

The ominous review and the lack of any reports from anyone about the first night have made me a little deflated.

Ring Robin who's also at the hotel. He confirms what I suspected – that last night wasn't so good. According to Robin the cast, over-complacent after a soft and successful time at Guildford, came out playing for their laughs rather than acting the play. He was just off to the theatre to give them notes. He didn't sound conciliatory.

Research trip to Africa for my never-completed novel *Uganda*. At the Equator with my guide, George Byomhumuza, Februray 1994.

One of the two good reviews of *The Weekend*. And we made the most of it.
Strand Theatre, Aldwych, May 4th, 1994.

Enjoying a Drink

LEFT: With Elena Salvoni, my all-time favourite maîtresse d', at Elena's L'Etoile.

BELOW LEFT: With Lena Rustin, the speech therapist whose work on stammering in children inspired the Michael Palin Centre; and (BELOW RIGHT) Travers Reid, who got me involved, at *An Evening with Michael Palin* at the Cambridge Theatre, London, April 17th, 1994.

RIGHT: *Sunday Times* photo for *The Weekend*. 'The photographer has some odd idea of me sitting in a dressing room and eating Mars Bars. The effort of not doing it is so much more draining than just getting on with it, so I borrow a dressing gown . . . and sit and eat Mars Bars.' Yvonne Arnaud Theatre, Guildford, March 26th, 1994.

Full Circle

Little Diomede Island in the Bering Strait. Where we started our journey round the Pacific Rim on August 28th, 1995 and ended it on August 14th, 1996.

Spectacular, almost unreal turquoise lake in the caldera of one of the many volcanoes in the Kamchatka Peninsula, eastern Russia.

ABOVE: On one of the longest, busiest filming days, I try my hand with the Kodo drummers. I'd already been running with them at 5 a.m. Sado Island, Japan, September 23rd, 1995.

RIGHT: On the Sado Island ferry.

BELOW: Filming in the monsoon is not to be recommended. Hue Station, Vietnam, November 23rd, 1995.

With Iban elders (and one-time head-hunters) in a communal
longhouse, Nanga Sumpa, Sarawak, January 1996.

Getting in the way of the tea harvest, Java.

ABOVE RIGHT: The one and only time I've looked
down into an active volcano – Mount Bromo, Java.

RIGHT: Helicoptering onto the Cook Glacier at the end of our
long voyage down the western rim of the Pacific, March 1996.

My morning in Alcatraz – with two men who'd spent a lot longer than that here. Now they take guided tours. 'A day described as "almost flawless" by Fraser at dinner'– San Francisco, August 2nd, 1996.

El Tatio geyser field. Spectacular steam effects at 4,500 metres. Calama, Chile.

Monday, April 4th

Drive to Wimbledon (rather enjoying *The Weekend* on tour – seeing one's play performed seems a satisfying reason to visit places – especially ones which would normally not be high on the list).

Richard is lying down, masked but awake. The last night at Brighton had been the best so far. Show him the new PM speech; he chuckles. He really is a very decent, patient man. Angela is making up, but very chatty. She has a different style to Richard. If something's wrong it's very wrong for Angela – 'This just *isn't* working,' and so on.

A backstage visit is really a series of diplomatic missions.

Tuesday, April 12th

Eric has sent a long, slightly manic fax trying to sell us a 'Python in Las Vegas' week, which will net us almost a million dollars each. John is back and working with Iain on 'Death Fish 2' – which sounds to be definitely going ahead in summer '95.

Despite the fact that Eric claims John as being the enthusiast for a Python stage show, John reacts rather irritably to the suggestion of such an event happening this Christmas, as he will be on the verge of production; Terry J and Terry G both quite intrigued, so I fax back to Eric offering my services, subject to everyone's agreement, over New Year '95.

Wednesday, April 13th: Crawley

Leave for Crawley – which I estimate will be my eleventh visit to the play in its 30 performances. David tells me that yesterday there was something of a panic – Richard still not there at the quarter – Medwin and Brian Moorehead, his understudy, walking around ashen-white – Angela taking a double dose of beta-blockers! Richard walks in just after the quarter cool as a cucumber. He has a telephone in his car, but every time he tried to ring the theatre all he got was a recorded voice telling him that all tickets for *The Weekend* had been sold!

Robert Fox has flown back from Rome to see it for the first time since Guildford. We're only able to sit right at the back on what they call VIP seats, and just as the lights go down we're evicted from those!

The audience reaction is warm, unequivocally good-humoured, and Richard is now very much on course, making the most of the audience's friendliness. Picking up just about everything.

Thursday, April 14th

To BAFTA where I've arranged to meet Terry G at a special French government-backed screening of Claude Berri's *Germinal*. Others there include Arthur Scargill – who shakes my hand, introduces me to his deputy and speaks admiringly of Ann Clywd, the Labour MP, currently sitting in a coal mine in S. Wales and refusing to come out until its closure notice is reconsidered.

Scargill is less of a ranter than he appears in public. He seems to have a sense of humour, and yet be completely single-minded – about his subject, his theory of working-class struggle, his place in history and his rightness. There just is no other side to the argument – which of course makes him very similar to M Thatcher. Their confrontation was of two bulls locking horns. Both believed they were right.

The screening is addressed by an endearingly scruffy Claude Berri. He makes a funny, self-deprecating intro, but the long three-hour epic that follows lacks, as far as I can remember, one single laugh. It is unremittingly worthy, epic stuff. *Germinal* as a national monument. I was about as moved as I am at the Royal Tournament.

Bernard Hill,[1] who himself looks a bit Scargill-like, with an obsessive stare, beards me about cars. What can he do about them? I'm very uncomfortable with this role of Mr Anti-Car, so let him know right away that I have a Mercedes.

Saturday, April 16th: Crawley

O'Rourke[2] at the bell again – first to tell me he's washed the pavement in front of my home, removed the weeds, and all I have to do is ring the council and get them to come and fill in the cracks. A moment later the doorbell sounds again and a more agitated O'Rourke tells me that Mr Osifu, his downstairs neighbour, is threatening him with court action for cleaning the street! They are both barmy.

At 5.30 a car collects me and then Robin L and we proceed down to Crawley.

Richard seems to be trying for a lighter, more naturalistic tone, playing much softer than before. Well, it doesn't work. The audience is subdued – well behaved, laughing at the usual places, only without the feeling of celebration which you'd expect from a Saturday night crowd.

1 Bernard Hill, actor who made his name in Alan Bleasdale's *Boys from the Blackstuff*.
2 A neighbour with an unfortunate aggressive stance on everything. Lived above Mr Osifu, a Nigerian, in a council house three doors away.

The second half is better – it's much more involving anyway – but I'm left at the end with some serious nagging doubts. If Richard can affect the play so much – it doesn't say much for the play itself. The first half, now so used to being played for laughs, is naked and vulnerable without them.

I ask Robin if he thinks Richard will return at Christmas. His reply is ominous and not terribly reassuring – that decision, Robin believes, will be based on 'your reviews, not his'. So back to how good is the play, and how much is it an average piece carried by a very special actor.

First time for a while I've felt negative about *The Weekend*.

Monday, April 18th

More interruptions from O'Rourke, who now accuses Osifu of trying to electrocute him by attaching electric wires to the letterbox.

At the RGS soon after six for the Wilfred Thesiger lecture. A distinguished gathering up in John Hemming's office. David and Jane Attenborough, Joanna Lumley and assorted medal wearers, the Duke of Kent and of course Thesiger himself. I don't like to thrust myself at him, so talk to David A (who is worried about having agreed to interview Thesiger for TV. 'I mean ... they all want to know about his homosexuality') and cast sidelong glances at Thesiger's remarkable time-encrusted aquiline features.

Thesiger is compulsively watchable and, being old and very famous, doesn't have to pander to the audience. He bemoans the way cars and oil have broken down the old way of life of his beloved Bedou, he thinks that the amount of guns now available in the country make the prospects for Kenya bleak; he pretends not to be able to either pronounce or understand the word 'ecological' – thus delivering a genteel put-down to an earnest young questioner. He doesn't accept the 'Greatest Living English Explorer' role – indeed he describes it as 'balls'.

Afterwards I'm Hemming's guest at the Geographical Club Dinner, held in an ornate villa off Queen's Gate. As lots of people with drinks fill the room around him, I go across to Thesiger and introduce myself and we have a few words.

Thesiger is only concerned about when we're going to eat. He waves his arm dismissively at the chattering crowds. 'It's always like this,' he grumbles, 'I want my food.'

Looking around I see thick thatches of white hair atop ruddy, regular faces – these are the faces of ageing schoolboys for whom life has been a rum old adventure.

Out of the dinner at 10.30; crowds streaming from the Albert Hall so no cabs to be found. Sir Vivian Fuchs[1] and wife said they'd watched all my *Pole to Pole* episodes!

In the spirit of Fuchs and Thesiger, I crossed Hyde Park by foot and picked up a taxi in Bayswater Road. 'Where you've been then, Michael, flashing in the park?' is my cab driver's opening gambit. I've a feeling Thesiger would have liked that.

Wednesday, April 27th

Richard Wilson has come from the Sony Radio Awards where he had to present Best Radio Performance (Male). I was shortlisted for *The Dresser* but it was won by Richard Griffiths. RW had begun his announcement 'And the winner is ... *not* Michael Palin whose play *The Weekend* opens next week ... but ...'

Thursday, April 28th

David rings at least three times during the morning to check on my guests for opening night. Apparently there have been a lot more acceptances than he expected and, as he put it, 'people who started off in the middle of the stalls are now in the upper circle'.

Kath comes round to do letters with me for an hour and a half. Apparently my recent high profile has resulted in deluge of phone calls asking for my availability – nearly 60 requests in the last two days. Kath says the transport people are the worst – their campaigners will not take no for an answer and seem to find it quite unjustifiable that I do a TV prog about transport and yet won't come and fight for their bypass, rail closure or whatever. I suppose they're a bit fanatical and fanatics are not renowned for taking the wider view.

Much better tonight. Richard playing sharp and hard, Angela wobbly to begin with but honest and effective at the end. Richard takes the audience on an emotional roller-coaster in the second half – with wondrous skill. Silences you could cut with a knife, in between big belly laughs.

Tuesday, May 3rd

Woke early enough to hear our milkman David at the milkbox and the sound of his float clinking off down Oak Village. Stayed awake. So much depends on today – the good name of the play for one – the critical seal of approval which

1 In 1958 Vivian Fuchs led the first team to cross Antarctica via the South Pole.

will so affect its future, keep Richard happy and secure a good replacement for the proposed summer tour.

Drive around collecting last presents. Cannot find what I'm really happy with for Robin – settle eventually for a fine malt whisky (after a tasting at Berry Bros and Rudd) and one of the silver, circular whisky flasks – like the one I found so useful on *Pole to Pole*.

Back home and finish wrapping up. Then organise delivery of presents to Pugh and Co. and several bagfuls which I take down to the stage door.

Backstage it's like Christmas – presents stacked everywhere – every dressing room a shrine.

The curtain goes up ten minutes late to a full house. As in all the previews, and unlike all the provincial performances, there is only mild laughter on 'Dear God! No ...' and I hold my breath, but things like Mrs Febble warm up well – good laughter on the Rebecca West line for the first time. Not a bad first half.

Scurry out at the end. David smoking furiously and looking desperately apprehensive. I reassure him. Drink with Jim Wilson, David's genial accountant, at the Waldorf. No-one's raving yet, but the second half is what makes the play.

I slide in after the dinner party is finished and watch with a growing feeling of panic as Richard's light, deft playing hardens up. I turn to find Robin right behind me. Our expressions say it all – he feels what I'm feeling, that Richard is having to work hard. My favourite scene, the one I'm most proud of and which, even in the darkest times, like Bank Holiday Mondays, goes well, is quietly received. I can't watch much more after that, and I turn and slip out. Robin has already left.

I push down the bar on the exit to Catherine Street and walk out into the fresh air. At that moment one of the autograph hunters spots me and they begin to run, pens and books raised, up the street towards me. I turn and shout at them very sharply. I don't want to be bothered, I want time to myself. They stop, clearly alarmed at this loss of affability. Then they slowly retreat back down to the main doors and I walk off around the corner into Tavistock Street.

I cannot control my frustration. I remember kicking at the stone dressing on the back wall of the theatre which hurts my foot quite badly. I feel utterly despondent.

Hear lightish but long applause at the end, then backstage to congratulate everyone. This is where acting experience comes in. Oddly enough they're all very happy, think it went well, etc. Richard, contrary to some nights, has no agonies of self-doubt. Maybe he's just pleased that it's over.

A grand party makes me temporarily forget my regrets and play the role of West End playwright in front of TV cameras and radio and press reporters. Don't see Robin all evening, but Pugh and Billy don't seem to share my doubts any more. For the moment, fuelled by champagne, adrenaline and famous faces, the atmosphere is of unequivocal celebration.

The Waldorf ballroom is a great setting for a first-night party – with its marble terrace surrounding the dance floor and discreet back bar. I've become very fond of the place over the last week.

Ian Hislop particularly complimentary – seemed to have struck something of a chord there.

Home, at a quarter to one on May 4th, knowing my worries are still there and sensing ominous rumbles of dissatisfaction beneath the layers of champagne.

Wednesday, May 4th

Deliberately treat this like any other morning – not reading the papers until I would normally read the papers. H has got to the *Guardian* first though and her grunt and then silence set the ball rolling on a day of almost unremitting critical gloom. 'Python With No Sting' (odd mixed metaphor) is the headline in a Michael Billington piece which is generally condescending and doesn't find Stephen Febble interesting and doesn't feel that we have understood him at all by the end – just 'luxuriated' in his rudeness.

Jack Tinker is destructive but ends with the odd proposition that had my 'name not been on the title page ... the play might well have surfaced to encouraging sounds in far less make-or-break circumstances'.

Today and the *Express* – the only other ones to carry reviews – are much more quotable but by no means raves.

David rings first and advises me not to worry as there are still plenty more to come and they have already made up an ad-ful of good quotes. An hour or so later Richard rings. He sounds lugubrious and though he shrugs off the bad reviews it's clear by now that the balance has tipped quite heavily towards the negative. He mentions the *Standard* as not being good, and this leaves me feeling decidedly uneasy. I'm due at a lunch held by Dewynters – the advertising agency for *The Weekend* – to discuss marketing etc. after the first night.

Take a cab, stopping off at a newsagent to pick up a copy of the *Standard*. It's far worse than I expected. The gist of Nicholas de Jongh's bilious piece is that Richard Wilson is a complete saint who does everything he can to save 'a boring little play' that isn't worth saving.

To Prominent for a meeting together with TG and TJ to think up funny captions for the Ink Group's Python cards. Both Terrys, but especially TJ, are enormously supportive, and my sense of humour returns and takes my mind off everything as we create a calendar with a free extra month called 'Derry and Toms' and featuring mainly rude days, viz. 'Arsehole Day (Tunisia)'. Good childish stuff, but wonderful to wallow in it again.

I'm going down to the theatre, for I feel I must show myself and keep up morale, etc. Park amongst the homeless in Lincoln's Inn Fields and take a quick drink with Robin L and Alan Bleasdale at the Waldorf.

Alan had loved the evening yesterday and roared with laughter. I feel much better for a dose of his warm, emotional, bear-like reassuring presence. Robert Fox has seen the first few minutes next door. Says it's a very good house and all the opening laughs are there.

Thursday, May 5th

Take Rachel to the Gatwick Express en route for her three-week trip to Mexico, with a tour group none of whom she knows. She's trying to put a brave face on it, but I can see that it isn't easy for her. Whilst Helen goes with her onto the platform I buy a couple of papers and look with appalled fascination at the reviews. The *Daily Telegraph* is angrily bad, *The Times* just unenthusiastic.

Drive back home. Pugh rings to wish me a happy birthday, and later faxes through an outrageous quotes page which finds enough from each review to make the play sound like a sure-fire hit! Very creative. Robert Fox also rings – tells me not to worry.

I'm tempted to throw the newspapers straight in the bin – but decide this would be avoiding reality. I carefully cut out the offending articles – which is rather like clearing up dog turds.

Walk over to the theatre – quick chat with each member of the cast. Medwin says John Osborne is in tonight – intrigued by the evocation of his name in Billington's *Guardian* review. He has bought me Osborne's book of essays for my birthday – *Damn You England*. Richard W had sent me some flowers earlier in the day with a note telling me how well the show had gone last night.

Pugh and Billy report good business – £170,000 taken already. No-one is anything other than indomitably cheerful.

To the Marquess of Anglesey then on to Groucho's with TJ. Though he is complimentary about the central characters in the play, his observations otherwise only add to the feeling that has grown in me since reading Wednesday's reviews – or perhaps since kicking the theatre on Tuesday night – that the last few months have been unreal. That what has been said and written about the play this week is the reality. It isn't a strong play. But then I knew that; and I also knew it could be a funny and moving play.

Friday, May 6th

As my cab bounces over the pitted surface of Camden Street, heading south, I reflect on how swiftly the bubble has burst. This time three nights ago I was full of excited expectation, the author of a first play that had virtually sold out its provincial tour and had played to 70% preview business in London.

Now I approach the theatre in a completely different mood. I'm guarded, apologetic, fearful of some fresh shock.

Try to put on a brave face for the cast – the workers at the coal face.

Slip in at the back of the stalls as usual and receive a shock. A dozen rows of empty seats. Up into the circle; lots of empty seats but central block pretty full. I should estimate a 60% house. On a Friday? For a new Richard Wilson play? The conclusion is inescapable – the critics have been listened to.

Saturday, May 7th

Simon A rings and makes the point that with R. Wilson and me on the bill there was an expectation which was perhaps not fulfilled by such a conventional play. He clearly felt the cast were predictable and familiar and would have liked more dangerous casting.

A dreadful and dramatic end to the season for Sheffield United, who are 2-0 up at Chelsea, then 2-2 but need only a draw for another season in the Premiership when, with the last kick of the League season, Chelsea score and United's grip on the parapet is finally loosened.

But to be set against United's relegation and *The Weekend*'s reviews, there's the election of a majority black government in South Africa, the thumping of the Tories in local elections (down to 27% of the vote) and the opening of the Channel Tunnel.

Woken by Rachel ringing from a call box on the main street of Mexico City. Thank God she sounds well and happy and has obviously fallen in with a good party. She's the youngest, and shares a room with a GP who is 30-something but behaves like a 20-year-old. Mexico does sound exciting.

Sunday, May 8th

I turn in cautious fascination to the arts pages of the *Observer* and the *Independent on Sunday*, holding the paper a little away from me, rather as a child might watch a particularly unpleasant scene on television from behind the sofa. Fortunately the reviews of *The Weekend* are confined to brief dismissals at the end of the columns. 'Dire', the *IoS* calls it. 'Dire', the *Observer* calls it.

Later I ring Richard W who seems to have taken it all with a glum jokiness. Apparently in *The Sunday Times* the review is the lead and written in dialogue form. 'You wouldn't want to see it,' is all R can say.

Robert Hewison's view of the savaging of my play was that RW and myself are both seen by the critics to be television people and there's nothing the critics like less than to have stars from another medium, heavily hyped and thrust into their world.

Monday, May 9th

At my desk at 8.30 and ready to grapple with the next big project, which will occupy the rest of 1994, and which should, if all goes according to plan, bring forth a first draft novel.

Realise that, though I've chosen 'Uganda' as the title and Anglo-African relations as a subject, these must never restrict me. The novel could, this morning, be about anything. What I must find is a voice which enables me to speak clearly and honestly and with the humour and understanding that I'm known for, about what really concerns me.

To a drink at the Nell pub opposite the Theatre Royal. David Pugh says he's only just now emerging from a deep and almost incapacitating gloom which affected him at the end of last week. Now, buoyed by the resilience of the booking figures (£10,000 taken just today) and, I suspect, by the backing of Robert and Archie, he is working on an ad campaign, which will concentrate heavily on radio and bringing in the sort of people who packed the Yvonne Arnaud at Guildford and the Hawth at Crawley.

Across Covent Garden and Soho to the Lexington restaurant for a comedy writers' get-together at which I'm sat next to David Renwick.[1] He is of the view that theatre critics are jealous and unforgiving when confronted by what they see as the alibi of success.

Barry Cryer says it is quite striking how indignant everyone is in my defence. Mind you, he was not happy about the opening night – didn't like the crowds and the hype and he and Terry avoided the party. He thinks that Richard Wilson was not the right casting because it is so similar to Meldrew and therefore will always be Meldrew.

1 David Renwick, creator of *One Foot in the Grave*, in which Richard Wilson appeared as Victor Meldrew.

Wednesday, May 11th

Look at the outline of plot of 'Uganda' and spend a moment or two idly wondering what I would come up with if I tried a different approach – i.e. to say serious things through a comic novel rather than comic things through a serious novel.

Well I come up with a title – 'The Man Who Woke Up as Cardinal Richelieu' – and this unleashed quite a little salvo of funny lines and developments. It could be about reincarnation. He could spend a lot of time in France trying to discover more about the man he was, or rather wasn't. And I liked the twist that the more he followed up his alter ego, the more he discovered to his satisfaction that Richelieu was as screwed up as he was, in fact that Richelieu was him.

Have been asked to do an appeal on BBC One for relief aid in Rwanda. For a moment I find myself thinking of saying no because people will say it's opportunism – a sort of instant rehabilitation after bad reviews. Then I'm quite appalled that I should be this worried about what people might think, and agree to do it.

Friday, May 13th

To my car, which is parked as close as I can get to the theatre, among the down and outs in Sardinia Street, off Lincoln's Inn Fields. Two men are beside it, talking. One is leaning against the passenger door. As I let myself in a crust of bread glances off my cheek and onto the ground. The fat mess of a man who has thrown it looks at me with undisguised hostility. The younger man he's been talking to has recognised me and is outraged – ''ere, you just threw bread at him!' He then asks for my autograph.

Saturday, May 14th

All four levels open tonight and R visibly relieved: 'So nice to get a really big laugh.' This sounds really heartfelt, and I'm reminded what he must have been going through these last two weeks. He could not avoid the play as I could. Julie says she feels 'the tide has turned', and it happened on Thursday night. As a result of all this I left the theatre happier than for a long time.

Sunday, May 15th

A very silly idea hatched between myself and TG for writing a comic novel. Take a standard like *Wuthering Heights* and reproduce it virtually in its entirety, except adding another character. Possibly Roger, an insurance salesman who would be glimpsed at a distance, at first, by Cathy or Heathcliff, then would gradually insinuate himself into the action.

Wednesday, May 18th

Long phone chat with Robin.

He says he never expected the critics to turn, as a pack, against me in the way they did. But he instances their recent attacks on Roddy Doyle,[1] previously a golden boy, for his series *Family*. 'They'll allow you so much success and no more.' Robin thinks there's nothing much wrong – reiterates his view that the play will be around in 200 years' time, and recounts a story of Pugh's, that Bill Kenwright[2] had rung him and said that he (Bill) would never have let the show get those reviews. Kenwright evidently wheels, deals, cajoles and usually gets what he wants. According to Robin he would have made sure Nick de Jongh didn't review *The Weekend*.

Saturday, May 21st

Visit Tom who is recording the work of a singer/songwriter called Andrea – from New York, early twenties, strong features, enormous eyes, brilliantined hair. Through her, Tom hopes for a lucrative publishing deal.

She says she wants an autograph. I laugh and point to Tom – 'That's who you want. I'm just a has-been.' She shakes her head firmly ... 'You're not a has-been, you're a has-now.' I like that.

Tuesday, May 31st

I woke early and lay awake with various anxieties but as soon as I was up I couldn't wait to get to the novel. All the aimlessness and diffidence that had been making the daily writing sessions such a grind seemed, for now at any rate, to have gone. Maybe the weather had something to do with it. Big clear

---

1 Roddy Doyle won the Booker Prize in 1993 for *Paddy Clarke Ha Ha Ha*.
2 Bill Kenwright, theatrical impresario who put on the long-running hit *Blood Brothers*.

blue sky. Started with determination, re-read the four thousand-odd words I'd already assembled, edited, elided and, liking the company of my characters, wrote on.

Rachel is all packed up ready for another departure. She doesn't like them and neither do I. Her plane to Greece leaves just before midnight and she will touch down at three a.m. our time. As I drive her through remarkably traffic-free streets to Victoria she says from the heart, 'I don't know how you do this, Dad, I really don't.'

Put her on the Gatwick Express for the second time in less than a month. All part of the learning process, I said as I held her hand at the train window. I'm proud of her.

Collect Richard W and take him out to dinner. I check that it's not one of his alcohol-free days, and he confesses that there haven't been many of those recently. He dresses carefully, taking time to make sure the handkerchief in the top pocket of his blazer is just right, then off we go.

The Ivy is not as riddled with the great and the greedy tonight. We end up bantering with Michael Pennington, just back from a very successful Pinterfest in Dublin, and Alan Rickman, who's just finished filming there and can think of nowhere better to live.

Richard confided to me that he has been offered an OBE and is to accept. He'd obviously agonised – 'Well I don't want to be seen supporting this government, or anything with the word Empire in it,' he explained gloomily. I'm very pleased – and it'll be good for box office!

Thursday, June 2nd

To the Ivy for supper with David P and his colleague Billy. They ask me earnestly whether the bad reviews have put me off playwrighting completely. They visibly perk up when I laugh off the reviews, which I feel I almost can now, pledge myself to giving *The Weekend* the best shot on a tour and affirm that I might indeed write another play. Well, says David, they would love to do another one with me. Jamie Barber is desperate to get it for Guildford and Robert Fox has talked of commissioning me to write something for Maggie Smith.

Opportunists that they are, David and Billy fly the kite of a possible acting role for me in a tour of *84 Charing Cross Road*, opposite Miriam Karlin ... oh, and endless other possibilities. It's nice, an occasion to talk more of the future than the past.

Friday, June 3rd

There is a letter in the columns of the *Ham and High* today headed 'Palin's Play A Pleasure' and is written by a recent visitor to the Strand who had found it a great night out and took exception to the critics stifling, or attempting to stifle, one of the few new West End plays.

Write a short 'Middle Word' for the Python songbook – pure relaxation. Create a rather nice, enthusiastic, chatty, not too bright character called E. F. God – who whinges on a bit about not being appreciated for the effort he put into the Creation, etc. Seven hundred words in an hour – faster than anything in the last month!

Monday, June 6th

A lot of D-Day 50th anniversary mania around. Charles Wheeler's documentary has the authentic ring of passion and despair. Wheeler has a completely unforced presentational style, the ease and naturalness you hear very rarely these days. Articulate without ever being verbose, reflective without ever being sentimental. He showed how rare it is to hear a simple, unaffected, documentary-style delivery.

His film pulled no punches and his observations balanced any sense of triumphalism. It was a hideously bloody offensive, in which we killed thousands of innocent French civilians in order to get at the Germans. The image of the inflated corpses of dead horses, grossly swollen, teeth bared, by the roadside cut very deep.

Tuesday, June 7th: Birmingham

Quite a decent review of *Palin's Column* in the *Independent* takes up most of the TV columnist's space – Charles Wheeler's infinitely more impressive and important D-Day prog being relegated to a paragraph at the end.

Run in late morning and down to Euston to catch the Birmingham Shuttle to give the keynote speech at the Women's Institute Biennial Conference.

Off at Birmingham International. Sinister hangar-like buildings of enormous size. In one of which are over 10,000 women, of, I'm told, an average age of 55.

I step up onto the platform, feeling like Billy Graham, and launch into my speech after a longish introduction through which I modestly keep my head bowed. I must say that I find myself not the least shy in front of this huge gathering. I've got a good speech (subtext of which is that we need to hear more women's voices in public life), with some successful jokes upfront, and I get quite a kick out of the whole thing. It's probably the most political speech I've ever made, and, as usual, one can't hear people thinking so I don't know how the serious stuff has been received.

Speak for over 30 minutes – great ovation, even though they've been squeezed onto uncomfortable chairs in sardine-like rows for more than two hours. Another interview, a cup of tea and back to London.

The speech took me two and a half days to assemble. Enjoyed delivering it and now feel the delicious calm after the storm.

Wednesday, June 8th

Surveyed the work in progress, then gave an hour's serious thought to an alternative to the novel – a memoir.

I think of all the fragments of childhood memory I've read and enjoyed. Michael J. Arlen's *Exiles* and J. R. Ackerley's *My Father and Myself* are two of my favourites. But then I begin to sway back towards the novel. I feel that I'm being cowardly in leaving it at such an early stage, and I must admit to myself that some of this cowardice is due to the last month's critical battering.

I feel worn out with the effort of not achieving a lot. To bed early with another delightful memoir – Blake Morrison's *And When Did You Last See Your Father?*

Thursday, June 16th

Nothing can really 'rout the drowse' (V. Woolf) today. Have to go up to Hampstead to buy some lunch. Whilst walking back to my car I'm greeted by the amiable grey-bearded figure who runs the Rainbow Alliance – George Weiss. He complains of how difficult it was to get publicity for his recent candidacy in the Euro-elections. In the end he got himself arrested. 'I walked into Hampstead police station with this huge spliff, took a puff and offered it to the sergeant in charge – well, they had to arrest me.' His party are committed to free public transport.

Mr O'Rourke came round this afternoon to tell me that he'd heard my play wasn't doing very well and that I should write a musical comedy. He even offered to find me a backer. A man he'd done some marble-laying for – 'a brilliant dancer, an excellent businessman, Wayne Streep'.

Friday, June 17th

To meet Terry Gilliam for lunch at the Lansdowne.

Terry talks about Hollywood, about his new lawyer, who is one of the three most powerful men in the industry, and his various projects, all of which sound to be dependent on some twist or turn or gamble.

He's full of ideas and images and wilfully refuses to tailor his talent to those he doesn't respect (i.e. most Hollywood studio heads). This makes life difficult for him but on the other hand keeps him fresh and sharp and combative. We bemoan the disappearance of silliness, surrealism, inconsequentiality. Everything now has to deliver, or as they say about movies in Hollywood, it has to 'open'.

At the end of a couple of hours of energetic talk I feel stretched and invigorated and anxious not only to finish my novel but to have something else on the go as well. 'The Adventure'? I worry that creatively I'm a sprinter, whereas someone like JC is a long-distance runner.

Sunday, June 26th, Sussex

Visit to Paul and Linda McCartney. We met them first at Frost's summer party, this time last year. Then again at Frost's dinner and today they've invited us to the depths of Sussex.

We leave at two and turn into the unassuming, unmarked concrete drive that leads to the McCartney farm at about 4.30. There is no gatehouse, radio link-up or fence or, as far as I can see, hidden cameras.

Paul confesses that he is sometimes embarrassed by the disappointment certain visitors try to conceal when they see no mansion or stately home, just a modest, liveable, red-brick, red-tiled house with carefully unmanicured gardens. Paul designed the house – 'first you take a sphere, then you take a triangle', he kept saying.

Paul in good shape. Hair less grey than it used to be; he runs, has done for a few years now. Takes the occasional drink of alcohol but prefers to share a joint with Linda. He's vegetarian, they both are, no meat or fish.

She's warm, open, direct and questioning in the American way – we're talking about Angela's death over the first cup of tea. A son, James, pale face, what looks like red hair, loose sloppy clothes, is introduced. He kisses Helen, rather sweetly, then disappears for most of the time. He goes to the local state school, which for a son of one of the richest men in England is remarkable.

We sit around a kitchen table and talk about anything and everything, but legend always intrudes and Yoko rings while we're there about some letter which John wrote to Paul after Linda had written to John who was, she thought, being beastly to her husband at the time.

We walk round the organic, non-fertilised wild meadow over which Linda is endlessly scattering wildflower seeds. They have a soft spot for animals – giving stable space to horses who are blind or with cleft palates.

About 8.45 we start for home, having left them some Python 'My Brain Hurts' T-shirts, and with a bunch of wondrously aromatic pink roses which were named Paul McCartney by the British Rose Federation or whatever.

I share many of Paul's views about fame, life and success, but am chastened by his work rate; his apparent lack of any wasted moments.

Monday, June 27th

A *Palin's Column* end-of-series party to coincide with the transmission of the last episode this evening. About 20 people. I make them all Pimm's.

I'm afraid there comes a point, when I'm in Parkhurst mouthing some inanity, that I have to get up and walk outside. I feel almost ashamed at my lack of penetration. There are excuses. I was tired – there was the hidden pressure of a column to be written (which was never seen), we were doing a lot on a very tight budget, and so on and so on. But I wasn't very good.

I was lazy. I let Roger create a series around me without ever really sitting down and asking if it was the best we could do. An air of crisis kept us blinkered.

The party in the garden, with excellent food and copious New Zealand white and South African red, lifted me from gloom. Candles lit, both parts of the garden used. Robyn compared the whole scene to a summer evening in Sydney.

Tuesday, June 28th

H and I take a taxi to the Frost garden party. We aim to stay only an hour or so and then go on to see the play nephew Jeremy has designed at the Royal Court Upstairs. However, it is almost impossible for anyone with a modicum of curiosity to sneak away from a Frost summer party. There are so many familiar faces – Kenneth Baker, Lord Tebbit, plus wife in wheelchair, even Lady Thatcher.

What you really need is someone to talk to whom you know awfully well and who won't mind your eyes swivelling and your gaze wandering. The Brooke-Taylors fit the bill perfectly and we work out a very effective reciprocal arrangement allowing us to scan the talent whilst appearing to be talking to each other.

The professional friendship is Frost's speciality. So at various moments I talk with Jane Asher, who is writing a novel and Gerald Scarfe, who's very happy and content to draw with one hand and hold their baby in the other. John Wells[1] is helpful and funny and kind. He urges me to make *The Weekend* for television, and reassures me about the novel, and encourages me to keep my resolve and push on with it.

Alyce Faye appears with Bill Goldman,[2] who gazes around the great chattering throng as if looking into the fires of hell. 'Eight people is my maximum,' he explains.

Largely egged on by the Brooke-Taylors, we've abandoned all plans to see *Thyestes*. It's after nine o'clock and we're among the stragglers. Richard Branson tries to grab our taxi, laughing and offering the driver First Class return tickets to New York if he'll turn us out.

Wednesday, June 29th

Watch Jonathan Dimbleby documentary on Prince Charles. 'Did you have sex with another woman while you were still married?' is one of the questions. Whatever shape the monarchy will survive in after the Queen goes, it is, because of accessibility and availability of this kind, certain that it will be very, very different from before. Charles, though decent, sounded tired and weary, as if almost admitting defeat.

Thursday, June 30th

At the theatre. An appreciative audience in the circle, large enough to warrant the presence of two large St John's Ambulance ladies with whom I share the row of seats right at the back.

Hugh Laurie is in Julie Peasgood's dressing room. Tell him about the St John's Ambulance ladies and he suggests that they're not the real thing, but people who dress up in the uniform to get in free.

Later, as we walk up Drury Lane looking for a taxi, Richard quite candidly points out that since rehearsals began he's spent 22 weeks on the play, half a year, and doesn't want to see it again for a while. I doubt if he will ever come back, frankly.

Good news is that Hampstead Theatre Club has approached David with a

---

1 John Wells, satirist, who created the 'Dear Bill' letters for *Private Eye*.
2 William Goldman, screenwriter who made his name with *Butch Cassidy and the Sundance Kid* and followed it with *All the President's Men*.

view to co-commissioning a new play from me. Now that's exciting. I have a title floating around in my head since yesterday – 'Love Bites'.

Friday, July 1st

In today's *Guardian* the feisty Suzanne Moore writes a column about the Charles interview. Throughout the 'embarrassing programme' she kept thinking of others who could do the Prince's job better.

'If his job is to be a roving ambassador, to amuse the natives, to conquer the world with reticent English charm, then why isn't Michael Palin king? He is not king because he was born at the wrong time in the wrong place.'

Saturday, July 2nd

Long chat with Derek Taylor – proponent of the triple whammy theory of press treatment. Derek fascinated by the phenomenon, as he saw the Beatles fairy story turn to reality. Once they've decided to go for you, it will be more than once. Well, *Palin's Column* was number two ...

Down to Terry J's for supper. He announces home-made samosas, of four different fillings, seared salmon, guinea fowl cooked in ginger and yoghurt and a selection of Mediterranean and tropical fruits – mangoes and an apricot which TJ bites and cries 'Shit! ... Oh shit ...' We all wait ... What on *earth* is wrong? ... 'This is *wonderful!*'

Saturday, July 9th

With Helen to the last performance of *The Weekend*. A good house, though not full. Three levels open.

The curtain call is, as ever, warm without being delirious. At the end, as we have done so often over the last five months, Robin and myself scuttle out, through the foyer and round the corner to the stage door.

Gather in Richard's dressing room for champagne. He has his god-daughter there – a sweet girl – and also Antony Sher,[1] a soft-spoken, quietly energetic character; he was interested in the autobiographical side of the play. That's another mess I've got myself into in the prelim interviews – giving the impression

---

1 Antony Sher, South African-born actor, writer and artist, who won a Laurence Olivier Award for *Richard III* (Royal Shakespeare Company). On television he made his name in an adaptation of Malcolm Bradbury's *The History Man*.

that Richard's character was my father. Real instance of cart before horse.

Marie[1] assures me that there have been 'tears in the wardrobe room'.

I go down to say my goodbyes to the stage staff – Lee and Peter and Trevor and Nicola. They're all busy striking the set. One side of the theatre has been opened up, exposing the Febbles' cottage to the world outside. The driver of a huge pantechnicon is arguing with the police over parking.

I'm sure I shall feel bereft and empty and sad about the ending of this adventure, but for now I just feel relief.

Tuesday, July 12th

There is little difference at the moment between the heat of the day and the heat of the night. A thick, damp, un-British warmth envelops the house.

Julian Schlossberg rings to invite us to his marriage to Merron – 'it'll be at seven p.m. and over by 7.06' – in NYC, July 21st. He feels that we should have a special place at the ceremony as it was with us that they shared their first date. He said he's already had the honeymoon, in Venice. We agreed that it was much more sensible to have the honeymoon before, rather than after the wedding.

Wednesday, July 13th

There seem to be a hundred and one things to do other than write the novel. I try to get to the bottom of this writing malaise – it's hardly writer's block, I can churn the stuff out quite easily – but I'm not sure where the reluctance to concentrate springs from. It is something I've felt before, and something I know I'm prone to: an inability to concentrate on one single area of my life, the ability to be easily distracted by a phone call, a book, maybe something more abstract – an emotion, some obligation remembered, a twinge of remorse or regret at some connection made, but not sustained. I seek inspiration from others, can't find enough of the real, intense stuff inside myself.

Later in the day I wrote a long letter to Michael Barnes, who is himself such a good correspondent and who wrote me possibly the most comforting, certainly most elegant, letter on the demise of The Weekend. Writing back made me aware of what a heavy, subversive weight the last five months have been.

In writing to Michael I feel the first lifting of this weight. I can begin to feel and say what I want. There is no longer in the back of my mind that fear

1 Marie Harper, wardrobe mistress.

of an audience not turning up, or another critic chewing up my work. I feel a little released.

Thursday, July 14th

Meeting up with Suzanna Zsohar at a restaurant off the Fulham Road called Aubergine. That part of the world doesn't half sparkle with the comforts of life. Antique shops, galleries, posh interiors shaded from the sun by wide blinds, everything in mint condition. Would I rather live here? Well on a summer's day it has a seductive quality but to really enjoy all this would cost a lot of money, and you would be surrounded by those with a lot of money to spend – and by and large they've never been my favourite income group.

Gazpacho in a coffee cup, little pieces of fish, superbly fresh and presented with such care and attention and colour and beauty and delicately patterned sauces that it's like eating a stained-glass window.

Good discussion with Suzanna, she understands my wish to avoid press publicity for a while (well, for ever, to be honest) and thinks that one trade occasion, plus a couple of signings, would do more good.

Taxi down to Camberwell, where the walls are decorated with graffiti rather than frescoes. 'Stop Graffiti' would be a wonderful piece of graffiti.

To Terry J's, to be interviewed for a *Guardian* Python 25th anniversary piece.

Talk, sitting under the shade of the trees, about how we met and how we wrote. 'Is it too early for a glass of wine?' Terry miaows invitingly at about ten past five, and soon a bottle of rosé nestling in an ice bucket appears beside the wrought-iron table and the reminiscences grow broader and more vivid, though not necessarily more accurate.

As so much of Python was born in or looking out over TJ's garden, I feel a sort of completeness, a rounding of the circle to be here talking about it.

Friday, July 15th

Meet Robin L at the Lansdowne.

We cover the usual ground and there is little he has to add to what he said before. Look at the pedigree of the people who read the play, liked the play and backed the play ... 'I don't do bad plays' was the closest he got to admitting his own status ... Given that these were experienced folk going into it with their eyes open, then I must understand that the extent of the critical clobbering was totally unexpected.

Not a lot of help, but it means I can accept the seductive theory that I suffered not because the play was bad, but because so much I had done in the past was so good!

Saturday, July 16th

Out to Maidenhead to the Flathers' 'At Home'.

Most of the guests seem to be Indian and there is a faintly post-colonial feel to the occasion. The Indians, being sensible, stand in small groups beneath the trees on the periphery of the lawn – the pink Brits, of which there are only half a dozen, tend to gravitate to the sun.

I'm introduced to the Indian High Commissioner – a dapper, erect man of middle age who looks as if he might well drink his own urine, and who, having been told who I am, directs me, somewhat regally, to a patch of shade and addresses me (this is the only description of his donnish technique) on the subject of two ideas he has for programmes about India. One quite good – all about the story-telling that's so much a part of Indian culture.

Ben Okri[1] was there with a tall, red-haired English lady called Rosemary. Okri is gently spoken, with big, round, slow, soft eyes. He talks earnestly but lightly. A big enthusiast of my work, recognises special qualities of naturalness and ease which he finds affecting.

We talked about writing. Don't feel self-conscious at the first-draft stage, he advised – write on, keep moving, write to explore and discover. It all may be rejected in a second draft anyway. 'Don't lose your natural playfulness,' he advises. Though I would imagine I'm 20 years older than him, I feel like the father-son role reversed.

Monday, July 18th

Look at two possible work places for August to the end of the year. A basement and first floor in Gloucester Crescent is just too big for one, largely absentee writer.

Even in the short time I was in the street I caught sight of Clare Tomalin pottering out to the letter box. Word of my arrival would spread like wildfire amongst the Frayns, the Millers, the Haycrafts, the Bainbridge and the Bennett.

On to 54 Delancey Street, not far away in Camden Town, which is much more like it. Top-floor flat in grubby state and a blue plaque on the front of the building announcing that Dylan Thomas lived here!

---

1 Ben Okri, Nigerian-born novelist and poet, winner of the Booker Prize in 1991 for his novel *The Famished Road*.

Wednesday, August 3rd

Returning home from a break down in the Lot Valley. Two thousand miles of French roads without cone or contraflow. On the 60-mile journey up from Portsmouth, three of the latter and many thousands of the former. Compensation is the surprisingly beautiful Hampshire landscape – a soothing and attractive balance of hills and trees and fields – through which the road curves and turns. There is a light, woolly mist around and, for a while, a good feeling of being up and about before the race begins.

With the energy of the recently re-returned I clear the desk and set to on piles of letters. Midway through the afternoon have something of a revelation.

Maybe it was provoked by the news that *East of Ipswich* is to be repeated a month today, but I found myself reaching for the 'Tea with Hemingway' file. Work done five to six years ago for Jack Rosenthal's 'Article For Sale' series and abandoned in favour of last rewrites on *American Friends*. I remember that I abandoned it reluctantly – and remember that Tristram was a great supporter of the story. Could it form the basis of a novel?

Quick read-through suggests yes. Plot and characters far more advanced than 'Uganda', and the territory, English small-town, much more familiar to me.

What was worrying me about 'Uganda' was its scale, its presumption. A novel about colonialism set in a country in which I have spent three weeks. I could see myself being shot down for choosing a big subject but producing a small book.

Thursday, August 4th

At ten I'm ready for my first day in the newly rented 'novel-only' apartment in Delancey Street.

Have to confront the consequences of my new thinking on the novel. This afternoon have a meeting booked with Geoffrey [Strachan] to discuss blurb and a book jacket design – for 'Uganda'.

Write down arguments against 'Uganda' and in favour of Hemingway and vice-versa. It boils down to the fact that 'Uganda' was a concept, never really a story, whereas Hemingway is a story, and the way through it much clearer.

By the time Geoffrey arrives, I've made my mind up. I shall write *Hemingway's Chair*.

Geoffrey is commendably unshocked, or appears to be; he gauges my mood and feelings and, being the gentleman that he is, refrains from a sarcasm that would be quite in order.

A couple of hours later the worst part of my volte-face is over. We talk more in two hours about the Hemingway idea than we have in three months on 'Uganda'.

Monday, August 8th

New regime.

Settle myself in at 54 Delancey, check the marmalade and white cat is in position on the top of Dylan Thomas's green caravan down in the garden below – it is. Soon after 9.30 set about *Hemingway's Chair*.

TG, who has been doing Python 25th anniversary interviews at the Studios, comes by, claiming to be a Dylan Thomas fan. I tell him to fuck off (through the intercom and in Welsh) and we walk down to the Delancey Café for lunch.

He says, gloomily, that he's the greatest living non-film-making director. Claims to have encouraged Tarantino to make *Reservoir Dogs*.

Friday, August 12th

To Southwold today to research small-town east-coast post offices for the novel. Leave at a quarter to seven. Roads going out quite smooth, traffic pouring in as there is another rail strike today. After Ipswich slow to a crawl behind caravans and hay lorries, but reach Southwold Common in almost exactly two hours.

Chris Richardson runs the post office, which he has bought, as a business, and it's dwarfed by an emporium of toys, stationery, books and sweets which extends at the back, converted from an old sorting shed.

My angle in the story seems instinctively right – modernisation is proceeding fast in the post office, hurting a lot of employees and confusing others. Everything now is about making money – the Post Office provides a business service which the government would like to put in competition with banks, building societies etc. Customers must be dealt with swiftly and a 'proactive selling policy' is encouraged to make them buy more than they want every time they come to the counter.

A fascinating glimpse of how much a centre of community life is being changed.

To the church to look at the gravestone of Mum and Dad – surrounded by wild daisies. A strange woman brushing up another grave claims to remember me, when I was 'so high, taking the best red apple from the front of Bumstead's window, with your school cap on and your socks rolled down by your ankles'. She must be a bit mad, though I'm quite happy to be mistaken for Just William.

On the way home make two visits – one to see my mother's old and trusty neighbour, Mrs Pratt; she's sitting in her glassed-in porch and can hardly see anything any more, but once she has recognised me, and I've taken her arm, she proves to be quite on the ball and delighted I've called in. Sit and talk with her for a while. We have a look over the fence to Croft Cottage, and when it's time to go her eyes have watered a little.

I've known her nearly 30 years. She doesn't want to go into a home. Won't even have a home help. Independence of a countrywoman.

Friday, August 19th

On Wednesday I sent the first two chapters – over 10,000 words – to Geoffrey S and received a fax next day which sounded happy with the characters, the way things were going and endorsing the decision to step aside from 'Uganda'.

This morning the character of Nick Marshall came to life – not just a symbol of modern, thrusting business, but something more manic and idiosyncratic.

In the afternoon I start on the American intellectual – she's now to be called Ruth – introduce her via a letter back to the US which I really enjoy writing.

A very clear idea of the potential of the characters and the course of the story comes to me. Almost feel I could go ahead and write the whole thing in a fortnight.

Tuesday, August 23rd

Cycle to Delancey Street, buy milk at the Portuguese shop on the corner; ease into the book and begin to get stuck into some of the conflict scenes.

Rang both Robin L and Alan Bleasdale to wish them well in shooting *Jake's Progress*, which they begin in Ireland next week for 26 weeks solid. Alan is being transported out there in a specially blacked-out Winnebago so he won't be able to see the motorway ahead.

He's been to another hypnotherapist who counselled him to think of something very good, when he had visions of something very bad. 'You know what? I thought of sex,' he admitted, bashfully, 'and I've been thinking about sex ever since.'

Alan is one of the few people I know who never forgets I keep a diary and at one point chuckled a lot at some gossip, but said he couldn't tell me because I'd write it down.

Wednesday, August 24th

Another early run sets me up for an excellent morning's writing. At one Tristram arrives. Inspects and approves the premises, especially the top room with its low, angled ceilings. 'I love properties, as you know.'

TP had actually met Hemingway on two occasions at the home of a wealthy American, Bill Davis, who kept a splendid house in Malaga which he liked to fill with, preferably literary, celebrities.

Remembers seeing Hem swimming – head bobbing up and down like a terrier. Legs were extraordinary. Knotted and gnarled like tree trunks.

Best story is of Tristram arriving back at the house after a long, incautious day in the sun. He was very burnt. Hem took him in hand and said he should rub vinegar all over the burnt area, soak in a hot bath and then rub some more on. TP said it worked.

Tuesday, August 30th

Cannot think how to go forward. Feel that what's gone before is just a whole bunch of words. Why would anyone want to put this inside book covers? I pace the room desperately. Sometimes on the verge of tears. There seems not only no way forward, but no reason for going forward.

Feeling awfully low I decide on an early lunch. Over my ham and salad sandwich from the corner shop I read some of Carlos Baker on Hem.[1] At the start of the chapter on *The Sun Also Rises* there is a quote from Hem to Scott Fitzg, which could have been spoken across the table to me. 'There is only one thing to do with a novel, and that is to go straight on through to the end of the damned thing.'

Which is what I do, and by the end of the afternoon I've put in a respectable day – with another thousand words added. I feel a little shaky but I just mustn't care. What I must do, however scrappily, is get to the end of the damned thing.

Wednesday, August 31st

The complete cessation of IRA activities to begin at midnight. It's a piece of news which could lead to something as momentous as the black majority rule in South Africa, the collapse of communism in Europe, etc. etc.

---

1 Carlos Baker's scholarly biography of Hemingway was published in 1969.

John Hume[1] has worked wonders. The Sinn Fein leadership – Morrison and Adams – looks fresh, comparatively young and acceptably intelligent. The Unionists look old and bitter – their voices sound shrill and bigoted and there is a complete refusal amongst them to accept any degree of Unionist culpability in the last 25 horrible years.

Tuesday, September 6th

Finding it easier to pick up and run with the story than I have for some time. Reading Hemingway has helped, which is rather neat and fortuitous. I respond well to his best writing – when it's clean and uncluttered and direct and robust and he's taught me not to agonise over being clever – searching for the adjective or adverb no-one will have heard of is not necessary – 'good' and 'fine' and 'big' and all those simple, strong words can be sufficient.

The first draft script of 'Wanda 2' is sent round and I start to read it as soon as I can. It is tremendously reassuring. The story moves on briskly, there is potential in all the characters and above all it is very funny. Good to see JC still on form.

Thursday, September 8th

To tea with Alan Bennett, who is awaiting the publication of a collection of his diaries and writings in early October.[2] *The Madness of George III* has just been filmed[3] but he didn't spend much time on location; there was a first-time director and Alan thought his job would be difficult enough without having the writer hanging around.

He makes some tea. I've bought two custard tarts from Ferreira (the Portuguese on the corner) which have welded together in my pannier. Alan sits at his desk and scoffs his enthusiastically. He still plays with his tie – today it's a knitted one in a rather lurid green. It seems he's as comfortable with a tie as I am without one.

Talk about how we write. Alan says he finds it difficult to work in complete isolation. At his house in Settle he watches people go by outside and it helps. I ask him if he's ever written a novel. 'Ooh no,' he says. 'I couldn't do that.

1 John Hume, founder of the Irish Social Democratic and Labour Party, who shared the Nobel Peace Prize with Ulster Unionist politician David Trimble.
2 The collection was called *Writing Home*.
3 *The Madness of King George* was directed by Nick Hytner and won a BAFTA for Best British Film.

I can hear what people say, I can see how they speak, but I don't know how they think. I don't know enough.'

Ramble through the latest doings of old friends. AB asks if I've read the Kenneth Williams diaries. 'Terribly depressing,' he says, 'if you think you're having a miserable time you should read these.' And he gives me a taste ... 'Came home, ironed sweater. And that would be all!'

He commiserates with me over *The Weekend* (which he never saw). He remembers them having a go at him over – what was it called, *Enjoy*? – so he's not entirely critic-proof.

Friday, September 9th

To Ladbroke Road for a meeting on 'Death Fish II'. JC, Iain J, Roger Murray-Leach, the art director, Robert Young, Hugh Laurie, Michael Shamberg. We sit round the boardroom table, with Lucy Willis' wonderful oil painting of a drawing class at some West Country prison mirroring our efforts.

John has prepared questionnaires for us all with headings such as 'What Doesn't Work?' 'What Needs More Work?' 'What Would You Cut?' 'How Would You Restructure?' and space below them for us to write in our opinions. And this is what we are asked to do for half an hour. Like schoolboys at exams (Hugh shields his paper with his forearm), we toil away trying not to take it too seriously, but anxious to be seen to be helpful, clear and concise.

Lucy Willis, artist of the prison picture, sketches us at work.

To Oakley Square in Camden Town to look at a possible flat for William. Big sturdy houses looking out over an un-exotic public garden studded with big chestnut trees. The 2-storey flat is big enough for two or even three. A new conversion. Reminds me of the way Sunset House was when first converted. Carpets down, all electrics provided; virtually ready to move into. A definite contender. Within walking distance of three main-line stations!

Saturday, September 10th

Come home to an urgent message to phone Denise Parry-Jones, Dizzy, Nigel's wife, Terry's sister-in-law. At last get hold of her, only to hear that Nigel died this morning of some stomach illness. Al is away in Italy. Diz doesn't know where Terry is in the US. I eventually track him down to the Sunset Marquis in LA. It's the middle of the night but I have to wake him and tell him to ring Diz. Can't give him the news myself. He rings back later. 'He had such a rotten life,' says TJ.

Friday, September 16th

Yesterday I took down 'A Bit of a Break', the novel I wrote in eleven weeks in 1977. (I think the title is awful and would like to rechristen it 'Nobody Here'.) It's much better than I thought in the sense that the writing is in parts authoritative and the central character a little more proactive than our Martin. Set it aside feeling gloomy on two counts – one that my writing style seems no better, and possibly worse than it was 17 years ago, and the other that 'Bit of a Break' seemed to ride the balance of humour and seriousness more satisfactorily than *Hem's Chair*.

The sun comes through. The two fat ginger cats spread themselves out on the wall of one of the gardens below and for a while it's like summer again.

Tuesday, September 20th

We leave about 9.45 to get down to Nailsea for Nigel's funeral. I have an imperfect image of Nailsea being this side of Bristol. In fact it's south and west of Bristol, off the M5 and near the coast of the Severn Estuary. We stop-start in the heavy traffic out of London.

It becomes clear as we make our way as fast as possible up a busy M5 that Nailsea is unattainable by midday – when the funeral starts.

Lightning stop at a filling station, off the motorway, then up to 120 mph on a curving gradient out of Avonmouth. Then into country roads, with solid elderly drivers who are not in a hurry and take great exception to others who are. Everything thrown in our way, but we reach the church only ten minutes late.

It's a neat old stone church with a tower. Almost full inside. Terry is on his feet giving a round-up of Nige's life – he waves us into the front row! opposite Diz and the children. Terry is energetic, restless, lots to say, but not much of a voice left to say it in.

Two local Labour Party men speak, one complete with red tie and red buttonhole. I speak, then Geoff Burgon, who wrote music for *Brideshead* and *Life of Brian*, speaks and plays 'Ain't Misbehavin' on the trumpet – very smoothly and mellifluously. Lady priest does prayers, we sing a hymn, 'Breathe through the heats' etc. then process down a lane to the graveyard. Despite the foul weather in London it is bright, with white scudding clouds, and the sun shines as Nigel is buried.

Then to the pub close by. Good chat and many memories. Some of the people in the local Labour Party didn't even know Terry was Nige's brother, so good was he at concealing his background.

Wednesday, September 28th

The novel has much greater momentum now. H asked me the other morning 'Is it funny?' and when I said 'No, not really' she said 'That's what you're good at.' Not judgementally or anything, but I think she's right and I must not forget there will be an expectation for me to provide laughs.

Meet Clem V for lunch.

There has been an awful ferry accident in the Baltic in the middle of the night. An Estonian ship keeled over and 800 feared drowned. Clem is concerned about safety in the transport services of the old Soviet Union. Planes are crashing with frightening regularity because there is no money for parts, or inspections or proper maintenance.

But, like me, he's looking forward to our third great journey together. Can hardly believe, as we sit congenially sipping American Sauvignon blanc and tucking into wild mushroom risotto, what we shall be putting ourselves through in the years to come.

Thursday, September 29th

Down to the RAC for a game of squash with Terry.

Afterwards we walk to the Chandos at the bottom of St Martin's Lane to have a pint before going on to the premiere of Ken Loach's *Ladybird, Ladybird*. In the pub, a young chap – regular features, well spoken, smart but unostentatious – comes up and shakes my hand. 'Congratulations,' he says, 'you keep many of us fighter pilots alive.' He's based in Coltishall in Norfolk. Apparently they give themselves 'hours' for their favourite comedy programmes. One hundred hours of *Blackadder* is pretty good, but he says there are people who've done 1,000 hours of Python!

Big crush at the Lumière. Ken, mild and retiring, shelters near the men's loo. He looks like a train-spotter, but his films are wonderfully powerful and this one, like the others, has the knack of showing you poverty and violence, but making you feel at the end of it that you understand these people more and pity them less.

Sunday, October 2nd

At 7.15 H and I arrive at the Dorchester for the Writers' Guild Awards in a Berryhurst car driven by a sinister, taciturn young man with a slight Central European accent, all in black with golden blond hair.

Welcoming committees of rather anxious, full-bodied, bespectacled women, but among them the reassuring presence of Alan Plater and his deputy chairman David Nobbs.

We are between Susannah York (co-host with Jimmy Perry) and the cartoonist Richard Wilson on one side and Honor Blackman, looking well-groomed, smart and still devastatingly attractive, on the other.

Susannah looks a bit nervous. We talk about how difficult it is in our business to remember the names of all those we've worked with and how we both fear these sorts of occasions for that reason.

Jimmy Perry, passing around us at the time, pats Susannah on the shoulder. 'It's lovely you could do this for us, Joanna.'

Colin Dexter, writer of *Morse*, is at our table. He's small, like a very old baby with a mischievous, gnome-like presence. In the gents before the awards begin he is confiding. The girl he's with is very excited to be on the same table as me – she's an ex-policewoman from Oxford. Dexter goes into rhapsodies hearing that Rachel is to go to Brasenose. Most of *Morse* filming is done there.

I see Richard Curtis and Emma Freud there and tell R that I'm presenting in his category and that I hope he wins, though I know I shouldn't say that. Well, he said, just read out my name whatever happens.

My piece goes well and Richard C is the winner for *Four Weddings*.

Monday, October 3rd

Rachel's first day at Oxford.

Lines of cars outside Brasenose, also unloading. Rachel in determinedly bouncy form. First good news is her room – number 5 on staircase 7.

If ever there was a room in which I might say my career began it's this one. The low beam, the window seat, the step down into a bedroom. This is where Robert Hewison and I wrote and planned our cabarets; where we ate Polish sausage and I learnt to love endive salad!

She's unpacked and the shabbily decorated room has taken on some of her life. We leave about 5.30. There are parents hugging their children all over the place. The men get a peremptory shoulder to shoulder, the girls something more lingering.

Monday, October 10th

The warm, settled days continue. On the very last lap of *'Hem's Chair'*, so in to work soon after nine. The final, apocalyptic sequence falls into place nicely and I race to the finish, spewing forth nearly 3,000 words in four hours flat.

Type 'The End' at ten minutes to two. No great traumas, but I shed tears for Martin as I write him off. Well, not so much Martin as the others left behind.

Then I have to start at the beginning again and work my way through. Corrections on every page and some quite substantial rewrites which I have spotted at early read-throughs.

H asks the uncomfortable question – 'Is it the sort of book you would want to read?'

Tuesday, October 25th

Have set myself up again at 54 Delancey, after eleven days away, re-reading the novel in the Hemingway locations of the Basque country.

Geoffrey, big in many layers of brown, arrives a little after ten. First of all we talk general points. Geoffrey, to his credit, is businesslike, thorough and doesn't attempt to disguise the fact that he feels there is work to be done. He finds the main characters interesting, contrasting and wants to know more about them. He feels the townsfolk should be better and more fully rounded. He is of the opinion that more cuts are necessary rather than extensive rewriting and that the book will take it, as it's at a good length.

I push as far as I can, without sounding alarmist or defeatist, my doubts about the weight and consequence of the book. Geoffrey plays a straight bat, refusing to supply false enthusiasms or countenance any convenient despondency. He reiterates its strengths – 'You've written some good scenes, and there is an effective story ...' and so on.

Back at the flat he fetches out his copy of the text which is peppered with pencil marks and we sit at the table together and begin a much more intense and fraught process than this morning's amiable chat.

The light goes and we huddle together around one lamp.

Wednesday, October 26th

The novel continues its relentless progress. We go to Michelin House to meet Angela Martin, slim, open and friendly Publicity Director, and Simon Westcott, conspicuously young Marketing Director.

There is a tremendous demand for this as yet unfinished work. Smiths want to give me a Hero Promotion – star of the month as it were, and sponsor a signing and reading tour in March. Both Angela, whom I like more and more as we go on, and Simon are expecting a bigger campaign than any I've done so far. Angela accepts my preference for provincial rather than metropolitan venues, and I'm able to steer Simon away, I hope, from cult-of-personality promotion. I'm mindful of the fate of *The Weekend* and want to make quite sure I get up as few noses as possible.

Friday, October 28th

The *Ham and High* runs a feature on Gospel Oak, trailed on the front page as 'Gospel Coke. Gospel Oak, a classic London village, home of Michael Palin ... and a cocaine and heroin problem as bad as anywhere in the capital.' Inside is a story of classic urban decay rather than classic villages. Whether it is worse now than it ever was I don't know. Drugs are more widely available, jobs and money less widely available, Camden, the great protector, is now rate-capped and reduced, so yes, it's hardly surprising it is worse.

I tell Helen that it's probably wiped ten thousand off the house prices at a stroke, but she thinks it all rather exciting! At least we live somewhere where something is going on.

To 54 and await Geoffrey. He says that he's just finished reading through to the end for a second time, and 'you know,' rubs beard ... 'it's very good'.

Monday, October 31st: London–Manchester

Off to Euston for the Manchester train.

Waterstones is busy. Joseph Heller is to give a talk and reading downstairs. Into a basement room where Heller is already at work, signing, surrounded by piles of his latest, *Closing Time*. Head down and writing his name time after time as books are thrust at him, he looks less the great author and more the toiling galley slave.

Our cab driver, with a Liverpudlian Irish accent, tells us that he too has written a book. He wrote it in prison. For the first ten years, he tells us, he wrote nothing, but he decided it was time to tell the story of how he ended up with a twelve-year sentence.

Good old Suzanna goes straight to the point. 'Excuse me, but what were you in prison for?' she calls through the grille. 'If I tell you,' he replies as if he's been asked the question many times, 'it mustn't go outside this taxi.' We all agree. He pauses, effectively. 'Murder.'

Tuesday, November 1st: Manchester–London

Joseph Heller and his wife Valerie are travelling on the same train with us. We stop and talk on our way to breakfast. She is slim and dark and a good twenty years younger than him I would think. He has broad, almost Geronimo-esque features and his complexion is pink and fresh and glowing. He looks healthy but confesses to demolishing much of a bottle of scotch during the signing and talk last night.

I compliment him on *Something Happened* and he says a lot of people are 'coming round to liking' the book. Published in 1961, it was the follow-up to *Catch 22*. He is in London for a week then to Oxford to be interviewed at the Union. Staying at Claridge's. He insists on the morning and most of the afternoon off. He was interviewed by Terry at Hay Festival. He'd caught a Python retrospective in the States and thought Terry looked better as a woman.

Tuesday, November 15th

To a PEN-organised reception at the slightly run-down Royal Society of Literature in Hyde Park Gate. A bevy of authors promised and punters pay £25.00 to come and mingle.

Ronnie Harwood describes the awful privations of writers in prison for what they have written and one thinks facetious thoughts about how many writers in this country you might like to see in prison for what they've written.

A very nice moment after the speeches end. Ronnie Harwood pushes his way through the throng towards me, grasps my hand and congratulates me on *The Dresser*. He had so many letters, he said, all mentioning the strength of my performance. He is wonderfully fulsome and to be congratulated thus by the author swells my pride in the best way. He asks if I would like to do it on stage. I waver. Am I too old? No, he says, two men in their 80s recently played it.

Renew acquaintance with La O'Brien – Edna,[1] who greets me with a soft brush of lips on cheek and a slow, enveloping stateliness which feels like being gently smothered by some naughty aunt. Tell her about the novel. 'What's the title?' she asks with breathy urgency. 'Good title.' Then she asks me how it begins. I start out on an explanation and she interrupts. 'No, no, I mean what is the first line?' She talks with loving intensity of the importance of 'first lines', and I rather pathetically cannot remember a word of mine.

Sunday, November 20th

JC has invited H and me round for a quiet evening. He's had a bad week. Film writing to do but also lots of tasks that took time without giving satisfaction

---

1 Edna O'Brien, Irish novelist who made her name with her first book *The Country Girls*.

– like talking about parking spaces on the filming! Jamie has decided to take on a film in early spring which has disrupted dates. Kevin has become concerned about whether he should play two roles.

Tuesday, November 29th

Must complete my second draft rewrite today, and do so.

To the *Literary Review* 15th anniversary party at Simpson's.

I think the *Lit Review* is more of a club than a magazine – perhaps even more a state of mind. Or a symbol. It loses money, has a modest circulation yet is something of a cause. Bron Waugh's helmsmanship and the generally constructive and generous tone of its contributions (viz. Beryl B's lovely review of *Pole to Pole*) attracts young and old writers. It's fashionable, a little exclusive.

Not that that word's the one that springs to mind as I climb the wide-carpeted stairs of Simpson's in the Strand.

The rooms smell of old gravy and the diners look, from a brief glimpse, like good territory for a George Grosz.

There is a competition, hosted by Bron, for the worst sex in a novel award. Last year it was won by Melvyn for *A Time to Dance*, and apparently he sportingly arrived to collect it. Award presented by Marianne Faithfull.

A flame-haired temptress asks me how P. J. O'Rourke was when I interviewed him on Saturday. She feels very foolish when I tell her that it was Melvyn Bragg who interviewed P. J. O'Rourke. 'Of course, you're Michael Palin! I much prefer you to Melvyn Bragg!'

I get a kiss from Marianne Faithfull, who says, before I can say the same thing to her, 'I feel as if I've known you all my life'!

Home by 9.15. More wine. H out. Realise I am drunk. Drink lots of water and crash out early.

Later H says she knew I must have been enjoying lavish hospitality as she could hear me snoring from downstairs.

Thursday, December 8th

This is the 13th consecutive day I have worked on the novel. Generally I have begun between 9.30 and ten in the morning, always at the Dylan house, except for last Sunday at home. Here I work until about two hours after it gets dark, i.e. about six o'clock. Drive home, have supper and put in two or three more hours before bed, usually at midnight.

There are notes in the margin about almost every character involved – 'let reader know more'; 'who is this, what is he/she wearing'. This aspect has been the hardest work, but I think Geoffrey right to pin me down to detail and precision. I've always had a lazy streak. 'Lines of Least Resistance' is my favourite autobiography title.

Friday, December 9th

If there were ever a time when I could say the novel is finished, this is it. Though Geoffrey will trawl through it with an even finer toothcomb next week, what I deliver today is essentially what *Hemingway's Chair* will be.

Began August 8th. Finished December 9th. Four months. Not enough. But what would be enough?

Thursday, December 15th

Dreamt about a land covered in white frost and my dream comes true this morning. Sun slowly pulling itself above the stagnant polluted air, but it's still a beautiful winter morning.

To 54 Delancey as Mary O'Donovan arrives at 10.30. Mary is the copy-editor at Methuen. She's brisk and efficient and confident in her judgements, though I should think she's not much older than Tom.

Have to go through the entire novel, page by page, one more time.

Home and, despite great weariness and the enormous attraction of an early night and a sleep of more than five and a half hours, we have to get ready to go out to George H's Christmas party.

George looks more like the garden gnome than the slim, fine-featured executive these days. He's wearing, he says, his 'Tibetan Book of the Dead Boots', which he last wore at the White House when George Bush was President.

Ade Edmondson wandering about clutching a beer and looking gently bemused. Very keen to know what I'm doing. I realise that I can't stop them treating me with respect, however much I want to pay it back to them. Harry Enfield calls me Mr Palin and I feel instantly like one of his Cholmondley-Warner characters. Feel more at ease with the Neil Innes and the Ray Coopers – my coevals rather than my admirers.

Sit next to Derek and Joan Taylor. Many laughs. Derek disappears to smoke a joint and comes back very bright-eyed.

The McCartneys' chauffeur-driven Mercedes limo is idling outside the front porch as we slip by and, feeling very good and comfortable, head back to town.

Monday, December 19th

To Portobello Road for a drink and view of the exhibition at Tristram's new gallery/shop up in the less trendy, but possibly emerging, fringes of Golborne. Trellick Tower looms a half-mile away. TP's gallery reminds me of a little Irish bar. The walls decorated with a sort of sponged yellow wash. A round green garden table and a red-leather bench give a carnival contrast to the lines of halogen lamps on wires which illuminate the works. It's quite chic, a mixture of high and low tech as Tristram says.

George Melly[1] is sitting comfortably at the table. He says we've met somewhere recently. I can't remember, and as I seem to have been the victim of mistaken identity cases so often recently – but I venture the *Passionate Woman* premiere – Melly doesn't think so. He says he never goes to the theatre – can't hear. Went to *Liaisons Dangereuses* and could hear the man's voice, because the pitch was right, but the woman's not at all.

Unload my heavy coat – for the weather has turned wintry at last – and my accumulation of shopping. TP shows me round. He's got a nice little office at the back, which has windows onto a yard and for some reason reminds me of the time-keeper's office at a factory.

Jonathan Miller arrives with his wife Rachel. He's having two days off between operas. Describes someone he's met in New York as having so diluted his Jewishness that he refers to him as having had a Jewdectomy.

Miller rants on about the critics. I mention my experience with *The Weekend*. 'I was away for that,' he adds hastily.

Monday, December 26th

Read slim Boxing Day papers. I detect a sense of national embarrassment over the royals and their revelations. Embarrassment and shame. As if we have allowed some unpleasantly prurient and titillating side of ourselves to be publicly exploited. I think there is a revulsion from the whole thing now.

Saturday, December 31st

Morning at various shops. London streets still quiet.

Drop in at No. 54 on the way back. The room in which I wrote *Hemingway's Chair* is much as it was as I worked there. Two big felt pin-boards on the walls in front of me and to my left, index cards of the chapters.

1 George Melly, writer, jazz singer, film and TV critic for the *Observer*, died in 2007.

Onwards, after a last lingering look at the modest, unspectacular premises, overlooking Dylan Thomas' caravan, where so much of my year was spent, to familiar haunts – the Persian dry cleaners, the Indian stationers, Renata and Rafael at Giacobazzi's Delicatessen.

Renata doesn't like the passing of a year. It generally makes her sad and regretful. I look forward so much to a new year that I never grieve for the old one, I say. 'I don't like change,' she says. This I can sympathise with too. But I'm a nostalgic with a fascination for the future.

Helen has cooked an Indian meal for our New Year's Eve party tonight. Everyone arrives about 8.30.

The old year slips away and 1995 is ushered in by Dame Vera Lynn on BBC One.

1995

Sunday, January 1st

Without really meaning to I find myself at my desk, with some Gene Vincent[1] playing, beginning to turn the pages of *Hemingway's Chair* yet again.

A rare and welcome feeling of optimism takes me. Maybe it's because I'm not yet again reading the book in rigorous silence, fearing doorbells and telephones, or in haste, aware of all the other things I should be doing. I'm reading for once because I want to read it.

The music seems to give life to the writing and the energy of the writing blends with the energy of the music. I keep replaying some of my loudest CDs, alternating Vincent with Southside Johnny and the Asbury Jukes.

Turn off the deck at midnight – after 'All Night Long' fades for the umpteenth time, and I feel at that moment that I have nothing to be ashamed of.

Tuesday, January 3rd

Rachel toils away upstairs, working as hard, now Christmas is over, as she ever did last term at Oxford, Tom is in a studio somewhere recording the work of a rapper called The Darkman and Will is enjoying the life of Riley on skis at Val d'Isère.

The roads are quiet. Drive across Hyde Park and down to the Michelin Building with unusual swiftness.

Simon and his assistant Jo at Reed Books are bright and helpful, but they have been conditioned into behaving and thinking in a straitjacket – determined by targets and flow charts. Dreams, hopes, inspirations must not be indulged in during office hours.

I ask them not to call it a 'brilliant' new novel, which they think very odd – but I feel that's for others to say, not ourselves. (The real reason for my reluctance is that I don't think they will!)

---

1 Gene Vincent, pioneer rock-'n'-roller, introduced to me by John Peel when we were both at Shrewsbury school together in 1957.

Sunday, January 8th

I wake quite soon after I first drift off. Was the sound of breaking glass the tail end of a dream or the first indication of wakefulness? Nothing to be seen outside the window. Back to bed.

Woken again by sound of letter box rattling. Then hear footsteps passing beneath the window – sounds like a man and a woman. No evidence of anything being put through door. Feel a little uneasy. Back to bed after checking the time. It's 4.15.

A few minutes later footsteps, faster and heavier, stop on our corner. Then I hear letter box shutter rattling again and subdued voices. Someone is trying the front door. Letter box rattles again. Tiptoe downstairs. Voices outside the door, though I can't hear what they're saying.

Clear view of two young lads – late teens – beneath the telegraph pole talking and glancing again at the house. What strikes me first is their appearance. Their shabby, ill-fitting clothes, the dirt on the face of one of them makes a classic picture of poverty. They look like they're from the very bottom of the heap.

One of them, a skinny, dark-haired boy with cadaverous features, is swaying on his feet. His eyes look slow and dead. Then the other one, a fairer, fleshier-faced lad, turns, holding what looks like a metal tape measure, open a foot or so, and they both come straight towards the window from which I'm observing them.

Tiptoe upstairs and ask H to ring the police. Can hear the metal being inserted between the window frames. Panto-esque farce now takes over as I move about the landing and into my room looking for paper and pencil to write down a clear description of the two. Don't want to risk switching light on or making any noise. Of all the pens and pencils I emerge with I choose the white one; back again, produce a biro that won't write.

Meanwhile the two would-be intruders continue testing the window. Then the phone rings. H grabs it quickly. It's the police. Probably because of their altered state the sound of the phone fails to deter the lads, and they are duly caught outside the house by a police van and four support cars.

Around 10.30 two Detective Inspectors arrive to take statements.

Would I be prepared to testify in court if the case ever got that far? I say yes.

The fingerprint lady arrives. She's number three in the Met, I was told by the Detective, in clear-up rate success. She does a thorough job, dabbing her brush at the window as H and I sit inside, giving statements at separate tables. Only at the end does her professional detachment waver. 'Could you sign my job sheet?' she asks.

Monday, January 9th

Lin Cook rings to tell us that Peter is dead. She can hardly speak. Once again that awful, palpable sense of loss, a feeling of time being called – but in Peter's case, called too early.

The news comes through about 10.15. Just after eleven I'm on Radio 5 Live with a hastily cobbled-together tribute.

The phone rings as soon as I've put it down; it's the *Standard* wanting my thoughts, then my nephew Marcus rings from *Newsnight* to see if I would come in and do a tribute. I feel that others knew him better, could say more about his professional career and that it might be presumptuous of me to turn up.

Helen goes up to see Lin. She is very distressed.

The death of anyone you know produces a kind of heightened introspection, and when it's someone you know and have become close to – and recently, driving them home late-night from parties, I feel we have become close to Lin and Peter – it's a momentary feeling of vulnerability, of the cold hand of the reaper coming very close indeed.

Meet Michael Barnes at Two Brydges.

Michael has not heard the news about Peter. He sits, long legs and long hands elegantly stretching across the sofa before the artificial flames of the fire, smoking and drinking a whisky. He is a thin version of Peter I think – what I mean of course is that he is an incorrigible and unrepentant smoker and drinker.

Michael then tells me two recent experiences – one, when he fainted in an Italian restaurant in Belfast and was taken to the City Hospital where, perhaps because of the way he looked, five days of tests were done. Brain scans and heart-rate monitors, etc. all revealed nothing.

Then just after Christmas he had a blackout whilst walking home, and remembers nothing of a fall which left him with head wounds that needed six stitches and an overnight stay in the City Hospital. He later discovered he had fallen.

I'm not sure why he tells me these stories at such length, but despite the underlying theme of basic good health, I think there is fear that something may happen again at any time. I notice that he put away two whiskies, a half-bottle of Côtes du Rhône and three measures of Armagnac before attempting the narrow, lethal stairs of Two Brydges.

We part in the street and I cannot help but feel as I press my arm around his bony shoulders that I fear for Michael's survival as urgently as I sometimes used to fear for Peter's.

Tuesday, January 10th

Work at home on various bits and pieces. *Observer* rings to ask if I would contribute a 700-word piece about Peter C for Sunday. Say yes.

Catch first episode of TJ's *Crusades*. A bit breathless and busy, but Terry is wonderful. He doesn't really seem to mind what he looks like.

Wednesday, January 11th

Outraged by news that John Marriott – the Governor of Parkhurst who so impressed me when we filmed there – has been sacked as a scapegoat for the Parkhurst escape.[1] I set my thoughts down in a letter to the *Independent*.

Wrestle with the Peter Cook obit. Very much aware that this is something I must get right. Temptation to assume I know all about his life – of course I don't.

Monday, January 16th

Feeling twitchily anxious about my *Tatler* phone interview re *Hemingway's Chair* this morning. The first proofs of the book have gone out to long-lead journalists and, I presume, to the *Omnibus* people, and this will be one of the first outside, upmarket reactions.

Their interviewer is Cressida Connolly, daughter of Cyril.[2]

'Your novel,' she begins, and follows this with a long silence. My heart sinks, and a drowsy numbness … She sounds kind, polite, not at all lofty, but I can't get any signals as to approval or disapproval.

Only at the very end of our amicable and sympathetic chat does she reveal that she liked the novel. Found it funny and also full of pathos and how nice it was not to have a relentlessly comic style.

She also revealed that Cyril was terribly pleased by the Pythons' reference to him at the end of 'Eric the Half a Bee' – 'Cy-ril Con-oll-ee?' 'Who?' 'Cyril Connolly'. They had the record and replayed it hungrily!

---

1 John Marriott was sacked by the Home Secretary, Michael Howard, following the escape from Parkhurst of three prisoners. He had been Governor of the Isle of Wight prison since 1990.
2 Cyril Connolly, influential literary critic remembered for his 1938 autobiography *Enemies of Promise*. His daughter, Cressida, is a writer and novelist, whose collection of short stories, *The Happiest Days*, won the PEN/Macmillan prize in 2000.

Tuesday, January 17th

Some interesting work offers, including playing Ratty to A Bennett's Mole in an animated version of *Wind in the Willows* being done for Carlton. The two other main characters to be played by Rik Mayall and Michael Gambon. Really can't resist. It's one and a half days and I'd do it for the lunch-break company alone!

Wednesday, January 18th

Lunch at Groucho's with Dan P. Catch up on things. In theory, I turn 'The Adventure' over to him now, knowing that I shall have no time until the end of 1997 to look at it in any concentrated way.

On the way out, I see Anna Haycraft talking earnestly to Jeffrey Bernard[1] who sits, white as a corpse, in a wheelchair beside the bar. I like the fact that the wheelchair is by the bar and in the main thoroughfare. No chance of any-one missing him, or vice-versa.

George H rings. He's back from India. He's most concerned that his post-card from the Udaipur Lake Palace hasn't arrived, but tells me what it says. 'There we were, hundred of us, living in't palace in't middle of lake. We 'ad to get up in't morning – lick palace clean wi'our tongues ...' Then he says 'I hear you've been seeing the bass player from our band.' Takes me a while before I realise he means McCartney. George has a good sense of silliness. Better able to send it all up than Paul.

Tuesday, January 31st

A letter from the BBC Radio Drama department. It's from one Duncan Minshull, Chief Producer, Readings, who has received an advance copy of *Hemingway's Chair* and thinks it would make 'a terrific and topical addition to *Book at Bedtime*, a real summer treat'. He proposes my recording it in ten 15-minute episodes, which would coincide with publication.

I spend the evening preparing for my debut as 'Ratty' in *Wind in the Willows* tomorrow.

---

1 Jeffrey Bernard, writer of the 'Low Life' column in the *Spectator*, who was immortalised in Keith Waterhouse's play *Jeffrey Bernard Is Unwell*.

Wednesday, February 1st

I am determined to walk to work – the recordings are being made at George Martin's 'Air' Studios. Step out with my umbrella. There just before nine.

Alan Bennett, who's playing Mole, is already in the studio sitting in splendid isolation at one of two long tables, each covered with a white, embroidered tablecloth, creating an effect (with all the hi-tech equipment) halfway between an operating theatre and a tea-shop. Actually the place is a converted church, and beyond the expensive shell of the recording studio are tall arched windows with stained-glass rose patterns at the top.

Alan and I try to gossip in between takes, but it's not easy with a half-dozen people in the box listening to our every word.

He'd recently been contacted by Dudley Moore's biographer, and thought it most peculiar that Dudley had clearly put about the story that he was a poor and put-upon working-class boy who had suffered a harsh, almost Dickensian upbringing.

And talking of Dickens, A tells story of David Hockney, who had been to see the musical *Oliver* and was disappointed that the homosexual nature of the relationship between Fagin and Dodger had not been brought out enough. 'Well, I mean,' says Alan, Mole-ishly, 'there's no sex in Dickens at all.'

By 12.15 we've completed all we had to do and A decides to go home for lunch.

Back up the hill again for two o'clock and Michael Gambon, as Badger, is already at the table. Big, crumpled, lived-in look. He's soft-spoken and affable, with no apparent actor's tricks or psychoses.

He and Alan B fall to talking about Michael Bryant (who played Ratty in the first National production of Alan's adaptation). Alan confesses that he was terrified of Michael Bryant the only time he'd worked with him, and Gambon confirmed that he is a hard man on stage. 'Tells you to "fuck off" as soon as you come on.'

George Martin makes a paternal appearance. (I don't have the cheek to ask him if he'd seen himself described in a magazine article recently as 'the Michael Palin of rock'!) He says the studio conversion cost about £15 million. 'Half the money was Japanese, so I feel I'd done my bit to pay them back for the Burma Railway,' he says, elegantly.

Thursday, February 2nd

The call has been delayed until eleven, so no great rush this morning. There is some very pale light outside at a quarter to eight now, which shows the winter slowly waning.

There is quite a chunk left for Alan and myself to do, which rather pleases me as I'm enjoying working opposite him. Slightly hysterical end-of-term atmosphere today.

Alan has, at one point, to do some wild-track 'fighting' noises. He screws up his face with effort – a sort of squeak comes out and he collapses into fits of laughter. 'Oh dear,' he laments, trying desperately to gather his concentration for another effort, 'this is why I never wanted to be an actor!'

All of us, I think even Alan, a little regretful to be told that it's all done.

Rik M has arrived for some publicity photos, and Gambon too. Rik is currently in a new Simon Gray play with Stephen Fry.[1] Gray is on a bottle of champagne a day, Rik says. 'I don't know if he drinks it all. He just likes to have it there.'

Monday, February 6th

The *Daily Mail* calls and asks if I would write them a piece about my feelings on the current state of the Labour Party. When I tell them I'm too busy they suggest me putting my name to a 'ghosted' piece. Tell them no, more vigorously.

Ring Alan Bennett to check if he is coming with H and myself to see Maggie Smith in Albee's *Three Tall Women* on Friday. When I ask if he'd like to bring someone, he says he hasn't anyone to bring. He laughs when I make sympathetic noises, and says it's not so much that he hasn't got anyone, but that there are very few people he would risk bringing along to meet, as he calls her fondly, 'the flame-thrower'. 'They'd have to wear asbestos suits,' he says, making himself laugh a lot.

Tuesday, February 7th

Down to Bush House to take part in an hour-long phone-in for National Public Radio.

Bush House, soaring skywards and grandly dominating the long, southward perspective of Kingsway, has still one of the finest exteriors in London, and the fact that it preludes a building devoted to nation speaking peace unto nation nicely combines the spirit and appearance of the place.

A slim young girl whose second name is Haybill takes me up and out and round the back and down an iron fire escape and eventually to a quite roomy

---

1 Stephen Fry disappeared to Belgium while appearing in the London production of Gray's play, *Cell Mates*.

studio from which I shall be able to talk to the American nation. That's precisely what does happen – the smooth, almost purring voice of interlocutor
Carl Suarez oozes through from Washington and introduces me to all sorts of
people from Tallahassee, Florida, to Seattle, who all want to talk to me about
the current running of *80 Days* on PBS.

Ms Haybill sits with me and occasionally fiddles with the controls. It's a
very intimate situation. Just the two of us and the whole of America.

Wednesday, February 8th

To Harley Street to have a combined insurance medical for 'Palin's Pacific'
and 'Death Fish 2'. Dr Forecast doesn't quite convince as a doctor. The whole
process over without me even having to take shirt or shoes or socks off. Rather
wearily, he hands me a small plastic container. 'Could you do a urine sample?
For the BBC.'

Friday, February 10th

To *Three Tall Women*. Wyndham's Theatre packed. Maggie's pulling power.
In the first act she looks a bit like the Thatcher dummy in *Spitting Image*, tight
and sharp and malevolent. But it's not she who is the unsympathetic character
in the play, whatever Albee might have intended. It's the young, hard lawyer.
So Maggie gets the laughs and carries us cheerfully on to the half. Second act
better but still not a good play.

Backstage and into Maggie's presence. Again, the disarming, purring lower
register of the voice. She hugs Alan – his raincoat flies everywhere. It's like a
scene on a station in the '50s. Then, with less abandon, she gives me a hug.

Then on to the Ivy. At one point Alan, who was voted Most Popular
Author of the Year at the Nibbies last night, professed that he rarely had phone
calls – 'I sometimes pick the receiver up just to see if it's working.'

Tuesday, March 7th

My first glimpse of the hardback of *Hemingway's Chair* – the finished work.

Turn it over and read a little. I keep doing this at various points during the
day. It gives me pleasure. Something about the artefact itself – the confidence
of the design, the printing, the binding, the price even – seems to elevate the
text, endow it with some distinction, some significance. Never have the words
felt less arbitrary.

Wednesday, March 8th

Angela Martin and Kath round to discuss 'HC' tour and publicity. Try to avoid exposing myself to too many of the 'big' celebrity articles which I find it so difficult to deal with, and at the other end of the scale avoid 'My First Kitchen' sort of stuff.

There are two photos in *Bookcase*, the W. H. Smith's free mag. One on the cover makes me look like a younger Warren Beatty – lashed in make-up on a beach, inside an extraordinary combination of quiffy, swept-back, wind-blown hair and someone else's sweater (I should be aware by now that if I wear someone else's clothes I look like someone else).

According to Angela Martin, Adrian Edmondson said I looked like k.d. lang.

Saturday, March 18th

Car collects me at 12.15 to go to my first official *Hemingway's Chair* function. Held at an anonymous modern pile of a hotel called Copthorne Tara, as if after the heroine of a tacky novel.

About 350 booksellers, currently in the middle of a conference, crowd in for this Reed Books-hosted event.

It's much more successful than it seemed likely to be. The food is good, and the four author speakers – Paula Danziger, the children's author, Dr Stefan Someone[1] (the obligatory gardening expert that every publisher likes to trundle out), Michel Roux and myself – are each allotted a course, rather than all kept until the end.

I'm the final speaker, accompanying the coffee, but sandwiched very close against the start of the England-Scotland rugby match.

I feel on top of my brief, as it were – the speech is very well received, mainly, I think, because I've talked less of myself and more about booksellers and bookselling. Know your audience. It pays off.

Brian the driver, who has had them all in the back of his car – 'John Cleese – he's much better now', Peter Ackroyd – 'well, he's a gay alcoholic isn't he' – drives me back via Museum Street in Bloomsbury so I can look for a J. B. Priestley first edition for Barry Cryer's 60th tomorrow. 'Boydy loves this street. I often have to bring him here' (Will Boydy, that is).

I've a feeling that I could find out a lot from Brian, who is genially, amiably indiscreet. I now know that Boydy, and Mrs Boydy, have a 'château' south of Bordeaux. Brian gives a grunt of wondering appreciation as if thinking of the Temple of Solomon.

1 Dr Stefan Buczacki.

Tuesday, March 21st

To the National Portrait Gallery, to which I have been invited for the private view/launch of the Richard Avedon show. A mass of photographers beehive around the entrance. No way of getting in except dodging through the traffic on Charing Cross Road.

Once in, herded upstairs to a 'reception'. Not allowed into the Avedon yet as Princess Di is paying a visit first.

Eventually we're allowed downstairs. Doors open, men with walkie-talkies push a way (unnecessarily) through our ranks and Lady Di, talking to, and towering over, little Dick A, walks past us. Does she double-take on seeing me? I had the distinct feeling she did; it made the whole shambles worthwhile.

Later I collar Avedon; he's very charming and remembers me. Our photo (the naked Pythons) is in the catalogue but not in the exhibition. Avedon, who looks like a little golden-haired doll, smiles apologetically – 'You're much more used to all this than I am.' Nice to have made contact. Twenty years on. Then some loud, proprietorial voice summons him. 'Richard! Over here!' No question of apologising for breaking into our conversation. It's not that sort of occasion.

Friday, March 24th

Into Holland Park to be interviewed on a bench by Frank Delaney.

Delaney, like a sort of Irish Ned Sherrin, burbles on, most agreeably. Feel he should be in a periwig for the bons mots and the little observations fall lightly and profusely. He does tell a very good story of Michael Winner banging on the door of a Portaloo and shouting to his lighting cameraman that he wanted him on set. The cameraman shouts back, 'I'm sorry, Michael, I can't deal with two shits at once.'

Brian drives me home. Is indiscreet about Ranulph Fiennes and Sir John Harvey-Jones. 'He likes to have two pints before every interview'!

Monday, March 27th

Interview with Andrew Duncan for *Radio Times* about my involvement in the launch of BBC's Mental Health Week (which I record on Wednesday). Offer information about Angela. Am amazed how fast journalists move in once you've volunteered some very personal information. No holding back. 'Does it worry you that you are now the same age as your sister was when she died?'

Friday, March 31st: London–Edinburgh

To the Caledonian Hotel, which I always feel is some sort of 'lucky' hotel. It was here that I heard that *Pole to Pole* had gone to No. 1 two and a half years ago, and here that I finished that extraordinary week when *80 Days* became a hit, and the book entered the charts, for the first time.

Tonight it came up trumps again – though in a more unexpected way. The Suzie Mackenzie piece appeared today in the *Evening Standard*. Apart from the awful headline 'How I Forgave My Father's Sins', it was a strong, moving piece.

Angela's 'gassing' of herself came up in the first arresting paragraph – but it was a good, fair piece, related to '*HC*', which she called 'a marvellous first novel', and which pieced together all sorts of small revelations about my relationship with my father accurately and with real sympathy. I read it twice, and with tears in my eyes both times.

Monday, April 3rd

Publication day.

To *Start the Week* studio. Talk to Tom Stoppard, big and slim and hardly a sign of conventional ageing on complexion or in the dense blackness of his thick, Byronic locks.

Melanie Phillips kicks the programme off with five minutes on hypocrisy – hardly designed to start the 25th anniversary edition with a bang. We all have to chip in. Nerve-racking really.

Then I have a few minutes on *Hemingway's Chair*. Melvyn murmured to me before we went in 'If I say the name Amis came to mind – Kingsley Amis – I hope you wouldn't take it amiss (*sic*)'. That's as close as he got to praise, but he's quite pleasant, jovial and indulgent with it on air.

Stoppard is like Martin, the hero of my book, something of a Hemingway addict. He says he's now weaned himself off the worst of the effects – buying every first edition he could lay his hands on, etc. 'You should have come to see me,' he advises afterwards. 'I could have saved you all that research.'

To the Victoria Station signing. It turns out to be the best attendance so far. For a solid hour there is a queue.

One man gives me his *Standard* to sign. 'Put "Roxy Music" at the bottom,' he orders. When I ask what on earth for he looks pained. 'You're Bryan Ferry, aren't you?' Much laughter from Angela. When I say no he looks cross, as if I've deceived him.

Tuesday, April 11th: Nottingham–Sheffield–Manchester

With breakfast comes a *Guardian* review of 'HC'. I brace myself. It's another man – why do they nearly always give the book to men to review?

The inevitable mixture – praise and punishment. But at least the praise rather warm and unexpected. He was very complimentary about my ability to write a sex scene and thought that the book was essentially a love story. No-one has seen it quite like that before.

It's a day of continuous, if not absolutely clear sunshine. Sheffield sprawls over the hills. We sign books at Blackwells – a lovely manager, keen staff, but hard hit by the removal of Sheffield's shopping centre to Meadowhall. Then out to Meadowhall.

It's the first time I've seen this legendarily successful complex that covers the site of Hadfield's East Hecla steelworks. Nearby are the remains of Edgar Allen's.[1] One long, black-sided shed still bears the name, but next to it just an empty, cleared area where the trackwork department used to be. The foundry's gone too – now part of the approaches to the shopping centre.

I'm just glad that I still have memories of pre-Meadowhall Tinsley, indeed of pre-viaduct Tinsley, memories of the grandeur and grime and the days when Vulcan really was the god of Sheffield.

Meadowhall is shopping as theme park. Spanish villages sprout for no particular reason – and it's quite in keeping with the whole surreal logic of the place that I have to be presented to the shoppers in a huge circular central hall, thick with the smell of burgers and chips, where crowds are eating.

Not only this but I'm interviewed as they eat. A smooth, alarmingly controlled man, who betrays not the slightest apparent awareness of the absurdity of what we're doing, asks me questions about Hemingway which I can barely hear above the noise of the throng. Our conversation is relayed onto a huge multi-panelled, closed-circuit TV screen above our heads. It is an awesomely pointless exercise and I take pleasure in imagining the least likely writers to be put through this ordeal. Anita Brookner? Nabokov?

Tuesday, April 18th

Breakfast, shower and at five to nine Graham Fordham, my driver for the next 16 weeks of *Fierce Creatures*, rings the doorbell.

Into Pinewood at twenty to ten. Meeting in the boardroom – English manorial library with real books behind latticed doors. So many old friends

---

1 The Edgar Allen company where my father worked as Export Manager until his retirement in 1965.

– Maria Aitken, Robert Lindsay, Robert Young, John, Cynthia, his daughter, Jonathan Benson[1] – a copious reunion. Neither Kevin nor Jamie is here yet.

A read-through begins.

As we read it occurs to me that this is Basil Fawlty time – John has created for himself a character more flexible, less tight and angry than Basil, but able to mine the same rich seams of physical comedy, outrage, double-take, double entendre. It is a return to the JC we know and love and roar with laughter at.

We read again, then lunch and there is a general feeling of satisfaction and indeed quiet excitement. It works. We trudge off to see the animals – ring-tailed lemurs – camply draping themselves in their Newcastle United-coloured tails, coatimundi – with long, ceaselessly enquiring noses. I try my tarantula, Terry. Soft, weightless and hairy. I like him.

Wednesday, April 19th

Collected at nine. In the boardroom all morning. John rather fond of statements like 'I think that all the problems occur in the following scenes' – so we are manoeuvred, skilfully but indulgently, towards certain group scenes at the end.

We're taken onto the site where the zoo will be, and with JCBs grinding past and lorries and dump-trucks and drills and hammers drowning out John's voice, he tries to explain to us all where we shall be on a set that hasn't yet been built. I applaud the generosity of his enthusiasm in taking us there but question the practical usefulness of the exercise.

Then back indoors and more reading and discussion of the end scenes. Much of Bugsy's role is not even written – the continuous chattering and ear-bending has all to be filled in. So I feel a bit out of it. The loner that Bugsy is seems to have become me.

To the Bush to see *Trainspotting* with Will. A squeeze, as the place is absolutely packed.

Very exciting – from the start the performance of Ewen Bremner as Mark rivets the attention. He speaks fast, broad Scots but with a range and clarity which is both soft and sometimes quite ferocious. His skinny body twists, turns and contorts into El Greco-esque attitudes, seemingly changing from foetal to stretched and staring heavenwards.

Two and a half hours of the most exciting theatre I've seen for a long time. Makes me very thankful that the little Bush theatre, above the pub, is able to

---

1 Jonathan Benson, First Assistant Director, *Life of Brian*, *A Fish Called Wanda* and *The Meaning of Life*.

present this uncompromising kind of work and proud to see my name as one of its 15 gold patrons.

Sunday, April 23rd

Run, feeling hearteningly agile. A keen, cool, south-westerly refreshes, but dies quite soon after I get home and the morning mellows into hazy warmth.

In mid-afternoon up to Helen's tennis club in Wood Vale to watch her play in a ladies' tournament.

Terry Turner, tennis coach, a man who if drawn would have been created by Raymond Briggs, is welcoming. He talks very seriously of Helen. 'She's a class player now,' he says, with an almost fierce pride.

At home ring TG in LA, where, I'd just heard, he had been kicked about the face by a horse. 'He isn't even arguing with anyone, that's what worries me,' says Maggie.

The fall, whilst out riding on his day off, sounds nasty, with hooves thudding into his face, and, more alarmingly, the back of his head. He said it was like being attacked with two baseball bats at the same time. Stitches back and front, and back on set the next day.

He is clearly driven mad by the stars on *Twelve Monkeys*. They seem to treat schedules and calls with disdain – ambling onto the set when they're ready. He sounds like someone who can't wait to get home – but film shoots are like that – however good, however happy or unhappy, you're always looking for that light at the end of the tunnel.

Wednesday, April 26th

At Hatchards' Author of the Year Reception.

I'm introduced to Laurie Lee. He is a solid man, an inch or so smaller than me, but a considerable presence in his heavy coat. His face is strong, quite fleshy, and his stance bold and confident, though I realise that he is holding a rather upmarket white stick, and must be blind.

Any feeling of awkwardness or embarrassment dissipated by the presence of Clare Francis, holding onto his left arm, and by Laurie Lee's reaction to being told who he's speaking to. He grasps my hand and tells me how wonderful my work is and how much pleasure I've given him and how he hates me because my books sell in such vast quantities!

All this is relayed with considerable humour and with such intense directness that I find myself seriously questioning his blindness. At last I manage to blurt out some corny compliment about *As I Walked Out One Midsummer*

Morning being one of my favourite books, and one of my favourite journeys. Laurie Lee, without any malice, says 'You got the title right.'

Ben Okri is there, in a striking, elegant white suit, all flashing eyes and big smiles; Edwina Currie[1] too, behaving just like politicians do behave – treating everyone with professional attention as though we are either constituents or would-be voters.

End up sharing a cab home with Rob Newman,[2] who is going to Leverton Street. We get on very well. He's a fan, but we talk about comedy and performance and about how difficult it is to always, effortlessly, hit form.

Thursday, April 27th

Helen asks if I'd had a lot to drink last night. Apparently she had come to bed to find my E. M. Delafield lying on the duvet and me, fast asleep, with my glasses on. When she'd removed the glasses I'd woken with a start. 'Thank you very much indeed,' I'd apparently said.

To work at Pinewood. JC is there but declares he's infectious and urges everyone to keep their distance. Within an hour he and I and Carey Lowell[3] are rehearsing what's known as 'The Farce Sequence' and John is sitting on my head with his hand over my mouth – having completely forgotten about the spread of his disease.

In the afternoon, at last, Hazel Pethig[4] and I decide on Bugsy's 'look'. The all-black, loner figure doesn't suit the words, so he's now looking more like an assistant BBC sound man, merged with a minor trade union leader. Sports jackets and cardigans – but long hair.

Monday, May 1st

Peter Cook's funeral. When we eventually reach Hampstead Parish Church, there are few people outside apart from Dudley Moore and legions of lenses. They form a thick gauntlet right up to the front door.

Once inside we're ushered right to the front by John's assistant Garry. Climb into the pew in front of John, who looks like the forbidding priest in

---

1 Edwina Currie, Conservative politician who lost her seat at the 1997 election. Her published diaries revealed a four-year affair with John Major.
2 Rob Newman, comedian who made his name alongside David Baddiel in the BBC series *The Mary Whitehouse Experience*.
3 Carey Lowell, American actress who played a Bond girl in *Licence to Kill* in 1989. Married Richard Gere in 2002.
4 Hazel Pethig, costume designer on all the Python TV shows and films.

Fanny and Alexander – all in black, tightly buttoned and black-tied. I hear him mutter something like 'no tie, I see,' as I squeeze past Alan Bennett, also in a suit, and into place alongside Michael Winner (blue suit, white shirt, no tie). In front of us are Peter's daughters, all in black. Everyone looks very serious, and I'm quite surprised. This doesn't seem true to Peter's spirit at all.

Various addresses and readings – Alan B funny and honest and free of sentiment. His line that 'as a young man, Peter's only regret was that he'd once saved David Frost from drowning' almost brings the church down. David Frost is behind me, in the pew with John and Alyce Faye and Dudley. He takes it admirably.

John's composed a poem and manages to deliver it, but only just. Both Peter's daughters dab their eyes profusely at this point. A short poem, read beautifully and directly by Eleanor Bron, brings the tears to my eyes, unexpectedly – and largely because it's really about Lin and the love Peter had for her.

Dudley, dressed dark in a musician's way and moving with that strange American-style power-walk which I observed in Kevin and Michael Shamberg – cool, apparently preoccupied with higher things, humbly aware of one's exalted status – plays 'Goodbye' at the end of one and a half hours, during which we've listened to Radley College Choir sing 'Love Me Tender' and a tape of Peter as E. L. Wisty.

An unexpectedly successful balance between the solemnity of the church and the sharpness of Peter's humour. Not nearly as relaxed and ribald as Graham's memorial, but affecting in a different way.

Friday, May 5th

Out to Pinewood and more rehearsals on the grass. Everyone seems to know it's my birthday and I'm given cards and presents by the three assistant keepers, Kim, Julie and Choy-Ling, who call themselves my Zoo-ettes! Choy-Ling, who, according to Julie, has three nipples, has given me a box containing two chocolate nipples.

At the end of the rehearsals I've ordered some bottles of Taittinger and the caterers have done a good job of keeping them iced. So the party goes on, under the trees and beside the rudd-filled lake (into which people occasionally toss slabs of French bread just to see the enormous numbers of fish who flock to eat it). It's a midsummer atmosphere. Everyone very happy and friendly.

Will rings from Venice where he has secured an internship at the Guggenheim. He's found an apartment, on the Campo San Margherita, and moves in there tomorrow.

To supper with Mary and Ed at the Ivy.

At the end of the meal Will Carling and Julia and Hugh Laurie and Jo come by on their way out. Carling jests that he could be out of a job tomorrow, having been heard on television calling the board of the Rugby Football Union 57 old farts.

Tell Hugh how well 'Death Fish 2' is going, which has the desired effect of making him dreadfully apologetic about pulling out.

Saturday, May 6th

Will Carling has been sacked as England captain.

Tuesday, May 9th

John has bounced back from the drawn anxiousness of the first two weeks of rehearsal and is looking well prepared for the start of filming next week. Kevin still away in the US. Jamie not yet comfortable with Willa; she falters, uncharacteristically, in scenes with the keepers. Must be daunting for her, confronted with a line of all-British actors. She is deep into *Hemingway's Chair*, and displays an almost childlike enthusiasm and relish for it. She advises that I must make a movie of it.

I feel sadly aware that there is not as much fun in Bugsy as there was in Ken. The work is largely ensemble, almost chorus, work about which I just can't get as excited.

Wednesday, May 10th

Richard Loncraine and Felice to supper. They arrive bearing that heightened sense of drama that always attends anything R is involved in. He has heard, literally on the way over here, that *Richard III* – or Richard 3-D, as a friend of his daughter described it – is to go ahead.

His reaction is similar to that of Terry J who heard, also this week, that *Wind in the Willows* is to go ahead – a sudden rush of doubt. In Terry's case whether the script is right (I read it over last weekend and though I don't think it's that strong, it has charm. The Americanisation of the story for Disney hasn't helped). In Richard's case it's a question he thinks of 'whether I can make Ian (McKellen) a star'.

Richard has pursued it without let-up. When Angelica Houston backed out at the last minute, he rang Warren Beatty (who'd called Richard after *The Missionary*, to say how much he'd liked it) and within a week had Annette Bening as Houston's replacement.

Thursday, May 11th

To Pinewood. A publicity blitz has been organised, which JC hopes will assuage the journalists and keep them off our backs through the shoot.

Some shots of the four of us recreating the *Wanda* poster – only with Jamie holding a wallaby instead of a goldfish. John gasps with pleasure at the strapline 'They're Older, They're Richer, They're Fatter and They're Back!'

Then we're led before the photographers of the world. It's almost royal baby time – a semicircle of lensmen, with video-camera crews prowling around the periphery trying to pick off any or all of us. It's easy to feel like an animal. Jamie cannot resist taking on the press. She strides up to them like a confident stripper to an audience of lager louts. Of course, they love it.

The movie is from today officially called *Fierce Creatures* – John has had his way – and oddly enough, as the day goes on and I hear more and more of the press mention the new title, the more acceptable it sounds.

Then a Japanese press conference. About 25 Japanese journalists applaud us as we come in, listen politely, laugh at the most bizarre moments. When JC, through the interpreter, is asked if there is any country in the world which does not know about Monty Python he says 'Papua New Guinea' and they all fall about.

After lunch we're put before the European press – some 70 of them – and then installed in hastily sound-baffled cubicles in four corners of a big room whilst the journalists are circulated, for four minutes only, to each of us. At the end the journalist is given a cassette of the recording, like a child being given a sweet after a visit to the doctor.

Friday, May 12th

Have contacted Hannah at Pilates again.

Hannah, who reckons she last saw me in February 1992, is as effusive as ever. She admits that she'd now like to get out of Pilates. 'If I have to say "pull your stomach in" much more, I may well scream.'

Anyway, I'm very glad to have gone back. My muscles are stiff and awkward in certain positions but on the whole I feel in good shape. Hannah is very encouraging and I book a series of sessions to help prepare me for the Pacific journey, on which we embark in less than four months' time!

Monday, May 15th

An easy start to the shoot, as I'm not called until midday.

Not too many thesps there – and some of my favourites – Maria Aitken, Carey Lowell, Michael Percival – so atmosphere becomes quickly like a good garden party. Occasionally, people come back from the set in the big, black Mercedes, looking a little shell-shocked. But mainly we talk and laugh and devise uses for some of the strange attachments I have in my coat of many pockets.

An orange rubber tube particularly excites Maria, who thinks I might use it to threaten M. Percival with an enema. So lots of 'Sleeping with the Enema', 'The Enema Within' jokes.

Midway into the afternoon comes the familiar news that they probably won't get to our scene today after all.

Tuesday, May 16th

Good news from Kentish Town Police that we shall not have to go to court over our attempted burglary. They've pleaded guilty, as one of the accused has just received eight months for another break-in whilst out on bail. I hear from various people who ring, during the a.m., that an account of the incident has appeared in several of today's papers. On my way out to shops I pick up a *Telegraph* and there I am: 'Michael Palin Foils Fumbling Burglars'.

Wednesday, May 17th

Out in the street Murphy's men are raising the paving slabs to lay the cable container pipes. Another Irishman is helping Mr Brown paint his house. 'You wouldn't think he'd painted the Sistine Chapel, now, would you?' says Mr Brown to Helen. The other man, young, thick-set, dark hair, florid face, protests from the top of the ladder. 'Paint it? I built it.'

Monday, May 22nd

My first big day on *Fierce Creatures*. The spider sequence in John's office.

Most of the morning spent, anti-climactically, waiting for re-shoots of last week's material, then giving lines off as John's close-ups are covered. Instead of getting on to me after lunch, the schedule is changed to film a quite different sequence.

All the extra keepers have arrived. A crowded, noisy afternoon in the rich, overgrown gardens of the house. At least I get a line and a close-up and everyone seems happy.

Wrapped by 6.30. Graham drives me to Bond Street for the Fine Art Society's Christopher Wood and Summer Show preview. A clutch of Sickerts – including a version of 'Ennui', which is one of my favourites.

Whilst I'm sipping a white wine and poking around the small and ill-attended Christopher Wood exhibition encounter Nigel, my cousin. After warning me about the Sickert – 'too clean' – he suggested we move on up Bond Street, as there seems to be a general open evening in the galleries.

Into Wildenstein's. Judge Tumim[1] is there peering, muttering and being generally jovial.

Ask Tumim about John Marriott at Parkhurst. He liked the man but believed he had no option but to take responsibility for the lax security. He also agreed that there was no way to run a long-term offenders prison without giving the inmates some autonomy.

Back home, as I clean my teeth, I listen to the first of the 'Book at Bedtime' *Hemingway's Chair* readings. Funny to hear myself filling the Radio 4 airwaves at this intimate time.

What is everyone doing while I tell them a story?

Tuesday, May 23rd: London–Lainston House, Hampshire

Out to Breakspear House and to my 'Prowler' caravan/trailer, with its slightly disconcerting sticker on the window advising that it's made of Trichloroethane, 'a substance which harms public health and the environment'.

Shoot my reverses on the spider sequence.

Unlike on *Wanda*, we have instant colour, sound video playback of every shot. This is alarming in some ways – an extra element of pressure – not just the cameraman watching but as many as can crowd around the monitor.

Home, pack my things, make some last phone calls and leave for Hampshire.

At about 8.15 arrive at the Lainston House Hotel.

Shown to a room called 'Walnut'. Woody, manor-house style inside. Big armchair, sofa. Four-poster with barley-sugar uprights. Plenty of space.

Ronnie Corbett is the next one to arrive. We meet for a drink in the libraried bar.

Order a Lagavulin – a rich, peaty, tarry malt. Sip it out on a terrace which overlooks a garden of tall, mature trees and a long grass strip which descends towards an avenue of limes – some of which they say are 250 years

---

1 Judge Stephen Tumim, Chief Inspector of Prisons for England and Wales since 1987.

old. There is not a breath of wind. Everything seems frozen, in a state of suspension.

Wednesday, May 24th: Lainston House

Breakfast rather graciously, with Ronnie. Still no sign of anyone else. Twenty-minute drive to Marwell Zoo. It's set amongst thick woodland (as is everything in this part of Hampshire). Plenty of animals – cheetahs, hippos, tigers – everything we tracked for so long across the South African savannah to see on *Pole to Pole* – here for the price of a ticket. And looking in much better shape than most of the animals in Africa.

Jamie's first day on the picture. She's shaken everyone up with her firecracker, no-holds-barred directness. She noticed my haircut and said 'That's a great haircut, it looks like a tarantula.' Then, after a pause, 'Mine looks like a vagina.' Now the dust has settled and she's ready for action.

Nothing very demanding. I'm wrapped at five.

To my woody room and write and learn my 'ad-libs' for tomorrow! Bugsy's spiel has to be long enough to fill the space required, but this does involve a lot more learning.

Over a drink in the lounge – she white wine, me Lagavulin – Jamie is subdued and serious. Serious about acting, which she loves. Talk about technique – different directors' styles – till all the others arrive.

Thursday, May 25th: Marwell Zoo

There are so many people working today – Steve Abbott [Producer on *Fierce Creatures* as he had been on *Wanda*] has counted 200 people on the week's payroll, and that's not including our own actors.

Jonathan Benson and Robert keep a good pace going despite casts of thousands – human and animal – and the constant presence of the public, as the zoo could not be closed whilst we work.

Otherwise the big story on the unit is that Cynthia and Lisa Hogan, two of our cast of keepers, apparently came across a couple making love on a grave in Winchester Cathedral's grounds, around midnight. The couple had not only not stopped, but on being seen had redoubled their efforts.

As I sit on the lawns at Marwell with hard bright sunshine alternating with chilly shadows as the clouds scud across, Steve A mutters darkly of major problems coming to the boil at a meeting tonight.

The construction team will not have the Pinewood zoo ready on time.

They are now weeks behind and there will have to be serious changes made in script and/or schedule.

Friday, May 26th

Arrive at the opening of Camden's newest library for seven o'clock ceremony.
Phil Turner, bloke-ish Head of Arts in Camden, speaks.
Turner is a politician. Perfectly nice, but still comes out with … 'Well, we'll have a new government soon.' This is the smug face of Camden Labour – the complacent cant that caused so much chaos, inefficiency and waste over the last 20 years … 'Well … it's the government's fault.' Bollocks, you lazy sod, I think, but smile sweetly and take my leave.

Sunday, May 28th

Another seven hours of sleep – alarm wakes me at a quarter to seven. Phone BA. Hear that the Boston flight, bearing Violet Gwangwa,[1] our one-time neighbour from South Africa, is on time. Dress, grab some orange juice and set off for the airport. It's raining.
Violet doesn't appear until nine. She'd waited one and a half hours to clear immigration. She's as stoic as ever though, and with her soft, intelligent voice chatters on about the women's group she's travelled to the States with, to learn how they can teach the poorest women to learn to help themselves, rather than rely on state handouts.
We eat lunch in the garden together as the clouds bluster about, illuminating us at intervals, like a lantern show. Jonas, her husband, doesn't make much money as a musician, though he's called upon all the time – V says it's unfair, but as one of the ANC brothers he's expected to give his services for nothing.
V says illegal immigration is one of the new and most potent problems. Three million crossed the border illegally since independence, attracted by the wealth and job prospects. If they're repatriated they come back again. The aching problems of Africa seem quite insoluble – by our criteria anyway.

Tuesday, May 30th

Wake, just after seven, with a sudden, tightening feeling of comprehensive anxiety. For a while I feel quite immobilised.
This weight does not lift until after I've washed, dressed, exercised (without

1 Violet, married to Jonas Gwangwa. Both ANC stalwarts during the apartheid years.

371

enthusiasm), breakfasted and left for Prominent Studios to meet Bobby Birchall, the designer we've chosen for the 'Palin's Pacific' book.

I have committed to a nine-part travel series, and a book to go with it, both of which have already paid me an advance. I have two people, well three, with Kath, waiting to hear what I have to say about book, design, working together. I have two options – one, to run screaming from the room, the other to run the meeting.

I run the meeting.

Sunday, June 11th

To the RAC at eleven for squash with TJ. Despite his increasing girth, which, together with recently Toad-shaved head, gives him more than a hint of Mr Creosote, he wins three games on the run.

They have put back *Wind in the Willows* for two weeks, and he's no further on with the cast. Nothing heard from Connery or Tim Roth. Turned down by Hugh Grant. TJ is going to offer Rat to Eric. He's asked me to record the voice of the sun!

Thursday, June 15th, Marwell Zoo

I can never remember such long hours and such hard work doing so little. I begin to allow myself some self-pity – feeling that, whereas I was intrinsic to *Wanda*, I'm marginalised on this one. Kevin slips in and out of character. Jamie paces like a cat – occasionally purring – more often than not hissing and showing her claws.

The crew seem tired. They watch it all, but I wouldn't say there was a close feeling of involvement. There is an uncomfortable whiff of elitism about the place.

Maybe I'm feeling jaundiced because I'm tired – maybe I'm tired because I'm feeling jaundiced.

The flamingos and ducks are brought along today – to make the lake seem idyllic – for a reputed £3,000 per day. The schedule slips and my day off tomorrow, Friday, is more likely to be a half-day after all.

Friday, June 16th, Marwell Zoo

Onto the grassy knoll, now worn thin by five days of movement, by nine o'clock.

John has a lot to do, concentrates hard, but also is clearly feeling on top of things – and these are some of his most difficult scenes. He sits beside me. We talk about my plans for the Pacific Rim. Earlier this week he told me of yet another film plan of his – not the sex comedy with he and me and Maria A, but a film of Peter Shaffer's *Black Comedy*, in which all the characters behave as if they're in the dark. This is the one he now wants to make – 'very simply – one stage at Twickenham – pretty soon after I've finished this'. My schedule will not release me until two years from now, at very earliest. John ruminates, sympathises and nods ruefully. 'Well, it looks as if I shall have to do it without you, little plum.'

When I think of *American Friends*, *The Weekend* and even *Hemingway's Chair*, I cannot avoid a feeling of having stumbled over the past few years. I wish I could say I had an irrepressible self-confidence, but I haven't. And this encounter just dampens the fire a little more.

Wednesday, June 21st

Talk to Robert Lindsay in his dressing room before the day's work begins. Says that he checked his part in the script which was sent out at the end of last year, and had 185 lines; he's now got 32.

John does his shots most of the morning. We talk a bit today. He asks for my advice on performance. Just relax, is all I can say. Avoid it becoming one-note.

Alyce Faye picks her way onto the set. She wears a new and expensive designer outfit every day – indeed one of the small pleasures of the filming is the arrival of AF – for not only is the outfit always different, she has in tow different celebrities – today Nicole Farhi and Eduardo Paolozzi,[1] big, thick, dark, with a massive face and built like a tree. His voice is deep like it's come from way underground.

John's new masseuse, a bespectacled lady called Wendy, gives my upper back half an hour's attention. Her fingers are extraordinarily strong and seem to pierce through to the deepest tissue. 'Deep-tissue' massage is what she's really about. She talks of 'opening people up'.

I can barely stop from crying out – and make feeble small talk about the trees to cover my pain. Later, I hear everyone feels the same. Maria A says she could hardly walk for a couple of days.

1 Scottish sculptor and artist, knighted in 1988.

Friday, June 23rd

We're shooting in the Pinewood zoo today for the first time, and will have lions, tigers and leopards working with us.

Enlivened by arrival on set of Charlie Crichton and Nadine. Charlie, his strong, long, handsome face well tanned, looks very little different from the way he was eight years ago. Nadine, however, seems much more frail.

Charlie is set down in front of the leopard's cage, and various members of the old *Wanda* team are ushered into or a trifle shyly approach his presence, as if he were ancient royalty – a revered icon. Amanda, John's assistant, brings him a large scotch in a small, chunky glass tumbler which he takes in his badly shaking hands. He's still the same slightly prickly, mischievous self, though. His face breaks easily into a smile, and he grips his walking stick with reassuring strength.

Monday, June 26th

A shot is being set up when Robert Y, today sporting a very British panama hat, marches up and says very loudly and emphatically that he is going to widen the shot 'because that's what Michael Shamberg wants!'. This was not meant to be funny. This was anger, exasperation and impatience combined.

Jamie has a copy of Janet Leigh's first novel. It's called *The Dream Factory*. She laughs about the sex scenes ... 'I just can't take all that you know ... I keep wanting to ask – was this how I was conceived?' She finds one of the offending scenes and is about to read it but breaks into giggles and asks me to do it. So I sit and read Jamie a very bad sex scene written by her mother.

Friday, June 30th

In at nine. Not called onto the set until a quarter to one. Have just avoided having to read the other character in a dreadful man–woman confrontation scene which Carey Lowell wants to tape as an audition for her next film. Sample line – Her: 'I'm a lesbian.' Him: 'How am I supposed to take that? I have a penis you know.' Her: 'I sure do. I've had it in my mouth enough times.' And Carey was about to have me record this with her in a studio full of carpenters making scenery!

Am wearing long johns and a vest, as part of my inside-the-tiger-skin costume, and this attracts whistles as I walk down to the zoo. A whole crowd of people around the camera; much admiration of my underwear. Then someone turns me round to be introduced. 'Here's someone you may know.' Find myself looking down at the screwed-up-against-the sun expression of the Duchess of York. Much laughter at our predicament. She takes it in her stride (probably quite used to meeting men in their underwear) and introduces me to her daughters – all prettily attired in bows and pigtails.

Saturday, July 1st

First shot is on Robert L and myself, and Bille Brown.[1] No-one else there – no featured keepers, 'B' keepers, 'C' keepers. In the chill grey of the morning we get the sequence together, quietly and thoroughly, and JC seems well pleased.

About midday we're in our stride when the set-up we have prepared has to be struck so that a jogging shot of Jamie can be covered before lunch. For some reason this causes another flare-up amongst the ruling body and I hear Jamie having a go at John; she's pouring out her indignation. JC fights back. Those of us near this drama tuck our heads deeper into our crosswords, and listen.

Sunday, July 2nd

To the RAC to play squash with Richard Wilson. He wins 3-1, though the games are close. The RAC is like a vast, elaborately decorated morgue this Sunday morning. RW suggests coffee.

The newspapers are laid out on a long, heavy oak table. On the front of them 'Divine' – the hooker in the Hugh Grant case – thrusts her body seductively off a bar stool. She's naked save for a 'censored' sticker across the genitalia. She's also sprawled across the *News of the World*, to whom she has sold her story of 'the incident'. Hugh Grant's manhood, we're told, was 'cute'. 'We're not going to read that are we,' says Richard severely, and we don't.

Monday, July 10th

Enjoy acting at last! Instead of a-line-a-day stuff – an actual exchange or two to get stuck into – and with Lindsay as well, so it's back to *GBH* confrontation time. One of the most enjoyable morning's work since shooting began. For once, I was completely surprised by the lunch break.

---

1 Bille Brown, Australian writer and actor. He died in 2013.

Tuesday, July 11th

Hot and sticky, especially in the small bar in which we're filming. Michael Shamberg's driver has head-butted another driver in an argument at the turn-in to the location.

Wednesday, July 12th

Up at 6.30, to ring Rose before I go to work. She says that my Aunt Betty, who died last night, had motor neurone disease and would not have lasted more than six months. When Rose had to go into her mother's end of the house and look for details of the funeral, she found an underlined instruction – '*No* female celebrant.' We both screamed with laughter at that. So typical.

Michael Shamberg announces to me that the poster is to be shot on Saturday August 19th – thus knocking out any real hope of a feet-up, sun-and-sand break before setting off for the Pacific.

Saturday, July 15th

Sleep well – up quite late. At 10.30 still at breakfast and the papers. Grim news from Bosnia as Srebrenica is 'cleansed'. Always uncomfortable to be reminded that our fellow human beings, the great brotherhood of man, are still capable of deliberate, brutal, callous cruelty, in the name, presumably, of some greater good. Feel v. pissed off with J. Chirac, latest in a long line of French poseurs, who is windbagging about action from the elegant comfort of the Elysée Palace. Still, after two weeks of Hugh Grant the newspapers seem to have realised it's time for some bad news.

JC rings. A rapid response to my fax of yesterday evening re my week off. Promises to sort something out. He's having a big scheduling meeting tomorrow. Can I wait? Touched by his concern. We talk a little about the film. Both of us felt last week was good.

Tuesday, July 18th

JC is very solicitous these days – doubtless aware of some tensions among the actors. So John takes time to tell me that things took longer today than expected – 'Kevin has to have time' – and that after a quick 'Tiger Terror' scene tomorrow a.m. we would get on to the 'Rollo's New Office' sequence – 'and knowing you and me, Mickey, we should have that knocked on the head pretty quickly'.

Wednesday, July 19th

It's around 5.30 when we begin the New Office rehearsals proper. By this time the air has grown hotter and heavier. It's a lumpy, lethargic atmosphere. Robert has decided to shoot the bulk of my lines – in effect a short monologue – in one single movement, without cut-ins, so I have to get it right. JC, with whom I practised it for the first time this afternoon, has suggested amendments which I have to try and remember. I'm suddenly having to call on reserves of energy and concentration that are by now dangerously thin.

We make several takes. 'Three in a row,' JC is fond of saying. Lots of heads nod sagely around the video screens, but JC and I both know that it could be easier, more relaxed.

Eventually, after two takes are aborted because of me, JC, who is being fanned down between takes with squares of cardboard, suggests we look at the best of them and if we think we can do better return fresh first thing tomorrow.

Leave the set disconsolately – though JC v. supportive. Brighten up as soon as I get home. After all, what am I doing but asking for time. Everyone else does. As JC says – if this had been a quick TV sketch show several of the takes would have worked just fine, but 'if it's going to be around in ten years' time we might as well get it right'.

Friday, July 21st

At lunchtime an assembly of 15 minutes' edited material is shown on the big rushes screen. It is impressive. The performances hold up and, though it is funny, it's also quite a lot of other things. Dramatic, touching, tense.

JC's scene with the animals in the loo, indeed all his stuff, is much better judged than I expected. The intensity he puts into the character is right, proper and very effective. In fact all the leading characters have an edge to them which is not just quick and cheap and phoney – it's based on truth and should sustain throughout the story. As I said to JC afterwards, even if the rest of the hour and a half's material is lousy, he's still got a great movie.

John Du Prez v. complimentary. Says I make tedium hilarious.

Tuesday, August 1st

Organise my unexpected day off – first down to Covent Garden, where I visit YMCA Adventure shop for things like mosquito nets, sleeping bags, bath plugs and waterproof leggings.

Then home and spend afternoon on Pacific preparation – checking supplies; reading; writing a sort of preface, a 'why' for the journey.

Thursday, August 3rd

To the set at Pinewood, which is wide and spread out and resembles the layout of a small school sports field. It's almost two weeks since I last saw everyone, and yet it seems as if they are all doing just the same things as they were when I left. It's like returning to a party that's been running for hours.

Jamie prowls, looking sharp, ironic, restless and edgy. 'There are just three words you need to know about this place,' she says through clenched teeth, 'Wasp! Wasp! Wasp!'

Friday, August 4th

Another morning of low-grade acting. A crowd growing ever smaller behind Kevin who is in his element – playing a big, bold, unequivocally central role – full of physical attack and extemporaneous embellishments.

In marked contrast to the rest of the sunburnt unit K has preserved an almost deathly pallor. He is followed around the location by his stand-in, Joshua Andrews, son of Anthony, bearing an umbrella like some punkah-wallah. K drives himself around in one of the buggies.

Jamie regards it all with ill-concealed impatience.

We talk more today – Jamie and me. I improvise some great 'Ifs' of history – If Joan of Arc had been deaf, If Hitler had been nice, If Shakespeare had been dyslexic, that sort of thing. Jamie insists that I call my agent 'within the hour' to sell the idea.

Some of the others are trying on their animal costumes for Monday. 'I'm giving my beaver,' shouts Robert L.

Monday, August 7th

So the panda cage scene gets under way. Find the morning hard work. It's one of those scenes that Robert seems to want to shoot every which way, and as the costumes are hot and quite uncomfortable, the process seems to go on for ever. Lines repeated endlessly in a variety of shots – and off screen for a variety of different actors.

Ronnie points out, without malice, that the scene is virtually a monologue for Kevin, with occasional interruptions from ourselves. Mind you, Ronnie, dressed as a sea lion, has as good a chance as anybody of stealing the scene.

John spends much of the day imprisoned in a kangaroo suit – but at least the hard tail serves as a sort of natural shooting stick and he sits back on it gesturing at people and making serious points about the filming with his short, shapely front legs.

Finish after seven o'clock. Graham drops me off at the Brackenbury for dinner and a chat with Roger and Clem about the Pacific Rim. This is the first meeting we've had together since they've come back from their various recces.

We have 50,000 miles to travel and 25 countries to pass through, in nine programmes. We will have to work hard to prevent it being rushed and sketchy.

All of us agree that the sit-down, set-up celeb interviews should be jettisoned in favour of the nuts and bolts of travel. Roger has already moved to cancel General Giap and Imelda Marcos!

Wednesday, August 9th

As ever, the end of the main shoot comes suddenly – and all those of us who at many points couldn't wait for it to end are now suffering the sharp emotional tugs of departure.

At the end of the afternoon I insist that they try a shot of me running towards camera, with Robert L in the tiger skin on my back, to intercut with the funny stuff they've shot running away.

Robert is hoisted onto my shoulders – or rather I lift him up as others take his weight. As soon as 'action' is given, there is a ten-second delay because a pile of cans is visible in shot behind me. Then I move forward. Realise this is very different from the rehearsal. This skin is much heavier. Robert has heavy boots pressing into my ribs. I need to run but know I can't. Stagger two or three paces then feel this huge weight pulling forward on my back and I subside and fall to my knees.

Feel very foolish, but enough has been seen on camera for JC to feel, as I do, that the sequence really needs it. But I equally well know my limits and I know that I cannot carry this weight at the speed which will make it work.

Thursday, August 10th

Watch rushes. The short, pre-collapse footage of myself and RL on my back is good. Shamberg asks if I would give it another go with a lighter skin. I agree and he goes off to fix it.

Next attempt is much better – actually reach the camera. However the tiger skin had fallen down and obscured my face – thus counteracting the one real reason for doing it myself. A third attempt is even better, but on the playback one of the assistants holding Robert didn't clear fast enough.

JC thinks they have enough. Only Shamberg is sufficiently unhappy with it to ask me for one last go.

Well, despite assurances, I know he is right. A good, long, clean five to six seconds would be better – the more of the run the funnier the sequence – it's as simple as that. I agree to a last attempt. It works perfectly. As I lower Robert one of the stuntmen pats me on the shoulder. 'That is not easy,' he says.

Friday, August 11th

The mild elation of the morning must be the left-overs from the last shot of yesterday. Whatever it was, it helped my confidence, and I began a rehearsal of the bugging of the Churchill Suite about 8.15, feeling steady and competent.

JC, seeing 16 pages to be shot by next Thursday, several of them involving motion control, is anxious to complete what he calls 'our stuff' as quickly as possible. It is planned to shoot the two long, bugging scenes in simple, single set-ups.

The outcome of the morning exceeds my wildest expectations. By one o'clock we have shot almost four pages' worth, including both my long dialogue scenes, and everyone is very happy.

In the afternoon we consolidate, with cut-ins and the first of the true farce moments with John and myself – then J, myself and Carey L, racing from door to door and so on. This very satisfactory day's work comes to an end at half past five when we break for the poster shoot.

I'm very hot – my shirt sticking to my back – as I descend the stairs from the set to the floor of the shooting stage where a BBC doctor – young and keen and wide-eyed – awaits with a serum of anti-tick encephalitis vaccine which I shall need for travel in Siberia. 'Was that John Cleese's voice I heard, by any chance?' he asks, in fascination.

Friday, August 18th

At the studio things are quite tense – though no-one puts direct pressure on, it's clear that they want to have the insect house finished by twelve so that the crew can pack up for the 24-hour trip to Jersey.

Except that the ants haven't yet made their appearance. They arrived the night before from Arizona via San Francisco – in a jar, accompanied by an ant wrangler on a Virgin Upper-Class ticket. There are 65 of them. By no means striking in size or behaviour: about three-quarters of an inch. Why we can't find British ants to do the job, I'll never know.

I have to be ready in tight close-up to start my speech as soon as the ants are in the right place – and they are there only very occasionally, when a sugar-water trail is marked out.

So I poise, the tongue-twister lines on the tip of my tongue – knowing that I have to be as cool and calm as at any time on the picture. It eventually works. Robert v. complimentary to me. Says my bottle held very well. 'But it usually does,' he adds.

Tuesday, August 22nd

The curly, bug-like hair-do and the thin, apologetic sliver of moustache applied, hopefully for the last time.

I end up, first as top-half of the character only, then, and finally, as the eyes alone. Bugsy fades like the Cheshire Cat and disappears at 1.20 on the 76th day of shooting.

I'm officially counted out with an announcement from John. 'You'll probably be delighted and deeply relieved to hear that this is Mickey Palin's last day of shooting.' Applause.

Sunday, August 27th: Anchorage, Alaska

So here I am, five days after finishing four months on *Fierce Creatures*, in another hotel room in another strange place, about to embark on a year's journey around the Pacific.

I know the alternatives. I know that I have made myself enough money – I know I could spend most of my life at home in London – eating and drinking well, reading, meeting friends, taking the Eurostar to France and beyond for the occasional long weekend.

But then I also realise that it's all relative: without the challenges, without the effort expended, peace and quiet and tranquillity don't seem as sweet or as intense. I am, whether I would admit or not, doing just what I often criticise others for – I am being competitive, I am playing my part in the endless, and especially Western drama of punishing self-advancement.

I kept a personal diary on Pole to Pole*, but it was lost in that dark and destructive last week in Zambia, in the days after Mpulungu and Dr Baela. I shall try again to keep a few notes of my own on this Pacific journey. Not to record everything I see – that's* *all noted elsewhere, on tapes and in my black travel notebooks – but what I'm feeling inside – how I'm bearing up.*

Tuesday, August 29th: Nome Nugget Inn, Nome, Alaska

The waters of the Bering Strait are lapping onto the sea defences 50 yards from where I write.

Yesterday the sun shone and a normally very cautious helicopter pilot decided it was clear to go out to Diomede Island. The weather improved during the day – we got all the shots we wanted; I coped with a long, semi-scripted to-camera piece on a hill overlooking the village and only a mile away from the International Date Line.

Last night jet lag settled and I slept pretty deep and pretty long. This morning a big interview piece done – my humour and nerve intact. I'm enjoying myself – and find Nome agreeable and friendly. I'm recognised everywhere – even on Diomede I was a 'star'! Bad for the romance, but helps with the people.

So, we're off and running. Only 50,000 miles to go!

Sunday, September 3rd: Westmark Hotel, Kodiak, Alaska

About to leave for the bears/camping sequence. Possibly, apart from the Nome beach sequence on Friday, this is the worst thing I could be doing at the moment. Stomach unstable after Ex-Lax last night and in the middle of a foul and fierce cold.

What I need is a day in bed. What I get is another plane flight, some more butch filming, standing in rivers and sleeping, at the end of it all, in a shared tent. Only good news is that where we're going, Camp Island on Karluk Lake, it's too cold for mosquitoes.

Wednesday, September 6th: Westmark Hotel, Kodiak

Returned from Karluk Lake, not one night later, but three nights later, owing to a shutdown of all air services out of Kodiak for two and a half days (fog). Considering how awful I felt when I last spent a night in this unprepossessing hotel, with smells, stains, slow service and fine views, I'm now remarkably well.

Camp Island was basic in some ways – no elec or running water, sleeping in tents (I shared with Basil) – but comfortable in others – very good, home-cooked meals, fresh air, a grand location, and, owing to the weather, enforced relaxation.

Apart from a dreadful night on Sunday (Nigel's 50th birthday) I slept extremely well. Only the occasional growl of a bear and the sound of the wind off the lake and the occasional patter of rain on the roof of the tent.

Tuesday, September 12th: Olga's, Yelizovo, Petropavlovsk, Kamchatka Peninsula, Siberia

Everything about Russia is difficult – the simplest arrangements and transactions are made complex. Olga's is, in itself, the sort of place that one feels could only exist in Russia – a big, quite handsome wooden house, built on traditional lines only two years ago – but lights, hot water, heating all quite mercurial. It's only September but I sleep now dressed like a paratrooper – socks, sweatshirt, tracksuit bottoms. Whatever cold there is the house seems to trap it.

But fortune shone on us yesterday – the weather was good, the light clear and we made an extraordinary journey in a big, grimy Mi-8 helicopter north to the Kronotsky Reserve – we circled the rim of volcanoes, we walked amongst hot springs in calderas and looked at plant life which has adapted itself to living in streams and waterholes at 90°C. We bathed in a filthy hot stream by a woodman's hut – we saw geysers erupt from a dozen holes in a cliffside. It was one of the greatest accumulations of natural wonders I've ever seen – and we concentrated it successfully into a day, and filmed it.

I'm gradually adapting, like the plant in the 90° stream, to the Russian way. It requires much more tolerance, patience and personal initiative than is ever asked of us in the pampered West.

Thursday, September 14th: Ocean Hotel, Magadan

Arrive back gloriously tired after three and a half hours' solid and concentrated filming in and around one of the last visible slave labour camps established in this remote and forbidding Kolyma region in the Stalin years.

Magadan is generally infuriating – full of dour and desperate Russian rules, gloomy corridors, curtains that don't draw, etc. Here in the Ocean Hotel there was a hint – or more than that – a manifestation of heavy, drunken violence in the dining room (after wonderful Magadan crab which Basil had encouraged Igor, our Russian guide, to buy in the market – the largest, spikiest crab I ever saw).

But this is a grim place, no two ways about it; the ugliest city I think I've ever seen – no, correction, the most featureless – and yet Ivan the prison camp survivor was wonderful and live on my TV at the moment Moscow Spartak are beating Blackburn Rovers

1-0, at Blackburn.

Another given in Russia – as the curtains don't fit the windows, so the sheets don't fit the bed.

Sunday, September 17th: Vladivostok

Tomorrow is the big end of prog one scene in which I dress as a sailor and sing with one of the finest choirs in Russia – the Pacific Fleet Ensemble. Roger tends to set me these tasks because they require a real stroke of inspiration and panache to bring off. Not easy, but unforgettable if they work.

The Russian diet is a bit of a plod. Breakfasts always uninspired. Only eggs, eggs, eggs. Have never eaten so many in my life. Miss cereals and fruit and the occasional sweet pudding.

Feel a bit out of touch with home – haven't spoken to H since Anchorage ten days ago.

Still, all in all, with my ivory walrus from Diomede as my talisman, this has been a good, strong start.

Have drunk more than I meant to these last few days – but drinking with the crew is a quick, effective way of rewarding ourselves.

Tuesday, September 19th: Vladivostok

Sunny, settled morning. Yesterday we completed the Alaska/Russian pro-gramme in some style – the song and the choir generally regarded as great success; so I am much relieved.

Sixty-eight rolls of film, 3,000 miles, three weeks.

Friday, September 22nd: Mano Town, Sado Island, Japan

Writing this in bed at Pension Nagakura, beneath fearsomely bright coiled strip light, at 9.10 on a Friday night. We shall be leaving here at five tomorrow morning to start one of the busiest days of this second programme's filming. Running with the Kodo drummers and working right through until seven or eight at night.

I took Basil's advice and tried a preparatory run before supper. Up into the wooded hills behind our hotel – gardens, women with straw bonnets held close in place by headscarves, working in the fields until the light begins to fade, harvesting the rice. When they've gone they're replaced by scarecrow likenesses of themselves. Smells were good – woodsmoke, drying rice stalks on racks, earthy, pungent, grassy odours.

Came back with all systems intact. A snort of grappa from the flask Graham Fordham gave me and sink beneath lurid green and purple smudged flower-designed blanket. Tomorrow an initiation for all of us.

Saturday, September 23rd: The House of the Red Pear, Ogi, Sado Island

Ten p.m: On my futon, on the tatami. As tired as I have ever felt on the trip. Was running with the Kodo drummers at twenty past five. Have been filmed eating breakfast with the apprentices, conducting interviews and hitting the big drum, now, fourteen hours after first sequence, still filming, this time dinner. Everything new to me – the ryokan quite unfamiliar – no chairs or bed in room, all washing communally downstairs. This is what has really exhausted me – being tired in somewhere unfamiliar, without understandable procedures and regular comforters to fall back on.

The film crew is noisy – the walls are thin – I've run out of good humour, tolerance and patience – I just want the world to shut the fuck up and let me sleep.

The pressure of work meant no further personal notes were kept as we travelled through Japan and into Korea over the next month.

Friday, October 20th

Back home.

Cleese rings, pretending to be a reporter from Aberdeen; he says the first of nine reels of the 'Death Fish' film look strong and he's very happy. He assures me that my performance is 'super'.

Out to *Wind in the Willows* wrap party down by the Thames at Westminster Boat House.

I don't immediately recognise the man with Alison. Only after I've greeted her effusively do I realise it's Terry. Eyebrow-less, almost hairless and his face an almost puffy yellow. He finished shooting as Mr Toad on the day we finished in Korea.

On the way out run into Steve Coogan on his way in. Shaggy head of curly dark ringlets confuses me for a moment but I'm glad to be able to rave a little over Alan Partridge. He raves in return. Says he used to record *Ripping Yarns* dialogue by pointing a mike at the telly. He'd then play it back to people, acting out the visuals as he did so.

To bed at 11.30 when the travel fatigue hits.

Saturday, October 21st

A beguiling, sunny autumn day outside and, without much of a plan, I drive into the West End to do some shopping.

Certainly there is a pattern to returning home – in my case anyway. First of all elation at being back – sometimes quite manic. This is accompanied by a fierce, potent energetic desire to catch up – on family, letters, work, people, the house. This lasts for most of my first day.

The day after there is an almost inevitable reaction. The extrovert, exhausted, collapses into the introvert. The feelings that all problems can and will be solved in a single day are ridiculed by cold reality.

Perhaps there are those, and I envy them, who never experience this emotional roller-coaster. Maybe their lives are uncomplicated, their minds, like their desks, uncluttered. Today, as the day wears on, I experience the ambiguousness of my feelings towards the work I do. The kick, the excitement, the richness of my working life is replaced by a formless, patternless arbitrary world in which nothing is exactly as I want it to be. Faces of friends neglected pressing against the window.

Friday, October 27th

After two months' solid involvement in the series and many early mornings spent musing on it, I still have reservations about 'Palin's Pacific' as a title. It's not *my* Pacific. But there never seems to be an alternative. As I'm bemoaning this, a sudden, quite clear image of what it should be comes to me. It should be simply 'Pacific' – 'with Michael Palin' or whatever as subtitle, but keep Pacific clear and strong. The problem with all the alternative versions – 'A Year in the Pacific', 'Pacific Circle', 'Pacific Progress' – is that the additional words belittle and reduce the only word that matters – Pacific.

Anne is taken with it and Kath too. I think, at last, and quite undeliberately, I've cracked it.

Monday, October 30th

Lots of traffic heading into town. One dirty, smoke-belching van makes me so angry that if I'd been alongside I think I would have had a go at the driver. I'd rather see pollution wardens than parking wardens but I suppose there's no money in pollution prevention.

Successful at last in finding some decent shoes. I was looking in the window of Paul Smith when Paul himself appeared, tall, birdlike, Notts accent still intact. He has the engaging, slightly old-fashioned look of a Midlands comedian. He's just come back from Japan – where he now has 150 outlets. Layers are in, he tells me. Not shirt and jacket so much, as T-shirts augmented with shirts, then if necessary a waistcoat or even a cardigan. Layers popular in Japan because of the Japanese aversion to perspiration, he says. He escorts me round the store, opening the shoe department especially early, just for me.

Thursday, November 2nd

To Gray's Inn Road at nine for my first BUPA check-up for over two years. The consulting rooms are cold and could do with a refit, but nurse very jolly as I go through tests. Always in the back of my mind is a determination to prove I am not on the decline.

Work terribly hard – blowing into tubes until I cough like an old man, straining to hear the faint sounds in the audio test, bending forward to an agonising stretch position – 'very good, above average' – oh, the magic words! Weight a fraction up on last time but negligibly so. My appearance clearly pleases the doctor. 'Believe me,' he says, warming to his theme, 'a lot of 52-year-olds I see look more like 72. They're bald, overweight and ...' I almost think he's going to say something like 'detestable', so enflamed has he become at health standards. He looks immaculate, needless to say. Not a nostril hair out of place.

Friday, November 3rd

I have accepted Simon Albury's invitation to visit him at the Grayshott Hall Health Club where he's spending this week.

Taxi to Waterloo, then train to Haslemere.

Simon meets me at the station. Drive to Grayshott – a big house, probably Edwardian, set around what could be a much older stone keep. Uneasy combination of country house hotel and sanatorium. Guests are in flannelled dressing gowns.

Lunch is definitely more of the sanatorium than the hotel. Food is buffet with calories marked on each dish, ranging from 'Spinach quiche, 250 calories' to 'Endive salad. Negligible'.

Harry Enfield is there. He's been down for a week trying to give up smoking again. 'But I knew,' he says with his ethereal smile, 'that all I want when I get back to London is a glass of wine and a fag.' Simon, who had not recognised Harry, now denounces him fiercely as the one who sets a furious pace on the Fitness Walk.

True enough, as Simon and I assemble for the walk after a copious low-calorie lunch, it is Harry who sets off like a rocket round the flower beds and down across the lawn to the woods. Simon, who has brought some leather boots in which he could climb Everest, keeps up with him for a while before falling back. Our instructor has to keep shouting directions to the fast-disappearing figure of Harry whilst at the same time dealing with a couple of stragglers.

The skies have cleared and are now as intense a blue as you'll get in November. All's well with the world, except that we're lost. Simon thinks he knows the way out and shouts into the woods behind him 'Hallo! We're going *up!*' and up the hill we go.

An hour later we cut, dangerously it seems to me, across a golf course and back to the house.

Harry, who seems to have barely broken sweat, is changed and leaving for London with a young blonde.

Monday, November 6th

Another fine, sunny morning after cold night. Brilliant sunshine bathes house and garden. TG calls during the morning and we meet at Odette's for lunch.

Twelve Monkeys is within two weeks of completion. Studio excited despite only OK test screenings. As TG says, with Brad Pitt and Bruce Willis they're guaranteed a good opening weekend and after that ... who knows.

Terry is already planning ahead to 'The Hunchback of Notre Dame' with Depardieu.

Back home to turn my thoughts to 'Pacific', the book. JC calls. Salutes my work on the film in less than hyperbolic terms ... 'I really have to say, Mickey, that I can see absolutely nothing wrong with it.'

Rachel works away at her essay on the Civil Rights Movement. A bookish quiet descends on the house.

Thursday, November 9th

To the David Hockney drawings exhibition at the Royal Academy.

Hockney there in the midst of them, chatting and signing for an endless stream of fans with great ease and apparent enjoyment. No sign of the tortured artist there.

Only as I was about to leave did I pass by the great man, resolving to shake a hand at least.

Hockney caught my eye and recognised me, which always helps. He came across, detaching himself from a hovering group hanging on his every word, and we shook hands. Talked about Salts Mill and the gallery project he supports there. He said he was going up to Bridlington to see his mother, but he could never stay long away from Los Angeles because of his dogs. Then he grabbed my arm and drew me to him and whispered close into my ear 'Bridlington's wonderful. Hasn't changed since 1953!'

Friday, November 10th

Rang Alan Bennett to get Hockney's address. I told him of Hockney's aside about Bridlington not having changed since the '50s. Alan is scornful. 'It could do with a bit of change, Bridlington. It's a terrible place.'

Out in the evening to Ronnie Scott's. I'd promised Graham and Maggie Fordham an evening out, as we never had time after the end of *Fierce Creatures* – also I thought it would be good to take Kath and John Du Prez to celebrate their engagement.

Welcomed like an old friend by the disparate group of large, slightly shambolic men who guard the door at Ronnie's. They look like fugitives from a jazz band themselves.

A Cuban group called Los Van Van. There are 16 of them, clustered on the confined stage, trombonists just about finding space for their slides, violinists for their bows, and charismatic straw-hatted lead singer containing an unstoppable dancing shuffle on a piece of floor the size of a sixpence.

Saturday, November 11th

For a haircut at ten. A playfully camp light-black boy called Alfie. Somewhat disconcertingly his hands shake and at one point, going for a razor, he cuts himself. He grins apologetically. 'I'm always doing that,' he says.

Feel I'm reliving the 'Barber Shop' sketch, except that Alfie doesn't appear to be shaking from fear – more likely from too much happiness the night before. He talks to me in the mirror. 'I love cutting hair,' he says. 'I love the feeling of power it gives me to know that I can ruin someone's sex life for the next six weeks.'

Monday, November 13th

After ten minutes of repeated re-ringing I get through to my doctor and book an emergency appointment to check out my gravelly chest.

At the surgery a young, good-looking man in dark glasses, coat collar pulled up, twitches and paces nervously. Two younger boys, early teens, who look as if they might be Arabs, with thick, curly hair, shout and jump about, apparently oblivious to everyone else around them. A mother tries ineffectually to stop a small, hyperactive five-year-old from ripping pages from one of the magazines. A big Indian or Bangladeshi woman, swaddled in scarves and coats, sways up to reception. Her eyes look dead, vacant, unconnecting. She communicates by nods and grunts. Her little girl is pretty and lively. A wild-haired man stares at the floor and mutters.

The staff are saintly – presumably achieving many small satisfactions in a day of intolerable pressures.

Out in the evening to a screening of *Fierce Creatures*. This is the first time I've seen all that summer work assembled. Eighty invited guests at Planet Hollywood's screening room. Very comfortable. John pacing around outside the theatre wearing his Cockney fruit-seller outfit. Cap pulled down low, big warm windcheater, jeans and trainers.

No shortage of laughter, and it was good and consistent too, right through the first 50 minutes of the movie. Then it began to sag as the plot became more convoluted and just about everything to do with Kevin's Vince McCain character failed – especially exposing himself to the tiger. But there were good moments, well received, right up to the end.

So everyone involved visibly relieved. Not least me, as Bugsy makes an impact. I get laughs and, apart from in the dreadful scenes with the keepers by the lake, I'm happy with my performance. That it took four months of my life is, on the other hand, barely believable from the amount of time on screen.

Flew back east after a month's break at home. The China shoot was postponed till next year for various reasons so we picked up the journey in Vietnam, continuing on to the Philippines before returning home for Christmas.

Saturday, November 18th: Saigon Hotel, Hanoi

Woke this morning at eleven. Slept nearly 12 hours after 36 hours' virtually sleepless travel from London via Hong Kong.

A cacophony of horns and children's voices rises from the street below, incessant except in the smallest hours of the night.

Hanoi is one of the most evocative place names. In the '60s and '70s it was more than just the name of a city, it was also a description of the enemy (if you were American), a state of mind – dour, hard-line, intransigent, severe but indomitable.

Well, from what I've seen last night – as our eight hired cyclos made their elegantly seedy way up the elegantly seedy boulevard to a rooftop restaurant – and what I'm hearing four floors below as I wake after my long restorative sleep, it is anything but severe.

There is a liveliness here, a tolerant and tolerable crush.

And in a couple of hours, after lunch, we shall be in the middle of it, beginning work on episode four of 'Pacific'.

Thursday, November 23rd: Century Riverside Inn, Hue

The rain which began as persistent drizzle this morning is now coming down in a series of increasingly heavy downpours. The silhouetted figures, hunched beneath capes, riding bicycles and scooters and pedalling cyclos, look like the stragglers of some retreating army.

The room is fairly shabby and small and has no bath or river view, but the bed's comfortable and I rather like its cell-like intimacy.

Vietnam is the most demanding country we've yet filmed. Though there are signs of accelerating modernisation and change it is still a modestly equipped Third World economy.

Beggars wait at all tourist pick-up points, extending bony, withered hands, or shuffling legless torsos towards the steps of the bus. Wherever we go where tourists are seen, there is a nudging at the elbow and an imploring look. Children, often beautiful and irresistibly bright-eyed, hold out their open palms, or demand pens or chewing gum. Along most of the inner-city streets there are open drains, and in Hanoi many ponds and canals clogged thick with rubbish and human waste.

One of the advantages of the raw, unpolished, Third World feel of Vietnam is that almost everything you point the camera at is interesting – and Roger has found a good number of English-speaking Vietnamese to be my companions.

This is good, purposeful travelling. Rough and ready, unpredictable, demanding but full of character and incident.

Saturday, December 2nd: Baguio City, Luzon, Philippines

Come on Michael, get a grip. There will be more times like this, when you've had to wake before six, travel for two or three hours, shoot, travel, arrive exhausted at another new town that's beginning to look the same as all the rest, be given an official tour of said town when all you want is sleep, soap and hot bath. Arrive at hotel to find yourself in dimly lit room, close to main road, next door to an aviary of very vocal caged birds, with no bath, and not even a towel.

Travel fatigue is insidious. Once it digs in you find that you concentrate with difficulty, operate automatically, move sluggishly and consequently feel you have not done your best – this leads to negativity, which itself adds to potential fatigue – and so it goes round again.

Well this is what I must snap out of. Must not let any vicious circles form around me. Here we go again.

Because the helicopter could not reach the Banaue rice terraces owing to poor visibility, a series of great strokes of luck gave us a spontaneous sequence involving landing on sports fields in the middle of a game, hailing Jeepneys, driving up past landslips and mudslides to the terraces – and finding the cloud so thick that I improvised a piece to camera in which I read about what they couldn't see from the guidebook.

We had pulled a sequence out of nowhere – and everyone felt duly elated. This was travelling and filming at its best. Emergency becoming the mother of invention.

So, apart from lack of quality sleep, a bright light and a bath, I really should not have much to grumble about. And indeed, after pouring all this out to my diary I feel I have begun to make sense of all this madness, to order my priorities, and that there is no reason why I should succumb, fall behind or cease to operate. I must, shall and want to go on.

Wednesday, December 6th: Pearl Farm Resort, Davao, Philippines

I'm sitting writing in small, curved-back wicker chair beside a wicker table with a hard laminated top. I'm drinking water, humouring my digestive system which has been unpredictable since Baguio, and have beside me John Berendt's *Midnight in the Garden of Good and Evil*, which I have just laid down after reading the opening chapters and being quite seduced by it. His early descriptions of Savannah seem to catch my mood at the moment, relaxed, curious, aware with pleasure of what I'm doing and where I am. In short, happy and comfortable.

Outside, only a patch of light caught by the hull of a small bobbing white boat indicates the gentle black expanse of water that laps up to and underneath my nipa-thatched, bamboo home on stilts.

I learnt the rudiments of scuba-diving in a sequence yesterday – in the swimming pool and in the sea.

I went into the water at about 11.30. A little awry to start with, I began to settle down. The coral was beautiful, lush and succulent and of wonderful extravagant designs. On it grew sexy purple plants moving like hair tossed in the wind.

I became more confident. Learnt to rely more on my own breathing. Filling lungs and holding breath to rise, breathing firmly and constantly to fall.

Suddenly, like learning to ride a bicycle, I could feel myself at ease beneath the water.

I think the turning point came at the end of the morning session, when at a depth of about 35 to 40 feet I had difficulty drawing my breath. The gulps got shorter and shorter. I gave my instructor Louie the wobbly hand 'something wrong' signal and he quickly checked my gauge, swapped my regulator for his spare, led me to the surface and changed my tank which was almost out of air.

The fact that I was able to cope, on my first real dive, with an emergency of this kind says a lot for Louie and his training yesterday, but also made me pleasantly aware that I was basically comfortable in an unfamiliar world.

Thursday, December 14th

Descend through a thick-ish bank of clouds into a damp, cold, pre-dawn London.

Graham Fordham meets me again. This time he's researched the breakfast situation and drives me only as far as the Hilton Hotel, the big, white, glass and steel rectangle next to Terminal 4. The interior is crisp and clean and modern and stylish – the breakfast isn't bad either.

Catch up on gossip. *Fierce Creatures* is in the States being test-screened over this week and the coming weekend. Word is that Universal are very happy with it.

Long, slow journey home.

Unpack and then work through piles of letters. Nothing nasty in the woodshed – and one very pleasant note from Richard Briers, who praised *The Dresser* and said that he'd listened to the tape three times!

I feel great pleasure at seeing my room again and being back in my own home.

Sunday, December 24th

Have to be strong-willed to get myself out and running this cold morning, but I'm rewarded with bright blue winter skies and virtually empty fields and meadows. As I run past Kenwood House there is not a soul about. For a minute or two I can almost feel that the place is mine.

After breakfast out to Camden Lock. At the bric-a-brac stall I buy a small, hand-painted bowl with a rather glamorous picture of Cardinal Wolsey on it. The man apologises for not recognising me straight away – 'You look so much younger. Have you stopped working or something?'

Wednesday, December 27th

Take Granny back soon after one. She is very concerned about the state of the roads and as we go north the fog lights are flashing, though the fog itself lurks no closer than halfway across the fields we pass. But it gives a grey, inhospitable aspect to the countryside and the ice is frozen hard onto Blacksmith's Lane as I pull into Church Farm.

A walk through the house brings on memories of past Christmases. Happy memories of being woken on cold, silent mornings by the children, barely able to contain their excitement. Sad, because things will never be quite like that again. Is it their innocence I'm missing? Is it that that's irreplaceable?

Must remember that there were all sorts of problems, crises, emotional ups and downs in those Christmases I'm so busy romanticising. But for a moment I stand in the bedroom upstairs and the smell and the look of it are so unchanged and evocative.

Sunday, December 31st

At three o'clock in the morning O'Rourke, probably in some sort of protest against a noisy party in the students' house between us, turns up his Caruso operatic collection to full-blast. The sound must have woken anyone who wasn't already partying and has absolutely no effect on the students, whose thumping beat goes on – though not nearly as loudly as O'Rourke's blasting opera. So 1996 is borne in on a note of hysteria.

I look out across the roofs of Elaine Grove. The fog that closed in last night hems in the day. It's a flat, lifeless aspect outside and in a way it reflects my own mood at the moment. I feel in abeyance. Coasting. Not consciously, but somewhere inside. I'm already beginning to prepare myself for another departure.

1996

Monday, January 1st

O'Rourke claims to have seen a friend of mine … 'MC'. 'Name mean anything?' 'Michael Caine. I met him down at the Harbour.' I ask O'R how he
knows Caine. 'I doubled once for him in a film. I've got eyes just like his you
see. It was only in long-shot, of course.' I really wonder where he gets it from.

Thursday, January 4th

Out to shops – Clem called and reminded me of how wet it is likely to be
from Borneo to North Australia, so buy myself a cape and some waterproof
trousers.

Then drive over to Whitechapel, where I eventually find the Art Gallery
– very handsome Art Nouveau stone façade – and take in Emil Nolde exhibition. His painting is big, vigorous, using very deep, strong colours.

Terrific thick oily seas and good too at the effect of clouds and smoke.
Don't much like his grotesque, fantasy works – but the exhibition is an eye-
opener.

As is a stroll around this part of East London. Spitalfields is nearby. Some
early-eighteenth-century terraced houses in reddish-brown brick – many very
well looked after. They cluster around Hawksmoor's cathedral-sized Christ
Church – like Nolde, H believed in adding a bit more. Neither man given to
restraint. And around all this is a Bangladeshi community which adds a rich but
disconcerting element to the mix.

I lapped it all up. More and more I find great pleasure in the city – in all its
nooks and crannies. London gets better. I must try to always organise myself
and my work so that I have time for it.

John C rings. This is the first time I've spoken to him since I returned, and
since he had the US screenings.

What he tells me is quite startling, though John makes it all sound businesslike and rather unremarkable. After three screenings in the US the problem
areas have come out clearly as being at the very beginning and the ending.

Almost all the last 20 minutes of the movie is to be jettisoned, thrown away.
'They hate Vince being killed.' So the rhino goes, the tiger skin, the scene by
the lake we rehearsed till it died. All go.

The re-shoot will take two weeks, it will be done in LA and JC estimates I shall be needed for no more than two of those days – 'three possibly, say four at most'.

On Friday, January 5th, myself and the film crew flew from Heathrow to Manila and resumed our Pacific journey at Zamboanga in the southern Philippines, and from there by ferry to Sabah on the island of Borneo. Two weeks later we had reached Sarawak on the western coast of Borneo. On our return from filming in the interior some very bad news was waiting.

Saturday, January 20th: Kuching, Sarawak

On Thursday 18th, around a quarter to five in the afternoon, we arrived back at the Holiday Inn from the longhouse up in the Ulu Ai. Three days and nights there had been more comfortable than I expected. The weather had been largely dry. Apart from a frustrating day stuck in a boat being, at times literally, pushed upriver, we filmed copiously and successfully and even Nigel reckons we have a ten-minute sequence.

On the bus on the way back from Batang Ai Dam I slept, dictated snippets into the records, read *Captain Corelli's Mandolin* and arrived back soothed, calm, clear-headed and even rested.

A fax was handed to me as we re-checked in. It was short and chillingly to the point. Please contact Helen as soon as you arrive as she needs to talk to you urgently.

My stomach tightened straight away. All the trivial little delays – in being processed, signing forms, waiting for the room card to be issued (mine was the last) – became barely tolerable. I rushed to the phone as soon as I had let myself into the room.

H had hardly begun to tell me that there was nothing to worry about – when the doorbell tinkled and I had to lay down the phone to let in an elderly bellhop who unloaded my bags unhurriedly and seemed a little disappointed at my brusque return to the phone.

So I learnt about her tumour, the cause of the splittingly painful headaches which had been at their worst whilst I was in the jungle. I learnt about the loss of control and feeling in the arm. I learnt that she had been unable to bear it and at her sister Mary's insistence had consulted a specialist at the National Hospital for Nervous Diseases, that he had given her an examination and found a sebaceous cyst called a meningioma between skull and brain, and that he had arranged for her to have it removed on Monday 22nd by one of the top surgeons, a Mr Powell.

She kept emphasising the word 'benign'. This sort of tumour is, evidently, always benign. It is not in the brain, but pressing on it. The operation is orthodox and straightforward and relatively common (though her particular condition is found in only one in 100,000 people).

The story of Helen's tumour is covered in the book Full Circle. *At risk of repetition I shall not tell the tale again in detail. The operation was indeed straightforward, but I never stopped worrying until it was over.*

Tuesday, January 23rd: Hotel Natour Garuda, Yogyakarta, Indonesia

12.45 a.m: To bed happy. I have heard from the hospital in Queens Square that Helen came out of the theatre at four UK, eleven Indonesian time, on the 22nd, that it was a 'textbook operation', the tumour is out and, although she still has a problem with movement in her left hand, she was conscious enough to send me her love and say she was fine.

Have rung Rachel and Tom (Will is at work) and will ring the surgeon this evening.

Wednesday, January 24th: Yogyakarta, Indonesia

Back at the hotel, mid-afternoon. Ring H again. She's recovering well, but I can tell by the fact that she's so pleased I've rung that the difficult time for her may just be beginning. She will not be able to go back to life as it was for quite a while and once the euphoria of having been rid of the tumour is over, the realities of tiredness, not to mention residual shock, will sink in.

Tomorrow I shall have to be up at six for a seven o'clock departure and another long drive on the stressful roads across to film Mount Bromo from the rim – a volcano up close.

But Helen is always in the forefront of my mind and I already find myself worrying that the hotel in Bromo (which even Clem thinks is rough!) will not have the easy telephone communication that has seen me through this extraordinary time. I shall ring again before I go to bed – after I've packed yet again. I can't quite take in that a week ago today I didn't even know she had a problem.

Friday, January 26th: Hyatt Hotel, Surabaya, Java

Fortune and the gods smiled at us this morning, and the superhuman effort of filming a complex sequence at a quite extraordinary location – an active volcano – almost entirely before 6.30 a.m. was blessed with good weather and clear visibility, and the very real possibility of having to stay another day there was avoided.

The last leg of the journey was completed by 1.30. Eko gave us a few last hair-raising moments as he raced back from Bromo to Surabaya. The road journey has dominated the week and much of it was hellish. To have it over is a huge and wonderful relief.

Have rung Helen and she sounds much stronger. She is having the 'staples' out later today, but the surgeon is so pleased he says there is nothing to stop her going home when she wants, and he added that when she does get home she's not to treat herself as an invalid!

Monday, February 5th: BA Flight 005, Heathrow–Tokyo

A catch-up on the last few days. Leaving the crew to take a temporary break in Bali, I reached home on the last day of January.

Graham dropped me at the house at half past seven and I made my way stealthily upstairs – feeling like a burglar in my desire not to wake anyone. So I had my first glimpse of H's shaved patch – gleaming, I swear, and giving her head the lopsided look of a monk whose tonsure has slipped.

At breakfast I note the scar, more than six inches long, which runs from the back right-hand side of her skull across the top and curves a little to the right again before it ends. Evidence, which H proudly points out, of the hole at one end of the scar through which a tube was inserted to draw off any bleeding after the op. I'm relieved at her colour, the normalness of her face. She doesn't even look tired. She shows me the scan pictures. The size of the tumour quite frightening.

Thursday, the 1st of February, is bright again, but there's a hard frost. Tidy up the garden, make phone calls, shop. My sore throat continues and wears me down.

Helen feels a little better and stronger each day. It's ironic that, having come all this way to look after her, I find myself croaking and snuffling wretchedly and H having to look after me.

Then a bombshell. A fax from Simon to tell me what he fears he would not be able to tell me in a phone call – that Derek Taylor has stomach cancer. He's been advised that it is malignant and inoperable. What timing – Derek heard the news on the same day that his son Dominic had his first big starring role on TV.

Did letters with Kath who told me Alison Davies[1] is getting married Sat-

1 Alison Davies, for years my assistant at the Mayday office, and before that assistant to the Pythons.

urday morning – the next day – at only 24 hours' notice. Find myself bitterly resenting the world's unwillingness to stand still when I want it to.

Slept well again on my third night home and had energy enough to buy a present (a double magnum of Château Talbot) with a card and tie some ribbon round the neck, and get myself to Sadler's Wells Theatre by 10.30 for the reception.

I have to give a father-of-the-bride speech and read telegrams from JC and Eric – 'I thought she was gay.'

Home, rather pleased with myself, only to find H seething. A *Mail on Sunday* reporter had doorstepped her whilst I was out, asking persistently about my return, the operation, etc. etc. He had a photographer with him and asked H if she wanted her picture taken. At first she didn't twig that he was a reporter – thought he was from the Residents' Association.

The combination of being duped and asked such personal questions left her angry and quite hurt. The latter made me take up the case. I put together a fax which I sent to the editor of the *Mail on Sunday*. It took two or three hours of precious time but within half an hour of transmission I received one back from the Editor, Jonathan Holborow – apologetic and concerned.

On the whole, though, the mercy dash home worked. I was glad I had been able to see Helen so close to the operation – see her cropped head and her scar and feel the little bristles growing on her scalp and our togetherness over the four days was important, though often low-key. She's happy to let me go back, though I wish I could have had a couple more days. She still seemed, beneath the solid, straight-bat, manage-anything veneer, to be a little dazed as I left.

Now, just after nine o'clock in the morning. I'm gazing down on Japan. Like seeing an old friend again – though the mountain ranges of central Honshu look more dense and impressive than I remember.

We shan't be long in Japan, maybe an hour and a half, if the flight to Darwin leaves on time.

We approach over an odd landscape of desiccated straw-yellow golf courses and small forested hillocks. Japanese – neat, precise, carefully arranged. A bonsai landscape.

Reunited with the crew in Darwin, we resumed filming with a north to south crossing of Australia, via Alice Springs.

Saturday, February 10th: Hilton Hotel, Adelaide

Roger this morning had heard on the news of an IRA bomb in London. Sinking feeling turned to something much more uncomfortable when I heard that the bomb went off at Canary Wharf, where Will works, and at night, which is when he works. There are many injuries apparently but no news of fatalities.

For a moment my senses reel, stagger, and I have to shut down for a minute or two, as I did when I received the fax to ring Helen from Kuching.

But there were no further details. I'd tried ringing H twice this morning and had received no reply.

From feeling vaguely pleased that she was well enough to have gone out, I went to the other extreme, imagining all sorts of sinister implications in her absence. Will hurt in wreckage, H at hospital or bedside.

Monday, February 12th: Flight AN93 Adelaide–Alice Springs

I rang Helen before I left. Bleary, unfamiliar voice of recently deeply sleeping wife tells me that it was Will's day off anyway, and he is fine.

The *Australian* has the only thorough report of the Canary Wharf bombing I've seen this weekend. It's now the South Quay Plaza bombing – and the big tower where Will works not affected.

We're in the last segment of a demanding run of filming days. We've worked and travelled on every one of the last eight days and now we're on the road again – squeezed aboard an Ansett flight to Alice and Ayers Rock. Prospect of long drive and more filming this afternoon followed by a night sleeping rough and one of the toughest days of all, at the camel muster tomorrow.

Our shadow races ahead of us as the 737 pulls off the tarmac and out over the jade-green surface of Gulf St Vincent. We've all got our heads down – knowing there's hard work ahead – but Australia has so far been generous in material and comfortable in the living. And not much time to think of anything but work.

Wednesday, February 14th: Alice Springs

Evening after one of our most memorable day's filming – the camel muster. Wind strengthening from the south-east and the 300-foot escarpment wall that rises a half-mile from my hotel window is in shadow.

This time yesterday I was in the overland vehicle to Alice, tired, grubby, bruised and bleeding after the camel mustering, one of the most extraordinary of filming days.

I haven't been worked as physically hard for many years. Nigel and Steve were working both cameras during the day – every sequence was well covered, none of them were mere duplications. It was a tough day, but should produce one of the great sequences, and last night I felt a tremendous sense of satisfaction and achievement. And quite a lot of pain.

Wednesday, February 21st: Sydney Airport

Confusing mixture of feelings as we prepare to leave Australia.

Various concerns nag away at my peace of mind. None of them has much to do with work, which has progressed well here. I thought the central desert area quite magical and we have plenty of material.

I've been most affected by the news from back home. For almost a week Helen has had a particularly virulent form of flu which has laid her very low indeed. When I rang she was either in bed or resting and her voice sounded tired and flat. I felt for her even more than during her brain operation, for this was a cruel blow just as she was recovering, and you don't get sympathy twice – and flu is less spectacular and frightening to people than head surgery.

Equally depressing is the resumption of the bombing of London by the IRA. Perhaps we shouldn't have taken the ceasefire for granted, but the return of pictures of bloodied faces, broken bodies, twisted, shattered property in places where I've walked and worked and know so well fills me, especially this morning, with another kind of helplessness. The awareness of how little we can do, for all our apparent sophistication and applied intelligence, to stop people killing their fellow human beings.

I shouldn't be surprised. The Provisional IRA have their own brutal, effective programme and little that has been said and done by John Major in the last 18 months can really have assuaged them. They don't kill as lightly and cynically as people like to make out – they kill out of an intensity, a fierceness, a dogged, deep, unshakeable belief, as people have done throughout history.

I'm beginning to think, like Vita and Harold Nicolson[1] in their letters on the outbreak of the Second War, that evil is gaining the upper hand. That goodness and decency are threatened. Added to that I felt a sudden closeness to my country. A protectiveness. As if, like Helen, it is suffering from an outbreak of illness, and I should be there.

Tuesday, February 27th: Kaikoura, New Zealand

It's a quarter to five in the afternoon; roughly twelve hours ago I got out of bed to begin the day's work, now, with the work well done, I sit sipping a cup of tea I've made myself at the Norfolk Pine Motor Inn, looking out from my room across a quiet-ish road, a line of robust Norfolk pines, complete with chunky, long-fingered leaves, a short beach to the sea. I'm a hundred yards from the Pacific Ocean (on which I spent most of this morning whale-watching).

1 Vita Sackville-West, novelist and her husband Harold Nicolson, politician and diarist.

The Norfolk Pine is run by Glenys and John – a lovely middle-aged couple of courteous, straightforward kindliness.

So refreshing, after many days of impersonal, system-designed, business-man-led accommodation, to encounter a place that expresses the taste and personality of the owners, that's unpretentious, and by the side of the ocean. I feel as warm towards it as I did towards the Nome Nugget Inn in Alaska, all those months ago.

News from home better. No more bombs. Helen making progress each day.

Wednesday, March 6th: Christchurch–Auckland, Air NZ

Highlight of the week was not Shotover-jetting or walking up through the natural beech forest above Paradise, it was a wonderful and quite unexpected adventure with Louisa Patterson and her husband and her helicopter which filled the middle hours of this departure day.

Louisa P one of the many NZ-ers who recognised me (in a café in Dunedin), but the only one with a private helicopter business and a confident, provocative free-spiritedness which combined to provide a glorious view and a most surreal lunch.

Our neat, black, fly-nosed Hughes helicopter deftly settled on a pinnacle of the Remarkable Mountains overlooking Queenstown and the snow-capped ranges beyond. A picnic hamper spread – ham, Brie, sliced tomato and avocado, kipper pâté, salami, fresh, thick, soft brown bread, fruit and a bottle of Bollinger champagne nestling in a bucket in the lee of one of the horizontal slabs of crumbly schist that stack up to the summit of the ridge.

Louisa disappears behind a rock and emerges triumphantly at the same moment as the strains of some crackly 1940s Hawaiian guitar. It comes from a wind-up gramophone, and is soon followed by a selection of some of the other 78s which had been thrown in as a job lot when she bought the gramophone.

So 'The Ballad of Davy Crockett' fills the silence at the top of the mountain, as our long journey south from Alaska comes to an end. Now we have to turn north again. Up the American coast, back to little Diomede Island to complete the circle.

Thursday, March 7th

Through a thin layer of cloud from brightness into gloom – fields, hedgerows, roads and rivers of Buckinghamshire drained of colour. My journey has lasted 27 hours or so. Only in the last four or five did I become impatient, fidgety and almost literally itching to be home, skin drying in the merciless air-con, sore throat and proto-cold beginning to dig in.

H comes to the door looking fine and pretty with blue beret at jaunty angle (to hide the patch where the surgeons went in).

Tom is there, having just taken H to M&S, and her Colombian friend Epi comes to visit. Main change in H's life is caused by her forced inability to drive for a year. Now people have to come and see her.

My room, my books, my house, the garden, my interest in everything around me renewed by absence. This little world suddenly special, no longer commonplace ... something to relish. It's a remarkable feeling and one which I count as paradoxically one of the great pleasures of travel. The almost sensuous delight in the ordinary and commonplace.

Friday, March 8th

JC's re-shoot seems to be in trouble. Kevin cannot make April or May and Jamie won't film in August. The location is now to be back in London, as Universal have found it too expensive to shoot in LA.

Tuesday, March 12th

Phillida rings to say that the news on Derek Taylor is not good. Chemotherapy not an option. Derek's days are numbered, but in what measure no-one can tell.

JC calls. He is still re-writing with Iain Johnstone; he has found this whole business of the re-shoot frustrating. When Shamberg suggested that if I couldn't make it in July, they shoot it without me, he finally said enough was enough and now they are working on late August, early September dates.

John sounds calm, composed, in control before letting slip that 'no-one liked the keepers, that's the problem'. First I've heard. 'In America?' 'No, no in England as well.'

What sort of revisionism is going on I dread to think – but if the opening scenes with Jamie and Kevin didn't work and 20 minutes of the ending didn't work, and they didn't like the keepers, what is left?

Thursday, March 14th

Drive H to the National Hospital for post-op check-up with her surgeon, Michael Powell. Queens Square is a long rectangle, quiet; as restful a thoroughfare as you'll find right in the centre of town. A most suitable site for a hospital for nervous diseases.

Mr Powell, tall, bony, Lenin-bald with a prominent skull with a distinct bump in the back as if a heavy object might once have fallen across it. Beard, cheap shirt, loose at the collar. His movements seem ever so slightly unco-ordinated. His eyes are soft and humorous, he behaves like a very physical man trying to be gentle.

This is the man who, a little over seven weeks ago, carved a side out of my wife's skull, removed a tumour, scraped, cleaned – 'sanded' as he put it with a smile – the piece of skull and replaced it. Hard to imagine such trauma being inflicted when I look at H sitting there serene and healthy – having been twice to the gym in the last few days.

Not that Mr Powell thinks this unusual. He avoids any sense of mystique or any air of superiority. He might have just sold her a new kettle or be offering an estimate for some kitchen work from the way he talks to her.

I want to tell him that his attitude, his reassurances, his refusal to dramatise or pontificate about the operation helped both of us cope with it better than we could ever have expected, but there isn't really a moment.

All he wants from me is the chance to dress up as a Gumby and pose with me outside the hospital. 'All neurosurgeons I know are enormous Python fans.'

Friday, March 15th

When I arrive at John's, Iain Johnstone and Amanda greet me warmly. Despite what JC later refers to as 'cash flow' problems, his little army of faithful retainers still seems to be in place. The court of Cleese still looks and sounds impressive.

JC appears, he looks tired and tense. With typical psychotherapeutic dir-ectness, he explains why he is indeed feeling a little tired and tense. He's just heard that his younger daughter Camilla has fallen from a horse in Chicago. She's not badly hurt but she's in hospital having tests.

He turns his attention to my trousers. 'Did you make them yourself?' I tell him later that they're rather expensive, from Armani, and I've got three pairs. JC looks down at them. 'Are you wearing them all at once?'

We walk across Holland Park Avenue, heading for a quiet lunch at the Halcyon.

The restaurant not full, but Simon Gray and Patrick Barlow were at one corner table and Prince Edward and two men at another. Edward looked across and smiled and on my way to the loo I stopped and chatted. He's the least regal of the royals I know, the least imperious.

He seems pleased to see me. He looks the same age as I remember him at the Royal Knockout – eight years ago? Very young and choirboy-like.

Whereas Simon Gray looks like a wicked choirmaster. Eyes flicking about the restaurant, features red and choleric.

Wednesday, March 20th

Talk to our Executive Producer Eddie Mirzoeff and tell him that I've decided on 'Palin's Pacific' as a title. He agrees with the same smooth and immediate readiness with which he greeted the news that I didn't want to call it 'Palin's Pacific'.

Friday, March 22nd

Papers full of the potentially appalling consequences of the BSE, mad cow affair, after scientists have gone public with their strong suspicion that BSE has leapt a species and infected humans who have eaten beef. No hard facts or advice. Everyone frightened.

As H says, the CJD disease takes ten years to incubate, and so our children, who ate beef in the late '80s, could, like us, be very much at risk if there is an epidemic. Apocalyptic news which vies with details of a huge increase in airborne tuberculosis, which is already on its way to becoming a new, life-threatening epidemic. There'll be some reading of the Book of Revelation tonight.

Sunday, March 24th

Reacquaint myself with *Hem's Chair* in advance of two busy days of paperback publicity. Made a list of reviews under Good, Equivocal and Bad. About 15 each under Good and Equivocal and only four under Bad, so feel less defensive about it all.

Monday, March 25th

Two television interviews at Carlton in late afternoon.

Carlton now inhabits the South Bank tower that used to belong to LWT and it is a great shock to see how completely the old television world has been broken down. Camera operators are young and nervous. They also have to act as sound operators – checking mikes, etc. The position of my lapel mike – not a complicated business – is changed three or four times in a minute.

The programmes are loose, rough, amateurish. The frothy waffle of the content is quite depressing, the ignorance and lack of pride in the job quite un-believable. It's as if all the qualified people had just been killed in an air crash, leaving the programmes to be made by a skeleton staff of students.

Tuesday, March 26th

Valerie Grove arrives to interview me.

The interview seems to fly off at various tangents – mainly because she is bright and curious and extrovert and we share many of the same concerns – about London lacking a central authority – even a mayor – about the shabby state of Camden, about the delights of the Heath. She does seem genuinely approving of *Hem's Chair* – being particularly complimentary about Ruth.

Wednesday, March 27th

Will round early evening. He has been offered a permanent staff job with the Mirror Group – £21,000 a year. He's pleased that it will offer him a chance to plan his employment, holidays, etc. for some months ahead. More security, but he doesn't think he will stay there for more than a year.

To dinner with JC at Alastair Little's new restaurant off Ladbroke Grove. Minimalist decor, minimal ambience – fierce eschewing of the candle-lit, tablecloth kind of atmos. John, big green Bentley spread out along the kerb in front of the restaurant – 'I can keep an eye on it' – is in reflective mood.

He once again expresses desire to make a walk-on appearance on the Pacific doc – preferably in some quite out-of-the-way place like La Paz. Says he'd do it for the price of an air ticket.

Wednesday, April 24th

To lunch with Will at Café Flo. A good catch-up with his news and his plans. He's coping well with the unsociable working hours at Mirror Group (where his official title is sub-editor). But he admits that he's restless, that he wants to keep on the move – doesn't want to be confined to one job or even living in the flat he has at the moment. He loves books and words too much to want to spend the rest of his life in front of a computer screen.

I see much of myself in Will – a need for constant change and stimulation grafted onto a deeply conservative sense of solidity and responsibility.

Sunday, April 28th

Epi, H's Colombian friend – full of warmth and infectious enthusiasm – comes round with husband and son for tea and a talk about Colombia, which is coming up on our itinerary. She has family contacts there. Brings coffee-table books which favour the great and strikingly beautiful interiors of some of the old houses.

Alongside this there is 'Narco' Colombia. A country where a drug baron wanting to strike a deal could offer the government the money to wipe out its national debt at one go. She describes the complete lack of political morality – the insidiousness of corruption running through every aspect of public life. But she still manages to make it sound unmissable.

Monday, April 29th

H and I spend several minutes trying to record a new message for the answerphone. It keeps recording things like 'Press this!' 'No, no, press that ...' followed by laughter and failed attempts to be serious. Like a pair of schoolchildren. Still.

To Groucho's to meet Dan Patterson and Ian Brown [his writing partner], who have some ideas and questions to ask on 'The Adventure'. Never feel altogether comfortable in Groucho's. To do the place properly you have to act a bit. You have to decide what role you're going to play before you go in. Generally quite ordinary people but occasionally someone larger than life looms up and you feel you should grasp their hand, then you remember this is Groucho's and it wouldn't be cool. Then you overcompensate and cut people dead. I muttered most unsatisfactorily at Clement Freud as we passed.

Monday, May 6th

To lunch with JC at Poons in Whiteleys (at his suggestion).

Much of the meal taken up with JC's renewed interest in the sex comedy. 'Small budget – ten at most, no American stars, shoot in Ireland, good for tax, you and me, maybe Julie Christie as your wife. What's not to like.'

407

Wednesday, May 8th

Over to Prominent for the first full Python business meeting since, according to Kath, 1989. I'm upstairs talking to her when I hear Terry G's boisterous arrival, bronchial laughter in return from Cleese and some squeaky sighs and groans from Terry J.

We all squeeze around the glass-topped table in the tiny meeting room. Eric is summoned up by phone from LA where it's eight in the morning. The phone call lasts three and a half hours, which is the time it takes for us to deal with the backlog of work.

The reorganisation of the Python companies is dealt with constructively. Clarifications necessary. Jokes keep diverting attention. Eric suggests that the 'B' shares be called Half-a-Bee shares. John adds an 'Eric' to this – so they will now be known as Eric the Half-Bee shares.

A lot of it is to do with who controls Python in the event of our deaths. After debate it is felt that only Pythons should have control over their companies – even down to the last one alive.

The only real contentious area is the dreaded Prominent Features. Terry G is greatly exercised about the way it's been left to run quite vaguely. John has taken 69,000 dollars of his money out, as has Eric, on projects which are manifestly not to be Prominent Features. Can they, should they do that?

I'm in favour, at a push, of keeping Prominent Features. It has a name, it has back product. But later, over a Japanese meal with the two Terrys, I feel Acrimony Films may be a better name.

On May 15th we left London for the last and longest of our Pacific filming legs. This one, from Cape Horn in the south to the Bering Strait in the north, took us away from home for three months.

Saturday, May 18th: Hotel Cabo de Hornos, Punta Arenas, Chile

It's half past five on a day at the end of a southern autumn, and it's almost too dark now to see the statue of Magellan, borne on the backs of Indians, which stands at the centre of the Plaza de Armas, seven floors below me.

Four years and a few months ago, on my way to Antarctica in the middle of a Southern summer, I kissed the bronze toe of one of those Indians, which traditionally means that you will return to Punta Arenas. I did return, safely, a few days later, after reaching the South Pole.

Now I've returned a second time, and I'm sure I shall have to kiss the lucky toe again, as we set out on the long journey to Alaska.

This is almost the first private time since our hurtling progress to the

Americas began at Heathrow last Tuesday night. We reached Santiago early on Wednesday morning, and within three hours were flying Air Patagonia to Punta.

We didn't stop there, but piled our 800 kgs of equipment and baggage into a twin-engined Otter and took off for Puerto Williams – a further hour's flying time to the south. Groggily unloaded onto a 130-foot Chilean navy patrol boat, the *Isaza*, where I spent my first night in South America, grinding out towards Cape Horn.

Barely rested, we had to take advantage of the weather to film our approach to and landing on Cape Horn.

Our second day of filming was along the Beagle Channel, taking advantage of generally clear weather and spectacular locations, then another night aboard the *Isaza*, tight and cramped and convivial, but no private space.

Now the wind howls outside my window, but for the time being we are home and dry; the last leg, which will seem endless at times, has begun with a severe test of stamina. The reward has been a chance to see lands very few will ever see, and enter a lonely, hard world which must look virtually unaltered since Darwin described it in his diary over 160 years ago.

Monday, May 20th: Costa Australis Hotel, Puerto Natales, Chile

Almost everyone else in the crew seems to switch the television on as soon as they get in their room. I like the time to think.

I think about the journey, what I've learnt and what I've seen and once that's in perspective – a mundane task of checking the tape-recorded notes and tidying up my notebook entries – I let my mind go and settle where it wants.

Called Helen last night and heard that our cat Betty was dead, her lungs had collapsed and the vet had drawn off ten millilitres of pus from them. Helen had tried to give her a healing pill but Betty had bitten her hard, leaving three deep incisions in her finger. Betty's legacy, as H put it.

It's only quite late in our conversation that I can tell her that I've been to Cape Horn, and stood on it too. What I want to exult about and share doesn't sound exciting any more. Betty's death sort of subsumes everything.

Sunday, May 26th: Chiloé Island, Chile

Have been awake for a long time. Outside the gale continues to blow, rattling the roofs and slapping rain against the windows. This is very bad weather indeed and we have a long, hard day's filming ahead. Now, just after my alarm goes, I find that there is no electricity. I want to curl up in bed and put the sheets over my head.

I can summon up nothing but resignation at the thought of cooking with the locals all morning, then having to listen to music and songs I don't understand for the rest of the afternoon. And, worst of all, having to look as if I'm enjoying it. All my systems – my mental and psychological systems – are at full stretch. Something will get me through, but after this – another two and a half months still to go.

Tuesday, June 4th: Calama, Chile

Dawn breaking at the El Tatio geyser field. Apart from being the highest place on which I've ever set foot, it was good to film, wondrous to behold, and the warmth of the steam and the sun slowly conquered the Arctic cold – it was minus 12 when we reached the geysers at seven o'clock. Roger's dire warnings of the headaches and nosebleeds that he and Vanessa had experienced on their recce were not fulfilled. Apart from flatulence, I suffered no effects of being, at one point, only 250 feet short of 15,000.

Fraser had the sound of the fumaroles to record, Nigel had pre-dawn, drifting steam and, after sunrise, brilliantly back-lit steam – in between huge swathes of mountainside turning a rich pink-brown.

I'd begun to get gloomy, thinking to myself that this last American section was a mistake.

Then along come days like today in El Tatio, and though I'm sore-eyed with tiredness after two very early starts and with the prospect of a long, late work and travel day tomorrow, I feel good enough to want to write up the diary. This is a most beautiful country. Press on.

Friday, June 28th: Hotel Sol del Oriente, Pucallpa, Peru

Bolivia and Peru have been more demanding. The altitude made everything hard work – I slept, and dreamt, in shallow breathless bursts, so was always quite tired.

Cuzco a brief and beautiful breather, then the long, nine-day hike to the Urubamba, and seven of those days and nights under canvas. Tents fine, slept extraordinarily well, but life at the horizontal, and sand accumulating in everything, and shitting supported on sandfly-bitten hands over a small hole full of other people's mess took its toll and we are all immensely happy to be through all that in one piece.

Monday will be the first day of July and (according to Nigel, who keeps these scores assiduously) the exact halfway point of our three months in the Americas.

Across the street professional letter-writers sit beneath colourful umbrellas waiting for business. Occasional blaring loudspeaker announcements announce the presence of a circus in town.

The food in Peru has been dull and generally unexciting. I miss good breakfasts particularly. Ask for coffee, even in this, the best hotel in Pucallpa, and you will be brought hot water, a spoon and an old, rusty-lidded tin of Nescafé.

My reading time has been prescribed by the pressure of the work and the nature of the places we've stayed recently, but I have finished Leigh Fermor's *Letters from the Andes* and launched into Hemming's *Conquest of the Incas* and Llosa's autobiography, but am currently caught by the great García Márquez – *Chronicle of a Death Foretold*.

Shaved for the first time in ten days. I'm ready for work tomorrow – Day 200 on the road.

Friday, July 5th: Hotel El Dorado, Iquitos, Peru

We are in limbo land at the moment, killing time very slowly as we wait for a boat to take us down the Amazon.

The crew, as Fraser put it, feels 'uncomfortable' when it's not working.

But this town has a charm and an atmosphere which Pucallpa lacked, and I enjoy walking the grid-plan streets – up Próspero, down Morona and onto the recently completed esplanade looking over the Amazon – which at this dry season looks less like a mighty river and more like a plain of flooded fields. The town has a colonial past, stretching back over two hundred years and culminating in the great rubber boom of the late nineteenth and early twentieth centuries. This has left behind a legacy of interesting, well-decorated town houses, with tall, arched French windows giving out onto classically pilastered balconies, and some eye-catching Azulejo tiling.

I've rung home and all goes on quite happily without me. I can almost hear Helen trying to scour her memory for some remarkable detail to feed me with when I ring from the back of beyond.

El Comercio is spread out on my bed; in it the news that Charles has offered 30 million to Diana as a divorce settlement.

Thursday, July 11th: Victoria Regia Hotel, Bogotá, Colombia

I feel as happy and contented and comfortable as at any time on this long, sometimes apparently endless journey. It's a euphoria which is bound at some point to pass away and return me to uncomfortable reality, but for now – 3.15 in Room 810 at the Victoria Regia – it's worth recording that I feel very happy indeed.

For what reasons? Firstly and mainly that 24 hours ago we reached the nadir of discomfort – on the *El Arca* where lights, water and air-con all ceased to function, leaving us, on the sweaty banks of the Amazon, trapped in a night of suffocating heat and rampant mosquitoes.

Crossing into Colombia at the small frontier town of Leticia, we discovered that our main sequence there – the coca plantation – was impossible to film owing to recent action by the DEA, the American Drug Enforcement Agency, and the Colombian government.

Decision taken to leave Leticia and fly straight to Bogotá. No-one complains. We are all pretty desperate to get out of the jungle.

So, at two this morning, to the Hotel Victoria Regia, a small, elegantly furnished, comprehensively efficient town-house hotel.

There is abundant hot water, dispensed from brass taps into bath tubs big enough for two. Lights work; hangers are unbroken, there are desks and tables with comfortable chairs to match.

Breakfast is a feast and there are luxuries like fresh milk, almost unheard of in Peru.

Awful things may lurk elsewhere in the city, but Oma Libros – a bookstore with English-language books, newspapers and a café – was a complete realisation of fantasies in which I had been indulging since we left Chile.

At the reception desk, the first four draft scripts of a sitcom by Roy Clarke which Geoffrey Perkins at the BBC wants me to do – and which Anne thinks the best thing she's read for me in ages.

Friday, August 2nd: Fairmont Hotel, San Francisco

It's nearly midnight. Have just closed the curtains on a magnificent view of the city skyline as seen from my room on the Fairmont Tower's 22nd floor. I'm a lucky boy. Only two more weeks to go; we have worked a day described as 'almost flawless' by Fraser at dinner tonight (we shot in Alcatraz and the Castro).

Steve Robinson and I had a good natter tonight about art and architecture. It began with him mentioning the Saltash Bridge and me saying that the victory of George Stephenson over Isambard Brunel was a significant portent of the way Britain was going to go. Opportunism and profit defeating style, flair, care and craftsmanship.

Friday, August 9th: Crest Motor Inn, Prince Rupert, Canada

Bands of light rain and wet mist drift across the fine, wide view of water and forested headland.

I can hear voices from the piers down below and occasionally a white float-plane will fly low out of the sound. Chunky, solid-hulled little fishing boats have been busy going in and out all day long.

Quite suddenly, it seems, the greatest journey I have ever undertaken, and probably ever will undertake, in my life, is coming to an end.

As I write, I'm aware in the back of my mind of that little nodule of apprehension that troubles me from time to time. We still have a lot of travelling left – several thousand miles and some potentially inhospitable locations – and many human elements leave margins for error.

Hanging over all arrangements is the start of *Fierce Creatures* re-shoots a week today, which will require my energy and concentration for 14 days on the run.

The script, in a black folder, is beside me on the neat, bottle-green up-holstered cushions of my alcove seat. There's a lot of new material to learn – 'Anywhere where you can see that Bugsy can talk more – just talk more' – John's written. It's clear that Fred Schepisi,[1] the new director, likes the Bugsy character, which is why I have so much work ahead. I approach it with greater confidence than before.

Tiredness has been the enemy since we left San Francisco. I was sorely tested by a long, damp day at the logging competition near Vancouver.

I performed, like a performing bear, doing what was expected, being a sport and deep down hating most of what I had to do and how I had to do it. And finally I fell in the water whilst running across a log and the ritual sacrifice was duly delivered and everyone was happy – though I showed my happiness in a howl of heartfelt indignation. Right in front of the camera, sodden and weary and trapped in the ring, I beat my hands on the grass and gave up. 'I want to go home!' was all I could shout, over and over again. I felt utterly, truly, completely broken. Everyone was delighted.

Monday, August 19th

After an unexpectedly sprightly three days, almost unaffected by jet lag, I find myself waking sluggishly on this fourth morning home.

To Pinewood for hair, make-up checks and to meet Fred Schepisi.

He's informal, no-nonsense, and any fears that working for a new master

---

1 Fred Schepisi, Australian director of *Last Orders* and *Six Degrees of Separation*.

might be uncomfortable are quickly dispelled. He says simply that if Bugsy is to be funny because of his monomaniac verbal persistence, then he has to talk almost all the time. He could see from the footage that Bugsy's part was underwritten – as were John's and Jamie's – hence his encouragement to John to beef up Bugsy, and the reason why I am on call for all but two of the 20 shooting days ahead.

I always felt it a weakness that Bugsy was not more intimately involved in the denouement. In the new script I am the *deus ex machina*, and have a much more complete role. So now it's up to me to make something of it.

Wednesday, August 21st

A good, brisk productive morning's work. Actually enjoy doing my close-ups and my delivery relaxes and Fred is pleased. Best of all, I did a professional job, and added to it that unparalleled feeling of having done something the best way it could be done – a feeling I rarely experienced on the last shoot.

What has helped me is that John no longer feels the need to direct, to whip up the cast's enthusiasm with his exhortations, songs, chants and the whole act he put on to make up for what he thought were others' shortcomings. Now John concentrates on his acting and Fred, with his mixture of ribaldry and Aussie bonhomie, runs the show and sets the tone. Ironic that Aussies should be brought in to save a film whose villains are Aussies.

Friday, August 23rd

Into the bee costume for the first time. I shall be wearing it for most of next week. Because of the weather we remain indoors and set to a short but complicated little scene involving Kevin being discovered stuffing a body in the freezer. Kevin and Jamie are both more relaxed and I'm pleased to have rediscovered the good working and non-working relationship we all had on *Wanda*.

Kevin wildly, richly, grandly inventive. Jamie told me yesterday that she'd been sitting out on the set minding her own business when she saw a penis appear from beneath the shorts of one of the crew. 'He just waggled it about a bit and stuck it back,' she claimed. Later, as I was outside on my way to work and she was returning to her dressing room, I asked her if she'd had any more visions. 'You better believe it,' she said, and as she added 'goodnight Michael' she swiftly pulled down her top and revealed her right breast.

It was only after she'd passed that I realised that one of the drivers was beside me, shammying the window of his Range Rover. 'Did you see that?' he said, adding regretfully, 'trouble is, if I tell anyone about it, they wouldn't believe me.'

Monday, August 26th

They've decided to move calls an hour earlier. To maximise daylight, I'm told. So I'm awake at five and picked up at 5.30.

Lines around the lemur cage at beginning and end of John and Jamie's first 'love' scene. Fred using Steadicam again. He gives me a couple of new thoughts for lines – just before the take. 'Keep talking,' he says. A challenge to be confronted then and there. And I must say I find that I do like working this way.

John thinks I should have a separate credit – 'endless additional dialogue by Michael Palin'.

Tuesday, August 27th

The morning taken up with a quick-fire, quite long dialogue scene between, largely, me and Kevin. We barely had an exchange in the original script. Now Bugsy's unstoppable drone has a chance to drive both Vince and McCain mad, with fatal consequences in the latter case.

Home to find a note from H to say that Jonathan Margolis has been commissioned to write a biography of me. He has already done one on John, which John asked us all not to co-operate on. My immediate reaction is one of indignation. I don't want him to write a biog of me and I resent the assumed confidence that I will co-operate.

Wednesday, August 28th

Kevin is high as a kite today – soaring off into sweeping voices, extravagant gestures, keeping himself going at a level of barely controlled manic intensity. He rarely comes down to earth. It's dazzling and exhausting.

'Anything you need Kev?' one of the crew asks routinely.

'Oh, a night's sleep, perhaps,' Kevin bats back tersely, only just joking.

Saturday, September 7th

As the various last shots are cleared up, the atmosphere becomes increasingly like that of a school on the last day of term. I wander the emptying studios, prompting Roger Murray-Leach to liken me to a boy whose parents have failed to turn up to collect him.

Jamie, who has given me as a parting gift a Paul Smith fish keyring, is drinking strawberry vodka from the bottle as I get made up around six.

There is red wine sloshing about the make-up area – a joyful reaction to a no-alcohol-on-duty clause in the employment contract. Bille Brown is bade farewell in the traditional manner – called to the stage, although still in his underpants, to receive our applause, hugs, etc.

Then it's Kevin's turn. Fred makes a short farewell speech calling Kevin 'a great talent and a pleasure to work with'. No-one would disagree with the first part, but like all great talents Kevin sometimes loses sight of the contribution of lesser talents. It becomes a solitary world when you're that talented – but he is still a kind, thoughtful, highly intelligent, serious man. I'd like to lark about with him though, one day.

Fifteen and a half months since the first scene of *Fierce Creatures*, John and myself are the only two left.

I know everyone wants to be done, but I still have three quite tricky little speeches to deliver, with the camera tight on my head and shoulders.

The clock is moving towards eight o'clock. Everyone is blearily staggering towards the tape, but I have to be clear and concentrated and remember that what I do now on this echoing, emptying stage will potentially fill screens all over the world.

All of which is my own self-congratulatory way of saying that my nerve held and I didn't slip a word on three takes. 'Check the gate.' And it's over.

Sunday, September 8th

It's a pleasure to lie and luxuriate in bed – until Elsie and Edith spring up onto the duvet and attack my radio during *Letter from America*. It's bizarrely like Alistair Cooke Being Attacked by a Duck (Python 1971) as the urbane 88-year-old purrs on whilst Edith chews the aerial and Elsie tugs the radio across the bed.

We lunch with John and Michael Shamberg and families at La Famiglia, off the King's Road. Michael S, heartened by the last three weeks, is more like the Shamberg I used to know on *Wanda*. He says he now has to go back to the States and 'start selling' the film. He does not anticipate much trouble – in fact he thinks the trailers that have been appearing over the last year might help.

John thinks I've been a 'really good stick' for working so hard so soon after my return. All is sweetness and light.

Monday, September 9th

After some debate with H I agree not to try and start work on the Pacific book at six in the morning (my thinking being that I have become so used to rising early over the last year that it would come naturally).

Look at the schedules again – estimate words to be done, time allowed. All of my books have, from necessity, been confined to a season – a spring or an autumn generally. Once again, I'm tight up against dates set by expectant publishers, and of course, in this case, expectant editors, directors and producers. Fourteen weeks is the time I have to complete a first and, virtually, last draft.

Friday, September 13th

Will comes by. We go down together to visit Tom at Whitfield Studios, where he, John and George are producing two tracks for a girl duo called Akin.

Tom and the boys look very much at home with the long, winking beds of equipment – the screens, digital controls and so on. Brockpocket, as he and his two partners call themselves, have a certain gentle swagger now.

Though Tom has not yet hit the jackpot, he clearly has style and substance. Next year will be their make or break year he reckons, with most of the work they've stockpiled coming onto the market. Tom has a good, straightforward, sensible attitude to it all. He's philosophical. He has H's calm centre.

Tuesday, September 17th

To BH to record my *Week's Good Cause* for the Prison Reform Trust. I wasn't much impressed by the original script, but the cause is a good one, and I spent time rewriting it so that it sounded more genuine and natural and less clichéd. No point in doing something like this unless you can do it with feeling.

To the South Bank for a private view of a new exhibition of Mel Calman's work at the National. Arrive early so get the cab to put me down on Waterloo Bridge and walk the rest. The underbelly of the South Bank Centre darker and more hellish than ever. The Royal Festival Hall has a presentation of Richard Rogers' plan for redesigning the area. It looks striking – great waves of poly-something or other will cover and unite the place.

Barely a day goes by now without some architectural muscle-flexing. Foster's Millennium Tower revealed at the weekend; the new British Library our entry for the Architectural Biennale in Venice. With the help of lottery money and the increasing wealth of rich patrons, architects are enjoying a sort of renaissance.

Thursday, September 19th

Good story in Alec Guinness' *Book of the Week* reading of his gloriously under-played diaries. Coral Browne on stage when asked if the wig was bothering her replied 'Darling, I feel as if I'm looking out of a yak's arse.'

Monday, September 23rd

Anne rings. She has been talking to Clem, who says he can do nothing more about graphics until he has a title. So must confront this one. Sometimes I sink back to the ease and convenience of 'Palin's Pacific'. If I wanted to please everyone this would be the one. But my own objections still stick. It's not *my* Pacific.

Monday, October 7th

Leave at ten o'clock for Oxford. Car loaded to the gunwales. It's a grey morning in London but the sky brightens as we reach Oxford. Usual combination of emotions. Oxford, more than anywhere else, and certainly more than London, reminds me of the ageing process. I mourn a little for my time here – which seems, at a distance, to have been full of promise and opportunity, freshness and self-discovery, a sort of golden time where everything was ahead of me.

At the same time I see Rachel's golden time (or so I presumptuously assume it to be) also fading. This is her last year. Already, the day I found her room in the Library Staircase was Robert's old room seems far away – lost for ever. So I sense the poignancy of both our lives either passing, or having long passed, important formative stages.

Rachel is swept away by her friends – her room is big, with en suite shower and bathroom, quite recently renovated and high, on New Staircase overlooking the quad and close to a big owl's head gargoyle. Desk before wide mullioned window.

At 12.45 arrive at St Edmund Hall to have lunch with Stephen Tumim, who asked me to drop in and see him if I were passing.

Stephen, whose first week this is as Principal, is like a child with a new toy. He greets everyone cordially, especially the lower members of staff, and is anxious that I should meet as many dons as possible. He's so enthusiastic about his various new jobs – including Fine Arts Admissions Tutor at the Ruskin. 'I'm hoping to get one of my ex-prisoners in. He's a lifer; rather good painter, I must say.'

He has old-fashioned ways and an old-fashioned appearance – half-moon specs and bow ties – but is lively, full of jokes, many at his own expense, and as bright and sharp as a 20-year-old. Except most of the 20-year-olds, struggling into their new rooms at the start of a new term, look far from bright.

Wednesday, October 9th

Need a suit for tonight's BAFTA 50th so, at last possible minute, drive to Grey Flannel in Chiltern Street.

Suit having been altered, trouser bottoms taken up, etc. – all in space of an hour – H and I are into a cab heading for Piccadilly.

This is a royal occasion, so there is much standing around and waiting and keeping spaces clear and announcements like 'the royal party will be arriving here in approximately eight minutes'.

Jim Acheson[1] and Julia and Helen and myself find ourselves in the row directly behind the Queen and the Duke. Their seats are marked by two fudge-coloured antimacassars. Jim has a plan to remove one of them at the end, and have me sign it to Julia's mother Valerie in New Zealand!

It turns out to be the one on the seat of the monarch herself. Not that the Queen leans back much. She sits bolt upright like a perched bird – as though at some horse trials.

Two Fellowships are awarded – one to Freddie Young,[2] the cameraman, who is 94 today and can barely move without help. He makes it to the microphone and between slow, laboured, emphysemic breaths gives brief thanks then, holding the audience spellbound with his breathing difficulties, he adds 'If you … want … to … see … any … more … of me … (long pause) I'm on *This Is Your Life* on Friday.'

Then a four and a half minute round-up of 100 years of British cinema in which I made the screen three times – *Private Function*, *Grail* and *Life of Brian* – and *Wanda* was in there too.

---

1 Jim Acheson, costume and production designer. Worked on *Brazil* and *Time Bandits*. Won three Costume Design Oscars for *Restoration*, *Dangerous Liaisons* and *The Last Emperor*.
2 Freddie Young, cinematographer, long-time associate of David Lean on his films *Lawrence of Arabia*, *Doctor Zhivago* and *Ryan's Daughter*, all of which won Academy Awards.

After the presentation, the Queen and Prince Philip leave for a private room and Jim Acheson swiftly pockets Her Majesty's antimacassar.

We're fetched to meet the Queen, who is showing admirable stamina. Her Majesty is turned in my direction and somewhat to my disappointment her face registers a complete blank. Eddie Mirzoeff prompts her about my recent travels.

I'm determined to get some reaction from her, and when I say that we were allowed home from filming for brief periods – 'to save our marriages and get our washing done' – her well-dusted face breaks into genuine jolly laughter.

Later, George Perry says that the only things she really enjoyed in the Best of British compilation were appearances by Sid James.

Tuesday, October 15th

Near-despair strikes mid-morning as, after cruising confidently along with the book, I accidentally press some odd combination of keys and the entire third section disappears.

For a half-hour or more I am utterly desolate. Helen's out, so I can't seek help and consolation. Will is very encouraging. He comes round, despite having been on night shift at the *Mirror*, and calms me down, says he's had whole essays disappear and that once he has resigned himself to rewriting – says the rewrite almost always an improvement.

So, keep the phone unplugged and get my head down. What makes it hardest at first is knowing that the 4,000 words or more that I've lost felt so clear and easy to write.

But by six I have completed over 3,000 of them and in most cases with greater fluency than when I first wrote them.

Sunday, October 20th

To Leicester Square Empire at 9.30 for screening of Steve A's *Brassed Off*.[1]

A heaving crowd, through which members of the Grimethorpe Colliery Works Band are dragging heavy instruments – kettledrums and euphoniums – for a pre-film recital. In the film they play the Grimley Colliery Band which, at the climax of the picture, wins the National Championships at the Albert Hall. Last night the real Grimethorpe band came second, by one point!

---

1 *Brassed Off* was produced by Steve Abbott and directed by Mark Herman: the same team that made *Blame It on the Bellboy*.

The film is well made and funny and quite gripping despite some spongily sentimental material when the goodies behave as too good to be true and the baddies as too bad. Reminds me of a *Ripping Yarn* sometimes. A good credit for Prominent.

Late start and finish because of the crowds. Back home as swiftly as possible, pick up H and out to Henley for lunch with Peter Luff.[1]

Fortunately, John Lloyd and wife Sarah are also late, coming from the other side of Oxfordshire. John reminds me of Lytton Strachey, or some eminent Victorian now his hair has receded and his face has lost its youthful glow. He is good company – intelligent, curious and infectiously world-weary. He shrugs off his achievements – *Not the Nine O'Clock* and *Blackadder* – and claims to have done nothing he's particularly proud of for several years. 'I make my money doing commercials with John Cleese.'

Big flag-floor kitchen and roast lamb around a refectory table. Feels like one of John's commercials. Lloydey, as they call him, says wistfully to me that 'I would like to meet whoever wrote the script of your life.'

Cross the road to drop in on George H. The spindly wrought-iron gates open and we roll up the green and gloomy drive with its trees so big on all sides it's like opening a door into British Columbia.

I always feel that what you see of George's house is just the tip of the iceberg – indeed there probably is an iceberg somewhere – but I do feel that he seems very small at the middle of it all, and yes, probably quite exhausted. He says he rarely comes up to town now – though Olivia likes to shop and meet friends.

Dhani is what one might call a fine boy. He's slim, good-looking, articulate and confident, without being a pain at the same time. He's one of the best coxes around and recently joined the Leander Club.

George is thinking of going to India 'to get healthy again', and then have a long holiday. I envy him that, but not all the rest of his life. As he is tucking himself away, I'm just enjoying getting back to people.

Wednesday, October 23rd

To lunch with Donald Woods. He's given up smoking but not drinking. 'I may be a fat drunk, but at least I'm not smoking.'

Donald is using me again to get money for his various Eastern Cape projects and particularly for his scheme to teach black journalists. 'I have to teach them to be confident enough to be critical,' he says. 'Critical of their own people.'

---

1 Producer of the first Amnesty International Charity Show *The Secret Policeman's Ball*.

Thursday, October 24th

Sid, who suffers from vertigo, comes to clean the windows. He tells H later that he is also an alcoholic. H asks if he is undergoing any treatment. He says there is an alcoholism unit at the Royal Free but he can't go to it because it's on the tenth floor.

Sunday, October 27th

To the 'BBC 60 Gala' at TV Centre. The Centre itself is lit with coloured floodlights and revolving spots and a makeshift doorway has been erected leading across the circular forecourt where Ariel stands on tiptoe, forlornly looking out over a fountain that never works.

A glut of celebs step out of rain-sodden taxies onto red carpet – BBC clearly aiming for Oscars feel. Charlie[1] from *Casualty* (H most excited here) then Robin Day and Alan Whicker – both nominated, like me, in Favourite Presenter section. 'We're in competition,' shouts Robin Day, who obviously takes the whole thing quite seriously.

I'm to give the first award for Favourite Sitcom Performer. My envelope contains the name of David Jason. Give him the rather skinny, skimpy likeness of Ariel and a hug for old times' sake. Next year will be the thirtieth anniversary of *Do Not Adjust*.[2]

Other winners, chosen by the public in a telephone poll, show that, generally speaking, it's the shows they remember most recently that win. So *Men Behaving Badly* collects the award for Favourite Situation Comedy Ever on the BBC – beating *Fawlty Towers*, *Porridge*, *Hancock* and *Steptoe* – and making a farce of the whole thing.

Des Lynam wins Best Presenter Ever, beating out Richard Dimbleby's challenge with the first report from Belsen in 1945.

Attenborough loses out to Des Lynam. Python to Victoria Wood.

Friday, November 1st

News of *Fierce Creatures*. Word is that the Monday screening and 'focus group' out on Long Island didn't go well. Only 58% returned the good to very good. Fred [Schepisi] then edited out ten minutes that weren't working and scores went up by 15% on the Wednesday screening.

1 Charlie Fairhead, played by Derek Thompson.
2 David Jason was one of the cast of *Do Not Adjust Your Set* (1967-9) along with Terry Jones, Eric Idle, Denise Coffey and MP.

So, after all these years of time, energy, money and hard graft, 'FC' looks likely to be a 90-minute quickie, its shape and content decided eventually by 20 people in Long Island. JC's 'message' scenes – all his indignation at the system, his invective against the modern management style – have virtually disappeared.

Saturday, November 2nd: London–Edinburgh

To King's Cross to catch the twelve o'clock.

Strong winds in Edinburgh. Walk from Waverley to the Caledonian through Prince's Street Gardens, quite an effort against Force-8 gale, but worth it just to take in the big, bold, jagged shapes of the city.

To the Scottish National Gallery of Modern Art in a very fine, august, black-granite classical building on Bedford Road.

The Anne Redpath Exhibition, to which I've loaned two works, is wonderfully rich – shows what a versatile, determined and talented woman she was. My 'Menton' has found two friends – both painted during the same visit in 1949 and the much-admired 'Blue Tablecloth' is next to one in similar ice-blue style. Feel rather like a proud parent at speech day as I eavesdrop on people pausing in front of my paintings.

Meet Eleanor Yule and Mhairi McNeill from BBC Scotland who want me to present a half-hour film on Redpath. Our feelings much the same about treatment – so agree to go next June.

Sunday, November 3rd: Edinburgh–London

Read the papers and look out over the grey slate roofs and stern stone walls of the city, and beyond them the scudding waters of the Firth of Forth. The view is bathed in sharp sunshine one minute, the roofs and walls black and oily with rain the next.

To the gallery at eleven. Philip Long, the young man whom I've dealt with on the exhibition, is there to show me round before it opens to the public. A more restful way to see the Redpaths – and in natural light as well. Philip says she was greatly influenced by the early Renaissance painters she saw in Florence, then later by Van Gogh, Vuillard and Bonnard.

Upstairs there is a fine, small selection of Picassos and good Scots Colourists like Peploe and Fergusson and the smoothly elegant Cadell.

A journalist from the *Scotsman*, a New Zealander called Susan Nickalls, arrives to ask me some questions about the pictures and Palin and art. She drives me to a café to talk. It is set on a cobbled hill near some of the most expensive property in Edinburgh. Sitting at the window with fresh flowers on the table and a stone wall and leafy patch of lawn outside, I feel we would fit into a painting rather well.

Tuesday, November 5th

BT ring to try and get me to do an advertising film – one of a pair – Whoopi Goldberg 'pretty certain' to be doing the other. Say no. Anne says that this same man rings almost every year to try and interest me in becoming a BT salesman.

Wednesday, November 6th

To the Royal Television Society Gala – dread word again – to mark 60 years of television.

Alan Whicker is one of the first people we see. After greeting each other, Alan stretches out a hand and tucks my errant collar down beneath my jacket. Somehow it was a touching gesture. Paternal really – as if I were his offspring and he was in some way responsible for me – which in a way is all quite true.[1]

Thursday, November 7th

Into the West End to have my photograph taken with Helen's surgeon, Michael Powell, at the National Hospital. Both of us, at his request, to be dressed as per his favourite Python sketch – the Gumby brain surgeons.

He's brought along what Gumby kit he can muster, in a carrier bag. So find myself in a most surreal situation; dressed in gumboots, knotted handkerchief and brandishing a surgical steel bradawl above the head of one of Britain's leading brain surgeons.

After it's done we remove our gumboots and hankies and he offers to show me the theatre in which H had her op. We go through into a small, narrow room, when he breaks off – 'Oh dear, there's someone in here.' We both peer round the door and there is indeed someone in there, shrouded in hospital green, laid at a 45° angle with a surgeon working in their spotlit head. Powell is quite unfazed; exchanges some boisterous greetings, which are returned from one of the masked figures around the body.

---

1 Alan Whicker was the first to be approached to present *Around the World in 80 Days*. He turned it down.

Sunday, November 17th, Suffolk

By 9.30, when we leave for Suffolk, the rain has begun. Progress is smooth and we are at Sudbury by eleven. Find Derek Taylor's turn-off, through low-lying meadowland on the road to Long Melford.

An old, weather-boarded Suffolk mill house, full of character, and with a tributary of the Stour running nearby. Today in the rain, with ducks ruffing and puffing and standing on their heads in the water, it seems almost to be floating. Comfortable rooms full of engaging bits of bric-a-brac as well as some good Clarice Cliff[1] pieces.

Derek is a little thinner maybe, but his complexion is ruddy and he does not look like someone who has inoperable stomach cancer. Of course they did operate and apparently his stomach is, as a result, up near his heart, but he had no chemotherapy, or further 'killer' surgery. Despite the Beatles offering him the best that money could buy, Derek ended up with the surgeon at the West Suffolk Hospital whom he liked and trusted.

The quality of his life, he thinks, is immeasurably better now than if he had had further, expensive chemical treatment. His wit isn't dimmed, but he is noticeably more frail.

He has several stacks of videotapes – many containing snippets of old news broadcasts or documentary programmes like *Yesterday's Men*, which with great prescience he recorded and kept.

He's still working on Beatle projects – setting up interviews with the Fab Three.

Monday, November 18th

A totally unsolicited catalogue from a coin dealer. I ring and complain that I have never bought coins and don't want any more catalogues from them. A bored man at the other end is quite unapologetic. 'We've recently rented some names from an outside agency,' he tells me, chillingly.

Friday, November 22nd

A rush of sorts in the evening as the lookalike BAFTA award which Helen's friend has made as our present is not ready until 20 minutes before the cab comes to take us off to Roger Mills' 60th birthday.

---

1 Clarice Cliff (1899-1972) was one of the best-known Art Deco ceramics designers.

First person I see as I pass Roger his mock award is Eddie Mirzoeff, Chairman of BAFTA.

Peter Bazalgette,[1] a life-and-soul-looking fellow with a colourful waistcoat, has arranged a *This Is Your Life* for Rog and would like me to take part. 'I'll point to you,' he organises, 'and then you can tell a few stories about Roger. That's all there is to it.'

I begin my contribution with Roger's immortal words – '"Michael, I wouldn't ask you to do anything I wouldn't do myself"' (pause). Which is why I've been dressed in drag, rubber, Maori loincloths ...' Roger roars with laughter throughout – he is his own best audience.

Thursday, November 28th

Shoulder pain wakens me again, in the night. Hunted feel – the end of a month looms – the *Full Circle* book is well behind targets.

Run, with difficulty. After the schoolboys shouting 'Knees up, Grandad' last week, I have an elderly passing stranger remarking 'Old feet getting flatter aren't they?'

Want to kill him, but can't stop.

Friday, December 6th

Evening out at Vasco and Piero's with Mary and Edward.

There are still some diners there from lunchtime. One, halfway through a stumbling phone call on his mobile, holds the phone up to me. 'Here!' he slurs. 'Say something to the wife!'

I lean into the phone and say 'You'd better come and get your husband, he's making an awful fool of himself.'

Friday, December 20th

To Pinewood in pouring rain. In Theatre 7 for a sound editors' final screening of *Fierce Creatures*. Wonderful way to see it for the first time. Big screen, empty theatre.

Jerry Goldsmith's music gives an immediate big-movie buzz. It isn't great music or anything, it just has a bustling, Dolby-filling confidence about it.

1 Peter Bazalgette, television producer, led the successful independent company Endemol, which produced *Big Brother*. Appointed Chair of the Arts Council in 2013.

It's a short film now – 93 minutes – stripped of all pretensions, and generally honed to comedy scenes that deliver good farce and well-hit one-liners. It's a solid, aggressive piece of work. Kevin and Jamie attack; John defends well; and I'm quite sidelined, stuck amongst the keepers. The keepers collective in *Fierce Creatures* fulfils the same sort of role as Ken Pile in *Wanda*.

Sunday, December 22nd

JC calls from Santa Barbara. Opinions of the film seem good. In fact he says the French distributor has predicted that it could do even better there than *Wanda* because it's broader comedy. There has been a review in a US magazine which calls it, not a sequel, but in every way an equal of *Wanda*, so JC feeling cautiously relaxed about it.

Out to dinner being given for Julian and Merron at the house of a friend. Turns out to be a very big house in Maida Vale. The host is a smooth, well-preserved American called John Knight, who is 56 and just back from a trek up Kilimanjaro, and his wife, Donna, attractive in a friendly, un-intimidating way. She has co-produced plays with Julian.

Tom Courtenay and his wife there. We touch briefly on the radio production of *The Dresser*, but it was clear that Courtenay found more satisfaction working with Albert Finney[1] than Freddie Jones.

Feel a sort of kinship to Courtenay. He, like me, prefers the quieter, more understated roles. He's not a shouter and prancer. I'm stunned to learn that he's 59. He has such a boyish, mischievous quality, I've always had him down as a closer contemporary.

1 Albert Finney was chosen to play 'Sir' in the film version of *The Dresser*.

1997

Wednesday, January 1st

Was preparing for another Far Eastern departure this time a year ago, and have hardly stopped since then; can look back on five episodes filmed and many thousands of miles covered, a three-week re-shoot of *Fierce Creatures* and over 100,000 words of a new book completed.

It's maybe too early to tell if it's permanent, but I have felt different after completing a year's Pacific filming. A great wave of relief came over me after that.

I have felt a real sense of freedom, and a sense that I am much more in control of things – or perhaps it's just that I'm happy with my life – I'm happy to be what I am and spend much less time on what I want to be.

Saturday, January 4th

The next worry doesn't take long to present itself. It slides into my bed, insinuates itself as I have my head still on the pillow – both H and myself confined to the house, our tennis and running cut short by the hard, unyielding winter weather.

It's the 'Palin's Pacific' problem that will not go away. I cannot reconcile myself to it as a title – just possibly for a TV series, though certainly not for a book – and I know that I must face my worries this weekend, and come to a conclusion, for after Monday I shall be off round the world on *Fierce Creatures* business and will have little time or opportunity to affect matters here. This is my last chance to put up or shut up.

I ring Roger. He is aware of my reluctance to go with 'Palin's Pacific'. Strangely, it was something he said when I called him at the end of the year which started this whole train of thought running again. Roger's mother hadn't liked the title at all. 'It sounds as if he owns it,' she'd said.

'Does Pacific have to be in the title?' he replies to my suggestion of 'Pacific Circle'. 'If it doesn't then we could go back to *Full Circle*.' This strikes an immediate chord, for some reason it sounds and feels right, even though it was Clem's original suggestion and had long been abandoned.

Sunday, January 5th

Wake with acute indecision in early hours of the morning. *Full Circle* can't be right, it's not strong enough, and has no notion of where we are. 'Pacific' has to be in there.

I now know exactly what is meant by an agony of indecision, for I suffered physical manifestations of my tortured internal debate. At one point actually got out of bed again and walked into the bathroom, silently moaning.

Pester H about the title. She advises me to stand firm on *Full Circle*. Doesn't like the compromise – 'Pacific Circle'. 'Too difficult to say.'

At a Twelfth Night drinks party, someone asks if I've heard this morning's *Desert Island Discs*. John has chosen me as his 'luxury object'. Feel vaguely disreputable.

Tom comes round. Without asking him I notice he looks at the two possible new titles which I've printed up and stuck on my wall. '*Full Circle*, I like that,' he says with gratifying and unsolicited enthusiasm.

So the day of doubt comes to an end, with family having the prime say in the matter.

Tuesday, January 7th: New York

Call Anne. *Full Circle* has met with varying degrees of approval – from the editing rooms who were unimpressed, through Eddie who liked it, through Paul Hamann, Head of Documentaries, who wasn't so keen right up to Michael Jackson, Controller of BBC One, who liked it most of all. He wants it, as it is, without a subtitle, which was what I had hoped.

Wednesday, January 8th: New York

Across the park by taxi to Julian Schlossberg's apartment in the San Remo building on Central Park West. Marbled reception area of serious munificence – like a dream of old New York wealth. Approach to apartment poky, but opens onto big, wide rooms which are prevented from being grand and impersonal by careful use of big pieces of antique furniture. A massive refectory table stands laid like an altar with candles already burning.

A young man, who I'm much surprised to hear is 50, engages me in that sort of sharp, slightly gruffly humorous way affected by well and privately educated East Coast Americans. It turns out he's squiring Elaine May.[1]

Talk to Elaine M about many things. She remembers *The Missionary* fondly – says that people should make movies like that which have the author's stamp and not the producer's. Not impressed by the *Fierce Creatures* subway campaign. 'The subway's for blacks and Englishmen.'

Thursday, January 9th, New York

At 11.30 Jean Glass from BBC Worldwide Americas and her Vice-President of Public Relations, disconcertingly called Joe Kennedy, come to the hotel to meet up before we all go to see St Martin's Press, who will be handling the *Full Circle* book in the US.

We taxi down to St Martin's to meet Thomas Dunne. He has an office in the Flatiron Building – right on the apex of the triangle. Exciting view of New York to the north and across to the Hudson. Views of the old wood-cladded water tanks on a vista of roofs gives this aspect of New York a nineteenth-century feel.

Tom is middle-aged, ruddy-complexioned and approaches with an amused, ironic expression on his face. Young men from surrounding offices have clustered in to meet me. 'We never had this with Joan Collins,' cracks Dunne, who looks a joker.

Friday, January 10th: New York

Picked up by car and travel with John C, huge, bearded, capped and wrapped in a great cloak like Nanook of the North. To the once very familiar 50th Street entrance of NBC in Rockefeller Center. We are to be guests on *Saturday Night Live*.

Up to the studio where rehearsals are under way. Bobby the floor manager is still there and lean, grey-haired, dour Phil on lights is now white-haired, dour Phil. Otherwise the writers are the usual preppy bunch of amiable twenty-somethings. The same cue-card technique still used. Kevin Spacey is the host.

Sit next to JC at a desk and rehearse through a longish cold opening which features JC, myself as anchorman with Lorne Michaels, explaining new censorship rules for TV. We're required later to rehearse the 'Dead Parrot Sketch'.

A small group of people, including Lorne and Spacey, gather around the set with something uncomfortably close to reverence on their faces as they

1 Elaine May, American actress, writer and director best known for her comedy partnership with Mike Nichols.

watch us work it through. It is still funny and we do play it well so I leave fairly happy that we shall cope tomorrow night, despite a heavy day on *Fierce Creatures* publicity.

Saturday, January 11th: New York

Car pick-up from my hotel at 8.15. Snow has fallen again – maybe only an inch or so, but enough to make Central Park look tempting. But I only see it from a window high in the Essex House.

Jamie didn't much like the film when she saw it in LA but this morning she concedes that 'people' will like it. As usual she paces like a lion, squawks like a mynah and exudes a terrific, irrepressible bubbling combativity. She wants something, or someone to take on.

We are all taken to our separate rooms (marketing, being the science it now is, has learnt that group interviews are costly and wasteful). In my room are two high chairs, two video cameras, the top of my bee costume, a big lemur photo, a poster of the movie and an illuminated tableau of stuffed lemurs.

In addition to the two camera operators there is a tape operator and a studio manager who explains the rules – six minutes only – and times each encounter.

The word is only good. The media saw the movie last night and, from what I can tell, all of them enjoyed it. So the questioning is curious but not hostile and by the end of a further 25 interviews I'm beginning to think, like the journalists, that we are a 'special group' – that there is 'a chemistry' between us.

At 6.15 back at the hotel. H has been shopping and spending the afternoon with Nancy and Tim. Only have half an hour with her before yet another limo pick-up and transported to *Saturday Night Live*.

At 11.30 we settle behind our desks, the red camera light shines and I start the edition of '*SNL*' for January 11th 1997 rolling with the words – 'Hello I'm Michael Palin. Please don't applaud, we're short on time.'

'Dead Parrot' duly executed about 12.40 a.m. The parrot bounces off the counter and falls on the floor when JC throws it up. This unsettles him and for a line or two he loses the rhythm. There isn't a lot of audience response, but we are performing it with our backs to them.

Head hits pillow at two a.m.

Helen's best memory is of walking out through the crowds of 20 or 30 autograph hunters, and hearing one of them turn gleefully away. 'I've got Michael Palin's autograph!' To which his friend says 'What about John Cleese?'

'Which one's he?'

'The tall one with the hat.'

Sunday, January 26th

Straight into the West End for the cast and crew screening of *Fierce Creatures* at the Empire Leicester Square.

Lots of people to clap arms around and celebrate with. It's only when I talk to Alyce Faye on the stairs that I hear the worst. The takings on the first night in the US were low. It sounds as if the unthinkable might have happened, and that the *Wanda* magic has not struck twice.

I accompany JC and Alyce to the Ivy for brunch. Everything seems suddenly sour. The Ivy is not serving for another hour, says a man at the door. JC says that an appointment had specially been made on his behalf. The man asks, 'Well, who are you?'

Inside eventually, we sit and hear the melancholy news. *Variety*, the *New York Times*, four and a half thumbs-up from Ebert, and a clutch of other good reviews did not seem to make much of an impression on Middle America, where awareness levels of the film amongst the young remained low despite TV campaigns, etc. So – good in San Francisco, bad in Detroit and Dallas.

Thursday, January 30th

Glum, grey weather. Torpid winter morning. Ugly smell to the air. At 8.45 off to London Zoo to be photographed for a *Daily Mirror* piece.

Warm, damp atmosphere at the insect house. Am photographed with a cricket-eating spider, smaller than Terry the Tarantula. Dave, in typical keeper fashion, tells me that tarantula is a word 'only those Americans' use. The spider I worked with in the film was a bird-eating spider.

Promised the insect man (sorry, the Invertebrate Conservation Officer) that if I made any money from this film I would put some of it towards expansion of the insect, sorry, invertebrate quarters.

Monday, February 3rd

I set to work on the commentary for the first episode of *Full Circle*. For a moment I'm immobilised, unable to face the first few frames, frozen by the significance of it all. What I write in these next couple of hours will probably be the most quoted commentary of the series. Critics usually watch first episodes only.

Saturday, February 8th

JC rings from Santa Barbara.

There is not much good news. Exit polls only average. He seemed surprised by the big drop in Australia – as though he might not have known about it. JC will not take a tax year out, but will sell Ladbroke Road and live, quite comfortably, he suggests, off the proceeds. He sounds almost relieved. He says there has rarely been a morning in the last two years when he has woken up looking forward to working on the film.

Thursday, February 20th

Bouncing out of my *Fierce Creatures* interview with Michael Owen in the *Evening Standard* has come an over-dramatised, much-embellished account of Helen's illness a year ago. It has now become, by turns, 'life-threatening' and I 'rushed to her bedside'. Michael O just about drew the conclusion that I would not be doing any more travelling because of H's illness.

The *Daily Mail* wants to put a reporter on to do a serious 'H tells the world' piece. H is not keen and wants to forget about it.

Friday, February 21st

Meet two UIP reps who tell me that *Fierce Creatures* has not done half badly here, taking 1.13 million in first week. All the bad reviews seem confined to the papers I read!

Thursday, February 27th

To the editing rooms to view prog five with Clem. He has a tape of some of the map sequences. My first impression of the opening swoop is that, in their primary-colour stylisation of the earth's surface, Australia comes out, perversely, as bright green. If ever there were a case for red, brown or even yellow, surely this was it.

Another problem has to be faced – the vexed question of an extra show to fit in all the wonderful material from South America.

We stay until nearly eight o'clock to look at programme eight in a rough 64-minute assembly. It is strong – Cuzco, train journeys, Machu Picchu – but only takes us to the other side of the Pongo Rapids and first sight of the Amazon. Logically this should mean that the next and last episode – nine – would go from Peru to Alaska, which is obviously ridiculous.

I suggest contacting the BBC as soon as possible to tell them that it does now look as if we have the material for another programme. I know Michael Jackson, Controller of One, will be at *Showcase* next week and though this might be a time to mention it, it might be best to ask Paul Hamann to sound him out first.

Friday, February 28th

At the editing rooms find Roger out of sorts. He's had a cold for three weeks and last night put his back out. Discuss the extra prog issue in the light of what I saw last night. Decide to call Paul H. Asks various questions and then agrees to have a word with Michael Jackson. Rings back a couple of hours later to say that Jackson would be prepared to find a ten-prog slot in return for a joke about me to use in his intro at BBC *Showcase* on Monday night!

Meanwhile, Eddie, whom we've called but has been out all morning, rings. Eddie is 'pissed off' that he was not consulted before we spoke to Paul. What a nightmare it is entering the minefield of an hierarchical organisation like the BBC.

Wednesday, March 5th

At 12.30 I'm picked up on a Limobike – a luxury motorbike taxi which has to take me swiftly through London traffic to the Park Lane Hotel to collect a special Python award from *Empire*, the film magazine. An outrider bike has a photographer snapping away as we wend our way round Cavendish Square and down Bond Street.

Elton John gives us an award for 'inspiration'. John and Eric on video from California. JC particularly good. Gives medical info on us all. TG already dead – being represented here today by his Mexican twin. Terry J has had series of massive heart attacks and has come here on one of his last days alive. I'm still around but have you seen these, he asks, and holds up what he claims are my latest chest X-rays. He taps a detail on the photo – 'This is not good.'

Thursday, March 13th

With H to see Mr Powell for a year's check up at the National Hospital. There is a hole where the tumour used to be which is now full of water. Powell says it was definitely orange-size. 'Won the award for best meningioma of '96,' he added cheerily.

Having reassured Helen that he wouldn't need to see her for another five years he gets down to the real business, which is having me sign some of the photographs of him and me as Gumbys in one of the operating theatres.

Sunday, March 16th

To the Barbican to see 'Modern Art in Britain 1910–1915' exhibition. A small collection of greats by Cézanne, Van Gogh, Gauguin, Picasso and Matisse, Derain, Vuillard, Bonnard and others is the bedrock of an exhibition which shows how English painting of the period was influenced.

It does make the English response to the outpourings of great work from Europe seem inadequate, mean, spinsterly stuff. Vanessa Bell and Duncan Grant do their best. Roger Fry is more homage than talent. Sickert comes out well – at least you felt a great unqualified appetite for life there – but no-one else seems to match Matisse's and Picasso's lusty enthusiasm and celebratory sensuousness, or Van Gogh or Derain's way with colour.

Basil arrives with the layout of *Full Circle – The Photographs* which he takes to the BBC tomorrow. It's a crisp, clean, cool book with photos of cloud formations which I fear will have BBC sales reps' hearts plunging.

Monday, March 24th

Out to supper at the Caprice with Richard Loncraine and Felice.

Unpleasant end to evening. Our taxi smashed into outside the restaurant by a van driven by a young peroxide-blond man with bare feet. Slammed quite hard into side of us, crushing driver's door and pushing us across Arlington Street. Then a strange and surreal slow-motion scene – or so it seemed – as one of the clutch of photographers outside the restaurant came across, stuck his camera up at the window and started taking flash photographs of a shocked Helen and myself, sitting in the back.

Then the photographer came round the other side, snapped happily away at the two of us – dazzling and further disorientating us. He then grinned at me and said in what sounded like a Spanish or Portuguese accent: 'Scare?' I'm afraid I let him have a piece of quite sustained verbal. Told him he should go and do something useful. He whined on about 'only doing a job' before retreating back to his pack.

Monday, March 31st

At 8.15 I climb up my spiral staircase and onto the gravelled roof and there, as H suggested, is the Hale-Bopp comet in the north-western sky. Quite clearly visible to the naked eye. The surprise is just how large it is – the tail, especially, is much fuller than I had expected. Put the binoculars onto it. Can see the nucleus – white and round and tiny compared to the billowing tail around and behind it – not long and slim but thick and chunky. I think this is the first time in my life I've seen a comet. It is as close to earth as it comes – around 125 million miles away – and will not be seen again for 4,000 years.

Monday, April 7th

Weekend spent working on commentary for seven. This is one process which can never be hurried. However fresh, bright and rested I may be, it is still a plod. Odd and perverse bits of editing trip me up and stall any momentum. Facts must be checked again. Maux mots turned into bons. And so on.

Rachel, revising modern British politics, came to 1979, the year Thatcher was first elected. The year of the last Labour government. She asked me what I remembered of it. I looked it up in my diary, found May 3rd, day of the election. Not a mention!

Tuesday, April 8th

Eddie calls to say he has spoken to Paul Hamann and *Full Circle* is now officially a ten-part series.

Friday, April 11th

To lunch with TG. Nick Cage, after being difficult for so long, is happy to do 'Defective Detective' next spring and in the UK as TG wanted. This left a gap this summer, but this appears to have been fortuitously filled for him by the firing of Alex Cox from *Fear and Loathing in Las Vegas*. Ralph Steadman and others have asked TG to step in and take over at the last minute – Johnny Depp is in place, they have money. TG off to the States to set it up – says it's just what he needs now – an injection of good, bubbling, last-minute adrenaline.

Tuesday, April 22nd

Mhairi and Eleanor, the two feisty ladies from BBC Scotland who want me to present a documentary about Anne Redpath, come round. They love the house and I can see (and hear) them occasionally slip into professional talk about lights, angles, etc. in that rather detached way, like doctors discussing a patient in bed.

Eleanor sounds a sharp director and Mhairi has excellent observation – noticing things in my paintings that I never have.

To Parkin's in Motcomb Street for Stephen Tumim's private view of paintings by prisoners. People spilling out onto the pavement. Looming above most of them is Patrick Procktor. He extends a long, bony hand and introduces me to some bewildered Asians standing beside him – 'This is our star explorer.'

Push my way into the throng. A familiar-looking man, tall, less elegant than Procktor, turns out not to be familiar at all. He's an ex-con who did four years for drug-dealing and learnt to paint in prison.

I ask which he's painted. One is a big, bold, red Bacon-like piece of three men and a door, called 'Bouncers'. It's a 'must-buy', and I struggle through the wonderful mixed crowd of Belgravians and crop-headed ex-prisoners and secure it for £1,100. Later Stephen goes round telling people I've bought the best picture in the place.

Wednesday, April 23rd

Family tree sent by relative shows Scots great-grandparents on Mum's side. Her grandfather, a Chapman, invented the lighthouse reflector.

Saturday, April 26th

In the evening we go round to the Tooks' for dinner with David Attenborough. His daughter Susan is there. Unmarried, very pleasant company – education consultant. Susan talks about inheriting and having to make sense of all the work that Jane used to do in running David's affairs.[1] He hasn't and never has had an agent.

David and I talk about making programmes – putting people at their ease, making contact, etc. D thinks that sex is a universal reference point. There is a bit of the schoolboy about him, which alongside his perception, intelligence

1 David's wife Jane died earlier in the year.

and articulacy could be seen as a bit of a character flaw, but makes for an attractive mix.

On our way out David pauses to enthuse over the marble panels by the front door of the mansion block. 'Look at those!' he cries, jabbing a finger at fossil shapes by the doorbell and running off a number of unpronounceable names. 'Four hundred and fifty million years old!' he declares. 'Isn't that the age of the earth?' 'No, no ... that's billion – four and a half billion.'

That's the difference between Attenborough and me. He knows it. I'm always learning.

Tuesday, April 29th

Prepare myself for the BAFTAs. I have agreed to present an award but not stay for the meal.

At the Albert Hall by 5.45.

Once inside shown to a hot, airless room below the ground where celebrity presenters gather. Richard Wilson is there. Beneath his jacket he has a fat Labour rosette which he is plotting to reveal on the podium.

Michael Caine, with Shakira, looms over everybody except Stephen Fry. Michael says it's a great time to be in England – 'snooker, cricket, football and the election, all on the same day'.

Frost and Clive James work the room briskly. Helen Mirren loves to give and receive attention. Eddie Izzard arrives, wearing nothing under his dinner jacket. His arrival animates almost everybody. They love him, especially Helen M.

I'm out fourth. My winner (for Best Comedy) is *Only Fools and Horses*. John Sullivan in a dreadful state of nerves, despite this being his third BAFTA for the series.

Thursday, May 1st

The six-week election campaign is over. The *Today* programme is completely devoid of any political stories and the result is rather eerie. Everything and everyone we've heard virtually non-stop for the past one and a half months has been silenced.

To the polling station at Gospel Oak. Almost everyone going in and out at this time of day is elderly. They greet me with great friendliness. It's like giving blood. We're all doing our duty and feeling virtuous. Consider Lib-Dems. I believe them to be the most honest and least divided of all the parties, but tactically as much as anything put my X opposite Glenda Jackson's name.[1]

Work on until the polls close at ten, then settle to watch the results. It's pretty clear from exit polls that the Conservatives have been walloped, and that I shall be witnessing something I haven't seen since I was 31 years old, the election of a Labour government.

The scale of the victory gradually unfolds. It's almost exactly as the polls had been predicting, for months and years. Still, the hours between one o'clock and Michael Portillo's demise around three are breathless and dramatic. Stories which would one by one have occupied the headlines for two or three days now come concentrated in a deluge of less than two hours.

Malcolm Rifkind and Portillo and Sir Marcus Fox, three faces representing the solid, confident leadership of the country, are all forced to eat humble pie[2] – not for once allowed the security of their own people, their own slogans, their own lighting, their own spin doctors; they are tonight, as near as possible, naked before the people. Reduced, in shabby public halls, to standing beside men dressed as chickens and other no-hopers who reckon the deposit will have been worth it just to stand on the stage behind a famous man.

Shy, almost apologetic little smiles are the order of the day. It's as if the game is up. They've been caught. They needed to throw a six to win but they could muster only a one.

Cecil Parkinson very funny. Asked if there will now be much squabbling amongst the Conservatives replies 'I don't think we've got enough people for a squabble.'

By the time my head hits the pillow my countrymen have elected the youngest Prime Minister this century. The once-groggy and near-dormant Labour Party, reeling after repeated blows from the electorate, has bounced back to reduce the Conservatives to their smallest number since, I'm told, the days of Lord Liverpool.

No wonder I can't sleep for a while.

Friday, May 2nd

John Major announces his resignation and goes off to watch cricket at the Oval, and little Blair, for whom the chipmunk comparison is quite the most accurate, goes to kiss the Queen's hand. A student of kissing would have had a field day watching the body language up and down the country last night.

1 She won the Hampstead and Highgate seat with 57 per cent of the vote.
2 Malcolm Rifkind, Michael Portillo, Sir Marcus Fox, Conservative grandees, all of whom lost their seats as Labour under Tony Blair ended eighteen years of Conservative government, gaining a majority of 179.

Cherie, awkward, feeling she had to be seen to be overwhelmed with a physical desire to merge with her husband. Would Kenneth Clarke kiss his wife?
It seemed inconceivable and was. The Kinnocks were the best public kissers.

Thursday, May 8th

We fit commentary ten on the Avid.[1] It's much faster in one way, no reel
changes, footage adjustments, unspooling to fit leader tape or rearrange a
sequence, but at the same time the material seems less precious and unique –
just a series of random images on an electronic machine.

The 'frame' is no longer as important as 'the look'. I, being a Romantic
where technology is concerned, miss working surrounded by the comforting background of celluloid strips, the outward and visible evidence of our
work.

Sunday, May 11th

Up for a run at eight. In West Meadow a harmless-looking beige Labrador
lollops towards me and delivers a sharp nip to the back of my left leg. I'm not
moving fast, there's no question of shock or surprise, or even aggression on the
dog's part; he just came over and bit me. His owner is a lean, quite elderly man
I frequently see. He doesn't seem much put out. 'I'll give him a good hiding,'
he says, with a grin.

Run on. Lloyd Dorfman[2] is walking up Lime Avenue. He's most concerned by the news, says I should go to hospital and have a tetanus jab.
Run on for quite a way in nervous apprehension of my body suddenly
freezing in mid-motion, before I remember that I'm covered for tetanus
until 1998.

Thursday, May 15th

To supper with JC. I remembered, at the last minute, that it was exactly two
years ago today that *Fierce Creatures* began shooting. John gave an ironic smile.
'Oh God, that film!' he said, affecting pain at the memory.

He's comfortable. He doesn't need anything else. He's finally shaken off

1 Avid, developed in America in 1989, is a computerised, non-linear editing system. This was
the first time we'd used it.
2 Lloyd Dorfman, founder of Travelex, the foreign exchange business.

As Bugsy in *Fierce Creatures*. With Robert Lindsay
and our tiger, August 9th, 1995.

Me as a bee with Jamie Lee, on the *Fierce Creatures* re-shoots, August 23rd, 1996.

Gumby brain surgeons. One of them really *is* a brain surgeon. With Michael Powell, the man who saved my wife, National Hospital, London, November 7th, 1996.

With my indispensable travelling companions: leather and canvas bag
with lots of pockets, notebook and pen. *Pole to Pole*, 1996.

Friends United

ABOVE LEFT: Palin's New Year Party team wearing a selection of my travel hats. Left to right: Phillida Albury, Ian Davidson, Anthea Davidson, Ranji Veling, Mary Burd, MP, Helen P, Simon Albury (where's his hat?) and Edward Burd. New Year's Eve, 1998.

LEFT: Family visit to Greenwich, Christmas 1998. Back row: Will, Tom. Middle row: Helen, Rachel, MP, brother-in-law Edward. Front row: Helen's mother, Anne Gibbins, and two sisters, Cathy and Mary.

ABOVE: New York pals. Left to right: Merron and Julian Schlossberg, Nancy Lewis/Jones, MP, Simon Jones, Sherrie Levy.

RIGHT: Alan Whicker presents me with Best Documentary Award for *Full Circle* at the National Television Awards: '. . . that Whicker should have to present me with the award does sort of bring things, well, full circle' – October 27th, 1998.

Pointing out my hero. With Spike Milligan at the Talkie Awards. The Goon shows were an inspiration and he was given a special award for *The Last Goon Show of All*, November 6th, 1998.

With my tall, funny friend. Almost anywhere – 1988–1998.

material things and seems on the verge of what he's always wanted – time to learn and listen.

I've heard this many times and know that John's ability to cut himself off from the world is about as likely as Tony Blair retiring from politics. But I do know what he's struggling to get away from – which is dealing with people of average intelligence and ability. JC is a thoroughbred and if he can't win, he'll pretend winning doesn't matter. He wants to do 'some trips' with me. 'Go on a few jaunts.'

Friday, May 16th

Call from Will to say that he has been offered a place at the Courtauld on their History of Architecture course. This despite an interview on Tuesday at which he admitted he did not shine. But they seem to have seen through his nervousness and he has achieved what he's been after for almost two years.

I receive a letter from the Royal Geographical Society inviting me to participate in some daunting seminar about the future role of Geography ... 'As you hold a key position in our national life.' Could this be me they were referring to? I've never felt less like someone occupying a key position in anything.

To celebrate Will's news at V and P.

Vasco is quietly chuffed about the election victory. I tell him that there could be a New Year's Honour on the way. He says John Cunningham has been in three times since the election. 'And he is the Minister for fish,' V points out, 'and that he comes here for his fish, makes me feel very good.'

Tuesday, May 20th

Ring Eric to check on time of arrival at Cliveden for the Python summit to-morrow. I have a glimpse of what to expect when I tell him that I met JC last week and didn't think he sounded keen on the new film project. 'Well he can write to *Time* magazine and explain why he thought it was such a good idea two months ago.' E clearly cross that JC had gone public to *Time* mag over E's film idea.[1]

Later out to launch of new publishing venture started by the *Modern Painters* people.

I fall into a chat with David Bowie, who is there as one of the co-financiers of the venture.

---

1 Eric had suggested a possible updating of *The Holy Grail* using the same knights twenty years older, embarking on a crusade.

He is very comfortable and relaxed, adept, I suppose, at creating around him an oasis of ordinary, everyday life, whilst being the goldfish at the centre of the bowl. Talk about Sickert. Bowie thinks his later work – like the graphic, inspired high-kicking chorus line, or the 'Camden Town Murders' – v. impressive. 'I mean, who would do that nowadays without howls of outrage from the newspapers?'

He looks good. Hair dyed carrot-orange and spiky, wearing a woolly purple polo-neck jersey – blithely confident that it doesn't matter what the hell he wears. He is the man. He sets the style.

He now lives in New York. He used to be in Switzerland. His wife Iman says that the beautiful thing about Somalia, where she comes from, is the people not the landscape. In Switzerland, she says, it's the opposite.

Wednesday, May 21st: London–Cliveden

Pack and drive up to Cliveden for the Python get-together. Terry G, hair drawn tight back in grey ponytail, is there with Eric and Terry J in the vast hall of this immodest house.

Eric draws up an agenda and we discuss the film idea first. Four of us clearly interested in proceeding, cautiously, with the 'Last Crusade' idea. John yawns a lot and at one point actually nods off. For half an hour the ideas pour out. Not always very good, but there is much of the old Python energy and mischief still there, and, amongst the four of us, a real comic empathy.

The stage show in Las Vegas is talked about on JC's return. I am the least keen on this one; everyone else, bar Terry G, moderately enthusiastic. I'd rather put our energy and efforts into new material which acknowledges that things have changed.

Nothing decided. JC has thawed out a little and four of us go on a walk down to the river and round the estate.

We stroll along past the red Victorian boathouses and gamekeepers' cottages where Profumo strolled with Christine Keeler. Terry J then goes for a swim, I go up to my room – the Prince of Wales Suite.

Have a bath in most wonderfully deep enamel, grey-marble-topped tub, and feel gloriously lucky and spoilt.

Can't remember much of the meal.

The usual mutterings about the accounts. TJ especially critical of the amount spent on management, which is almost a third of total profit.

John goes to bed and the rest of us seek out the snooker room and Eric and I take on the Terrys. They are even worse than Eric and myself, who are coasting home to victory when TJ is suddenly transformed into Steve Davis and pots almost everything that's left.

Friday, May 23rd

Anne comes round and we share a taxi down to the Ritz to meet Tom Dunne of St Martin's Press.

Tom is good company, congenial, a little mischievous but enthusiastic. He compliments Anne on the impression she made on everyone at St Martin's when she went to NY two weeks ago, buys us martinis, and is grateful for all our help on publicity, delighted that the PBS schedule has been fixed, delighted to hear that we now have an extra episode and concerned only as to whether he has enough books.

He asks me if I'm ever going to write a novel. I tell him I'll send him a copy of *Hemingway's Chair* to read on the plane back to NYC.

Saturday, May 24th

This is what I have been looking forward to. A plateau of peace and quiet after a week scrambling over rough, unknown terrain.

Ring JC and get Alyce Faye. She's wonderfully indiscreet and seems to say just what comes into her mind.

According to Alyce, John had driven down to the Cliveden meeting 'like thunder'. He hadn't wanted to go and was very worried that we should force him to do things he didn't want to do. He came back, evidently, much happier.

JC attempts to explain his 'contradictory' position. 'If someone like Robin Williams offers me three weeks' work with practically no lines, I'm happy to do it. I just don't think I'm up to another long shoot with all the work that has to go with it.' I point out that the advantage of the Pythons is that we are a group, we have a director, a designer, and several writers with whom he can share the load. And anyway we're not talking about a film till '99.

Tuesday, May 27th

My morning is cheered by a report in the *Guardian* of a man who fell a hundred feet down a hillside trying to avoid a 'bouncing 8lb Double Gloucester cheese'. Actually, his injuries sound quite severe, so I shouldn't really have smiled so much.

Receive a fax from Tom Dunne – handwritten, which is his style – to say that he has read *Hemingway's Chair*. 'Good clean fun' is his three-word assessment. He would like to publish it in the US next spring.

Friday, May 30th, Chilton

Leave home around quarter to ten and stop at Stoke-by-Nayland after an hour and a half. Hottest day of this present high, dry, sunny period.

Sit on a grassy bank in the churchyard, beneath the 120-foot, four-stage tower, and read up my Pevsner. It's been so long since I've done something like this. I suppose my father's constant 'churching' could have put me off, but quite the opposite – it's an appetite of his which I happily share – and have passed on to Will as well.

But this is not a complete, drift-where-you-want day off. I have to check my watch as I stand before the 500-year-old tomb of Anne Windsor, as I'm due at Chilton for lunch.

Oddly enough, I hadn't decided to come here because of the tenth anniversary, yesterday, of Angela's death, but now I'm here, it seems right. I'm not too good at remembering people on special days – my memories of Angela come, unbidden, at pretty regular intervals, and with varying degrees of intensity.

Valerie opens some wine and we eat salmon and new potatoes and raspberries from the garden. More and more of the land surrounding Chilton is being sold off to the burgeoning industrial estate.

Walk round the garden and then go, on my own, across the field to St Mary's Church, which stands, solid and red-bricked, at the very edge of the sea of development. But the approach from the house is still countrified and soothing, and the old church retains its dignity, despite some doors and windows having been boarded up.

Realise, with a shock, that this is probably the first time in ten years that I've seen Angela's grave. A solid, small stone with her name and the name of Mum and Dad on it.

A few minutes later, drive along the pot-holed track to Brundon Mill to see Derek T.

He's in blue-denim shirt and trousers, has lost weight since I last saw him, but his head and mane of well-cut grey hair still striking and not at all bowed by what must be considerable pain. He has his legs on a stool in front of him, and leans back on a pointed cushion which he calls the V-sign. 'Two relatives have already died on it,' he points out. The Taylor smile still firmly intact – eyes and mouth very much alive.

He's listening to a selection of Eric Coates's music. The strains of 'In Town Tonight' and 'Music While You Work' – immortal memories lightly fill the room and outside the sun shines hard on the grass and the surface of the water as it spills over the weir.

After a bit we sit outside. Derek selects a panama hat for me. In the garden he stretches out on a slightly lopsided plastic recliner. He says that now he has to realise that he could be at the top of a steady downward spiral. The cancer is still there – though a couple of recent operations have relieved some of the pain.

His regrets are clearly expressed – emotion well held in check. 'Why me?' is, he says, 'the ignoble thought that does occur'.

But we laugh a lot. Talk about the flashers of our youth. 'Go into any air-raid shelter in West Kirby,' Derek remembers, 'and you'd find a 30-year-old man with an erection.'

Tuesday, June 10th

Redpath documentary filming at the house.

George Bruce, an 88-year-old who made a film on Redpath in 1961, arrives to be interviewed. He is an unstoppable talker. A lively man, great self-dramatist, working poet, Python fan – he genuinely came near to hysterics when I recited 'Parrot Sketch' as we sat out on the benches in the garden.

Eleanor Yule, the director, who has a good, inventive, imaginative way of shooting, was finding it hard work with all the reflecting glass surfaces. And the phone kept ringing.

Friday, June 13th: Cap Ferrat, French Riviera

Today we get to see what lies behind the high stone walls of the Château St Jean, which was the Château Gloria at which Anne Redpath's husband worked as an architect in the 1920s and '30s for an American carburettor millionaire called Thomson. There is a sign on the great timber gates reading 'Chien Très Méchant'.

But the Dubai Ambassador who currently owns it is only here for a month or so and we have been allowed to film in and around it. Two Finnish people act as housekeepers and there is a gardener and a huge, black Great Dane.

The house is more like a pavilion. It's full of objets d'art. Many of the Rococo or Louis Quinze style. Dripping gilt.

Saturday, June 14th: Roquebrussanne

Drive west to the Var. Into green, wooded countryside; wide, flat plains ringed by low forested ridges.

Spend the afternoon filming up at a Carthusian monastery. Father Bruno, one of 14 middle-aged men who live at the monastery, proves to be a hermit of the Python kind. Immensely voluble, humorous, gregarious and apparently worldly. He gives us permission to film inside the monastery itself. It's a celibate order so the producer and director have to wait behind in the 'public' tower at one end of the complex.

Father Bruno laughs heartily as the doors close – 'Now you won't have to obey the ladies for a while.'

Sunday, June 15th: Roquebrussanne–London

Wind rustles the leaves and sets my shutters creaking and banging. Up at eight. Bright morning of clear Provençal sunshine. Breakfast, then set off for Nice Airport.

Full flight arrives back at Heathrow just after lunch. Into taxi, complete with *Sunday Times* which runs the 'Relative Values' piece showing Tom and myself, apparently fused together, growing out of Primrose Hill like Anne Redpath's houses grow out of the hills of Spain, Corsica and the Canary Islands.

Not a bad piece – nothing that makes my heart stop or my face blush. The writer has put words into our mouths and inscribed her own demotic on us. I refer at one point to Tom having been 'such a timid kid'. Eurgh. I'd never say 'kid' like that. But names, details and the general summing-up is accurate and sympathetic.

Monday, June 16th: Edinburgh

A series of shots in and around the New Town – starting in London Street, where Anne came to live at the end of her life (funnily enough, I find myself uncomfortable saying 'Anne'. I have the feeling that she was the sort of person from whom you would have to earn the right to such familiarity). Pass Johnston Terrace and the Castle Arms. It's now 32 years since we met Eric Idle of the Footlights for a drink there during the Edinburgh Festival. End up in Newington, a stylish but less flashy end of Edinburgh, where David Michie, Anne R's son, lives.

David Michie paints and I talk to him. With the Digibeta[1] silently working away we can record for 40 minutes without a break, and without the sound man ever having to complain about camera noise.

---

1 Digibeta short for Digital Betacam, a cassette video camera developed in 1993. Film cameras, which we used for our travel programmes, could only shoot ten minutes of material before changing magazines, but were thought to produce better-quality images.

He's an imposing man with a fine, handsome, strong face. A respectable man of Scottish arts, OBE and wary of any indiscretions. But wheedle out a few good stories and quite a moving last admission about the funeral, and the mistake that he and his brothers might have made in keeping it so plain and simple that no-one even spoke in his mother's honour.

Tuesday, June 17th: Edinburgh–London

An interview with Eileen Michie, who sat for many of Anne's pictures. She says she's always depicted reading a book – which she did because she was so bored. A very lively, intelligent woman, quite a high-powered scientist in the field of hormone research. Born in Hawick, like AR, and married David, her second cousin. They're a busy, aware, alert, rather loving couple. Absolute salt of the earth.

Interview, and my last shot of the film, complete around 1.30.

It has been a pleasure. As good as I hoped. Eleanor, Mhairi and the crew excellent company – Eleanor with a good, fresh eye for the material, a refreshing lack of bullshit and an admirable tenacity in getting what she wants. I think she will do very well.

Wednesday, June 25th

Monster book on 'Success' by Martyn Lewis arrives, via the office. No wonder it wouldn't slip through the letter box, it's a great, fat tome that looks rather like those big sex surveys (Hite, Masters and Johnson) that the Americans were fond of producing in the '70s.

At the start of my interview contribution I resolutely express my unease with the whole premise of the book, but am still accorded 20 pages – more than most of the illustrious, rather worthy, mostly male contributors.

Friday, June 27th

Helen is to collect Rachel's things from Oxford this a.m. I'm off to record more commentary.

Then hear just before eight o'clock news that the M40 to Oxford is closed in both directions as a power cable has come down.

Ring H immediately on the mobile, but as I'm doing so, am followed into my parking spot opposite Dillons by police van with flashing blue light. A police lady gets out and, quite pleasantly but firmly, informs me that I'm to be booked for using a mobile while driving (a very new offence, of which I heartily approve).

Into the van as the rain patters down on the roof. Particulars taken. When she asks me to spell my name, the two young policemen with her (v. fresh from cadet school I would think) apologise that 'she's not a Python fan'. As she gets out to check my number plate they apologise again. She's very zealous. Had two people already this morning. They'd have let me off, they assure me!

Monday, June 30th

Basil rings from Hong Kong, ten minutes before the handover. I've been watching solemn Chris Patten, puzzled Prince Charles and inscrutable Tony Blair on the podium for a half hour or so. Rain sheeting down on the outgoing Brits.

Basil is on Cheung Chau and has a crowd of people there for a handover party. 'What you drinkin' Mike?' Bas demands to know. 'Tea,' I lie. I'm not drinking anything. I'm working. He persuades me to fill a glass at this great moment and then, as the National Anthem is played for the last time and the Union Jack descends after 156 years at the top of the Hong Kong masts, to stand up. 'We're all standing up here, Mike.'

So, half stood up at my desk with a glass of grappa, I salute the end of British rule in Hong Kong. Feel no great tugs of emotion, despite the bands and the *Britannia* and the kilts. I wish the PLA didn't goose-step, and I wish I felt the slightest sympathy for or compatibility with the Chinese who have taken over. But I don't understand them and I feel no real sense of common purpose either.

Change into DJ and out to the Hatchards 200th anniversary party. Suppose I should draw some comfort from the fact that a bookshop has lasted longer than the British in Hong Kong.

A motley collection. Melvyn and Salman move around with the world-weary ironic smile of senior prefects. I'm introduced by Roger Katz, the manager, to Princess Margaret (who, he says admiringly, still comes into the shop to buy her books 'during open hours'). Big wide eyes, an element of flirtatiousness in her responses. A very large tumbler of whisky and water is produced for her.

Find myself thrust into line as she leaves, alongside John Major, who has been eyeing the shelves in a distracted way, frequently alone save for a big girl who is his private secretary. She seizes my hand and introduces me, for the first time in my life, to the ex-PM. His handshake is cool, his face pale and he affects a rather debating society defensiveness – trading cool, patronising quips as though he perceives me as a threat of some sort.

Perhaps he would have thawed out if we'd had more time together, but that is the nature of these events. They are useful for networking, or for making and keeping up superficial acquaintance. Not much more.

Thursday, July 3rd

Low, scummy skies. Clem here at nine just after arrival of rented palm and bamboo plants which he's ordered, in some megalomanic burst of inspiration, for background in one of the video introductions we are to shoot today. He says Eddie Mirzoeff was a changed man after seeing prog nine. Almost sentimental about the series and lyrical about its pleasures – even enquiring as to whether we might do another!

Two of the three introductions are completed quite swiftly – though I do make a Freudian slip – referring at one point to 'only 25,000 meals' instead of miles, to go. This leads to some rapid calculations and the conclusion that Nige and I ate around 850 meals together on this journey.

So quite possibly my last filming with Nige is completed, eight years and ten months since he first filmed me in Stanford's, at the start of *80 Days*.[1]

Wednesday, July 16th

Invited to lunch by Geoffrey Strachan at Frederick's in Camden Passage.

Geoffrey keen to pin me down on my writing intentions for next year. Talk over ideas – a possible memoir instead of a fully-fledged novel. Possibly even an 'In Search of Hemingway' travel book.

Heard this morning that Rachel gained a 2:1.

Tuesday, July 22nd

Have promised the day to *Time Out*, who have an idea of doing 'Around the World in 18 Hours' – a tour of all the different cultures in London.

So a big Land Rover arrives for me at ten – with photographer and Scots girl called Elaine Paterson who is Features Editor and reporter on this assignment.

Down to Brixton Market – which is impeccably well kept, clean, attractive and very friendly. If this is what a good riot brings then one wonders why there aren't more of them.[2]

1 We were to do five more series together.
2 There had been major racial disturbances in Brixton in 1981 and again in 1985.

Such delights as The Souls of Black Folk bookshop – a West Indian sec-ond-hand bookshop where I pick up a '30s English novel called *Black* and a copy of Charlie Mingus' autobiography which made such an impression on me 25 years ago.

Armenian church in Kensington – and talk to the Archbishop. Incense and Gulbenkian money. Lunch at an Iranian restaurant opposite Cibo. Then to huge Japanese supermarket on the Edgware Road, where Elaine and I play automated electronic downhill ski-racing, eat sushi and drink Kirin beer. Then to the wonderfully elaborate Hindu temple in Neasden. Fantastic building skills opposite the crummiest houses of north-west London.

To the Polish Hearth Club, where the pre-*80 Days* departure dinner was filmed.

High-ceilinged rooms, waitresses with blonde hair and high cheekbones, slouching men – an air of prosperous negligence.

Then out into the hot and steamy West End. Eat fish, sweet potato and plantain at the Africa Centre – as true to my memories of Africa as the Japanese supermarket was for Japan.

Then out of Africa, and drag our tired limbs to Shaftesbury Avenue and a salsa club, down below street level. A dancing partner is provided for me. This is like *Full Circle* all over again and I have the same mixture of exhaustion and relief when we have done our final duty and climbed the stairs.

Home by 11.30. Have earned my publicity today.

Saturday, July 26th: Sunset Marquis, Los Angeles

To the Villa Pool and there is Michael (official designation: Villa Pool Butler) who shakes my hand warmly, shows me the three-week-old kittens who have made their home beneath a palm tree and tells me that the old rock and roll bands are using the hotel again. The Eagles are checking in later. 'They're quiet as church mice now,' he adds.

Call Eric and arrange to see him after lunch.

Eric's house looks even bigger on second sight. But big in a sort of disor-dered, profligate way – rooms spread, sprout and extend all over the place. Dogs yap at my heels. Eric's daughter Lily romps around after them.

Eric is limping – he shrugs off my enquiry. Sit out by the pool. The Con-nollys call. Billy is a neighbour.

We talk about the film. John remains against it, what do I feel? I still think it offers the best prospect for a Python reunion.

We decide that instead of making the next movie we should spend the money on an ad campaign and trailers only. 'I want you to write some more jailers,' Eric says with feeling.

Sunday, July 27th: Los Angeles

The Ritz Carlton Pasadena is a chillingly well-ordered place – a sort of luxury penitentiary on which the outside world seems hardly to impinge. Thick carpets, lush but characterless gardens, an attempt at French classical style for no real reason.

Then the centrepiece of the day, and my raison d'être for the trip – the *Full Circle* presentation. I'm on stage before 60 or 70 journalists who have been through three weeks of such presentations. Kathy Quattrone, Chief Exec of PBS, tall, in powder-blue suit, introduces me as a 'Renaissance man' in a long, droning preamble which means I have ground to recover right from the start. But we get some laughs and they applaud at the end, which I'm told happens very rarely.

A party out on the terrace at which I meet an ebullient black man with chest and stomach vying with each other to see which can burst out of his clothing first. His job is to check the tapes received by PBS for any sign of naughty bits, in particular white men's willies.

He it was, he said, who was alerted to the sight of a full-frontal Michael Palin in the Odessa mud baths sequence in *Pole to Pole*. He had to re-run the tape to see if my member 'wobbled about at all'. 'Movement is what they don't like,' he assures me. Having judged it to be indeed moving, he proudly tells me that he became 'the man who pixelated Michael Palin's pee-pee'.

Wednesday, July 30th

Will picks up H and myself at 9.30 and we drive down to Spitalfields to see the house he so enthused about last week.

The house, in Hanbury Street, is on what the current owner describes as 'the Front Line' between old Spitalfields and the rest of the world. Bare brick walls, wooden-board floors. Much of the building has lasted since it came into existence in 1717.

A dank, earthy, unconverted basement, some sizeable rooms on ground and first floor. Big, tall bedroom windows look out over the tiny backyard and on top of the house is the old silk weaver's attic with long glass lights on either side. These are the special feature of the area – originally settled by the Huguenots.

Across the other side of Hanbury Street is the ugly brick and steel roof of Truman's Brewery, extended in the '70s at the expense of a row of Georgian houses. Spital Square had already fallen. In the seventies – that infamous decade for London architecture – John Betjeman and others squatted what remained of the old houses and that is the only reason they're here now.

By the time we've walked the area and are taking coffee in Commercial Road Market even H has come round to the qualities of the place. When I get home I call the agent and register a cash offer, ten grand short of what they asked.

Thursday, July 31st

Am at my desk taking care of business when the estate agent rings about my offer for the house in Hanbury Street. He ums and aahs and generally suggests that they might take it off the market if they don't get what they want. Other people in the running, etc. etc.

It sounds like the estate agent mess I don't want to be part of, so I ask him the question straight – 'What would clinch it?' 'Three-oh-five,' he says ... 'perhaps.' I don't want to wait or mess about so I offer 305 and he will call them later.

H back at 11.45. It's still raining. She is not at all pleased by the news on the house. The jump of 15,000 she sees as a complete con.

Perhaps she's right. I'm too positive, too easy to please, too eager. Perhaps I've made a terrible mistake.

Friday, August 1st

I'm on the point of ringing the estate agents to reduce my offer – but when I do get through they tell me straight away that the offer has been accepted.

Saturday, August 2nd

In the evening to Simon and Phillida's for a barbecue. Ben Okri and Rosemary there.

Talk of America. Ben says he feels uncomfortable there – especially in New York – and thinks colour is still a significant issue. After all the political advances in our lifetime the blacks in America have more rights – but they remain different, uneasily integrated. He much prefers London, where there is a cosmopolitan feeling which derives much more from celebrating differences than fearing them.

I like Ben, but he's canny too.

On our way down Kilburn High Road we talk about writing. He thinks knowledge of the area you want to write about is most important. Know your subject – want to write about it. In two days I shall be in France, with time to think about what I might want to write about next.

Monday, August 4th: London–Prayssac

The terrifically clammy air clears by evening; we swim, lie on bed in declining sunlight and doze as if we'd crossed half the globe to get here. Unwinding it's called. All will not be complete relaxation. Edward has a brochure for the Cinéma Louis Malle announcing a 'soirée exceptionnelle' tomorrow night with Michael Palin, in person, 'parmi nous lors de séance de *Creatures Féroces*'.

Tuesday, August 5th: Prayssac

Outside the theatre is a big *Fierce Creatures* poster and two good French reviews, plus an inked notice announcing my presence tonight. Michel Legrand, the theatre manager, is a likeable man with neat, greying hair, round specs in metal frames and a lazy, attractive smile. He suggests I turn up at the cinema at 8.30 for a drink and a few words before the film. He says he has a 'traducteur', but I tell him I'm happy to give a short speech in French.

Down to the Cinéma Louis Malle by 8.30. The small foyer is hung with all sorts of MP-related posters, including one very rare one for the French version of *Private Function – Porc Royal*. Marcel tells me there is a strong market in pig posters.

The audience seems mainly British on holiday or with homes here. Young girls with names like Olympia and Romilly gather round for autographs.

Despite early misgivings there is a half-full theatre for me to address at nine. Michel makes admiring opening speech. I give my two-minute oration, regretting that the film has 'pas de frites dans le nez, pas de chiens morts et, malheureusement pour moi, pas de baisées avec Jamie Lee'. (Use of word 'baisées' carefully checked beforehand as Edward says it may mean to 'go down on someone'.) They show a trailer for *Brazil* and then the Prayssac premiere of *Fierce Creatures*.

Wednesday, August 6th: Prayssac

By chance, have bought *Le Figaro* and there is yours truly standing, bag on shoulder, beneath a shaft of sunlight in an Istanbul bazaar, and above it a long review of *Pole to Pole – D'un Pole à L'autre* – which begins a 16-part run on Arte this evening. It calls it an 'excellent' series and notes approvingly that I do not make judgements or condescend, and that I let people speak for themselves. Best of all (which I ask to be read several times), it likens me to such travellers as Lord Byron!

This is a great tonic at the breakfast table as we look out over the dripping woods and hills, on whose higher slopes still trail patches of mist.

Thursday, August 21st

Lunch at the invitation of Karen Wright of *Modern Painters*. She has commissioned a cover from Tracey Emin. 'The first cover we've ever commissioned,' she says proudly. Unfortunately Tracey's contribution is an embroidered square reading 'Fuck Modern Painting'. Karen is distraught. Her husband says he'll leave her if she puts it on the cover. W. H. Smith will refuse to stock it. I really can't understand her pusillanimity. If you commission from Tracey Emin, this is what you get. Anyway, it's rather colourful and sweet and quite a good joke.

Tuesday, August 26th

My upturned face stares out at me from the cover of the *Radio Times*, under the massive headline 'Palin's Pacific'! Serialisation of the book covers four pages inside – there are endless details of books to be bought and tapes to be won – a whole MP industry blossoming ahead of next Sunday's premiere.

Sunday, August 31st

Preparing for a run, I put on the radio about ten to nine and am aware at once that something is wrong. Instead of the laid-back semi-news or charity appeals that usually fill this time on a Sunday I hear Jeff Banks talking of someone who has clearly passed away – a woman, a Royal, someone of style.

My immediate reaction is that it must be a special edition marking the death of the Queen Mum. Just my luck, I feel ruefully, on the day we've waited for for two years, we're upstaged by the Royal Family. How utterly unfair.

Then at the end of the interview – Banks is hustled off – I hear the quite paralysing news that Princess Diana and Dodi Al-Fayed have been killed in a car crash in Paris. I can't move for a moment. Half dressed, I stand there by the basin, staring down at the radio as if it might have developed some technical fault. The words coming out couldn't surely refer to real life.

Then I realise it's true and this is one of those 'Where were you?' moments

– like in the tiny dark back room at 24 Parker Street, Oxford, where I heard about the Kennedy assassination, or on Gospel Oak Station when Holly Jones told me of Lennon's death.

The radio coverage repeats the news like a mantra, as if only constant repetition will make it a reality.

I wonder whether I should run – whether or not anything less than sitting stunned and sombre will match the ugliness of the moment. I decide to go, of course, but hope there won't be too many people I know, because in a way I feel embarrassed to have heard what I've heard.

It's a grey, characterless day – not much light in the sky.

People pottering about on Parliament Hill, walking their dogs as if nothing had happened. Perhaps, I think, they don't know what I know.

Up to Maersh, our newsagent. Collect some of the papers.

Late editions carry the news of her death, though it was not confirmed until three or four in the morning; the *News of the World* headline reports her injured – the *Independent on Sunday* does not even have mention of the accident.

Paparazzi are blamed for causing the high-speed chase which sent her car out of control. It all seems appallingly likely. The photographers chased her to death. And apparently some of them stood and took the final photographs. There's an awful primal feel to the whole thing – mixed in with Greek myth – with the beautiful and the damned.

At about 12.30 Will Wyatt rings to give me details of how the extraordinary events of the day will affect the launch of *Full Circle*. The BBC has decided to keep BBC One clear throughout the evening for Diana news. *Full Circle* episode one will still premiere at eight o'clock, but on BBC Two. The whole series will begin again on BBC One, from the top, next Sunday.

Monday, September 1st

The Diana story dominates. There is, at the moment, no other news.

I feel, in one way, cheated of our moment, our launch, our chance to make a bold start and the strongest possible impact after two and a half years of preparation. On the other hand I feel less affected by that tightening apprehension that always follows a big launch. We'll be lucky to be reviewed at all.

Over to Mayday for a meeting re our will, finances, etc. We're joined by a tax-planner from Ernst and Young.

No sooner has our man begun to explain the intricacies of forward tax-planning than the phone rang with the first overnight ratings, hot from Eddie M. We pulled in an average of 4.5 million, a little more than the Jonathan Dimbleby Diana fest, for which we were cleared from BBC One. *Heartbeat* on ITV scored thirteen and a half million.

Wednesday, September 3rd

Rung by a lady from the *Daily Mail*. Slight foreign accent, delivery tired and lacklustre as though her heart isn't in it. 'We're asking famous celebrities (*sic*) where they were when they heard the news about Diana.'

I tell her I was in the bathroom.

'Were you in the bath?' she asks tentatively.

I can only be honest. 'No, I was halfway between the basin and the door.'

This is becoming wonderfully surreal. But she's not giving up. She's under orders, clearly.

'And what did you do when you heard, ring friends? Switch on the television?'

'I went running.' Also the truth.

'What were you thinking about when you were running?'

I couldn't take any more of this and gave a quick, probably rather clipped summary of my feelings and the call ended.

Frightening. Maybe I'll hear from the Compassion Police if I don't conform to the required State of Grief.

Saturday, September 6th: London–New York

It's the day of the Princess of Wales' funeral. Crowds have turned out in greater numbers than any day since the end of the war. This may be right or wrong, but considering the press coverage, which has effectively accepted a week of mourning, and a mounting mood of public adoration (and by implication, condemnation of the cold-hearted Queen for remaining at Balmoral), it's not surprising. Whatever it is that Diana is seen to represent, it's something more unequivocally good in death than it ever was in her life.

There are strong letters in the *Guardian* and the *Independent* bemoaning this sentimental selectivity but they are drowned out.

I can't help getting caught up in it. Diana's coffin, draped by the Royal Standard (was this a concession by the Queen?), is making its way on the back of a horse-drawn carriage with mounted Hussars and scarlet-tunicked guardsmen with black busbies walking along beside.

And the huge crowd is quiet. If you close your eyes you could think that, apart from the Hussars' horses and the occasional sound of sobbing, there was no-one else there.

The most unexpectedly moving moment for me (I didn't shed a tear until Spencer's address) was the commentator's observation, as the hearse finally reached the gates of Althorp Park, that 'this is the last any of us will see of Diana, Princess of Wales', and in through the gates went the car. Ridiculous really, it's not as if we can see her anyway, but after this extraordinary week which has rendered almost all other national and international events unimportant – Mother Teresa died yesterday and Jeffrey Bernard too, and Georg Solti this morning – this marks the end of it all. A finality.

Fly out to New York. Concorde is full of American luminaries who must have attended the funeral. Dr Kissinger and his beanpole wife towering over him are in the second row, behind Rupert Murdoch and his son. Anna Wintour is tucked up under a blanket in the back row of the front cabin.

I shall not easily forget standing beside Kissinger and Murdoch (surely two of the most demonised figures of our generation) at the baggage retrieval in JFK on the day Princess Di finally disappeared.

Monday, September 8th: New York

Lunch with Tom Dunne in the Post House. We talk of how utterly Mother Teresa's death has been eclipsed by Diana. Christopher Hitchens[1] – 'he's a naughty boy, and I like naughty boys' – is a friend of Tom's and two years back was excoriated in some circles for writing a damning article about Mother T – her refusal to support the Indian government's birth control measures, her willingness to take money from dictators like Duvalier and other insalubrious characters. From the brief coverage of her demise it's clear that she was admired more than loved.

The morning's news – a phone call from Helen to tell me that Derek Taylor has died. Apparently he had had enough of the pain and turned over one last time and that was that. The family all with him. There's a funeral on Friday which, sadly, I shan't be able to make. Write a letter, then and there, to Joan.

Tuesday, September 9th: New York

Slept uncomfortably. Diana didn't pervade my dreams but Derek's death did. I lay there, awake from the still dark hours, thinking about this latest loss – another light out of our lives. Knew that I must do my best to try to get to the funeral.

There isn't a lot for me to do on Friday which can't be done on the phone from the UK. By the time my first interview rolls up, just before eleven, I've booked myself on the 9.25 Virgin flight out of Newark on Thursday night, and feel much better for it.

Meet Mike Myers who tells me that despite the Diana week of grief his

1 Christopher Hitchens, British-born polemicist, long resident in the United States.

comedy *Austin Powers* has done well in England – but not before every print was first recalled to have a reference to the break-up of the Royal Family removed.

Wednesday, September 10th: New York

To Fox Television for *Vicki Lawrence Show*. Willie Nelson and someone who's written a book about him, and Chuck, a big, all-American hunk and game show host – *The Dating Scene, Love Connections*.

Chuck delivered a most eloquent and generous tribute to my shows and Willie Nelson held up a copy of *Full Circle* to camera and then began to slowly open the pages! This American legend, with a face half ravaged by a full life and as noble as an Indian chief, managed to carry this off with dignity – all I could do was fall to the studio floor and bow a few times before him.

Friday, September 12th: Newark–London

Slept, though all my joints seem to ache from the effort, until woken for breakfast about an hour out of London.

We're 45 minutes late touching down – but the weather is good, and the bags are through swiftly. The office have done a good job and found me Brian, a friend of Graham F's, to drive me to Sudbury and back. We're out of the airport with two hours still to go.

Everything fine until the M25 eastbound fills, slows and finally comes to a halt.

Brian stays cool, finds a turning off and we cut through the rural lanes of Hertfordshire.

St George's Sudbury is very fine – perpendicular with wide side aisles and fine tombs and brass plaques and a delicately painted ceiling in the chancel.

As Derek's body is brought in, a soft patter of rain strikes the roof; the shower intensifies into a small storm, with accompanying thunder, as the service goes on and stops as the coffin leaves.

Derek, apparently, planned the service carefully, chose the readings and the music and the guests. Some Kathleen Ferrier, 'Danny Boy' by Phil Coulter and James Galway – Stéphane Grappelli as a recessional.

It's a good service – as Derek would have wanted it – literate, eclectic, dignified.

Back to the Mill. Jonathan Clyde asks if I would like to say anything.

But there's not much left to say when I get to my feet. I point to the irony of having to choose between publicity and Derek, the supreme publicist, to get here.

Wonderful tributes from the likes of Brian Wilson and Van Dyke Parks are read out – showing how much this very English man was loved in the USA.

But for me the star was Derek's brother, reminiscing about how Derek once kissed him – for reassurance – on his first day at prep school. His tone, his wit and his timing all eerily echo Derek's.

It's almost 6.30 when we're shown out of the side gate by Dominic to find Brian waiting patiently in the Jaguar. He said he'd heard the piano being played. I said that it was Jools Holland, who remembered Derek saying that the best way to clear a room was to start playing the piano.

Saturday, September 13th

It seems at last that O'Rourke has gone. The windows on which he stuck his defiant notes of protest against the council have been sealed with dark, vaguely sinister metal frames, and the lavatory bowl in which he grew flowers is dumped at the kerbside awaiting collection.

Monday, September 15th

Overnight figures for the Japan/Korea episode were 6.4 and 25% of the audience. *Heartbeat* strides away with 14.4 and 56%. The highly praised Hawking and the long-awaited Alan Clark *History of the Tory Party* cobble about 2.5 million between them.

Eddie confirmed that we have removed the Diana reference in programme four.

Wednesday, September 17th

To Charlbury with H to see Geoffrey and Susan S. We decide to take the train.

Charlbury is a tiny, immaculate station with one of the old Great Western wooden signs – big, bold, bulky brown lettering – and a goldfish pond maintained by the Women's Institute.

GS and I talk about the prospects of a book from me next year.

Geoffrey is keen on a comic novel. I don't think he wants me to be too introspective. I tell him of 'Glasgow y Valencia' – the drain-cover salesman idea. He likes that.[1] Also my thoughts on some sort of Hemingway book – in time for Hem's centenary in '99.

Friday, September 19th

Anglia Trains have been pressing me for some time to agree to have one of their trains (not locomotives sadly) named after me. I agreed a while ago and now, on this drizzly mid-September morning, my bluff has been called.

At Darsham Station – so full of private memories. Television crews, radio reporters, pressmen all waiting for me where once there was only my little mother.

Drizzle abates long enough for a speech of welcome from Andy Cooper of Anglia. Then I reply and, uttering the immortal words 'I name this train Michael Palin', pull a curtain cord to reveal my likeness, or rather a shadowy outline of my likeness – made up of lots of white and black dots. ('It looks really good from 100 yards away,' Andy reassures me.) Beneath this spectral depiction is my name. The whole lot is stuck on the side of a one-coach unit.[2]

Still, my mother and father would have been proud and they keep coming to mind, especially poignantly when Andy presents me with two framed photographs of Darsham Station over the last 100 years. In both of the sepia snaps it's virtually deserted, which is how I remember it.

We're rocketing home through the eastern suburbs of London when someone whispers in Andy Cooper's ear and he heaves a sigh and turns to me – 'Smidgeon of bad news ... there's been a train crash outside Paddington.' He adds, 'It affects all of us, a thing like that, we know how it feels.'

Tune in to six o'clock news. A high-speed train is spread all over the line at Southall, coaches entangled with a line of yellow goods wagons. Eight people reported killed, 170 wounded. Overhead wires dangling. Words like 'carnage' bandied about. It's described as the worst rail accident since Clapham, in December 1988.

Feel sorry for Anglia – they worked hard and could not have treated me better today. They went all-out for publicity for themselves, the East Suffolk Line and the railways. Now all that publicity has been negated.

---

1 The idea came to me as I was sitting outside a café in Segovia in Spain. In front of me I noticed a drain cover with the words 'McNaughton and Sons, Glasgow y Valencia'.
2 The class was named after famous East Anglians. I've quite often found myself sitting on 'Delia Smith'.

Tuesday, September 23rd

To the Soho House for a long interview for the *Daily Telegraph*.

At the end of a reasonably agreeable, non-invasive interrogation a photographer arrives and we go out into Romilly Street for some snaps against a garage door. Norman Balon, notorious landlord of the Coach and Horses,[1] ambles up the road.

He casts a dyspeptic eye in my direction and wheezes out a half-cough, half-laugh. 'What are they photographing you for, eh? You're so fucking ugly.'

I'm chuffed that he even recognises me, let alone feels me worthy of abuse.

Saturday, September 27th

Driven down to the LWT Tower on the South Bank for an interview with Clive Anderson.

Shown to a tiny, dim dressing room. Just relax, I'm told, yet when I try to I'm subjected to a constant series of knocks on the door; the last of which is quite bizarre. Standing in the passageway is Chris Eubank, the boxer, clad only in white underpants and holding up a pair of trousers. 'I'm going to show the world a new Chrith Eubank tonight,' he promises and asks if I know where the wardrobe lady has gone.

Friday, October 10th

To TV Centre, where I'm to appear on *Blue Peter*.

All goes well, except that during the 'make', as they call the 'now here's something you can make at home', I used 'God!' as an expletive and was apparently caught on camera sniffing the glue pot.

Friday, October 17th

Paul Lambeth, clean-limbed, well-dressed lawyer dealing with the Paragon litigation,[2] comes to see me, as he needs some details before preparing my deposition – i.e. my statement to the court.

1 The Coach and Horses pub was the long-time venue for *Private Eye*'s fortnightly lunches, and the setting for the play *Jeffrey Bernard Is Unwell*.
2 A company called Paragon claimed worldwide rights to *Life of Brian* after they bought the HandMade Films back catalogue. Python went to court to win these rights back.

I like him, and have no trouble in backing up with facts and personal experience those things he would like me to say. The case has been set for March 9th 1998. There seems no way in which Paragon can win, but 'points of law' could be enough to prevent us from winning.

Friday, November 14th: The Grand Hyatt, Hong Kong

Bas and I talk about future travel. Cuba seems a must in the spring. Bas has printed out a proposal for an Islands series. I enlarge on the type of shorter-distance, stay-longer travel that I see as a new direction after the mega trips. Suggest calling each one 'Living In' (as in 'Living In Calcutta', 'Living in Ouagadougou', 'Living in Bahia'). I would stay in a place for six weeks, living with a local family.

We take a couple of martinis to celebrate the past, the present and the future of Palin and Pao as night falls and the sheer sides of the buildings around us are transformed into jewelled columns of light.

Sunday, November 23rd: London–Salisbury

H and I leave the house at 10.45 for lunch with Sir Edward Heath at his house in Salisbury. Curious to know why I've been invited and what sort of occasion it is. We've been sent a guest list which looks rather grand – Kenneth Clarke the last Chancellor and some 'Excellencies'.

Arrive a bit early and draw into a service station for some petrol. The Indian cashier's eyes are shining and, as he hands me a receipt, he blurts out 'Kenneth Clarke was just here!'

Arundells is a handsome Georgian house, long windows, solid, square and built of stone with a columned portico projecting from the front door.

The door is opened by Sir Edward himself. He resembles a great big soft toy. Face pink and wide, hair white and neat, eyes alert and very bright. Disarmingly reassuring.

We are offered Dom Perignon in a small sitting room, walls hung with Chinese watercolours.

Meet the other guests. The Clarkes, Richard Webber, a wild-haired academic, I think. Very easygoing, down-to-earth – reminds me of Richard Hoggart. Heath's secretary – young, dark, attractive in a tomboyish way and her 'young man', a surveyor. The American Ambassador and his wife are announced.

We move into a dining room, a well-proportioned room, quite tall, not grand. Food exquisitely served – butter in silver-lidded dishes, cut glass, etc.

Cabinets of fine china on one wall – watercolours (he has two in the hall by Winston Churchill – not very good).

The American Ambassador, Philip Lader,[1] is keen to get to know the country (he's never been ambassador anywhere else). Asks direct questions to the table, in most un-British manner, like 'May I ask all of you what you feel has been the greatest change in Britain over the last ten years?' Some say food, I suggest the growing awareness of being a multiracial community.

Heath, who likes to speak in well-judged, weighty sentences, feels that it is the deference to the consumer. 'Everything must be available for the consumer. The consumer is king.' He enlarges on the point that excellence has suffered. If 'the people' do not understand something it can't be done. Mr Webber concurs. He feels the last ten years have seen a 'dumbing-down'.

Ken Clarke, a gourmet, says that, whereas you used to have Chinese restaurants and Indian restaurants, taste now has become so sophisticated that people demand to know if it's Cantonese or Szechuan, or South Indian or Rajasthani.

Every now and then Sir Edward rings a small glass bell and a fresh course is produced.

His house reflects a real interest in the rest of the world – which is why perhaps he invited me. In front of everyone he praised the series for opening minds and extending horizons and says that he was very sorry to hear me say that I was doing no more.

I hear him telling the American Ambassador that he was once asked by Mao Tse-Tung what he thought of Kissinger. 'Well I told him,' Heath begins in typical anecdotal style, 'I thought he served his government well. That he was a man of intelligence with a good grasp of affairs and a devotion to his work.'

'He was shaking when he came to meet me,' Mao replied.

'Coe-niac?' asks Sir Edward as we assemble, efficiently, in another room – this one filled with photographs, stood in serried ranks upon every flat surface like gravestones. He doesn't push his experiences, nor his contacts, except in a quietly startling way – viz. handing round the cigars from a polished wooden box he's clearly very proud of, 'They're all Havanas, Castro sends them to me every Christmas.' The American Ambassador's eyes are out on stalks.

I feel a growing awareness that being a world leader makes you eligible for a special club – the World Leaders' Club – with its free gifts, discounts and fraternal Christmas greetings. Tory or Communist, it doesn't really matter, as long as you've been a Leader.

I'm slipped a message asking if I would kindly look in at the kitchen before I leave, as some of the domestic staff would like their books signed. Sure enough there are eight *Full Circles* laid out on the kitchen table.

---

1 Before becoming US Ambassador to London, Philip Lader, a lawyer, held various posts in President Bill Clinton's administrations.

Sir Edward bids us goodbye at a few minutes after four. We're the last to leave. Across the gravel drive and out through the wrought-iron gates, at which stands a tall blonde with a machine-gun. 'I 'ope you signed my book for me!' she calls after us as we walk into the Cathedral Close.

Saturday, November 29th

Last day of my out-of-London signings. A week in which I estimate, conservatively, that I've signed five and a half thousand books, and in which we hit the No. 1 slot on the *Sunday Times* list in some style, with figures of 31,700, 11,000 more than Bryson in second place and considerably more than even the big Christmas paperbacks – Pratchett and Francis and *Bridget Jones's Diary*.

Wednesday, December 3rd

Talk to Cleese.

He says, triumphantly, and with a great wheeze of anticipatory laughter, 'I bet you can't guess who I'm having lunch with on Sunday.' When I say Edward Heath, he's quite chastened.

Wednesday, December 10th

To the RGS to give a lecture on Peru.

Try not to look at the front row – apart from Hemming, the great Peruvian scholar and South American expert, there is the author and travel writer Redmond O'Hanlon, Tim Renton the old Arts Minister and his wife, and the Peruvian Ambassador at the Court of St James's.

I drew the sting by saying that for me to be addressing myself to things Peruvian in such company was like the Spice Girls giving advice to the Royal Opera House – laugh – mind you, I think they'd take advice from anyone these days – not a great line, but an even bigger laugh!

The talk lasts just about an hour – then I take questions, and eventually I'm extracted from the throng and driven back to John Hemming's for dinner.

Small, pretty house in Edwardes Square off Kensington High Street. Upstairs are the distinguished guests – the Rentons, the cadaverously elegant Sir Anthony Acland, Provost of Eton (his wife tells me Princess Anne is a great fan of the journeys!), O'Hanlon, John Hatt of Eland Books, John Julius Norwich and wife Mollie.

There's also Princess Alexandra and Angus Ogilvy – both of whom apologise profusely to me for not having been able to attend the lecture.

Acland's wife talks about a book she's reading in a weary way – 'Why do they always have to deal with, well ... what I'd call the sordid things of life. I mean the books seems to me to consist of,' she touches her finger as she rattles off each word – 'menstruation, masturbation, motherhood and murder.'

I ask Princess Alexandra what's the most dangerous thing she's ever done. 'Oh, that's a *very* difficult one.'

Tuesday, December 16th

In the evening of an undemanding day I go round with Will to Hanbury Street – first time I've seen it since it became my property – or Will's to be legally accurate – seven weeks ago.

Walk right up to the top. There's no light in the weaver's attic, and there are glimpses of a broody, ash-coloured winter sky between the rafters. Out of the northern window rises the industrial skyline of the old brewery – great tubes and vents and piping running above the roof levels, a striking Gilliam-esque silhouette; on the southern side are the gardens and back walls of the old Princelet Street houses, and to the west the emphatic stone spire of Christ Church looms over what remains of old Spitalfields – a curious mixture of benevolence and malice – or have I been too affected by Ackroyd's *Hawksmoor*?

At a quarter to ten Brick Lane is buzzing. Like a Martin Amis novel come to life this is London raw and nervy. Bright lights like an Eastern bazaar, narrow, crowded streets along which a big Mercedes noses through.

It's a heady atmosphere down here. I'm muddled and confused and enthralled by it.

Wednesday, December 17th

To the Ivy for one of TG's 'celebrity in town' evenings. Tonight it's Johnny Depp who is over here looping *Fear and Loathing*. Ray Cooper makes up a foursome.

Depp is an interesting, quietly attractive character. Like Kevin Spacey, whom I met on *Saturday Night Live* at the beginning of the year, Depp is physically undemonstrative, soft-spoken, but his whole manner, and the way he will snap into someone else's voice to make a point, suggests that there is a lot there. Contained energy.

He's a Python fan, needless to say, born in Kentucky – and he seems to have a touch of that attractive Southern politeness.

He, like Simon Albury, was present at Allen Ginsberg's memorial service. He'd seen Ginsberg a couple of weeks before he died (Ginsberg must have loved him – a successful, competent, vulnerable, pretty boy). He told Depp he was looking forward to meeting the Grim Reaper 'and getting in his pants'.

Thursday, December 18th

Out to supper with JC at the Halcyon. It's really a catch-up opportunity. John rang me yesterday to tell me that Alyce Faye has gone to America ahead of him and that he has invited along a female companion – 'tall, blonde, American,' he sighs 'inevitably'. He's happy to supply a 'blind date' for me, he says solicitously.

So I meet up with Caroline Langrishe,[1] who played a scene with John in the latest Michael Winner film.

'Langrishe Go Down' I found myself saying, without thinking it other than a cleverish literary reference.

'Yes, I'm afraid that's something I have to live with,' she replies.

Almost a year ago exactly I saw the final cut of *Fierce Creatures* for the first time, out at Pinewood. 'We made 45 million,' says John, tonight. 'Not bad.'

JC off to California on Saturday. He brings up the subject of the Python film – and despite seeming to be the black person in the woodpile last May, has obviously been thinking about it. He gives an alarmingly precise rundown of the character he seems to now want to play in it – organiser of a women's crusade. It's very funny and just confirms in my mind that John, like the rest of us, and possibly more so than the rest of us, doesn't really know what he wants.

Wednesday, December 24th

Once again we have our Christmas Eve party. Over 40 people from the neighbourhood plus some of Helen's and Rachel's friends.

Richard Lindley asks if I'm going to become one of 'the great and the good'. 'Some form of acknowledgement is well overdue I would have thought.' I tell him that I'm not really interested in all that – committees, charities, patronships, university degrees. They're all on offer, but I prefer to stay free of these ties. I don't want to live my life to someone else's agenda. I tell him I was never head boy, or head prefect – I never took things seriously enough.

---

1 Caroline Langrishe, actress well known for appearances in series such as *Lovejoy* and *Sharpe's Regiment*. *Langrishe Go Down* was the first novel by Irish writer Aidan Higgins.

Tuesday, December 30th

Fall to reading the Jonathan Margolis biography for the first time.

He has a significant observation about an aspect of my 'development' which still puzzles me, namely, how I managed to perform so confidently at Oxford. Though this confidence in front of an audience was there – I'd won the Bentley Elocution Prize at Shrewsbury (one of many things he missed in a dismissive chapter) and acted regularly with the B & C Players on my 'gap year' in Sheffield – he notes 'Where the remnants of Michael Palin's shyness disappeared to in the autumn of 1962 was anybody's guess, perhaps it had never really been anything other than a childish trait exacerbated by his father's crushing lack of encouragement for all but the most humdrum of ambitions.'

Much skimping (Shrewsbury very thin), some inaccuracies of detail and over-emphasis on trying to compare the origins of my career with those of JC. But generally his instinct leads him to the right places.

Wednesday, December 31st

The year ends very quietly. Almost too much so. For the first time in many weeks I find myself waking earlier than usual and staying awake. It's part of a process I know well enough now. Hard work – like the production and marketing of *Full Circle* which has dominated my year – fills all one's working hours, leaving little room for idle thoughts – for the mind to wander. Decisions have to be taken swiftly, and they're limited to and conditioned by the task in hand.

Once the pressure's off, as it has been since my last book-signing in Manchester, there is a period of sheer and wonderful elation, the incomparable pleasure of not having to work hard. This quite quickly replaced by the often unsettling speculation about what lies ahead.

One thing is clear after *Full Circle* – that I could make travel programmes like this until I die. I've carved out a piece of the market that is now unquestionably my own – as much as Monty Python was to the six of us who made it.

So, should I accept that this is what I'm best suited for, and stop trying to be an arts presenter, or a novelist, and just get on with bringing people the sort of pleasure they derived from *Full Circle* – the sort of pleasure that no-one else seems quite able to purvey? I don't know. All I can say as '98 strikes, is that I shall continue to need to provoke and possibly punish myself into not resting on any laurels; *Full Circle* was a considerable achievement, but it's over. That was last year.

1998

Monday, January 5th

What the newspaper calls 'a family of deep depressions' continues to produce spectacular weather. This morning starts grey and mouldering, another morning which gives hibernation a good name. Then the weathervane swings round to the east and much colder air tugs the temperature quite rapidly down, before finally settling in the north-north-west from which comes a most dramatic deluge; this eventually passes, leaving a short respite before semi-night returns again – accompanied by rumblings of thunder and hailstones scattering onto the garden table.

Drive over to Islington to meet Mike Slee and Martha Wailes of Principal Films who want me to make a film about Cuba with them.

Mike Slee is a slim, neat man with tight, well-cut greying hair – not far off my age I wouldn't have thought. Martha is younger. The pair of them look very English.

I have to hedge my enthusiasm for Cuba with reservations about time, availability and the fact that so far I have not made any plans beyond the novel this year (and even this is not contracted).

Wednesday, January 7th

Have been asked to lunch at Anna Haycraft's. She has a project she wants to talk to me about.

To Gloucester Crescent. Normally casual garden gate replaced by large cell-block door with remote control lock. Anna, small, pearly-white skin, big TV screen spectacles emphasising rather than disguising the tragic look in her eyes, apologises. 'We've had lots of burglars, I'm afraid. A big Rastafarian just walked in and took the television!'

She shows me Henry Mayhew's book on London.

I give her some advice – suggest that if it is done as television, it should be shot in the style of the current fly-on-the-wall docs – impressionistically, quick fades in and out.

Anna says she refuses to go on programmes like *Start the Week*, or anywhere where she can't say fuck. She's most interested in the death of a lady who was struck by a falling lamp-post in Cavendish Square during the weekend's gales. Darkness, literal and metaphoric, seems to cheer her up enormously.

About eight we drive down to Tower Hill to see Fiona Shaw's *Wasteland*, which she's performed nightly over the last few weeks at the unheated, barely lit shell of Wilton's Music Hall on the corner of Cable Street and Ensign Street. Have invited Ray Cooper and Dearbhla Molloy along.

Tall chamber, with barleycorn cast-iron columns, freshly painted in gold, supporting the gallery. Narrow stage. Like Sickert's music hall paintings come to life.

She speaks the difficult poem very well. Clear, strong and, although I miss most of the references, I feel she understands what she's saying completely. Her confidence carries the evening.

Dearbhla is on good form and looks very well – her red hair well cut and shining almost gold. Ray rubs his bare scalp and tells wonderful stories about acupuncture. He had needles in his forehead when the acupuncturist stuck one in a tender part of Ray's anatomy, causing Ray to cry out in pain and involuntarily slap his hand to his brow – driving the needles already there deeper into his skull.

Tuesday, January 13th

Letters, phone calls, then set to work to implement changes to end of *Hemingway's Chair* for Tom Dunne. He has asked if I would rewrite the ending to make it clear my hero hadn't perished. I enjoy doing it. I have no feeling that the end is sacrosanct; rather the opposite, I relish the chance to play around with the words again. It was always ambiguous and ambiguity is quite bad for a writer, I think.

I look forward to concentrated writing again. The offers of television documentaries – the ideas about religions, Cuba, Hemingway, railways – have come in such a flood that it is almost impossible to select one from the other. It feels increasingly sensible to say no to the whole lot – this would reduce the agonising at a stroke.

Sunday, January 18th

Out in the evening to what promises to be a dauntingly intellectual evening. We've been asked by Sarah Hawkins to 'meet' Steven Pinker – the American with big, wild, 1970s hair who's just written a much-publicised book on language called *How the Mind Works*. Doris Lessing, Richard Eyre and academics Colin Blakemore and Steve Jones are promised as light relief.

As it turns out Pinker is very polite, un-stuffy and not at all pompous. More like a very clever kid than a professor. Colin Blakemore had cancelled earlier in the day – last night his windows were smashed by animal rights activists who have been giving him and his family a hard time since he made some public statement of support for tests on animals.

Doris Lessing is the greatest surprise. I had her down in my mind as a severe woman (the weathered face, hair pulled back from her forehead), rigorously intellectual and somewhat ascetic in her approach to life.

'We all know you,' she said as we were introduced, as if her own strong features weren't iconic. She's modest and realistic and though she was always very much against the arrogance of white Africans, accepts that the blacks have made mistakes 'of a quite different kind'.

Talk to Pinker about stammering. He thinks that there is a genetic cause – it's something that's passed on through families. I tell him that I know of no other stammerer in my father's family, before or since.

Tuesday, January 20th

A chance to read *You've Got Mail* – the new Hanks movie, their first together since *Sleepless in Seattle* – in which there is a part they want me to do. It's quite a bright, cool, witty, up-to-date script – v. middle-class, A–B readership, and my character William Spurgeon is clearly based on Thomas Pynchon (reclusive novelist). Three scenes; quite fun. Seriously tempted to break my rule on cameos.

Thursday, January 22nd

To Camberwell for squash with Terry J. Best game for a long time. Hold on at 2-2, then fall apart in the last game. Traditional ritual of a beer, and then a meal.

He's enmeshed in a number of projects which aren't making him any money and says he's been quite badly affected by the hold-up of Python monies – which are currently being used to finance the case against Paragon.

Friday, January 23rd

Anne rings to say that the new dates for *You've Got Mail* seem clear. She's also managed to up my fee from an initial offer of 50G to 100G. As usual, I feel a frisson of nervous indecision here. Normal, retiring MP would settle for 50G and not rock the boat, but another part of me knows that everyone else will be trying to negotiate up. That's what I pay Anne for, I suppose, to be all the things I'm not.

Saturday, January 24th

Read some of the depositions on the Paragon case and speak to Terry G. He has heard rumours that John Slan and Paragon – the chief villains of the affair – may both be taken over by another company – a week or so before the hearing. How does that affect us? Why can't this all be settled out of court?

Monday, January 26th

Make calls, including one to Nora Ephron, co-writer and director of *You've Got Mail*. She repeats her, and everyone else's, delight at my acceptance of the Spurgeon role. 'When I called Tom (Hanks) and said, well, guess who we've got for Spurgeon? "Bill Clinton" was the first name he came up with.' (Spurgeon makes a pass at Meg Ryan's Kathleen.)

I in turn tell her I'm glad to play a character with no redeeming moral virtues.

Rachel is back from France for a few days. She's going to sort out future plans then return to do casual work and attend a French conversation class for two weeks.

Wednesday, January 28th

To Lincoln's Inn by a quarter to nine. The same quiet quadrangle that featured in *Wanda*. A meeting has been called by Anne and Paul Lambeth, our solicitor, with Mr Munby, who will be our counsel at the hearing in March on the Paragon case. He's a short, smiling, welcoming man in an ordinary sort of suit. Looks like he'd be very good company.

He thinks that we have an above-average chance of winning on all counts. He has one area of doubt however. This concerns the presence of a side-letter between Denis O'Brien's company EuroAtlantic and Python relating to but separate from the two main contracts on which he will base most of our case. Only in the side-letter is there a mention of forfeiture – of the film returning to the Pythons in case of breach of contract.

Munby feels that there may be a problem in proving that Paragon ever saw the side-letter. So, though we may be able to prove breach, we should not necessarily get the film back.

Over weak coffee and biscuits, in a very small room, he goes over the case. If any Python is called it will be me – attendance by any of us at the hearing would be appreciated as proof of our interest/seriousness in the case.

To see Kevin Kline at the Dorchester, where he is to promote *In & Out*, a comedy with Frank Oz directing.

Upstairs to his palatial suite and we have a half-hour or so to talk. He has an interesting observation about *Fierce Creatures* – that the problem was that John is at his best when creating awful people (Fawlty, Otto, etc.) and least convincing when trying to write warm, friendly, decent ones (his own character as Archie in *Wanda* an exception). I think he's right. John is happiest when he's on the attack. And funniest too.

Thursday, February 5th

Into the DJ and off to the Hilton for the *Publishing News* Awards. I'm one of the four nominees for Book of the Year.

There is a reception upstairs for celebrity guests which turns out to be a slightly deceitful way of putting us all to work. Champagne is handed out and just as you see a friend you'd like to talk to – Benedict Allen, Jane Asher, Jilly Cooper or whoever – you're hauled away, made to stand in front of a microphone and camera.

Some good questions – some completely silly. 'What's your favourite word in English?' 'Carpathian,' I say – the interviewer looks quite lost and rather put out. 'And the worst?' 'Stub.' 'Why is that?' There's no scintilla of humour behind it all.

Then to the tables. Whenever there's a quiet break for conversation, disco music blasts out over the 900 guests.

Ned Sherrin explodes into his monologue. It's all delivered at a desperate and relentless pace. For some reason the name of Leni Riefenstahl comes to mind as the music, the flashing lights, the manic exhortations from the man on stage are all piled together to create a sort of crowd hysteria.

Book of the Year, presented by Jane Asher, goes to Helen Fielding for *Bridget Jones's Diary*. It has been a phenomenon, and though issued only in paperback, has sold 700,000 copies.

Not winning always makes these sorts of evenings seem even more pointless, but, as usual, met some good people. Helen Fielding, a quite solid, northern lady, says she wished I'd presented her with the award as she'd always been 'insanely jealous' of me. By the time I asked why, someone had come up and badgered me with an autograph book.

Kathy Lette[1] wondrously, almost crusadingly, physical. She wraps herself around me and announces that she'd like to put her hand on my bottom. I'm about halfway through telling her a hand-on-bottom story when John

1 Kathy Lette, Australian-born writer, married to lawyer Geoffrey Robertson.

Mortimer approaches. Kathy transfers her sinuous embrace to Mortimer as briskly as in the 'ladies' excuse-me' dances that were popular in my teenage days!

Sunday, February 8th

Only thing of real interest from the outside world are faxes from Anne and Steve which suggest that Paragon are at last realising that their own legal action could do them a great deal of harm. As from last Friday, they have made 'without prejudice' suggestions of a settlement. They have offered us their share of the rights in *Life of Brian* for £500,000. We would still have to pay our legal costs as well.

I call Steve. He, like me, agrees that this is pretty outrageous but if taken as the first position in a compromise, not as bad as it looks. If they reduce the purchase price to say £150,000 he thinks it will be worth serious consideration.

Thursday, February 12th

Down to Rathbone Place to record some introductions and promos for a Python weekend that a small cable channel, Paramount Comedy, are planning for April.

I was struck again by the number of people around the crew; there seems little change from the great days of BBC over-staffing, though in this case the superfluous staff are young and probably quite badly paid, whereas the BBC was over-staffed with the middle-aged and well paid.

They have all sorts of bright ideas for serving up the Python episodes, films, etc. The new electronic capability has greatly increased the potential for deconstructing Python.

Then lunch with Paul Hamann and Peter Salmon.

I end up saying all I want to say – that I am not contemplating any 'big' TV involvement for 18 months at least, that I am happy working with the BBC, that I have no wish to become a pet presenter for them or anybody else (I've turned down hosting both BAFTA ceremonies this year) – that when I do do something it must be special, it must involve adventure.

Hamann plugs away at the MP-J.Cleese co-travel prog, but I'm wary. Sometimes two presenters can seem a bit cosy, and run the risk of cutting out the audience.

Friday, February 13th

There has been no response from Paragon to our rejection of their settlement proposal, and it looks as if we are now committed to spending another slice of money – £70,000 or so – in preparing briefs.

Thursday, February 19th

Out to dinner with Suzanna Zsohar and Michael Ignatieff. Salman Rushdie, wife Elizabeth and baby Milan are there.

Salman talks a little about his situation. The fatwa has been reasserted, nine years after it was imposed – and he is bitter that New Labour has promised so much – a meeting with Robin Cook[1] – but delivered so little. He says united international action is required but the French and Germans don't want to rock the boat with Iran.

At the end of the evening after vodka, and borscht and thick pasta and cabbage and plenty of wine and even some fierce brandy, we get up to leave and suddenly there are two young men with us.

Only later does H tell me that they had been there all evening, eating in the bedroom. They are, of course, Salman's police protection team. Young, strong, polite, well turned-out.

Elizabeth, Salman's wife, pretty in a sober way, with pale skin, goes off with the baby. Salman moves quickly downstairs (quite contrary to his discursive, rambling style in the flat) and into one of the two cars parked in the almost empty Clare Street. The two cars, keeping close to each other to avoid any interception, move away as if there is a magnet between them.

We're going the same way – up to Islington. They wait at a set of lights in Goswell Road and let us pass. And I feel a little guilty – well more than a little guilty – as I speed on over the hill and down towards the spires of St Pancras – that, as a fellow writer, I've done so little to help him. Because Salman is so full of life – so obviously delighted to be the focus of attention – and such a performer – I tend to forget his predicament.

Friday, February 20th

Head for the sun and light of the Bonnard exhibition at the Hayward Gallery.

For an hour I concentrate on the canvases. The effect of a brace of Bonnards is to bring time to a standstill. His is an unhurried world – a listless, languid,

---

1 Robin Cook, Labour MP, Foreign Secretary since the General Election.

slow pattern of relentlessly repeated events, actions and scenes. It creates an almost palpable sense of a quiet, shuffling world, broken only by the sound of soft splashing bath water and the occasional sigh of wind in the trees.

Everything about it is *sotto voce* – nothing violent, swift or sudden intrudes. I never was aware of this before, but today the feeling is strong and gives me the sort of satisfaction I drew from a film like the *Quince Tree Sun*.[1] Understated, closely observed, diurnal detail.

Tuesday, February 24th

Out to a dinner at Daphne's in Draycott Avenue hosted by Michael Bloomberg, whose name is all over the place now on financial and other news services.

He's a shortish, trim man in mid-50s, tanned and professionally healthy. He has a much taller girlfriend – Mary-Jane, with big, red, Pre-Raphaelite hair but an almost gawky manner which is appealing but lessens the impact of her striking looks.

She's marvellously indiscreet. The picture she painted of her inamorata – 'Do you work with him?' I open the conversation. 'Oh no,' she gives a slightly cackling laugh ... 'I just sleep with him' – is of a hard, sharp, clever businessman – 20 years with Salomon Brothers – who has quite hawkish economic views. And later, I hear, aspirations to be Mayor of NYC.

She seems obsessed by the backwardness of Europe – 'All these guys thinking all they have to do is a 30-hour week?' she asks incredulously.

Thursday, February 26th

To do my duty for the Prince's Trust – this involves hosting a fund-raising lunch with successful businessmen and women.

Tom Shebbeare, who runs the Trust, hails me in the street. He's busy lashing his bicycle to a lamp-post, which is too thick to take his locking clamp. I help him secure it higher up where it hangs like a tutu.

I've evidently pulled in a star guest – Elisabeth Murdoch, daughter of the Dirty Digger and second in command at Sky-BSB.

Murdoch is slim and seems serious. She has what looks like natural blonde hair and a bone structure and complexion which is as prominent as it is delicate. When the host retells my story of how Kevin Kline's character in *Fierce Creatures* was moved to New Zealand and officially modelled on Sam Chisholm to avoid offending Murdoch, she seems to take it, if not with a laugh, with a

---

1 Released in 1991, about the painter Antonio López. Directed by Victor Erice.

quite unoffended ease – as if she hears stories about her father every day.

I make a short speech at the start of the meal – without notes, I've decided – and it's the right decision as notes would have looked rather over-formal. A good discussion about helping young people find work, begin businesses, etc.

The whole event takes about two and a half hours of my lunchtime, and they all seem to think it's been a success. Tom stares in fascinated appreciation of my phrase 'children are born enterprising'. He loves that.

Saturday, February 28th

Call Basil. He's suddenly being offered good Hong Kong work – ironic, as he's on the point of moving out. Tourist board want him and, more excitingly for him, so does the new airport company.

In course of our usual mix of business and banter he suggests that a possible way out of the Hemingway for 1999 impasse would be for him to do a photo-book of all the places Hemingway worked and lived in, and I would only have to come up with the text. This sounds a marvellous idea. A real breakthrough.

Immediately plunge into research on Hemingway places. This keeps me occupied until supper.

Rachel arrives back from Paris at six, with two bulky suitcases, her five-month study time there now finally over. Half an hour later I have to run her to Belsize Park, on her way to a party.

Monday, March 2nd

Wake early. I wonder if I've not been too impulsive in my reaction to the Hemingway idea. After all, it's less than 48 hours since Bas floated it and from my reaction he would be right to presume that it will all soon be sorted out and going ahead.

How much do I really want this? Hem's 100th anniversary is next year. We shall have to move fast.

Paul Hamann rings to follow up on things talked about at our lunch in mid-February. Wants me to float the idea of a Python evening on the BBC (which followed on from my enthusiasm about Paramount's weekend of Python), and after some tentative probing suggests that I might like them to commission a researcher to go and do some preliminary work on the Sahara idea!

Wednesday, March 4th

Anne collects me by cab and takes me for a catch-up lunch at Damien Hirst's Pharmacy in Notting Hill Gate.

It's a wonderful joke – only because it's carried through so completely. The windows that flank the entrance are full of carefully displayed preparations (true or false I don't know) and the reception desk is a counter attended by young men in white pharmacists' jackets. The downstairs bar looks and smells like a dispensary and must be a pretty awful place for a drink – but earnest unsmiling couples sitting with champagne buckets beside them seem to take it seriously enough. I like the obsessive detail and the carrying-through of the idea. As I say to Anne this is the first restaurant that's really made me laugh.

Upstairs the chemist motif is more diluted – but the walls are papered with pharmacological charts and there is a small picture on the menu of a pill being dropped out of a bottle and proffered on the hand. The generous bright sun is screened by white blinds.

Tell Anne of the Hem idea. She is of the opinion that the photo-book on Hemingway Trail/Places/Travels is a substitute for the obvious idea which is a TV series, of which the book would be the spin-off. She observes that I talk about Hem's places with such enthusiasm that it feels to her a much stronger bet than the novel.

Her other piece of news is that I may be called to court after the Python reunion at Aspen.[1] Life seems to be getting complicated.

Friday, March 6th: Aspen, Colorado

In the afternoon the first meeting with all the people involved in our show – which is around a dozen people apart from ourselves.

First surprise is when we're handed a 30-page 'script' of our spontaneous appearance, with pink cover. On the whole it's cordial, but TJ the most uncomfortable with prepared links and set pieces.

Earlier in the day we've bumped into Eddie Izzard – who has a show here. It's suggested he be the mystery skier who comes on stage with us when we're first introduced.

I think much will be sorted when we rehearse at the theatre tomorrow. 'Rehearse?' says Terry with indignation. I fear there will be tears before showtime. Terry G has already run into flak after asking if the journo Giles Smith, who is travelling with him for a *New Yorker* article, can attend the planning

1 The surviving five Pythons had been asked to the Aspen Comedy Arts Festival for an on-stage interview and to receive an American Film Industry Award.

meeting. Eric is not happy. 'We don't want bloody Boswells in here.'

Terry G has asked if I'll come to Hunter Thompson's ranch with him this evening. The idea appeals in a kind of diary-filling way but my head tells my heart that I'm short of sleep already and tomorrow will be a long day.

End up going to see three short Steve Martin sketches and an Alan Zwei-bel playlet down at the Jerome (the only really interesting hotel in Aspen). Amused to see that Eddie Izzard also has a *New Yorker* scribe in attendance. Such is Eddie's stature these days that he gets John Lahr.

Saturday, March 7th: Aspen

Breakfast with TG and the Joneses. Al's off skiing for the second day running and I envy her. Seems ridiculous to be in one of the great ski resorts of the world and confined to corporate hotels and meeting rooms.

Meet beside the Terrace Restaurant in a completely unexceptional private room. The five of us plus our new manager Roger Saunders.

In a couple of hours some positive decisions are taken. To investigate syndication (i.e. cutting the shows into 65 22-minute chunks, with our con-sultation) and to use the 30th anniversary of Python – October next year – as a commercial springboard.

JC proposes a stage tour for the 30th anniversary. Six weeks, end in Vegas, clean up, etc. etc. He's got the time to spare to organise it – 'with a committee of us' he suggests airily.

So, remorselessly, the stage show '99 seems a front runner. Terry G, who wasn't back from Hunter T's until two this morning, hunches into his seat, fiddles with his ponytail and does his best to be non-committal in the face of John's persistence. Terry is hoping to get 'Defective Detective' up and run-ning by then. I voice my worries – lack of GC bad enough, but without TG involvement, disastrous.

Nothing is allowed to slow the process of a Python relaunch, and by the time we pack up it's even suggested we announce the show during the taping tonight.

On to the Wheeler Opera House for a run-through. It's an unusual and quite beautiful interior with a roof painted night-time blue and dotted with golden stars. Seating for 350–400 in well-kept maroon velour seats. A curved balcony and boxes – occupied by the cameras.

The set is good – a series of overlapping panels covered in bold Python images, the foot, various TG faces, all give colour and depth to the stage. There is old-fashioned English country house furniture around, tea and biscuits on a trolley – upholstered Edwardian-style chairs.

Eddie Izzard there to rehearse the opening. We decide it's better if he doesn't wear a ski outfit, just appears as himself, and it's only as he begins to answer the first question about how we got together that we become aware of him and drive him off the stage. Robert Klein, the moderator, asks anxiously if someone is at least going to mention Eddie's name. 'No, fuck him!' is the general response – which Eddie thoroughly enjoys. Klein can't quite see the joke. 'You're hard men,' he mutters.

All seats sold, a video-feed set up to the foyer – all seats sold there, another video-feed to 1,200 people in an adjacent hotel.

To the theatre. Hair, make-up, Lahr shadowing Izzard, Giles Smith hovering around Gilliam. John sits bolt upright in his dressing room, an oxygen mask clamped over his face and two cylinders beside him. A frightening sight. Although it's a quite acceptable way of dealing with the altitude, it nevertheless looks like some chilling glimpse of mortality.

The show begins recording a little after 9.15. All goes well with the clips, the entry and Eddie's moment. Then Robert K, who doesn't look at all at ease, asks some quite unanswerable question about what it is 'in your gut' that makes you want to do comedy. I mumble something, Terry J bravely launches into a school reminiscence. TG, with consummate timing, kicks over the urn with Graham's ashes in. From then on, we're invincible.

After it's over, there is mayhem on stage. The press have been given half an hour to get their stories and the camera crews from CNN and *Entertainment Today* and NBC News and God knows what jostle with the *Aspen Times* and students with tape recorders and an incongruous middle-aged public school man from the *Daily Telegraph* and people like Ted Danson and Kelsey Grammer from *Cheers*. Those who come up to me have evidently heard that the stage show is happening – though we didn't mention it on the recording.

Eric wasn't surprised by the rush to confirm the stage show. He says John told the press last Thursday.

Sunday, March 8th: Aspen

Should have slept the sleep of hard work rewarded – in fact, at first light I'm lying awake consumed by an indignation that both causes, and grows with, my wakefulness. John should never have told the press that we were doing a 30th anniversary tour when we had barely considered the details and problems.

He had done exactly what he would have violently and vociferously objected to in anyone else – he'd steamrollered us into a course of action purely because it suited him, then created a fait accompli by announcing it publicly.

Rang H and let off steam, then I cheer Rachel up when I tell her I'm hoping to go skiing with Eddie Izzard later in the day.

Later I call Eric who talks me down in his best and most persuasive style. No harm is done, he says, by announcing the tour – it gives a focus to the enormous enthusiasm for and appreciation of Python as evidenced by last night's event.

We should take advantage of JC's positive mood.

I talk to John, briefly. He's the only Python staying in Aspen tonight so I shall have dinner with him and hopefully have time to at least register the criticism.

Then hire ski gear and climb on the bus to Buttermilk Mountain. Can't be sure I'll remember how to ski (it must be about six years since our last holiday in Switzerland).

Eddie arrives a little late, gesticulating wildly to someone at the other end of his mobile phone. Have a beer together then up the chair lift.

Some good runs down – long, wide, safe slopes. Eddie on his snowboard – or sometimes skidding flat on his face. As he says, with snowboarding there is no halfway point between looking good and a complete idiot.

We ski until the light begins to go and the black shadows become dangerous and, like a pair of happy, slightly battered schoolboys, catch the bus back to Aspen.

Have a half-hour massage, which is a wonderful complement to the skiing, and, by now thoroughly relaxed, leave for supper with JC and Eddie.

I can't really in the circumstances give full vent to the anger I woke with this morning, but as we pick our way carefully across the road and down the slippery sidewalks I voice my doubts as to the wisdom of announcing a stage show we don't know we can do.

John shrugs off the problem, says that it's not fixed, but it's worth letting people know we're keen; he says that clearly he wouldn't want to do it without everyone's involvement. He himself is prepared to work hard on co-ordinating it.

To a smart, cramped little restaurant called The Renaissance.

Eddie says that women seem more, rather than less, attracted to him when he's dressed in women's clothes; John's fascinated. Eddie suggests he might start gently, say, by wearing some eye-liner.

Tuesday, March 10th: Aspen–London

The purser has to shake me quite violently before I wake. Have slept five deep hours over the Atlantic and we are an hour from Heathrow.

Have breakfast and return to Hem's *The Dangerous Summer*, which has only strengthened the resolve I made as I lay in bed in Aspen on Friday morning to do something on film for next year's Hemingway anniversary. His writing still hits home and without too much artifice, just concentrates and engages the mind and the senses.

So, dropping into London once again – Python revived at Aspen, a new direction for the year ahead, and an awards ceremony at the Grosvenor House in four hours' time.

Awards ceremony organised by TRIC – Television and Radio Industries Club – 960 people squeezed into the Great Room.

I pick up BBC Personality of the Year Award, and have to stay as we're also nominated for BBC Series of the Year which is the last award. It's announced, to my complete surprise, by Baroness Thatcher, who is roared to the rostrum by the suits.

'And the winner is,' I hear her voice intoning, '*Full Circle with Michael Parlin*.' Is this 'Parlin' a joke – or, like JC's 'Pallin', a way of having a dig? Gasps and laughter from all around. I urge the directors and Anne to get up and help me, but they are nowhere to be seen as I move through the tables and up into the presence of Baroness T.

Thatcher is small, bony, her face white and waxy, her handshake cool but a little damp at the same time. 'The only programme to win the double,' she says to me, quite pleasantly, with a touch of the schoolmistress in the tone and sentiment.

After referring to my award announcement as 'probably the shortest speech Baroness Thatcher ever made – but, as far as I'm concerned, absolutely the best' – I begin to tell the story of the old ladies in the Amazon village and the saliva-spiked cocktail, only to become aware of Mrs T standing close beside me and breathing 'Steady!' every time I mentioned the words 'old lady' and 'cocktail'.

I struggle on with the story as the audience begins to warm to our double act. I steal a look to one side and her gaze bores into me. 'I can see why she stayed in power for ten years,' I confide to the audience, who love it. I take another look at Thatcher. Still staring, with almost primal intensity. 'Steady!'

Somehow I got to the end of the story. I understood then what had happened. Baroness T thought the story had to be about her – relating, probably, to her well-known appreciation of a glass or two. But she didn't seem to know what exactly was going on any more than I did, and I felt confusion, rather than anger, emanating from her as we had our photos taken by a barrage of cameramen on the side of the stage. Me with my arm round Baroness Thatcher.

Thursday, March 12th

To Court 18 at the Royal Courts of Justice which manages to feel very large and very cramped at the same time. Most of the volume is in the height.

Squashed along narrow benches, one behind the other, are about 20 people. On our bench is the genial, wise-cracking Norman Horowitz, our main witness. John Goldstone is up in the witness box, which is on the same height as the judge, who is called, memorably, Justice Rattee.

The court rises, but the tape-recording doesn't work, so the court adjourns whilst the machine is fixed. Modern technology including tapes and computers has been unceremoniously stuck onto G. E. Street's Victorian Gothic woodwork – lengths of black cable secured to delicately carved cornices and architraves with gaffer tape.

Just when I think I'm set for the afternoon session I'm called up.

The Channel 4[1] lawyer speaks in soft, insidious tones – far worse than being shouted at. He leads me into defending *Life of Brian* despite the censorship and Church disapproval, then smoothly turns my far too helpful reply into some sort of judgement that *'LOB'* may now be less successful because it is no longer controversial.

As I had had no preparation for any of this I felt quite helpless and afterwards realised I'd been tricked into saying all sorts of unhelpful things.

But I'm away after lunch. General feeling being that they don't have much of a case and that the judge is very impatient of the time they're taking with witnesses.

Friday, March 13th

Rachel off to work at At-It Productions – could this possibly be the first day of a television career?

To TV Centre to see Peter Salmon, the new Controller of BBC One, and pitch 'The Hemingway Travels'.

For the first time in any of my 33-year dealings with the BBC top brass I feel I'm treated, unequivocally, as an asset. We talk for three-quarters of an hour. Peter makes little notes about H as I go along. 'Four wives eh?' – he scribbles something down. 'Lust for life,' he mutters approvingly at one point.

There is some distraction in the back of his mind – I know that. I know I'm sharing his time, but he's remarkably positive and likes the idea of four 50-minute progs – Palin on Hemingway – for autumn 1999. BBC One.

Leave the BBC at three. Home. Should be feeling elated but I've been through all this before and part of me is heavy with the awareness that this will mean being tried in front of a television audience again, rather than enjoying the quieter pleasures of novel-writing.

---

1 Channel 4 with Paragon were co-defendants.

Sunday, March 22nd

Today apply myself to Hemingway. Put together a 'sales pitch' for the series – as much to convince myself as anyone else. Take down the Pacific map that's dominated my wall since the summer of 1995, and replace it with 'The Ernest Hemingway Adventure Map of the World'.

There are many ifs and buts to the series. I'm no further on with decision on director, or whether to go for old friends or new blood.

Monday, March 23rd

Feeling unsettled this morning. Spring equinox has brought thick, low cloud cover and a cool day – which doesn't help raise optimism. So many issues unresolved, from Python's stage show proposal with Tom Hoberman[1] to my insecurity over the Hem series.

I was on the verge of offering Roger Mills the Hemingway job this a.m. His knowledge of Cuba seemed important. But Paul Hamann calls to suggest I contact David Turnbull, whose work on the Jonathan Meades[2] series I saw and greatly admired last year.

Turnbull rings and, though I waffle a lot, I hope I give some impression as to how and why I came to this project and how I want to proceed. He's soft-spoken, makes erudite quips, but I know there is a keen intelligence there. We agree to talk at the weekend when he returns from filming Meades in Birmingham.

This cheers me up somewhat. At least it's a positive lead in the 'new broom' direction.

Terry J's response to Hoberman's proposal is a bouncy, enthusiastic account of how he's dreamt the opening sequence of the new stage show and is now v. enthusiastic towards it. At the same time he reckons it probably isn't possible without TG – which to me means it probably isn't possible, period.

Thursday, March 26th

Meet Roger at the Yorkshire Grey – a pub-brewery close to ITN where he's editing his film on Yeltsin.

A chance to talk and catch up over a few pints. He's been offered a series

---

1 Tom Hoberman, Eric's lawyer in the States, was putting together a deal for the stage show.
2 Jonathan Meades is a writer, broadcaster, actor and critic, who specialises in polemical, cultural documentaries.

on cricket with Mick Jagger which may or may not happen. Alex Richardson, our editor, is soon to be busy on a new Jeremy Mills 'docu-soap'.

So I don't feel so bad telling them of my plans for the Hemingway series. As I say to Roger, 'I've taken the advice you gave me before *Full Circle* and gone for a completely new team.' But, as a sop, I suppose, I can't help speculating about the next travel series – beyond Hemingway – 'Sahara 2000?'

Friday, March 27th

Martha Wailes,[1] who has also worked with Jonathan Meades, is next to come by. She has a quiet, understated determination. I liked the feeling that she has for Hemingway – think I could work well with her, and it may be very good to have a female perspective.

To a room in the bowels of the Law Society in Chancery Lane for a Python meeting to discuss all the moves since Aspen. Eric is, once again, on the phone in the middle of the table.

JC, I felt, had cooled on Eric's Hollywoodish pressure and come closer to my more cautious view of what we should commit to. He's also adamant that he would feel most uncomfortable doing it without Terry G.

After preliminary chat amongst ourselves an agreement is reached on enquiring further into a three-city, nine-week maximum, less than 2,000-seater auditorium deal. TG's involvement not to be taken for granted.

The discussion is amicable and concentrated and businesslike. Eric brings up Las Vegas because he says so much more money can be made there (in return for a very short engagement). I'm not keen. 'Not for a million?' Eric comes back. I should have said no, not for a million, but that would be selfish!

Tuesday, March 31st: London–New York

Ten-thirty Concorde slips out of Heathrow on time. Met at JFK by 'service and greeting' staff and briskly out to a car and into my second metropolitan rush hour of the day.

In Central Manhattan 15 minutes early for my *You've Got Mail* fitting.

To a costumier called Grace in the theatre district. Met by Albert Wolsky, short, balding, civilised and very sweet. 'Everyone's so excited you're here,' he keeps saying, without affectation.

Takes an hour or more to refine the look Albert has planned for me into

---

1 Martha Wailes, producer of *Hemingway Adventure*, who had also previously worked with James Burke.

something I'm comfortable with. Do I have enough energy left to go over to the set? I do, and at the hottest part of the day I find myself on the corner of Columbus and W69th. Cables, cranes, makeshift shelters, trailers, girls with headphones and mouthpieces carrying coffees across a side street littered with chairs.

I find Nora only after she's pointed out. She doesn't look like or come across as an archetypal director. She's short, physically slight, with an intelligent face framed by dark hair and dark glasses. Nice and easy – possibly a little tortured round the edges – more like an academic than a filmic.

'We're all so excited that you're here,' I hear again. I meet Meg Ryan – slim, quite delicate, though her face in some odd way gives off light – a friendly, uncomplicated first impression.

A wearying process as I try to select the right glasses to wear. This involves some hanging about, waiting for Nora to come and approve.

She and I talk a little while about the character. She doesn't want Spurgeon to be American; she thinks people shouldn't be forced into unfamiliar accents and she rightly observes that if it's not spot-on, an American audience will notice and it will distract from the comedy.

Go away relieved.

Thursday, April 2nd: New York

To Nora E's trailer where we are to read my two scenes (it's the second, more complex one we shall start later tonight). Meet Delia, Nora's sister and co-writer. She's gentle, likeable, undemonstrative. Defers to her sister but I suspect is influential. Meg is there and Greg Kinnear, good-looking young actor who was in *As Good As It Gets* – nominated I'm told later.

Always find read-throughs demanding. They're absolutely unimportant to the final result, but absolutely important at the same time. This is the first moment Spurgeon comes to life – and these early stirrings have to feel right.

I'm not yet absolutely comfortable with the lines as written or the level at which to pitch Spurgeon, so the response is muted. Maybe a dose of reality after all the expectations.

Not ready to work until 9.30 – by the time the rain machines have all been tested and the lights set. Opening of the scene – 'loitering, lurking, skulking, stalking' are my first lines.

A little uneasy to start with but good notes from Nora enable me to gradually focus the character and capture a vanity and a detachment – cocooned in self-belief – which feels right. Meg Ryan is solid, dependable, she has the ease which comes from having been with the team and the project from the beginning. Thoroughly professional.

Despite eye-aching fatigue I manage to keep my own professional standards up. I have the words tight, and make the right moves at the right time and hold the umbrella in the precise best way – and see to all the mass of other concentrational details that make up a film performance.

At midnight I'm released.

Friday, April 3rd: New York

Good news as I arrive at the set at five o'clock this afternoon. The dailies have been seen and liked and Nora is already hatching plans to extend my first appearance in the scene in the shop.

It's exciting in a way I've never experienced before. Being on a big film, outside my own country, the only non–American in the cast, working under the cranes and gantries on the busy streets of New York. Life goes on around us – restaurants and cafés are Friday night full. Clusters of people stop at the end of the street, rubbernecking.

As the night wears on, only serious night owls are still out and about. At half past three I walk down to the other end of W69th, onto Broadway where the yellow cabs are flying by and look back up the street we've taken over, a whole row of brownstones lit for my close–up, and as I walk slowly back up I can see Meg, wrapped in a big, black jacket coming towards me for the next shot, and I think to myself that only New York and Paris have this legendary quality – this alchemy about them – that ability to transform ordinary life into something infinitely more dramatic.

At four o'clock I'm through. The rest of my scenes to be shot in a month's time. Fond farewells, back to the Lowell and pack and set the alarm for 9.30, which, as I turn the light out, is four and a half hours away.

Tuesday, April 7th

Anne round for a Hemingway series meeting. We go over the crewing plans. Turnbull, obviously, but Martha as producer. Eddie Mirzoeff already installed as BBC Executive Producer. I spoke to Nigel last night and he is very keen to shoot it. Still necessary for the various parties to meet and check each other out.

Thursday, April 9th

Rang Michael Katakis, the Hemingway rights manager, in Montana. V. positive. He has already spoken to Patrick Hemingway – eldest son who will be

70 this year – and they are happy to bless the project and help where possible.

Katakis sounds serious, sensible and sympathetic. He is a writer himself and photographer, his wife an anthropologist and they are currently working on their own documentary. He clearly doesn't like New York, and is very keen for me to come out to Montana and do some fly-fishing and meet Patrick and talk.

He is at pains to point out that he is not keen on mythologising Hemingway and feels that what I do or write myself about Hem should not be censored by the family.

Friday, April 10th

Have the rolling news on in my workroom at 5.35 when news of an agreement in the Ulster peace talks comes through and the unfamiliar sound of concord, however temporary, is heard around the table as each of the chief participants sums up and is applauded.[1] I wonder, though, if what was undoubtedly made possible by George Mitchell's skill as chairman, and the last-minute efforts of Blair, Ahern and Clinton, can be sustained when they are all gone.

Tuesday, April 21st

To studios near the Westway to film my contribution to an ad for the new BBC digital service. It will use various 'friends' of the Beeb, from Stephen Fry to Alan Partridge to Harry Enfield, to extol the virtues of digital TV. I have the pay-off line, the last appearance in the commercial, pushing my way up to camera through the jungle.

The jungle that's been assembled for me in Olaf Street W11 is more convincing on camera than the one we filmed in by the Urubamba in Peru. And it has no bugs and is temperature-controlled.

Thursday, April 23rd

Supper at the Commonwealth Club as guests of Peter Luff. Paddy Ashdown is amongst the fellow guests.

He tells stories about Northern Ireland (where he is from and where, in 1977, he was commanding a force of Marines) with superb renditions of the

1 This was to become known as the Good Friday Agreement.

Irish accent. He thinks Prescott and Blair a good team and was impressed by how bright Prescott was.

There is a general feeling that New Labour has been, over the last year, a good government. Paddy recalls Blair telling him early on just how much they wanted to do. But he adds that the 'openness' is a misapprehension. He says he has known no government 'more secretive'.

The service is quite bizarre. All of us who order liver are brought quail and my cheese has custard on. What part of the Commonwealth are the staff from, I ask Peter. He seems to find this hugely funny – 'Spain!'

Saturday, May 2nd

Various local chores – to the recycling depot. Bill Oddie's there. Draw his attention to a new bin for 'Spectacles'. He said one for 'Scripts' would do well round here.

Monday, May 4th: London–New York

Arrive on time to a JFK shrouded in warm, low mist and semi-dark at half past six. Into the terminal behind a jet-load from Haiti – thin old men in white suits and blue trilby hats, children in bright dresses and ribboned pigtails. Make us look so boring.

To the Inn on Irving Place by a quarter to eight. Mine is top-floor room of this three-storey brownstone, converted and full of tasteful nineteenth-century pieces of furniture. I'm in 'Edith Wharton' and have three windows which look down on Irving Place – which has restaurants, greengrocers and a bustle that is quite different from that outside the Lowell. Rarely a suit in sight.

There are new pages for my scene on Friday – just completed by Delia E – and quite difficult too – plus a letter from her saying that she's halfway through *Hemingway's Chair* and 'loving it'. So, back into the warm bosom of the Ephrons.

Tuesday, May 5th: New York

Woken periodically by constant street noise three floors below me. Cars, cabs collecting diners from the clutch of restaurants along Irving Place, then dust-carts crunching up the waste, street cleaners swishing slowly along the kerb, then delivery trucks and vans starting the whole process going again.

Breakfast in the tastefully furnished parlour downstairs. Good, fresh orange juice, strong coffee and croissants.

Work on the new lines and make arrangements with Michael Katakis to visit Montana if and when I'm released from *You've Got Mail* next Tuesday morning. He's just come back from Cuba – says Gregorio Fuentes, Hemingway's boatman, is 101 and still going strong!

Wednesday, May 6th: New York

Filming over on the Upper West Side. Myself and Greg Kinnear – as he tails me out of the subway, etc. Skies overcast, which is helpful as this is supposed to be Fall. Occasionally whole trees in autumn colours can be seen being hauled across intersections.

In the afternoon we move to a big sports store on Broadway. Here, to my complete surprise, I'm presented with a cake and the crew stand around the displays of sportswear and sing 'Happy Birthday'.

Thursday, May 7th: New York

The new lines from Delia E are a gratifying show of confidence, but as they're meant to be bad poetry they're hideously difficult to learn. Run through them as I pump the treadmill at the Equinox gym on Broadway.

Across town to the Chelsea Piers, a massive complex built around the renovated White Star Line jetties – where, amongst other things, the *Carpathia* arrived in April 1912 bearing the survivors of the *Titanic*.

My trailer is in the car park beside the murky waters of the Hudson. Onto the set of the bookshop. Meet up with Meg again. She's very interested to hear I may be going to Bozeman next week, as she and Dennis [Quaid] have a house there.

Rehearse. Without light or costume and the crew hanging around, but it's still a performance and these first impressions, so deceptively casual, are very important.

They release me, after one more rehearsal and block, around seven o'clock.

Sunday, May 10th: New York

Collected at 7.15 for what I hope will be my last day on *You've Got Mail*. At our location, just off Wall Street, in a quarter of an hour.

We have a subway train and three stations at our disposal to shoot the scene in which I make my first appearance. Complicated by need for 30 or 40 extras to be deployed, plus awkwardness of wielding the camera in confined space as the train moves.

Shuttle our way between Fulton and Broad Street covering the scene thoroughly.

I'm finished by two in the afternoon. Traditional movie farewell – 'That is Mr Palin's last shot' (of what I reckoned must be my 14th film).

Up into the rain again, distribute presents. John Linley, the DP, even offers his services should I need some emergency shooting done on *Hem's Chair*. He's an exceptionally nice man who looks like Aubrey Beardsley.

Back to the hotel. The few days I've spent on the picture have been hard, concentrated work, made more difficult by a long lay-off from movie acting, over 18 months, a strong character who needed to be played forcefully, and, of course, a completely new group of people to work with. All tremendously helpful and friendly – but the prize goes, I think, to Albert, the costume designer and the first member of the crew I dealt with when I arrived at the beginning of April. A sweet and good man. I gave him a book and signed it with feeling!

Tuesday, May 12th: New York–Bozeman, Montana

An uneventful flight to Denver – whose brand-new airport stands on the plains, waiting, it seems, for some enormous influx of non-existent passengers to materialise. Thoroughly modern, everything matching, lots of space – even a copy of *Hemingway's Chair* in the bookstore.

The flight north to Bozeman is a twin-engined turbo-prop Dornier and reminds me, with its enormous engine filling the frame of the window beside me, of the flight to the North Pole.

Bozeman on a wide plain, surrounded on every side by snow-capped ranges. Michael K is waiting for me. He's a big man with a gently bulging midriff, a greying moustache and dark, intense eyes which remind me of another Greek, Michael Angelis.

His house is unremarkable. A recently built grey clapboard bungalow in what we would call a close, at the end of a newly built road. Inside it's light and spacious and I can see from the copper skillets and the gleaming stainless steel pans that they're serious about food.

This is borne out by a fine meal preceded by smoked salmon with peppercorns and a glass of Laphroaig.

Last thing I remember is Michael telling me the sensational news that there is a new Hemingway book coming out – an African memoir – written in mid '50s – edited by Patrick H. Material never seen before.

Wednesday, May 13th: Bozeman, Montana

Aware of much moving around – and am not surprised to hear that Michael gets up and runs a mile and a half at five-thirty, then either he or Kris takes their insatiably energetic black retriever, Angus, across the golf course.

Breakfast – slices of Ogen melon, cafetière coffee and National Public Radio. Michael likes to talk and talk seriously. Conversation (which he claims is hard to find amongst his American friends) is to him like water in the desert.

Thursday, May 14th: Bozeman, Montana

We spend a very productive morning at the solid old wooden table discussing the Hemingway project in depth. With a little trepidation, I give Michael my first synopsis to read. He's complimentary and approving. As far as he's concerned this is the best Hemingway proposal he's seen. Neither over-adulatory nor cynical – and as he sees it the key to it is that it is Hemingway seen through my eyes – the eyes of another traveller, and not an American.

In the afternoon Michael drives me up to Buffalo Jump, a section of rocky escarpment over which the Indians, sorry Native Americans, used to drive herds of buffalo, who were then finished off and cut up for food, pelts, etc.

We climb to the top. Magnificent views; huge spaces. Big, wide plains, the presence of snow-capped peaks evoking the altiplano of the Andes. The weather, ever changeable, dumping rain here and there, alternating cloud and sun in glorious light patterns.

Well whipped by the wind and rain we return to Bozeman for a couple of beers at Boodles. Useful input from Michael on the best dates for shooting. He thinks we should do the Gulf Stream and Cuba soon – preferably in September. He rings a friend in Key West – 'Have you had your martini yet, Fitz? When's the Gulf Stream colour at its best?'.

He enthuses about Michigan – is so glad I'm doing that because many people under-rate that early part of Hemingway's life. Plays me a tape of Hemingway reading his work.

Friday, May 15th: Bozeman–Chicago

News of Frank Sinatra's death on the radio. Eighty-two. Somehow one thought people like that immortal.

To the airport and onto the two o'clock flight – with Michael and Kris watching me onto the plane. Michael is an unusual man. Shy but successful – son of a Greek immigrant who made good in Chicago property, a musician good enough to be the solo act for Tina Turner and Joan Armatrading in his touring days. A vulnerable man who has done tough deals for the Hemingways. He and I could almost have an Al Levinson/MP relationship, I feel. He likes writing letters in fountain pen, he warns me.

Saturday, May 23rd: Oxford

Rachel's graduation.

Installed in the Sheldonian by 10.50 – there's a fight for places on the hard wooden tiered seating. We clamber up to the very top row and settle in an alcove with a good, if precipitous, view of the open arena beneath and the tall oak doors through which the graduates will enter in their new robes.

We enjoy the various deans who have to introduce their prospective candidates in Latin; some have it memorised and deliver it confidently, smoothly, co-ordinating the bows and turns to the Vice-Chancellor and Proctors, others have to read part of it. One of them, an elderly man with flowing white hair, reads each announcement from a card stuck in the centre of his mortar board.

Rachel is the first of her group so has to hold the hand of the silver-haired, rather natty Dean of Aen Nas, The Brazen Nose.

About one o'clock it's all over and we mill outside. Make our way to college.

Rachel, now with the white fur trim of a BA on the neck of her gown, sits at High Table.

I have someone opposite who used to live in Belfast and much of the talk is of the imminent disclosure of the referendum result in Ireland.[1]

Actually, I first hear it in the car on the way home, and the news is good – 71.12% 'Yes' in Northern Ireland and 96% 'Yes' in the South. More importantly, it's estimated 55% of Prods have voted yes.

Sunday, May 24th: London–New York

Across the Atlantic for the fourth time this year.

Welcomed, quite touchingly, at the Inn and I must say my room – my Edith Wharton – looks fabulous with the late-afternoon sun angling through my three street-side windows.

There are four boxes of *Hemingway's Chair* books to sign – which I set to after unpacking.

---

1 Two referendums were held in Northern Ireland and in the Republic to gauge support for the Good Friday Agreement.

Read my review in the *New York Times* – 'Not the Full Monty' – 'MP's latest novel owes more to Kingsley Amis than John Cleese'. It's a prominent review taking up most of the page next to that of John Irving's latest novel – so I can't complain of not being taken seriously.

By odd coincidence, one of the few other books extensively reviewed is a new biog of Gerald and Sara Murphy.[1] All being well I shall be meeting up with their daughter Honoria tomorrow at twelve. As ever – things happen in New York.

Monday, May 25th: New York

Honoria Donnelly Murphy is a striking woman – over 80 with patrician white hair and a nose that is hooked like a Roman. Her face is heavily powdered and she wears elegant black. Her daughter, Laura, is 30-something, perky. A single mother by the sound of things.

She has brought photos and slides of Hemingway, and two or three letters (copied) – one the very moving letter he wrote to Patrick Murphy when he knew the boy had little chance of recovering from his second bout of TB. 'No-one you love is ever dead.'

'Everyone sought his approval,' she said, 'he was that kind of man.' Once she remembers pulling her hair in a bun and securing it with 56 different pins. When she asked Hem what he thought he nodded – 'Too many pins.'

Honoria moves quite slowly, but purposefully, with the aid of a stick, along to the Blue Water Grill in Union Square where we eat well.

She has liver cancer but is in remission, which makes me very sad for she's a warm, friendly and easy companion.

A good day, in which the most remarkable piece of information was possibly that this exquisite repository of Victorian taste called the Inn at Irving Place was a Rasta flophouse 15 years ago.

Saturday, June 13th

Note death of John Marriott, the energetic, friendly and liberal Governor of Parkhurst, who entertained us with such generosity when we filmed *Palin's Column*. He was 51. I wrote a letter to the paper protesting against his dismissal from Parkhurst after the break-out. Can't help feeling another life force snuffed out whilst meaner, lesser men survive.

1 Gerald and Sara Murphy were Scott Fitzgerald's models for Dick and Nicole Diver in *Tender Is the Night*. Their biography was called *Everybody Was So Young*.

A fan has sent me a copy of the *Dandy* – in which I'm now immortalised as Michael Railin – Famous World Traveller, complete with notebook, pencil and shoulder bag. The family especially like the way my nose is drawn. I just like appearing in the same comic as Desperate Dan. One of those magic, not quite believable connections with my childhood. On a par with hearing Elvis Presley loved Monty Python.

Sunday, June 14th

I've had an odd, hovering sense of dislocation over the last few days, maybe even weeks.

I'm sort of echoing what Michael Katakis was trying to say when we talked in Montana. Where is home? This is not a question that troubled me, but recently it's been on my mind – as I stare out of aircraft windows at the world below.

Perhaps it's partly to do with my reconnection with America – well, the USA. This year's work – on Hemingway, on the Ephron film, on the Hemingway book tour – has put me back in touch with the American way of doing things. The enthusiasm they have shown for my work – and my work with Python too – is infectious and rather gratifying. The likes of Norah, Sherrie, Michael K and Nancy have reminded me how bright and stimulating the Yanks can be.

Then back to England, and its fields and neat old rural patterns seem oppressive; the city, as usual, a little frustrating. Car alarms, more graffiti-ed scribbles, wanton destruction and Tube strikes threatened.

And, oddly, and though it irritates me to have even noticed it, let alone allow myself to be pricked by it, there is the latest Honours List. June Whitfield, John Peel, etc. all given some sort of recognition. What services does one have to give to be recognised? I can only assume that the Pythons are on some sort of blacklist, otherwise the group's work would have been recognised as having as universal an effect on TV comedy as the Beatles did on music.

I spend a couple of hours in the afternoon composing three letters to the Travellers Club, who have, after Frank Herrmann's promptings, finally elected me as a member.[1] I was prepared to accept, if only for access to one of the most beautiful buildings in London, but how much time do I want to spend with a body of men who regularly vote against the presence of women, except on sufferance and on the peripheries of the club?

1 Frank Herrmann, retired publisher, influential member of the Travellers Club.

Monday, June 15th

I hear that Anne has had an offer accepted for premises in Tavistock Street in Covent Garden. She's not certain when she will move the Mayday office there. Eleanor and Gloria — mainstays of my financial management — are both leaving. This succession of bombshells (not all unexpected) leaves me dazed and confused.

Worried too as to where Tom will find work. Talks of picking up with Sheridan again — his working life, as he comes up to 30, increasingly resembles a record that's stuck.

Rachel is only on the payroll of At-It for another ten days. Will is working to finish his thesis for his MA by the end of the week.

Thursday, June 18th

A proposal from Hoberman about the Python tour and marketing in the US has come through on the fax. I scan it quickly and am not encouraged by what I see — 54-show, nine-week tour in the US alone — some of the theatres well above the 2,000-seat capacity we preferred.

To dinner at Robert Young's. John Mortimer and his wife Penny among the other guests. Mortimer, who has become Sir John Mortimer in the latest Honours List, lies back in a chair with a stick alongside him and apologises for not being able to get up. He'd had a fall and twisted his ankle.

He and I were both at Brasenose. He was there with Archbishop Runcie, and recounts with some amusement a mention of himself in Runcie's auto-biography. Runcie, who has apparently seen Mortimer with girls 'at the bus stop' on frequent occasions, refers to Mortimer's 'irrepressible member'.

Asked John about writing. He does all his work longhand on a legal pad. 'I never learnt to type.'

Good food, immaculate decoration. Mortimer drank well and ate little and we all packed up around midnight.

Sunday, June 21st

Call Marianne, wife of John Marriott, ex-Governor of Parkhurst who died last week. I ask if he'd been ill. She says, sounding shockingly cheerful, that he'd been upstairs, on a rowing machine, had come down, walked round the garden and 'fell dead at my feet'.

What with news of Tumim leaving Teddy Hall after only two years as Prin-cipal (difference of opinion with unpleasant bursar) I feel that my two Great

White Hopes for a sensible attitude to prisons and prisoners have suffered from the forces of reaction.

Marianne says that John was on verge of a breakdown after his Parkhurst dismissal. 'Look at that footage you shot,' she advises, still with a chuckle, 'in the recreation area there's a whole group of prisoners saying what a good bloke the Governor is – well at least two or three of them went over the wall that night.'

Thursday, June 25th

Spend much of the morning reading through Justice Rattee's judgement on the Paragon/Channel 4 case. It's 92 pages long and, like many of the best novels, it demands early concentration and repays it with great drama later on.

Rattee is clearly appalled by the behaviour of Paragon and Jon Slan – 'a thoroughly unreliable witness' – and singularly unimpressed with their solicitor – 'evidence extremely unsatisfactory ... impulsive carelessness'.

Channel 4 hardly come out of it well. They have still not exercised their right to appeal – only 24 more hours to do so.

Saturday, June 27th

This morning I put my mind to the Gospel Oak tree-planting. Should I rely on off-the-cuff or write down my thoughts on the inspirational nature of the event?

The public garden – about 80 feet by 20 feet – where the oak is to be planted is little more than a strip, but it has been carefully and painstakingly prepared.

A bossy, blonde lady with 'Steward' written on a yellow badge secured to her left breast stands up and addresses the small crowd, then asks me to plant the tree. She's taken half the words out of my mouth already and does not seem to consider it worth asking me to say a few words.

So once the oak is planted (and it is a sapling descended from the oak tree at Hatfield House under which Princess Elizabeth was sitting when told she was to be Queen Elizabeth I) I uncharacteristically have to ask to speak.

The bossy blonde bemoans the 'negativity' of the local residents, but I wonder if she ever gives them a chance. I suggest, obliquely, that gardens like this, places where people can get together and meet naturally – pubs, cafés, libraries – are more important than people going round banging on doors and asking people to join this or that.

Tuesday, June 30th

As England's next 'hour of destiny' arrives in France[1] I make my way up to a lecture hall behind the Royal Free Hospital, with the running order of my slide show rolled up and tucked away in my inside pocket.

Helen Marcus of the Friends of Hampstead Town Hall is looking worried – a lot of people have called in to say they'll send the cheque, but they have to stay and watch the football.

A small handful of punters fill the first few rows of the hall. But I do my best for them.

When I finally walk back down an eerily quiet Agincourt Road and past the flats, the game's obviously entered extra time for there is a telly on in nearly every house I pass.

Golden goal period. David Beckham off. England only have ten men but are holding the Argentinians. They hold on until penalties. Enormous relief, impossible tension. A's second goal saved, then Ince saved. Neither side looks that comfortable.

There's only H on the sofa and me, just arrived, in the hall, when Batty's poor shot is saved and he joins Waddle and Southgate in the growing group of those who have had the final word in another – glorious – English failure.

Thursday, July 2nd

A conference call to discuss reactions to the Python tour proposals.

A BT voice comes on and links us up one by one – first me, then TJ in Wales, 'from where I'm talking I can see a sheep', then Eric in Venice, at the Cipriani, and finally JC, sounding already a wee bit testy, in Montreal where he's filming with Bette Midler. TG can't be found. He's gone to Italy but I relay his general unwillingness to the rest. No-one thinks his lack of performing is completely disabling, provided he's involved in other ways.

Over a period of 40 minutes we agree on certain specific requirements with which Hoberman's people should go back to the producers. Nine weeks max; six shows a week; four different venues all in the USA; average size around 2,500 people.

Eric is happy to do it on a rock concert basis – big side-screens enabling us to play enormous halls. JC and myself most keen on performing in a pleasant atmosphere where we have some control over the audience.

---

1 England v Argentina in the World Cup.

Monday, July 13th

A phone call over the weekend from Robert Agnew asking me to come to Belfast for the festival. At a time when the news is all of people leaving the province as the Drumcree siege[1] persists, his invitation has a certain perverse attraction and I agree in principle to a one-nighter.

I ask about Michael Barnes. He's been in hospital and is now at a nursing home. His short-term memory has almost gone. I think of him this morning and feel a short, sharp choke of despair at the ruthlessness of ageing, sometimes you want time to stop and people to be always as you want to remember them.

Wednesday, July 15th

At eleven I drive to the Stammering Centre for a photocall with children for a magazine article.

I never really mind coming to the Centre. Not only is the welcome enthusiastic but the atmosphere is always upbeat and positive, and it's good to meet the parents and the children who've benefited. A mixed bag today, articulate, confident private-school boy from Chelmsford (without parents), and a local father with cropped haircut and stitches down his forehead with wife and, equally articulate, son.

Roger M, my *Daily Telegraph* correspondent, has rung to tell me that there is a review of last night's Mike Wood programme on Alexander the Great headed 'In the Steps of Palin the Great'. One of *Full Circle*'s best reviews, he says. A year late.

Thursday, July 16th

Ann Jefferson[2] arrived just after I left this morning. She's very easy to chat to, and we eat in and listen to her horror stories of life in Wilton, Connecticut. She was diagnosed as having Lyme's Disease just before she flew over. From deer ticks. It's what Kevin had at the start of *Fierce Creatures* filming. Seems particularly prevalent at the top end of the property market.

Makes me quite relieved that I live in a city. 'Much healthier than the countryside.' 'Oh, much!' says Ann with feeling.

---

1 The 1998 Drumcree siege was inflated by a decision from the new Parades Commission to ban the traditional route of the march. Three children died in the protests that followed.
2 Ann Jefferson, one of Helen's oldest friends, who was living in America.

Monday, July 20th

Good news from the Law Courts. Damages have been discussed today and as Paragon are in receivership we're pursuing Channel 4 for most of the money. They claimed today that as not all points against them were proven they were prepared to give no more than 50% maximum. The court considered this and ordered them to pay 80%. Very good news for us – and prospect of something like two-thirds of our £500,000 costs being reclaimed is not a distant one.

Tuesday, July 21st

A list in this morning's *Independent* of the 100 books of the century chosen by the editorial board of Modern Library, a division of Random House. In the opinion of Gore Vidal, A. Schlesinger Jnr, W. Styron, A. S. Byatt, John Richardson and others, Hem's Nobel Prize-winner *The Old Man and the Sea* doesn't rate. In fact EH barely scrapes into the top 50 (*The Sun Also Rises* is at 45). He would doubtless have whizzed round in his grave to have seen Scott Fitzgerald at 2 (*Great Gatsby*) and 28 (*Tender Is the Night*).

Watch *42 Up* – remarkable continuation of the *7 Up* series begun in 1963 by Michael Apted. The most odious of the seven-year-olds has grown up to be the most successful – a QC now so prominent that he would not appear in the programme.

All the encounters had an intense and revealing power. There was nowhere for the interviewees to hide, one felt, because we know them too well. A dozen plays there.

Sunday, July 26th

To Henley with H to see George H.

George is in amongst his recently planted trees – he's put in 150 in the last couple of months. He emerges from beneath an arch made from old tree stumps – a wonderful, elaborate, fantastical construction. He's looking good. Trim figure. Hair shortish.

On the broad, green, sloping curve of grass, as we shuffle about trying to find patches of sunlight coming through the trees, he launches into a long description of what he calls with a rueful smile 'my little brush with cancer'.

He tells, quite matter-of-factly and unemotionally, the story of connections and revelations – discovery of a spot on the lower inside surface of the mouth leading to discovery of a spot on the upper part of one lung. Most of it happened in the last year, and though the lung treatment (removal of what did turn out to be a malignant spot) was done at the Mayo Clinic in America, the six weeks of acutely uncomfortable laser therapy on his neck and throat was done at the Royal Marsden in Sutton, Surrey.

George drove himself every day, five days a week, for six weeks out along the M4 and the M25 to have his 30-second zapping.

George leavens all this with his Indian wisdoms about the transience of this bodily life – 'We have always been here and always will be here' – and praises the Self-Realisation Fellowship for their help and prayers.

We move on up to the house for tea. The little front room, where Olivia keeps her glasses in a silver metal case like my own, with a label reading 'Kitchen' stuck on it.

It seems every corner and every detail of Friar Park is preoccupying them. George admits that the Matterhorn's not in great shape and the Rockery is a wilderness. But he's had carpenters build a small Russian 'dacha' complete with onion dome and cross, and a ring of stones he calls Friarhenge.

We end the evening sitting near Friarhenge, whilst George stokes a campfire.

It's extraordinary in a way – this restless, creative, inventive multi-millionaire ending up, happy as Larry, sitting round a fire of twigs and branches.

It begins to rain. We're shielded for a while by the trees but around 10.30 we strike camp and begin to start back.

Tuesday, August 4th

Call Terry J and put to him my views on the Python tour. I'm as frustrated as everyone else by the lack of hard detail on the offers – or realistic detail anyway – and suggest that we scale down the whole project, and instead of nine weeks on the road, play one week (say five shows) on one stage with making of film or TV deal added on.

This way we could make some money without committing to the slog and complication of a tour, and try out a show that could be exciting but not have enough time to become boring in the playing. We could always then play it elsewhere in 2000. TJ adds that under this shorter arrangement TG may become fully involved.

The house is quiet as I pack once again, for a Hemingway recce in Havana. I feel a touch of loneliness. A reminder of how much fun I have with the family, and the prospect of leaving home yet again at 4.45 tomorrow morning on a project which I know will keep me away from them for much of another year.

Then I realise that I've been through all this before – on Python films, *Ripping Yarns*, *80 Days*, etc. etc. It's part of my life and probably always will be.

Saturday, August 8th: Ambos Mundos Hotel, Havana

It is ten to ten in the morning as I write, here in the building, indeed on the very floor, in which Hemingway was turning the Spanish Civil War into *For Whom the Bell Tolls*, 60 years ago.

Notes before leaving Ambos Mundos, and Havana, for cooler climates on the Great Lakes. The great sweaty heat reducing all human movement to a slouch or a stroll. The weight of the humidity bowing the shoulders. Only one street away from Obispo and O'Reilly, both prepared for tourists, are potholed road surfaces, torn wiring, houses that look abandoned but are lived in – bicycles and tricycles, thin, almost emaciated old women – the smell of human effluent.

Street traders, people waiting, squatting, crouching. Awful prison of language – not knowing enough Spanish to really respond to these people. Are they all trying to sell me something, or is it just a natural openness which I've mistaken for hassle?

Hemingway never wrote about life in Havana – he always wrote about one country whilst in another.

Monday, August 10th: Petoskey, Michigan

Petoskey itself is a comfortable, well-behaved, well-looked-after town. Last night David [Turnbull] and I found a micro-brewery and drank wheat beer – tonight we're booked in at a restaurant called Andante – which, ominously, promises 'eclectic gourmet dining'. The word gourmet frightens me enough – God knows what the eclectic will involve.

Tuesday, August 11th: Petoskey

Am quite shattered by the concentration of a one-hour Python conference call prompted by reaction to my last week's proposal for one week in Vegas. More later, must pack now – but it was one of the more bitter Python altercations. I've made a dent in the nine-week option, and won a few days' breathing space to consider a less Hollywood-driven alternative. JC also off the nine-week option, but only because it won't raise him enough money.

Cloud thickening out over Little Traverse Bay. Temperature down. Time for a coffee on the terrace which looks across to where the railway station once stood and from which EH drew inspiration for a story or two. What an unlikely place to be deciding Python's destiny!

Monday, August 17th

Run for first time since my morning plod by the shores of Little Traverse Bay, followed by the Python conference call in which the relentless forward momentum to a megabucks, money-at-all-cost Python tour was checked. Today, it's followed by a meeting of the British Pythons – Terry J, John, myself and Terry G – at Nico Central to discuss a possible new direction.

The meal is rather bad. Terry J has taken against the place from the start and becomes especially heated when they can't find him a toothpick.

Gilliam is a little subdued. He says he's 'numb', but it's good to have him back in the group discussion. JC clearly doesn't fancy a long tour and in the end we agree on two weeks' preparation and rehearsal, and two weeks at Las Vegas.

Over in Washington President Clinton goes on TV to admit his fling with Monica Lewinsky.

Wednesday, August 19th

Terry J calls. Eric has sent an email reply after hearing news of the meeting. As we both agree, not a friendly response and certainly not an understanding one.

So, for a moment, the process is stalled. EI suggests we pay off the lawyers and forget the whole thing. The first seems something devoutly to be wished.

Stay at home all day and, despite mugginess inside, and tempting sunshine outside, I try to focus down on an order of filming for the Hemingway series. A script and a structure for the USA and Cuba.

Thursday, August 20th

Finish up my Cuba notes and put it all together for a production meeting.

David arrives at 12.30 – wearing a music biz T-shirt and carrying his Hem papers in a plastic bag and bearing the news that Clive James is about to film one of his 'postcard' series in Havana. They'll be there from mid-September.

When Martha arrives clutching a vast amount of paperwork, I make them sandwiches and we sit down to examine all the various problems of time, location, budget, etc.

It's a good session. After two and a half hours I feel that we have come further than in all our previous discussions.

No fancy special effects – we don't have time; will attempt to shoot Cuba for the marlin-fishing tournament and before Clive James, then have a rest back here for two clear weeks before going to USA. Return to Idaho for Sun Valley/Ketchum ending to the series at end of the filming.

The clearing of the air on 'HT' and a conciliatory fax from EI agreeing to the two-week Las Vegas proposal has lifted my mood from sluggish pessimism to real enthusiasm for the task ahead.

Clinton, in whom I'm afraid I've lost much faith after Monday's weaselly Lewinsky performance, is in front of the American people again – telling them with the same firm jaw and steely gaze why he has ordered air strikes on Sudan and Afghanistan without consulting the United Nations.

He's now punching some foreigners – only this, we all know, will affect our lives far more than his devious dismissal of Lewinsky.

Friday, August 21st

Have arranged Damien Hirst's Pharmacy for a boys' night out with TG and Ray. The Medical Council challenged the name Pharmacy and it has been changed by anagram to Aram Cyph.

Ray becomes very vociferous about the destruction of the old East End and predicts that the Millennium Dome will be the ruination of Greenwich. TG has been approached by the Dome Fillers. It's clearly a big corporate clean-up in there and what TG would like to do (a version of his Human Body fairground ride) would be in far too poor taste for any big sponsor – so that's that.

Sign the bill with a pen shaped like a hypodermic. Pick our way through packed crowd of young who are now dancing downstairs amongst the pill cabinets, past the wannabees clustering round the entrance and then a long natter by the car in Ladbroke Terrace. So long that TG has to go into a neighbouring garden to relieve himself behind the hedge.

Thursday, August 27th

Drive to TJ's for squash. He looks even more harassed than me and has evidently had a very similar day of phone calls, demands, etc.

The game is probably therapeutic. Forty minutes devoted to one subject only. I'm unable to overcome my serving shortcomings and lose yet again – my last victory seems to recede into the mists of time.

Home at eight. Am reading A. E. Hotchner's memoir *Papa Hemingway* at exactly the point where he recounts a long, rambling, bitter phone call from Hemingway about the intolerable demands of celebrity – the photographers, the requests for interviews; the impossibility of getting any work done. Fax the page to Terry.

Saturday, August 29th

To Covent Garden to augment wardrobe for the filming ahead. Entering the Emporio Armani at 10.30 on a Saturday is a pretty intimidating experience. The 'assistants' (perhaps storm troopers would be a better description) are ranged across the threshold; unsmiling, dressed in black, like some sort of personal army (Giorgio's of course) of cool. Very fascist and thoroughly unpleasant, until you actually talk to Giorgio's soldiers and realise they're rather nervous and from South Shields.

Monday, August 31st

A year ago Princess Diana died and *Full Circle* went before the public for the first time. Feel as if I haven't done much that's new since then.

Publicity, publicity, publicity – revisiting work of the past – Python revisited in Aspen, *Hemingway's Chair* revisited in the USA in May and June.

Tuesday, September 1st

Work on the Chicago/Michigan ideas. David T arrives. I make sandwiches for lunch and we talk through material. Halfway through our discussions the phone rings – it's Nora Ephron. Pleasantly but efficiently she lets me know that my contribution to *You've Got Mail* is on the cutting room floor.

Apologies – it was too long, impossible to cut – 'we tried triage', look forward to working together again. I'm no wiser by the end. Except that I had doomy feelings about the character even while we were shooting. He seemed a clever idea but rather an alienating character. I think I was too heavy. 'Everyone loved having you around.' Well that's something. Maybe I could just visit film sets in the future.

On to André's studio. Record 80 limericks to coincide with reissue of my 1985 collection. Cassette should be ready by November.

Wednesday, September 23rd

Taxi down to Covent Garden. Walk over to the Orion HQ in St Martin's Lane.

Michael Dover, the editor/publisher of Weidenfeld Illustrated Books – which is the imprint bidding for 'Hem's Travels' – is a smooth operator – tall, blond hair falling onto forehead, upper-crust accent.

We talk. They show me some of their books, which are certainly no better than the BBC, but they do sound to be a highly focused company, with books as their priority and a good international network. Dover is a friend of Tom Dunne's which helps, and I have a feeling that they will be much less fazed by Basil's input than the BBC.

At the end of an hour together I meet Anthony Cheetham, who is the head of the company. He beams, listens and tells me 'I just wanted to shake your hand before you left the building.'

As we walk back Anne and I talk through the pros and cons. We stop for a coffee at the Seattle Coffee Company on Long Acre. Both of us have some reservations over Dover's manner – the soft words of encouragement sounded oddly abrupt and businesslike – but we liked the feel of the company. I think that the Basil factor is important – more than ever if he's designer – and I remember how irritated he always was with procedures at the BBC.

I like Cheetham and I think, because of the money they're prepared to spend, that they will sell it well. Anne confirmed that they have no options on any future books of mine.

By the time we're back at Tavistock Street I've made my mind up to try Orion/Weidenfeld for 'Hemingway's Travels'.

New director, new producer – why not new publisher. Only way to learn.

Home for lunch. Halfway through afternoon Rachel rings to say she's been offered a job at Choice, on the new BBC Digital service which began this morning.

Saturday, September 26th

Good news that Will has got a job at the Georgian Group for three days a week. Their remit is to protect and preserve Georgian architecture. Like Rachel with the BBC, there is the feeling of being on the first rung of ladders that both of them want to climb.

Thursday, October 1st

To Tavistock Street for a long letter session. Among the many requests is one asking me to join the Millennium Dome experience. I've been rather dreading some approach from them, but this one is couched in such obscure millenno-babble that I have no difficulty in saying no. 'We feel your talents would be best suited to The Mobility Zone'!

Friday, October 2nd

A letter from Alan Bleasdale begins 'You wrote to me on New Year's Day' and ends by offering me the part of Brownlow in his adaptation of *Oliver Twist*.

He says 'there has been something stopping me from writing to you, until I'd written for you'. Filming will be Feb–June next year. I hope my dates might fit.

Saturday, October 3rd

Work hard to clear as much of my desk backlog as possible, and set to packing for US. A small celebration of Tom's upcoming 30th which will fall when I'm in Petoskey next week.

I'm very proud of him – he's come through 30 years as well as any son of a celebrity. He's his own man – quite stubborn, but persistent and hard-working. Of course I often think I should have pushed him more in this, that or the other direction, but he doesn't strike me as angry or frustrated with where he is now. Precious little angst in the boy. Possibly too little. He's much more of H's temperament than mine.

Tuesday, October 27th

By car to the Savoy – an invitation to a celebratory lunch for Schuyler 'Skye' Jones's[1] CBE, with which he has been invested this morning.

A wonderful mix of guests – Wilfred Thesiger, David Attenborough and a large tribe of Skye's in-laws.

Attenborough is on good form. He asks me, in mock horror, about the news that I am leaving BBC Books. He left them years ago, except as sales-man. He is so baffled, as I am, by the new management terminology at BBC Worldwide that he actually shows me his notebook in which he has written down his editor's new title – full of words like 'genre' and 'global', and no mention of the word books.

The jolly party breaks up around four o'clock. Time to get back home and dress up for the National TV Awards at the Albert Hall.

About halfway through the long event the documentary award comes up and out comes Alan Whicker, tiptoeing gingerly through the silver gossamer set to announce and present.

---

1 Schuyler Jones, curator of Oxford's Pitt Rivers Museum while teaching cultural anthropology at the university.

'And the winner is' – professional pause – '*Full Circle with Michael Palin.*' I am so convinced that this will follow the BAFTA pattern that I'm already clapping for the camera trained upon me, in case I should look churlish. Takes a moment or two to sink in that I'm actually applauding myself.

Complete surprise, but this voted for by the viewers rather than the secretive, insider committees of BAFTA. And that Whicker should have to present me with the award does sort of bring things, well, full circle.

Friday, October 30th

Talk with David Turnbull and Martha Wailes before Martha goes to Milan, Sunday, to begin two-week recce in Italy.

I feel now that I know the dynamics between the three of us a little better. I had been cautious with David, not wanting to stifle his own thoughts and his independent perspective on the series. Now I think that he has said probably all he wants to say about basic approach, i.e. avoid anything that smacks of conventional arts biography, and is happy to sit back and be led by my enthusiasm – which he regards as less suspect than Martha's enthusiasm.

Martha still straitjacketed by her careful, linear approach to H's life – but she seems to have relaxed and accepted that what comes out will generally be my preferences and perceptions.

To Tristram and Virginia's for supper. Georgia there with new baby Hope. Tristram cooks veal knuckle.

Talk turns to diaries. Tristram confesses to keeping one in his teens. 'Deeply, deeply embarrassing,' he says. 'Everything was either "pleasant" or "boring".'

A pleasant evening. Not at all boring.

Monday, November 2nd

To a reception for BBC 'performers' and 'contributors' up on the 6th floor of TV Centre.

Think of Rachel and wonder how her first day at BBC Choice is going.

At the reception I encounter Peter Salmon, who's talking to Richard Wilson. Peter talks of the continued agonies of supporting Burnley – 'I'm getting really tired of failure.'

Frost appears – we talk about his family – all the boys are going to Eton. I ask him if he knew Diana as well as he knows Charles. He says that he and Carina used to see her for a while then she would disappear from their life for long periods. She was godmother to their youngest child, though. Now she's been replaced by David Seaman![1]

Peter makes a short speech, the main drift of which is to announce, in awed tones, that in just over a year's time the BBC will be embarking on its greatest single programme ever. The Millennium. Oh God. Thirty-six hours of continuous presentation. Oh God. And many presenters will be needed.

Much muttering and looking away from the assembled Frosts, Deaytons and Attenboroughs. What does this forebode – MP on a Pacific island?

Leave around a quarter to eight. Rachel back at home an hour later. A good first day. Her team all women.

Tuesday, November 3rd

Alan Bleasdale rings. 'Brownlow's getting bigger and bigger,' he confides. All of which is quite painful as I shall have to squeeze even more time out of tight 'HT' schedule. 'You get to do a pistol-whipping in episode six,' AB tells me, as if this might really sway it.

To Orion, to first meeting with Michael Dover since the decision to go with Weidenfeld & Nic's for 'Hem's Travels'.

It's 3.30 and prematurely dark outside. The red neon lights from the St Martin's Theatre across the road stand out like a slash of lipstick.

Talk through thoughts on the book so far. Dover is hoping to meet up with Basil in New York in early December. There has been a lot of foreign interest since Frankfurt and he clearly wants to try and get as much of the book blocked out a.s.a.p. so the foreign translations can be given time to produce the books in Hem anniversary year.

As we discuss dates there clearly is a problem. I undertake to write the Cuba section by mid-December, but cannot concentrate on the rest until March 22nd. Eyebrows raise. I had hoped to be available for Bleasdale's *Oliver Twist* during that period. Eyebrows bounce off ceiling. I know now that I'm not destined to play Brownlow.

Thursday, November 5th

Ring Alan B and tell him I can't do *Oliver Twist*. He says he lost me and Robert Lindsay in half an hour and now he's slipped a disc.

JC calls; he's in London to make a series of commercials for Sainsbury's at Christmas campaign – then he returns to US.

1 David Seaman, England and Arsenal goalkeeper. Frost himself was a pretty good goalkeeper.

We talk a little about the Vegas stage show. Roger Saunders told me that it is still being prosecuted and the MGM Grand, with capacity reduced to 2,900 seats, may be the best.

'I'm not going to cry myself to sleep if it *doesn't* happen,' says John.

Friday, November 6th

To the Landmark Hotel for second award ceremony since return from filming in Montana. These are The Talkies – awards for the spoken word. I'm at Table 2, right in front of the stage, with various BBC Worldwide luminaries and next to me Mary K – Alan Bennett's long-time producer. She says Alan is getting a lifetime achievement award but will not be coming along. There has been some development 'in his illness' as Mary K puts it.

But Spike Milligan has come along and I'm put next to him for most of the meal. He comes in, with his manager Norma Farnes in attendance, looking very frail.

A female acquaintance comes across to pay homage. She squats down beside his chair. Spike turns to her. 'You used to be much taller.' To a cheery greeting from radio producer Jonathan James-Moore, Spike replies with an equally cheery 'I've been looking for your name in the obituaries for the last five years.'

I'm up for Best TV or Film Spoken Word Tape for *Full Circle* and win the category jointly with the doyen of all readers, Martin Jarvis.

A few awards later, Spike is named winner of the comedy award for *The Last Goon Show of All*. He receives an instant and unanimous standing ovation and when he steps down and returns to the table Norma tells him he should have said something. Spike shook his head and said softly, his eyes still wide, but a little moist as well now ... 'I was overcome.'

Later, I ask him what he reads – 'Biographies, autobiographies. Anything about the war.'

'Why are you so interested in the war?' I ask him.

'Well, I was in it, wasn't I.'

Thursday, November 12th

Sort through correspondence; think about my Belfast Festival performance tomorrow night. Had planned a first half of *Full Circle* slides and second half of readings and chat, but feel this wrong for the occasion and settle on an hour of reading and biographical reminiscence (I've given them the title '30 Years Without a Proper Job').

Friday, November 13th: London–Belfast

Seventeen years on from my first appearance at the Festival, the city feels very different. No longer a gauntlet of vehicle checks and security inspections. Very little sign now of a city under siege.

The Hilton is the latest state-of-the-art hotel. Prada-style black uniforms look a little odd on chunky Ulster bodies, but my suite on the eighth floor is comfortable, bright and has everything working.

Then across to the Whitla Hall at Queen's. This is from the old Belfast and is a big institutional hall designed for exhortations and degree ceremonies rather than intimate comedy.

I'm on, eventually, at 8.15. The theatre is sold out – 1,200 people. Bad start as the radio mike begins to crackle. The sound man, who seems to have been expecting the worst, brings another up to the front of the stage. Change the mike. The second one seems to be better but then it too begins to hiss and screech and I abandon both, to loud applause from the audience.

Saturday, November 14th: Belfast–London

To East Belfast to a gallery called The Engine Room, part of an old mill building. There is a Bill Viola installation. A baby being born on one side, a man dying on the other.

At one moment the newborn baby (apparently Viola's grandchild) and the dying, skeletal man (his father) seem both to share the same expression of patient suffering with this thing called life which neither of them ever demanded.

I'm driven out to the south of the city to see Michael Barnes. Modern, gabled bungalow accommodation for elderly people who have lost or partially lost their minds.

Michael is at a table with a couple of elderly ladies.

His beard has gone and he looks a little hunched, but he recognises and embraces me and smiles his generous smile and begins to laugh.

I've been advised to ask him if I can see his room – this gets him away and into some privacy. So we sit on his bed and look through books on trains and old photos of Armagh and so long as he sticks to the present he's fine. He laughs, and we make each other laugh, just the way we used to, but any attempts at personal reminiscence just peter out. He waves his long elegant hands dismissively ... 'Oh well, never mind.'

I didn't see doctors and couldn't ask whether things might change, because if this is premature senility, then it's come awfully early. He's not yet 70.

Monday, November 30th

Try and decide which of my dwindling supply of 'lounge suits' I should wear for the John Birt dinner this evening.

When I'm shown into the upper room at Broadcasting House where the drinks are being served, he shakes my hand warmly – and checks the suit. He is encased in some very modern black number which looks like something archdeacons wear – with no opening visible down the front at all.

A few guests already there including Germaine Greer, looking wild and woolly – grey hair erupting around her fine, strong head and with little metal glasses on she looks, for a brief moment, like John Cleese in drag.

I break the ice by, first of all, kissing her warmly, which she doesn't seem at all prepared for, and remembering the days on *Twice a Fortnight* when I carried her through Kenwood. 'Carried Germaine?' picks up Birt, with rather unflattering incredulity.

We're joined by a man called Charlie Whelan, an amiable, law-unto-himself presence – with a roguish, teasing line in banter, an ever-present mobile phone. He's Gordon Brown's adviser.

When all 20 of us are present we're sat at a long table and the lights are dimmed very low. Birt stands up and hits a glass for silence and assures every-one that this is not a seminar or a chance to talk about the inner workings of the European television code of practice – we should enjoy ourselves. He does add something about being a chance to thank some of the BBC's most suc-cessful contributors – and mentions myself and David Croft by name.

Talk travel for most of the meal to Jane Birt. John is deep in conversation with Lord Falconer – a minister of state – whom I later see chatting intensely to Anthea Turner, who has one long leg stretched out across a row of chairs.

Bill Oddie gives me a ride home, confesses that he doesn't really like things like this – always feels like a naughty schoolboy and finds no-one ever talks about the things he enjoys – music and, well, Bill, I suppose.

Home around midnight.

Tuesday, December 1st

John C calls from America about the Python stage show.

He signals that ten nights in a 2,000-seater at Las Vegas doesn't look as if it will provide enough capital to make up for the time spent preparing the show which he estimates as three weeks. So, he's backing off. Asks me my opinion of the alternative – big audiences, relying on TV screens to see us. I'm not keen and neither is he.

Thursday, December 3rd

A note from St Martin's, congratulating me on *Hemingway's Chair*'s appearance on the *New York Times* list of the Year's Notable Books.

Friday, December 4th

Ten years ago today I was leaving New York on a container ship, a week away from the end of my *80 Days* journey.

Today I'm up at 7.30 and down to the Tottenham Court Road to film another Clem Vallance travel epic. Only this time my involvement should be a maximum of 80 minutes. Have agreed to start a Comic Relief relay which will take a videotape through Africa, filling it on the way with images of Comic Relief work, messages from Mandela, etc. I'm to be filmed collecting the tape from a humble Tottenham Court Road hi-fi shop and setting up the next step, which is to take it to Rolf Harris, who will design the cover.

Because what we're doing is fundamentally so easy, it takes for ever.

Eventually complete the shot, and later a trailer for Comic Relief night in March. Farewell to Clem – who's on very benign, good-humoured form. I feel gently regretful that we aren't planning anything else together. Still, ten years is a neat, comprehensive period. Time to move on.

Sunday, 6th December

Largely working day. Pushing on to complete 8,000 words on Cuba.

Monday, December 7th

In that half-hour or so before I get up, the unsatisfactory Python stage show business pushes itself, once again, into the front of my mind. Try to push it back as I have done many times recently, but this morning it is dogged and demands to be taken seriously before it will go away.

Talk to H about it at breakfast. 'It' being my continued concern about the creation of a completely new show. Who will organise it and will it work? Eric and John are both over in California, Terry J, whom I spoke to recently, is busy rewriting 'Mirrorman' yet again and TG doesn't care.

Nothing seems to be happening between us.

So I must seize this beast and I know I shan't be able to settle to any other work until I have. Spend the morning composing a fax to send out to all the

Pythons explaining my worries about the sort of thing we are planning and suggesting we do a much less formal 'Evening With' show or shows in New York or LA. In other words, stating the position I've always held but have twice compromised under pressure from the others.

Oddly enough, when I ring Roger Saunders to check if he's heard much from the others (which he hasn't) an offer of six days at the Beacon Theater in New York has just come in.

This sounds a lot better than the Millennium Dome which JC mentions a lot.

Wednesday, December 9th

To the Overseas Club in St James's Place in time for the Declaration Dinner, being organised by the Medical Foundation for Victims of Torture to announce fund-raising plans for a new centre.

I am sat next to Brian Keenan,[1] whose head is shaped like Enoch Powell's and who has a look of Enoch in the intense, slightly fierce, set of the eyes. Talk about their days of imprisonment. He calls them 'our holidays' – 'when we were on our holidays' etc. He didn't take the offer of psychiatric help after their release – 'I felt if there was something that needed to be done, I'd better do it myself' – and he is sceptical of the good it did.

He says his captors thought America was the Great Satan, yet they wore bandanas to make them look like Sly Stallone in action.

He's disgusted by the level of violence in entertainment. Also pretty disgusted by David Trimble – 'Oh don't get him onto Trimble,' says John McCarthy. He thinks that in an Ireland united the Protestants would probably be more secure and successful than they are in the divided Ireland they're so anxious to promote.

Thursday, December 10th

Python developments – a fax from John via Roger. He feels that there isn't enough 'energy' in the group for a stage show. Terry G doesn't want to do it – 'Eric is on the sidelines' – Terry J will go along with whatever anyone else wants to do, and my new proposal ('for a rehash of the old show' as he puts it) doesn't interest him at all.

So, as John goes on his travels, all bets seem to be off. I feel unhappy and

1 Irish Republican who, with John McCarthy, was held hostage in Beirut from April 1986 to August 1990. McCarthy was not released until a year later.

uncomfortable about my role in all this, yet ultimately I think I was right to sound continued warnings. I could, and indeed hope to be persuaded that we should do some sort of reappearance together, but the way things are at the moment, as John rightly recognises, there is no central driving force trying to make the show happen.

Thursday, December 17th

More cards, send first slice of the 'Hemingway's Travels' book to Michael Dover, and into town for lunch at Neal Street Restaurant.

Antonio Carluccio looms up, gives me a big bear hug and tells me that he's been to ITV to set up a series of travels. 'Like you do, only with food.' He mutters dark criticism of BBC Books. He has left them and will work for Hodder Headline until 2003.

He tells us all a joke about the Mafia – little Mafia boy writes to baby Jesus – 'if you ever want to see your mother again' – and goes off to do his Christmas shopping.

News of bombing raids in Iraq, and postponement, by two days, of impeachment vote on Clinton.

Friday, December 18th

Talk to Michael Ignatieff, who has been travelling with Richard Holbrooke, the US special envoy who brokered peace in Bosnia and has been currently struggling to hold the Wye Agreement (aptly named) between Israel and Palestine together. Michael, who is writing a piece about him for the *New Yorker*, asked how he approaches his task. Holbrooke apparently quoted the haggling scene from *Life of Brian* as his inspiration!

Will tell Eric this when I reply to his email, which has a severe go at me for changing my mind on the stage show and suggests therapy.

My morale improved by a complimentary fax from Michael Dover who says he wouldn't change a word of my text (this bodes well for the rest).

Monday, December 28th

Day of the post-Christmas river trip, so no long lie-in. Rewarded by quiet streets and have time to show Granny our new office location in Tavistock Street and Waterloo and Blackfriars Bridge views before gathering with the others for the 10.30 boat from Embankment Pier to Greenwich.

Full family turnout. Eleven in all. Onto a barge with chairs and a plastic hood. It's a quarter full, almost entirely of foreigners, as we turn under Charing Cross railway bridge and head downstream.

A Cockney commentary, full of jokes of the corniest sort and not even told with any charm, just routine taxi-driver sort of prejudices. Edward and especially Catherine Burd, both architects, made apoplectic by references to the National Theatre – 'thought by most architects to be the worst building in London'. Piers Gough's Cascade Towers – 'they say they were designed to look like a boat under full sail. Well all I can say is he's obviously never been on a boat in his life', and the Millennium Dome – 'biggest waste of taxpayers' money this country's ever seen'.

In a way I prefer this batty bigotry to a recorded message, but that's quite a perverse view to take.

An hour to Greenwich and the changes along both banks are considerable. Housing runs in a broken line on the south bank and an almost continuous line on the north, all the way to Greenwich. Canary Wharf is expanding again, after its dodgy hiatus in the late '80s and the bombing in the '90s. London's eastward spread looks inevitable and unstoppable now.

The Dome, a strange new shape, a blister amongst the strips of housing and the fingers of the tower blocks, looms beyond Greenwich's elegant seventeenth- and eighteenth-century façades.

We climb up the hill to the Observatory, following an ant-trail of visitors. There is a space on the wall below Flamsteed's Wren-designed building where the zero line of longitude runs. It's covered in graffiti.

Tuesday, December 29th

Low cloud, grey dawn. I think of Cleese in Barbados, or Eric in his pool in LA. What am I doing stuck here in this grubby, graffitied corner of dour, cold England, when I could be in the sun too?

This is much too complicated a line of enquiry to unravel, and anyway, it just makes me depressed lying there, playing the where-could-I-be-now? game.

Complete U-turn in mood as I switch over to hear Darren Gough's last over of the Fourth Test in Melbourne. Australia defeated!

Thursday, December 31st

If last year was a big one (*Full Circle* completion and transmission), this was its much-reduced younger brother. *Full Circle* echoed through until March,

when Aspen revived Python (only for it to be put back in its box), and stim-
ulated me into the Hemingway project. Sidetracked, and ultimately sidelined,
by *You've Got Mail* (currently No. 1 in US). Surprised, very pleasantly, by the
success of *Hemingway's Chair* in America.

A sputtering firework of a year. I hope that it will lead to a better display to
end this millennium.

Index

Index

Index

Index

Index

Index

Index

Index

Index

Palin, Michael—*contd*

discusses *Great Railway Journeys* trip to
Ireland, 214

reads book by Raymond Briggs for audio
cassette, 214

and *A Stab in the Dark* programme, 215

discussions about *The Weekend* with
Robert Fox and David Pugh, 215

at Will Wyatt's BBC party for writers, 216

interview with Susie Mackenzie, 216, 219

addresses AGM for Association of
Stammerers, 216-17

works on commentary for *Pole to Pole*,
217, 218, 224

at wedding of his brother-in-law Veryan,
218

invited to be a judge on NCR non-fiction
panel, 219

goes to Presidents Evening of RSNC/
Wildlife Trusts Partnership, 219-20

resigns from board of Meridian, 220

at Joan Sanderson's memorial service, 221

invited to present *Literary Review* Poetry
Award, 221

visits printers where *Pole to Pole* is being
printed, 221-2

agrees to supply documentary material for
Meridian, 222

visits John Hughman in hospital, 222-3

at *Literary Review* lunch, 223

at Tom's black belt grading, 223-4

meets Gary Lineker, 224

goes to see *Someone Who'll Watch Over
Me*, 224

talks about *The Weekend* casting with
David Pugh, 225

attends production meeting on *A Class
Act*, 225

Meridian advertiser's launch at BAFTA,
225-6

receives doctorate from Sheffield
University, 226

at screening of *Pole to Pole*, 227

on *Start the Week*, 227-8

discusses his documentary commitment to
Meridian, 228

appears as Transport 2000 President
at House of Commons Committee
Room, 228-9

appears on Frank Bough's programme,
229

reads *Pole to Pole* reviews, 229

at Gardners warehouse for *Pole to Pole* sales
and book-signing, 229

and filming of *A Class Act*, 229-30

good viewing figures for *Pole to Pole*, 230,
231, 234, 241

in Edinburgh for talk at Usher Hall, 231

Pole to Pole book becomes No.1 best-
seller, 231

meeting with Rebecca Eaton from
Masterpiece Theatre, 231-2

learns about high sales figures for *Pole to
Pole* book, 232

at TG's birthday party, 232-3

offered a part in *An Immaculate Mistake*,
233

receives request to play role in *The Dresser*,
233

discussions about *Fierce Creatures*/'Death
Fish II', 233-4

at NCR for first meeting of Book Award
judges, 235

recording interviews for 'What's On
Meridian' programme, 235-6

at Aspreys Christmas party, 236

goes to Liverpool for friend's birthday
party, 236-7

goes to Sickert retrospective, 237

visits John Hughman, 238-9

in Southampton for Meridian's opening,
239

and John Hughman's death, 240

does piece for *TV Weekly*, 241

on *Wogan* show, 241

talks about Angela at dinner party, 242

considers idea of Pacific journey, 242

and Rachel's 18th birthday, 242

at John Hughman's funeral, 242-3

at Denholm Elliott's memorial service,
243

unsure about undertaking a third travel
project, 244

at dinner party with the Cooks and
Cleeses, 244

works on *The Dresser*, 245-7

interview with Hunter Davies, 247, 249

discussion about Tom's work, 247-8

wins Travel Writer of the Year Award,
248

in Sheffield for its 100th anniversary as a
city, 248-9

goes to Vice Presidents lunch for RSNC,
249

watches *Howard's End*, 250

congratulates JC on success of *Life and
How to Survive It*, 250

meets Molly Dineen, 250-1

Index

scripts put together for Methuen to
  publish, 39
discussion between MP and Anne James
  about 20th anniversary, 43-4
meeting for group photo and screening of
  Python material, 47
follow-up meeting and photo, 48
MP gives interview on 20 years of, 49
Graham Chapman watches videotapes of
  shows, 65
portraits by Tom Phillips, 68,70
20th anniversary piece filmed, 70-1
Thatcher uses 'Parrot Sketch', 144
reaction to Thatcher's use of sketch, 146
repeat cancelled after outbreak of Gulf
  War, 163
and dubbing, 201
John Cleese's attitude to possibility of
  stage show, 313
cards and calendar, 318
songbook, 324
25th anniversary interviews, 332, 335
and Cyril Connolly, 353
meeting about Python companies, 408
award from *Empire* magazine, 434
meeting at Cliveden, 441, 442, 443
idea of new film project, 441, 442 ,443,
  450, 466
stage show in Las Vegas talked about, 442
case against Paragon, 461-2 and n, 470,
  471, 473, 474, 496, 499
and Paramount Comedy, 473
in Aspen, 477-80
and idea of 30th anniversary tour, 478,
  479, 483, 484, 495, 497
MP suggests scaling down to one week,
  500
reaction to MP's proposal, 501
further discussion about options, 502
proposal for two weeks at Las Vegas, 502,
  503
John Cleese backs off from Las Vegas idea,
  512
MP expresses concerns in fax about stage
  show, 513
reactions to fax, 514
brief mentions, 46, 228, 255 and n, 281,
  341, 422, 476, 481, 494, 504, 516
*see also Life of Brian; Monty Python and
  the Holy Grail;* Prominent; Python
  sketches; names of individuals
Python sketches
  'Blackmail', 46
  'Cheese Shop', 33

'Hearing Aid', 71
'Parrot', 88, 93, 144, 146, 151, 430-1, 445
'Spanish Inquisition', 46

Q

Quad Cinema, New York, 255
Quaid, Dennis, 489
Quattrone, Kathy, 451
Queen Mary, 12 and n
Queenstown, 402
Quince Tree Sun, 475 and n

R

RAC Club, 307, 341, 372, 375
Radio Drama Company, 245
Radio 4, 164, 369
Radio 5, 175, 352
Radio Kent, 185
Radio Sport, 263
Radio Times, 242, 247, 288, 359, 454
Radley College Choir, 365
Rainbow Alliance, 326
Raine, Craig, 229
Random House, 288, 290, 499
Rank, 144
Rantzen, Esther, 67
Raphael, Freddie, 268
Rattee, Justice, 482, 496
Raven, Abbe, 160
Redpath, Anne, 423-4, 437, 445, 446, 447
  film about, 423, 427, 445-7
Red Sea, 3
Red Sea Hotel, Suez, 3
Red Sea Palace Hotel, Jeddah, 4
Redwood Recording Studios, 42, 72, 219
Reed Books, 350, 358
Rees-Mogg, William, 17
Reeves, Vic, 198
Reform Club, 14, 15, 39
Regent Hotel, 291
Reid, Travers, 85, 216 and n, 282
Relph, Simon, 51 and n, 53, 57, 60, 100-1,
  114, 123
Remarkable Mountains, 402
Remenham, 76
Renaissance restaurant, Aspen, 480
Renoir Cinema, 118, 196
Rensselaer, 12-13
Renton, Tim, 464
Renwick, David, 321 and n
Reservoir Dogs, 335
Restaurante El Landó, Madrid, 27
RGS (Royal Geographical Society), 269,
  315, 441, 464

Index

Index